# Behavior in Organizations

*Prentice-Hall*
*Behavioral Sciences in Business Series*

Herbert A. Simon, Editor

Prentice-Hall International Series in Management

# Behavior in Organizations:

## A Multidimensional View

SECOND EDITION

ROBERT E. COFFEY

*University of Southern California*

ANTHONY G. ATHOS

*Harvard University*

PETER A. RAYNOLDS

*University of Southern California*

PRENTICE-HALL, INC., Englewood Cliffs, New Jersey

*Library of Congress Cataloging in Publication Data*

Coffey, Robert E
Behavior in organization.

(Prentice-Hall behavioral sciences in business series) (Prentice-Hall international series in management)
First ed. (1968) by A. G. Athos and R. E. Coffey.
Includes bibliographical references.
1. Organization. 2. Social psychology.
I. Athos, Anthony G., joint author. II. Raynolds, Peter A., joint author. III. Athos, Anthony G. Behavior in organizations. IV. Title.
HD31.C58 1974 301.18'32 74-12372
ISBN 0-13-073148-X



Case material of the Harvard Graduate School of Business Administration is made possible by the cooperation of business firms who may wish to remain anonymous by having names, quantities, and other identifying details disguised while maintaining basic relationships. Cases are prepared as the basis for class discussion rather than to illustrate either effective or ineffective handling of administrative situations.

Printed in the United States of America

10 9 8 7 6 5 4 3 2 1

Prentice-Hall International, Inc., London
Prentice-Hall of Australia, Pty. Ltd., Sydney
Prentice-Hall of Canada, Ltd., Toronto
Prentice-Hall of India Private Limited, New Delhi
Prentice-Hall of Japan, Inc., Tokyo

Prentice-Hall, Inc.
Prentice-Hall International, Inc., United Kingdom and Eire
Prentice-Hall of Canada, Ltd., Canada
Dunod Press, France
Maruzen Company, Ltd., Far East
Herrero Hermanos, Sucs., Spain and Latin America
R. Oldenbourg Verlag, Germany
Ulrico Hoepli Editors, Italy

To HAROLD S. SPEAR

# Contents

# Cases

# Foreword

In studying chemistry, physics, or biology the real world can be brought into the laboratory. The student need not rely on verbal descriptions, or even pictures, to tell him about the force exerted by a weight on a lever arm, or what happens when you mix hydrochloric acid with sodium hydroxide in a test tube. He can see for himself. If he doubts Galileo, he can replicate his experiment of rolling a ball down an inclined plane.

In the laboratory, the student also learns how to *do* science: he acquires skills in the basic processes for carrying on a scientific investigation; he takes the first steps toward developing the knowledge and technique that a professional scientist or engineer needs.

A major problem in teaching the behavioral sciences effectively—and a major problem for the student in learning them—is to provide an effective counterpart to the laboratory. Of course we live all our lives immersed in a sea of human behavior. We can use that experience as one part of our behavioral science laboratory, to test out abstract concepts and to exercise skills of living with others. First-hand experience in particular kinds of social institutions—especially organizations—is harder to come by. We cannot always find a factory or a store that will allow full access to the behavior of the members, or that wants to be "practiced on."

Professors Coffey, Athos, and Raynolds make a frontal assault on this learning problem in their book. They have been imaginative in discovering and suggesting ways of applying knowledge about organizations, and ways of practicing the skills that are essential to effective management.

Among others, they deal with the vitally important skill of seeing what is going on around us, and getting the meaning of what we see. A manager repeatedly finds himself in new social or organizational settings, where he has to understand the pattern of human interaction around him — the relations between people, where power lies, the kinds of people who are part of the situation, the feelings people have about their work and about their relations with each other.

It is sometimes thought fashionable, in academic circles, to disparage the learning of "mere skills." One might argue, on the contrary, that the natural sciences owe their spectacular successes to never separating "knowing" too far from "knowing how." In this book, the authors take the position, quite rightly in my view, that understanding human behavior in organizations requires the ability to see in the actual behavior before us the concrete realization of the concepts and theories we hold about organizational phenomena. As Professors Coffey, Athos, and Raynolds state in their Introduction, the value of the book to the student will depend on his willingness to practice his growing skills of observation and behavior, and to view new concepts as providing those skills with a framework of guiding ideas.

HERBERT A. SIMON

# Introduction

Much of what we have come to believe and understand about learning in the area of behavior in organizations has resulted both from our own administrative and consulting experiences and from being with undergraduates, graduate students, and managers while they dealt with the ideas posed in this book. We are grateful to these people who have bravely forced us to experience our own teaching failures along with our successes, for they taught us most, even if at times we didn't particularly want to learn what they were teaching us!

It may be that you will have similar experiences in using this text. All of us love to do what we are already good at, and find it less attractive to proceed beyond new insights to the development of new human *skills*, especially when "the rules of the game" are unclear or rapidly changing. We hope you are ready and willing to explore some ways of thinking that may be new to you, as well as to practice *using* them in a personal way to illuminate your own experiencing. For this book can be of help only if you give it life. It will be worthwhile only if you make it your own, for intellectual constructions that are not used until they are as comfortable as an old sweater are at best temporarily ornamental.

Our hope is that you will actively scrutinize, select, and possess as your own some of the ideas that follow, so that they become a part of your natural skill as a human being functioning in the world. In a way, what we are saying here is akin to learning to drive a car. Simply knowing the rules of the road, how to shift, signal, and steer is not the same as being skillful at driving. The latter takes enough practice that shifting, for example, requires really no conscious thought at all. It becomes a natural intuitive skill that permits attention elsewhere. If you recall the sometimes painful effort of first learning to drive, and then the pleasure and usefulness of being skilled at it, you will know something of what we hope for you in this book: the excitement of personal growth and increased mastery in grasping the complexities of real behavioral situations. For us, it has been a deeply satisfying and, at times, a moving experience to be involved with persons like you who have given enough of themselves to grow a great deal.

The second edition was accomplished without the direct participation of one of us, Tony Athos, but with the assistance of a new co-author

Pete Raynolds. The contribution of both men will be apparent to users of the first edition. Tony helped considerably in preliminary conceptual discussions, and his original contribution continues importantly in this revision. This book is divided into three basic parts: text, readings, and cases. The text material has been expanded and brought up-to-date. Eleven more timely cases have been added, and two articles emphasizing the future have been included, not as a forecast, but to provoke your thought about how the future may be and what meaning it has for you and others. We have drawn from the recent minor explosion of new terms, theories, empirical research and points of view those that we think strengthen the conceptual framework of this book. We have felt no compulsion to include everything, and we are already aware of some outdatedness. For example, we are now much more sensitive than before to some of our unintended, but inappropriate, "male chauvinistic phraseology." Unfortunately, we could not make changes because of printer deadlines. They remain as a reminder to us and others of the importance of growth and sensitivity to social change and new awareness.

The ideas in the text and readings are helpful in understanding the cases and classroom exercises, as well as your own experiences. In turn, the cases and exercises can breathe life into the ideas. In this second edition we have tried to clarify and deepen the conceptual frameworks, but our main thrust remains an emphasis on *situational analysis*; i.e., the diagnosis of each behavioral situation as at least partially unique. The conceptual frameworks employed in the text are designed to help you fill in the specifics of any behavioral situation so that you can understand better what is happening. These frameworks provide you with ways of looking at the determinants of behavior, actual behaviors, and the consequences of behavior. Our approach stems implicitly from an "open-systems" orientation.

Skill at diagnosing behavioral situations is achieved only through persistent effort. Thus, we hope that as you go back and forth between concepts, exercises, and cases your skills at using the ideas will develop so that you can begin to look at the actual behavior of yourself and others, first for understanding, and then for action on your part. We suggest that you record (perhaps in a diary) your own insights, comments, and examples, and note questions you may wish to raise in class—in short, *participate* in your own learning, which is, of course, necessary if you are to achieve skill in addition to knowledge.

Participating with us in this way is also useful in that what we hope for you involves importantly the richness of your own personal experiencing. The area to be explored here is simply not yet well enough "mapped" for us to offer you a sure way to negotiate it without your involvement. The field itself is changing rapidly. That makes it all the more exciting for us, in that the frontier for every person, is as Hemingway knew, "A Moveable Feast."

So to pick up the metaphor again, we invite you to take a trip with us and your instructor and your fellow students. Your instructor will be your personal guide, being perhaps more familiar than you may be with such trips and the territory to be explored. Our book will be your reference material and will mark many of the major points of interest. But you and your instructor and other students will see things relevant to you that we have slighted or missed, and thus you may pause for a longer look at a few things than we have done. So it should be. The journey will be what you make of it. We hope you care enough to give a lot of yourself so you will not only learn more knowledge *about* the area but will also gain *skill* in it. We wish you well.

# Acknowledgments

Like all authors, we are keenly aware of the many contributions to our book by others, and we wish to thank those whom we know about and ask those we inadvertently overlook to accept our apologies as well as our thanks.

For the intellectual stimulation and guidance that their writings have provided us, we are grateful to George C. Homans, Fritz J. Roethlisberger, Arthur W. Combs, Donald Syngg, Carl R. Rogers, Abraham Maslow, Rensis Likert, Eric L. Trist, and William B. Wolf.

We thank Harold S. Spear for significant help with the first edition. Peter Vaill also made most useful comments. Dr. James Gatza of the Insurance Institute of America has made helpful suggestions in this revised edition.

For being with us so importantly in the development and testing of the materials in the book in courses at the University of Southern California, we warmly thank the professors and students who unfortunately are too many to be identified by name here, though we do extend special thanks to our colleague, Robert Turrill.

For permission to use the articles included in the book, we thank the authors and publishers listed in the text.

For excellent support and assistance, we thank the people at Prentice-Hall, especially Ann Marie McCarthy, who has been both effective and pleasant to work with, and Mary Allen, who provided many helpful editorial suggestions. We also thank Donald Schaefer and Cecil Yarbrough, who contributed so much to our first edition.

For prompt, accurate, and cheerful typing, we thank Lyndell Martin, Sally Hamer, and Martha Pattison. For permission to take and use the pictures in Chapter 1 we thank Regional Vice President Arthur Brenneman of State Farm Insurance Companies and President Merel Hilliard of the Sonnet Group. For taking those pictures we thank Susan Jones and William Jollitz.

For the cases they have written so that others might learn, we thank all the casewriters, especially Paul R. Lawrence and John A. Seiler whose cases and help with course design were of significant value to us. For permission to use many of the cases in this book, we thank the President and Fellows of Harvard College, and express gratitude to former Dean

George P. Baker, Deans Lawrence Fouraker and George F. F. Lombard, and Mr. Charles N. Gebhard and the late Professor Robert W. Merry for making the permissions possible. Copyright information appears at the beginning of each case.

# CHAPTER 1

# The Entire Organization

The aim in this book is to develop an understanding of behavior in organizations. To do this, it is necessary to achieve a sense of an organization's entirety by studying and, hopefully, grasping the complex interrelatedness of its parts; for the character of any organization, and the variables that determine that character, obviously determine its behavior as an entity and, to a great extent, the behavior of the people within it as well. For example, the organization's character influences the degrees of freedom people within it have to behave, the kinds of opportunities they have, the types of control imposed on them, the nature of their communications, and even the way they feel and think. Identifying the critical parts of an organization and their interrelationships enables us to bring about change and to predict the consequences of change.

We can approach the study of behavior in organizations by relating the results of the four following learning methods, which we will later refer to as the Sherlock (Holmes) Process: (1) observation, (2) intuition or insight, (3) knowledge, and (4) induction and deduction. By *observation* we mean what one sees; by *intuition* or *insight* we mean the ideas and/or feelings that flash into consciousness in connection with what one is observing or recollecting; by *knowledge*, what meanings, information, and facts one has available to draw upon; by *deduction*, that mental process by which one reasons from the general to the specific (All living human beings breathe; this man is a living human being; therefore this man breathes); and by *induction*, the mental process of reasoning from the specific to the general (Every dog I have ever seen wags its tail when happy; therefore all dogs wag their tails when happy).

What is needed here is knowledge, skill, and inquisitiveness. Neither the attempt to grasp a sense of the organization as a whole with interrelated parts nor the effort to understand the climate or character, behaviorally speaking, that diffuses an organization is regularly "taught," probably because these two avenues of approach are difficult and do not readily reduce into a simple set of principles or categories.

Although our emphasis in this book will necessarily be on the more systematic conceptual approaches that embrace both analysis and synthesis, it is important to realize that what we cannot understand by intellectual processes, we must try to understand by intuitive ones. Therefore, we will start with a look at the more neglected approach to emphasize that it is a very real, powerful, and legitimate tool to be used in conjunction with more familiar intellectual processes of systematic analysis.

## THE INTUITIVE APPROACH

We want you to practice gaining a sense of the whole of two distinctly different organizations by looking at some pictures of them. The camera stops time for just an instant and thus allows us to look for clues that may help explain the totality of what is happening both in the individual picture and the entire organization. We will ask you to identify what you think is important in these pictures. Then, as you accumulate your observations, we want you to synthesize them to gain an initial intuitive sensing of each organization's character. Remember, though, what seems valid to you will not necessarily appear so to others.

Begin by looking at the pictures of the parking lots and buildings shown in 1A and 1B. Then (1) jot down briefly the first phrases that come to mind relative to each organization based on what you see, feel, and know; (2) decide what factors in the pictures and yourself evoked your responses; (3) identify important environmental elements relating to space, working conditions, things, and people. What impact will these have on the organization's success and the satisfaction of its members?

People will, of course, react and respond differently. Here are some sample reactions.

1. *Initial impressions.* For Company A words such as the following have been given: stark, dirty, functional, square, unattractive, old, dingy, prosperous, and physical. For Company B: clean, spacious, pleasant, pretty, inviting, new, bright, mental, and potentially exciting.

Company A
Picture 1A.
*a*) Side view

*b*) Front view

*c*) Parking lot

**4**

Company B
Picture 1B.
*a*) Front view

*b*) Back view

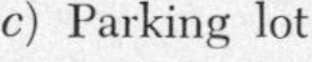

*c*) Parking lot

2. *Factors evoking responses.* A variety of responses were given. For example: Company A is surrounded by cement, asphalt, and telephone poles; B is ringed with grass, a patio, and trees. A is walled in and has small windows; B is more open with more abundant and larger windows. Company A's building has an architectural design dating about 1940 to 1950; B utilizes a modern poured concrete slab construction, and its design dates in the 1960 to 1970 period. Company A's building has some decor in the vertical strip siding bracketing the windows; B has much more glass, external pillars, and large overhangs, all of which combine to give it a more aesthetic appeal. A's building has uneven coloring suggesting fading, which suggests aging; it also has high double doors and few windows, which suggests a factory or warehouse. B has no signs of capability of handling large physical objects, thus appearing to be either an office or a primarily knowledge- and work-oriented company. A Cadillac and new cars in A's parking lot suggest some prosperity, at least for some of its members.

3. *Environmental factors, success, and satisfaction.* Now we will consider in more detail several environmental factors and their possible impact on the success of each organization and the satisfaction of its members.

SPACE. Company A's environment is crowding in all around; it is not crisp, but run-down and unattractive. This may mean that A has a relatively high dollar-per-square-foot cost for space. The relatively few cars in the parking lot indicate it may have a fairly low number of people per square foot. Emphasis appears to be on efficient, functional use of space with little concern for "frills" or aesthetics. B is surrounded by open land and a large parking lot. It probably could expand and may even own contiguous land. This would imply a dollar-rich company, and its generous use of space may imply relatively low dollar cost per square foot of space. The large parking lot indicates a relatively high number of people per square foot of interior space.

WORKING CONDITIONS. Company A may experience an awkward plant layout and cramped space caused by the hypothesized high dollar cost of space. It is probably below average in conditions such as lighting, heat, noise, dirtiness, fumes, and dust. This is reasoned from its age, the assumption that it is a factory, and the hypothesis that emphasis is on getting output with few frills. Company B could be either textured, pleasant, soft, and varied, or plastic, sterile, hard, and monotonous. In terms of space, lighting, cleanliness, noise, and aesthetics, working conditions in Company B are likely to be above-average.

THINGS. It was hypothesized that Company A has relatively few employees per square foot, and further that it has a high dollar cost for equipment. Its rather functional façade, showing no clear sign of company identification, may mean the company does subcontract work for others rather than making products under its own brand name to be marketed directly to consumers. Things inside A would be relatively old, traditional, and inexpensive. The cars, truck, and motorcycles in the parking lot indicate the wide variety of people that work at A. In contrast, the cars in Company B's lot actually appear to be generally of lower market value, with a few exceptions. Company B is likely to have newer, more modern, higher-quality furniture and things inside than is A. It is even possible that some waste will be evident. A tentative hypothesis is that Company B may be more concerned with impressing its public than is A.

PEOPLE. Company A's urban location means that it is probably close to transportation and labor sources. We infer that Company A is more likely to have blue-collar workers and B white-collar workers. A is likely to have a lower proportion of college graduates than B, and B a larger proportion of females than A. Data used in making these inferences include the fact that eight out of nine people in picture 1B are young females. There is a large number of Volkswagens in 1B, which often connotes economy. This may indicate that many of Company B's personnel are young females who are just starting to work or who are married and drive second cars. Additionally, the façade and area of Company B may be more appealing to women. Company A is more likely to appeal to male blue-collar workers who care more about their work than about working conditions and aesthetics. Only tentative inferences can be made about race. Company A's city location would suggest that minorities would be hired, although until recently craft unions have historically been restrictive about minority members. However, A's small size may mean it is nonunion. Tentatively we would infer that some minorities work for A. Company B's area may not be populated by many minorities, but it may be concerned with its public image and social responsibility. Thus, we would expect minorities to make up a small part of B's workforce.

CLIMATE. Company A's assumed small size, no-frills environment, and few signs of concern for status lead us to infer an atmosphere of informality, friendliness, and concern for work. On the other hand, it could also mean the atmosphere is tense and hostile. Its employees, especially if they are skilled as we inferred, may embody and conform to the ideologies of the Protestant Ethic; i.e., they value hard work, frugality, and skill. Men earn respect, and tender emotions are largely hidden. Little attention is likely paid to formal organizational structures because of the small size and assumed informal climate. Workers are very likely self-contained and self-disciplined. The climate in Company B might be either busy, efficient, and boring, or, in contrast, creative, exciting, and synergistic. The nature of the product or service will influence this. We might hypothesize a formal or semiformal atmosphere in B based on its size and decor, although the informal dress of the people in the parking lot and the suburban atmosphere may offset this and encourage an informal atmosphere.

IMPACT ON SUCCESS AND SATISFACTION. Company A probably has poor working conditions. However, it may emphasize efficient, no-frills use of resources, which may be conducive to successful productivity. The sign on Company A indicates that it may be an old company moving to a new location, or it may be a young company that is either failing or succeeding and moving to a new location—we cannot tell which with certainty. People in A may be either quite satisfied or dissatisfied. Although working conditions are poor, these may be offset by higher than average pay and benefits. Also, if the atmosphere is informal, friendly, and close-knit, people may enjoy working there. Further, the small size may be conducive to relatively easier recognition, independence, and achievement. On the other hand, the opposite of these conditions might exist. We would hypothesize that people in A all know each other, and that variations within rank are few, status differentials modest.

Company B appears to be successful. Its attractive appearance and generous use of space denotes success. Its pleasant conditions are likely to be appealing to people. However, satisfaction depends on other factors, including the nature of the work, supervision, pay and benefits, and general atmosphere. Whether the work is boring or interesting, whether the supervision is supportive or stifling, and whether the atmosphere is friendly or repressive will all influence people's feelings. One might hypothesize that a company that shows concern for its physical appearance will also show concern for its people, but this would have to be tested carefully. Because of B's apparent size, we would hypothesize that many people do not know each other and that more differentials exist with respect to both rank and status.

## Companies A and B

Company A is actually two companies, Sonnet Tool and Sonnet Supply. Both are housed in the same building located in Hawthorne, California, which is an industrial-residential area located south of Los Angeles. Today both companies exist separately but under the same president, Dr. Merle Hilliard, who is also the principal owner. The combined companies, housed in separate parts of the same building, together employ about a hundred people. Sonnet Tool specializes in unusual cutting tools but also has a line of standard products that are sold through distributors in every major industrial area in the United States, Canada, Europe, Japan, and Australia. Sonnet Supply numbers among its customers some of Southern California's leading manufacturers of metal and electronic products. It also distributes specialty lines through local distributors west of the Rockies. Combined Sonnet sales in 1972 were $3 million.

Company B is the Westlake Village Regional Office of State Farm Insurance Companies. It is located about thirty-five miles west of Los Angeles. State Farm has been the largest auto insurance company in the United States for the past thirty years. It also is a leading seller of fire and casualty insurance and more recently of life insurance. In 1972 it employed 25,000 people, 11,000 agents, and was organized into twenty-five regional offices throughout the United States. Its corporate headquarters is in Bloomington, Illinois, where the company was started in 1922. The Westlake Regional Office employs 450 people in its office and 315 claims personnel located throughout five counties in Southern California. Over 340 agents are associated with this region. The Westlake Region office was started in 1970, when the Southern California Region was split in two.

You can see that some of our inferences came close to being correct and others did not. Note that we were not trying to reach conclusions. Instead, we were only developing hypotheses that would enable us to determine what further information we needed and what hunches might be tested. The Sherlock Process, which Figure 1 summarizes, is an accumulating process. It encourages us to get progressively better "fixes" on the nature of the organization being studied. It helps us get a feel for the probable error, or zone of uncertainty and unknowability, based on information at hand. Thus, the process assists in deciding what further kinds and amounts of information are needed to answer the questions we have.

Several pages of pictures of Companies A and B follow.[1] Do they resolve some of the questions you raised? Do they suggest new questions? We suggest you first go through the pictures rather quickly. Then (1) jot down briefly the words or phrases that come to mind and then ask why these reactions were evoked. As you look, also ask yourself which company you would prefer to work for and why. (2) Note again the relevance of space, working conditions, things, people, and activities and note their probable effect on success and satisfaction.

There are really no right and wrong answers to these questions, although some hypotheses may be better supported than others. In later chapters we will develop ways of thinking that will help in selecting, interpreting, and relating data to the questions. But for now we are more interested in your continuing with experiencing the Sherlock Process in a

[1]The pictures used in this chapter were obtained through the cooperation of both the Sonnet Companies and State Farm Insurance Companies. The deductions in this chapter are the authors', not those of the companies. Remember, too, deductions should not be thought of as facts. The photographs were taken by Mr. William Jollitz (Sonnet) and Ms. Susan Jones (State Farm).

9 comparative analysis. We return to the pictures comparing companies page by page. To provide a few examples of data that exist, there are a few observations that might be made on page 28–29.

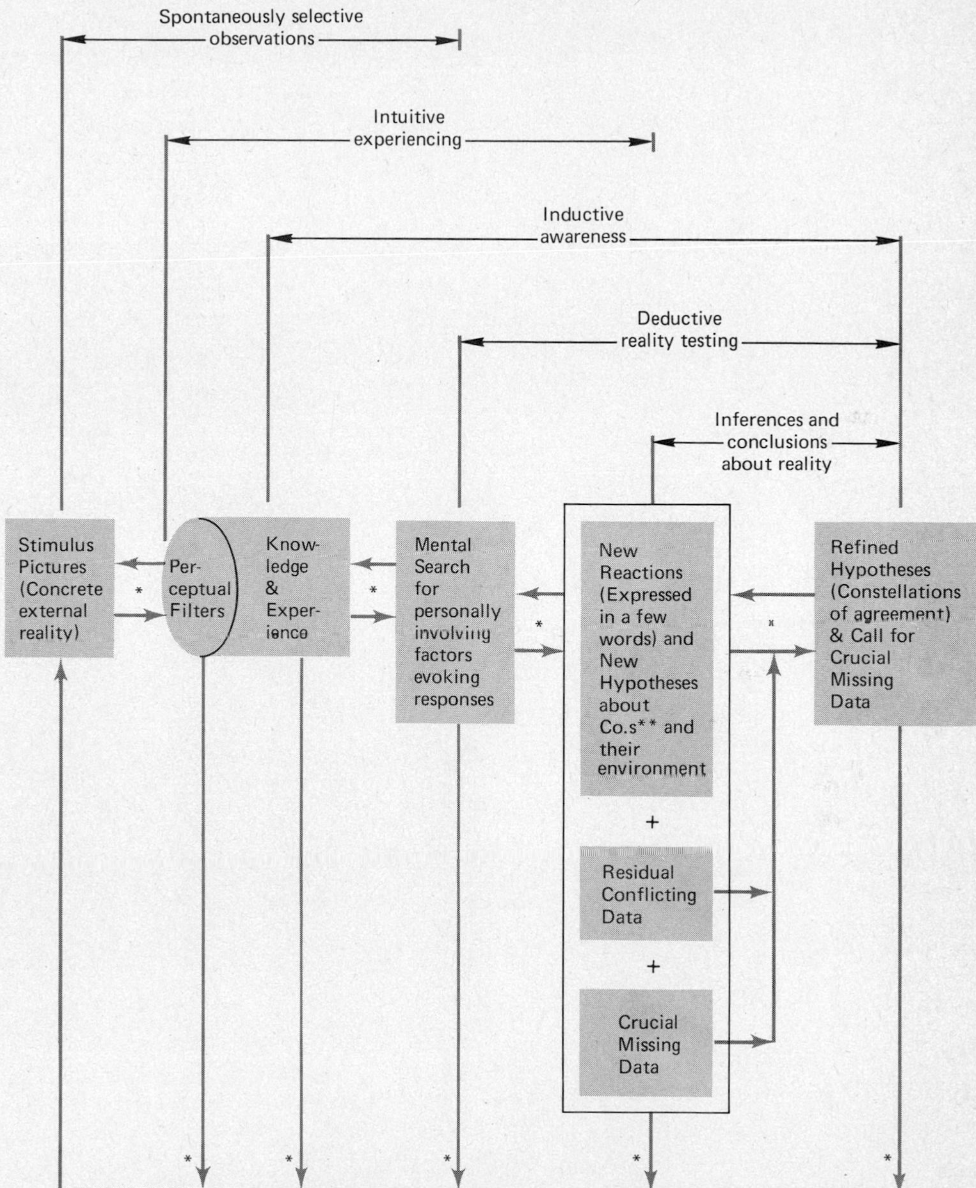


Notes: * A complex recycling of sub-processes continue until ambiguities, incongruities, and matches between what is expected and found reach tolerably low levels.

** For example, how factors such as space, working conditions, facial expressions, behaviors and things affect each company's productivity and worker satisfaction.

**Figure 1** Development of Refined Hypotheses and Constellations of Agreement through the Sherlock Process

## Company A

Picture 2A. *a*) President's Office

*b*) President's Door to Office

*c*) Marketing Vice President's Office

Picture 2B.
*a*) Regional Vice President's Office

*b*) Regional Vice President's Office

*c*) Personnel Manager's Office

Picture 3A. *a*) Shop Meeting

*b*) Coffee Time

*c*) Coffee Break

*d*) Coffee—Women's Room

**13**

*a*) Lunch Break

*b*) Lunch

*c*) Lunch Recreation

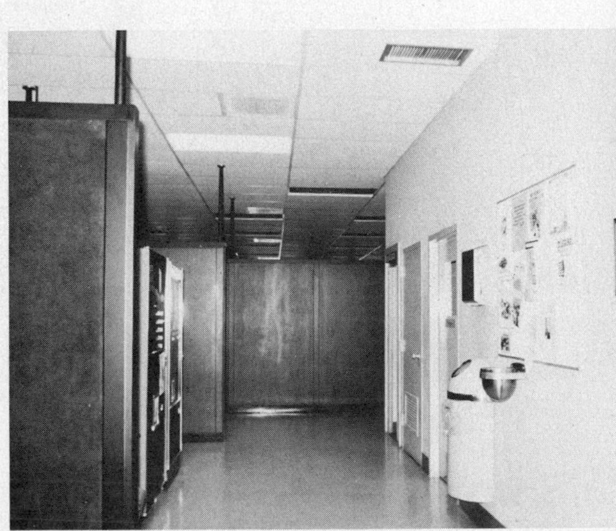

*d*) Snack Center

Picture 4A. *a*) Production Planning

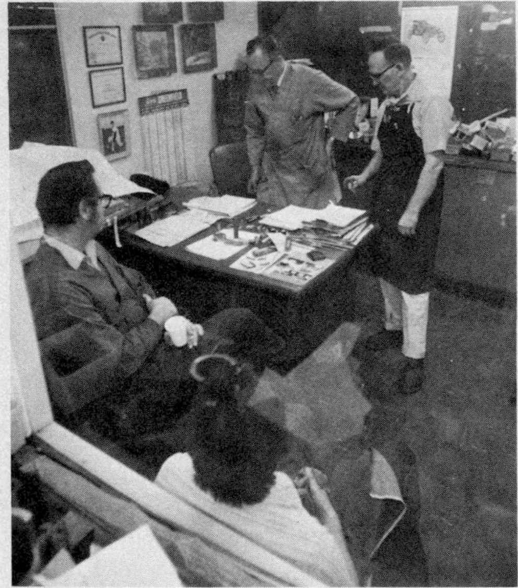

*b*) President

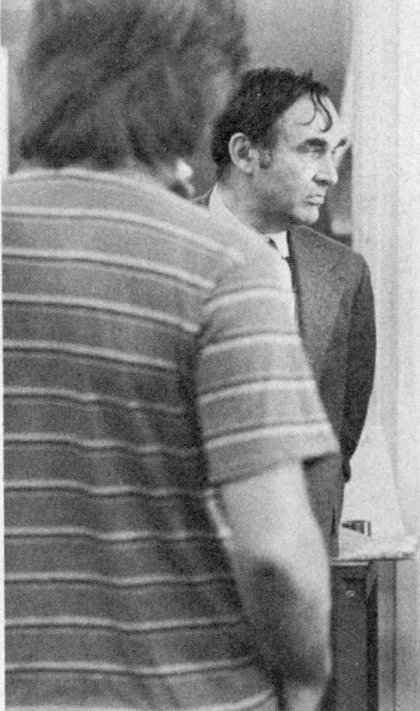

*c*) President and Vice President, Manufacturing

a) Two Managers

Picture 4B. b) Office

c) Regional Staff Meeting

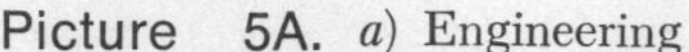
Picture 5A. *a*) Engineering

*b*) Accounting

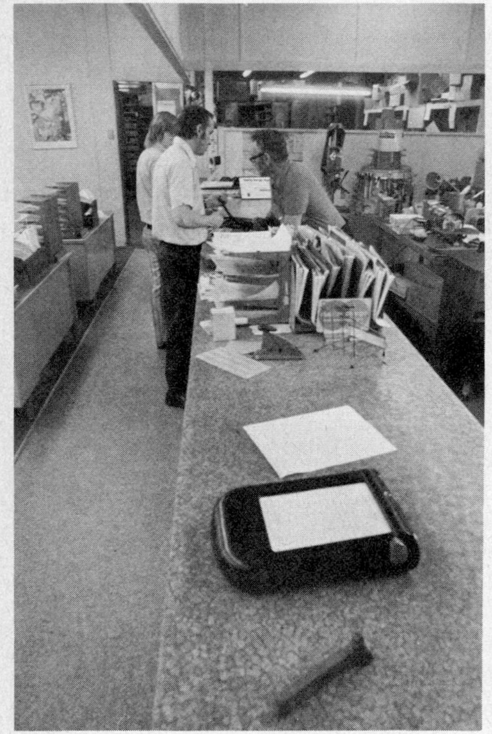

*c*) Sonnet Supply Pickup Counter

Picture 5B. *a*) Computer

*b*) Reception

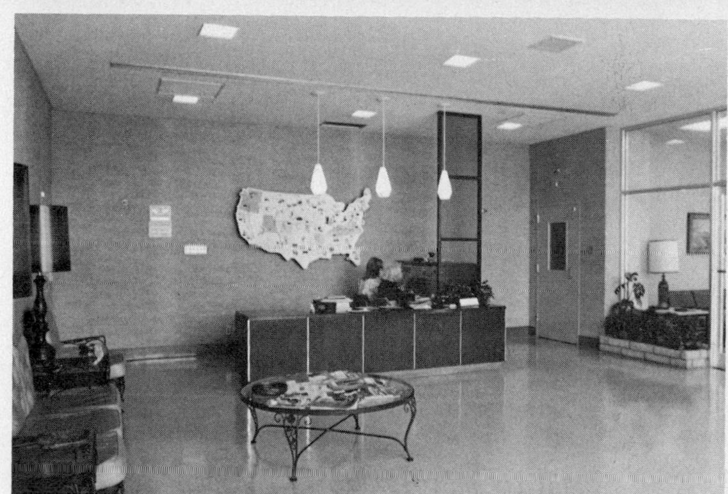

*c*) Accounting

Picture 6A. *a*) Parts Storage

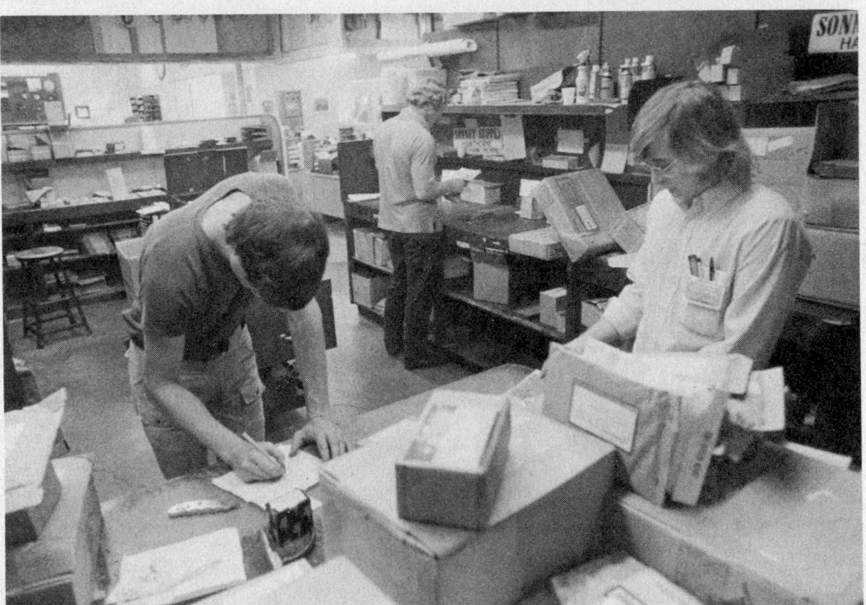

*b*) Shipping and Receiving

Picture 6B. *a*) Current Files

*b*) Non-Current Files

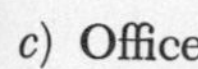

*c*) Office

Picture 7A. *a*) At Work

*b*) At Work

*c*) At Work

Picture 7B. *a*) Work Management Control Office

*b*) Work Management Control Office

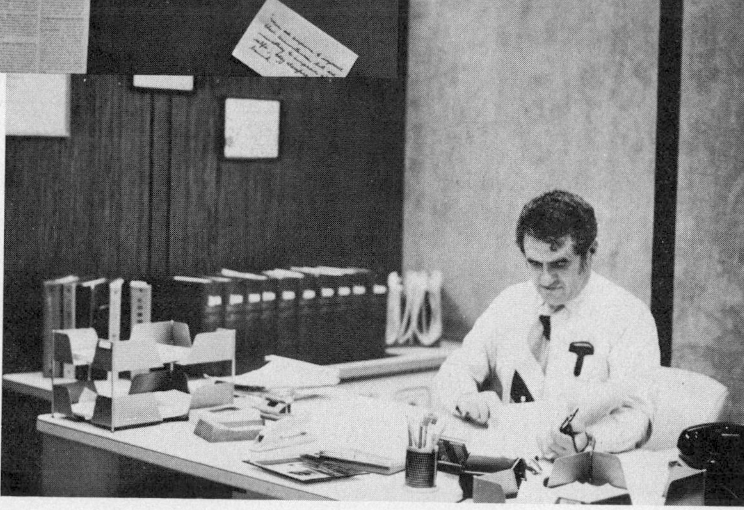

*c*) A Manager

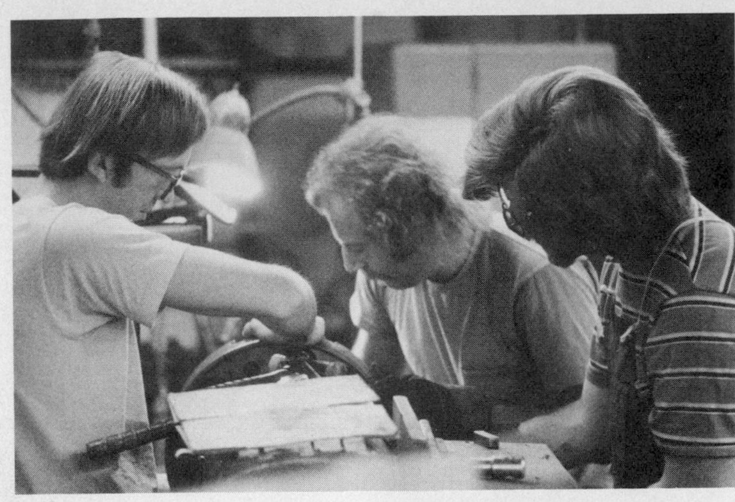

Picture 8A. *a*) At Work

*b*) At Work

*c*) At Work

Picture 8B. *a*) At Work

*b*) At Work

*c*) Personnel Reception

*d*) At Work

Picture 9A. *a*) Work Discussion

*b*) Production Shop

Picture 9B.
*a*) At Work

*b*) At Work

*c*) At Work

Picture 10A. *a*) Xeroxing

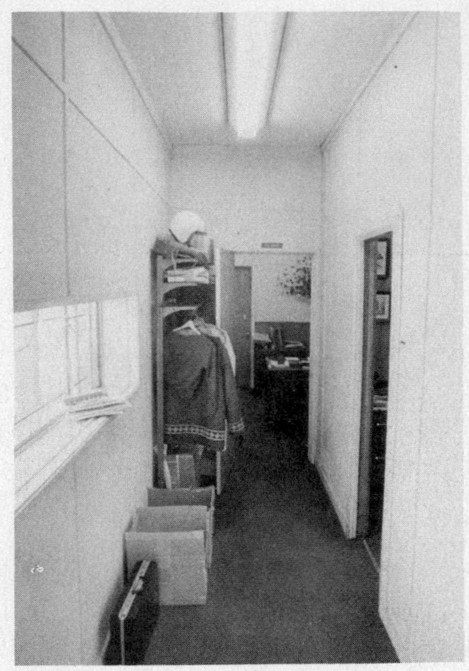

*b*) Front Hall

*c*) Sonnet Supply Office

Picture 10B. *a*) At Work

*b*) Day's End

*c*) Interior Hall

STATUS. In picture 1C notice the Cadillac parked in the first spot under a cover. Whose car is it? (You are right if you hypothesized the president.) What status differences do you note between the offices of Company B's regional vice-president and personnel manager (pictures 2B)? (Example: the VP has a couch; the PM does not. The VP has a wooden desk and cushioned chairs; the PM has a metal desk and plastic chairs.) In picture 9B notice the three different types of chairs. One is a heavily cushioned armchair, a second is a smaller armchair, and a third has no arms. Each type of chair is assigned to particular job-level classifications. You can partially tell a person's status by seeing his chair!

THINGS. Compare the pictures in 2A and 2B. Note that there are many more in the office of A's president than in that of B's top manager. The variety and kind in A's office is quite different than the landscape in B's. (Closer scrutiny would reveal that some of those hanging in A's office are by his wife.) Do these differences suggest anything about either the men or their companies? For a sharp contrast, note the calendar in picture 8A. Notice the wall hangings in the marketing manager's office in 2A. Is there the beginning of a pattern relating it to the modern pictures in the president's office? Family pictures suggest something about a person's values. Notice them in pictures 4A, 2B, and 9B. Notice the pictures of two men in 4Bc. Does this suggest an emphasis on past company leaders?[2] If true, this suggests something about the age of the company and its identification and concern with its history. Compare the notices on the walls in 4A and the bulletin board in 3B. Does the degree of orderliness of each fit other patterns in each organization? Notice the quantity and type of wall hangings in each organization and the way they are hung. Given the existing patterns, it would be relatively easy to pick out those belonging to each organization even if they were out of context. (Note how much can be seen just by looking for one type of thing such as wall pictures. We will not belabor other things to the same extent, but hope our few examples suggest the richness of data available for those who seek it.)

The computer in 5B and the size of the accounting department in 5B compared with 5A says something about the quantity of data handled by each organization and their technology for doing so. Although too little data is available to suggest a firm hypothesis, it appears that the equipment in B tends to be newer and more abundant than in A.

Compare 3A and 3B. The visual evidence in 3A suggests that coffee may be free in Company A. Also, notice the number of clocks in B. Do you see any in A? Does this have any meaning?

SPACE. Notice how the desks are organized in A and B. In 5A and 10A desks face different directions. Do you see this in B? How do you account

[2]Note the *assumptions* here: (1) that the men are associated with the company; (2) that they are past rather than current members; (3) that they are leaders. These appear reasonable, but nevertheless they are assumptions, not fact.

for these differences; do they have any meaning? Does the order of desk arrangement and machine arrangement fit with other factors to form a pattern? What about "clutter"? Notice the contrast in the halls of 10A and 10B. Notice pictures 3B to 6B. Is there a pattern of how things are placed in space?

Notice in Company B where supervisors appear to be in space compared with subordinates. They are in back. What significance, if any, does this have? What does this use of space communicate? Notice the marketing manager's "space" in 2A. The relatively small office and few chairs may mean that much of his contact work is done outside his office, whereas his office is used primarily for paperwork. Notice that in Company B relatively few supervisors are in enclosed offices. What does this infer about the company and its approach to supervision? What does the openness of space utilization and the way in which it is utilized tell about each company?

PEOPLE. Notice the contrast in age and race in Company A. What differences might they make for employee communications, interactions, satisfaction, and behavior? What likely differences and similarities of values might be encountered?

Notice in 3B that men and women sit separately. Does this suggest a pattern? (In fact, the pattern is frequent, though not absolute.) Notice also the variety of dress and appearance. Would you be surprised to see some of the people from A working at B? Why? In which company would you expect to find the greater variety of dress and appearance? Does this fit other variables to form a pattern? What significance do the patterns have, do you suppose?

Now that you have observed and reacted to considerable data, indicate the degree to which you associate each company with the bipolar adjectives in Figure 2. Mark "A" in the space seeming most appropriate for Company A, and "B" for Company B. Now, count and note the number of scale divisions separating A from B for each adjective pair. Second, circle the more extreme rating (A or B, versus neutrality) for the eight to twelve scales showing the largest differences. Do these adjectives capture some of the "character" of the companies *for you*? Does this process indicate any patterns for you? We hope that you now have a good feeling for the character of each organization.

The pictures we have seen have provided us with abundant data from which we have drawn or suggested a variety of inferences, some probably sound and some less than sound. We are sure you realize that both the data selected and the inferences made are only a *sample* of what could be available and utilized. We hope you questioned some of the inferences we made, and thought of some that we did not. Our purpose, again, has not been to analyze each company exhaustively but rather to illustrate the process of sensing the wholeness and uniqueness of organizations. By now perhaps you can see how many variables in each company fit together to form the unified whole.

| | 1 | 2 | 3 | 4 | 5 | 6 | |
|---|---|---|---|---|---|---|---|
| Valuable | ____ | ____ | ____ | ____ | ____ | ____ | Worthless |
| Slow | ____ | ____ | ____ | ____ | ____ | ____ | Fast |
| Tight | ____ | ____ | ____ | ____ | ____ | ____ | Loose |
| Complex | ____ | ____ | ____ | ____ | ____ | ____ | Simple |
| Interesting | ____ | ____ | ____ | ____ | ____ | ____ | Boring |
| Unpleasant | ____ | ____ | ____ | ____ | ____ | ____ | Pleasant |
| Not demanding | ____ | ____ | ____ | ____ | ____ | ____ | Demanding |
| Control Oriented | ____ | ____ | ____ | ____ | ____ | ____ | Expression oriented |
| Nonthreatening | ____ | ____ | ____ | ____ | ____ | ____ | Threatening |
| Orderly | ____ | ____ | ____ | ____ | ____ | ____ | Chaotic |
| Tense | ____ | ____ | ____ | ____ | ____ | ____ | Relaxed |
| Obsolete | ____ | ____ | ____ | ____ | ____ | ____ | Current |
| Formal | ____ | ____ | ____ | ____ | ____ | ____ | Informal |
| Personal | ____ | ____ | ____ | ____ | ____ | ____ | Impersonal |
| Growth-oriented | ____ | ____ | ____ | ____ | ____ | ____ | Static |
| Not well regarded by others | ____ | ____ | ____ | ____ | ____ | ____ | Well regarded by others |
| Friendly | ____ | ____ | ____ | ____ | ____ | ____ | Unfriendly |
| Successful | ____ | ____ | ____ | ____ | ____ | ____ | Unsuccessful |
| A place I'd like to work | ____ | ____ | ____ | ____ | ____ | ____ | Not a place I'd like to work |
| Dissatisfied employees | ____ | ____ | ____ | ____ | ____ | ____ | Satisfied employees |
| Resistant to change | ____ | ____ | ____ | ____ | ____ | ____ | Not resistant to change |
| **Fill in other characteristics** | ____ | ____ | ____ | ____ | ____ | ____ | |
| **important to you** | ____ | ____ | ____ | ____ | ____ | ____ | |

**Figure 2** Character Analysis of Organizations A and B

Quickly (3 seconds each) place one mark for *each* organization ("A" and "B") on *each* line at the location you think most appropriately describes the organization.

Now that you have experienced something of the process we are exploring, we will turn to some ways of thinking that may help us to become more skillful in using it.

## A SYSTEMS APPROACH

### Levels of Analysis

A key perceptual problem in observing behavior in organizations is knowing what to look at or for. You can start by trying to see the "whole" organization, or you can begin by looking at small parts of various sizes and configurations. Whether you go from whole to part or part to whole is unimportant. It's probably a good idea to practice doing both many different ways.

To understand the whole you must reduce what you observe into conceptual parts or levels. This can be done by observing *entities* in their *environments*. By entity we mean something that has separate and distinct existence and either objective or conceptual reality. Examples of entities in this sense include individuals, groups, organizations, and even societies.[3] Using the concept of entities along with the interactions that occur between entities, we can break whole organizations into the following *levels of analysis*:

1. the individual
2. person-person (dyad) or person-person-person (triad) (interpersonal)
3. small groups of persons
4. more than one group relating to the other groups (intergroup)
5. a total organization
6. the larger society

### Multidimensionality

Of course, focusing on a level of analysis only partially solves our problem of observing and comprehending our world. Each of us experiences a variety of internal needs and feelings as we try to observe, com-

[3]Note: Groups and organizations are not *concrete behaving* entities. Only individuals within them behave. We should remember that, if and when we ascribe human characteristics to groups and organizations, we may be either consciously or unconsciously reifying or "making abstractions human," which they are not. Although groups and organizations acquire a "climate," they do not behave. Only people do.

prehend, and cope with our worlds. Each of us wants to be "ourself"—i.e., we want to express our feelings, abilities, and beliefs in consonance with the way we see ourselves. Most of us also want to relate to certain other people. We like them and want them to like and appreciate us. We want to gain their respect and belong to certain groups. Frequently, we also need to accomplish tasks, and most of us feel at least some need to achieve a degree of success in our job endeavors. Most of us also have a need to learn and grow as human beings. We want to experience new places, people, ideas, and activities; we try to gain more competence and dominion and satisfaction in our world as we experience it. Most of us also experience an internal need to conform to many of the important ideals of our society. We want to be "good citizens" and worthy members of society. Virtually all people's internal needs and overt behavior are influenced by cultural values and customs.

These many dimensions of internal experiencing sometimes engender conflict within us. We can experience this conflict both within and between the dimensions themselves. For example, you may see yourself as a "good student" and as a "friendly person." If a very good former school chum calls you to say he is visiting in town for just the evening while you are preparing for the final examination in a borderline course, you may experience some conflict within yourself about whether you want more to be a good friend or a good student. This same example illustrates a potential conflict between your need to be yourself and your need to have friends and belong to groups.

We will have more to say about the multidimensionality of behavior in our final chapter. You may want to read it before you proceed with the rest of the book. Our only reason for mentioning these concepts now is to warn you of something you already know; namely, that our experiencing of our worlds can be very confusing and complex. One important reason for this is our multiple internal needs and how they influence our observations of our world and our decisions about how to cope with it. The problem of optimally integrating our various needs in confusing, complicated situations is central to most of our lives.

## Systems and Environments

Our objectives here ultimately are to learn how to be better able to observe what goes on around us, comprehend it, make predictions, decide what to do, and finally, to act. We have suggested that it may be helpful to focus on certain levels of analysis, and we have warned that making our observations is made more complex by our multidimensional internal needs. Now we will suggest the value of first focusing on the whole of a situation and then sensing the interrelationships of the multidimensions and multilevels of our world.[4] In other words, it is useful to take a systems approach to observing and understanding.

By *system* we mean a set of interdependent and interrelated elements existing in an environment. We assume that each organization is a functioning system; i.e., a group of parts united by some form of regular interaction or interdependence in such a way that they form a unified whole. The word *system* is applied to varied phenomena—mechanical, business, political, and solar. We will use it mainly in reference to social systems, but organizations can be thought of as including other subsystems, such as work-flow structures, authority-power structures, communications structures, reward structures, and role structures. All of these, functioning together, constitute what we call *organization.* The concept of system is crucial to our understanding of organizational behavior. It emphasizes the interrelatedness of parts and suggests the importance of interpreting an individual part only in context of the whole.

What constitutes a system is a matter of definition. You, or anyone else, can define the boundaries of a particular system. You could make the assumption that a particular system is self-contained and is not particularly affected by its environment. This is called a closed system. Because no social system of any importance is closed, we will be concerned only with open systems. These are open to inputs and influence from their environments, and in return produce outputs that flow into and influence the environment.

We make the assumption that behavioral entities partially determine their own behavior, and their behavior is partially determined by their environments. Thus, to understand behavior, it is essential that we observe and understand as well as we can both the entity and its environment. Environment includes the surroundings of the entity. Some of the environment is important, or relevant, and some is nonrelevant to the behavior of a particular entity. Further, some of the environment is immediate, or within view of the entity, and some is more distant and even remote, or beyond immediate view. Thus we can distinguish conceptually between different parts of the environment as shown in Figure 3. These concepts can serve as guides for questioning the relevance of what we see in an environment, given some system definition; change the system definition and we change the environment!

Environmental elements include space, time, things, conditions, entities, behavior, and events. Because there are so many, the classification in Figure 3 takes on central importance. If you are a manager in the personnel department you may not be concerned that the chief engineer is talking with the president about the design of a new heating system,

[4]This is the familiar "gestalt" approach, which suggests that it is also useful to study whole patterns of behavior as well as discrete elements, under the assumption that the system as a whole is more and distinctly different from the mere sum of its parts.

| | Relevant | Nonrelevant |
|---|---|---|
| Immediate | | |
| Intermediate | | |
| Remote | | |

**Figure 3** The Environment

but you might be quite concerned if they are talking about the design for a new building that will include your department. One is more relevant to your behavior than the other. If you live in California an earthquake in Nicaragua may seem remote and relatively nonrelevant. A prediction made by a mystic in California that an earthquake would occur on a specified date might be immediate but nonrelevant. A similar prediction made by a noted scientist might take on more relevance. You can easily see the variety of possibilities that can fit in each of the matrix boxes.

In observing and assessing the impact of environment on a system we should know both what kinds of elements to look for and what different kinds of general environments exist. We will explore key specific environmental elements in detail in Chapter 2. In order to develop a simple way of identifying the kinds of relevant environments, we suggest that you note three key "qualities," which are caused by the typical behaviors by individuals alone or as members of entities inhabiting the system environment.

**Some Important Qualities of Systems Environments**

1. Hostile ............ Supportive
2. Static ............ Dynamic
3. Certain ............ Uncertain

To sense the "whole" environment and its impact on a system you will have to know what "qualities" to look for, decide or observe how they relate to one another, and then assess their impact on and relationship to the system under observation. Observing data that will help make this kind of assessment will help in identifying and understanding the assertive, adaptive, and coping behavior of any system. This kind of thinking process also can be useful for determining different, and hopefully more effective, ways of behaving and how such behavior might be induced.

Our assumption is that each individual partially determines his own behavior and that his behavior is partially determined by his environment. So it is with other social entities such as groups, organizations, and even societies. Thus, to understand why an entity behaves as it does, we must know something about both the person and his environment.

## Organizational Character

Individuals and social entities behave so as to cope with their environment in ways that maximize their own need satisfaction and the achievement of their goals. Thus, patterns of behavior for coping with opportunities and problems arising in the environment are developed. These patterns, plus the motivation and reasoning behind them, are different for each person and social entity. The differences produce what can be referred to as an enduring organizational character (analagous to personality at the individual level).

Another important assumption we make is that each organization is unique; i.e., it has a personality or character of its own, just as do human beings.[5] Each entity is unique. In the two companies we just observed we found differences in physical facilities, things, people, the use of space, and other variables. The combination of these and other elements contributed to very different organizations, each with its unique "character."

In order to heighten awareness and understanding of a total system with its unique character, it is helpful to seek information about its important parts. By looking at these parts, obtaining relevant information about them, responding to them, and interpreting their meaning based on our past and present experience, we can often get a feeling or intuitive sensing for the totality of the whole system. This process does not enable us to achieve a systematic understanding of the whole, but it can be useful in developing *working hypotheses* for further attempts to understand the organization more completely. By *working hypotheses* we mean tentative explanations and understandings that can be examined as new data and interpretations are gathered.

One important step that can be used in the analytical process of diagnosing organizational character is that of looking for *constellations of agreement* among our observations and inferences. Where the in-

[5]We are indebted to Professor William B. Wolf, who first introduced us to many of the concepts and techniques used in this section. See his *Management: Readings Toward a General Theory* (Belmont, Calif.: Wadsworth Publishing Co., Inc., 1964), pp. 315–26, part of which is reprinted in this book.

ferences from one variable are supported by inferences from other variables, this reinforcement, or constellation of agreement, may reasonably lead to a tentative assumption that the inferences are useful. (Note: not true, just useful; i.e., they continue to be working hypotheses.)

It is equally important to identify those variables that do not appear to fit. While the clusters of agreeing variables can serve to reinforce our conclusions, the *conflicting* ones help warn that more data or thought is needed for more accurate understanding.

Something we have already strongly implied but want to stress is the *danger in the process we are describing*. Sherlock Holmes was often conveniently correct in his conclusions, but the same, alas, cannot be said for the rest of us. This is why we must be aware of the *tentative and incomplete nature of our understanding of organizational character*, and why we should defer judgment and resist assuming that our observations and deductions have led us to "the answer." This danger is why we need to be as aware of the *conflicting variables* as we are of the agreeing ones. Although the process is tentative and uncertain, we are convinced that our observational skills, our knowledge, and our ability to reason can all be improved with practice. And the improvement, in turn, will enhance our ability to diagnose organizational character and behavior even more skillfully.

As we practice sensing the whole of several organizations by inferring from partial data about them, you may see that the process has a double utility. First, it permits us to seek constellations of reinforcing inferences *within* a given company. Second, it permits us to become sensitive to crucial differences *between* companies. This is important, for it helps us to judge better the usefulness of those managerial suggestions that are offered as "answers" for all companies. Such suggestions must be evaluated in terms of a specific setting, and our sensitivity to the differences between companies may protect us against accepting the seductive simplicity of the newest managerial panacea. Consider the suggestion that good physical working conditions are essential for employee satisfaction. Is it valid? In some companies the opportunity to engage in interesting and challenging work with attractive people may more than offset poor working conditions.

The process of looking for similarities and differences between specific behavioral situations is important enough for us to give it a name. We will call it *comparative analysis*.

## SUMMARY

The process explored in this chapter should be useful to you in furthering your understanding of organizations and behavior in them. Yet it should be clear to you that it is an uncertain process at this stage in our treatment of it. In Chapter 2, we will consider in some detail a more systematic way of thinking about the parts. But even then the "reality" of the whole of an organization will elude us to some extent, because

1. *Opportunities to observe* and gather data may be limited.
2. *Awareness of and sensitivity to sensory data* may need heightening.
3. *Feelings* about the phenomena observed may color the meanings attached to them.
4. *Knowledge* relevant to the observations may be incomplete.
5. *Skill in inferring and deducing*, and in perceiving constellations of agreement, may be limited.
6. *Familiarity with a way of thinking* that relates parts to a system may be insufficiently developed.

These limitations are admittedly irritating, and they must be overcome if we are to become more competent; but the point of this book is precisely that it permits you to confront many of your needs in order to achieve better understandings. Although you will not find absolute truth, you can increase your awareness of, feeling for, knowledge about, and familiarity with behavior in organizations. All of these are of a piece and thus cannot be neatly separated.[6] The kind of learning they involve is often accompanied by feelings of uncertainty that are best expected and accepted as reasonable, for accepting them, though not very pleasant, is more likely to lead to growth than finding ways to avoid them. Ours is, after all, a search for human skill. And skill in dealing with the real world takes practice and talent and tenacity.

[6]See "Personal Perception, Involvement, and Response," pp. 59.

# CHAPTER 2

# Background Factors for Behavior

## Introduction

In the previous chapter, you looked at pictures of two organizations. We considered with you the importance of many variables that could be observed or known about to help sense the overall pattern—the "whole"—of an organization. Yet for the most part, we excluded discussion of behavior itself, as we will do in this chapter also. To employ a simple metaphor, we want to focus still further upon those variables involved in producing a play up to the point in time when the curtain goes up. Then in Chapter 3 we will turn more directly to actual behavior.

The aim of this chapter is to refine the largely intuitive approach we used in Chapter 1 by identifying those variables that are of significant importance in most organizations. In Chapter 1 we were concerned mainly with observation, intuition, knowledge, and thought process. In this chapter we set forth a vocabulary that helps us identify and discuss some of the significant environmental elements that make up an organizational setting. We will discuss these categories and their interrelationships with others. In short, we will be developing a more orderly and systematic *way of thinking* about them which can enhance your capacity to make use of the process you have just experienced.

We will call these important variables *background factors*, to emphasize their separateness from behavior itself and to permit easy reference to all of them with a single phrase. You might tentatively think of the background factors as given, and of behavior as what is to be explained. In a book on marketing, your focus would be directed toward the product and customer, whereas in a book on behavior, those variables become background factors. Each of the background factors we discuss could be the main subject of an entire book, of course. In this book, however, the area to be studied and understood is behavior. The background factors are considered only because they determine or influence behavior.

### Sensing the Whole

We begin with the general assumption that all of an organization's background factors will fit together in a unified system (even though we know full well they do not always do so). Thus we will be looking for what "fits," while we also keep an eye out for what does not fit. The latter often will help us explore more deeply for better explanations and understanding. We will hypothesize that (1) a given external environment and (2) a given organization of people, things, space, and activities will all fit into one unified (if imperfectly integrated) whole.

So we can reason back and forth between 1 and 2, and 2 and 1. If you know about the environment, you can predict about the organization. If you know about the organization, you can predict its internal variables. You might think of this as two kinds of threads woven, woof and warp, into a fabric with occasional irregularities.

## THE EXTERNAL ENVIRONMENT

What is inside and what is outside an organization is sometimes ambiguous and must be categorized arbitrarily. Organizations do not have skins like people, and the line between them and their environments is a shifting one. But it is useful to accept an approximation if it gives us greater clarity, and so we will offer one way to think about what is "outside" an organization. (Thus, this *way of thinking* is a *tool* that is better than none—a useful guide even though not a perfectly accurate description of *reality*.)

Because what we conceive of as "outside" an organization is so vast and complex, it is impractical to discuss it in any detail. And we prefer to assume that you will know enough of what we mean by "external background factors" to make any oversimplified detailed discussion of each superfluous. But take a good look at the left side of Figure 1. Think about how the *industry* to which an organization "belongs" determines many aspects of that organization. Hence, just knowing the industry involved can provide important tentative inferences about the organization (pro-

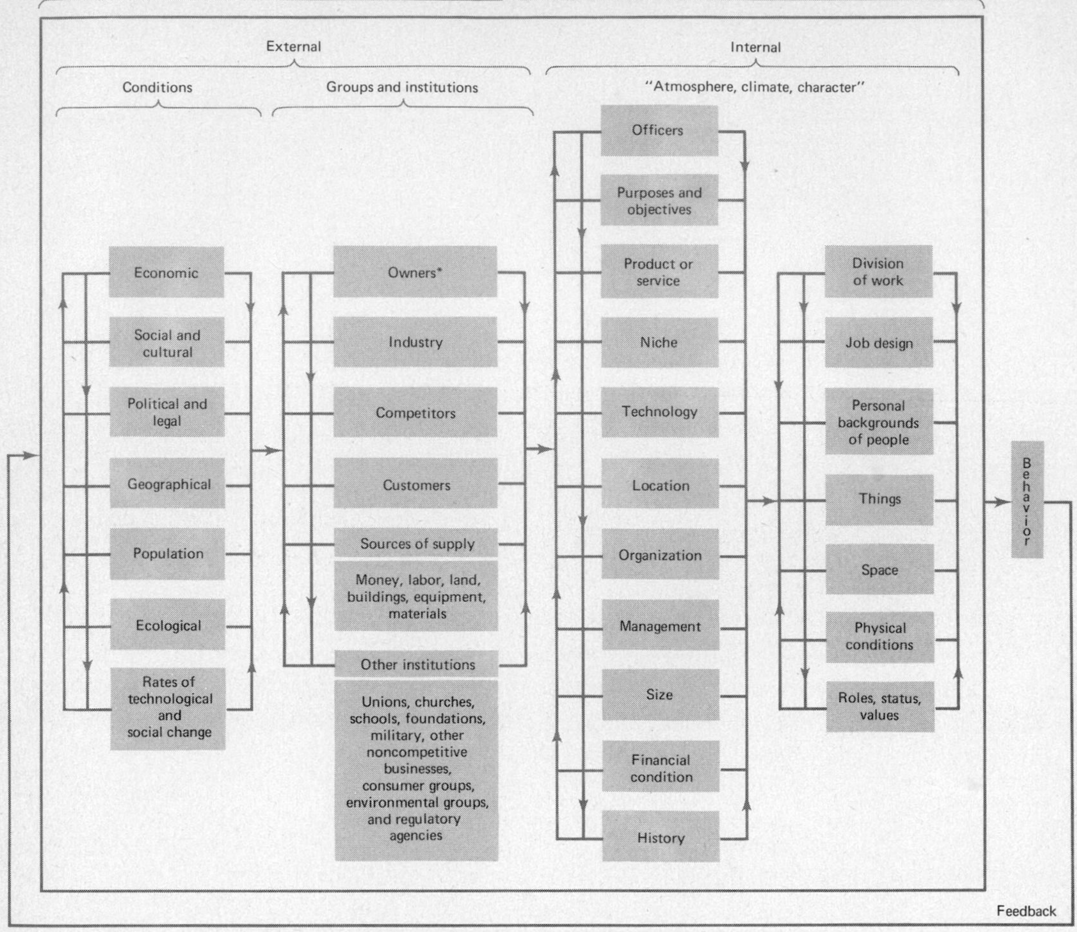


**Figure 1** External and Internal Background Factors

*Here is a perfect example of how the neatness of concepts can distort what is real. The owners may be considered outside the organization, say, in the instance of General Motors Corporation. But an owner may be the manager of his organization, as is the case with the Sonnet Companies. Our chart separates the owning from the running (to be seen later), which is conceptually useful but arbitrary.

vided, of course, you know something about the industry itself). For example, if one were to consider banking as an industry, it would be helpful to know that banking institutions operate within complex legal restraints, are necessarily concerned with accuracy and reliability, have much detailed work to accomplish, have only recently moved from clerical to computer methods, have often selected their chief executives from outside their organizations (because centralized decision making in the past permitted little opportunity for growth from within), and have attracted career employees who often put a high value upon security, stability, and social status. Simply knowing these things would help you explore further any specific bank, because virtually all of them share the industry's situation to some extent.

We will now turn to a much more careful consideration of internal background factors and will occasionally relate them to external ones. It would be good if you would now look at the right side of Figure 1 and then refer back to it as we proceed. The whole of the figure shows both the internal and external background factors and their relationships.

## THE INTERNAL ENVIRONMENT

### Officers

The "people at the top" may be the most important influence of the many that shape an organization's character. These people may be the owners, or the top managers, or both. General Motors is owned by thousands of shareholders, none of whom holds a controlling percentage of G.M. stock. In such an organization, top managers are likely to have more impact than owners. In a smaller organization, on the other hand, or in any organization where a few people own a major portion or all of the stock, owners may have considerable impact, even though they may not be the top managers.

Those responsible for the initiation, development, and survival of an organization constantly monitor its environment and decide how to change it and/or adapt to it. Their decisions vitally affect the organization. Some of these include the following: (1) What industry the organization will enter; (2) within the industry, how it will compete (e.g., quality, price, depth and breadth of product line or service); (3) where it will be located; (4) how large it will be; (5) the kind of organization it will be (e.g., proprietorship, partnership, closed or public corporation); (6) how aggressive it will be in various areas (such as price competition, product innovation, and promotion); and (7) who will be the top managers. All of these decisions have to be made in the context of the relationship between the environment and the personal orientation of the entrepreneurs involved.

Organizations often seem to have a philosophy, just as individuals do. Of course, organizations per se are nonhuman; it is the people within them—normally, the owners and/or top managers—who generate the organizational philosophy. The objectives, values, and personal philosophies of these people will be reflected throughout the organizations they direct. Thus, in order to understand any organization, it is helpful to know who the top managers are and something about them.

## Purpose and Objectives

Normally, an organization cannot survive and prosper unless it fulfills some useful *purpose* in its environment. That purpose is very largely determined by external environmental factors, such as economic, political, and social conditions, the tastes and needs of customers, the availability of resources, and the number and quality of competitors, to mention a few. The *product* or *service* that an organization offers in order to fulfill its purposes and achieve its objectives is in large part determined by the external factors mentioned above. In turn, the characteristics of the product or service pervasively influence the entire organization and its component factors. For example, think how many differences it makes whether an organization is a bank, or a grocery store, or a shoe manufacturing company, or an oil transportation company. Think what a difference each makes in terms of people, space, things, and activities.

To understand any organization, then, it is important to know its purpose and how it is influenced by and fits in with its environment. Many business leaders see their prime objective as making the most profit possible for the owners, while others seek to "optimize" their profits given other goals, while still others seek only enough profit to satisfy the owners. (Of course, there are other organizations, such as government bodies, universities, philanthropic organizations, and the like, that are nonprofit.) Most organizations have a hierarchy of overlapping objectives including such goals as profit, growth, survival, civic contributions, and innovation. It is the way these are ranked and interrelated with an organization that is significant, because such rankings are important determinants of how decisions tend to be made when conflicting values and goals are at stake. The relative importance of each goal differs from organization to organization and, from time to time, within a given organization.

## Niche and Technology

Within each industry, each organization tries in some way to find a *niche* that distinguishes it from its competitors. It may do this in the products or services it offers (price, quantity, quality, location, convenience, service, etc.) or in the way it offers them. Noting the ways in which an organization attempts to distinguish itself is useful, both for understanding its place in its environment (and predicting its chances of survival and prosperity) and for understanding the impact these differences may have on the people, things, activities, and space within the organization.

*Technology*, to a large extent, can be related to the industry a company chooses to enter. By *technology* we mean the knowledge, skill, and things required to accomplish specific kinds of work. The technology required in a bank differs greatly from that required in a grocery store, or a chemical plant, or an insurance company. Can you see how many internal factors are influenced significantly by the technological requirements of the organization? Consider the impact on the people hired, the things and space required, and their cost, as well as the work to be done and how it is divided.

## Location

*Where* the organization is located (oversimplifying for a moment and assuming it is in one place only) is often influenced by external factors such as customers, sources of raw materials, labor, transportation facilities, and other resources. A quality leather-goods manufacturer with national distribution might be expected to locate in Chicago where hides, labor, and transportation are easily obtainable. A new research-oriented aerospace firm might be expected to locate in Los Angeles, Dallas, or Boston, where many technical personnel already live. A retail store is likely to locate where its customers can easily shop.

What region of the country, what state, what city, what part of the city, all can be relevant in adding to understanding of an organization. For example, the way a given business is conducted in Texas may well differ from the method of its counterpart in Maine. The way savings and loan associations in Massachusetts operate is probably different from the way those in California do. Even the part of a city in which a firm operates can make a difference. The variations in the cultural and social patterns in various parts of the country and the differences in economic and social conditions within the cities are generally important.

Thus it is that many organizations, once located, consciously try to fit into their environments in terms of their exterior appearance. Recall that the building façades of the two organizations we observed in Chapter 1 differed in ways that were appropriate for their own environments.

The importance of fitting in the community in terms of appearance is now recognized by many chain stores. During the thirties and forties, some grocery chains attempted to establish their unique identity and to simplify and economize by using a standard store façade and layout. But over the years many grocery chains have changed their policy and construct buildings that "blend in" with the local environment. Of course, not all companies have adopted such a policy, as the standard architecture often used by McDonald's hamburger chain illustrates. Nevertheless, the immediate environment can strongly influence how the façade of a building may look. The reverse is true too. Consider how a petroleum refinery affects its environment.

Noting where the company is located can help you infer something about its character and market niche. The nature of the area and surrounding buildings, including their appearance, cost, and function, and the types of people they attract, all say something useful about "who" the company is.

## Organization

As soon as any organization grows large enough so that work is divided and individuals and groups begin to specialize, coordination must take place. This coordination is achieved partially by establishing formal organizational relationships and by assigning the job of managing and supervising to specific people.

All organizations of any size have either explicit or implicit policies, procedures, methods, rules, and standards that help achieve coordination. *Policies* serve as general guides for thinking and acting in specific situations. *Procedures* define the sequence of operations that are to take place in order that work can be accomplished. *Methods* prescribe how a task is to be accomplished. *Rules* specify certain behavior that is either required or prohibited. *Standards* provide a basis for evaluating the performance of required tasks. All of these taken together influence and direct much of the required behavior in organizations, and they are designed primarily to achieve coordinated, efficient behavior.

The work of an organization can be separated conceptually into mental decision making and physical action. Generally, specific individuals or groups are assigned the task of making certain decisions or of performing certain work. The various *decision and activity "centers"* are connected by *communications networks* designed to achieve coordination, to help relate people and groups separated in space but interdependent in function. Who gets what information, when, how, and from whom is generally established in most ongoing organizations.

Coordination is also partially achieved through the establishment of a formal *authority hierarchy*, which specifies who can tell whom to do what.

Another aspect of the formal organization that we should note is its system of *rewards and punishments*. This system includes more than the payment of money, although that is a common and important part of it. How much people are paid for their work, in relationship to others both in and out of the company, has obvious impact on behavior. Whether a person is paid piece rate, or a straight hourly wage, or a weekly, semimonthly, or monthly salary can also make a difference. But people and groups within the organization are also rewarded or punished with, among other things, the work (and titles) assigned them, the resources provided them, and by their relative positioning in the communications network and authority hierarchy.

We will discuss the subject of formal organization in more depth later in this book. For now all we need note is that the several factors making it up all influence behavior within it and that the organization itself is influenced by several external and internal factors we have already been discussing, including the nature of the product, industry, technology, people, space, activities, and things related to the organization.

## Management

Another important factor in understanding the nature of an organization and the behavior in it is its management. Of course, managers, being human, are not all alike, and their differences, as well as their similarities, are important. For example, many managers in the same company share certain important values, including those related to how work should be done, how goals should be achieved, and how people should be treated. Can you see why many of these key values would be shared? What causes this to happen? Can you also see why there are some differences among the managers in both values and actions? Can you see why some want to make all decisions and others let their subordinates make some? Or why some want to oversee closely the work of their employees and others do not? Or why some are friendly and warm with their subordinates and others are cool and distant? These differences and similarities are worth noting in observing any organization.

## Size

The sheer *size* of an organization, especially in terms of the number of people employed, influences both the kinds and types of coordination and control required. The 26,000 employees of State Farm Insurance Company differentiate that organization from Sonnet Tool with its one hundred employees. The kinds of policies, controls, and organization needed for the former will be unlike, in many ways, those needed for the latter. In general, the larger the size, the more impersonal will be the proceedings of policy formulation, the greater will be the problems of identification with the organization and the tendency to think of people in terms of groups rather than individuals. On the other hand, large size means more opportunities for breadth of training, more avenues for promotion, and, usually, more resources available for purposes other than sheer survival. One is not better than the other, but they are different; and size, therefore, is a variable important to our understanding of any given organization.

## Financial Condition

A company is influenced in several ways by its financial condition. Firms comfortably beyond their survival point financially are very different from those that are not, and the difference is one that is often easily observed. The financial statements of a company, when available, can tell much—including how prosperous it is, how it has grown, how it uses debt, how it distributes its profits, and numerous other things. Noting the relative proportions of liquid and fixed assets may also suggest something about the company's character.

If financial statements are not available, the relative financial strength can often be inferred by looking at the kinds of buildings, equipment, things, and other resources within the company. The age and history of the company may also be relevant in inferring the financial condition. In turn, knowing the financial condition can be one bit of useful data in making inferences and predictions about company behavior patterns.

## Company History

Knowing or observing the age of a company is usually easy and relevant. Companies with long histories have present patterns that are partial outcomes of their past. The scandals that hit the insurance industry in the late nineteenth century, for example, led to federal and state legislation that complicates the functioning of insurance companies to this day. One reason that the salaries of top officials are often less than those of the better salesmen, it has been suggested, is that top-officer salaries, which are usually published, are still a sensitive matter.

Whether a company grew internally or by merger or acquisition is often important to know. A subsidiary that was acquired five years ago may still operate differently and feel separate from its parent unit.

Values and ways of operating develop within organizations over time and, once established, frequently become rather rigid. These factors obviously influence present behavior. Knowing how these values and methods of operations have developed can be useful not only in understanding why the organization operates as it does but also in attempting to bring about change.

## Summary

Keep in mind that in this chapter we have not been looking at behavior (which we will begin to do in the next chapter), but only at the environment of behavior. We are looking at some of the important background factors in the environment that, when observed, interpreted, and related, tell us much about the total system. Relating the variables facilitates making tentative predictions about the behavior that will take place in the organization, and further observations enable such hypotheses to be tested.

Remember our assumption that the various parts of a whole "fit" and that we can either make inferences about the whole from the parts or vice versa. This is because of the many mutually dependent relationships that exist between the parts. To understand behavior in organizations you need to develop skill both in sensing the totality of a given organization and in sensing how specific behavior influences the pattern of the whole. Keep in mind the *complex interrelatedness* of these internal background factors, as well as the influence on each of them of numerous *external* background factors. To add an increasing element of complexity to the rather static model we have been developing, add just a dose of dynamics; i.e., assume some of the changes that take place in each of the factors as time passes. Can you see the problem of keeping all the relationships in mind at once? Impossible? Yes, but persisting in the effort can lead to increased understandings, for the comprehension of parts, one by one, and their interrelatedness, can help you usefully apprehend the whole.

## Division of Work and Job Design

People working are people behaving, and it is useful to note what they are doing. However, for now we will only consider the way the work itself is divided and grouped, and, more specifically, how individual jobs are designed. Noting these things will, of course, help explain much of the behavior.

The nature of the product or service and the related technology heavily influence how work is divided. What work is required and how it is divided varies significantly between organizations. Hotels that sell services are organized differently from firms that manufacture things, and factories that produce products individually or in small batches, are organized differently from those that mass produce products. In a bank work is often divided according to functions such as loans, savings, checking, and safe deposits. Can you see what influences these divisions would often have upon people, things, space, and, thus, upon behavior?

Within the grosser divisions of work just mentioned, work is divided more specifically into *jobs*, the set of tasks assigned to an individual. The *job design*, combined with the related technology, is an important influence on behavior. Can you see some of the job designs in a tool company? Think about who does what, how, and with whom. Both the design of any given job and the design of the relationship between it and other jobs are important to note. The sequence of activities prescribed for doing a particular job and what those activities require of the person doing them are important in understanding that person's behavior at work. In turn, the relationship of one job design to others is a kind of system. In assembly lines, each person's work is dependent upon the work of the person ahead of him. The same work can be accomplished by a different system, in which each person does all the various operations. The two systems require different rules and regulations. The controls necessary to make certain the assembly line continues to move smoothly are probably greater than those needed where each employee functions as a separate "unit" that is not dependent on others. In general, the greater the dependency built into the job designs, the greater will be the controls required, because any one person's failure affects the total group's production.

Some jobs are designed so that their performance by any one person is very difficult. An example might be the typical bank teller's job, which most banks see as including strict attention to detail and accuracy; friendly, warm responses focusing upon the individual customer's needs; awareness of opportunities to sell other bank services to customers who may be able to use them; caution in dealing with transactions that might subject the bank to losses; speed in accomplishing each customer's transactions so as to provide fast service. It would be an unusual person indeed who could do all of these aspects of the job well all day long. Knowing this would help an observer better understand the behavior of tellers in a busy branch.

Other jobs are designed so that two or more people are forced, in order to accomplish their tasks, to work very closely with each other. Take the obvious example of two men using one saw to fell a tree. To do the work demands a kind of interrelationship as close as that which used to be required by dancing.

Some jobs can be done well with little concentration; others demand close attention. Some permit much opportunity for the employee to decide what he will do, when he will do it, and how he will do it. Others are so carefully prescribed that the employee has virtually no opportunity to vary the design. Jobs can be categorized in many ways. They may vary along dimensions represented by the following extremes: mental (specialized or broad) or physical (skilled, semiskilled, or unskilled), simple or complex, repetitive or nonrepetitive, technical or nontechnical, supervisory or nonsupervisory, autonomous or nonautonomous. These variations in design affect what people on the jobs will *do*, who they will *be*, and how they *feel*.

## Personal Backgrounds of People

We eventually are to be concerned in this book mainly about people behaving in organizations. So, as we enter a specific organizational setting, such as Company A in Chapter 1, we might ask "Why are these people here?" We have already pointed out three important influences. One is the environment in which the organization is located. The people working usually live either nearby or within reasonable commuting distance. A second factor is technology. The employees must have the skills and

knowledge necessary to do the various kinds of work required. A third factor is the type of customers served. (Consider how cultural differences between regions in the United States might alter this.)

People display many cues that help us sense who they are and how they fit in an organization. What they do, where they are located in space, and the kinds of things they have and work with all tell us something about them. Personal characteristics such as age and sex are easily identifiable. Think how age and sex, as well as space, help distinguish one employee from others. Can you see how you might be misled in identifying an assistant manager in a bank because she is a woman? What assumptions, relevant here, do many people make about the kinds of jobs women do?

The technological knowledge and skill required to do specific work is usually obtained either through education or experience or both. Thus, knowing a man's educational background may tell you something about what he does, and vice versa. In addition, what he does is influenced by his attitudes, aspirations, and values, which, in turn, stem from his family, education, work, religious and socio-economic background, and experience. Again we usually expect most of these to fit with what a man does, and they all combine in particular settings to say something about the man's role and status in the organization.

The people within a business, or within two or more businesses, can differ in ways that seem fairly obvious but have great meaning for the organization. The *educational level* of employees and the *kinds* of education evident are important to notice. A business that employs high school graduates for eventual managerial positions must have patterns of background factors different from one that seeks only graduate degree holders. Within an organization, the number and grouping of different people by kind and level of education can often be well worth noting. If one sees that every important position is held by men who have graduate degrees in science and engineering, and if one notices that large numbers of high school graduates are hired, one might deduce that the latter group has small chance of attaining an executive position in the future (although this hypothesis would need further checking, of course).

Ethnicity is another important variable. People have different personal backgrounds, and their ethnic origins are often important in the way organizations function. In retail selling, the ethnicity of sales personnel is often complementary with the ethnicity of customers. Within a business, a group of twelve people may include three ethnic groupings, and we would expect some tendency for the whole group's functioning to be influenced by the ethnic divisions. Prejudice along ethnic lines is as real as it is deplorable, and, as observers, we would be naïve to miss such important data.

Similarly, *religious* groupings are relevant. The life orientations that various formal religions encourage in their members are sometimes quite different, and, thus, division of groups into religious subgroups is not

uncommon. In some smaller Eastern cities, the Catholics, Jews, and Protestants live largely within their own religious groupings. But virtually everywhere, men are more comfortable "with their own kind," and, thus, religious orientation becomes to some extent a focus for groupings.

*Family* is important also, in that kinship ties still influence organizations. "Marrying the boss's daughter" may sound like a phrase from the innocent past, but it is still a helpful event in many men's careers. The relationships of father to son, brother to brother, etc., can also be of great importance within companies. It is said that blood is thicker than water, and it can count more than money. In addition, kinship ties are often a means for the passing on of skills, especially at the craft level. Family relationships within a business often make a difference and are worth noting.

There are many other personal variables that help differentiate people and explain some of their characteristics and behavior patterns. Some, such as age, sex, skill level, physical characteristics, aspirations, and values are sufficiently easy to identify and understand the implications of that we will not dwell on them here. We only wish to stress that the personal backgrounds of people, "where they are from and what they are of," are highly relevant variables in understanding behavior. The American often believes the only acceptable question is "Where are you going?"; but "Where have you come from?" is, as the European knows well, still an important variable. Look for both.

## Things and Space

Both things and space can provide useful information about people and behavior in organizations. For example, we can make inferences about the financial condition of a company by observing the kinds and quality of things in it, including equipment, machinery, furniture, and decorations. The kinds of things people have at work often suggest clues about their status and even their personal values and interests. Space, too, suggests information about various things such as status, rank, and function. For example, in many companies the higher and bigger a person's office, the higher will be that person's status, in all likelihood.

Things, space, and time all "talk." We urge you to read "Time, Space, and Things" on pages 69–81 for a more thorough discussion of this.

## Physical Conditions

People and things in space include various physical conditions. Most of these are easily discernible, and even their impact on behavior is not difficult to comprehend, though they are so "natural" that we often are unaware of their full significance. For example, compare how you might react to working near the furnaces in a steel plant with how you would

react to working in an air-conditioned office upstairs; or imagine your reaction to working or talking midst the thunderous pounding in a tin can factory and then think of working in a small office; or think how the odor of a paper mill or chemical factory compares with that of a bakery; or imagine the difference in reaction of clerks in a crowded department store and clerks in a quiet suburban bank. Color, cleanliness, noise, newness, light, elegance, and countless other factors that make up the conditions of a given setting influence how people feel and what they must cope with, and it is usually not difficult to sense how this might affect behavior. Stop for just a moment to think how heat, noise, color, and crowding affect your own performance.

As with the other factors we have been considering, we can infer several things about the organization from our observations of conditions, and we can make certain predictions about what impact those conditions will have on behavior. For example, what relationship do conditions have to technology? to management concern for employees? to the organization's financial condition? to customers? You can see that many factors combine, generally, to influence what conditions prevail and that those conditions, in turn, affect the behavior of people.

## Roles, Prestige, and Organization Values

A role is a part or a function performed by a person in a particular position or situation. With most roles there are associated certain expectations of behavior. For example, we expect anyone who is a president to behave differently from a junior employee, or the foreman to behave differently from the workers, or the coach differently from the player. Thus it is that if we know someone's role (which is often indicated by his job title or assignment), we can make some reasonable predictions about some of his behavior, even though we do not know the person. If a particular person behaves differently than is generally expected of someone in his role, uneasy feelings, often negative, frequently result.

In a given organization, various roles have to be performed, and each of them is likely to carry a certain prestige, the amount of which will depend on the importance of that role to the achievement of goals and on preconceived expectations of the role. For example, we expect the role of president to be more important than that of general manager, and more prestige is accorded to the president. The roles and prestige of individuals and groups are useful to note because they help influence behavior and interrelationships in significant ways. Think how role expectations might affect a general manager as he deals with the president, a shop foreman, a worker, and his secretary. If you think his behavior might differ, why do you think so?

You can predict rather easily the prestige accorded certain individuals and groups and the roles they perform. We have already indicated how things and space give us many cues for making such observations. Think for a moment how both things and space serve as status symbols in a business organization. Observation of such symbols helps identify the relative value assigned both individuals and groups.

By noting the resources, things, and space allocated to work groups and people, and the nature and conditions of their work, and by considering these factors in the context of the total organization, we can often get good understandings of both their relative status in the organization and some of the factors influencing them. In addition, such observations indicate something about the values of the organization. By noticing the quantity and quality of various facilities and people, and by observing the things and help high-status people have (and low-status people do and do not have), you can make reasonable deductions about the values of the organization. For example, you can tell something about the college that has a large new library and no stadium as compared with one that has a large stadium and a small library.

## SUMMARY

We suggest that you go back to Figure 1 in this chapter, and, beginning at the left, consider the meaning of each of the background factors listed, as well as their interrelationships. We hope you can begin to see the intellectual ordering of the intuitive process experienced in Chapter 1, the interrelatedness of all the background factors into a unified system or whole, and the great influence of these factors and their interrelatedness upon the actual behavior of people in specific settings.

In the next chapter we will extend this somewhat static model to a more dynamic one that is very useful in helping you better understand *behavior* in organizations. As you move into this new model and practice using it, keep in mind the relevance of asking frequently: What is influencing the occurrence of the behavior described, or that which I see in my own life? When you go out to dinner or to the bank or grocery store or whatever, keep your eyes open and be aware of what is going on. It can be quite exciting to see well what has long been taken for granted. And this is really step one on the tour we are taking in this book.

# Strategic Factors in Diagnosing Organization Character

*William B. Wolf*

. . . We are caught in the parts-versus-whole dilemma. Organizations are too complex to be studied as totalities. Yet, to study only their specific parts is unsatisfactory; for if we are really to understand the parts, we must see them in relation to the whole of which they are part, and in relation to one another.

One compromise that is a useful way of mitigating this dilemma is to study the strategic factors (that is, those that are of major importance in determining or revealing organization character). For example, we might analyze the strategic factor *style of supervision* as an independent variable, such as was done by Lewin and his associates. We would then discover certain patterns associated with different styles: for example, under autocratic supervision, a tendency for subordinates to manifest low morale, repressed hostility, increased tension, and accident proneness. Similarly, we could define settings in which specific leadership styles are most effective; for example, autocratic leadership tends to fit certain situations where specialized technical knowledge is essential to the carrying out of a task.

Thus, our procedure is to examine strategic factors as independent

•From *Management: Readings Toward a General Theory*, edited by William B. Wolf. © 1964 by Wadsworth Publishing Company, Inc., Belmont, California. Reprinted by permission of the publisher.

[1] Ronald O. Lippett, "An Experimental Study of the Effect of Democratic and Authoritarian Group Atmospheres," *University of Iowa Studies in Child Welfare*, XVI, No. 3 (1950), 43–195.

variables, and then to reason through the impact that each may have if other aspects of the organization are held constant. Thus, we do study the individual parts of an organization—but in such a manner that we also gain an awareness of the important dimensions of the whole.

The procedure is to examine strategic parts one at a time. For each part, we make the following assumptions:

1. There is an explanation for the condition or dimension of that part as it exists in the organization: that is, we assume causality. Every aspect of an organization can be explained and its purpose or *raison d'être* discovered—provided we have adequate knowledge.
2. There exists a functional relationship between each strategic factor and various dimensions of the organization; consequently, given a strategic factor with specified dimensions, we can derive tentative but reasonably sound hypotheses about other dimensions of that organization.
3. The inference drawn from an analysis of any one specific strategic factor may be reinforced or contradicted by analysis of other strategic factors. Where constellations of reinforcing or consistent inferences are drawn, one may tentatively assume that the inference is sound.

By analyzing a number of strategic factors and noting reinforcing as well as contradictory inferences, one can develop a perspective of the organization as a whole.

. . . . .

Many of the [strategic] factors, external to the organization, are aspects of the broader environment—e.g., social role of the institution, economics of raw-material markets, economics of consumer's markets. Some of the factors are internal to the organization—e.g., layout technology used, formal organization structure. However, these internal and external forces are closely related; moreover, external forces tend to dominate and shape many of the internal ones.

Probably the easiest way to bring together the concepts presented here is to give a short illustration. First, we will list a number of facts about a company; then we will relate them to the manner in which that company is managed:

1. The company manufactures briefcases, wallets, and men's travel kits for toilet articles.
2. The business experiences large seasonal variations in demand for its products.
3. All of the company's products are made of leather.
4. The policy of the company is to compete on the basis of quality rather than price.
5. Raw materials used constitute approximately 38 percent of manufacturing costs.
6. The demand for the products varies widely from season to season on the basis of style factors such as colors, shapes, decorative stitching.

7. The company has only one manufacturing plant, and for its industry it does a volume business.

From facts such as these, we can draw a number of inferences about the management of the firm: the organization is (or should be) sales oriented; it has difficulty maintaining a steady flow of production; it doesn't use many mass-production techniques. The logic underlying these inferences would run as follows: The company manufactures leather products. Raw-material costs are a significant part of total cost. Because the company produces a "quality" line, and because each leather hide has to be selectively cut to get maximum utilization, it is unlikely that highly automated procedures are used. Furthermore, if the company is to be successful, it will have to have a strong sales organization; in a business such as this, with low fixed-capital requirements, it is easy for new producers to go into business; moreover, since there are few cost advantages to be gained by volume production, the key to a competitive advantage is aggressive sales and distribution.

The seasonal nature of the business, the variations in styles, and the high cost of raw materials indicate problems in maintaining a stable work force in the manufacturing plant, although ways of dealing with this problem (through subcontracting work or development of compensatory lines) may be utilized.

Several additional facts—(a) that the management of the firm is profit motivated and doesn't identify closely with its labor force; (b) that the manufacturing facilities are located in a neighborhood with a large reservoir of marginal labor; (c) that workers on the payroll ninety days or more become permanent employees and have collective-bargaining rights to recall after layoff, as well as to pensions, vacation pay, and other fringe benefits—all lead to the inference that management would tend to dilute job skills, discourage workers from becoming permanent employees, and otherwise keep labor costs low by varying the size of the labor force to meet seasonal needs. One way to cope with wide seasonal variations in a manufacturing business is to simplify jobs and dilute skill requirements, so that a marginal worker may be brought up to peak performance in a short period of time. The fact that this company located its plant in a labor market where many unskilled people from minority groups are available would reinforce this inference.

The soundness of the inference that the company tries to discourage workers from becoming permanent employees would be determined by analyzing other aspects of the organization. Supporting evidence would be a tendency to minimize personnel service activities—personnel picnics, bowling teams, etc.,—as well as designing jobs to discourage worker interaction.

In contrast, we might postulate that management wants the manufacturing plant to be a "big happy family." If this were so, jobs would probably be set up to encourage interaction among employees, personnel techniques would be used to increase the camaraderie in the organization, and seasonal variations in production would be met by varying the hours of work, and/or calling back to work people who have left the organization for good reasons (such as pregnancy or family responsibilities). Moreover, the manufacturing plant would probably be located near a stable labor market.

The above illustrates the type of analysis suggested for building a theory of management. At this stage in our knowledge of management, we are quite limited. We lack a formalized body of knowledge of the various strategic factors and the implications to the total organization of each variation in a strategic factor. Thus, there are a number of tasks to be done. First, we need a systematic analysis of each strategic factor. Here we need to ask what kinds of variations in that factor may be encountered. Second, we need to build a body of illustrative materials demonstrating the manner in which the impact of different strategic factors gives character to the organization as a whole.

The problems of building such an analytical structure are great. We can illustrate the approach by taking the factor of formal organization structure (specialized departments and their relationships) and examining its dimensions and its effect on the total organization.

How do formal structures vary? We can perceive variations in terms of:

1. Number of interdependent units established within the total organization.
2. Number of levels of formal authority designated in the hierarchy.
3. Size of each formally designated unit within the organization.
4. Kind of authority formally delegated to the various units.
5. Kind of work done by the formally designated units.
6. Location of work.
7. Degree of autonomy granted to each unit.

There is reason to believe that the *span of control* of supervisors (the number of subordinates reporting to one supervisor) influences the nature of supervision, the types of subordinates who "fit in," morale, and efficiency. Where a supervisor has only a few subordinates, and where his superior also has relatively few men reporting to him, one is apt to find close supervision. Such a structure encourages subordinates to adhere closely to established rules and regulations. This and related tendencies are reported in the studies conducted by Sears, Roebuck and Company. Sears studied its class-B retail stores and, on the basis of a thorough analysis, concluded that formal organization structure was a significant factor in determining the character of a store.[2] They found that retail stores with many layers of authority (numerous levels of supervision) were more rigid, less adaptive, and less satisfactory to employees than retail stores of comparable size but with few levels of supervision. These "flat" organizations tended to keep formal controls at a minimum, whereas in the organization with many levels of supervision the employees felt restricted, controlled, and policed. The "flat" organizations exhibited greater

[2]The Sears studies isolate the impact of a flat organization structure with an extended span of control. It should be recognized, however, that retail selling is a separate species of organization, and Sears is a special case in this species. It is unlikely that a flat organization would be more efficient in an organization where there is a close interdependence between departments, or where morale is less directly related to profitability such as in mail-order sales.

creativity and flexibility and were more profitable. Moreover, Sears found that deep hierarchical organizations tended to weed out employees with self-reliance and initiative.[3]

Another dimension of formal structure is seen in the relations between line and staff units. . . . friction may develop between the line and the staff: and this apparently stems from forces inherent in such a structure.[4]

Similarly, where interdependent departments come under different supervisors, one often encounters frictions between those departments.[5]

Similarly, the specific location of work enters into the broad character of organizations. For example, if a department is placed near the central headquarters of a firm, that department's functions very probably carry status or are otherwise considered important within the total system.

Where work is divided between a central headquarters and regional units, one encounters what appear to be common patterns in the problem of managing. For example, the subunit tends to develop a character all its own and tries to preserve its own integrity. The central office, feeling a need to maintain formal control, specifies procedures and policies. The local unit, in turn, interprets these policies as it sees fit. Thus, suspicion frequently develops between the leadership in the central office and that in the local unit. One device used to remedy this problem is to have a local manager report directly to the top manager in his unit and also to a staff officer at central headquarters. However, the manager who must report to two bosses is in the precarious position of violating the confidence of one of his superiors. Of course, the outcome of such an organization structure is intimately tied to the interpersonal relations of the men involved. Yet, the fact is that the basic nature of the structure releases tendencies toward such a conflict.

The location of the supervisor's work station relative to his subordinates also relates to the character of the organization. For example, if the supervisor's work station automatically gives him a full view of his subordinates, an accepted part of the work climate is to have the boss make visual inspections of what is going on. However, if the boss's office is located in an isolated corner or at a distance from the workers he supervises, then workers may interpret inspection trips of the boss as "snoopervising."

Before leaving this illustration, it is important to point to the fundamental problem encountered in this type of analysis; namely, that our knowledge is incomplete, so that we are dealing with tendencies or trends rather than precise facts. Hence, only as we note reinforcing tendencies released by other strategic factors should we give weight to what we have inferred.

[3]James C. Worthy, "Factors Influencing Employee Morale," *Harvard Business Review*, XXVIII, No. 1 (January, 1950), 61–73. See also "Democratic Principles in Business Management," address given at the Industrial Management Institute, Lake Forest College, May 27, 1948; and "Organizational Structure and Employee Morale," *American Sociological Review*, XV, No. 2 (April, 1950), 169–79.

[4]See Douglas McGregor, "The Staff Function in Human Relations," *The Journal of Social Issues*, IV (Summer, 1948), 5–22.

[5]Cf. F. J. Jasinski, "Foremen Relations Outside the Work Group," *Personnel*, XXXIII (September, 1945), 130–36; C. R. Walker et al., *The Foreman on the Assembly Line* (Cambridge, Mass.: Harvard University Press, 1956).

Numerous other "strategic" factors should be considered in any given situation. The following are some of the more commonly encountered ones. However, the significance of any one factor is a function of the field in which it occurs; thus, what is considered "strategic" in one setting may not be in another.

*Strategic Factors*

1. Charter
2. Location
3. Physical facilities
4. Size
5. Ownership and control
6. Labor force
7. History of organization—age, rate of growth, changes in character
8. Competing organizations
9. Leadership
10. Labor market
11. Economics of markets for supplies
12. Public image of the organization—its social role or place in the cultural environment
13. Technology
14. Formal organization structure
15. Status systems
16. Cliques and interpersonal interactions
17. Communication systems
18. Finances
19. Formal systems
20. Supervisors
21. Job design
22. Strategic policies

## Organization Health

Implicit in this discussion is a concept or point of view toward organizations that needs to be made explicit; namely, that we are viewing organizations from the point of view of executives (those who manage). Our criterion of organizational effectiveness is survival. We view organizations as dynamic cooperative systems. Their survival involves change and adaption, as well as economic performance and the distribution of incentives to members.

The presentation is organized to help the executive understand the dimensions of his job in contributing to organizational survival. As mentioned elsewhere, we hold that the manager should have awareness of how organizations in general function, as well as an understanding of the character of his specific organization. In short, the organization is seen as a "system" with needs for its own security, stability, and continuity. Managers perform the functions of organizing, directing, and controlling within the system.

The criteria for judging managers (i.e., organizational health or effectiveness) are not measures such as performance, morale, lack of conflict, or profit per se. These are important but insufficient criteria. Rather, we have to evaluate managers in terms of the total dynamic system represented by the organization. In this framework, it is more important to judge managerial effectiveness upon the basis of how the organization handles its problems (i.e., adapts and changes to pressures), rather than whether or not it has problems.

### Conclusion

What is present here is a rudimentary theory of management. It is a theory in the sense that it is a conceptualization that provides a way of ordering and understanding the multitude of facts related to managerial actions. The theory is not new or startling. A similar approach is now used in all sciences dealing with complex organisms: abandonment of the traditional mechanistic or atomistic approach and, in its place, emphasis on the organism as a whole. This orientation is clearly discernible in Gestalt psychology, field theory in physics, systems theory, and organismic theories of personality.

This approach is not without weakness. Perhaps a major problem inherent in it is that one must accept a concept of relativity that is tremendously complex and, when followed through logically, leaves one with little firm ground upon which to stand. Absolutes vanish, and events and happenings have to be explained in relation to other aspects of the situation. With respect to this, Chester I. Barnard's comment is worth noting:

> It seems to me quite in order to cease encouraging the expectation that human behavior in society can be anything less than the most complex study to which our minds may be applied. However desirable clarity and simplicity of statement, it is not desirable to underestimate either the difficulties of observation and experiment or those of constructing hypotheses that may prove helpful.[6]

[6]*The Functions of the Executive* (Cambridge, Mass.: Harvard University Press, 1938), pp. xii–xiii.

# Personal Perception, Involvement, and Response

*Robert E. Coffey and Peter A. Raynolds*

The focus of this book is on the individual, his relationships, and his world. We hope you share our goals of wanting to become more aware and understanding of yourself, your relationships with others, and your world. An important step in this direction is to review how centrally important are one's own perceptions. Some of us are more perceptive than others; i.e., some of us "see" more, and all of us see somewhat differently. Consider Figure 1; how many squares do you see?

Typically, most people respond "sixteen." Then someone sees another. Then people begin to catch on, and some quickly see thirty. This simple exercise partially illustrates what happens in life; that all of us see every situation differently.

## Selection

One important reason for our differences in perceptions is that we select different stimuli on which to focus. These differences depend on such things as the clarity and familiarity of the stimuli, the observer's physical characteristics, his needs and values, his knowledge and feelings, and in general his past experience. A three-year-old child views the world from an entirely different perspective than an adult, partially because of height differences, partially because of needs and motives, and quite significantly because of differences in experiences.

We are aware that our needs and motives influence what we select to focus on. If you need to buy tires you are much more likely to focus on tire advertisements than otherwise. If you are a sport enthusiast you look for and find information and stories on sports more than does someone whose interests are different. A man hurrying down the street, late for an appointment, is more likely to notice a clock than are two lovers enjoying a leisurely stroll. One well-known experiment revealed that poor children tend to overestimate the size of coins.

Selection is just one part of the perceptual process. Look at Figure 2 and count the number of squares. Some of you will see six; some seven. Can you see it both ways? (If not, turn the page upside down.) Some will find this difficult. One reason is that once we have "locked into" a way of organizing what we see, it is sometimes very hard to change that view.

**Figure 1**

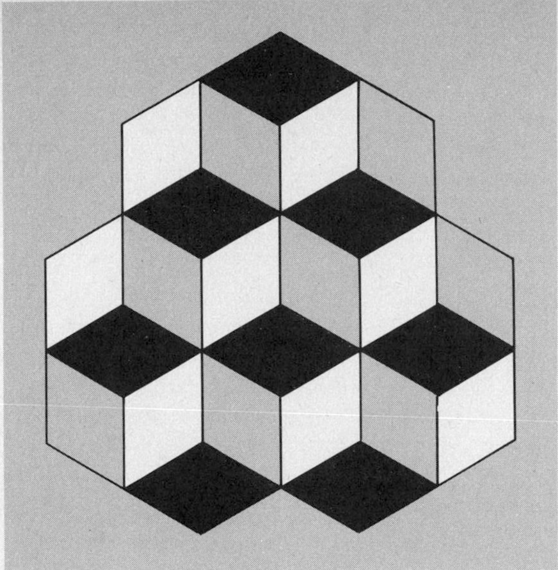

Figure 2

## Frame of Reference

Consider Figure 3 below. What do you see?

Figure 3

Many people see two faces; others see a goblet. The concrete stimuli are identical for everyone, yet people perceive them differently. The differences are a function of what we term an individual's *frame of reference*, which is the way each person sees and interprets his world at a given time. Each person's frame of reference is unique, being the result of his past experience, and including his accumulated needs, values, aspirations, feelings, and knowledge. Try now to see if you can visualize the gestalt (the whole picture) you did not see at first. This requires that you change your frame of reference; something happens in your head that determines which perception you have. In other words, it is you who makes the sense or meaning out of an ambiguous picture, and in everyday affairs this is usually done unconsciously.

Both our needs and expectations influence what becomes *ground* (as in "background") and what becomes *figure* (e.g., "object": person, feature, thing upon which we focus). When we enter a dark movie theater looking for a seat, we often are relatively unaware of what is happening on the screen. We may focus on the seats immediately near us. As our eyes become more adjusted to the dark, we may scan in a wider range looking for empty seats, still not focusing much on the screen. Once we find a seat, the other seats in the auditorium switch to ground, and the movie switches to figure.

Look at Figure 4A. What do you see? Is it clear which is ground and which is figure in your perceptions? Now look at Figure 4B. Is it clearer which is ground and figure? The obvious reason for the difference is that the white patterns in Figure 4B are familiar; in 4A they are not. Familiar

**Figure 4A**

**Figure 4B**
Bernard Berelson and Gary A. Steiner, *Human Behavior: An Inventory of Scientific Findings* (New York: Harcourt, Brace, and World, Inc., 1964), p. 110–11.

patterns are more likely to be figure and unfamiliar patterns ground in our perceptions.

## Organization of Stimuli

Another important aspect of perception is that we tend to fill in missing details—to organize our perceptions into wholes. For example, you have no trouble identifying what Figure 5 represents. You are quite aware in this instance that you are filling in some of the necessary data, but it is not so easy to see that we do the same thing when we fill in or block out data about the personality or behavior of a friend or enemy, or when the reasonableness of one of our pet theories, values, or beliefs is challenged. We tend to add data we need to make our perceptions "fit," and eliminate data that contaminate our views of what we expect or think should be. Thus it is that some of what we think we see is as much or more in us than it is in the world outside us.

**Figure 5**
Roy F. Street, *A Gestalt Completion Test: A Study of a Cross Section of Intellect* (New York: Columbia University, 1931), in Berelson and Steiner, *Human Behavior*, p. 107.

## Interpretation

In addition to selecting and organizing external stimuli, we select and interpret internal stimuli in terms of our needs, values, and past experience. Usually our interpretations are made instantaneously and unconsciously, and we are unaware of how much of the reality out there we make ourselves. Over a period of time we build the unique frames of reference through which we filter current, incoming stimuli. We also tend to modify our models after comparing them with those of others. Consequently, much of what we perceive is the result of interpersonal influence.

Perceptual misinterpretations of external stimuli sometimes occur because of visual distortions. In Figure 6 the lines appear to be of different lengths, although they are all the same. This points up our need to be-

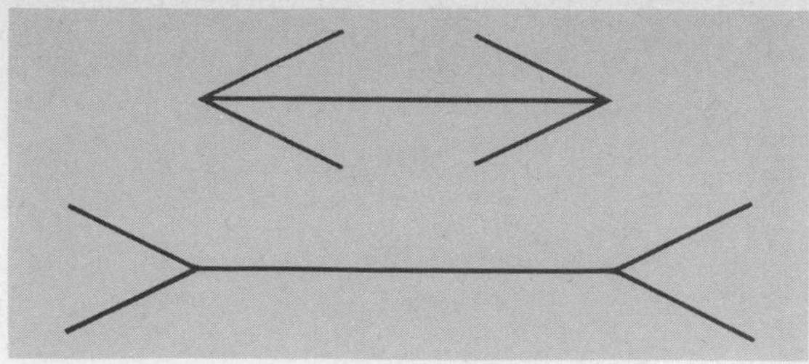

**Figure 6**

come more aware of the times when we are subject to similar perceptual distortions.

Some of the stimuli we apprehend through our senses are ambiguous, and may even appear to be unexplainable, such as in Figure 7. What are some of the things that come to your mind when you look at Figure 8? Some people see one or two ladies standing, others see clouds, some see dancing Indians with feathered headpieces. Often a viewer will first see parts of the inkblot, and then he may see a pattern that encompasses the entire inkblot. Many people see more than one gestalt before settling on a final one; a few refuse to see anything other than an inkblot. The point is that the more ambiguous the stimulus, the greater our need to reduce the ambiguity by "making a meaning." Also, the greater the ambiguity in what we see and experience, the more room there is for our unique interpretations.

Most of us find ambiguity difficult to tolerate. Thus, when we are faced with stimuli that are susceptible to more than one interpretation, we tend to search for the "right" one, and, having reached this goal, we tend to shut out the other possibilities. People vary in their tendency to change their own frames of reference. Some will stick with their first gestalt no matter what; others seem to vacillate endlessly. Where would you place yourself on this continuum?

## Learning and Perception

Concepts, theories, and other learnings strongly influence our perceptions and behavior. We tend to interpret ambiguous stimuli in terms of

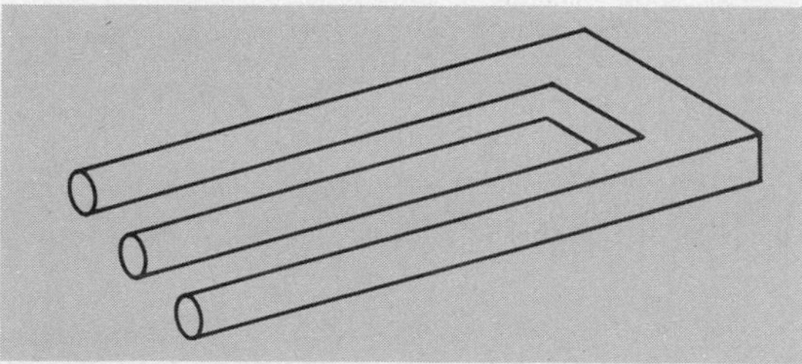

**Figure 7** "Magic" triangle

**Figure 8** Inkblot
Bruno Klopfer and Helen H. Davidson, in *The Rorschach Technique: An Introductory Manual* (New York: Harcourt, Brace & World, Inc., 1962), p. 8, offer a readable summary of the scoring and interpretation of inkblot responses. The inkblot illustrated in Figure 8 was made at one of USC's Management Creativity Workshops.

our past learning, and our resulting perceptions influence our behavior. This phenomena is so important that it may be referred to as the "law of behavior change"—as we learn more about behavior and become more aware of it, we tend to change in both predictable and *un*predictable ways. As we do so, our original learnings tend to become less valid because their original bases have become altered.

As an exercise demonstrating the law, first study the following statement: "Research has shown that more intelligent and mentally active persons tend to utilize the entire inkblot, rather than disregarding major portions, in forming their perceptions. Additionally, they tend to incorporate more explicit inkblot details in relating their responses to the inkblot stimulus." Then go back to Figure 8 and again ask yourself what you see.

We can predict that many readers will now utilize more of the entire inkblot and specify more of its details because of the influence of the new information about how more "intelligent" persons tend to behave.

How one feels and what the state of one's mind is at any particular time influences significantly how the more ambiguous aspects of the relevant environment will be perceived. Also, it is helpful to realize that we have several choices. One is that we choose when to stop looking for new gestalts. Another is that we choose which gestalt goes with which particular stimulus (situation). We also choose when to shift to new gestalts as new data (parts) are made available to us or as old data are shown to be unreliable or invalid.

In Chapter 1 we were concerned with sensing organizations as wholes. We observed certain data, used our knowledge, and made inferences about the meaning of the observed data. We looked for constellations of agreement among important variables, and we also looked for those variables that did not fit, in order that we might know where to strive for deeper understanding.

## Feelings and Responses

When you observed the pictures in Chapter 1 and made inferences about what you saw, you were engaging in what might have seemed to be primarily an intellectual process. Like Sherlock Holmes, we stressed observation, knowledge, and deduction. However, we did not emphasize a fourth important variable that influences our personal responses to what we observe and interpret. That variable is *feeling*.

In observing and interpreting the pictures, you probably did not experience many strong feelings, although you may have felt somewhat elated or frustrated, depending on how accurate were your inferences and how involved you were in the process. Each reader could respond to the pictures out of his past experience—his knowledge and ways of thinking—but it is unlikely that many brought intense feelings to the experience.

It is not difficult, though, to imagine yourself in situations in which you might have intense feelings. Suppose you asked a question in a classroom and the professor rather irritably replied "That's a *stupid* question!" Think how differently you would feel if he had said "That's a fascinating question to explore!" In either situation, most students would feel quite involved, and their perceptions of either being attacked or complimented would undoubtedly trigger pretty intense feelings. These feelings would in turn influence both their perceptions of what was happening and their behavioral responses.

Feelings depend on the individual observer and how he perceives himself and his situation. His perceptions, in turn, depend in part on his past experience. For example, if you were to see a picture of a policeman, and then were asked what you saw, you might respond rather neutrally. However, if you had strong feelings about policemen as symbols of an oppressive authority and power structure, you might respond quite differently. In addition to the observer, his past experience, and the stimulus observed, the *setting* in which something is observed also influences the response to it.

An important fact in any behavioral situation in which you find yourself is your own involvement. It is useful to learn about other people and their behavior, but it is essential to learn more about yourself, your own behavior, and your own involvement. In fact, it is difficult to understand others better without also understanding yourself. It is for this reason that we are examining here in some detail the process of your own involvement in behavioral situations. In Chapters 1 and 2, we looked at "things out there." Now we need to look at what is inside us to see better what is "out there."

## Experience and Experiencing

In understanding your own response to a stimulus in a setting, it can be useful, if you can do so, to differentiate between past experience and present experiencing. *Experiencing* takes place only in the present—an instant later, it is a past *experience*. One significant difference between experience (past) and experiencing (present) is that feelings take place only in the present. They are influenced by feelings you *have had* in the past, however, just as your present knowledge and ways of thinking are influenced by your past knowledge and ways of thinking. And, of course, your present experiencing will influence your knowledge, ways of thinking, and feelings as they become part of your experience. Thus there is a mutually dependent relationship between experience and experiencing.

You may be wondering what reason we have for differentiating between experience and experiencing. We will answer with an illustration. Suppose you have been raised in a family that values free enterprise and individualism and abhors unionism. Assume further that you have been taught that most union leaders are untrustworthy and greedy. You might even have had a few contacts with union people that tended to substantiate these beliefs about them. Now, suppose you meet the president of a local union in an unexpected setting—say, at a party given by a mutual friend. The man is regarded by your friend as pleasant, intelligent, and dedicated. But because of your past knowledge and ways of thinking, you may have feelings of dislike and distrust for him. On the other hand, if you are able to distinguish between your past experience and your present experiencing, you may be able to see the man as being pleasant, intelligent, and dedicated in at least that setting.

Your present experiencing depends on that part of your past knowledge and feeling and ways of thinking that you select for use in interpreting present feelings. What you know influences your feelings, and your feelings influence what you know and your ways of thinking. A young child who knows nothing about rattlesnakes and happens to encounter one may feel no fear. But adults who have been taught that rattlers are poisonous are likely to have intense feelings of fear if surprised by one. And their feelings of fear and revulsion about rattlesnakes will influence their ways of responding to all snakes, whether they are harmless or not.

## Process of Observation and Response

Figure 9 is a summary of the process we have been discussing. Briefly, you select and observe external phenomena in settings with your senses. These sensory perceptions are filtered through your present experiencing and past experience in such a way that you interpret their meaning. Each person filters the sensory inputs differently, thus leading to differences in interpretations and responses. In fact, some data are badly distorted in this filtering process. After an individual interprets the meaning of his sensory inputs, he then behaves covertly (internally) and overtly (externally)—and this behavior ultimately becomes part of his past experience. As the diagram suggests, past experience and present experiencing constitute a mutually dependent relationship, just as do the relationships between knowledge, ways of thinking, and feelings. Behavioral responses are categorized here as covert and overt, and it is important to recognize that they may differ. (A student may respond covertly with boredom to a professor's lecture, but behave overtly as though he were fascinated.)

Although we have attempted to set forth a diagrammatic description of the perceptual-response process, it is important to recognize that the result constitutes some distortion of reality. The whole process—from observation to response (input to output)—happens instantaneously and simultaneously. For this reason, we do not *experience* the process happening as conceptualized in the diagram.

In general, at any given moment no two people are likely to perceive "reality" in essentially the same way, especially if ambiguity is relatively high. A built-in perceptual gap separates people at the outset. Communication is merely a fantasy unless all parties disclose something of their perceptions and are flexible enough to make perceptual adjustments a fuller and richer shared reality. We will find that much of behavior in organizations is concerned with reducing perceptual gaps and ambiguities in behavioral situations.

We can draw several important implications for learning more about behavior in organizations from our exploration of perceptions.

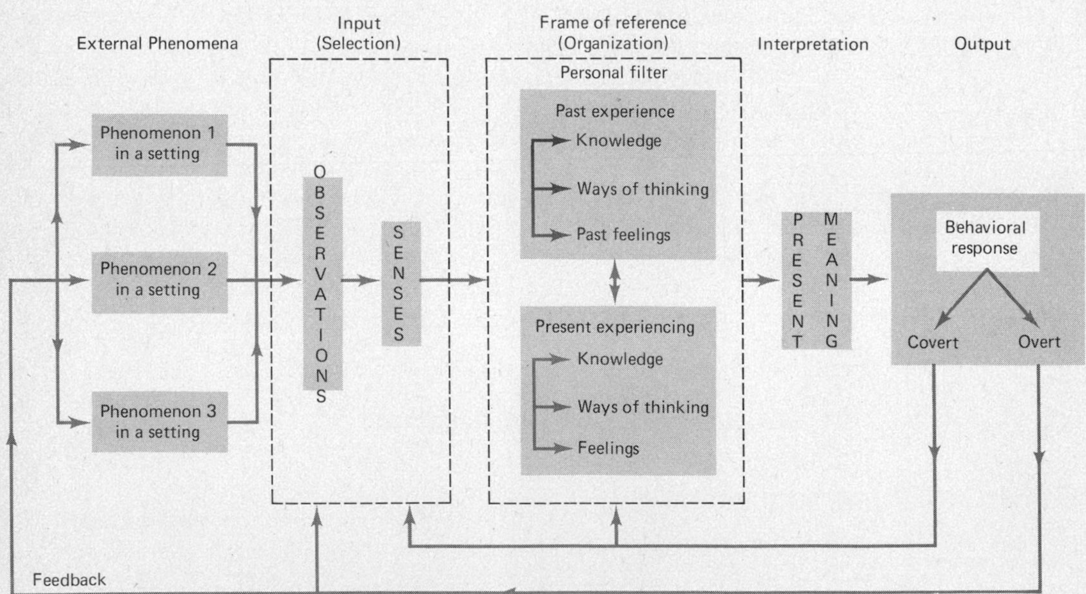


**Figure 9** The Perceptual-Behavioral Process

1. We are frequently confronted with ambiguous situations and stimuli, and the meaning we make out of ambiguity influences our behavior. Some of the world "out there" is really in us.

2. We select, organize, and interpret external stimuli in terms of our needs, values, feelings, and experience, including past learning. We tend to believe what we see, but we also tend to see what we believe.

3. We often "read into" ambiguous situations what we expect or want to see, and block out opposite kinds of stimuli.

4. Because we each have a unique frame of reference, we perceive many things differently. Thus, communication is essential but hazardous, difficult, and challenging.

5. We must be continually on guard against making inappropriately rigid interpretations of what we experience so that we can try to develop more flexibility and accuracy in our own perceptual and communication capabilities.

Each of us may interpret what we see a little (or a lot) differently. However, this is not at all defeating of our purposes. There is no one "right," "true" way available to any of us, and each of us will have to live with our own perceptions in the real world. So we assume it is useful to begin practicing now. Personal skills can be sharpened by practice with others under supervision. So it is with all arts.

# Time, Space, and Things[1]

*Anthony G. Athos*

It was amazing to me to discover how many ways we have of talking about time. We have time, keep time, buy time, and save time; we mark it, spend it, sell it, and waste it; we kill time, pass time, give time, and take time; and I hear that some of you, every now and then, even *make* time. With so many ways of dealing with time in the English language, we must be as sensitive to it as Eskimos are to snow, for which they have many words and no small respect.

Our American[2] concepts of time are that it is *continuous, irreversible*, and *one-dimensional*. Recent movies that shuffle the sequence of events so

[1]This reading is a lecture stimulated by Edward T. Hall's *The Silent Language* (Doubleday, 1959; also available in paperback as a Premier book, 1961), an excellent book recommended for additional reading to anyone who finds the subject interesting. Hall's *The Hidden Dimension* (Doubleday, 1966) is an interesting further statement much worth reading.

[2]"United States" and "America" refer here to the whole country, ignoring the rich and exciting differences in the culture of Hawaii, Alaska, Texas, and other parts of the whole.

that they do not proceed in the same order as they "do" in time, including flashaheads as well as the old standard flashbacks, are effective in disturbing us into powerful experiencing precisely because they deny our long-standing assumptions about time. We often seem to think of tomorrow as spatially in front of us and yesterday as almost literally behind us. With some effort we might be able to think of today as the space we were just in and the space we will very soon be in as we walk in a straight line. "Now" is even harder for many Americans, and it seems we experience it as the space filled by our bodies.

Perhaps that is why such interesting variations exist in different parts of the United States in orientations toward time. My personal experience in New England leads me to see people there as more oriented toward the past and the future than toward the present. Southern Californians seem more present- and future-oriented, with some important emphasis upon now (and thus greater familiarity with their bodies). The Latin Americans I know about seem more past- and present-oriented. My only point here is that we differ in our experiencing of time, focusing upon different aspects of it, yet there is a tendency for us to see it as *linear*; i.e., as a "straight line" from the past through the present into the future.

Of course, those of us who live more in touch with nature, say, farmers or resort operators, might also see time as cyclical. The earth makes its daily round of the sun; the seasons, like circles, "each mark to the instant their ordained end" and cycle again. And many of us, on an island vacation, for example, "unwind" like a corkscrew from what we left behind, slowly lose our concerns for tomorrow, and relax into letting days happen so that each merges with the one before and into the one after as an experienced, continuous present. The loosening delight of such vacations is in contrast with our more usual patterns, wherein our concerns about time can easily become compulsive.

## Accuracy

I can recall being in Athens, Greece, and asking my Greek cousin "How long does it take to walk from here to the library?" I was staying with her family and I wanted to spend the afternoon at the library and leave there in time to get back home for a 6 p.m. appointment with an American friend. She said "Not long." I replied with some irritation "No. I need to know so I can stay there as long as possible. How long does it take?" She shrugged and said "It's a short walk." I said with a frown "Come on. I want to know exactly. How long?" With great exasperation she finally dismissed me with *"A cigarette!"* Well, I felt a bit defeated, if a little amused, for to her a ten- or even twenty-minute error in estimate would have been simply irrelevant. Any greater precision would *confine* her. Yet we want to know *exactly*. Our concern for accuracy is enormous. Where else but in the Western industrialized world would watches get advertised as not being off more than a few seconds a month? Where else would people literally have timepieces strapped to their wrists so they can be sure they "keep on time"? Because of our concern for accuracy, the way we use time in our culture "talks" to other people.

Can you remember the first time you ever drove to pick up a girl for a date? It's not surprising to find that many of us got there a bit early and drove around the block awhile so as not to communicate our anxiety or eagerness too openly. To arrive at 7:00 for a 7:30 date is to "tell" the girl about these feelings and may result in your seeming naïve, unless you can explain it away. To arrive at 8:00 for a 7:30 date "says" you feel somewhat indifferent, and a decent explanation is required if the evening is to make any sense at all. I remember, all too well, a situation in my own life that illustrates this painfully. A mutual friend had tried for months to arrange a blind date between me and a girl, but neither of us was particularly interested and we avoided the matchmaking. Finally, I agreed to phone her, did so, and arranged a dinner date for a Saturday night at 7 p.m. I arrived at her house at 7:20 or so, only to find her slightly embarrassed parents offering me a drink because their daughter had not come home yet from wherever she was. At 7:30, she came into the house, exclaimed that someone had stolen her new blouse at the hairdresser's, that she couldn't get a cab to come home, and that she was sorry to be late but would hurry to get ready. (*Implicit message*: I feel harassed. I cared enough about this date to have my hair done and buy a new blouse, and the theft and lack of cabs and walking all the way home has me upset and hot and worried about what you will think.) I said airily "Take your time." (*Implicit message*: I don't care one way or the other, so your being late doesn't matter to me.) She said "Thanks, I will," and she took a long bath and appeared at 8:30 finally ready to go. War was declared! It took awhile to overcome our mutual resentments (which I am glad to say we did).

We also use time to tell how we feel and see others in terms of *relative status*. If the president of the United States called you to Washington to talk with him next Tuesday at 3 p.m., it is very likely that you would not arrange your flight to arrive in town at 2 p.m. You would most likely want very much to be *sure* you were there *no later* than 3 p.m., and might very well get there on Monday to be certain nothing would go wrong. Because of the great difference in the status of a president and the rest of us, we would feel that any inconvenience in waiting ought to be ours.

The same is true in companies. If the president of a large organization calls a young salesman to his office for a 3 p.m. meeting, the chances are awfully good that the salesman will arrive well before 3 p.m., even if he walks around the block an hour, so as not to arrive "too early."

Imagine two executives in the same large company, whose respective status is virtually the same but who are very competitive in many ways. One calls the other on the phone, and asks him to come to his office for a meeting at 1 p.m. that afternoon. (Notice that one man is initiating, which generally indicates higher status, that he is specifying the *place* and the *time*, which diminishes the other's influence on those decisions, and that the "invitation" comes only a few hours before the intended meeting, which may imply the other has nothing more important he must do.) The chances are good that the second man will not arrive before or even at 1 p.m. for the meeting, unless his compulsiveness about time in general is so great that it overcomes his feelings about being "put down" (in which case he has lost a round in their competition and may be searching for a victory during the meeting). He might well arrive late, perhaps five to ten minutes, which is enough to irritate but not openly insult, and then offer either no apology or only a very casual one. By the way he handles time in this setting, he will communicate to the first executive, and so he is likely to work out his response as carefully as a choreographer does a ballet. Yet little of the process may be fully conscious for him. As Hall says in the title of his book, these are often truly silent languages for many of us.

Perhaps you will see more clearly why men in public life are so concerned with such matters. The complex and delicate negotiations between President Johnson and Premier Kosygin during the latter's visit to the UN in 1967, about *where* they might meet, led each to come "halfway," to a small college that was neutral territory belonging to neither. For President Johnson to have come to New York or for the Premier to have gone to Washington would have communicated something neither wished to "say." This may look silly on one level, but laughing at a culture can ring hollow in the end. Yet I am getting ahead of myself, since I will discuss the uses of space later on. Let's get back to time.

The longer a man is kept waiting the worse he feels, because he suffers increasing damage to his ego. If the young salesman who was invited to his company president's office for a 3 p.m. meeting arrives at a "respectful" 2:50 and is told by the secretary to have a seat, he remains relatively comfortable until 3 p.m. If the secretary waits until 3:10 to phone the president and remind him the salesman is there, she communicates that she thinks a ten-minute wait is about all she can handle without feeling that the salesman will be feeling the first pangs of being unwanted. If she hangs up the phone and says "He'll be right with you" and the clock continues to tick until 3:25, she might feel impelled to say something about how busy the president is today (i.e., "Don't feel bad. It's nothing personal."). By 3:45 the salesman is likely to be angry, because he is likely to assume that the president doesn't *really* care about seeing him. If the president comes out of his office to get the salesman and apologizes for being late and explains why (especially if the explanation includes information about "the top" that the salesman is not usually aware of), the salesman may "forgive" his boss ("That's all right. I don't mind at all. Your time is more important than mine.") and all can go well. If the president buzzes his secretary and tells her to send the salesman in, and then proceeds directly to the business at hand, the salesman is likely to be torn between the anger he feels and the fear of expressing it, which may ruin their meeting without either one knowing why. In short, then, the longer a man is kept waiting, the more "social stroking" he needs to smooth his ruffled feathers. Awareness of the process can reduce its power to discomfort when you are on the receiving end, and can increase your skill at helping others to realize when you were not deliberately, with intent, trying to "put them down." If you were doing it deliberately, with malice aforethought, then I suggest there is something wrong with you that is not particularly related to culture.

Using time to manipulate or control others is common, even if we who do so are unaware of it. I once hired a Mexican-American gardener on a monthly contract to care for my yard. When we were discussing the arrangements, I felt somewhat uncertain that he would do all I wanted done or do it to my satisfaction. My feelings of mistrust were expressed by focusing upon time. I wanted to know precisely what day of the week he would come and how many hours he would stay. He seemed to understand and said "Thursdays. Four hours."

Well, he actually did come on Thursdays once in a while, but he also came on every other day of the week except Sunday and Monday. He never to my knowledge stayed four hours even when I happened to be home. I was sure I was being taken until it occurred to me that the yard had never looked so good and that everything really needing to be done was done.

The gardener apparently thought in terms of planting and cutting and fertilizing cycles. He felt his duty was to the *yard*, not to me. He sent me bills about every three or four months and then he often had to ask me what I owed him. He trusted me completely to pay him what he deserved. He worked in terms of seasons of the *year*, and I was trying to pin him down to an *hourly* basis. My attempt to replace my insecurity with the brittle satisfactions of controlling another person would eventually have led him to quit or me to fire him. I was lucky to see what was going on, and I left him alone. We got along fine.

## Scarcity

Perhaps you have already seen that my dealing with the gardener introduced another notion about time: *scarcity*. I wanted at least his four hours. We seem to see time as a limited resource for each man, so we think that what a man chooses to do with what time he has is a signal about how he *feels* about us.

You are already experienced with the application of this notion. We all have notions about how frequently we "ought" to see certain persons in order to express a "suitable" amount of affection. Take visits home to see your parents. Some students go home every weekend, some only on vacations, some only at holidays, some never. But almost all parents are pleased, assuming they like their kids, to find that their offspring choose to come visit them rather than do something else. There is a mutual exclusivity operating here. If you go home to see your parents they know you did so at the expense of some other option. If your other options were attractive, they hear that you care enough about your relationship with them to forego some other pleasure. Simply choosing to "spend your time" with them is thus a gift of sorts and a signal about your sentiments.

Even when the choice of how or with whom we spend our time is not really our own, others may "hear" a communication about our feelings. If you and two other persons begin to meet after class once a week for coffee and then you take a part-time job which forces you to go directly from class to work, your missing coffee will be "understood" as out of your control (given the choice you made to work). But the loss of interaction must be made up elsewhere or your friends will probably feel that you "withdrew."

Some people are really tough on this one. You may have three final exams to study for and a broken leg, and like most professors some mothers will insist you come to the appointed meeting and bring your leg with you. And there need be no unreasonable demands involved for misunderstandings to occur. Perfectly reasonable people can think we don't care for them because we do something else rather than see them. They can misjudge the importance to us of the something else. A supervisor who spends more time per day with one subordinate because the tasks being done temporarily require closer supervision may communicate to his other subordinates, especially if his time with them is temporarily reduced, that he "cares" more about what the one subordinate is *doing*, and perhaps will come to care more about *him* than them.

There may be more than a little truth in this. Sociologists have noted that it is not uncommon for positive sentiment to increase as the frequency of interaction increases, albeit with several important exceptions (including the problem of formal authority[3]).

But even in our informal relationships, we often experience with new friends an increase in frequency of interaction that accelerates beyond the point of equilibrium, given the importance the relationship comes to have for one or both persons. Then, if one person begins to withdraw a bit in order to adjust the frequency to the kind and amount of the sentiment, the other person—especially if he is lonely or flattered by the former attention—tends to feel hurt. This hurt can lead him to react by further reducing the frequency of contact, and until someone says openly what they are feeling, the cycle can proceed to the destruction of the relationship.

The point of this is, again, that time is seen as scarce, and thus who you choose to "give your time to" is a way of measuring your sentiments. Simply being more aware of this can help you recognize the usefulness of simply *saying*, out loud, what the meaning of your choices is for you. And, of course, such awareness also helps prevent you from assuming the meanings of other persons without checking their intent.

## Repetition

Finally, time has meaning for us in terms of repetition of activities. Some of our personal rhythms are so intimate and familiar to us that we are unaware of them. Most of us eat three meals a day, for example, not two, not five. The culture assumes lunch is at noon for the most part, and this was probably in response to what people experienced in terms of hunger. But the convention also becomes a structure to which we adapt and with which we become familiar. When we experience an interruption of our pattern we often become irritated. I can recall, for example, that I found it difficult to adjust to a change in schedule on my first teaching job. For several years as a doctoral candidate I had had coffee at 10 a.m. with a group of congenial colleagues. The coffee hour became one of the central social functions of my day, in addition to a means of getting some caffeine into my reluctantly awakening body. When I began teaching I had a 9 o'clock and a 10 o'clock class three days a week, and I was troubled by the 10 o'clock class and adjusted intuitively by bringing a cup of coffee

[3]See Chapter 8.

into the class with me. The pattern was so well developed and so valued within me that I was willing to "break a norm" (and, in fact, a *rule*) against food in the classrooms in order to have my 10 o'clock coffee. It sounds like a small matter, and in one sense it is, but it makes my point even if it is a trivial example. There *are* daily cycles we are used to, and while there are many we share, there are others relatively unique to each of us. The closer to the *body* any repetitions of activity come, the more important they are to us.

Take seasons of the year, for example. In areas that have weather rather than climate, say, New England rather than southern California, the use of time varies from season to season as activities change. People in Boston not only put away their silver and use their stainless steel in August but they give different kinds of parties with different time rules than they do in winter. In general, the rules are relaxed, more variety is "allowed," and time is less carefully measured for meaning.

Our rhythms are also influenced by our feasts and holidays and rituals. Christmas, Easter, Father's Day, Thanksgiving, Memorial Day, and the like all have their "time" in the year. It has been hypothesized that Christ was really born in August, and that the December celebration of his birth came about because the peoples of northern Europe had long had a pagan winter festival which they were used to. In any event, we are accustomed to certain activities and feelings in connection with each "special day."

Take Christmas, for example. Most businessmen know that there will be less work done just prior to Christmas and afterwards than is usual. People experience a need for closeness, for family, for ritual, for the nostalgia of past Christmases, for gift-giving and midnight services. They eat more and drink more and even get fond of their old Aunt Minny. It is a time set aside for warmth, affection, children and family, friends, and ritual.

The Greeks, however, celebrate their Easter much as we do our Christmas, and mark their Christmas almost as casually as we do our Easter. If you were to spend Christmas in Athens you would likely sense something as missing. If you were there on Easter you would get a "bonus." If you were working on a job that peaked in volume between December 20 and January 3 and you had to work long hours, the chances are you would feel quite resentful. The rhythms of our days, our weeks (the weekend having become an institution), our months, our years are all deeply familiar to us even if we are unaware of them. Any serious disruption of any of them is felt as deprivation. Just being aware of this can help you in many ways—planning changes, for example. Can you see why major changes in work design or location or personnel are particularly resented during the Christmas holidays?

Then, for students (and nowadays nearly everyone in the country spends at least twelve years as one and more are spending sixteen or even eighteen), certain rhythms that matter are established. Where else in our culture do people get promoted every year for anything better than dreadful work? Where else can people choose their bosses (professors) so as to avoid certain ones, and where else can they drop out from one of them with no penalty after several weeks' work? If you look at the assumptions students naturally take with them to work from school, you can see why the yearly immigration of graduates into business is such a trauma for both students and companies. Subculture shock is what it is.

And a subsummary may help here. Basically all I am saying so far is that time is important to us in many ways, that *when* you do what you do says things to others about what you feel, and that the "rules" about time vary from setting to setting. If you will just watch for one day what is going on in your life vis-à-vis *time*, I think you will see some interesting things.

## SPACE

Space is a language as expressive as time. It seems that we have five general notions about space which I will discuss here.

### More Is Better than Less

The chances are good that you have all seen various business organizations. If you have, the chances are even better that you found the size of offices related to the status of persons there. It is rare indeed to find a company president occupying a smaller office than his subordinates, and it is not uncommon to find the top man ensconced in a suite of rooms. One of the ways we "tell" people about the importance of persons is by the amount of space we assign to them. Space is scarce and a limited resource like time.

I recall a distinguished senior professor returning to a school after a long and nearly fatal illness. He was being moved from his old office to a new one in an air-conditioned wing of the building, largely because the dean of his school believed the air-conditioning would be of help to him. The professor may have thought he "heard" something else, for as I passed his office one day I found him on his hands and knees measuring the width and length of his new office with a twelve-inch ruler. It was a good deal smaller than his prior office, and I think he was "learning" that his illness had diminished his importance to the school, so that he was reduced to a smaller office. It would be amusing if it were not so painful.

Another time I was being toured through a new and beautiful office building of a large corporation. The president's office was handsome indeed, but when I was taken next door to the executive vice-president's office, I realized that the VP had a larger and recognizably more stunning space in which to work. I asked my guide, an officer of the company, how long the president and executive vice-president had been vying for power. He looked surprised and defensively asked "Why do you ask?" I told him what I saw in the use of space. He laughed and said "Another theory bites the dust! The VP's office is better because he has charge of sales in this district and his office is our best example of what we can do for customers."

A year later the VP and president came into open conflict in seeking the support of the board of directors, and the VP left the organization. Of course, the offices alone were not the *cause*. But they were a signal that something was off. There are few organizations that can accept incongruence in the use of space when it communicates so clearly to hundreds of employees. In the company mentioned, I heard later, the most frequent question in the executive ranks prior to the VP's departure was "Who is running this place?"

Of course we observe this in everyday life. We want *larger* houses on *more* land. We want lots with a view. (Although I swear I never see anyone with a picture window looking out at the view. What we want, I suspect, is simply the illusion of an enlargement of our space.) Yet other people are more comfortable in smaller spaces. Latin peoples love to be awed by cathedrals and vistas in parks, but they seem to enjoy being "hugged" by smaller rooms at home and at work. The smaller space apparently is associated with warmth and touch and intimacy, while larger spaces are associated with status and power and importance. Perhaps that is why entering a huge office intimidates many of us. We almost physically inflate the man who occupies it, as Negro children in the deep South do white kids when they draw them next to Negro kids. In any event, there is a strong tendency in organizational subcultures to relate the amount of space assigned to individuals to their formal status or organizational height. Check this out in your own school or in any business. When the pattern doesn't hold, something interesting is going on.

### Private Is Better than Public

As a doctoral candidate I was first given a desk in a large room with many other desks, then was upgraded to a cubicle with six-foot walls and an open top, then to a private office. It was minuscule, but I could shut it up and be alone or private within it. Then as I began working as a professor, I shared an office with two other men, then I shared it with one other man, and again I have my own private office, roughly twice as big as my last one. The sequence and size are what matter here. It is "better" to have your own space than to share it, and it is "better" if it can be closed off for privacy than if it is open to the sight or hearing of other persons.

And we use much the same thinking about country clubs or pools or university clubs. By excluding *some* others, on whatever criteria, we make it feel more private to us. And we like that. The very process of exclusion marks the boundaries of our space both physically and socially, and, of course, psychologically. When we say a person is "closed" we mean we are excluded from him. Thus the process of defining the extent to which our various spaces are private is complex. As we set our boundaries we also exclude. And we need our own space as we also at times need to be "open." Yet in organizations, it is clearly the rule that private offices are better than public ones. To go from a large but public office to a smaller but private one is a mixed blessing, but often the balance is favorable. For we are not like Miss Garbo who wants to be alone, but we do want to be *able* to be alone or private when we wish.

A powerful illustration of the value we place on privacy took place in the 1920s. A coal company in West Virginia owned the houses in which its miners lived. When the miners struck, the company took the doors off the houses. Another example is the automobile company that took the doors off the men's room stalls in the 1950s to discourage workers from long toilet breaks. The response in both instances was pretty strong, and understandably so. When a space is designed for activity that is close to our body, we value its privacy all the more. Our free-flowing modern houses almost always have doors on at least two rooms—the bedroom and bathroom. Perhaps that famous "key to the executive men's room" is of more utility than arbitrary status.

Given the importance we attach to privacy, the way we use the space we have "talks" to others. If we have a private office and shut its door to speak with a man, we announce a message to him and to those outside. We are saying "This conversation is important and not to be overheard or casually interrupted." Neither the man nor those outside know whether the news is good or bad, but they do know that you care about it. For we close off our space for more intimate behavior. Whether it is angry or loving, we intend to *focus* importantly.

## Higher Is Better than Lower

Only last week I watched my three-year-old daughter playing "I'm the king of the castle" with friends. They laughingly fought each other for position at the top of a small steep hill. Each wanted to be on top, to be higher up than the others—in this instance, quite literally, in space. When they grow up, I fell to musing, they'll jockey for height with less laughter and more discomfort.

Perhaps our desire to be higher rather than lower comes from such childlike games, or rather from the important business of being little for so long, and thus less powerful than we might wish. In any event, houses higher on the hill, from Hong Kong to Corning, New York, are "better" (and usually more expensive) than those below. The view is often cited as the reason, but I don't believe it. It's a residue of our childhood that probably reaches back in evolution far beyond the Greek who built the Acropolis on a sharp-rising rock for protection as much as grandeur. Much as dogs still circle about before they lie to sleep (a still visible link to their wild forebears who circled to crush tall grass into a kind of nest), we seek height for reasons in large part lost to us.

We move *up* in organizations, or *climb the ladder*. We go *up* to the head office and down to the shop. We call the wealthiest people the *upper* classes and the poorest the *lower* classes. Much of our imagery for what we value is in terms of up and down. People from Boston go "down" to Maine, although it is north of Boston. Allegedly this is because early travelers were referring to tides, but it also fits the notion of many Bostonians that Boston is the apex, the Athens of America. One can only go down from Boston!

On a more concrete level, the ground-floor, walk-in legal aid centers that have opened their doors in deprived neighborhoods are less frightening to prospective clients partly because of their ground-level location. Here again space speaks. To be higher than you is to be better than you.

## Near Is Better than Far

Really, this one can be just the reverse of what it says. It depends upon whether sentiments are positive or negative. Near is better if the sentiments are positive. Far is better if the sentiments are negative.

In a business organization, it is not uncommon for the offices near the boss to be more highly valued than those farther away. If the chief executive officer is on the third floor, the others also on that floor are assumed to be privileged. They are closer to the top man and thus have more opportunities for informal interaction, as well as the formal designation of spatial assignment near the boss's space.

The same principle holds at formal dinner parties, where nearness to the host is valued. The further down the table one is placed, the lower one's status at the dinner. In branch organizations that cover large territories a common problem is that each branch develops internal loyalties greater than the loyalty to the head office. The distance from the center of the organization impedes communication.

Thus when the sentiments are positive, being near is better than being far away. As I mentioned, the reverse is also true. People prefer to increase distance when their sentiments are negative.

## In Is Better than Out

We seem to assume that people who work inside are better than those who work outside, perhaps because of the respective associations with mental and manual work. Baseball teams prefer to be in their own field, their most familiar space. Often when we are uneasy or anxious we move to our own space. In it, we feel more secure.

The basic difference between in-out and near-far is that the former works from a specific point while the latter is a matter of degree. But they are closely related. Let me give an example in my own life. A wedding was to take place in the side chapel off the main seating area of a church. The number of guests exceeded the number of seats in the chapel. So decisions needed to be made about who sat *in* the chapel and who sat *out*side it. There were thus created two classes of guests: those sitting inside and those sitting outside; yet within each class there was a sliding scale at work. How close to the front of your class were you seated? I can tell you those who sat at the back of the second class felt like relative "outsiders." Certainly, they were not among the "in-group."

Naturally these five dimensions of space are related. An office that is *smaller* but *private* and *near* an important executive may be highly desirable in spite of its size. When you consider the impact of space, you must look at the possible influence of each of the five dimensions, and at how they can balance each other out in specific settings.

## Interpersonal Space

On a more personal level we have another silent language related to space. We have the general notion that we own the space around us, much like an invisible bubble. Others are to stay outside the bubble except when powerful feelings—of intimacy or anger—are being expressed. Touch is especially to be avoided in our culture with the same exceptions. How many times have you sat next to a stranger in a movie theater and jockeyed for the single armrest? Because touching is out, it often ends up under the arm of the bolder person who risks touch. The other will usually pull away.

I recall an amusing yet painful incident at a recent cocktail party. An atractive woman, newly arrived from Israel, was talking with an American male of Swedish descent. Her conception of the proper distance from her face to his was about half the distance he in turn would feel comfortable with. She would step in, he would step back. She virtually chased him across the room before they both gave up. She dismissed him as "cold." He saw her as "pushy." Each had a different notion of the appropriateness of distance given their relationship, and neither could feel comfortable with the other's behavior.

When someone with a different notion of the use of space interpersonally steps into our bubble we feel crowded, aggressed upon, and we intuitively expect either anger or affection to be expressed.

In addition, in our mouthwashed, deodorant-using culture the idea of smelling another's body or breath is often repugnant. The experience is avoided except in lovemaking, and even there many perfume away all traces of personal odor. Yet other peoples enjoy being close enough to others in public settings to feel their body warmth and smell their natural odors, and they touch others much more often then we do. When we meet such people we have a terrible time because they "say" things, in the way they use space, that we do not appreciate or understand. They, in turn, find us as difficult as we find them.

Yet within this huge country there are many subgroups with variations in their use of interpersonal space. Men walking down the street in the Italian district of Boston often do so arm in arm, something one would seldom if ever see in the New York Yacht Club. And in any large business organization, you can see the effects of variations in the use of space complicating relationships. A warm, expressive executive who feels comfortable touching the arm or shoulder of a subordinate may make him exceedingly uncomfortable if he is the nontouch, keep-your-distance type. You can watch your own behavior here to see how you use your own space and how you react to others who behave differently. Just being aware of it helps a great deal.

In summary, then, remember that people use space to say things that they are often unaware of, but highly responsive to. To the extent that you can become aware of your own patterns, you can be more skillful at saying what you mean to others and hearing what they mean. It is a fascinating exploration.

## THINGS

This aspect of cultural communication is so easily grasped that I will just briefly present the ten generalizations I have. Each points to what I see as the *major* assumption operating in our culture. Each naturally has exceptions which I will largely leave to you to document.

*Bigger Is Better than Smaller*. The automobile is a perfect example in the U.S.A. Except for small sports cars, it is clear that bigger is regarded as better than smaller. The exceptions prove the rule.

*More Is Better than Fewer*. Two cars, houses, etc., are better than one.

*Clean Is Better than Dirty*. The American fetish.

*Neat and Orderly Is Better than Messy and Disorderly*. A clean desk may communicate efficiency, while a messy one may "say" you are disorganized in many settings.

*Expensive Is Better than Cheap*.

*Unique Is Better than Common*. Original works of art are "better" than reproductions.

*Beautiful Is Better than Ugly*.

*Accurate Is Better than Inaccurate*.

*Very Old or Very New is Better than Recent*.

*Personal Is Better than Public*. One's own object, say, chair or desk, is valued as a possession. When a person brings personal property to the office he is saying something about the extent of his involvement with what goes on in his office.

## SUMMARY

Just as the various aspects of space are interrelated (remember the *little* but *private* office *near* the boss?) so, too, do they overlap with our use of things. If that same little office has an expensive, one-of-a-kind Persian rug in it, and antique furniture, it can become even more valued even though it is small.

The way we and others use time and space and things *talks*. If you are deaf to the messages, you miss much of the richness of what is being said by you and others. If you start "listening" consciously, you can appreciate all the subtle harmonics that are available and increase your personal skill in being with other persons in and out of organizations.

# CHAPTER 3

# Basic Concepts for Small Groups

The background factors listed in Chapter 1 and briefly explained in Chapter 2 were useful for sensing the totality of organizations at a fairly general level. To increase the depth of our grasp of behavior in organizations, we need to develop our ability to comprehend in detail some of its parts. We will go about this by studying the way small work groups function within the organization.[1]

We will focus at considerable length on *behavior in small groups* for several reasons. One is that people often behave differently in groups than they do when alone; groups are important determinants of behavior. Second, many of us spend much of our time in groups, and the average person belongs to as many as five or six important groups at any one time in his lifetime. Third, groups are relatively easy to study; they are small enough to be observed and understood, at least partially, and

[1]The basic way of thinking about a social system presented in Chapters 3 through 5 is derived from George C. Homans, *The Human Group* (New York: Harcourt, Brace & World, Inc., 1950). The diagram of the conceptual scheme presented in this chapter is similar to Arthur N. Turner's in Paul R. Lawrence and John A. Seiler et al., *Organizational Behavior and Administration*, rev. ed. (Homewood, Ill.: Richard D. Irwin, Inc., and the Dorsey Press, 1965), p. 158. Other useful sources on small-group behavior include Marvin E. Shaw, *Group Dynamics, The Psychology of Small Group Behavior* (New York: McGraw-Hill Book Co., 1971) and Dorwin Cartwright and Alvin Zander, eds., *Group Dynamics Research and Theory*, 3rd ed. (New York: Harper and Row, 1968).

much research has already been done on them. Fourth, small groups are easily affected by leaders and managers, in contrast with whole organizations, which usually are much more difficult to influence. Finally, skill developed in understanding small groups helps one better understand large social systems, such as those of whole organizations.

## Types of Groups

There are, of course, many different kinds of groups. A person might belong to a primary work group, but he might also be a member of one or more committees or a project team or an ad hoc task force. Some of these might be permanent, and others temporary. Some, including many primary task groups, operate continuously, while others (e.g., committees) function intermittently.

Although multiple group membership is common, most people usually identify more with one group than others. This one is called a *primary* group. Other groups with which a person identifies, but not as strongly, are called *secondary* groups. How closely a member identifies with a group will influence his involvement, commitment, and motivation.

Groups can also be classified or described in terms of their general purpose. Table 1 suggests several different kinds of task groups, which will be our main concern. It is useful to be aware of the differences between these groups and to assess the significance of these variations for behavior. Attempting to distinguish the most important function of a group at a particular time helps in diagnosing and evaluating the behavior of its members.

Groups also vary with respect to their stages of development. These stages include formation, early development, ongoing operation, and

**Table 1 Task Groups Classified by Broad Purpose**

| | |
|---|---|
| Production | Coordinating |
| Processing | Planning |
| Problem solving | Brainstorming |
| Decision making | Information dissemination |
| Advisory | Discussion—exploration |

major change periods or termination. The particular stage a specific group is in affects the kinds of problems it is likely to face. We will examine this important aspect later. But first we will turn to the development of a model of group behavior that will help you focus on the functioning of small work groups.

## Basic Concepts

By *small group*, we mean a number of people who regularly communicate with one another (usually face to face) over a period of time, who think of themselves as a group, and who differentiate their group from others, either implicitly or explicitly.[2]

To focus on the functioning of small work groups requires that we bring more concepts to bear upon the phenomenon being studied. It may help, as before, to regard the background factors previously discussed as elements in a play about to open. All the people and props are ready. The entire production is poised for the curtain to go up and for the players to actually begin to *behave*. Our work so far could build from snapshots. Now we begin to deal with behavior in the settings we have observed and interpreted, and we would need, to burden the analogy further, moving pictures to catch much of the complexity of the actual behavior.

Instead of movies, we will use case studies and our own experiences. But before we go further into the cases, we need some basic concepts to use in ordering the behavior to be studied. These are:

Interactions

Activities Sentiments

By *activities*, we mean the physical movements people make that can be observed by an outsider; some examples are dictating a letter, swinging a golf club, running a mimeograph machine, or walking down a hall.

By *interaction*, we mean the mutual response of people participating in an activity. The stimulating activity may be verbal or nonverbal: Two men talking to each other would be an example of the former; two men simply shaking hands, an example of the latter. When we observe interactions, we look for three aspects of them: *frequency*, *duration*, and *order*. When you look for frequency, you will want to know how often the people interact. Ten times a day? Once a month? When you look for duration, you will want to know how long the interaction goes on.

[2]The meaning of "small group" will be elaborated in the next two chapters.

Do the people interact for ten minutes or for an hour? The order of the interaction has to do with who initiates it. Does Joe always approach Pete? or does Pete always approach Joe? or do they share the initiative to some extent?

By *sentiments,* we mean all of the internal feelings, attitudes, and drives that exist within a person. Unlike most activities and interactions, they are not directly observable, but must be *inferred* from the activities and interactions that express them. We infer that someone is angry from how his face looks and what he is saying and how he is saying it. We *infer* from his observable behavior that which lies within him. When we analyze sentiments, we look at the *number of people who share them,* the *degree of conviction* they have, and the *intensity* they feel. For example, a group of ten men may share a feeling of irritation because they believe that a certain management practice is wrong and be absolutely *convinced* they are right but not feel very *intensely* about the matter personally.

Although the three concepts—activity, interaction, and sentiment—are separate, they are closely related. The drawing may help you to understand their mutual dependence. Let us illustrate them, in sequence, with one encounter. Suppose Joe sees Ann at a party. Sentiments of attraction occur in him, and so he walks over to where she is sitting (sentiment-activity). He strikes up a conversation (activity-interaction), and as they talk, he finds he likes her better (interaction-sentiment), so he asks her to dance (sentiment-activity-interaction). They dance and enjoy it (activity-interaction-sentiment). Can you see the relationship between the concepts as clearly as you can the one between Joe and Ann? We hope so, for we are leaving the illustration but not the concepts.

We have identified each of the three key concepts (activity, interaction, and sentiment) and their mutual dependence. We will explore them in more detail in the next chapters, but first we must continue our overview by introducing what we will call the required system, the personal system, and the emergent system.

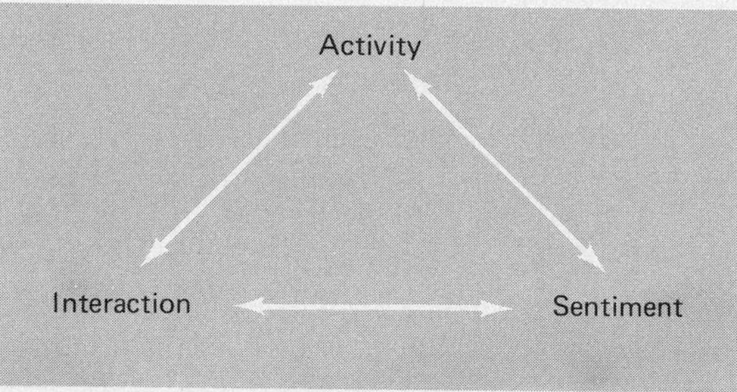

## Required System

By *required system*, we mean those activities, interactions, and sentiments that are *essential*, or *required*, in a group if it is to survive as a group. That is, the background factors are related in ways that produce certain requirements of a group. For example, the tellers in a branch bank simply *must* count money (required activity), talk with customers (required interaction and required activity), and feel their job is sufficiently satisfying to keep at it (required sentiment), or something will happen to a member of the group or to the entire group. Management will often rapidly force changes upon a group when the system's requirements are not met.

The required system is a result of all the background factors, but it is especially important to management because it relates most directly to the task necessary for the accomplishments of the organization's purpose. One can imagine how long a teller who refused to count money would have to wait before her supervisor did something about it.

## Personal System

By *personal system*, we mean the values, beliefs, aspirations, knowledge, ways of thinking, sentiments, and perceptions that each individual in an organization brings with him from the wider culture. Management may not require them at all. In fact, managers may wish they were not entirely as they are. But people have feelings and values and beliefs—in other words, entire internal emotional systems—which they do not leave behind when they come to work. In a sense, this system is the *psychological* one in that it relates to each person's inner life. However, it also includes the individual's whole being, and so is a physiological system as well.

A group is often composed of people who have common *values*, but the particular value orientation of each individual is largely his before he joins the group.

An example of how an individual's personal system affects a group in an organization is not hard to imagine. Say a man *feels* and *believes* that neatness, personal order, and cleanliness are very important and "good." His problems in a group of people who appreciate the "warmth" of personal clutter should be apparent.

The personal system is one of great complexity, and we will deal with it in more depth in Chapter 7. For now, let us simply note that behavior in organizations has as one of its important components the personal, inner world of each of the people involved and that their individual sentiments influence what goes on in any part of the organization. Although we do not need to know *all* of a person's psychological makeup to understand his behavior in organizations, we do need to know something about it. The personal system concept helps to identify the essential relevant psychological phenomena.

### Emergent System

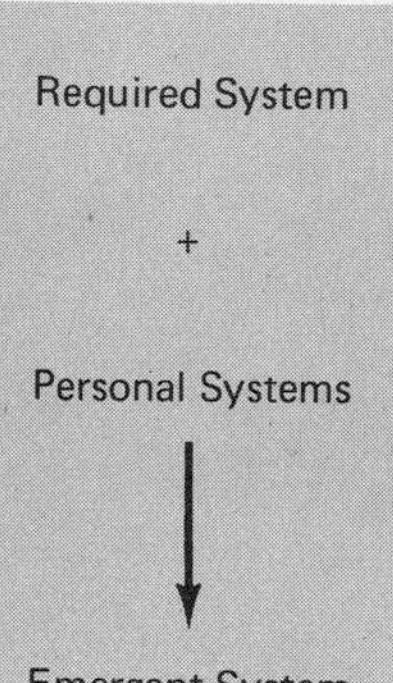


As the background factors determine the required and the personal systems, so the latter two determine the *emergent system.* By this we mean the behavior of people in a group that is not required but is in addition to what is required and thus related to the personal needs of people. Consider the bank tellers again. Their personal needs for such things as friendship and self-expression will prompt them to talk with one another, for example, or go for coffee together. This "extra" behavior *emerges* out of personal need (personal system) within the limits and opportunities of the required system. When it interferes with the required system, managers, as we have said, often act fast. But when the required system is designed so that the personal needs of people for social relationships are thwarted, making little emergent behavior possible, the deprivation to the individuals can be severe enough to cause rapid employee turnover or to produce hostile behavior. When emergent behavior supports the required system, managers are likely to say, "We have a fine group. Our people get along well together."

The emergent system is composed of emergent interactions, emergent sentiments, and emergent activities. Remember Joe and Ann, our young couple at the party? Their behavior was certainly not required but was clearly emergent. Joe's sentiment-activity in walking toward Ann, his activity-interaction in beginning a conversation, his activity-sentiment in dancing with her, and his sentiment-activity-interaction in ultimately asking her for a date, *all* were emergent. His and her personal systems led, within the required system of the party, to their emergent behavior.

NORMS. When a group of people are working together over some time, their emergent behavior tends to become their customary way of behaving. Out of this extended emergent interaction, activity, and sentiment develop notions shared by all about what the members of the group *ought* to do under given circumstances. We will call these notions *norms.* Norms are *not* what people most often actually do (the average, for example)—they are what people in a group think they *ought* to do under given circumstances.

A group of ten members may have a norm that could be stated as "Each member ought to produce 500 parts a day." If we were to count each person's production, we could very well find a range like the one in Table 2, in which workers 3 and 4 come closest. If you assume that these

**Table 2**

| Worker | Output |
|---|---|
| 1 | 590 |
| 2 | 511 |
| 3 | 507 |
| 4 | 496 |
| 5 | 491 |
| 6 | 488 |
| 7 | 463 |
| 8 | 455 |
| 9 | 452 |
| 10 | 400 |

outputs are typical, you might also deduce reasonably that worker 1 is a "ratebuster," workers 2 to 6 are "regulars," workers 7 to 9 are a subgroup of deviants, and worker 10 is an "isolate."

Each norm, then, will be an *ought* with a *range* of actual behavior in relation to it. That person who best meets all the norms, or best meets the ones most important to the group, often becomes the informal leader of the group. Others in the group will emerge in a hierarchy in terms of the decreasing degree to which they meet the group's norms.

We will call this hierarchy of informal rank, together with other patterns of relationships that emerge within the group, the *internal social structure* (to be discussed further in Chapter 4). This structure is usually implicit, but it nevertheless exists. Thus, within a group, social structure will develop in relation to the norms, which in turn grow out of extended emergent interaction, activity, and sentiment.

The norms developed in the emergent system will relate to both the systems that influenced it—namely, the required and the personal systems. In other words, groups will develop norms for all of their important behavior, whether required or personal. The way a group functions in terms of its individual needs (the personal systems) is important to it; the way it responds to the required system is important to management and thus to the group as well. The group will develop norms about how much to produce, how to relate to bosses, how to behave with one another, what to wear, etc. So the emergent system is obviously of great importance to our overall scheme. Emergent behavior adds greatly to the richness and variety of life in organizations; it also makes the problem of administering human beings complex, challenging, and often difficult.

## Behavioral Consequences

From behavior of people within an organization come such important consequences as *productivity*, *satisfaction*, and *revitalization*. Productivity refers to the quality and quantity of products and/or services, i.e., the output (in relation to inputs) that is ostensibly the organization's "logical" or formal purpose. Satisfaction refers to the positive feelings of the people in a group about themselves and their situation. How much of what kind of satisfactions are they getting? Revitalization refers to the increased ability to cope with and adapt to changes in both the internal and external environments. For the individual this includes growth, in terms of emotional health or skill or learning of various kinds. For the social system in which individuals behave, it means the capacity to change internally to permit more productivity and/or satisfaction in the long run.

We will refer to productivity, satisfaction, and revitalization collectively as *effectiveness*. This term implies that to be effective a system must produce all three. The complexity imposed by these multiple criteria for effectiveness demolishes any meaningful idea of maximizing effectiveness—at best, an organization can only approach an *optimization* of these criteria. Table 3 suggests that each of the components of effectiveness may

**Table 3 Behavioral Consequences: Effectiveness**

| | *Effectiveness* | | |
|---|---|---|---|
| Entities | productivity | satisfaction | revitalization |
| Individual | | | |
| Group | | | |
| Organization | | | |

be viewed from the vantage point of any of the principal entities; namely, the individual, group, and organization. The consequences of behavior may vary by entity and category.

A second major behavioral consequence of importance to small groups is *cohesiveness*. By cohesiveness is meant the tightness of the interpersonal bonds that hold a group together. Cohesiveness and effectiveness are essentially different concepts and both will be discussed later in more detail.

**BEHAVIORAL CONSEQUENCES**

*Effectiveness*

Productivity

Satisfaction

Revitalization

*Cohesiveness*

## Social Systems Conceptual Scheme

A chart of our entire scheme follows on page 91. Note, however, that the final outcomes—productivity, satisfaction, revitalization, and cohesiveness—*feed back* into the background factors. If productivity is insufficient, management will know and presumably take some action (most often by changing the required system). If satisfaction is high but based on dangerous and costly horseplay, again management may well act. If satisfaction is low, required sentiments may be negative and workers may be absent often or even quit.

The point is that the feedback line closes a circle that proceeds again to move across toward the consequences. Our scheme is of a *dynamic* system. Each variable in it is related to other variables, and many of the relationships are mutually dependent. As one variable changes, so do others as a result, and the latter changes may, in turn, affect the first variable. Our task is to try to grasp some understanding of the dynamic, complex, ongoing functioning of specific behavioral systems by *using* the concepts. The concepts are of value only if they can be used to achieve better insights and greater understanding.

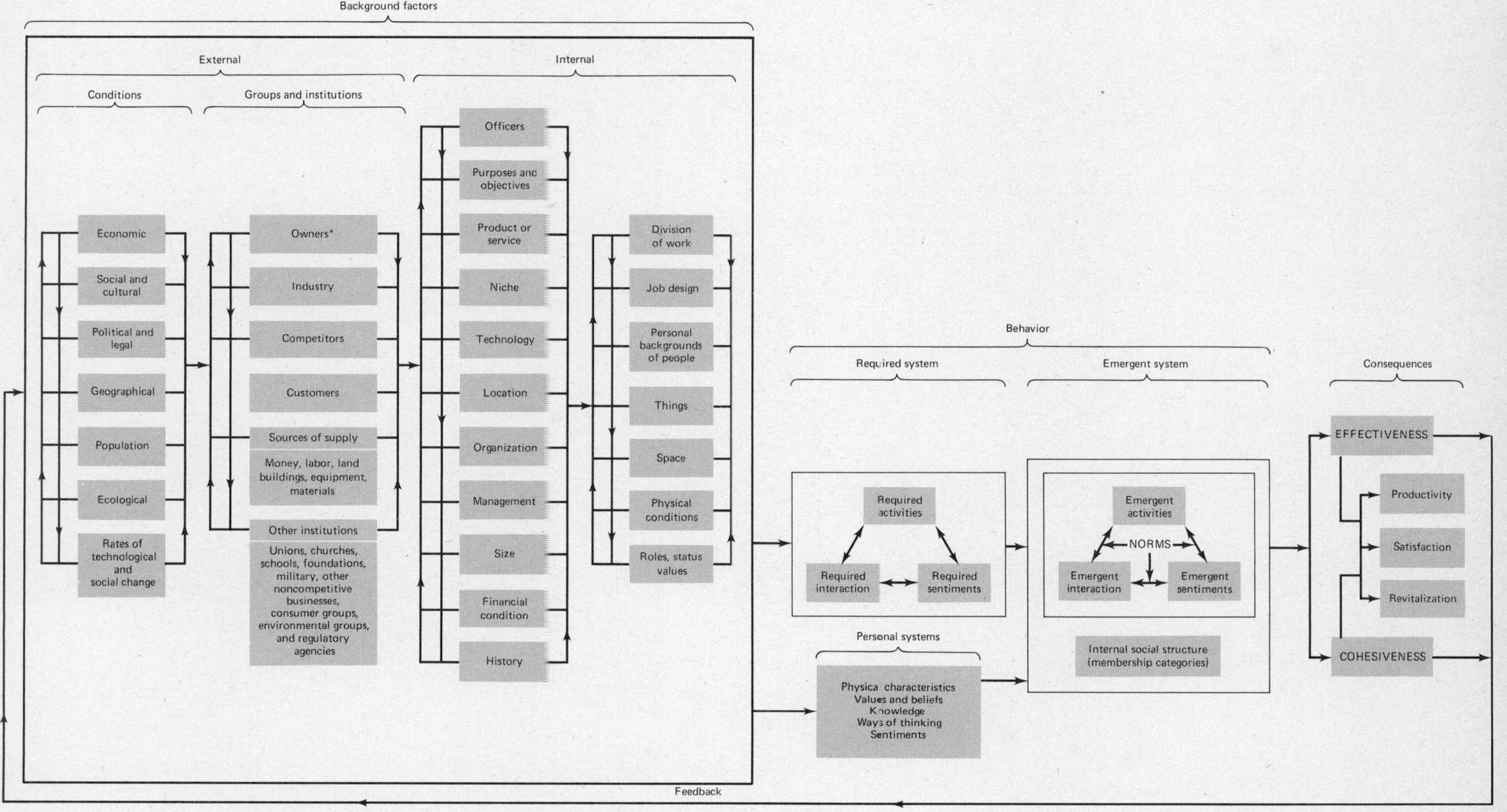


**Figure 1** Social Systems Conceptual Scheme

The required system in business settings is designed by managers primarily to achieve productivity. If a particular group of people were willing and able to behave *only* in the required system, those managers concerned only with productivity might well be satisfied. But people are not willing to live only in the required system. They have their own personal systems to satisfy, and when options are available to them, they will seek settings in which their needs for satisfaction and revitalization (both, in part, a function of productivity, of course) are met. So the manager who sees only the required system simply has his head in the sand.

As we have discussed, the required system, along with the personal systems, sets in motion a third system, the emergent. The relationship of these three systems to the subsequent consequences (productivity, satisfaction, revitalization, and cohesiveness) is complex. Those who care only about productivity and thus see the required system as "good" and the other two as nuisances try to control people to force them to produce and *only* produce. Such control is rarely achieved in any society, and especially not in ours. The ability of people to defy it is amazing and results in a responsive range of emergent behavior that proceeds from minor—e.g., restriction of output—to major and violent—e.g., outright sabotage.

On the other hand, those who care only about satisfaction and revitalization, and see the required system as necessarily "inhuman" or "bad," tend to accept every "inadequacy" as "understandable" and refrain from pushing for productivity. The resulting inefficiency can be a threat to the very existence of a group (and organization), making survival its problem or at least reducing the satisfaction of the group in terms of pride in accomplishment.

Clearly, caring only about one consequence to the exclusion of the others leads to an imbalance in groups with tasks to perform. The behavior of people is affected by aspects of *each* of the three systems, and that behavior is the determinant of *each* of the consequences. The truly "practical" man is concerned with both people and productivity, because both are both means and end. Their relationship is complex, to be sure, and yet the way of thinking that we are developing is one way to grasp the complexity of an ongoing organizational system.

## SUMMARY

Behavior in small groups includes activities, interactions, and sentiments. Externally imposed *required systems* influence each group member's *personal system* and behavior to form a group *emergent system*, which gradually incorporates both the external factors impinging on the group and the internal factors introduced through the members' behavior.

The emergent system evolves from a relatively spontaneous system to one which grows increasingly normative and structuralized.

A succinct framework for organizing information relevant to how well a group is doing is provided in the behavioral *consequences* of *effectiveness* (productivity, satisfaction, revitalization) and group *cohesiveness* (mutual close-knittedness, unity, and involvement). The *Social System Conceptual Scheme* (SSCS) provides a powerful tool in the Sherlock process for organizing information about any group. The scheme focuses attention on the dynamic nature of groups by explicitly including a *feedback* loop. Thus, the impact of recent events are traced through their behavioral consequences back to likely changes in internal and external backgroup factors, and ultimately to the required and personal systems evoking the next round of emergent behaviors.

In the next chapter, we will focus largely upon the emergent system. First, we will consider certain factors in small-group functioning that tend toward *uniformities* across groups and produce *standardization* of behavior within them. Then we will explore *factors* that produce *differentiation* of behavior within groups, resulting in internal social structures and ranking that, in turn, further differentiate the behavior of members.[3]

[3]See "Territory, Maps, and Cases," pp. 131–38, and "Using the Social System Conceptual Scheme," pp. 139.

# CHAPTER 4

# Uniformities and Differentiations within the Emergent System[1]

In Chapter 3, we saw that the three major systems of behavior (required, emergent, and personal) are mutually dependent. Required systems generally permit certain emergent behavior to exist, and, in fact, almost encourage it. If the required system includes interaction among people and if their personal systems produce positive sentiments among them, then it is likely they will initiate further interaction and activity in the emergent system. The point is that the design of the required system can both encourage the beginning and influence the nature of the emergent system, just as the sentiments of the personal system do. Thus, the nature of the required system, combined with the members' needs (personal systems) for more psychological and social satisfaction than the required system alone normally can provide, inevitably leads to emergent behavior.

[1]For a detailed exploration of uniformities within groups, see George C. Homans, *The Human Group* (New York: Harcourt, Brace & World, Inc., 1950), Chapter 5. Much of this chapter is based on the theories in this book. For a further discussion of this topic, including reports on specific research, see Dorwin Cartwright and Alvin Zander, *Group Dynamics*, 2nd ed. (Evanston, Ill.: Row, Peterson & Co., 1960), especially Part Six. The interaction of job design (required system) and emergent social systems as culminating in the study of "sociotechnical systems" has been recently collected in Louis E. Davis and James C. Taylor, *Design of Jobs* (Middlesex, England: Penguin Books Inc., 1972).

If, for example, two workers find themselves newly hired to work in a department, standing close to each other and doing work that after a few hours' practice can be accomplished proficiently without close attention, we might predict that some form of emergent interaction or activity will occur if either man has (1) even mildly positive feelings for the other or (2) neutral feelings for the other but a need to express some internal sentiment of his own that is not necessarily directed toward the other. (For example, he might say: "Boy, this is a lousy place to work" or "This is a pretty good place to work, huh?")

## Relationship between Interactions and Sentiments

We might state a general hypothesis about the relationship between interactions and sentiments:

> If interactions between members of a group are required or permitted by the required system, and if sentiments of liking exist or develop between members of the group, these sentiments will lead in turn to further interactions and activities in the emergent system.[2] These interactions and activities *may*, in turn, increase the positive sentiments, leading to still further elaboration of emergent interaction and activity.[3]

And so the emergent system develops, round after round. The process does not, however, proceed at the same rate indefinitely. There are forces at work to slow its acceleration as the increasing sentiment and further elaborated activity and interaction reach a point of *equilibrium*. Perhaps the most obvious restraint is the required system. At some point, the freedom for emergent behavior on the job permitted by the required system will have been depleted by the developing emergent system. Should still increasing positive sentiment exist, off-the-job behavior may well develop. Should there be factors restricting off-the-job emergent behavior, there will be an excess of emergent positive sentiment over and above possible expression of it in further emergent interaction and activity.

The chances that this excess positive sentiment will remain unexpressed are low. One might more reasonably expect either further emergent behavior at the expense of the required system or the development of negative sentiments and corresponding behavior toward either the required system or the managers who represent it, because

[2]Because sentiments are crucial, we should be more precise, if we can, than just to say that they are *either* positive or negative. Sentiments exist along spectrums; the *intensity* of feeling at either end is high, while the middle intensity is low.

[3]If people are required to interact frequently in the required system, they may develop sentiments of *disliking* for one another. In such cases, interactions are usually limited to required ones, and emergent behavior is minimal or hostile. A clarifying theoretical integration of these dynamics may be found in William H. McWhinney, "Synthesizing A Social Interaction Model," *Sociometry*, 31, No. 3 (September, 1968).

they may appear to be the causes of the restricted opportunities for further emergent elaboration. In either instance, the resulting equilibrium is likely to be an uneasy one, because of the tensions between the two systems. Managers may increase pressure on the required system for more productivity, but some people may press for more freedom to enjoy emergent behavior. Individuals may feel forcibly the resultant conflict.

Given all of this, you may be wondering if nothing can be said about behavior that is at once more simple and less uncertain. The answer is, sadly, "no." The best we can do is to simplify at the loss of usefulness. Thus, we can only say that *interactions and activities will tend to increase as positive sentiments increase, and vice versa, until some equilibrium is approximated.*

We have already seen some restraints on the process described in this hypothesis, and at least one exception to it must be noted. When one member of a group has authority in the formal management structure or is so highly ranked in the internal structure of the group that he is very distant from certain members, then the fear of his authority or awe of his role will keep emergent behavior at a lower level than it would be otherwise. For example, frequent interaction between the higher-ranked member and another might not lead to increased liking or satisfaction, because of the subordinate's feelings of dependency or of "having to be on guard."

Let us review what has been said thus far. The mutual dependence of emergent interaction, activity, and sentiment leads to an elaboration of behavior, but that elaboration is limited by certain forces so that some point of equilibrium is probable. The precise path of equilibrium will depend on the opportunities derived from the required system, the kinds of sentiments brought in by the personal systems, and how any inhibiting factors such as formal authority affect the behavior. In group behavior there seems to be a "natural" tendency toward equilibrium between the emergent, personal, and required systems. But the movement toward and away from equilibrium is frequently a continuous one. In some groups the equilibrium remains relatively stable for long periods of time; in others it is more unstable. Changes in one or more systems, such as change introduced by management in the required system or changes within the group itself, tend to upset the equilibrium. Although the dynamics of social systems sometimes make them difficult to comprehend, some disequilibrium seems useful in protecting groups from falling into a state of stagnant stability.

## PRESSURES TOWARD UNIFORMITIES

### Standardization

As any group proceeds to increase its emergent interaction, there is a tendency for the members to become more alike in their activities and sentiments—in what they do and in how they feel about things.[4] One need only consider any student group, for example. The special language, the sentiments toward any number of people or ideologies, the clothes worn, the activities undertaken will be more alike within a group than between groups. In short, there is a tendency for a group to move toward similarity in its activity and sentiments.

This mode of standardization is, of course, complemented by a mode of differentiation, which will be considered later in this chapter. There are forces working for both. The standardization forces are useful for a group in that they tend to generate expectations about behavior that help people know "how to behave" and anticipate others' probable behavior. In other words, groups tend to formulate, out of their emergent interactions, activities, and sentiments, a set of "oughts" for behavior. As a group comes together, it generates ideas about how members ought to behave under certain conditions. We briefly discussed these "oughts" in Chapter 3 and have referred to them as *norms*. We will now discuss this aspect of emergent behavior in more detail.

## Norms

GROUP NORMS. Norms are *ideas*, often unconscious, in the minds of members of a group that specify what the members or others *ought to do under specific circumstances*. They are *ideas*, not actual behavior. They are concerned with what men *ought* to do, not necessarily what they actually do, under *specific* circumstances, not all circumstances.

For example, a group of workers might have a norm that could be stated "One ought not to talk to the boss, or help him, any more than necessary." Another group's norm on this matter might be "One ought to be friendly with the boss and help him as long as neither action results in hurting the group." In both instances, the "ought" is stated in a way that makes the individual determine in the specific setting what behavior of his would come close to the group's idea of desirable behavior. In other words, he has some "wiggle room" that may seem either pleasant or unpleasant to him, depending on his concern for acceptance by others in his group and his clarity in understanding the implications of the specific situation.

Most groups will develop in their emergent systems a number of norms that they find useful in guiding members' behavior. One of them may be about productivity, while others may be about various activities or interactions, such as helping others or sharing equipment or information. The point is that these norms are very powerful in tending to standardize behavior in the group. Anyone who fails to meet them within the

[4]Of course, the members of some groups are alike in their desire to be different, but even within such groups the ways in which differences are expressed often tend to be similar.

accepted range of variation will tend to be "attacked" and then isolated from the group if the undesired behavior continues.

The differences in actual behavior are as important to group members for self-differentiation as the norms are for setting acceptable ranges of behavior for all. The norms act as a force for standardization, and thus are important outcomes of the emergent interaction, activity, and sentiment.

Of course, "norms," as the word is used here, are abstractions. One cannot see them as one can see the activities and interactions. They must be *inferred* by an observer or participant from the emergent activities, interactions, and sentiments that produce them. If one sees members of a group borrowing tools from one another, one infers that the group has a norm about sharing that might be stated "One ought to lend tools to friends." If one hears a group member breaking in a new employee say "We figure about 700 parts a day is what you ought to produce," one can easily guess at the output norm.

"CULTURAL OUGHTS." While the norms are ideas about what one ought to do under *given* circumstances, there are also ideas in the broader culture about what men ought to do under *all* circumstances. These "cultural oughts" are often so thoroughly ingrained in the culture that the members are no longer aware of them. They, too, tend to standardize behavior.

Yet, because they apply to all circumstances and to all men, they are frequently stated at even higher levels of abstraction and thus leave more "wiggle room" than do norms. An example is the sentence "All men ought always to be honest." Now, the specific behavioral conditions surrounding any individual's decision are sometimes so complex and ambiguous that he is not sure which, if any, of the options available to him is "honest." And even if he is sure in his own mind, the norms of his specific group may be in conflict ("One ought to take home a few tools now and then") with his "cultural oughts." In addition, the "cultural ought" as stated may be so widely abused that the actual behavior establishes a newer "ought" that is really the influencing one. For example, while both the culture and the law forbid one to cheat on taxes in the United States, there is allegedly widespread padding of certain deductions. If the practice is so widespread as to make the "cultural ought" a piece of "yesterday's innocence," then the new "cultural ought" for some persons might be "One ought to pad one's deductions a little." The latter could be the influencing one.

Certain gross "cultural oughts" operate in virtually all groups. "One should not squeal on peers" is a very powerful one. So is "One should not curry favor from authority figures." Most groups assume that everyone accepts such "oughts." Those who do not are rejected even more vigorously than are those who break norms.

Different subcultures within the total society have somewhat differing "cultural oughts." It is common for owners of small businesses to believe "Men ought to have individual initiative" and for certain union groups to believe "All for one, and one for all." The resulting conflict between the two groups is understandable, especially when the "oughts" in question are cultural and thus frequently further out of awareness—i.e., not very conscious—than norms (which are hard enough to state explicitly).

SOCIETAL ASSUMPTIONS AND VALUES. There are additional forces besides group norms and what we have been calling "cultural oughts" that tend to standardize group behavior. These forces result from assumptions made and values held in the society. We will use the word *assumptions* to refer to *ideas* that most people in a culture *accept as being true*. Some assumptions frequently made are that a person who is paid more than another has a better job; that a person who gives orders has a better job, or higher rank, than one who doesn't; that an older person knows more than a younger one; that a person with more seniority than another deserves more company benefits; that a person with more education than another is better off. There are many others. To the extent that people accept the assumptions as reasonable, they will act upon them, and the group's behavior will reflect them. Many undergraduates are aware of what can happen when they behave in a way that denies some of them. Say they reject a professor's "right" to assign them work. He is likely to be angry, because they are not behaving according to the assumptions about an older person being more knowing, education making him better, and rank permitting him to initiate activities. In any event, such widely held assumptions usually tend to standardize behavior.

We also hold *values* that are important in standardizing behavior. By *values*, we mean *ideas about what is desirable*. In our culture, there are many: It is desirable to be young (or at least to *look* young, if not act it), to be rich, to have power, to be successful sexually, to achieve significant worldly accomplishments; there are hundreds of others. (In other cultures, the list would be quite different. For Buddhists, for example, it is more desirable to withdraw from the world than to achieve dominion over it.) The gross influence of our own Protestant Ethic upon what we think is desirable is worth noting, as is the difference between what we think is desirable and what we actually desire. Conflict between the two is frequently experienced.

## Group Pressures toward Uniformity and Conformity

We have been looking at some of the factors that help explain why uniformities of behavior develop within groups. Now we will look briefly at the pressures a group exerts on its members to conform to its various standards. These pressures create tension, and sometimes friction, both within individual members and within a group. Tensions often build within an individual member when he perceives that his own ideas or behavior are not conforming closely enough with group norms, although he may simultaneously want to conform. Tensions build within a group when one or more individuals are clearly deviating from its norms.

The tension that develops within an individual in such cases arises when he perceives a conflict between his need to be true to his own needs and values and his need to adhere to the norms of the group. For example, a student who wants to perform well scholastically and achieve high grades may belong to a social group that has the norm, "It's better to hang out with the group than to study alone." The student may feel the pressure of his conflict on the night before an exam when he wants to study but the group wants to have a few beers.

A group will exert pressure on its members to conform to its norms for several reasons. First, it does so *to protect and maintain the group*. If individual members all do things very differently, there is less chance that the group will remain alive and cohesive. Second, sufficient conformity to standards *facilitates the achievement of the group's goals*. (If the objective of the group mentioned above is to have fun and to provide social belonging and security for its members, it must have members who are willing to engage in activities that will achieve these objectives.) Third, a group can *help its members perceive validity for their behavior and opinions* if there is considerable conformity to its norms. Such conformity can give members a feeling of security in knowing what is "correct" and "good." For example, the members of the group described above might feel little guilt about not studying the night before an exam. In the comfort and security of their shared norms, they might rationalize collectively that they were not wasting their time on "book learning" that had little to do with real life—that is, as long as no member insisted on studying and disrupting their comfort and security.

Individuals who deviate too frequently or too severely from the group's norms are usually "punished." The group has at its disposal a variety of penalties, ranging from gentle kidding to harsh ostracism, for pressuring deviant members into line. The individual may react in a variety of ways. The student in our previous example may rationalize his conforming to the expectations of the group by deciding that good grades are not important after all. Or he might decide to go ahead and break the norms by studying and incur the resulting pressure from his peer group. If that pressure becomes too great for him to endure, he may leave the group.

There is little doubt that group pressures are an influence causing conformity in the perceptions and behavior of people. S. E. Asch conducted an experiment in which group members were asked to match the length of a given line with one of three unequal lines.[5] All except one

[5]S. E. Asch, "Effects of Group Pressure Upon the Modification and Distortion of Judgments," in *Groups, Leadership and Men*, ed. Harold Guetzkow (New York: Russell and Russell, Publishers, 1963), pp. 177–90.

member of each group was told to give the same incorrect answer. The uninstructed member was asked to give his answer after the others, and was thus confronted with the dilemma of either reporting what he saw as being correct or of reporting what all of the others had said in order to avoid appearing ridiculous. Asch reported that "one-third of all the estimates in the critical group were errors identical with or in the direction of the distorted estimates of the majority." If group pressures can cause distorted perception of objective, nonvalue-laden lines, think what it can induce with more subjective political, religious, moral, and social values!

Both the personal system of the individual and his attachment to the group will influence his ability to withstand group pressure. For example, some people are sufficiently inner-directed to prefer to rely on their own judgments rather than those of others, even if many others are united in disagreement against them. In Asch's study two-thirds of the estimates in the critical group were correct despite the pressure of the majority. The more an individual identifies with a group and feels attachment to it, the more likely he is to let himself be influenced by group pressures and norms. When an individual feels free to leave the group, he may be much less responsive to group influence.

Dealing with deviants can be a difficult and frustrating experience for a group. Most people have had enough experience to know that the deviant is sometimes "right" and "useful" and that the majority, even when overwhelming, is sometimes "wrong." There is little doubt that deviants can play useful roles, because they can prevent what might be an overly self-satisfied, conforming group from straying off on "wrong" behavior paths. A group that is always in agreement, or in which there is little dissent, may be less effective than one that experiences considerable disagreement among its members. On the other hand, it is also clear that a lot of nonconformity is sometimes detrimental. Although some people frequently admire the inner strength and courage of the deviant, and although it is recognized that dissent is often the catalyst of progress, it is also true that some conformity is essential to any kind of orderly social behavior. Conflict can spur progress, but cooperation is needed to consolidate, maintain, and enhance the fruits of progress. Neither one is sufficient in itself.

## PRESSURES TOWARD DIFFERENTIATION

### Internal Social Structure

In prior sections we looked at some factors that contribute to uniformities of behavior within and between groups. Now we will turn to some of the aspects that make groups different from one another and that differentiate members within the same group. We have seen that as emergent groups endure much of their behavior is repeated, norms quickly evolve, and highly stable patterns of relationships tend to emerge (partly because most people want and seek stable relationships).

We will call the patterns of relationships that emerge within groups the *internal social structure*. Although all groups have internal social structures, they have them uniquely; i.e., each group tends to form its own patterns and structure of behavior. It is useful to sense what these structures are because they affect behavior in the required, personal, and emergent systems of specific groups.

The internal social structure is made up of members with different rank, status, and roles. These, along with the differences among individuals, all contribute to the differentiation of members within groups. These differentiations constitute part of the internal social structure. The factors that contribute to conformity, including norms, common goals, and shared values also contribute to the structure.

Differentiation within an internal social structure can be either horizontal or vertical. For example, members play different roles in a group and have different status in the eyes of the other members. A given group may have its sports "expert," its old-timer and historian, its amateur lawyer, and its "garbage collector" who is in on all the gossip. These unique roles, called to the fore from time to time, are important components of a person's overall position in a group.[6]

RANK AND ITS DETERMINANTS. Rank is a vertical form of differentiation within the internal social structure. Group members have different informal "ranks," to the degree that sentiments (feelings) by the members indicate that another member ranks higher, lower, or the same as himself. There is an important mutuality between a member's rank and many of the group's expectations about his behavior and its impact upon the group as a whole (as well as upon individual members). Rank is one of the major factors in accounting for the differentiation of members within a group, and it is also an outcome of differentiation.

There are several ways of thinking about or explaining why certain people are ranked as they are in the internal social structures of specific groups. All of them are useful to explore even though a synthesis resulting in a new theory is yet to appear. Here are five key areas which are listed along with additional ones in Table 1, that help account for rank.

1. *Objectives, activities, and resources.* Members who most help a group achieve its objectives tend to be ranked highest. Their help often takes the form of performing essential activities or of providing necessary resources.
2. *Role.* Each member will tend to be ranked within the group ac-

[6]We thank Dr. James Gatza of the Insurance Institute of America for his help in formulating this section.

**Table 1 Characteristics of those Group Members Frequently Associated with Higher Ranks in the Internal Social Structure of a Group**

1. *Exhibiting high degree of conformity to group norms* (often substantially unconscious and especially relevant during formation, early development, and middle developmental stages of a group's life).

2. *Having wide range of interactions* (known and generally liked by a relatively large proportion of a group's members).

3. *More likely to initiate interactions* (relatively often the first to undertake conversation, nod recognition, or greet a member of the group).

4. *Assisting required and/or emergent system goal achievement.*

5. *Assisting personal systems goal achievement.*

6. *Having access to scarce resources.*

7. *Having centralized access to critical communications and/or information.*

8. *Having high external status in the eyes of group members.*

9. *Having high formal rank via job or position in the group.*

10. *Having positive sentiments toward the group.*

cording to how the other members perceive and value the role he plays and the function he performs.

3. *Communications Network.* Members who are placed strategically in the emergent group communications network and who have access to useful information are likely to be ranked higher than those who are not so positioned.

4. *External Status.* The higher the status a member carries into his group from either the formal organization or outside, the higher his internal group status is likely to be. This assumes the group values the outside activity from which the member derives his status. (A

high-status gambler is unlikely to be ranked higher in his church group merely because of his gambling status!)

5. *Adherence to Norms.* How closely a member conforms to the group's important norms influences his rank.

Because adherence to norms is frequently important in group rankings, we will elaborate some on this. Those groups that have the clearest norms are also likely to have the clearest internal social structure. If the norms are unclear, so will be the ranking.

However, in many groups we find that the middle-ranked members adhere most conformingly to the group norms, the leaders next, and the lowest level least. The lowest-ranking members usually deviate because of apathy, inability to perceive, or unwillingness to behave according to the norms. The leaders are likely to be members who early in the group's life behave most closely of any in the group to its norms, or strongly influence the establishment of group norms and by doing so become accepted as informal leaders. However, once having reached the top ranking, they may, and in fact are sometimes expected to, innovate and initiate new norms. In such cases, the leaders' "deviations" are seen as being helpful rather than detrimental to the group. The leaders are fulfilling role expectations of members by playing their role as expected. However, they run some risk of undermining their position if they deviate too drastically from the established norms or from what the members think is appropriate.

Leaders, it should be said, are likely to be more successful in influencing the *means* for achieving goals than they are in altering those goals. Although an established leader may influence some shift in norms, a new leader would often encounter considerable resistance in doing so.

In conclusion, it should be noted that rank in the internal social structure is seldom influenced by only one or a few of the above variables. More frequently, a combination of several or all of them influence a member's rank.

## Dynamic Relationships between Rank and Internal Social Structure

A group's internal social structure can affect an individual's degree of autonomy, achievement, recognition, association, security, and, thus, his general satisfaction. A member's rank in a group can have considerable impact on his satisfaction, and his rank, in some instances, can be determined by factors over which he has little control.

The internal social structure can influence how well or poorly a group functions in achieving its objectives. If members perform functions, play roles, and are assigned ranks that correspond well to their interests and abilities, the group is likely to function better than one in which this is not the case. How satisfied members are with the internal social structure may affect the cohesiveness of the group. This may directly influence the amount of energy available for achieving goals and/or may reduce the efficiency of the available energy through wasteful competition and fighting among members.

### Required and Emergent System Interrelationships with Rank

An emergent group's internal social structure often has important impacts on the required system. You are probably quite aware by now that much of what has been said about structure within the emergent system is also applicable to the required system. However, at this point we need to emphasize that, within a given organization, the two structures may be quite different.

For example, authority in the required system is usually thought of as a delegated right; it comes down from above. Authority in the emergent system is clearly permitted as a privilege by the group members; it must be earned. Rank in the formal organization may not be parallel to that in the emergent system. For example, the worker in a group who produces most would likely be ranked high according to the *formal organization's standards*, but by the *emergent system's norms* that same worker might be ranked low—and regarded as a "ratebuster." This is because the goals and standards of the formal organization may not only differ from, but be at variance with, the goals of the emergent system.

What effects do the required and emergent systems have on each other? Do they help or hinder each other? The answer, of course, varies with different situations. People join organizations with the expectation that certain of their personal needs will be satisfied. After joining, they usually become members of one or more emergent systems that also satisfy certain personal needs. It is usual, then, that individuals expect to find some kinds of satisfaction from both the required and the emergent systems,[7] but these satisfactions need not be the same. For example, a man may expect to satisfy some of his economic and achievement needs through his participation in the required system and some of his social needs through the emergent system.

The required system is primarily concerned with achieving productivity, and the emergent system is mainly concerned with achieving satisfaction. Sometimes these consequences can be achieved simultaneously. For example, a group of top executives who closely identify themselves with the formal organization and its success may find great satisfaction in joining together to find ways of enhancing the productivity of the required system. Their emergent behavior, in this case, will actually reinforce and add to their required behavior.

[7]We are assuming here that we are dealing only with voluntary organizations; some of these generalizations would not hold for a nonvoluntary type, such as a prison.

On the other hand, sometimes the consequences of productivity and satisfaction are at odds. A small group of office workers may find that the required system prevents them from engaging in certain satisfying behavior such as talking with one another, eating lunch together, or taking coffee breaks together. In such a case, the emergent system may include behavior that attempts to circumvent the restrictions of the required system or that expresses hostility to it. The behavior of the emergent system may thus have impact on the required system, and the latter may be altered.

These examples are suggestive only. In actual cases, the combined required, personal, and emergent systems all coincide to make up an infinitely complex behavior system. Changes in one lead to changes in the others. Each system has impact on the others, and that impact may be positive, neutral, or negative. If the impact of one on the others becomes too negative, friction that demands attention is likely to develop in the total system. To reduce friction, managers may make changes in either certain background factors or the required system. If in so doing they do not perceive adequately the effects these changes may have on the personal or the emergent system, a variety of unexpected and unintended consequences might ensue.[8]

## SUMMARY

This chapter has explored complementary forces among group members that develop into an equilibrium level of interaction in the emergent system. *Internally* generated pressures toward standardization, group norms, and conformity, as well as *externally* imported cultural oughts, societal assumptions, and values further contribute to uniformities that evolve in the emergent system. On the other hand, a group tends to become ordered into a differentiated ranking of members. Patterns of emergent system behavior reflect continuing pressures from required and personal systems. A deeper analytic treatment of this is the main topic of the following chapter.

[8]See "When Human Relations May Succeed and the Company Fail," pp. 293–300.

# CHAPTER 5

# Types of Behavior in Small Groups

Much of your time at work in organizations will be spent with other people in group endeavors. You will want to know how you and others fit together, what you need to do to achieve your own satisfaction and to influence the effectiveness of the group, and what to look for in accomplishing these goals. Our objective is to provide you with analytic tools for use in diagnosing behavior in groups and to provide a better understanding of the ingredients that make some groups more successful than others.

## BASIC TYPES OF BEHAVIOR IN GROUPS

It follows from our assumptions about the needs of a group and of a required and an emergent system that some of a group's behavior is directed toward accomplishing the formal tasks, and other behavior is directed toward maintaining the group's ability to function. A third kind of behavior is directed toward satisfying solely the personal needs of the members. We label these three types of behavior:[1]

[1]This section draws heavily on Kenneth D. Benne and Paul Sheets, "Functional Roles of Group Members," *The Journal of Social Issues*, IV, No. 2 (Spring, 1948),

1. *Task behavior*—directed toward helping the group to select, define, and solve its problems.
2. *Building and maintenance behavior*—directed toward helping the group to function as a group, and in doing this, to help alter, regulate, support, strengthen, and perpetuate it when necessary.
3. *Personal behavior*—directed toward satisfying an individual's own needs without regard for the needs of the group as a whole.

Behavior often cannot be classified this neatly; some behavioral acts can fit all three, some two, and some one of these categories. Usually, though, one of the three seems most dominant.

SOME EXAMPLES. Suppose a group is working to meet a deadline for a contract proposal. The hour is late, the people are tired, and tension is mounting. They are all working in a room around a large table. They exchange information, ideas, and opinions. They occasionally clarify their objectives, analyze the problems in reaching them, and develop alternatives for achieving their goals. These activities and interactions are mostly required task behaviors. However, some of the inflections and gestures may also reflect traces outside the boundaries of pure task.

As you continue to observe this group, you notice that some of the remarks exchanged are increasingly tense and sharp. Finally, you see the project leader look up, put down his pencil, and say, "Hey, let's have a break." You hear general assent to the idea, and before long most of the group is congregated around the coffee machine in the hall talking about a variety of things, little of which pertains to getting out the proposal. This is predominantly building and maintenance behavior—it is emergent. In one respect, it is not immediately required to accomplish the task. But because it is very useful in helping the group to remain emotionally stable and able to work together, it may be essential to the eventual completion of the task.

You might then observe one member in the meeting off to one side making notes for an unrelated community project he has to present. He is with the group physically, but at the moment he is behaving to satisfy his personal needs and is not contributing to the group.[2]

You will notice in real experience that most people in a group exhibit both task and building and maintenance behaviors, although some

42–45. For further elaboration, see Rensis Likert, "The Nature of Highly Effective Groups," in *New Patterns of Management* (New York: McGraw-Hill Book Co., 1961), Chapter 2, and William B. Wolf, "Small Groups in Large Organizations," in *The Management of Personnel* (San Francisco: Wadsworth Publishing Co., Inc., 1961), Chapter 12.

[2]Personal behavior is not necessarily dysfunctional for a group. For example, sometimes friendly inquiry into personal behaviors provides data of high relevance for the group. It may open the way for involving a member in the group by utilizing his special interests and capabilities. Such inquiry may also shed light upon new alternatives that an excessively task-oriented group might otherwise miss.

tend to be more task-oriented and others more group building and maintenance-oriented. For example, John may usually be concerned with getting the job at hand done. He may say things such as "Well, where do we go from here?" or "Let's do it this way," or "Let's get started." Joe, on the other hand, may be more concerned with the group members getting along well with one another and having some fun. He may interject occasional jokes, suggest a break, ask the group to pause and respond to a member's ignored but serious input, or attempt to smooth ruffled feelings. Most group members are relatively unacquainted with building and maintenance behavior such as this—however, most people can, if they try, develop their skill in diagnosing the current needs in a group situation, and also in behaving functionally for the group's success. This kind of behavioral skill and flexibility is a rich asset for any group.

### Leadership

The identification of the different but necessary needs of a successful group leads to an important implication for leadership, especially in informal groups. Because some people usually are more task-oriented than others, and some are more building and maintenance-oriented, and because both are usually essential, it follows that a given group may have different leaders or even more than one leader at different points in time. For example, let us return to John (task behavior) and Joe (building and maintenance behavior). When the group is concentrating hard on achieving its task, John may be the leader. Later, when the group needs a break, Joe may assume the leadership. The person who senses the group's need at a point in time, whether it be task-oriented or group-oriented, and then acts to meet the need will probably be the group leader, at least at that moment. This shift is referred to as leadership flexibility, and the group has *shared leadership*.

It follows that some groups, especially peer groups, will often have more than one leader over time. Some groups will have a clearly predominant leader; others will not. Neither pattern is necessarily better or worse than the other. The essential point is that both the task and building and maintenance needs of the group must be satisfied. Furthermore, successful groups normally allow sufficient slack for members to indulge in personal behaviors at times.

## EMERGENT TASK BEHAVIOR

The required system for an effective task group varies considerably with the type of work to be performed. For example, some tasks are primarily physical and some mental. Some involve production, such as the manufacturing of machine parts, some involve batch processing, such as handling insurance papers. We have already identified several different kinds of mental task groups (see Chapter 3) and Table 1 suggests further classifications of tasks.

Although requirements vary importantly, there are certain aspects of task behavior that are common to almost all groups. In a larger organization one common aspect is that some of the task requirements and constraints are imposed by others in the organization but external to the group. It is common that the work to be done, schedules, methods, controls, and organizational arrangements are prescribed by managers outside the group. Within these constraints and requirements certain further requirements may be established by internal formal and/or informal leaders in the work group. The emergent group also furnishes additional detail about how to do the work within the already prescribed constraints. These details are fed back into the group's background factors and become a part of the required system.

LEEWAY. Some groups have considerable leeway in determining their task behavior; others have little. Normally, groups with standard, repetitive tasks have less freedom to determine how to do their work than do those with nonrepetitive jobs, because the emphasis is upon efficiency

**Table 1 Task Classifications**

*A. By Nature (Four Bipolar Continua)*

| | |
|---|---|
| Simple ........ | Complex |
| Structured ........ | Unstructured |
| Familiar ........ | Novel |
| Judgment ........ | Problem Solving |

*B. By Function (Six types)*

| | |
|---|---|
| Producing | Processing |
| Exchanging | Transporting |
| Problem Solving | Deciding |

often achieved through interfaces with other groups. The stability of the external environment's inputs and/or requirements may also influence the freedom groups have to fix the degree of their work patterns or "required systems." Groups working in very dynamic environments are much more likely to have more freedom than those in more stable environments, because it is difficult for outsiders to specify all the variations required to respond to environmental changes.

Ambiguity usually increases with more freedom to determine how a job will be done. This kind of freedom appeals to some groups and is a source of difficulty to others. Some find challenge in developing their own approaches; others find comfort in the security furnished by a structure designed by someone else. How well a group can furnish its own job detail in fulfilling environmental expectations and their own member satisfactions influences how they respond to the opportunity. How successful a group is in furnishing this kind of detail also influences external managerial decisions on how much freedom will continue to be given the group.

PURPOSE AND RESOURCES. Another common aspect of task accomplishment is that successful groups normally achieve a clear sense of purpose and direction. If clarity is lacking, the group should strive to determine what it is trying to accomplish. For example, a group may find it useful to identify whether it is planning, discussing, deciding, brainstorming, or disseminating information. If there is ambiguity, identifying the output the group hopes to achieve is a useful exercise that provides direction, limits, and motivation.

Most groups require information and resources. A problem-solving group, in particular, needs to determine what information is needed, whether or not the group has it, and if not, how it will be obtained. An analysis of the data should lead toward the development of various alternatives for solving the problem or achieving the group's goals, and each of these would ideally be assessed in terms of costs, benefits, time constraints, and other pertinent criteria.

If the group's task is to solve a problem or to develop a plan, a selection must be made from various alternatives that have been developed. At this point plans for implementation must also be carefully considered and possibly authorized. Such plans normally include control milestones or checkpoints for measuring progress and obtaining feedback on how the plans and their implementation are going.

TASK DIAGNOSIS. The goal of the diagnostician, manager, or group member often will be to find ways to maintain and improve task operations. In doing this, three time dimensions can be used: Past patterns of recurring mistakes, shortages, miscommunications, and other difficulties should be identified; present trouble spots and blocks to immediate task ac-

**Table 2 Partial Checklist for Task Accomplishment**

*Do we have adequate*

*1. Clarity of purpose and objectives*

a. short and long-run
b. overall and subunit

*2. Detailed plans*

a. schedules
b. procedures
c. methods
d. rules
e. policies
f. budgets

*3. People resources*

a. skills
b. knowledge
c. attitudes

*4. Physical and Financial resources*

a. facilities
b. materials

*5. Organization*

a. division of work
b. integration of work

complishment should be noted and their causes sought; future problems and opportunities should be anticipated. The more absorbing current problems and involvement are, the more difficult it is to take time for future forecasting and planning.

Table 2 suggests some of the elements that constitute successful task achievement. The diagnostician can look for their presence and quality. Gaps or inadequacies may suggest areas for task improvement. You can also note whether these elements are prescribed by the required system, either external or internal, or whether they are furnished by the emergent group. Supervisors and groups toward the bottom of an organization are often unaware of the power and discretion they *can* exercise.

In addition to the various task elements we have mentioned, the way in which members interact will significantly affect the group's effectiveness and cohesiveness. We will turn next to the building and maintenance concerns of a group.

*6. Controls*

a. criteria or standards of performance
b. checkpoints
c. methods of performance measurement
d. communication feedback
e. implementation of corrective action

*7. Direction*

a. work assignments
b. rewards and incentives
c. discipline
d. training
e. counseling
f. appraising
g. trouble-shooting

*8. Decision process*

a. data quantity and appropriateness
b. alternatives explored
c. analysis
d. evaluation
e. choice consensus
f. implementation

*9. Communication patterns*

a. content and direction of flow
b. number and capacity of channels
c. accuracy
d. timeliness

## BUILDING AND MAINTENANCE BEHAVIOR

How people relate to one another within a group influences its consequences. Do they work well together? Do they like one another? Do they trust one another? Do they enjoy working and being together? Do they find personal satisfaction? These are some of the questions the diagnostician needs to ask. Table 3 suggests some of the important problems groups encounter, and each of these represents an area to observe and assess. We have selected only three of these elements for discussion here: commitment, communications, and leadership.

### Commitment

One particularly important aspect to observe is that of commitment or involvement. This can be determined partially by observing the amount

**Table 3 Problems Encountered by Small Groups**

1. *Competence*—How to achieve increasing competence in accomplishing tasks and in satisfying member needs.
2. *Commitment, Caring*—How to achieve commitment, involvement, and participation in achieving group goals.
3. *Integration*—How to integrate the goals of the larger organization, the group, and individual members.
4. *Communications*—How to achieve authentic open, clear communications and the freedom to express ideas and feelings, whether they be negative or positive, conventional or far out.
5. *Trust*—How to achieve trust among members, so that they feel free to be authentic and so that they can count on one another for performance.
6. *Leadership*—How to achieve leadership and an equitable, workable distribution of power and influence.
7. *Collaboration, Conflict*—How to achieve collaboration, and how to manage conflict and competition.
8. *Adaptability*—How to adapt appropriately to the changing requirements of both the external environment and the group's internal needs.
9. *Liking*—How to achieve mutual respect and friendly feelings among group members.

and intensity of participation and interaction. Are most members deeply involved, or just a few, or are most only mildly involved? Do people appear committed to achieving the group objectives, or are they passive or even resistant? The answers to these questions lead to the important question, *why*? Looking for an explanation of either positive or negative involvement can be helpful in finding ways to maintain or improve the group's capacity to function successfully.

### Communications

Another critical aspect of how a group functions is its communications, including both content and process. Content usually includes both cognitive and affective elements. The cognitive elements refer to the intellectual meaning, and the affective elements refer to feelings. For example, one group member might direct a critical comment to another, and the latter might "hear" either caring or hostility along with the cognitive message. What he hears is likely to influence his own feelings, which are likely to be embodied in his own response. The essential point in observing and diagnosing group behavior is to watch for both feelings and ideas. Also, it is important to observe and "hear" the nonverbal communication along with the verbal and written. Tone of voice, facial expressions, gestures, posture, and various other behavioral movements often communicate more than words.

The direction and pattern of communications are also important for both the satisfaction of the members and their ability to accomplish their tasks. It is useful to note whether or not communication flows primarily through a leader, or through all members, or one to one or one to group. Research has indicated clearly that the structure of communications networks affects both the speed and quality of work and the feelings of people. In order to see how this might be true and what kinds of factors are involved, study the two simple communications networks shown in Figure 1 and then answer the following questions.[3] Assume that the lines represent two-way communication; i.e., all persons connected by lines can talk to each other. B represents the boss of each group; S represents a subordinate. Assume the groups are attempting to solve a problem that requires each man to give and/or receive some information before a solution is reached. Now answer the questions:

1. Which group will solve the problem faster?
2. Which group will have the higher morale?
3. Will Group I have a leader? Who?
4. Will Group II have a leader? Who?

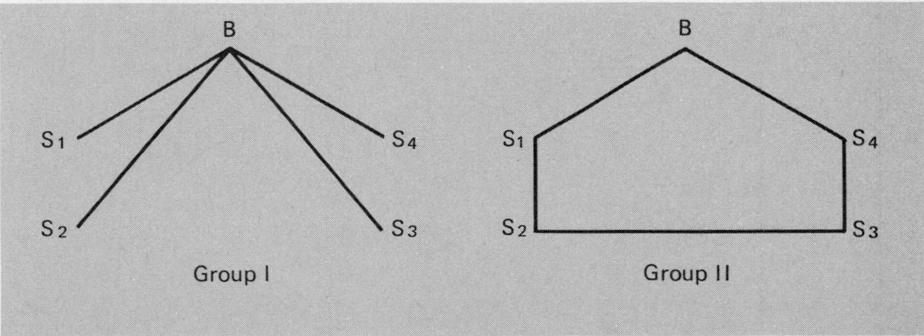


**Figure 1** Some Alternative Communication Networks

[3]We have drawn heavily in this section on the excellent work of Harold J. Leavitt, *Managerial Psychology*, 2nd ed. (Chicago: University of Chicago Press, 1964), Chapter 9, pp. 5–17.

5. Will Group I have some high and some low morale positions?
6. Will Group II have some high and some low morale positions?

Experiments have been conducted simulating the conditions just described. The results indicate that the answers to the above questions are as follows:

1. Group I will solve the problem faster.
2. Group II will have the higher morale, and the people in that group will be more enthusiastic about their work because they feel more deeply involved.
3. Group I's leader will be B, primarily because the others must all work through him to communicate with one another.
4. In Group II, the leader is likely to be the person who first arrives at the answers, and that could be any one of them. In fact, the leader might be a different person on different problems.
5. B in Group I will enjoy his work, but the others are likely to feel bored, dependent, and largely uninvolved.
6. In Group II, each person communicates with two others and is equal with all the others in this respect. Thus, each position is about the same as it relates to morale.

Now look at the communications networks in Figure 2. How would you compare it to the two in Figure 1?

Harold Leavitt summarizes a few of the conclusions reached after studying various research data as follows:

> Groups whose problems require the collation of information from all members work faster when one position is highly centralized and the others relatively peripheral. But the morale, the self-correctiveness, and perhaps the creativity of such groups may be better when the com-

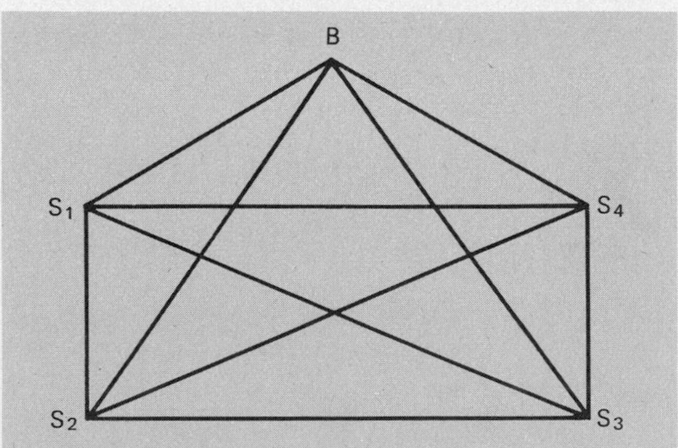


**Figure 2** A Star Communication Net

> munication network is more equalitarian and when each member has more than one source of information.
>
> Highly centralized groups may often be used for their consistency with general organizational designs, their speed, and their controllability; but they are also used as psychological defense devices to protect superiors' "weaknesses" from being exposed to subordinates, and vice versa.[4]

Of course, it is possible for a group to use a variety of communication patterns depending on the group needs. However, these networks often emerge without conscious design or even awareness of how they operate and of their importance. Thus, the diagnostician should observe the kind of net being used and evaluate its appropriateness for task performance and group satisfaction.

### Leadership

Also important in influencing how a group builds and maintains itself is the way leadership emerges in each specific group. Some leaders are able to influence the group toward eager participation, while others get such results as resistance, lack of enthusiasm, and low commitment. One variable to observe is the leadership style of behavior. Some leaders encourage wide participation and group involvement (democratic style). Others tend to take charge, issue orders, gain a position such that communications all flow through themselves, and they make a majority of the group's decisions (autocratic style). Still others let the group members go pretty much as they wish but are influential as resource persons when called upon by the group (laissez faire style). None of these styles are good or bad per se, and their appropriateness depends on the leader, the group members, and the group situation. However, observing the style is the first step required in assessing its impact on the members and its appropriateness in a given situation.[5]

Another observation to make is how well the members like the leader and each other. The degree to which members like one another has important impact on the cohesiveness of the group, and often on the effectiveness, too.

## PERSONAL BEHAVIOR

Organization and group behavior is, of course, a complex summation of the behavior of individuals. How people behave depends partly on organizational and group constraints and requirements and partly on in-

[4] Leavitt, *Managerial Psychology*, p. 241.
[5] For a more detailed discussion on leadership, see p. 193.

dividual needs, orientations, and perceptions. It is on these individual differences that we will now focus.

We assume that individuals behave to achieve satisfaction of personal needs and avoidance of discomforts, some of which are conscious and some unconscious. Needs vary in intensity and priority, but most people feel some need for achievement, power, status, belonging, friendship, and safety. Although some believe that these needs are genetically determined, we assume that most of them are predominantly learned as an overlay upon genetic factors. We further assume that most individuals are not fully aware of the presence or power of the motivational forces that influence this behavior.

From personal needs develop patterns of individual behavior, which can be conceptualized into emotional styles, cognitive styles, and personal orientations toward people and tasks. These behavioral manifestations of personal needs significantly influence how an individual behaves in a group and how well he "fits in". Our purpose in identifying these ways of conceptualizing individual behaviors is to help understand how and why particular individuals do or do not contribute to the success of certain groups.

## Emotional Styles[6]

People vary tremendously in how they express and respond to emotion. Figure 3 illustrates one way of conceptualizing the emotional styles or orientations of people. Clearly, no one is totally one type or the other. Almost everyone is capable of expressing both tough and tender emotions, and most people do so at one time or another. Nevertheless, many people do *tend* to express and to feel comfortable with one type more than the other.

Any particular emotional style is neither good nor bad per se, but in connection with group behavior, the relevant question is whether or not a particular style is functional for the group. People can become more aware of their own feelings and emotional styles. Further, they can, through effort and practice, become more aware that some of their feelings do not fit easily into their "style," and they can, if they want, learn to express these feelings at least to some degree. The friendly helper can learn to recognize and deal with conflict when it exists; the strong achiever can learn to give and accept warmth; and the logical thinker can learn to recognize the part his own and others' feelings play in group behavior. Thus, people can develop more *emotional flexibility*. If people are to enjoy their own preferred emotional styles, they must be able, in some degree, to express and deal with all kinds of emotions. Developing this kind of ability is a slow and sometimes painful process, but it is

[6]This material is taken from the National Training Laboratories Institute for Applied Behavioral Science Summer Reading Book, 1961, p. 18. This paper was originally prepared for a theory session at NTL Institute's laboratories.

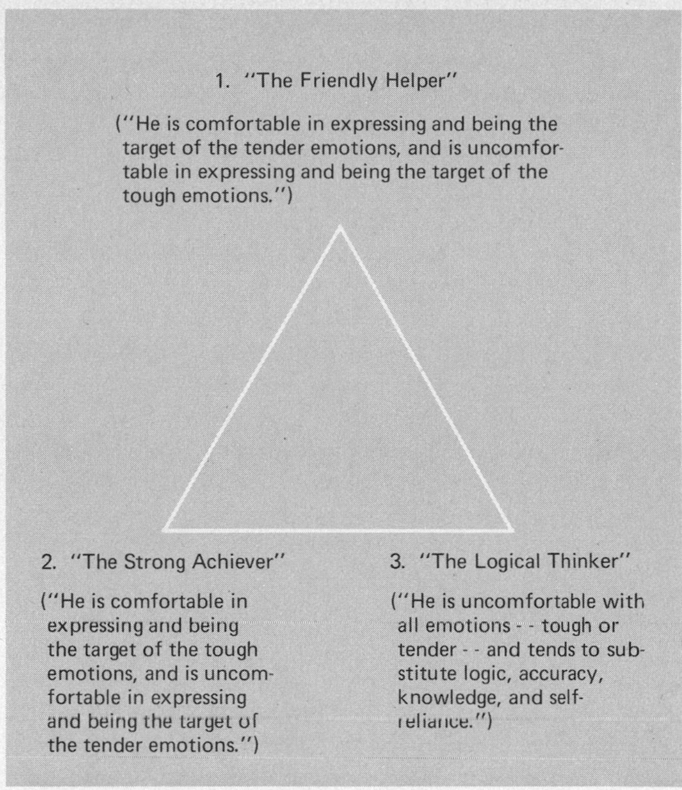


**Figure 3**

usually rewarding to those who have the courage to experiment and to learn.[7]

## Cognitive Styles[8]

Individuals also vary in how they think and solve problems. They tend to develop patterns of thinking when they encounter problems, and these patterns are termed cognitive styles. Some styles are more functional than others for certain kinds of tasks.

[7]This kind of experimentation is often very difficult in everyday relationships. As a result, some people have found it helpful to join T-groups or sensitivity training laboratories, and team building workshops, in which they feel freer to take the risks involved in trying out new patterns of behavior.

[8]For a more detailed treatment of this relatively new viewpoint, see: M. J. Driver and S. Streufert, "Integrative Complexity: An Approach to Individuals and Groups as Information Processing Systems," *Admin. Sci. Quarterly*, XIV, No. 2 (1969), and H. M. Schroder, S. Streufert, and M. J. Driver, *Human Information Processing* (New York: Holt, Rinehart & Winston, Inc., 1967).

The theory and concepts on cognitive styles are relatively new, diverse, and undeveloped. The main utility of any cognitive concept for most people is that it points out that differences exist along certain new dimensions, and that the differences are very important for understanding behaviors of individuals and groups.

Table 4 shows three dimensions along which cognitive information processing styles can be differentiated. Each represents a continuum.

The *decisive thinker* tends to make fast decisions and, more often than not, hold onto them. He comprehends a situation quickly (not always accurately) and says yes or no, stop or go. The *flexible thinker* views data from various points of view. His thought moves freely, uninhibited by a need for a single, permanent order. The *simple thinker*, as the term implies, tends to see in terms of black and white, good and bad, yes and no. He blocks out the complexity of various situations and reduces his perceptions to simple dimensions. The *complex thinker*, on the other hand, tends to see many shades of color and to make fine distinctions in meanings, possibilities, and alternatives. The *hierarchical thinker* tends to categorize his perceptions and data. He orders his experience, events, and knowledge into neat, hierarchical systems. He tends to be both mechanistic and authoritarian. The *integrative thinker* looks for more data, ponders more, evaluates longer, and is adept at synthesizing and creating new arrangements.

It is easy to see that people with varying styles might not fit compatibly with one another. For example, someone with a flexible complex style might feel quite uncomfortable, or at odds, with someone with a hierarchical complex style. In some groups, the composition of members' cognitive styles may be functional or dysfunctional for the group, depending upon the tasks at hand and specific conditions.

Individuals would do well to become more aware of their own cognitive styles in order to be able to identify those organizations, groups, and tasks that are most suitable for them. They can also utilize their awareness to develop more flexibility in their personal cognitive styles.

**Table 4 Some Bipolar Extremes of Cognitive Styles**

| | | |
|---|---|---|
| Decisive | ........ | Flexible |
| Simple | ........ | Complex |
| Hierarchical | ........ | Integrative |

## Preferred Personal Orientations

Some people feel more comfortable with people, some with things, and some with ideas. Those who are more oriented toward people are generally more concerned with how people feel and react both toward themselves and others; those who are more work-oriented focus more on work to be done than on how people feel. Of course, people express many variations of behavior along these two dimensions, but most have a tendency more toward one than the other. These orientations can be related to our early concepts of task and building and maintenance.

## Orientations toward Others[9]

We all vary importantly in our personal orientations toward interactions with other people. These orientations are influenced by deep inner needs and feelings about ourselves and others. Some theorists contend that many of these feelings are unconscious, although it appears that many of them can be brought to at least a partial level of awareness. Such awareness can be very helpful in determining why we behave as we do and to help indicate what is required to behave differently if we choose to do so.

Each of us has experienced being in a group with someone who dominated and overparticipated, often much to our annoyance. Or, contrariwise, we have worked in groups in which some members behaved passively and dependently to the detriment of the required effort. Although people vary in these respects along many dimensions, Table 5 suggests a few that are very important in group activity.

Again, let us reiterate: none of these traits are either good or bad per se, although some are more functional than others for specific individuals in specific groups. Some individuals feel more comfortable behaving passively rather than actively; with respect to control, some prefer to let others take charge, while others want to take charge. Some people value one type of behavior more than another, but such estimates are based on their own value systems and do not necessarily concur with the values of others or the reality of a group situation.

People also vary along the dimensions suggested in Table 5 in terms of their preferences for expressing or receiving. By expressing, we mean the desire to give or initiate behavior. By receiving, we mean how much is desired from others' behavior. One individual might find it difficult to

[9]For a more detailed discussion of this topic see William Schutz, *FIRO: A Three-Dimensional Theory of Interpersonal Behavior* (New York: Rinehart & Co., Inc., 1958), or Schutz's "Interpersonal Underworld," *Harvard Business Review* (July–August, 1958), pp. 123–35.

**Table 5 Bipolar Extremes in Personal Orientations toward Others**

| | |
|---|---|
| Dominant | Submissive |
| Active (aggressive) | Passive |
| Independent | Dependent |
| Sociable | Nonsociable |
| Personal (intimate) | Impersonal |

express his own innermost thoughts and feelings but find it very easy to listen to others. Another might have a strong preference for being included in group activities (social—receive) but a weak preference for joining such activities on his own (social—express).

The mix of people and their various characteristics may make a difference in how a group operates. Two common, apparently contradictory statements are: "Birds of a feather flock together" and "opposites attract." Which is true? As you might suspect, there is some truth in each.

Consider two people with reference to dominance or control. If both like to take charge of things and be in control, they are similar, and you might predict conflict. If one of them prefers someone else to take charge, they are opposites, but likely to get along well, at least on the control dimension.

Consider another example of two people with respect to sharing their deep, personal feelings and thoughts. If both feel comfortable with such sharing, they are similar and likely to get along well on this dimension. However, if one feels uncomfortable, the opposite is likely to result.

Many groups in formal organizations are formed with little consideration for personal preferences and orientations such as we are discussing. However, awareness of these dimensions of behavior can be helpful in understanding why people behave as they do and what impact each has on the other. Awareness of our own preferences can help each of us to achieve satisfaction and to contribute to group effectiveness.

## Role-Taking Preferences

We have seen that individuals differ in their emotional styles, cognitive styles, and orientations toward people and work. Thus, we normally expect to find people behaving differently, and taking different roles. Most groups require several different roles to be played, and how well the individual role preferences fit with the required roles of the group affects the success of the group.

*A role is a function, set, type, or pattern of behaviors either assumed by or assigned to a person. People often expect certain behaviors from those taking various roles, and this is "role expectation."* How people actually behave in their roles may vary from the expectations of others, and in such cases it is common to experience dissonant feelings ranging from mild to intense. Sometimes the dissonance is curiously pleasant; at other times it is annoying. Dissonance can be reduced or eliminated by changing expectations, by trying to change the behavior of the role player, or simply by being accepted.

Groups are often characterized in the simplified terms of various manifestly labeled roles including "leaders," "deviants," "isolates." Additional roles may be required and may or may not be played. Table 6 suggests several. These can be used to diagnose roles being played or to suggest what roles need to be filled. You can see that many of these can be related to the *task, building and maintenance*, or *personal* behaviors of group members. Again, none of the roles is either good or bad. The relevant question is whether or not a particular role is functional for a specific group at a certain time. For example, in some situations the role of "information blocker" may be functional and in others dysfunctional. If members of a group need to generate more information, ideas, and views, the blocker role could be dysfunctional. On the other hand, if members of a group were saturated with ideas or were running out of time and needed to get closure, the blocker role could be highly functional.

The roles people take may be determined largely by others. For example, the required system may assign an individual to the role of "leader," "secretary," or "trainer." Assignments can also be made by the emergent system through the implicit expectations and assumptions of other group members. The external characteristics of an individual may influence such assignments. Some may expect that a large man with a booming voice will be leader, and their behavior toward him may influence significantly his assuming the leader role. Appearance, education, titles, and similar characteristics may influence the expectations of others about what roles specific individuals will tend to play. Sometimes the expectations are ill-founded and lead to inappropriate behavior.

The requirements of specific situations also may influence what roles are played and by whom. Sometimes such requirements are obvious, such as in an emergency like a fire or accident or crash project to meet a deadline. However, the requirements are not always obvious, and the ability of the group members to sense and anticipate the needs of the group influences the group's effectiveness.

Of course, individuals themselves influence which roles they take. Their personal preferences and abilities influence the roles they assume.

**Table 6 Some Group Roles**

| | |
|---|---|
| Leader | Innovator |
| Follower | Clown |
| Initiator | Coach |
| Information-Seeker | Negotiator |
| Information-Giver | Arbitrator |
| Information-Processor | Pace-Setter |
| Tension-Reducer | Overseer |
| Tension-Stimulator | Agenda-Maker |
| Clarifier | Recorder |
| Harmonizer | Timekeeper |
| Evaluator | Process-Observer |
| Coordinator | External-Communicator |
| Dominator | Representer |
| Recognition-Seeker | |

How a person sees himself, his more enduring or more transient needs, and his deep inner makeup, all influence the roles he seeks to play.

## Conclusion

We have mentioned only a few of the important personal determinants of behavior in groups. A key problem for most groups is to integrate the needs and expectations of the group with those of the individual members. The ideal group would be one in which most members were aware of both the task and building and maintenance needs of the group and who had the emotional flexibility and personal skill to help meet the varying needs as they change over time. When this ideal situation does not exist, the group needs to confront and try to resolve the conflicts involved, or else it will suffer from dysfunctionally directed behavior and energy leading to a downward spiral of negative sentiments and less interaction.

## SUMMARY

In this chapter we explored three basic types of behavior in groups: task, building and maintenance, and personal behavior. Task and building and maintenance behaviors were discussed from the context of the group's dependence upon them for success. Various personal system characteristics were examined for their relevance for behavior in groups.

# Readings

## Committee Behavior*

You may have experienced some of the pleasures as well as frustrations associated with working with a committee. Committees are formally constituted bodies characterized by periodic, intermittent, or temporary rather than continuous functioning. Purposes for conducting a committee meeting almost always include an objective of gaining or maintaining intergroup coordination and/or cooperation. Staff or subgroup meetings have analogous purposes on the group level of analysis.

Committees *integrate* organizational behaviors vertically in the authority hierarchy and/or horizontally across group boundaries. Committees may function primarily as a formal *communications medium* for one-way dissemination of information from above at one extreme all the way to omnidirectional informational sharing (e.g., new projects, problems, etc.) at the other. Two other common committee functions are *problem solving* (e.g., performing a technical design, cost and schedule feasibility assessment) or *decision making* (e.g., adjusting and approving departmental overhead budgets for the upcoming three months).

There are both advantages and disadvantages to employing committees for any, or any combination, of these functions. The net effectiveness is emergent and is no doubt influenced by the nature of the tasks to be performed, the time available, the people involved, and primary task groups represented as well as other situational factors. However, some of the advantages and disadvantages can be generalized and are listed.[1]

*This reading was prepared by the authors as a supplement to the chapters on behavior in small groups.

[1]These advantages and disadvantages are drawn from those discussed by Harold Koontz

### Advantages

*Group Deliberation.* The saying goes: "Two heads are better than one." Of course, this may not always be so, as in the case in which one head is so weak that the other head must devote too much time to strengthening it. But generally, a group of people brings a breadth of experience and judgment to a task that individuals do not have. This enables the group to see more possibilities and to evaluate them from a broader base of experience.

*Representation.* Many organizational problems cut across several groups or departments, each with its own point of view. Committees often make it possible for these views to be represented.

*Balancing Authority.* Delegation of too much authority to one person may be avoided, or a gathering or consolidation of sufficient authority may be accomplished through a committee.

*Communication.* Information can be transmitted quickly and effectively to people who do not normally encounter each other in their daily routines. Two-way communication is made possible when it takes place in committee meetings.

*Coordination.* Tasks requiring the efforts of several groups can be coordinated through a committee because representative members are more clearly aware of the task requirements and how each group relates to them.

*Motivation.* Committee members frequently feel involved in what the committee does, and this involvement often increases the motivation of individuals to perform the related tasks better.

*Delaying Action.* Appointing a committee offers a means for a manager to delay or avoid action when he wishes to delay closure around a problem.

### Disadvantages

*Costs.* Committee work is often time-consuming, and time costs money in business and is valuable in all organizations. Time spent in inefficient committee meetings is time away from what might be more fruitful endeavor.

*Indecision.* Normally, opinions differ, and reconciling these differences can absorb time and lead to postponing a final decision. A minority coalition or even a single member can block or dominate committee decisions.

*Compromise.* In an effort to reconcile conflicting views, committees frequently resort to compromise. This may mean that the committee approves the conclusion that is least offensive to the most people. Such a conclusion may not represent the best one.

*Responsibility.* When a committee acts, it is difficult to pinpoint responsibility in cases of failure or success.

---

and Cyril O'Donnell, *Principles of Management: An Analysis of Managerial Functions*, 5th ed. (New York: McGraw-Hill Book Co., 1972), Chapter 19.

It is true that some of the advantages and disadvantages mentioned above may be just the opposite in given situations. From the viewpoint of a manager who wishes to delay or prevent action on a certain matter, the fact that committees consume time and are indecisive may be viewed as an advantage. Committees are sometimes appointed for this very reason—to delay or avoid action. And it is sometimes considered desirable to hide responsibility. When decisions regarding promotions and salary adjustments are to be made, the split or hidden responsibility may be considered an advantage. Thus it is that the advantages and disadvantages of committees must be weighed in terms of specific situations.

## Diagnosing Behavior in Committees

When observing behavior in a committee you may find it advantageous to review the background factors of the Social Systems Conceptual Scheme (page 92) as a way of more quickly grasping the aspects that will be relevant to you. Usually of particular importance are the committee's formation, setting, task, people, size, goals, and involvement—with the latter three deserving special mention here.

*Size.* The size of the committee may have some impact on behavior.[2] A very large committee—say, nineteen members—can be expected to break up into subgroups; it may become rather unwieldy for the accomplishment of certain tasks. On the other hand, a very small group—say, three members—may have power struggles in which two members oppose the other, or it may lack the resources necessary to do its job effectively.

In addition to size, how the committee members arrange themselves is sometimes important. Who sits next to whom may be an indication of feelings of liking or security. Whether someone sits near the door, at the back of the room, in the center of the group, or some other spot may give some clues about his attitude toward the group and its work. As with all such clues, the observer must be cautious about misreading or overreading what he sees.

*Goals and Involvement.* Presumably, the committee has some kind of task to perform, and its goal is to accomplish that task efficiently and effectively. How interested each member is personally in the committee's goal is likely to influence his behavior. Normally, the more a person believes that the committee's work is important to him, the more he will be involved in the committee's work.

Every committee member has a variety of personal goals, one or more of which conflict with the committee's formal goal. Some members bring with them to the meetings what have been termed *hidden agendas*.[3] The personal hidden agendas are based on the individual's own needs;

[2]See Dorwin Cartwright and Alvin Zander, *Group Dynamics*, 2nd ed. (Evanston, Ill.: Row, Peterson & Co., 1962), pp. 80–81.

[3]William B. Wolf, *The Management of Personnel* (San Francisco: Wadsworth Publishing Co., 1961), pp. 161–63.

although they are important to him, they are often not expressed openly. Thus a committee member might appear to be dealing with the group task when actually he is attempting to satisfy his own personal goals.[4] For example, member X may enthusiastically endorse an idea that has recently been introduced and that has not been discussed thoroughly. He may do so not so much because he thinks the idea is the best possible one, but because he is in a hurry for the meeting to adjourn so that he can go on to an activity more interesting to him. Member Y may keep finding fault with an idea that most members approve. He may do this not so much because he thinks the idea faulty as because he enjoys being in the meeting and wants it to continue so that he will not have to return to a less pleasant activity. Member A may vigorously attack an idea presented by member B, but it may be B rather than B's idea that he wants to hurt. Hidden agendas—i.e., the unexpressed or hidden feelings of group members, which, in part, motivate their behavior—can be disruptive and unsatisfying. The disruption can sometimes be minimized by recognizing and openly identifying what is believed to be someone's hidden agenda. This may mean that the group will have to stop dealing with its task behavior and turn to a consideration of its own functioning as a group. For example, if a group has been working hard for a long time and some members are beginning to talk among themselves, it may be useful for someone to relate the two facts and suggest a break.

*Behavioral Diagnosis through Interaction Analysis.* When a meeting begins you can listen carefully to what people say, watch what they do, and infer how they feel. This may be difficult for you to do because most of us tend to be engrossed in the *content* (the subject or task) of the meeting and tend not to concentrate much on the *process* (how the content is dealt with). Both are important, and through practice you can become more skilled at dealing simultaneously with both content and process.

You can better understand the group process by observing the group's *interaction patterns.*[5] This involves observing who talks to whom, about what, and how frequently. If the group works together long enough, you may begin to see certain patterns of behavior. For example, you may notice that Joe frequently asks the entire group questions about how to proceed and that group members look mostly at Joe when they answer. Bill may raise difficult questions that annoy the group because they must be dealt with, and some members may either direct hostile remarks toward Bill or ignore him. You may notice that Tom seldom says anything that helps the group solve its problem but that he occasionally cracks jokes that the group enjoys. You can easily see that the number and variety of interactions within a group is great. The problem is to sense the patterns that emerge from the numerous individual interactions and then to interpret and assess what the patterns mean for a specific group.

While watching for the interaction pattern of a specific group, you may be able to diagnose which members perform which group functions

[4]Hidden agendas also can be based on the needs of a primary group, and we can think of these as *group hidden agendas*.

[5]See "Markham Instrument Co. A", pp. 448–68.

and roles. In addition, you may be able to evaluate, as being either positive, neutral, or negative, the contributions to both the group's task and its building and maintenance needs.

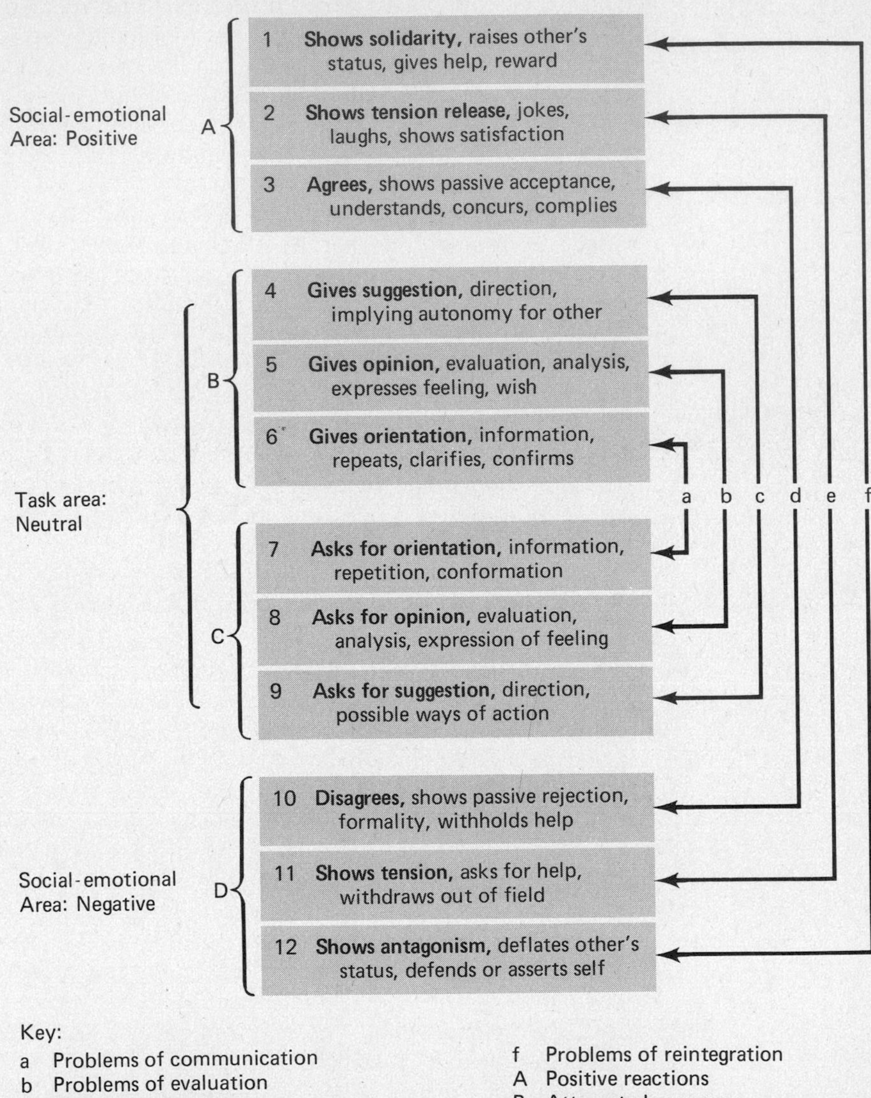


Key:

a Problems of communication
b Problems of evaluation
c Problems of control
d Problems of decision
e Problems of tension reduction
f Problems of reintegration
A Positive reactions
B Attempted answers
C Questions
D Negative reactions

**Figure 1** The System of Categories Used in Observation and Their Major Relations.

Redrawn from Robert F. Bales, *Interaction Process Analysis* (Cambridge, Mass.: Addison-Wesley Publishing Co., 1950), p. 9. See also Robert F. Bales, *Personality and Interpersonal Behavior* (New York: Holt, Rinehart & Winston, Inc., 1970), especially Appendix 4.

Robert F. Bales has provided a framework for summarizing some of the concepts we have discussed in this section. This summary is shown in Figure 1. The first three categories shown are positive group *building and maintenance functions*, the next six categories pertain to the group *task functions*, and the last three are group *inhibiting functions.*

It is much easier to understand intellectually how to observe and interpret the interaction patterns of a group than it is to put this knowledge into practice. In the abstract you can understand the concepts, but in real situations your own involvement with the content of the group, as well as with its process, makes observation and comprehension of the process difficult. In addition, your perceptions of other members—their emotional styles and the roles they play—and how you interpret and evaluate them are influenced by your own feelings and values. *One of the most difficult aspects of understanding a group often is to recognize and evaluate "objectively" your own part in it.*[6]

Although observing and understanding groups and committees is difficult, it is clear that one can develop and improve skill in doing so. Fortunately, you live in a world that furnishes you with a living laboratory that provides plenty of practice. In developing this skill, it is helpful to become more aware of relevant factors and what to look for; to become more sensitive in observing; and to become adept at interpreting and assessing what you see.

# Territory, Maps, and Cases

*Robert E. Coffey*

## Territory and Maps[1]

Most people want to develop their skill in observing and understanding the world around them and in behaving "appropriately" in specific situations. The "Sherlock process" (observation, knowledge, reasoning) approximates what we all try to do to some extent in living in a complex and often confusing world. We observe what is around us, decide what part of all we see is important, try to relate it so that we understand what is there, make decisions about what alternative actions we might take to satisfy our own and others' needs, predict the consequences of those alternatives, and finally behave. Of course, we sometimes skip some of these steps, and most of the time they occur almost simultaneously so that we are unaware of their taking place as described above.

[6]See "Personal Perception, Involvement and Response," pp. 59–69.

[1]These terms are taken from Alfred Korzybski, *Science and Sanity* (1933), as used in S. I. Hayakawa, *Language in Thought and Action*, 2nd ed. (New York: Harcourt, Brace & World, Inc., 1964), pp. 30 ff.

The world we behave in is made up of concrete phenomena, that is, of tangible, observable people, things, and events, which are perceived through the senses rather than through intuition or reasoning alone. We will refer to this world (or the specific parts with which we happen to be concerned) as "territory."

In order to comprehend the territory around us, it is useful to have some ways of thinking about it. By "ways of thinking" we mean words, concepts, and theories (abstractions) that help us to know what to look for when we observe territory, and how to analyze, how to relate, and how to interpret what we see. We will use the term "maps" interchangeably with "ways of thinking." Maps enable us to make predictions and action decisions in the territory around us.

Maps are oversimplified abstractions that represent concrete territory. They are designed to help people understand and find their way through that territory. Simple maps help, but sometimes not very much. For example, you might look at a road map and observe that City A is only 100 miles from City B. You might therefore allow about two hours to make a trip by car between the two cities. However, if it happens that the route goes through a mountainous area much of the way, and the road is winding, and there are many trucks on the highway, your estimate is likely to be off by an hour or two. Your map gives you only a partial representation of the territory, and in this case might prove to be inadequate for your purposes.

The territory of human behavior is wondrously complex. Suppose, for example, someone were to ask you to map the territory of a roomful of people. You could quickly and easily draw lines representing the room and its dimensions, and you could indicate where furniture and fixtures are located. But "mapping" the people "completely" would be an insurmountable task. It is true that you could depict some things easily—the number of people, their size, age, color, sex, and even such things as their education, religion, and economic status. But the dynamic feelings, motivations, and assumptions of each individual, which are of utmost importance for behavior, are impossible to map completely.

What happens when someone who lacks either an education or interest in art looks at an abstract painting? Reactions will differ with the individual, of course. But it would not be surprising if the response were rather neutral, or even negative, including such comments as: "What is it? What is it trying to show? It's just a blob of color." Someone more sophisticated about art, looking at the same painting, would probably react quite differently. He might respond by talking in terms of design, balance, color, rhythm, texture, brush technique, and other similar dimensions.[2] He would also probably talk in terms of his personal feelings about the total impact the painting has for him. Because he has some ways of thinking about the painting and the process of looking at it that the less sophisticated observer lacks, his experience is likely to be a richer and more meaningful one.

[2]The word "design" is an example of a map. It is an abstraction, but for some people it has meaning that enables them to observe, analyze, interpret, and respond to certain territory more fully and accurately than they could if they did not have that concept as one of their personal ways of thinking.

One of the dangers inherent in learning words and concepts designed to help observe and understand territory is that we sometimes fail to distinguish between the words and the territory, or else do not know how or when to apply the words to the territory.

> Let us call this world that comes to us through words the *verbal world*, as opposed to the world we know or are capable of knowing through our own experience, which we shall call the *extensional world*. . . . The human being, like any other creature, begins to make his acquaintance with the extensional world from infancy. Unlike other creatures, however, he begins to receive, as soon as he can learn to understand, reports, reports of reports, reports of reports of reports. In addition he receives inferences made from reports, inferences made from other inferences, and so on. By the time a child is a few years old, has gone to school and to Sunday School, and has made a few friends, he has accumulated a considerable amount of second- and third-hand information about morals, geography, history, nature, people, games—all of which information together constitutes his verbal world.
>
> Now, to use the famous metaphor introduced by Alfred Korzybski in his *Science and Sanity* (1933), this verbal world ought to stand in relation to the extensional world as a map does to the territory it is supposed to represent. If a child grows to adulthood with a verbal world in his head which corresponds fairly closely to the extensional world that he finds around him in his widening experience, he is in relatively small danger of being shocked or hurt by what he finds, because his verbal world has told him what, more or less, to expect. He is prepared for life. If, however, he grows up with a false map in his head—that is, with a head crammed with error and superstition—he will constantly be running into trouble, wasting his efforts, and acting like a fool. He will not be adjusted to the world as it is; he may, if the lack of adjustment is serious, end up in a mental hospital.[3]

Some people are so set in their ways of thinking that they try to fit new territory to their thought patterns rather than vice versa. This can be as helpful as using a map of Los Angeles to find one's way around St. Louis. The point is that in addition to developing ways of thinking, we also need to develop some skill in knowing *which* ways of thinking to use appropriately in specific situations, and then *how* to use them.

Say that we have different ways of thinking about individuals, people behaving in pairs, people behaving in small groups, and people behaving in larger organizations. It is probably most useful for us to use our interpersonal map when we are observing and trying to understand two people communicating with each other; but that map might be less adequate for understanding the behavior of a small group—it would not include several pertinent elements. In no way do we want to imply that there is one way of thinking appropriate to a particular situation. Several may be useful. But some discretion must be used in deciding which ways are *most* helpful in given situations.

The degree of specificity of maps varies. A general map can be helpful for understanding territory in gross terms, but when we want to find our way in concrete territory in more detailed fashion we need to use more specific, less inclusive maps. Thus the scale of the map ought to be related to our purpose in the territory. For example, the concept of "sentiments" is a general map. We know that a man's sentiments influence his behavior,

[3]Hayakawa, *Language in Thought and Action*, pp. 30–31.

and so to understand him better we may ask ourselves about one aspect of his sentiments: what is he feeling? This may be a useful question as a starter, but we need to become more specific, as a rule, to achieve more depth of understanding. For example, we may need to identify whether the person appears to have positive or negative, intense or weak feelings. Even if we were to identify them as intensely negative feelings—even more specifically, anger—we would still appropriately try to understand the phenomena underlying the anger. Thus, "sentiments" is a very general, inclusive map; several more specific maps are needed to grasp more specific phenomena. The closer to concrete territory we wish to get, the more useful specific maps become. If we avoid the territory, we are likely to be thinking about abstractions as if they were "real." If we avoid maps, we are likely to be much less skillful in dealing with the territory.

One of the problems people encounter in observing and interpreting territory is that they can only see and think about a limited number of things at a time. There are usually many ways of looking at and thinking about territory. Recall our art analogy—one might look at the painting in terms of line and design, or of color and texture, or of personal feelings and images. None of these ways are "wrong," although for a given painting and a given observer with a given purpose some might be more rewarding than others. The observer who has several ways of thinking can look through the "lens" of one way of thinking, then through another, and then another, and then he may try to put loosely together in synthesis all that he has seen. In sum, he has gone through the process of analysis (mentally looking at parts) and synthesis (relating the parts to form a whole). The more ways of thinking he has at his command, the more likely he is to see and understand and experience the territory in ways that are relevant to him.

## Using Cases for Learning

One of the major types of learning tools used in this book is the case study. A case itself is not territory. It is a case writer's abstracted description of territory. However, a case can serve as a useful substitute for territory, and using several cases has the advantage of providing, partially vicariously, a variety of different experiences. Reading and diagnosing cases that describe different people in different settings provides us with substitute, second-hand experience that can help develop our skill in observing and understanding actual territory when we experience it. That is why there is an advantage in reading cases that describe a variety of people, events, settings, and time periods.

As you have exposure to a variety of cases you are more likely to recognize the importance of situationally interpreting each piece of territory you encounter. It is true that situations have similarities with others, but it is also true that they have differences that make each unique. For this reason we stress the importance of *situational analysis*—the observation and interpretation of each behavioral situation more in terms of its own uniqueness than in terms of its similarities to other situations. It makes no sense, of course, totally to ignore the similarities, for that would be to reject maps needlessly.

One way in which case studies can be used is to give students an opportunity to find "their own order" in a description of territory. The cases, as simulations of concrete territory, often include a variety of data. The challenge is to decide which of the data are relevant, how they relate, and what they mean. The ways of thinking developed in this book and in other places guide our observations and reasoning, but none of them give surefire guarantees of reaching pat answers. This is true to life. We all face many situations that require us to "make order" out of what we see. Doing this often raises feelings of doubt, anxiety, inadequacy, and frustration. When some of us experience these feelings in trying to "figure out" particular cases, we can find some consolation in knowing that these feelings are as shared as they are useful.

Some students experience frustration because they do not easily comprehend cases or because they see things in a different way from others. These students frequently look to the professor to provide the desired order and answers. That is not surprising, because teachers have provided the structure and solutions for most, if not all, the courses and problems students have previously encountered. On the other hand, some students seem to thrive in unstructured discussions and enjoy the freedom to do their own exploring. Most students experience both feelings. The comfort and security of structure (e.g., memorization) is rewarding, while the lack of freedom confines; the openness of freedom (e.g., discussion) is exciting, while the lack of structure induces uncertainty. Too much of either freedom or structure is ultimately dysfunctional in learning situations.

One of the most difficult aspects of diagnosing many cases is to determine what the problem is. Many cases include several problems, and it is difficult to determine which should be dealt with and in what order. In this respect such cases are similar to real experience. All of us regularly face the problem of observing our partially unordered environment and of deciding what we should do in it. Deciding what to deal with is often difficult. Thus, although it is irritating not to have the problem defined or presented in obvious form, it is useful for practicing what we encounter in actual experiencing.

It is clear that life itself presents to each of us many complex and confusing situations. It is equally clear that we often have to provide our own order—we sometimes cannot turn to teacher, parent, minister, or friend to find that order for us. There is thus considerable merit in having experiences in school that simulate these real-life conditions—i.e., partially unordered, reasonably unstructured situations in which we discover our own modes of initiation and response. Experiencing the process of learning this way may be frustrating and uncertain, but it is also both practical and realistic.

Although you may have some difficulty in finding order in the cases you read, you will undoubtedly recognize after you have read several of them that the cases themselves are partially ordered abstractions of reality. This fact underlies the potential danger of becoming proficient at *just* analyzing cases. Because they are not real territory, but rather a reduction of it, it is quite possible to become proficient at analyzing them and still remain unskillful at finding order in one's own experiencing of his world. The ways of thinking one develops in analyzing cases are often helpful in diagnosing real territory, but that is just the point: Case diagnosis is not an end in itself but rather a means of developing skill in observing and understanding real territory.

Diagnosing cases can be different from diagnosing real territory in still another way: we are not likely to be so personally involved in cases as in real territory. It is possible to become proficient at analyzing cases quite objectively and at the same time be unable to maintain that objectivity in one's own experiencing, where one's own feelings, assumptions, and values are involved. On the other hand, you have undoubtedly seen people becoming very involved in case discussions, and expressing their own feelings and values. The point is to remain aware that personal involvement or its lack can make a difference in how we respond to cases and to real territory.

Questions commonly raised by students new to the "case method" of learning (as it is often used in business schools) are: What is the answer? What actually happened? What would *you* do? Considerable letdown and frustration often ensues when the response is: There is no *one* right answer; we don't know what happened; what *you* would do is what matters. Again, this is to be expected. Students have for years been given problems in school for which there are clear and precise answers, and they expect that to continue happening, as it can and does in some areas. However, we all know that in real life there are usually several alternative courses of action open to us and others in specific behavioral situations, and often more than one of these is right, "okay," or "good." Further, we usually do not know whether they are "good" or "bad" decisions until we have implemented them and seen the results. Even then, what was a good decision at the time may be interpreted as bad because of unforeseen events—at least unforeseen at the time the decision was made. The problems in life that matter are more for living with than solving.

One reason frequently given for wanting to know what happened is that a basis for comparison is provided. However, the assumption cannot be safely made that the people in a particular case made either the "right" or the "best" decision. Even if the results were good, there is no guarantee that the decision made was the only possibility. Further, what was an appropriate decision in a past situation is not necessarily appropriate for any other decision, if we accept the assumption that each behavioral situation is likely to have at least some differences that make it unique.

The question might naturally follow: Well, then, what use is there in studying cases? One answer is that by sharing our perceptions with others, and by trying together to find order in cases, we can begin to see more and understand better. We learn better what to look for, how to relate various elements, how to interpret them, and how to consider the consequences of our various action decisions. We can learn to identify the implicit, often unconscious, assumptions and inferences that both we and others make, and that in turn blind us from seeing more and deeper. In sum, we can develop our analytical and diagnostic abilities, which in turn help us make better decisions in our own experience. To ask for security and sureness is to seek "hard knowledge" which can armor us against the uncertainties and thus lock us away from living our life.

Another answer to the question "Why study cases?" is that a group of people who can communicate well with one another can study a case and arrive at fairly high agreement about what they perceive and what the consequences of certain actions would be. The potential reward awaiting an involved group exploring a case and trying to communicate with one another is a breakthrough to richer understanding.

## Shoulds versus Ises

All of us have values and make value judgments about much of what we perceive. But making value judgments can sometimes cloud our observation and understanding of behavior unless we understand the process involved. For illustrative purposes assume that a young man and woman are seated on a park bench in the moonlight and that they are kissing. Assume three people walk by, witness the scene, and later tell you what they saw. One says "As I was walking in the park, I was shocked to see two wild youngsters violating all standards of decent conduct." The second says "As I was walking in the park, I was delighted to see two fine youngsters enjoying each other so much." And the third says "As I was walking in the park I saw two people, a man and woman, each about 20, sitting next to each other on a park bench, kissing." Obviously, the first two descriptions are value-laden; the third is purely factual and nonvalue-laden. In developing our skill in understanding behavior it is helpful to become aware of the differences between the value-laden and the non-value-laden type of description. Doing so may enable us to perceive both phenomena and our personal reactions to them more accurately, and this increases our chances of achieving a better understanding of what we observe about the phenomena and ourselves. A closely related skill is that of being able to separate our shoulds from our ises. To illustrate what is meant by this, assume that Supervisor A observes some of his workers indulging in horseplay or deliberately slowing down their work pace. He may think to himself "Workers *should* not indulge in horseplay," and thus he might quickly step in to stop the behavior because it is "wrong." (The workers may not perceive what they are doing as wrong, or they may see it as partially wrong but justifiable for offsetting reasons, such as unpleasant work conditions or harsh treatment by the supervisor.) He has observed by means of his shoulds, judged, and acted. In sum, value judging prematurely can lead, as it did in this illustration, to reversing the old adage "seeing is believing" to "believing is seeing" and thus to taking action upon symptoms directly without considering the causes of behavior.

Supervisor X may face a similar situation and share Supervisor A's values about horseplay and work slowdown. However, he sees objectively that the behavior *is* occurring, whether or not he believes it should. Thus, he will try to understand *why* the behavior is taking place and to determine what alternatives might be implemented to change it by dealing with its causes. He would observe, *ask why*, consider alternative actions, predict consequences, and then act.

It is apparent from the above illustrations that one of the key words is "why." Behavior is always caused. Thus, in trying to understand behavior, it is usually appropriate to ask *why* it is as observed. Asking this simple question can greatly improve our chances of understanding and dealing with the causes of our own and others' behavior, rather than just the results.

## Assumptions and Inferences

Most of us, at least sometimes, accept without awareness assumptions or inferences as fact. Becoming more aware of our own assumptions and inferences (as well as those of others) can help us become more accurate observers and understanders of behavior. You might hear one man saying to another: "Joe works very hard, so he must really love his work." This statement may or may not be true. The assumption that Joe loves his work does not *necessarily* follow from the fact that he works hard. He may dislike the work but want to keep his job, maintain his self-image of being a hard worker, or merit a promotion. It may make a difference which is true. For example, if Joe's boss were to assume that he worked hard because he loved his work, he might decide to keep Joe on that job instead of promoting him or transferring him to a new and, to Joe, more appealing position. This could be unfortunate if the reason Joe worked hard was to get out of his present position.

The difficult problem we all encounter in distinguishing between facts, assumptions, and inferences is that we often are unaware of the assumptions we make. Being unaware, we do not know to question the assumptions.

Identifying assumptions is only part of the skill we can develop. Another aspect is to become more adept at using data to check the assumptions and inferences we make. What frequently happens is that a person making an assumption selectively perceives the data that support it but disregards or minimizes those that contradict it. And sometimes no data exist to support or deny our assumptions or inferences. Being open to both supporting and contradicting data, and being aware when we lack data of either kind, are helpful in more accurately observing and understanding behavior.

# Using the Social System Conceptual Scheme

*Robert E. Coffey*

The Social System Conceptual Scheme described in Chapter 3 (hereafter abbreviated SSCS) is a way of thinking that can help you understand concrete behavioral territory by suggesting pieces of phenomena that can be observed and how they can be related and interpreted. The scheme is a high-level abstraction of territory; it comprises several different elements each of which can serve as a way of thinking about a particular part of the territory.

One question that frequently arises is: Where do I start? The answer generally is either "It depends on the phenomenon" or "It doesn't matter." The SSCS represents a dynamic system of mutually dependent background and behavioral elements. For this reason it may not matter where one begins mentally to observe, analyze, and interpret what he sees in the territory. For example, the observer might begin by observing the "consequences" of behavior. He might ask himself: What is the productivity of this group? What is its degree of satisfaction? Is there any personal growth taking place? After observing data available to him to get some answers to his questions, he might then ask: What were the significant elements that led to these consequences? He might next turn to the required behavior, and observe the nature of the required activities, interactions, and sentiments. Or he might look at the emergent behavior. Or he might begin with the various background factors. On the other hand, he might have started his observation and analysis with any one of these concepts. It is less important where he starts than that he eventually consider the total system as a dynamic, organic whole.

Although there is no one way to use the SSCS, we can identify certain steps that are generally taken in using it. The first one is to look in the territory for data related to specific elements—the SSCS serves as a guide for knowing some of the elements that *may* be usefully observed. The second step is to determine whether or not the data for a particular element (if there are any) appear—at least tentatively—to be useful in understanding other elements and the system as a whole. This second decision should not be made precipitously. It often turns out that the meaning of certain elements is not fully understood until one senses the system as a whole and begins trying to find the relationship between the elements.

Thus, a third step might be to search for relationships between the elements. One might ask such questions as:

1. How do the technological requirements of this social system affect the required activities and interactions?

2. How do the technological requirements influence the kinds of people selected by this company?
3. How do the kinds of people hired by this company (with their attendant skills, values, and attitudes) influence the emergent system of behavior?
4. How do the required interactions in this social system influence the emergent interactions? and sentiments? and norms?

The number of questions that can be asked is large. One of the main values of the SSCS is that it helps the observer know what kinds of questions to ask. It serves as an observing and questioning guide or checklist. The SSCS is designed to help us observe and identify the *parts* of a functioning social system and to *relate* them in such a way that we can achieve new meaning (additional insights) and a deeper understanding of that particular territory. Some mechanical skill can be developed in using the SSCS, but *insight* is also required. It is only a way of thinking; you are more than a blind user of it. What *you* see is what matters to you in the "real world."

## Considering the Total System

Before we take action in any specific situation, it is important to consider several different possibilities. The statements "The only thing that can be done is . . ." and "Either . . . or . . . has to be done" are common but both should cause automatic warning buzzers to sound in our brains. Seldom is there only one thing to do, and usually there are more than the two implied by "either-or." The key is to develop several alternatives.

The next step is to assess them by predicting the consequences of the behavior they will bring in the total system. What often occurs is that a student or manager sees Problem A and decides to take Action X to solve it. However, while concentrating on Problem A, he may neglect the impact Action X will have on Factors B, C, and D; and as a result his action may lead to several unintended consequences. Even if it solves Problem A, it may create other problems, some of them more severe than the one it solved.

For example, a manager might decide that productivity (a consequence) could be improved by redesigning the work-flow (job design) and by adding some new machines (technology). His reasoning might be correct if these were the only elements involved. But he might find after implementing his decision that productivity was not (at least initially) at all as high as he had anticipated. It may be that he did not consider that the changes he made caused alterations in some of the emergent behavior of the workers, which in turn reduced some of their satisfaction, which in turn led to new emergent behavior that resulted in less than optimum production. More specifically, the workers may have found their customary interaction patterns altered. Say they had been used to talking with one another on the job and had enjoyed it. If the new job design made such interaction difficult, they might have begun to leave their positions occasionally to talk with others. This, in turn, might have led to less than the maximum productivity expected. If, to illustrate the continuing dynamics of the social system, management were to observe the new worker interaction and take steps to prevent it, emergent negative sentiments might be caused in the workers which would result in their slowing down their work pace in more subtle fashion. They might even try to sabotage the new process.[1]

It should not be implied that changes should be avoided if they conflict with worker emergent behavior and satisfaction. This frequently happens and is sometimes inevitable. The point is that, in predicting the consequences of certain actions, the entire social system, both required and emergent, must be considered. It is not uncommon for managers to make changes in either the background factors or required system without regard for the impact such changes will have on the emergent system. This oversight often results in surprising and unintended consequences. A change in one element usually reverberates throughout the system, and the resulting changes in other elements may induce further changes. Thus, one change may cause the social system to reorganize itself toward a new equilibrium over some period of time.

## Analysis and Description

The SSCS is a way of thinking that can facilitate analysis. Before showing why this is so, let us first look closer at what is meant by analysis and how it differs from description. Analysis, as we know, means separating (in this instance, mentally) a whole (piece of territory) into its component elements and relating them. The purpose is, of course, to gain a deeper understanding of the whole.

Here is an illustration of what analysis is not, and of what it is. Most of you are familiar with a corporation balance sheet. (Incidentally, the balance sheet, too, is a "way of thinking" about a corporation.) Table 1 is a simplified sample. Quite obviously, it considers only a small part of the total territory of a specific corporation, but it can be a very helpful way of thinking about the anatomy of the territory. Now, if we were to tell you that ABC Company has current assets of $1,000, fixed assets of $4,000, current liabilities of $500, long-term debt of $1,500, and net worth of $3,000, we would have told you only what you already knew from the balance sheet. We would have *described* the *map*, which is in this instance a balance sheet. However, if we were to tell you that ABC Company has current assets of $1,000 and current liabilities of $500, and this means it has a current ratio of 2:1, which indicates, as a rule of thumb,[2] that for a company of this size, in this industry, it has a healthy liquid position, we would have *analyzed* the data. We would have *taken out* two of the parts

[1]The "shoulds versus ises" concept might be appropriate in this illustration. Some might say workers *shouldn't* leave their positions and *shouldn't* talk on the job; they are paid to work. But the workers in this case *are* doing this, and they *are* concerned about their own personal satisfaction as well as the organizational productivity. The problem is how to reconcile the two in optimum fashion.

[2]Another useful, if less than precise, map.

**Table 1 ABC Company Statement of Condition, December 31, 19–**

| *Assets* | | *Liabilities* | |
|---|---|---|---|
| Current | $1,000 | Current | $ 500 |
| Fixed | 4,000 | Long-Term | 1,500 |
| | | Net Worth | 3,000 |
| Total | $5,000 | Total | $5,000 |

of the whole balance sheet and *related* them in such a way that we would now have *new meaning* and a *deeper explanation* of what the balance sheet gave in its original form. We could continue our analysis by "taking out" other parts and relating them to help us find further meaning and explanations of the territory the balance sheet represents. Those of you who know more about accounting will recognize how variations in the choices of maps for corporations can obscure or illuminate the territory.

## Some Misuses

One way the SSCS can be misused, and often is by those learning about it for the first time, is to use it to describe only a certain piece of territory. For example, a student who decides to use the SSCS to help him understand a case may write down on paper all of the background factors data in the case, then the required system data, the emergent system data, the personal system data, and finally the consequences of behavior. This is a painfully repetitious way to begin to understand the territory (case) involved, and in any event it clearly does not represent the ultimate goal of the analysis. What the student has done so far is analogous to our *description* of the ABC Company balance sheet. It is best to begin looking for *relationships* among the various elements that you see; this will enable you to achieve additional meaning and deeper understanding of the territory under consideration. You may then go back to the SSCS to see if you missed any of the elements. The SSCS can help you to separate the various elements of the social system, and it can help you to find relationships between the elements that help explain the total functioning system. In sum, it helps you to look at the territory and see and understand more than you would without it.

Another way to misuse the SSCS is to try to force all parts of it onto a particular piece of territory. An observer of a particular piece of territory may look for data on each of the background factors, but it does not at all follow either that he will be able to obtain data on all of them (in the case or in the real world) or that all the data he finds will be equally important to his understanding of the particular social system being observed. The skilled observer is the one who looks for the data, but then *discriminatingly* determines which of them are important. He does not dwell on or elaborate those pieces of data that are not fruitful in analyzing and understanding a particular system.

# CHAPTER 6

# Individual Frame of Reference and Interpersonal Behavior

By now you have spent some time studying and discussing some of the cases in the back of this book. As you have done so, it may well have occurred to you how varied were the perceptions of different persons about the same material. Each of you tended to see the same case somewhat differently, yet all of you were presumably using the same intellectual framework to help understand the same case phenomena. The differences among you as people, the differences in what you saw in and thought about cases, the differences in how you behaved in class and in your own small groups, and the differences in your perceptions of your own groups and yourselves are all important if you are to begin to understand yourselves better. The differences between and the similarities among human beings are at least as important as and perhaps more difficult to grasp than the differences in and similarities among companies or small groups. This chapter will present some ways of thinking about yourself and your interpersonal (two-person) relationships that may be helpful in initially exploring how you see yourself, the world around you, and the relationship between the two.

## THE INDIVIDUAL

It is worth stating at the outset that, although our immediate goals in this chapter are in a sense quite modest, our ultimate hope for your learning is far from it. We are seeking initially increased awareness, experientially and intellectually, of ourselves and others in terms that relate our individual uniqueness to other men. We are doing so because such awareness may lead you, eventually, to value for learning others' differences from you as much as you value for comfort others' similarities to you. Such, ultimately, is the stuff of wisdom, which will be reflected in greater interpersonal, small-group, and larger social system contexts, as well as personal relationships with family and friends.

### Seeing Other People

All of us use many categories to group individuals who seem alike in some ways. For example, we say "Those guys are fraternity types" or "That group is made up of athletes" or "Engineers drink beer" or "Teachers live in ivory towers." The grouping of individuals into a category meaningful to us is often helpful in conceiving of others. It also tends, frequently, to limit our view of the differences between the people we lump into our category. Sometimes, sadly, we tend to deal with an individual as if he *were* our category for him, and thereby miss much of who he is and who we could be with him.

If we wish to understand the behavior of any one person, it is useful to be aware that the ways we have of thinking and feeling about him may be very unlike the ways in which he thinks and feels about himself. His behavior will be far more a function of his own view than of ours. Our task, then, is to seek to understand how he sees *himself* and *his* world, because his behavior will then seem "logical," *given his view*. In short, everything he does is making sense to him when he does it, even if we may see his behavior as "wrong" or "irrational" or "illogical."

In order to understand another's behavior, we have to be willing to suspend, at least for a time, *judgments* about him, and be willing to try to understand how he sees *himself* and his situation and what needs *he* is trying to satisfy at the moment. We must try to see as *he* sees, not as an outsider might see him. His view of self and his situation we will call his "personal frame of reference." Each of us has one, and it is to some extent unique. Yet there are enough similarities between many frames of reference for people to communicate and share ideas and experiences. The similarities are relatively easy for us to deal with. It is the differences that usually trouble us.

Take two students in a discussion class. The desire of the teacher for students to participate in discussion may be seen by one student as an exciting opportunity and by the other as a threatening requirement. The reason will be that the students have different frames of reference, which, in turn, are outcomes of their prior experiencing. The way they see themselves, the teacher, the classroom situation, and their relationship to other students is different, and each will behave so as to *protect, maintain*, and *enhance his own adequacy* in the situation *as he sees it*. Both will strive for their own adequacy, and in that sense they will be similar, but they may go about it in very different ways. All of us, then, want to be and feel adequate in our frames of reference (i.e., our self-concepts and our view of a situation).

## Individual Frame of Reference

Let's dig into what is meant by "differences in our frame of reference." We must consider (1) our bodies as means of perceiving; (2) our experience over time in accumulating and relating perceptions; (3) our learnings about values, feelings, goals, and techniques; and (4) our development of our concepts of self and others.

If you were asked how many windows there are in the building in which you live, it is unlikely you would know. You probably have never needed to know, and so you likely have never noticed. We simply cannot deal with all the phenomena that are available to our senses. We must learn to select, out of all that is "out there," that which is useful or important to us. Men who are born blind must learn to get along with fewer available stimuli; yet there are frequent stories of how such men function well by learning to rely, more than others might, on nonvisual data. So all of us are dependent upon our bodies as our means of perceiving what is outside us. Because we differ in our physical endowments, so, too, we differ in our raw ability to respond to external stimuli. But most of us are sufficiently endowed to have many similar physical experiences.

As a baby first comes to distinguish itself from its mother and first recognizes her as "not-me," the process of receiving stimuli from the outside world increases. Anyone who has tried to keep a curious child from touching a hot oven by saying "No, no. Hot." realizes that the words have little *meaning* to him until the actual physical experiencing of the sensation of unpleasant heat occurs *in the child*. Then the body reacts to the experience with sensations of pain, and the baby begins to associate the oven with pain, maybe even with the word "hot," and learns to avoid it. The *learnings*, or meanings one attaches to physical experiencing, accumulate at a bewilderingly swift rate in children. And these learnings tend to encourage behavior that protects, maintains, or enhances the individual and to discourage behavior that hurts him. Our instinct for survival and avoidance of pain is strong, and our desire for pleasure and enhancement of self follows quickly.

As we grow older, we "learn" different things about ourselves and our world. One child, after repeated falls, finds the steps in front of his house threatening, while another, perhaps more coordinated, learns that they offer opportunities for delighted climbing up and down. One child learns that a certain gesture on his part wins the approval of parents, and so he keeps producing the rewarded behavior. Another may find the same movements ignored or punished, and so reduce or eliminate them. The point is that, as children, we learn to avoid doing what hurts us physically and emotionally, and to continue doing what pleases us or gains rewards for us. In other words, we learn to *protect, maintain, and enhance our own adequacy in our settings as we see them.*

## Self-Concept

From parents primarily, but from others too, we learn much about our world and how to see it, and much about ourselves and how to see us ("who we are"). The view we come to of ourselves (our self-concept) may be anything from the essentially positive—we learn to like ourselves and feel that we are good and loving and lovable—across a scale of great complexity to the essentially negative—we learn to feel ugly or dirty or worthless or bad.

Most of us seem to carry within us a number of views of self, ranging from an idealized view (often of who we wish we were) all the way to a diminished view (often a fear of who we are afraid we might be). Yet all the views have a kind of "center of gravity," at which imaginary point the various views focus in frequency and importance to produce *a* view that is central for us. This latter, central view is what we will call the self-concept. It may fall anywhere along the scale from idealized to diminished, but for most of us it will probably be somewhere in between.

However it develops, each of us has a view of himself that is a mixture of notions, some of them out of our awareness, that combine into a self-concept. This self-concept tends to resist change. Indeed, we protect ourselves from any attempts to change it, even if our view of self is a painful one. "At least it is *me*," we seem to be saying, "and I'm going to hold onto what I've got." Yet much learning takes place nonetheless, and we are all torn at times between the need to know and the fear of knowing—especially if the "knowing" forces changes in our self-concept.

We also learn what others think and feel about the "not-us," and over time we come to share their behavior, and their reactions in effect become our own. For example, if a child lives in a family where affection is expressed physically, he tends to learn that one *ought* to demonstrate and express that feeling physically. If anger is not expressed openly (and indeed is thought to be a "bad" feeling), he may learn that his experiencing feelings of anger is "bad" even if he does not express them. One learns to *value* highly the technical or religious or aesthetic or numerical or other aspect of experiences; one learns one *ought* to want to achieve certain goals and not others, such as graduation from college or journeyman's status in a trade, or freedom from responsibility; and one learns certain *techniques* acceptable to use, such as certain language forms, or professed superiority over other human beings, or postures of aggression.

These beliefs about what behavior, feelings, values, goals, and techniques are *desirable* also become internalized. (Later living is complicated often because one desires what one has been taught to feel is *un*desirable.) Thus an individual builds his *value system*. He learns, in addition, what *goals* are to be highly valued (i.e., status as a professional man or competence in a trade) and what techniques for achieving those goals are acceptable (i.e., skill in getting good grades or certain kinds of social behavior).

Out of all this comes a view of self (not all of it in awareness), of one's own specific behavior, and of other people and things and places, which has been laboriously built up over time. This view is our "personal frame of reference." And each man continues to behave so as to avoid pain and to maintain or enhance himself—given his view of himself, his behavior, and others. Even if our view of ourselves and others leads to behavior that results in little satisfaction or sometimes even in pain, we tend to hold onto our frame of reference tenaciously and to continue to behave in light of what we see because to each of us, what *we* see is real. What we perceive, we take for reality.

Those two students in the discussion class mentioned earlier are a case in point. One may have found in the past that his behavior in discussion classes was rewarded, that teachers were helpful and accepted him, that school was a place where he felt good. For him, the opportunity to recite may be a chance to further enhance his adequacy in a potentially rewarding setting. But the class may be a threat to the other student's adequacy, because his past experience led to learning that his recitations were rejected or laughed at by other students, that teachers were punishing and dangerous, that he was inarticulate or even mentally slow. He would understandably perceive the situation as threatening his adequacy. Thus, staying quiet may be the most "logical" behavior, given his frame of reference.

Everyone's frame of reference is an abstraction. We cannot observe it or measure it. And constant experiencing tends to keep it changing somewhat. But we can try to infer what it might be, given the behavior we see exhibited. Our problem, of course, is that it is difficult for us to see others' behavior without filtering it through our *own* frame of reference. Conscious attempts to hear another without judging him in terms of our own values can help much—to understand better not only the other's frame of reference and behavior but our own as well. The point to remember is that you are behaving so as to protect, maintain, and enhance your own adequacy, given your frame of reference, and that your behavior is, therefore, internally logical. *So is everybody else's.*

Respecting another's need for adequacy as we want him to respect ours does not mean that we must accept, as either most fruitful for him or satisfying for us, his means of satisfying that need. Nor should we expect others always to accept our own behavior as either most enhancing for us or satisfying for them. Most of our growth takes place in interpersonal relationships, and each of us can see in the other only what our own frame of reference permits us to see. We can, therefore, enter upon a lifelong process of growing if we will but continuously explore with others our own perception of reality (our frame of reference). The process requires awareness of and concern for ourselves and others. The outcomes can be exciting personal insights. Yet all of us know that interpersonal relationships are also complex and at times far from rewarding.

### Summary

We will explore interpersonal relationships in the next section of this chapter, working from the individual frame of reference developed above. But first a summary:

1. The way in which a person perceives himself (and only part of his view of self may be consciously available to him) is his *self-concept.*
2. The way a person perceives his world at any given moment (including the people, places, and things in the situation about him) *and* the way he perceives himself in that setting are, together, his *personal frame of reference.*
3. Each person behaves so as to *protect, maintain, and enhance his adequacy* in any situation (i.e., to protect, maintain, or enhance his self-concept in the situation as he perceives it).

So we can say, then, that an individual's behavior is a result of:

1. The way he sees himself
2. The way he sees his situation
3. His need to protect, maintain, and/or enhance his adequacy

Thus, any person's behavior is, *from his point of view* (of self and situation), perfectly "logical" and sensible to him at the moment.

## INTERPERSONAL BEHAVIOR

By *interpersonal behavior* we mean the behavior of two people in a relationship. Each of us has a wealth of experience with such relationships, and they constitute an integral, essential part of our lives. Each interpersonal relationship has many dimensions, a few of which are shown in Figure 1.

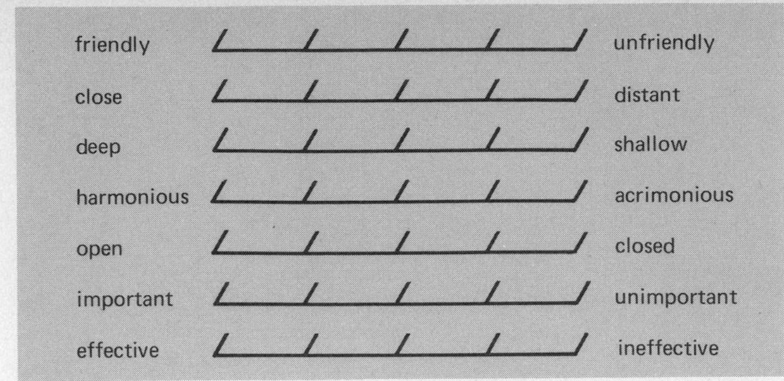


**Figure 1** Some Dimensions of Interpersonal Relationships

## The A-B Model

What interests many of us is why our relationships are as they are, how they got that way, and at times what it requires to make them different. The fundamental answer to the question of what causes relationships to be as they are is two people and their individualized perceptions. We have already developed in the preceding section the basis for understanding interpersonal relationships.

Figure 2 illustrates part of the chain of rapid events that happen between two people.[1] Assume that these people are A and B. Each has a self-concept, a view of the other, and a view of how the other perceives him. Couple this model with the assumption that each individual behaves so as to maintain, protect, and enhance his self-concept. Then, ask: Do interactions with the other enhance or diminish the self-concepts of each? If the answer is that the relationship is enhancing, it is likely to rank toward the left column of Figure 1, and vice versa.

Assumptions and feelings influence perceptions, and it is easy to see

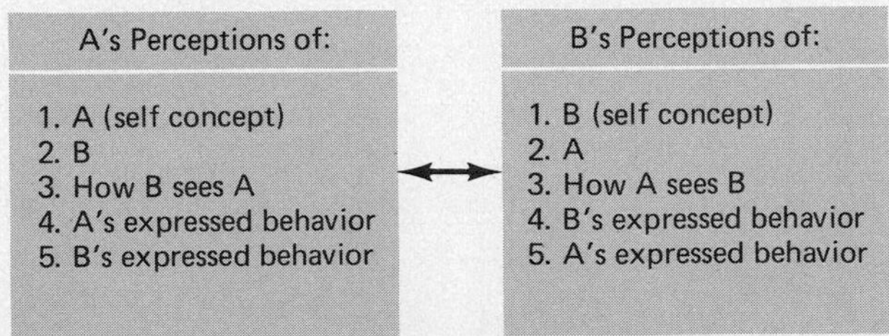


**Figure 2** The A-B Model

[1]This model is adapted from A. N. Turner and George F. F. Lombard, *Interpersonal Behavior and Administration* (New York: The Free Press/Collier-Macmillan, 1969).

the importance of this fact for interpersonal behavior as depicted in the model shown in Figure 2. For example, if A *assumes* that B sees A negatively, A may *feel* diminished. It would not be surprising, then, if A perceived B negatively and interacted with him accordingly. If he did that and if B perceived this correctly, B would likely be left with negative feelings and perceptions of A. It is useful to note that in such an example A's first assumption may have been incorrect. If this were the case, his subsequent behavior probably helped make his incorrect assumption come true.

The A-B model suggests that it is helpful, if not vital, to be as aware as possible of the other person's self-concept and how the relationship of each other affects that concept at a given time, because mood, strain, recent events, etc., all change with time. In some cases it will be apparent that the behavior of one is threatening or diminishing to the other. If such awareness exists, that individual can then choose whether or not to continue behaving that way. Threat, per se, is neither good nor bad, but, as usual, the appropriate question to ask is if it is functional or dysfunctional for the relationship. Sometimes threat might lead to constructive conflict that ultimately would strengthen the relationship, while at other times the opposite could occur. The key is to understand the rapidly moving process that leads to longer-lasting behavioral consequences.[2]

## Need Compatibility

Behind the self-concepts of each individual is an array of needs. In Chapter 5 we saw that individuals vary in their personal orientations to other people. The intensity of need to express and to receive varies along certain dimensions such as belonging, dominance, and intimacy. If one individual has a high need to express dominance, or control, and another has a high need to receive direction, they are likely to get along well, at least on this one dimension. On the other hand, if they both have high needs to express dominance and low needs to receive it, conflict is probable. This kind of analysis suggests why married couples who are quite different sometimes have very successful marriages, while some couples who are quite similar do not. The key is whether the important needs of each person in the relationship are complementary or not, and to what degree they are satisfied in the interpersonal relationship.

[2]R. D. Laing, Fritz Heider, Eric Berne, and F. K. Harris have delved into these rich kinds of dynamics in great detail, although their immediate applicability appears to fit more in the realm of individual growth than organizational behavior. For example, see Thomas H. Harris, *I'm OK–You're OK: A Practical Guide to Transactional Analysis* (New York: Harper & Row, 1969), or Eric Berne, *Games People Play: The Psychology of Human Relationships* (New York: Grove Press, 1964).

## Interpersonal Attraction[3]

Considerable research has been done to determine what influences one person to be attracted to another. Although the findings are not startling, the evidence is rather convincing. We will only review very generally the major findings.

One theory that has received some empirical support is the "social comparison theory."[4] It indicates that one reason people are attracted to one another is to help decide how they do or should feel and or think in certain situations, especially ambiguous, anxiety-inducing ones. In such situations people tend to be attracted to people in similar psychological states or conditions. They seek those similar to themselves apparently because of the assumption that such people are better able to help them understand their own feelings and beliefs. An example might be two people who both are under the supervision of a domineering boss and feel humiliated by him. They might be attracted to one another to better understand their feelings and to determine how they will behave.

The major determinants of interpersonal attraction are *nearness, similarity*, and *rewardingness*. The nearer two people are together in space and the more exposure they have to one another, the more likely they are to be attracted to each other. Evidence is also strong that the more similar two people are in their basic values, beliefs, and attitudes, the more likely they will be drawn to each other. Rewardingness is a generalized term that means that we like to be with people who either reward us directly or are rewarding to be with. It means that we are attracted to those who say nice things about us (assuming we do not perceive them to be ingratiators) or help us to feel enhanced. It also means we are attracted to people who are interesting, friendly, physically attractive, humorous, competent, or virtuous. Obviously, a specific individual might find any of these traits unattractive in another individual, but generally such traits are appealing to most people.

Most interpersonal relationships that endure involve what is termed *reciprocity*. Most people expect a reciprocal exchange of benefits in interpersonal transactions. For example, physical and mental effort and skill might be "traded" for dollars, power, or status. Affection, interest, respect, knowledge, and emotional support are all examples of benefits that can be exchanged. The exchange need not be "equal," but unless it is perceived as "fair" by both parties, tension likely will arise. Enduring relationships include expectations of continuing reciprocity.

[3]This section draws heavily on *Psychology Today: An Introduction* (Del Mar, Calif.: CRM Books, 1970), Chapter 34.

[4]Leon Festinger, "A Theory of Social Comparison Processes," *Human Relations*, VII (1954), 117–40. See also Stanley Schachter, *The Psychology of Affiliation* (Stanford, Calif.: Stanford University Press, 1959).

## Roles and Behavior

Each of us has a wealth of experience in interpersonal relationships, and often they involve us not only as experiencing persons, but also as role occupants. For example, student-teacher, mother-son, pledge-member, boss-employee, male-female relationships—all have a role component that one feels.

Social roles are useful to us in that they increase our security in being able to anticipate the behavior of others; they also provide some guidelines for our own behavior so that others (and we) may feel reasonably sure of what we will do. But when we experience the role aspect of our behavior as so important to us or others that we do not feel free to express ourselves in ways that do not fit our own or others' conception of the role, we often feel diminished as people and sometimes get angry at roles in general. And we sometimes refuse to "go along," and so disrupt the social dimension with the "satisfaction" of reaction, or else we decide to "play the game" and become conforming and cynical. If we believe the roles are "right," we may even come to feel that our impulses to behavior outside the roles are "bad" and suffer guilt as a result.

Roles have the utility of increasing our anticipation of others' behavior and of guiding our own, but it is important to recognize that their utility does not constitute some kind of commandment for us *all of the time in any relationship.* If you are being interviewed for a job by a person whose job is only to screen applicants initially and who seems to be uneasy and relying heavily on his role as "interviewer," you might decide to "go along" and act as if you *are* an interviewee. But if your fiancée acts as if she is a concept in a woman's magazine and the two of you are only actors in a play about two about-to-be-marrieds, you might decide to risk the results and behave outside her role expectations. The importance of being a person in marriage, which is closer and lasts longer than an interview, might appropriately demand your not "acting as if you were," but rather "acting as you are."

## Behavior Beyond Role Prescriptions

Roles are frequently thought to be a form of reductive restriction on behavior. It seems clear to us that any person in a role who *overemphasizes the role component of his behavior to the serious diminishing of his own personal expression of self is indeed being "reduced."* If he is a teacher or parent or therapist or boss, he can, as a result, reduce others too. Yet the opposite extreme is equally reductive in the long run. A father who refuses any aspects of that role in order to be "free" of the social structures or a manager who insists that all the formal titles, roles, and hierarchies are "so much phony baloney" simply reacts against structure and produces confusion and chaos. In short, if you live too much *inside* your roles or too much *outside* them, you are threatened, respectively, by rigidity and reduction or confusion and chaos.

You are, as a student, *a person in a role*. You are not just the role, nor has the role no relevance for you. It is part of who you are, perhaps even a very important part, but *only* a part. Once we asked a group of students to tell us who they were in five nouns. One replied "A man, a student, a lover, a son, a Sigma Chi." Another said "A human being, a man, a husband, a father, a poet." Still another answered "Me, myself, and I." Only the last one failed to include any roles, and, for what it is worth, he seemed to be a very difficult person to relate to, albeit a very gifted one.

Our first point here is that roles are like food. Too much or too little is to be avoided. In addition, we are saying that your different roles in relation to other people can be a means for usefully structuring some aspects of your relationships; i.e., they *can* be "good." And finally, we are implying that any given person will see some of his roles as more important to him than others and will value those roles highly because they help him live better rather than confine him unduly.

Keeping in mind the relevance of *roles* in providing some structure for interpersonal behavior, it is important to explore further the felt need to express oneself as one is as a *person* in these relationships. When you and your father are talking, the two of you are more than just son and father, and much of the rest of each of you needs to be expressed also. It is a not uncommon complaint of sons who are also students that their fathers ask "How is school going? What were your grades?" and fail to ask additionally "What's new with *you*?" Fathers sometimes feel that their sons, when asked this last question, choose to exclude them by replying "Nothing much. Same old things." In short, each locks the other out and himself in by dealing primarily with the other as a role occupant.

For any of us to relate to another as a person beyond the expectations of the roles we are in is a complicated, uncertain process that can include both rewarding and punishing experiences. To open ourselves somewhat to another can indeed be painful, if we are rejected; but it can also be wonderfully rewarding. The fact that it can go either way sometimes frightens us into hiding behind our roles. But at other times the courage to express what is personal within us (and yet not in keeping with role expectations) allows us to reach another person in ways that are deeply meaningful for both of us. An example of this was reported by a therapist as follows:

> In a recent incident during a group therapy session, a patient whom we will call Tom stood thundering over another, whom we will call George. Tom was shouting at George that George was not going to make him leave the room and that he, Tom, would show George that he couldn't

> boss him around. While he was shouting, he was swinging his arms and George crouched, ready to defend himself. I found my heart beating very fast *and told Tom that, and that I was experiencing fear and was afraid of him.* Tom stopped, looked at me, and after a moment he said that he too was feeling fear. We went on to talk about his fear. (Our italics)[5]

The therapist, by openly expressing his fear (an action that some of his colleagues think ought not to be taken by someone in his role), helped Tom to realize his impact on another and to hear more clearly what was going on inside him. In short, by behaving "outside" his role, the therapist took a risk that made a useful difference.

With persons less accepting of such an extent of openness outside a role, or in settings in which strong expectations mitigate against it, one might feel it wise to proceed slowly and "test the water" before jumping in. For common sense, that rare commodity, tells us that many of our interpersonal relationships are of such an order that significantly or suddenly increased openness is either inappropriate or seriously threatening to the relationship and/or us and/or the other.

## Openness and Closedness

When and how much and with whom to be open are questions that each of us asks. The decision is sometimes difficult because to be open involves both rewards and costs. However, we sometimes forget that closed behavior can incur costs just as can openness. Both too much and too little openness can be dysfunctional for interpersonal relationships.

Two M.D.'s named Joe Luft and Harry Ingham developed the well-known "Johari Window," which is shown in Figure 3. We all have a part of our selves that is known to both ourselves and others; we have another

| TO OTHERS | TO SELF: Known | TO SELF: Not known |
|---|---|---|
| Known | I. Public Self<br>area of free expression | II. Transparent Self<br>growth area accessible via feedback |
| Not Known | III. Private Self<br>undisclosed or hidden area | IV. Unknowable Self<br>area of totally unknown activity |

**Figure 3** Johari Window

[5]Gerard V. Haigh, "Some Reflections on the Concept of Unconditional Positive Regard," *Voices,* II, No. 1 (Spring, 1966), 60.

part known to us but not to others because we consciously keep it hidden; another part is known to others but not to ourselves, because we "block out" such data, usually for ego or self-defense reasons; and finally, there is a part that is unknown either by ourselves or others.

An assumption we make is that the "better" an interpersonal relationship is, the larger will be discoveries in area II, often leading to decreases in areas III, area I, and presumably IV. This assumption is based on the premise that good interpersonal relationships include a trust and a caring concern that encourages and facilitates open and honest communications. When we "hide," or cover, some of our thoughts or feelings, we generally are afraid of exposing and hurting ourselves or possibly of hurting important others. Sometimes we excuse covering our true feelings under the guise of not hurting another person, when actually we may be protecting ourself from the hurt we think might come from the other's negative, reactive feelings toward us.

## Strategic Openness

Growth and depth of relationship is often hindered by covering true feelings and thoughts. Assume that a professor is boring, and his students find his class of little value. They may feel afraid to express their true feelings to the professor for a variety of reasons, including, for example, their concern for how he might then evaluate them at final grade time. So, they cover their feelings of boredom and may even put up a front of interest. If this is done, consider the "cues" the professor gets. The feedback to him is that he is doing fine, which is probably easy for him to accept! What is his incentive to change? If a student risks giving him feedback he is more likely to recognize the need for change.

Too much openness can be as dysfunctional as too little. Too much can hurt, embarrass, and arouse anxiety. The problem for each of us is to choose when and how to try to be more open and authentic in our relationships with others. One approach to making such choices is called *strategic openness*.[6] In choosing how open to be, it is wise to consider our own motives, the probable effects our remarks will have on the other person, and the recipient's readiness to get our views.

Our motives for openness vary and can include helping, impressing, seducing, punishing, or exploiting. Some people who are open in expressing their feelings and views use the guise of helping for one of the other motives. If one's motive is to punish or exploit, the interaction is likely to be destructive. If remarks are judgmental in nature, they are likely to be detrimental to a relationship and to evoke a defensive response.

Effective openness requires sensitivity to the other person, and developing this skill requires some risk-taking. People vary in their capa-

[6]This section draws heavily on J. William Pfeiffer and John E. Jones, "Openness, Collusion and Feedback," in *The 1972 Annual Handbook for Group Facilitators* (Iowa City, Iowa: University Associates, 1972).

city to cope with open, honest communications. We each make assumptions about the other person's capacity in this respect, but our assumptions may not always be accurate. When possible, such assumptions should be sensitively tested.

Some of our communications to those with whom we have important relationships involve "feedback" about our reactions to them, their behavior, or things of importance to the other person. Feedback is more likely to be constructive if it has the following characteristics:[7]

It is descriptive rather than evaluative.
It is specific rather than general.
It takes the needs of the system (two-person, multi-persons) into account.
It focuses on modifiable behavior.
It is solicited rather than imposed.
It is well-timed.
It is validated with the receiver.
It is validated with others.

Openness can involve both positive and negative feedback. Some people have as much difficulty expressing or receiving one as much as the other. For example, in our society many men find it more difficult to express affection and tenderness than anger. And, of course, some are just the opposite. It is not safe to assume that people have difficulty only in expressing negative or tough emotions and views.

## CONCLUSION

The articles by Carl Rogers and Harold Spear explore this problem of expressing more of ourselves in our behavior, and with such lucidity that we strongly recommend that you read them. We think many of you will also be interested in the reading by Sidney M. Jourard, which relates the concept of role and openness to health and becoming.

In general, we believe that the more *important* a relationship is to you, the more need there is for you and the other to behave beyond role expectations. The larger your commitment to a relationship with another, the more risks in openness are justifiably taken. Not all of your interpersonal relations can be deeply meaningful beyond role expectations. But some of them have to be if you are to live a rich and healthy life. There may well be a scale for the extent to which interpersonal relationships are personally meaningful beyond role, ranging from intimacy to formality. Not all, indeed, not many of our relationships at any one time can be fully intimate. But to settle for none and to live completely toward the other end of the scale is to *exist* as an object, an ugly condition for any man.

[7]Pfeiffer and Jones, *1972 Handbook*, p. 199. These items are adapted from theory session material contained in the *NTL-IABS 1968 Summer Reading Book*.

CHAPTER 7

# Individual Frustration and Interpersonal Conflict

How do you feel in a conflict situation? Do you feel comfortable or uncomfortable, enjoy it or not? Of course, each of us responds differently to some extent depending on the situation. But think a moment about your own reactions in several conflict situations. Chances are high that you will notice a pattern. Some people attack, while others tend to defend. Some relish conflict situations, while others abhor them. How aware are you of your own customary feelings and reactions to conflict?

How each of us thinks, feels, and behaves in conflict or potential conflict situations is significantly influenced by assumptions that are often deep-seated and even unconscious. Some of us think conflict is "bad" and to be avoided; if this is not possible, it should be resolved quickly and prevented from recurring. Others assume that conflict is "normal" and "good"; it need not be avoided, and in fact, should sometimes be encouraged.

Conflict is the tension- and energy-inducing opposition of persons or forces to the achievement of goals. It can be good or bad, functional or dysfunctional, for a person, group, or organization. If there were no conflict, there would be little change. Conflict goes hand in hand with change and usually is related to adjustment in the status quo. A group or organization entirely without conflict would tend to be dull and stultifying for most of us, but one with constant conflict would be anxiety-inducing, debilitating, and destructive.

Conflict includes recognition, awareness, and choice. The following discussion will develop a conflict model that indicates some of the choices to be made.

## An Individual Conflict Model

Conflict is common at all levels of analysis. It occurs within and between individuals, groups, organizations, and societies. Here we will emphasize the individual level. We have already identified two key elements in a conflict model: the individual and his goals. We assume that the behavior of each individual is directed, consciously and unconsciously, toward various goals. Some of these goals are manifest and others are latent. The latter are more basic in that they are intrinsically important to the individual, whereas the manifest goals are more extrinsically important. A *manifest goal* is an openly stated, openly sought goal (e.g., to develop a good plan, make an important sale, accomplish a penetrating analysis, or achieve some worthwhile job objective). A *latent goal* is often unstated, and an individual may even be unaware of it himself. Examples would be recognition or advancement or a competitive edge over a colleague. It is useful to be aware that when individuals direct their behavior toward achieving manifest goals, they are probably also striving for more personally important latent goals.

None of us can achieve all our goals without encountering some barriers.[1] These may take the form of conditions, things, or people, including both others and ourselves. If a barrier is unyielding, we may begin to feel insecure and dissatisfied. This feeling is called frustration, and often leads to a stronger feeling of displeasure and sometimes antagonism. We respond to frustration consciously and/or unconsciously. At the conscious level we assess the importance of our goals, the strength of the barriers, the probability of our reaching the goals, and the appropriate behavioral response. The latter can be selected from alternatives such as increasing effort, decreasing effort, redirecting effort, changing goals, or withdrawing.

At the unconscious level our response may be determined at least partly by our feelings and psychological defenses. If our frustration is very great, we may begin to feel anger, which often leads to offensive and hostile actions called aggression. People or things can be the targets of aggression, and they may be either warranted or unwarranted recipients of the hostile feelings and behavior. If the target(s) of aggression are people, they may "fight" back. This interaction leads to strife or discord called conflict.

Figure 1 summarizes the elements of the conflict model we have de-

[1]Note that we are not always fully aware of either our goals or the barriers we encounter. Sometimes the barriers are obvious, but sometimes they are not, especially when our self-concepts are deeply involved.

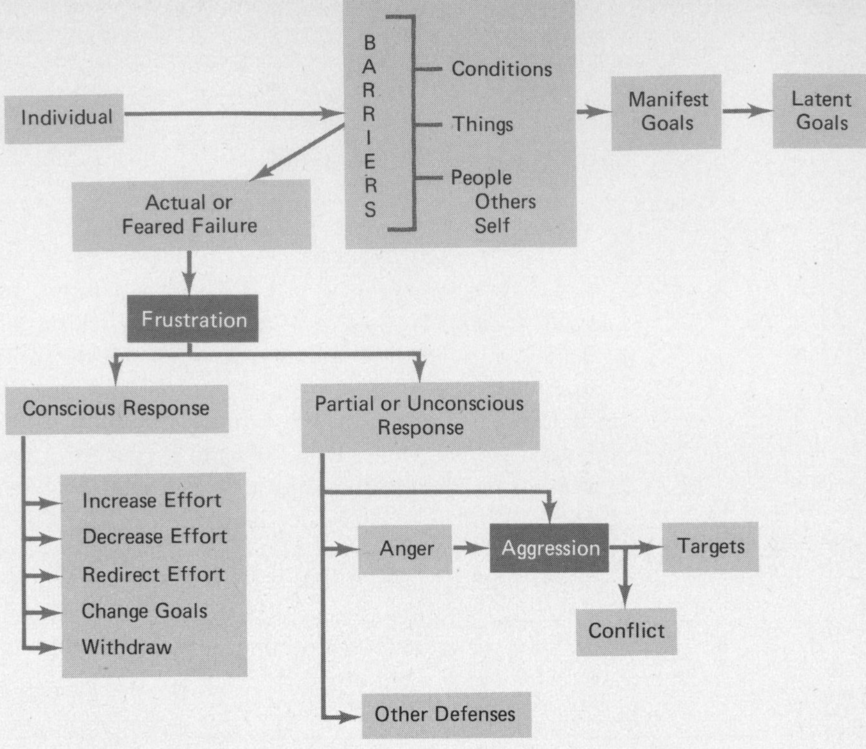


**Figure 1** Personal Conflict Model

veloped so far. It implies several choice points with which we will be concerned later, including how we choose to express our aggression and toward what targets. Our model also implies the importance of being aware of our feelings of frustration and anger and of recognizing what barriers are causing these emotions. Our behavior flows from our feelings and choices, and we continuously assess results of behavior to determine our new action decisions. The importance of perceptions based on feelings and assumptions becomes apparent in conflict situations.

## Coping with Frustration

There are three general approaches to coping with frustration: (1) to ignore it, (2) to recognize it, and (3) to attack a nonrelated target. The first approach is sometimes labeled smoothing-over or covering. The second approach includes several choices. One is to retreat or to give up seeking the desired goal; another is to change the goal or to downgrade its importance; a third is to attack the barrier to eliminate or move it aside; and a fourth is to change strategies for reaching the goal by going around the barrier, developing new skills, or acquiring new resources. The third general approach—attacking a nonrelated target—is normally dysfunctional and utilized by those unable or unwilling to accept their frustration and confront their sources directly.

Our responses to frustration can be consciously rational, unconscious, or some combination of both. Although purely rational responses are desirable, our assumption here is that we need to spend less time considering them than the other types of responses.

We may respond unconsciously to frustration with one or more of a variety of psychological defenses. We utilize these, usually unconsciously, to protect our self-concepts. Figure 2 identifies and illustrates some of the more common defenses we use. These defenses help us block off the force of more "reality" than we can take at a particular time. Such defenses can be functional if they protect us from being overwhelmed, but they can also be dysfunctional if they are used too frequently or block us from coping with our problems in more direct and effective ways. A desirable learning goal is to become more aware of the defenses we use and to avoid those that prevent us from dealing with our frustrations as well as we might.

Mild frustration may not lead to anger and aggression, although intense frustration often does. However, it is possible to experience anger without expressing aggression; one can behave aggressively without experiencing anger. An example of this is a football player who is trained to behave aggressively without feeling anger toward his opponent.

Some behavioral scientists claim that much of our aggression is genetically based and instinctual. Others say that it is learned from conditioning by the environment. The answer is probably that both contribute, but our assumption is that much is learned. A more pessimistic view would imply that little can be done about choosing when and how we express our frustration. We think much can be learned.

## Sources of Conflict

Conflict flows from frustration and aggression. We will be concerned here mainly with conflict involving people who interact aggressively to achieve their goals, often at the perceived expense of others. The causes of conflict may be found in people, things, or conditions. It is important to diagnose as correctly as possible the underlying causes of conflicts, because sometimes they are not what they appear to be on the surface. For example, some conflicts between individuals are hastily diagnosed as mere "personality conflicts," when in fact structural factors may be the basic cause.

PERSONALITY. We frequently hear about personality conflict, and yet we find that many people do not really understand what causes it. Some say

**Figure 2** Defensive Responses to Frustration

| Adjustive Reactions | Psychological Process | Illustration |
|---|---|---|
| Compensation | Individual devotes himself to a pursuit with increased vigor to make up for some feeling of real or imagined inadequacy | Zealous, hard-working president of the Twenty-five Year Club who has never advanced very far in the company hierarchy |
| Conversion | Emotional conflicts are expressed in muscular, sensory, or bodily symptoms of disability, malfunctioning, or pain | A disabling headache keeping a staff member off the job, the day after a cherished project has been rejected |
| Displacement | Re-directing pent-up emotions toward persons, ideas, or objects other than the primary source of the emotion | Roughly rejecting a simple request from a subordinate after receiving a rebuff from the boss |
| Fantasy | Day-dreaming or other forms of imaginative activity provides an escape from reality and imagined satisfactions | An employee's day-dream of the day in the staff meeting when he corrects the boss' mistakes and is publicly acknowledged as the real leader of the industry |
| Identification | Individual enhances his self-esteem by patterning his own behavior after another's, frequently also internalizing the values and beliefs of the other; also vicariously sharing the glories or suffering in the reversals of other individuals or groups | The "assistant-to" who takes on the vocabulary, mannerisms, or even pomposity of his vice-presidential boss |
| Negativism | Active or passive resistance, operating unconsciously | The manager who, having been unsuccessful in getting out of a committee assignment, picks apart every suggestion that anyone makes in the meetings |
| Projection | Individual protects himself from awareness of his own undesirable traits or unacceptable feelings by attributing them to others | Unsuccessful person who, deep down, would like to block the rise of others in the organization and who continually feels that others are out to "get him" |
| Rationalization | Justifying inconsistent or undesirable behavior, beliefs, statements and motivations by providing acceptable explanations for them | Padding the expense account because "everybody does it" |

**Figure 2 (continued)** Defensive Responses to Frustration

| Adjustive Reactions | Psychological Process | Illustration |
|---|---|---|
| Reaction-formation | Urges not acceptable to consciousness are repressed and in their stead opposite attitudes or modes of behavior are expressed with considerable force | Employee who has not been promoted who overdoes the defense of his boss, vigorously upholding the company's policies |
| Regression | Individual returns to an earlier and less mature level of adjustment in the face of frustration | A manager having been blocked in some administrative pursuit busies himself with clerical duties or technical details, more appropriate for his subordinates |
| Repression | Completely excluding from consciousness impulses, experiences, and feelings which are psychologically disturbing because they arouse a sense of guilt or anxiety | A subordinate "forgetting" to tell his boss the circumstances of an embarrassing situation |
| Fixation | Maintaining a persistent nonadjustive reaction even though all the cues indicate the behavior will not cope with the problems | Persisting in carrying out an operational procedure long since declared by management to be uneconomical as a protest because the employee's opinion wasn't asked |
| Resignation, apathy, and boredom | Breaking psychological contact with the environment, withholding any sense of emotional or personal involvement | Employee who, receiving no reward, praise, or encouragement, no longer cares whether or not he does a good job |
| Flight or withdrawal | Leaving the field in which frustration, anxiety, or conflict is experienced, either physically or psychologically | The salesman's big order falls through and he takes the rest of the day off; constant rebuff or rejection by superiors and colleagues, pushes an older worker toward being a loner and ignoring what friendly gestures are made |

Source: Timothy W. Costello and Sheldon S. Zalkind, *Psychology in Administration: A Research Orientation* (Englewood Cliffs, N.J.: Prentice-Hall, Inc., 1963), pp. 148–49. Reprinted by permission.

it is caused by differences in values. This is true to some extent, but we know that many of our close friends have some values that are different, and yet we don't have personality conflicts with them. Further, some personality conflicts occur between those who have similar values. One way of thinking about the underlying cause of personality conflict is to realize that one or both individuals involved feel threatened or diminished in some way when they interact with the other. Often the feelings of threat or diminution are suppressed and unconscious, and the involved individuals tend to attribute any clash to the other person without realizing either the extent or nature of their own involvement.

GOALS. Mutually exclusive goals are a frequent cause of conflict at all levels of analysis. You can see problems that arise within yourself if faced with two attractive goals, only one of which is possible to reach; or one attractive goal that can be reached only if an unattractive one is also attained. Such dilemmas are the source of psychological conflict. A single shared goal can also be the source of conflict if it is limited and more than one person or group is competing to reach it. A common example is the competition between peers for a single higher-level position. Multiple goals can also be a source of friction. For example, if too many desirable goals are being sought, and not enough resources and energy can be directed toward their attainment, conflict may develop over the priority of the conflicting goals.

MEANS. How work is accomplished and how goals are sought can also be a source of conflict. For example, many tasks can be achieved in more than one way. You may have the beginning of conflict if you think the job should be done one way and your boss or subordinate thinks it should be approached differently. This kind of conflict might also involve a struggle to exert dominance and independence, both of which are latent goals. Standards of performance are also a common source of conflict. Bosses and subordinates often disagree on what is reasonable or fair output. Another source of friction is competition for scarce resources necessary for doing a job. Resources can include tools, space, and various other things useful or desirable in getting work done. Incentives also trigger conflict. People compete for limited incentives or for larger proportionate shares of desired incentives such as salary, vacation time, higher position, and various amenities.

STATUS. Competition for status can lead to conflict. People without status may try to get it from those who possess it. Status incongruence can also lead to conflict. A common example is that of a new, young man (or, worse, a young woman!) supervising an experienced, older man. Another example is that of a bright young subordinate who develops better ideas and receives more praise than his superior. Such are the makings of conflict.

PERCEPTIONS AND VALUES. Much conflict is the result of differences in values. Three managers may look at the same problem and perceive it quite differently. The sales manager may call it a marketing problem; the production manager may see it as a production problem; the personnel manager may label it a human or organizational problem. Each may have difficulty perceiving the problem from the other's point of view. Differences in important values are also an obvious source of much conflict. A manager who values making a profit at any cost is likely to come into conflict with one who highly values social responsibility. Such conflicts usually involve perceptual differences too. For example, the man who values profit is likely to see making a profit as synonymous with social responsibility, whereas the other might see it quite differently, depending on the manner in which the profit is earned. Different groups of people may value differently such things as time and structure. For example, both production and sales people tend to have a short time horizon compared with research people. Production people value higher degrees of structure and research than do sales people. When individuals or groups from these areas interact, conflict sometimes arises because of their differences.

## Coping with Conflict

People respond differently to conflict just as they do to frustration. Here we will look at some of the responses and their underpinnings. You can help by doing some fantasizing with us. Imagine yourself driving a brand-new sports car. You approach a red light, slow down, stop, and bang! You lunge forward, your chin bounces against the steering wheel; you look in the mirror and see that you have been rear-ended. Jumping from the car, you see a slight, besmudged, and long-haired teenage boy glowering at you. He shouts "Why don't you look where you're going!" What is your reaction? How do you feel? What do you think you would say?

Do you think you would respond differently if the other driver was an old, gray-haired lady? What about a burly, tough-looking man in work clothes? Or an attractive member of the opposite sex? Would it have mattered if the other person had lowered his head in embarrassment and said, "I'm sorry. How stupid of me!"?

We could develop some further scenarios, but it is probably more useful for you to pause and think back to four or five conflict situations in which you have been involved. They may not have been as dramatic as our fantasized collision, but they were real. How did you feel and respond in your real situations?

PERSONAL FACTORS. How a person behaves in a conflict situation is, of course, a function of his perception of himself, of other people, and the specific situation. Most people tend to develop a pattern of responses to conflict. Some withdraw from or entirely avoid conflict situations; some defend themselves and then retreat from the situation. Others attack; some attack inwardly (themselves), and some attack outwardly (others). All these responses depend largely on how adequately a person perceives himself. Those who feel inadequate are more likely to retreat or to attack inwardly than those who feel adequate.

If the conflict is between two people, how each person perceives the other and his role in relationship to himself will influence the behavioral response. I might feel inadequate, but compared with someone else I might feel stronger and relatively more adequate, and these feelings might cause me to behave more aggressively and assertively than I would with someone I perceive to be stronger or more able. However, if I clearly perceive myself to be more adequate and dominant than the other, I may suppress outwardly aggressive behavior. For example, in our car collision scenario, if the other driver had been a frail-looking old lady, I might have restrained my aggressive feelings because of my perception of how to behave "properly" toward defenseless old ladies.

SITUATIONAL AND ENVIRONMENTAL FACTORS. Situational and environmental factors also influence our behavioral responses to conflict, sometimes in important ways. You are likely to respond differently to conflict situations in your own home than you are at school or work, and your responses may vary depending on whether you are with friends or strangers. Some situations and conditions are more conducive to the expression of strong feelings than are others, and our perceptions of these differences in situations will influence the degree to which we express our hostile, aggressive feelings and the manner in which we do so.

Figure 3 indicates that we have choices as to how, when, and where we express our aggression and as to what targets we attack. This assumes, of course, that we are aware of our feelings of frustration and anger. This is not always the case. Some people are fearful enough of such feelings that they block them from awareness. In such cases the feelings may motivate in ways the individual concerned does not understand. But assuming awareness, we can choose between expressing or not expressing our feelings. If we choose to express, we can attack either inwardly or outwardly. We can also choose our targets. If we choose to attack outwardly, we choose a specific manner of expressing our feelings from a variety of possibilities, ranging from nonverbal to verbal to physical and from subtle to blatant. These may be either appropriate or inappropriate, depending on their relationship to the source of our frustration. We may choose inappropriate targets because they are safer or more available than appropriate ones.

Our discussion of choice in relation to conflict so far appears to ignore the emotional, nonrational aspects of conflict behavior. If only they could as easily be done away with in real life! We temper our cognitive mapping of conflict with an awareness that in specific situations holding onto the rationality is not easy. Nonetheless, we think rational mental tools can help even in emotionally heated situations. To be effective, though, these tools need to be internalized and utilized.

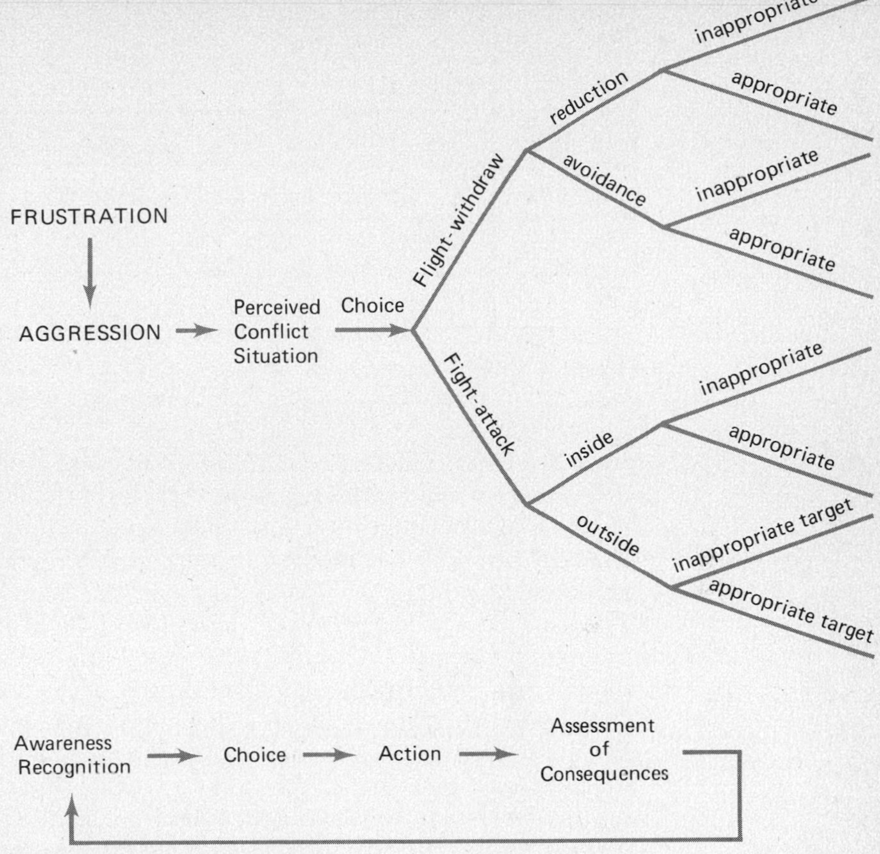


**Figure 3** Conflict Choices

## Fighting[2]

Conflict and fighting mean different things to each of us. For example, we can think of fighting as a behavioral continuum ranging from harmless assertion to hurtful hostility. The former involves a usually verbal declaring of intent, to make a demand or to try to cause another to change relationships or conditions to what you consider to be better or more appropriate. Hurtful hostility, on the other hand, involves the inflicting of injury or destruction, sometimes physical, and may even include violence. Thus, we can differentiate fighting in terms of whether it is verbal or physical, in terms of whether the objective is to improve a relationship or situation or to injure or hurt another, and whether the ex-

[2]Much of the following material is derived from George R. Bach and Peter Wyden, *The Intimate Enemy: How to Fight Fair in Love and Marriage* (New York: Avon Books, 1968).

| Nature | Harmless assertion | Hurtful hostility |
|---|---|---|
| Instigation | Mutual consent | Uncontrolled frustration and aggression |
| Objective | Change for better | Hurt or eliminate |
| Expression | Verbal | Physical |
| Feeling | Mild annoyance | Rage |

**Figure 4** Fight Continuum

pression of the conflict is controlled or uncontrolled. In our discussion of fighting we will be talking about verbal, controlled behavior with the objective of changing a relationship or situation for the better. Persons prone to physical uncontrolled fighting usually do not last long in organizations.

STAGES OF FIGHTING. When we think of fighting most of us have images of emotional outbursts and a lack of control over what is said and done. This is indeed a common aspect of fight behavior. But it represents only one of several stages. Think of a fight as taking place over time and going through four stages: the buildup, the blowup, the reconstruction, and the resolution. By looking at a fight going through these stages we see that the emotional outbursts and lack of control take place in the blowup stage. Most of us cannot sustain such outbursts for long. In fact, we usually experience quite a cathartic draining of energy and feel almost subdued after such outbursts. It is after this stage that we get hold of our reason and self-control and can then work through with another to a

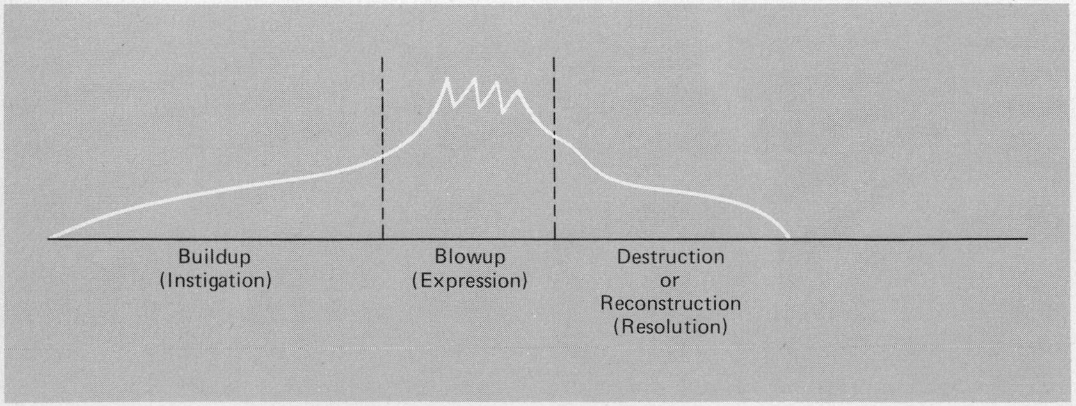


**Figure 5** Fight Stages

better understanding of why we are experiencing the conflict and what we might do together to reconstruct our relationship in a way that would be to our mutual enhancement.

The reconstruction stage is obviously difficult and vital to an effective resolution. Much skill, courage, sensitivity, and self-control is required for a successful passage through this stage. Most of us have had no training in how to handle this part of a conflict, and much of what we have learned through experience may be dysfunctional for effective resolutions. There are some guidelines we can try to keep in mind. One is to work hard to clarify the issues in the conflict so that it is clear what is causing the problem. The use of specific data and examples is more helpful than generalizations.

It is vital that each person in the fight reveal as much as he can his relevant feelings and thoughts. This is called "leveling." If important data is withheld, the other does not know fully what is causing the conflict and may not know how to develop an appropriate resolution.

A third guideline is to scale the fight or conflict to the size of the provocation. Have a little fight about a little issue, and a big fight over a big issue! Unfortunately, what often happens is that we have big fights over little issues, and little squabbles over big issues. This usually happens because of our reluctance to "get things out" and we store up feelings that surge forth when the walls are lowered. We tend to unload stored-up feelings, often on some innocent victim who had little to do with putting them in our storehouse.

A fourth guideline is to pick an appropriate place and time to fight if this is possible. You may think this is impossible (and sometimes it is). One approach is to avoid the blowup stage by recognizing seeds of a new conflict in the buildup period. If this is accomplished, the blowup stage can be bypassed and you can move directly into the reconstruction and resolution stages. If this doesn't happen, and usually it won't, you may decide to postpone the reconstruction stage for another time and place. It is often advisable to have a cooling-off period before attempting this difficult part of the conflict; immediately after a blowup may not be the time.

Another important guideline is to try being empathetic and sensitive to the needs of the other person. This is difficult in a conflict situation, but it is very helpful. Each person will have to work skillfully to help the other to level, and this in turn will require an acceptance of the other person, though not necessarily agreement with him.

## Individual Responses to Fighting[3]

People respond to and cope with conflict differently. Some withhold their feelings, tending to feel uncomfortable with frustration and anger,

[3]Much of the following material is based on J. William Pfeiffer, "Transcendence Theory," in *The 1972 Annual Handbook for Group Facilitators* (Iowa City, Iowa: University Associates, 1972).

and may even deny to themselves as well as to others that they have them. They avoid conflict when possible, and if it cannot be avoided, they frequently "turn the other cheek." Outwardly such people often appear cool and calm; inwardly they are sometimes churning. Usually they burn much energy in suppressing their hostile feelings, and the suppression can be damaging physically if it occurs too frequently or intensely.

One reason that some people withhold hostile feelings is that they have learned it is "bad" and "unsocial" to express anger or hostility. They want to be polite, and more often than not they want very much to be liked. They reason: How can he like me if I am angry at him? Sometimes the reluctance to express hostility is related to deep-seated feelings of inadequacy and weakness. Few of us are willing to take on someone we think or feel is stronger. Those who feel particularly uncomfortable with anger, hostility, frustration, and conflict face a double problem, because they have to deal not only with the conflict situation itself but also with the feelings they have about the kinds of emotions they are experiencing.

Some people are able to express their hostility and anger openly. This may be learned behavior, and such learning (or unlearning) may come hard—most of us have deeply ingrained learning and behavior patterns that need to be broken before we can express our hostility openly. For most people there is almost a feeling of exhilaration when they "let loose." Congruently, letting out angry and hostile feelings has somewhat of a cathartic result. The recipient of such expressions, however, may not share the catharsis. Although learning to express hostile feelings openly is an important step for many of us in personal growth, it does not necessarily lead us to an ideal point. In fact, most of us who reach this stage encounter numerous interpersonal problems.

To deal with the problems engendered by arrival at this stage, some people arrive at a level that Pfeiffer calls "introspective sharing."[4] At this level a person is able to identify his hostile feelings, to acknowledge them as his, and to express them openly. But he is also aware of the other person involved, and his goal is to express and share his feelings with the other so that together they can explore what is going on between them. They seek together to find out why one or the other feels upset and where each other is emotionally.

An example will illustrate these three levels. Suppose you are to meet a friend at 9 A.M. for an important engagement. The appointed hour arrives, and you are at the meeting spot, but he is not. He does not arrive until 9:30 and by that time you are fuming. He greets you with a friendly hello and asks how you are, casually mentioning that he is sorry he is late, but that he overslept.

You have several action possibilities open to you. If you have grown very angry during your waiting period, you may not be as rational as you normally are. One option is to contain your anger and say "Oh,

[4]Pfeiffer, *1972 Handbook.*

that's OK." In such a case, you store your anger, leaving your friend feeling that everything is all right. Strangely enough, though, it is not safe to assume that he will always feel good about such a smoothing response. It may be that he is feeling guilty and would have preferred a "chewing out" as just payment. In such a case a smoothing response leaves him with his guilt.

A second response, of course, would be to vent your feelings. You could tell and show your friend just how angry you are. This is likely to leave him feeling angry, too, and he then has the same kind of response-choices to make that you do. Once you get your feelings out (and he may get his out, too), where are you? Your angry feelings have been released, but your new situation has not necessarily been improved.

The third possibility is to engage in introspective sharing. This option embodies the step of expressing your feelings, but it adds an additional important facet. You consider the other person and the effect your expressions might have on him, and you indicate you want to explore with him why you feel so upset. Your goal is to find out why you feel as you do.

You may think the answer is obvious. However, it may not be. Anger is a second-order emotion. That means there is a more basic feeling underneath, such as hurt, fear, humiliation, inadequacy, resentment, or jealousy. The anger lets you (and maybe others) know you are upset, but it does not automatically tell you the emotion behind it. That may have to be searched out. In the previous example your friend's lateness may signal to you: "He doesn't care about me" or "I'm not very important to him." Or you may be afraid that the lost time will threaten you with the loss of an important event.

Introspective sharing does not work unless both participants are advanced beyond the first two levels described earlier. If one wants to share and explore but the other is afraid or unwilling to express himself openly, useful introspective sharing is unlikely. Even if the other is willing to express himself, he may not be willing to go further to explore why each feels as he does and what meaning that has for their relationship.

Expressing angry feelings openly is not easy for most people. And it is often risky, because the receiver's reaction may not be entirely predictable. But there can be both physical and psychological rewards for learning when and how to express feelings, even if they involve hostility and anger. However, there are some considerations to make in assuming whether or not to engage in a "fight."

First, to fight well with someone, you should care about him. This is true because fighting is risky, scary, and draining. You normally have to care about someone before you are willing to take the requisite risks. Note that many people fight most openly with those closest to them and about whom they care most.

Second, in most instances you would expect to have a relationship that would endure over a reasonable period of time. "Reasonable" will be defined differently, of course, but conflict that is evoked between two people who will only associate for a brief time may not be worth working at. The importance of the relationship will also influence a decision as to whether or not to engage openly in conflict.

Third, the other person should have similar values, beliefs, and experience to your own about the value of conflict and how to engage in it. Open expression of hostility and anger with the expectation of a constructive fight may take an unwitting or unknowing participant by surprise.

Fourth, entering into conflict assumes the participant's acceptance of the other's right to rejoin with expression of his genuine feeling.

Finally, the willingness to take personal risks is essential for entering conflict situations. The potential payoff for taking the risk is personal growth and improved interpersonal relationships.

## CONCLUSION

Conflict is natural and unavoidable. It can be functional or dysfunctional for a person, group, or organization. Some conflict is needed, but it must be managed and controlled. Managing conflict may mean stimulating and creating it as well as diminishing or channeling it. The key problem is how to control aggression constructively. This can be attempted by modifying and regulating the instigation of conflict, channeling its expression, and facilitating its resolution.

# A Tentative Formulation of a General Law of Interpersonal Relationships

*Carl R. Rogers*

*During a recent summer I gave some thoughts to a theoretical problem which had tantalized me: Would it be possible to formulate, in one hypothesis, the elements which make any relationship either growth-facilitating or the reverse. I worked out a short document for myself, and had occasion to try it on a workshop group and some industrial executives with whom I was conferring. It seemed to be of interest to all, but most stimulating to the industrial leaders who discussed it pro and con in terms of such problems as: supervisor-supervisee relationships; labor-management relationships; executive training; interpersonal relations among top management.*

*I regard this as a highly tentative document, and am not at all sure of its adequacy. I include it because many who have read it have found it provocative, and because publication of it might inspire research studies which would begin to test its validity.*

I have many times asked myself how our learnings in the field of psychotherapy apply to human relationships in general. During recent years I have thought much about this issue and attempted to state a theory of interpersonal relationships as a part of the larger structure of theory in

• Reprinted from Carl R. Rogers, *On Becoming a Person* (Boston: Houghton Mifflin Co., 1961), pp. 338–46, by permission of the publisher.

client-centered therapy. . . . This present document undertakes to spell out, in a somewhat different way, one of the aspects of that theory. It endeavors to look at a perceived underlying orderliness in all human relationships, an order which determines whether the relationship will make for the growth, enhancement, openness, and development of both individuals or whether it will make for inhibition of psychological growth, for defensiveness and blockage in both parties.

## The Concept of Congruence

Fundamental to much of what I wish to say is the term "congruence." This construct has been developed to cover a group of phenomena which seem important to therapy and to all interpersonal interaction. I would like to try to define it.

"Congruence" is the term we have used to indicate an accurate matching of experiencing and awareness. It may be still further extended to cover a matching of experience, awareness, and communication. Perhaps the simplest example is an infant. If he is experiencing hunger at the physiological and visceral level, then his awareness appears to match this experience, and his communication is also congruent with his experience. He is hungry and dissatisfied, and this is true of him at all levels. He is at this moment integrated or unified in being hungry. On the other hand, if he is satiated and content, this too is a unified congruence, similar at the visceral level, the level of awareness, and the level of communication. He is one unified person all the way through, whether we tap his experience at the visceral level, the level of his awareness, or the level of communication.

Probably one of the reasons why most people respond to infants is that they are so completely genuine, integrated or congruent. If an infant expresses affection or anger or contentment or fear, there is no doubt in our minds that he *is* this experience, all the way through. He is transparently fearful or loving or hungry or whatever.

For an example of incongruence, we must turn to someone beyond the stage of infancy. To pick an easily recognizable example, take the man who becomes angrily involved in a group discussion. His face flushes, his tone communicates anger, he shakes his finger at his opponent. Yet when a friend says, "Well, let's not get angry about this," he replies, with evident sincerity and surprise, "I'm not angry! I don't have any feeling about this at all! I was just pointing out the logical facts." The other men in the group break out in laughter at this statement.

What is happening here? It seems clear that at a physiological level he is experiencing anger. This is not matched by his awareness. Consciously he is *not* experiencing anger, nor is he communicating this (so far as he is consciously aware). There is a real incongruence between experience and awareness, and between experience and communication.

Another point to be noted here is that his communication is actually ambiguous and unclear. In its words, it is a setting forth of logic and fact. In its tone, and in the accompanying gestures, it is carrying a very different message—"I am angry at you." I believe this ambiguity or contradictoriness of communication is always present when a person who is at that moment incongruent endeavors to communicate.

Still another facet of the concept of incongruence is illustrated by this example. The individual himself is not a sound judge of his own degree of congruence. Thus the laughter of the group indicates a clear consensual judgment that the man is *experiencing* anger, whether or not he thinks so. Yet in his own awareness, this is not true. In other words, it appears that the degree of congruence cannot be evaluated by the person himself at that moment. We may make progress in learning to measure it from an external frame of reference. We have also learned much about incongruence from the person's own ability to recognize incongruence in himself in the past. Thus if the man of our example were in therapy, he might look back on this incident in the acceptant safety of the therapeutic hour and say, "I realize now I was terribly angry at him, even though at the time I thought I was not." He has, we say, come to recognize that his defensiveness at that moment kept him from being aware of his anger.

One more example will portray another aspect of incongruence. Mrs. Brown, who has been stifling yawns and looking at her watch for hours, says to her hostess on departing, "I enjoyed this evening *so* much. It was a delightful party." Here the congruence is not between experience and awareness. Mrs. Brown is well aware that she is bored. The incongruence is between awareness and communication. Thus it might be noted that when there is an incongruence between experience and awareness, it is usually spoken of as defensiveness, or denial to awareness. When the incongruence is between awareness and communication, it is usually thought of as falseness or deceit.

There is an important corollary of the construct of congruence which is not at all obvious. It may be stated in this way. If an individual is at this moment entirely congruent, his actual physiological experience being accurately represented in his awareness, then his communication could never contain an expression of an external fact. If he was congruent he could not say "That rock is hard"; "He is stupid"; "You are bad"; or "She is intelligent." The reason for this is that we never *experience* such "facts." Accurate awareness of *experience* would always be expressed as feelings, perceptions, meanings from an internal frame of reference. I never *know* that he is stupid or you are bad. I can only perceive that you seem this way to me. Likewise, strictly speaking, I do not *know* that the rock is hard, even though I may be very sure that I *experience* it as hard, if I fall down on it. (And even then, I can permit the physicist to perceive it as a very permeable mass of high-speed atoms and molecules.) If the person is thoroughly congruent, then it is clear that all of his communication would necessarily be put in a context of personal perception. This has very important implications.

As an aside, it might be mentioned that for a person always to speak from a context of personal perception does not necessarily imply congruence, since any mode of expression *may* be used as a type of defensiveness. Thus the person in a moment of congruence would necessarily communicate his perceptions and feelings as being these, and not as being facts about another person or the outside world. The reverse does not necessarily hold, however.

Perhaps I have said enough to indicate that this concept of congruence is a somewhat complex concept with a number of characteristics and implications. It is not easily defined in operational terms, though some studies have been completed and others are in process which do provide crude operational indicators of what is being experienced, as distinct from the awareness of that experience. It is believed that further refinements are possible.

To conclude our definition of the construct in a much more commonsense way, I believe all of us tend to recognize congruence or incongruence in individuals with whom we deal. With some individuals, we realize that in most areas this person not only consciously means exactly what he says, but that his deepest feelings also match what he is expressing, whether it is anger or competitiveness or affection or cooperativeness. We feel that "we know exactly where he stands." With another individual we recognize that what he is saying is almost certainly a front, a façade. We wonder what he *really* feels. We wonder if he knows what he feels. We tend to be wary and cautious with such an individual.

Obviously, then, different individuals differ in their degree of congruence, and the same individual differs at different moments in degree of congruence, depending on what he is experiencing and whether he can accept this experience in his awareness, or must defend himself against it.

## Relating Congruence to Communication in Interpersonal Relationships

Perhaps the significance of this concept for interpersonal interaction can be recognized, if we make a few statements about a hypothetical Smith and Jones.

1. Any communication of Smith to Jones is marked by some degree of congruence in Smith. This is obvious from the above.
2. The greater the congruence of experience, awareness, and communication in Smith, the more it is likely that Jones will experience it as a *clear* communication. I believe this has been adequately covered. If all the cues from speech, tone, and gesture are unified because they spring from a congruence and unity in Smith, then there is much less likelihood that these cues will have an ambiguous or unclear meaning to Jones.
3. Consequently, the more clear the communication from Smith, the more Jones responds with clarity. This is simply saying that even though Jones might be quite *in*congruent in his experiencing of the topic under discussion, nevertheless his response will have *more* clarity and congruence in it than if he had experienced Smith's communication as ambiguous.
4. The more that Smith is congruent in the topic about which they are communicating, the less he has to defend himself against in this area, and the more able he is to listen accurately to Jones' response. Putting it in other terms, Smith has expressed what he genuinely feels. He is, therefore, more free to listen. The less he is presenting a façade to be defended, the more he can listen accurately to what Jones is communicating.

5. But to this degree, then, Jones feels emphatically understood. He feels that insofar as he has expressed himself (and whether this is defensively or congruently), Smith has understood him pretty much as he sees himself and as he perceives the topic under consideration.

6. For Jones to feel understood is for him to experience positive regard for Smith. To feel that one is understood is to feel that one has made some kind of a positive difference in the experience of another, in this case of Smith.

7. But to the degree that Jones (a) experiences Smith as congruent or integrated in this relationship; (b) experiences Smith as having positive regard for him; (c) experiences Smith as being empathically understanding; to that degree the conditions of a therapeutic relationship are established. I have tried in another paper to describe the conditions which our experience has led us to believe are necessary and sufficient for therapy, and will not repeat that description here.

8. To the extent that Jones is experiencing these characteristics of a therapeutic relationship, he finds himself experiencing fewer barriers to communication. Hence he tends to communicate himself more as he is, more congruently. Little by little, his defensiveness decreases.

9. Having communicated himself more freely, with less of defensiveness, Jones is now more able to listen accurately, without a need for defensive distortion, to Smith's further communication. This is a repetition of step 4, but now in terms of Jones.

10. To the degree that Jones is able to listen, Smith now feels empathetically understood (as in step 5 for Jones); experiences Jones' positive regard (a parallel to step 6); and finds himself experiencing the relationship as therapeutic (in a way parallel to step 7). Thus, Smith and Jones have to some degree become reciprocally therapeutic for each other.

11. This means that to some degree the process of therapy occurs in each and that the outcomes of therapy will, to that same degree, occur in each: change in personality in the direction of greater unity and integration; less conflict and more energy utilizable for effective living; change in behavior in the direction of greater maturity.

12. The limiting element in this chain of events appears to be the introduction of threatening material. Thus, if Jones in step 3 includes in his more congruent response new material which is outside the realm of Smith's congruence, touching an area in which Smith is *in*congruent, then Smith may not be able to listen accurately; he defends himself against hearing what Jones is communicating; he responds with communication which is ambiguous; and the whole process described in these steps begins to occur in reverse.

## A Tentative Statement of a General Law

Taking all of the above into account, it seems possible to state it far more parsimoniously as a generalized principle. Here is such an attempt.

Assuming (a) a minimal willingness on the part of two people to be in contact; (b) an ability and minimal willingness on the part of each to receive communication from the other; and (c) assuming the contact to continue over a period of time; then the following relationship is hypothesized to hold true:

> The greater the congruence of experience, awareness, and communication on the part of one individual, the more the ensuing relationship will involve: a tendency toward reciprocal communication with a quality of increasing congruence; a tendency toward more mutually accurate understanding of the communication; improved psychological adjustment and functioning in both parties; mutual satisfaction in the relationship.
>
> Conversely, the greater the communicated *incongruence* of experience and awareness, the more the ensuing relationship will involve: further communication with the same quality; disintegration of accurate understanding; less adequate psychological adjustment and functioning in both parties; and mutual dissatisfaction in the relationship.

With probably even greater formal accuracy, this general law could be stated in a way which recognizes that it is the perception of the *receiver* of communication which is crucial. Thus the hypothesized law could be put in these terms, assuming the same preconditions as before as to willingness to be in contact, etc.:

> The more that Y experiences the communication of X as a congruence of experience, awareness, and communication, the more the ensuing relationship will involve: (etc., as stated above).

Stated in this way, this "law" becomes a hypothesis which it should be possible to put to test, since Y's *perception* of X's communication should not be too difficult to measure.

## The Existential Choice

Very tentatively indeed, I would like to set forth one further aspect of this whole matter, an aspect which is frequently very real in the therapeutic relationship, and also in other relationships, though perhaps less sharply noted.

In the actual relationship, both the client and the therapist are frequently faced with the existential choice, "Do I dare to communicate the full degree of congruence which I feel? Do I dare match my experience, and my awareness of that experience, with my communication? Do I dare to communicate myself as I am or must my communication be somewhat less than or different from this?" The sharpness of this issue lies in the often vividly foreseen possibility of threat or rejection. To communicate one's full awareness of the relevant experience is a risk in interpersonal relationships. It seems to me that it is the taking or not taking of this risk which determines whether a given relationship becomes more and more mutually therapeutic or whether it leads in a disintegrative direction.

To put it another way. I cannot choose whether my awareness will be congruent with my experience. This is answered by my need for defense, and of this I am not aware. But there is a continuing existential choice as to whether my communication will be congruent with the awareness I *do* have of what I am experiencing. In this moment-by-moment choice in a relationship may lie the answer as to whether the movement is in one direction or the other in terms of this hypothesized law.

## REFERENCES

Rogers, Carl R., "A Theory of Therapy, Personality, and Interpersonal Relationships," in *Psychology: A Study of a Science*, Vol III, ed. S. Koch. New York: McGraw-Hill Book Company, 1959.

———, "The Necessary and Sufficient Conditions of Therapeutic Personality Change," *J. Consult. Psychol.*, XXI, 95–103.

# Notes on Carl Rogers' Concept of Congruence and His General Law of Interpersonal Relationships

*Harold S. Spear*

*Note to the reader: I assume that you have read the preceding reading by Carl Rogers, in which he defines congruence and its relevance to interpersonal relationships. What follows are my own understandings of congruence, based upon my experience and what I understand Rogers to be saying.*

It is important to keep in mind, when working with Rogers' concept of congruence, that he is concerned with growth-facilitating interactions—ones in which the people in the interaction are, in some way, gaining more accurate knowledge and/or skill about themselves-and-the-world-around-them. He is *not* talking about attaining satisfaction in interactions, nor about getting a task done—at least in the first instance. Indeed, the satisfactions experienced from growth-producing interactions may be quite different from the satisfactions we often experience in relationships; they may have a fair proportion of discomfort, even of pain and hurt. These latter satisfactions are likely to be from a sense of having perceived, felt, understood, etc., something new and deeper. Our usual satisfactions are more likely to be merely feeling "good"—often from being pleased, or from having our wants satisfied, or from being affirmed just as we are, rather than growing towards something new.

Likewise, there is no simple, immediate connection between growth-facilitating relationships and getting the task at hand accomplished. Indeed, an interaction which becomes growth-facilitating *may* involve a diversion of immediate attention from the task directly to the persons themselves, though it may also allow for an improved attention to the task but at some later point in time. Over a longer period of time, growth, satisfaction, and productivity *may* be very much positively related, but at any instant of time in a relationship, they may well not be.

Looking at this from a slightly different point of view, we are here concerned with those interactions in which change, growth, something new, meaningful, and more real may emerge—for the persons involved and for the relationship. That means we are not particularly looking at "equilibrium" relationships, ones which carry on relationships as they have been in the past. These latter may or may not be satisfying relationships and they may or may not facilitate productivity. But they do not have any explicit aim toward personal growth and change.

Rogers sees congruence as having central importance in facilitating growth. It is a complex concept to understand. In the next several paragraphs, I will try to explain and clarify what it is, what it is not, and what some of the dilemmas connected with it are.

There are two different aspects of congruence—one internal to the person and one concerning the connection of what is internal to what becomes external. The first involves whether the person is aware of what he is, in fact, experiencing. In other words, this is a question of whether there is in the person's awareness perception of what is going on inside of him, in his body and mind. (Stated in older, classical psychological terms, this is a question of whether the person's defenses—denial, rationalization, projection, repression, etc.—are preventing something from coming into awareness or whether the person is free to be aware of all he is experiencing.) The second aspect concerns whether the person consciously communicates what he is aware of as fully and clearly as possible or whether he consciously withholds or distorts what he is aware of. Incongruence with respect to the latter aspect is usually much easier for us to recognize in the behavior of both others and ourselves; we tend to know when someone is purposely being a liar, deceitful, phony, or even what we call usually "tactful" but not frank. The first kind of incongruence is likely to wear much more subtle disguises; we are likely to have lessened conscious sensitivity to picking it up in others, while with ourselves, we are,

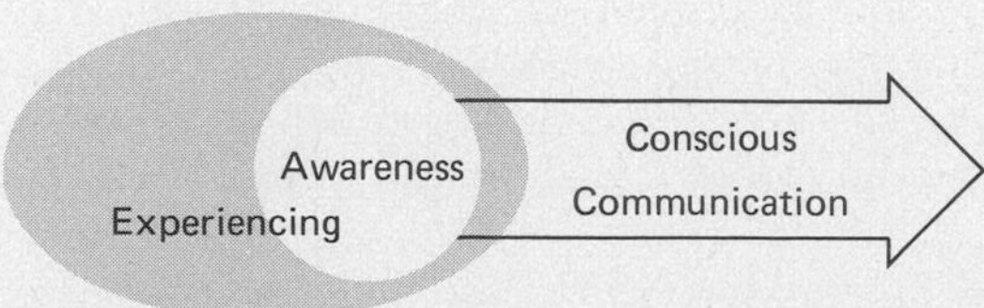


**Figure 1** Internal and External Aspects of Congruence

by definition, unable to see it clearly at the immediate moment of time in which it is occurring, although later on we may recognize in what way we have been defensive or denying something from awareness. When a person is fully congruent, his awareness matches his experience and his conscious communication matches his awareness; hence he is communicating fully what he is experiencing. In that sense, he is being fully genuine or real or transparent. Note, this is different than being frank or honest. These last terms refer to the connection of awareness and communication. A person who is very "honest" may, in fact, be rather incongruent much of the time, for he may not be aware of many important feelings that he is experiencing but that are too threatening to come into his awareness (see Figure 1).

As Rogers notes, we tend to use cultural labels for congruency and incongruency between awareness and communication: the person is being honest or dishonest; frank and straightforward or phony; etc. But for internal incongruency, we need psychological labels, such as a person's being defensive or free from defensiveness; denying, projecting, rationalizing, etc., or not doing these; etc.

To make this discussion more concrete, let us look at a person with negative feelings to the other person he is interacting with—a difficult situation in which to be congruent. When a person experiences some kind of negative reaction to another but is not aware of that reaction within himself, then quite clearly what he communicates must be incongruent. He will talk and (consciously, at least) behave as if he is calm, objective, not having any emotions, etc. There are, however, several consequences of his lack of awareness of that negative reaction. It is highly likely that he is with*out* awareness (i.e., "unconsciously") emitting behavioral cues—tone of voice, gestures, facial expression, bodily movements, etc.—which the other person will experience. If the other person is *aware* of these, he may respond with negative reactions of his own to the latent feeling of the first person; and since there exists in the first person some need *not* to be aware of his feelings, he is likely to feel further threatened. Thus, if I experience a situation in which you threaten my concept of myself so that I "need" to defend it by attacking you, but I am not aware of those feelings of threat and consequent anger at you, my total behavior is likely to be communicating anger. If you are aware of this, you are likely to attack back. I may then perceive your angry attack and respond to that. The circle will continue to reinforce itself. Yet, in the first instance, the problem started from feelings of threat to my own concept of myself, a threat of which you had no intention or awareness in your original behavior.

It is also possible that you may *not* be *aware* of those aspects of my behavior which are *unawarely* signaling my anger. But this will mean that you are experiencing an angry attack, though hidden, from me. Within yourself you are experiencing threat and counteranger, even though you don't "know" it. Both of us will continue to behave consciously as if we had no feelings of threat or anger. But because of the way our minds will be functioning, our talk will be directed at "getting at" each other. Each of us, in hearing the other, is likely to interpret even further the other's talk as counter to our own perceptions. Our calm, "logical" talk may remain a never-ending argument, driven on by unaware feelings of threat and counterattack.

Clearly, if either person could become aware of his anger and say "I am angry at you," it would make the conversation more accurate. As it is, the interaction at the level of experiencing is one between two angry people, but it is carried on as if it were between two wholly logical, "factual" people when the "logic" and "fact" are being largely determined unconsciously by the anger. Expressing the anger would obviously change the nature of the interaction. We would be getting "off the subject" to examine what causes the anger. If either of us could go one step further and recognize that we felt threatened (before the consequent anger) and say "I feel threatened by what you say," it would be even more congruent and more likely to lead to an understanding of what is going on.

Another aspect worth noting is the way in which we become aware of our feelings. We may be more or less congruent in the way we are aware of them. For example, when inside me there is some irritation or anger with you, in the form "You're a pain in the neck," this is not truly congruent. The more accurate symbolization of this for me is "You give me a pain in the neck." That may sound like only a slight twist in words, but if I really understand the difference, it locates the phenomenon far more accurately. The "pain" is in me and you are outside of me. When I say "You're a pain in the neck," I am projecting my feeling onto you. Even more accurate would be "I have a pain in the neck while listening to you," or "I am irritated while listening to you."

If I am aware that I am experiencing such a feeling, there is an obvious difference to you in which way I am aware of it and communicate it. If I say "You're a pain in the neck," rather obviously this is a threat to your self-concept, which is quite *un*likely to contain a "pain in the neck" aspect as a major part of it. You are, therefore, likely to feel threatened, and whether consciously so or not, likely to respond to this threat. If, however, I am more congruently aware of what I am experiencing and communicate this as "You give me a pain in the neck," then you have something different to work with in understanding what I am saying: you have me, you, and the relationship to look at, rather than just you. (This may seem to be a very small difference, but we tend to look at where the words point. If they point to you only, you will look first there; if they point at you *and* me, you will tend to look at both.) There is, thus, at least a greater opportunity for *you* to perceive the situation as: "I'm not a pain in the neck, but the way I'm behaving towards you gives you a pain in the neck. What causes that? Something about you and me taken together." Obviously, the thinking process may not be this explicit, but at least they are more than likely to be nearer this than they are to be a simple defensive reaction to "being" a pain in the neck.

Actually, to be precisely congruent, I should not say you are causing pain but rather something like "I am irritated while listening to you." That is what I am experiencing; whether and how your talking and behavior is, in fact, "causing" the irritation is an explorable question. If I say that to you, I am being not only more congruent but also less threatening to you. You would then likely be most able to focus on my irritation, and help both of us find out more about the irritation—which may very well, of course, involve you.

Thus, we have been looking at different degrees of congruency of expression:

- "You are a pain in the neck," which places my feelings "out there," which is more congruent than my sitting, listening, with a false, pleasant smile on my face.
- "You give me a pain in the neck," which connects you with me and my feelings but implies that you fully "control" and "cause" my feelings.
- "I am irritated while listening to you," which connects what is occurring in me in relation to you in an experientially accurate fashion.

The question is not one of finding "perfect" words; it is one of *owning* our feelings as being our own feelings, not as something "out there" or as something automatically caused by the "out there," but as something that is the result of our involvement with the "out there."

Congruency applies as well to positive states of experiencing others as it does to negative states. My feelings of warmth, liking, enjoyment, friendship, satisfaction, love, etc., toward you are also influences on my behavior in the interaction. If I am unaware of them, they may be influencing me toward agreeing with you, etc., when I do not, in fact, agree with the actual thought content of what you say. Also, I may be aware of my positive feelings toward you, but not communicate them consciously toward you. In that case, you may keep at a greater psychological distance, act more closed and guarded toward me, and find the interaction less satisfying, rewarding, and learningful than if I had communicated those positive feelings.

Hence, congruency and its importance in interpersonal relationships does not refer only to negative feelings. It refers, as it says it does, to whether experiencing, awareness, and communication are congruent, whatever the nature of that experiencing may be.

The last paragraph of Rogers' article raises the question of taking the risk of communicating what I am aware of, even though it may not be congruent with what I am experiencing. Should I communicate my feelings, even though I may not be aware of them in a fully congruent fashion? Much of the time, if we are aware of any feelings in ourselves, they are in "projected" form—we see the phenomena outside of ourselves as being "bad," "unfair," "irresponsible," "pain in the neck," etc., but are not aware that we are feeling angry, irritated, or whatever. The judgments and the feelings are in us, but we "see" them as being "out there." And, of course, the person "out there" may see himself in just the opposite way—as being "good . . . fair . . . responsible . . . a good guy . . . etc." If we express what we are aware of, we directly threaten what he is aware of.

What will happen, then, if we express our "feeling," which really isn't our feeling, but a projected version of our feeling? Will that improve communication, facilitate growth, etc., or will it do the opposite? It might get us a figurative or literal punch in the face; it might lead to a break in the relationship; etc. Certainly, if we do not express it, we are behaving incongruently—we are withholding the data of our own awareness from the other person. Yet, communicating it is also incongruent, for we are communicating something which is discrepant with what we are really experiencing.

The answer, to me, is ambiguous. Sometimes the expression of such a not-fully-congruently-perceived feeling is fruitful, sometimes it is not. Sometimes it does clarify the situation; the expression of it indicates that emotions are present and need to be looked at and worked through. Sometimes it leads only to further threat. It therefore seems to me that the person must make his own choice (assuming he is even aware of the choice of communicating or not communicating his feelings), making his own best estimate of the risks involved. It is risky, but the risks are often worth it, *if* we are willing to "hang in" and work through the problem aspect of the relationship.

Taking those risks may lead to real difficulties—hurt, rejection, etc. Yet it can also lead to beautiful growth and relationships. An effort at being congruently open may help more openness, richness, and warmth grow in the person who makes the effort and in the other as well. The following excerpt from a sensitive person's paper indicates what may happen when someone takes the risks. It was written by Nancy L. Reordan, a member of a training group. She refers to expressing her feelings about another person at a time in the group when the members were being asked to form work groups from the total membership:

> One example that was very meaningful to me in terms of the whole process was what happened between myself and John. I risked expressing to him a strong negative feeling I had about his smile and something completely turned around from where it started out. We found it relevant to work through the feelings related here, and it turned out that we eventually wanted to work together—and ended up this way. There is something about taking the risk of simple expression of those feelings that are within awareness—no matter how congruent they actually are—and also communicating in a way which contains enough positive regard so that the other can hear it. I did not feel a lot of unconditional positive regard toward John, but I must have communicated some that he could hear, and I also must have been open enough myself so that the feeling grew in me.

Restating this from a slightly different perspective, we are dealing with the question of the importance of taking responsibility for our feelings as being *our* feelings and not something "out there," and for our values as being just that, *our* values. It is the question of whether we will own and take responsibility for our own experience as being just that, and not something else. Yet, if we could do that well, it would mean that we had already grown a great deal. Hence the road to growth means behaving not fully grown; it means the probable expression of not-fully-congruent behavior, with all its attendant risks, in order to learn how to be more fully congruent.

Finally, there is an interesting and very central question about congruence: If being more congruent helps facilitate growth, how come most people behave relatively incongruently most of the time and do not try to be otherwise? In a sense, Rogers is only rediscovering in modern words an age-old concept and precept; in Shakespeare's words it was, "To thine own self be true/And it must follow as the night the day/Thou canst not then be false to any man." The answer to this question, for me at least, is intellectually simple but emotionally very difficult. Rogers says "The sharpness of this issue lies in the often vividly foreseen possibility of threat and rejection." And this is sharp, indeed. When we are behaving quite congruently (at least as we are aware of ourselves) and the other person does not accept what we are communicating, it seems no longer to be a simple rejection of what we say, but a rejection of our "self," of our "person." We have exposed our self and it has been rejected—at least that is what we often tend to feel. Few of us have the inner sense of our being acceptable—of self-acceptance—sufficiently to hold to it in the face of rejection from the outside. Hence we "duck," either consciously or unconsciously. We do not expose ourselves. We maintain an "appropriate" role behavior, one that leaves things smooth and avoids the risk of our inner self being rejected. Life remains, in such cases, with the everyday façades and the "games people play."

Yet, paradoxically enough, the development of that very sense of self-acceptance at a deeper level—not just a surface self-assurance—depends on our being willing to try to behave congruently and risk whatever happens. It involves the growth of confidence—in the sense of having trust and faith in life, rather than certainty. To Shakespeare's question, "To be or not to be," we can only reply with the question from Tillich, "Do we have the Courage to Be?"

# Some Lethal Aspects of the Male Role

*Sidney M. Jourard*

Men die sooner than women, and so health scientists and public health officials have become justly concerned about the sex difference in death age. Biology provides no convincing evidence to prove that female organisms are intrinsically more durable than males, or that tissues or cells taken from males are less viable than those taken from females. A promising place to look for an explanation of the perplexing sex-differential in mortality is in the transactions between men and their environments, especially their interpersonal environments. In principle, there must be ways of behaving among people which prolong a man's life and insure his fuller functioning, and ways of behaving which speed a man's progress toward death. The present paper is devoted to an overview of some aspects of being a man in American society which may be related to man's acknowledged faster rate of dying.

The male role, as personally and socially defined, requires man to appear tough, objective, striving, achieving, unsentimental, and emotion-

• Adapted from a paper presented at a symposium entitled "The Compleat Man" held at the Southeastern Psychological Association, Atlanta, Georgia, April 1960. Printed in Sidney M. Jourard, *The Transparent Self* (Princeton, N.J.: D. Van Nostrand, Inc., 1964), pp. 46–55. Reprinted here by permission of the publisher.

ally unexpressive. But seeming is not being. If a man *is* tender (behind his *persona*), if he weeps, if he shows weakness, he will likely be viewed as unmanly by others, and he will probably regard himself as inferior to other men.

Now, from that we can fathom about the *subjective* side of man, as this has been revealed in autobiography, novels, plays, and psychotherapists' case histories, it seems true that men are as capable as women at responding to the play of life's events with a broad range of feelings. Man's potential thoughts, feelings, wishes and fantasies know no bounds, save those set by his biological structure and his personal history. But the male role, and the male's self-structure will not allow man to acknowledge or to express the entire breadth and depth of his inner experience, to himself or to others. Man seems obliged, rather, to hide much of his real self—the ongoing flow of his spontaneous inner experience—from himself and from others.

## Manliness and Low Self-Disclosure

Research in patterns of self-disclosure has shown that men typically reveal less personal information about themselves to others than women (Jourard, 1961a; Jourard and Lasakow, 1958; Jourard and Landsman, 1960; Jourard and Richman, 1963). Since men, doubtless, have as much "self", i.e., inner experience, as women, then it follows that men have more "secrets" from the interpersonal world than women. It follows further that men, seeming to dread being known by others, must be more continually tense (neuromuscular tension) than women. It is as if "being manly" implies the necessity to wear neuromuscular "armor," the character armor which Reich (1948) wrote about with such lucidity. Moreover, if a man has "secrets," "something to hide," it must follow that other people will be a threat to him; they might pry into his secrets, or he may, in an unguarded moment, reveal his true self in its nakedness, thereby exposing his areas of weakness and vulnerability. Naturally, when a person is in hostile territory, he must be continually alert, hypertonic, opaque, and restless. All this implies that trying to seem manly is a kind of "work," and work imposes stress and consumes energy. Manliness, then, seems to carry with it a chronic burden of stress and energy-expenditure which could be a factor related to man's relatively shorter life-span.

If self-disclosure is an empirical index of "openness," of "real-self being," and if openness and real-self being are factors in health and wellness, then the research in self-disclosure seems to point to one of the potentially lethal aspects of the male role. Men keep their selves to themselves, and impose thereby an added burden of stress beyond that imposed by the exigencies of everyday life. The experience of psychosomatic physicians who undertake psychotherapy with male patients suffering peptic ulcers, essential hypertension and kindred disorders, seems to support this contention. Psychotherapy is the art of promoting self-disclosure and authentic being in patients who withhold their real selves from expression, and clinical experience shows that when psychotherapy has been effective with psychosomatic patients, the latter change their role-definitions, their self-structures, and their behavior in the direction of greater spontaneity and openness, with salutary consequences to their bodies. The time is not far off when it will be possible to demonstrate with adequately controlled experiments the nature and degree of correlation between levels and amounts of self-disclosure and proneness to illness and/or an early death age.

## Manliness: The Lack of Insight and Empathy

There is another implication of the fact that men are lower self-disclosers than women, an implication that relates to self-insight. Men, trained by their upbringing to assume the "instrumental role," tend more to relate to other people on an *I–it* basis than women (Buber, 1937).[1] They are more adept than women at relating impersonally to others, seeing them as the embodiment of their roles rather than as persons enacting roles. Women (often to the despair of businesslike men) seem to find it difficult to keep their interpersonal relationships *im*personal; they sense and respond to the feelings of the *other* person even in a supposedly official transaction, and they respond to their *own* feelings toward the other person, seeming to forget the original purpose of the impersonal transaction.

Now, one outcome that is known to follow from effective psychotherapy (which, it will be recalled, entails much self-disclosure from the patient to the therapist) is that the patient becomes increasingly sensitized to the nuances of his own feelings (and those of the therapist) as they ebb and flow in the relationship. The patient becomes more adept at labeling his feelings (Dollard and Miller, 1950, pp. 281–304), diagnosing his own needs, and understanding his own reactions. Coincident with this increase in insight is an increase in empathy into others, an increase in his ability to "imagine the real" (Buber, 1957). Studies of leadership show that the leaders of the most effective groups maintain an optimum "distance" from their followers, avoiding the distraction thereby of overly intimate personal knowledge of the followers' immediate feelings and needs (Fiedler, 1957). But not all of a man's everyday life entails the instrumental leadership role. For example, a man may "lead" his family, but he is not a father twenty-four hours a day. Personal life calls both for insight and for empathy. If practice at spontaneous self-disclosure promotes insight and

[1]There is an interesting implication of these observations for the training of male psychotherapists. It seems true that effective psychotherapists of whatever theoretical school are adept at establishing a warm, bilaterally communicative relationship with their patients, one characterized by a refraining from manipulation on the part of the therapist. The effective therapists do not "take over" the patient's problems, or "solve them" for the patient. Rather, they seem to "be and to let be" (Rogers, 1958). This mode of being is quite alien to the modal male. Indeed, it can be discerned among beginning therapists that there is often considerable dread of such passivity, because it constitutes a threat to masculine identity. Beginning therapists seem to be most fascinated by "manly," active techniques such as hypnosis, reflection, interpretation, etc.—the kinds of things which will be difficult for them to master, but which will make them feel they are doing something to the patient which will get him well. These techniques, however, leave the self of the therapist hidden behind the mask of his professional role, and have limited effectiveness.

empathy, then perhaps we have here one of the mechanisms by which women become more adept at these aspects of their so-called "expressive" role. Women, trained toward motherhood and a comforting function, both engage in and receive more self-disclosure then men (Jourard and Richman, 1963).

Let us now focus upon insight, in the sense that we have used the term here. If men are trained, as it were, to ignore their own feelings, in order more adequately to pursue the instrumental aspects of manliness, it follows that they will be less sensitive to what one might call "all is not well signals" as these arise in themselves. It is probably a fact that in every case of outright physical or mental illness, earlier signs occurred which, if noted and acted upon, would have averted the eventual breakdown. Vague discomfort, boredom, anxiety, depression probably arose as consequences of the afflicted person's way of life, but because these signals were "weak," or else deliberately or automatically ignored, the illness-conducive way of life persisted until breakdown finally forced a respite, a withdrawal from the illness-producing role. The hypothesis may be proposed that women, more sensitized to their inner experience, will notice their "all is not well signals" sooner and more often than men, and change their mode of existence to one more conducive of wellness, e.g., consult a doctor sooner, or seek bed-rest more often than men. Men, by contrast, fail to notice these "all is not well signals" of weaker intensity, and do not stop work, nor take to their beds until the destructive consequences of their manly way of life have progressed to the point of a "stroke," or a total collapse. It is as if women "amplify" such inner distress signals even when they are dim, while men, as it were, "tune them out" until they become so strong they can no longer be ignored.

Accordingly, manly men, unaccustomed to self-disclosure, and characterized by lesser insight and lesser empathy than women, do violence to their own unique needs, and persist in modes of behavior which, to be sure, are effective at changing the world, but no less effective in modifying their "essence" from the healthy to the moribund range.

A curious exception to these patterns has been noted among college males. Mechanic and Volkert (1961, p. 52) have proposed the term "illness behavior" to describe "the way in which symptoms are perceived, evaluated, and acted upon by a person who recognizes some pain, discomfort, or other sign of organic malfunction." Visiting a physician at a university infirmary following perception of some malaise thus qualifies as a type of "illness behavior." Some as yet unpublished research at the University of Florida Student Infirmary has shown that male students consulted the infirmary one and one-half times more frequently than comparable female students during the year under study. A breakdown according to religious denomination showed, moreover, that of the "high users" of the infirmary, Jewish male students were represented with nearly double the frequency of males affiliated with Methodist, Baptist, Catholic, and other religious groups. A completely independent study (Jourard, 1961b) of self-disclosure patterns among members of different religious denominations on the University of Florida campus showed that Jewish males were significantly higher disclosers than were comparable Methodist, Baptist, and Catholic males, none of the latter three groups differing significantly from one another. These findings imply that college males in general, and Jewish college males in particular, may depart from more stereotyped patterns of masculinity which prevail in the general population for the age range between 18 and 23.

## Manliness and Incompetence at Loving

Loving, including self-love, entails knowledge of the unique needs and characteristics of the loved person (Fromm, 1956). To know another person calls for empathy *in situ*, the capacity to "imagine the real," and the ability to "let be," that is, to permit and promote the disclosure of being. The receipt of disclosure from another person obviously must enhance one's factual knowledge about him, and also it must improve one's degree of empathy into him. But data obtained in the systematic study of self-disclosure has shown, not only that men disclose less to others than women, but also that of all the disclosure that does go on among people *women are the recipients of more disclosure than men* (Jourard and Richman, 1963). This fact helps one better understand why men's concepts of the subjective side of other people—of other men as well as of women and children—are often naïve, crude, or downright inaccurate. Men are often alleged, in fiction, to be mystified by the motives for the behavior of others, motives which a woman observer can understand instantly, and apparently intuitively. If this conjecture is true, it should follow that men, in spite of good intentions to promote the happiness and growth of others by loving actions, will often "miss the target." That is, they will want to make the other person happy, but their guesses about the actions requisite to the promotion of this goal will be inappropriate, and their actions will appear awkward or crude.

The obverse of this situation is likewise true. If a man is reluctant to make himself known to another person, even to his spouse—because it is not manly thus to be psychologically naked—then it follows that *men will be difficult to love*. That is, it will be difficult for a woman or another man to know the immediate present state of the man's self, and his needs will thereby go unmet. Some men are so skilled at dissembling, at "seeming," that even their wives will not know when they are lonely, bored, anxious, in pain, thwarted, hungering for affection, etc. And the men, blocked by pride, dare not disclose their despair or need.

The situation extends to the realm of self-love. If true love of self implies behavior which will truly meet one's own needs and promote one's own growth, then men who lack profound insight or clear contact with their real selves will be failures at self-loving. Since they do not know what they feel, want, and need (through long practice at repression) men's "essences" will show the results of self-neglect, or harsh treatment of the self by the self.

It is a fact that suicide, mental illness, and death occur sooner and more often among "men whom nobody knows" (that is, among unmarried men, among "lone wolves") than among men who are loved as individual, known persons, by other individual, known persons. Perhaps loving and being loved enables a man to take his life seriously; it makes his life take on value, not only to himself, but also to his loved ones, thereby adding to its value for him. Moreover, if a man is open to his loved one, it permits two people—he and his loved one—to examine, react to, diagnose, evaluate, and do something constructive about *his* inner experience and his present condition when these fall into the undesirable range. When a man's self is hidden from everybody else, even from a physician, it seems also to become much hidden even from himself, and it permits entropy—disease and death—to gnaw into his substance without his clear knowledge. Men who are unknown and/or inadequately loved often fall ill, or even die as if suddenly and without warning, and it is a shock and a surprise to everyone who hears about it. One wonders why people express surprise when they themselves fall ill, or when someone else falls ill or dies, apparently suddenly. If one had direct access to the person's real self, one would have had many earlier signals that the present way of life was generating illness. Perhaps, then, the above-noted "inaccessibility" (Rickers-Ovsiankina, 1956) of man, in addition to hampering his insight and empathy, also handicaps him at self-loving, at loving others, and at being loved. If love is a factor that promotes life, then handicap at love, a male characteristic, seems to be another lethal aspect of the male role.

## The Male Role and Dispiritation

Frankl (1955) has argued that unless a man can see meaning and value in his continuing existence, his morale will deteriorate, his immunity will decrease, and he will sicken more readily, or even commit suicide. Schmale (1958) noted that the majority of a sample of patients admitted to a general hospital suffered some depressing disruption in object relations prior to the onset of their symptoms. Extrapolating from many observations and opinions of this sort, the present writer proposed a theory of inspiritation-dispiritation. Broadly paraphrased, this theory holds that, when a man finds hope, meaning, purpose, and value in his existence, he may be said to be "inspirited," and isomorphic brain events weld the organism into its optimal, anti-entropic mode of organization. "Dispiriting" events, perceptions, beliefs, or modes of life tend to weaken this optimum mode of organization (which at once sustains wellness, and mediates the fullest, most effective functioning and behavior), and illness is most likely to flourish then. It is as if the body, when a man is dispirited, suddenly becomes an immense fertile "garden" in which viruses and germs proliferate like jungle vegetation. In inspirited states, viruses and germs find a man's body a very uncongenial milieu for unbridled growth and multiplication.

Now, from what has been said in previous sections, it seems clear that the male role provides many opportunities for dispiritation to arise. The best example is provided by the data on aging. It is a well-documented observation that men in our society, following retirement, will frequently disintegrate and die not long after they assume their new life of leisure. It would appear that masculine identity and self-esteem—factors in inspiritation for men—are predicted on a narrow base. If men can see themselves as manly, and life as worthwhile, only so long as they are engaged in gainful employ, or are sexually potent, or have enviable social status, then clearly these are tenuous bases upon which to ground one's existence. It would seem that women can contribute to find meaning, and *raisons d'être* long after men feel useless and unneeded.

Thus, if man's sense of masculine identity, as presently culturally defined, is a condition for continued existence, and if this is easily undermined by the vicissitudes of aging or the vicissitudes of a changing social system, then, indeed, the male role has an added lethal component. The present writer has known men who became dispirited following some financial or career upset, and who fell victims to some infectious disease or "heart failure" shortly thereafter. Their wives, though affected by the husbands' reverses or death, managed to find new grounds and meaning for continued existence, and got on with living.

## Discussion and Summary

It has been pointed out that men, lower disclosers of self than women, are less insightful and empathic, less competent at loving, and more subject to dispiritation than women. The implication of these aspects of manliness for health and longevity was explored. As a concluding note, it seems warranted to step back, and look briefly at the problem of roles from a broader perspective.

Social systems need to delimit people's behavior in order to keep the systems functioning. No social system can use all of every man's self and yet keep the social system functioning well. This is what roles are for—sex roles as well as occupational, age, and familial roles. The role-definitions help men and women to learn just what actions they must perform, and which they must suppress in order to keep the social system functioning properly. But it should not then be thought that just because society cannot use all that a man is, that the man should then strive to root out all self that is neither useful, moral, or in vogue.

If health, full-functioning, happiness, and creativity are valued goals for mankind, then laymen and behavioral scientists alike must seek new ways of redefining the male role, to help it become less restrictive and repressive, more expressive of the "compleat" man, and more conducive to life.

## BIBLIOGRAPHY


Buber, M., *I and Thou*. New York: Scribners, 1937.

———, "Elements of the Interhuman" (William Alanson White Memorial Lectures), *Psychiatry*, XX (1957), 95–129.

Dollard, J., and N. E. Miller, *Personality and Psychotherapy*. New York: McGraw-Hill, 1950.

Fiedler, F. E., "A Note on Leadership Theory: The Effect of Social Barriers between Leaders and Followers," *Sociometry*, XX (1957), 87–94.

Frankl, V. E., *The Doctor and the Soul: An Introduction to Logotherapy*. New York: Knopf, 1955.

Fromm, E., *The Art of Loving*. New York: Harper, 1956.

Jourard, S. M., "Age and Self-Disclosure," *Merrill-Palmer Quart. Beh. Dev.*, VII (1961a), 191–97.

———, "Religious Denomination and Self-Disclosure," *Psychol. Rep.*, VIII (1961b), 446.

———, and M. J. Landsman, "Cognition, Cathexis, and the Dyadic Effect in Men's Self-Disclosing Behavior," *Merrill-Palmer Quart. Behav. Dev.*, VI (1960), 178–86.

———, and P. Lasakow, "Some Factors in Self-Disclosure," *J. Abn. Soc. Psychol.*, LVI (1958), 91–98.

———, and P. Richman, "Disclosure Output and Input in College Students," *Merrill-Palmer Quart. Beh. Dev.*, IX (1963), 141–48.

Mechanic, D., and E. H. Volkert, "Stress, Illness Behavior, and the Sick Role," *Amer. Social Rev.*, XXVI (1961), 51–58.

Reich, W., *Character Analysis*. New York: Orgone Press, 1948.

Rickers-Ovsiankina, Maria, "Social Accessibility in Three Age Groups," *Psychol. Reports*, II (1956), 283–94.

Rogers, C. R., "The Characteristics of a Helping Relationship, *Pers. Guid. J.*, XXXVII (1958), 6–16.

Schmale, A. H., "Relation of Separation and Depression to Disease," *Psychosom. Med.*, XX (1958), 259–77.

# CHAPTER 8

# Leadership and Authority

You have been learning about leadership all your life. During your childhood many adults, especially your parents, influenced your behavior and served as models for your own becoming. And in your relationships with peers you probably experienced leading and being led, each to varying extents depending on your own personality, the nature of your peers, and the settings in which you found yourself.

We suggest that the ideas in this chapter will be more meaningful to you if you stop a moment and try to recall the various instances in your own life, from early childhood to the present time, that involved your leading or being led. Especially try to find those instances in which you led, in which you much wanted to lead but failed, and in which you were happy to be led. Make a note of each of them, so that at the end of this chapter you can go back and examine your own life data to see if any patterns appear that help you to understand better your own leadership behavior and aspirations. We can only offer you some modest maps to use in such an examination; but you bring a wealth of territory for understanding more about leadership.

## LEADERSHIP

In this chapter we will look at some ways of thinking about leadership that we hope will help you more consciously observe, interpret, and assess people, including yourself, behaving as leaders. Thus, in a sense, our hope is that you will gain some conceptual tools that will help you to continue to carry on your own research in an area in which much remains to be learned. Some of the questions we will consider are: What makes a good leader? What is the best style of leadership? What influences leaders to behave as they do? We warn you that our answers are far from complete, but we hope to help you further along your own path to discovery.

## Leaders and Managers

A leader is one who influences his followers to achieve an objective in a given situation.[1] The followers may be the superiors or peers, as well as the subordinates, of the leader; the essential thing is that the leader is the one who *influences* the others to achieve given *objectives* in a certain *situation.* It is sometimes useful to distinguish between *formal* and *informal* leaders. Formal leaders hold positions in the required system that give them certain formal authority and status. In this respect, the term "formal leader" in a business organization is synonymous with that of "manager." The informal leader, on the other hand, often holds no formal organizational position, and achieves his leadership results solely by his ability to influence others. His authority depends on the willingness of his "followers" to accept his "directions."

A leader does not require formal authority, according to our definition, although he may have it and find it most useful. For just a short while, we will make a somewhat artificial distinction between a manager and a leader. The manager has the *right*, as a function of his formal position and role, to *direct* or *order* people to behave so as to achieve objectives; the leader without any "formal" authority *influences* people to behave so as to achieve objectives. The reason we want to distinguish temporarily between manager and leader is to emphasize the difference between achieving possibly forced responses and necessarily voluntary cooperation. In actual behavior, of course, cooperation often includes both elements simultaneously.

We can emphasize the distinction being made even further by asking: Is a manager a leader? You have already seen evidence in some of the cases you have read that a leader does not have to be a manager. Does

[1]For a more detailed discussion of leadership, see Robert Tannenbaum, Irving R. Weschler, and Fred Massarik's *Leadership and Organization: A Behavioral Science Approach* (New York: McGraw-Hill Book Co., 1961), Chapters 1 through 8; especially Chapter 2, "Leadership: A Frame of Reference." Our own definition of leadership is substantially the same as that given on page 24 of *Leadership and Organization:* "interpersonal influence, exercised in situation and directed, through the communication process, toward the attainment of a specified goal or goals." See also Paul Hersey and Kenneth H. Blanchard, *Management of Organizational Behavior*, 2nd ed. (Englewood Cliffs, N.J.: Prentice-Hall, Inc., 1972).

it follow that a manager need not be a leader? (We will define a manager here as one who is recognized formally as being a manager and who performs managerial functions such as planning, organizing, staffing, directing, and controlling.)

The answer to our question has already been implied. It is "Not necessarily." The terms are not synonymous, at least as we are using them here. It is true that an effective manager actually is a leader as well as a manager, but it does not follow that all managers are leaders. The important distinction hinges on the concept of authority. The manager may *direct* people through the use of formal authority only; the leader *influences* people through the use of personal power or informal authority. The *effective* manager usually does both.

## Effective Leadership

What makes a good leader? Men have thought and talked about this question for centuries. Unfortunately, no clear answers have been found yet, and it is apparent that, so far, leadership remains a rather illusive art practiced more on the basis of "feel" than cognitive knowledge. Nevertheless, researchers and thinkers have developed findings and concepts that are helpful in *better* understanding what is involved in leadership. It is the purpose of this section to review some of these findings.

LEADER TRAITS. Possibly one of the most often explored questions is: What qualities or traits does an effective leader have? Today, it is largely agreed that no single trait or cluster of traits can be used to predict leadership success. For example, one study that reviewed over one hundred other studies that individually examined various physical, intellectual, and personal determinants of effective behavior showed that only 5 percent of the traits appeared in four or more studies.[2] Research has pointed to so many traits in an attempt to describe and predict leadership that, in effect, nothing of much concrete use has resulted. One writer concluded that "fifty years of study have failed to produce one personality trait or set of qualities that can be used to discriminate between leaders and nonleaders."[3] The traits approach has been barren because it does not consider the people being led or the *settings* in which "leaders" lead. The man, his job role, the other people, and the setting in which he leads are all related. The traits any given role and setting demand are not necessar-

[2]R. Stogdill, "Personal Factors Associated with Leadership: A Survey of the Literature," *Journal of Psychology*, January, 1948, pp. 35–71.

[3]Eugene E. Jennings, "The Anatomy of Leadership," *Management of Personnel Quarterly*, 1, No. 1 (Autumn, 1961), 2. See also Alvin W. Gouldner, ed., *Studies in Leadership* (New York: Harper & Brothers, 1950), pp. 31–35, where Gouldner concludes: "At this time, there is no reliable evidence concerning the existence of universal leadership traits."

ily those of another situation. Although researchers have not discovered single traits that identify and predict leadership, it does not follow that charismatic characteristics are illusional. The fact is that some people have clusters of traits that give them a charismatic personality. Nor does it necessarily follow that people are completely unable to identify and predict leaders. In fact, some people often are able to recognize those who are, or have the potential for being, effective leaders. The ability comes more from an intuitive sensing than from the use of a scientific predictor.

There is some evidence, though it be tentative at best, that leaders can often be seen to display within the "situation" of a group, the following relative characteristics:[4]

1. *Awareness of group attitudes.* Leaders tend to be more socially perceptive than nonleaders, especially on issues relevant for the group's goals and values. They tend to be more empathic and are better able to judge the relative popularity of group members.
2. *Ability in abstract thinking.* Leaders tend to be a little brighter than others in their group and have better than average conceptual ability.
3. *Emotional stability.* Leaders often tend to be more stable emotionally than others in the group, even though they operate under more stress at times.

There is also some evidence that a leader tends to have a relatively positive self-concept, and his own self-perception tends to be close to that of the group. Leaders are frequently attractive personally. Although many are seen as friendly, this does not seem as important as the power and ability to help individuals and groups achieve their goals.

FOLLOWERS' NEEDS. Another approach to studying leadership has been that of focusing on followers rather than leaders. The assumption is made that the followers have basic needs and that they tend to follow those leaders who best help them satisfy those needs. For example, the single "A" student in a group of students cramming for an exam may emerge as the group leader because he can be the most helpful to the others in preparing for the test.

Yet another approach has been that of considering the characteristics of the particular group being led. The assumption is made that the leader is not free to determine the group's actions at will but is limited considerably by its needs and norms. Thus, the leader must be aware of the needs, norms, and behavior patterns of his group in order to structure the activities and interactions in such a way that the needs of the group are

[4]These findings are elaborated in Floyd L. Ruch, *Psychology and Life*, 6th ed. (Chicago: Scott, Foresman and Co., 1963), pp. 424–33.

satisfied. George Homans hypothesizes that the way a leader maintains his social rank is by living up to the norms of the group he is leading.[5] In fact, the leader of a group is often one who abides most closely in his actual behavior to the group's norms, particularly if the group is an informal one.

The "follower approach" and the "group approach" are closely related. The group may in one sense be considered the "follower." Also, both approaches emphasize the leader's understanding and helping to satisfy needs, in one case the individual follower's, in the other case the group's. One difficulty that is pinpointed in distinguishing between these two approaches, however, is that the leader must sometimes be aware of his followers as both individuals and part of a group.

SITUATIONS. Another approach to studying leadership is that of examining the situation in which it occurs. The assumption is made in this approach that the demands of particular situations are what determine the kind of leadership needed. Similar to the group approach, the situational approach emphasizes more specific environmental and situational factors, such as physical phenomena (space, light, noise), time, individual and group goals, cultural factors, and organizational settings. Thus, a worker who is a scoutmaster might lead on a company picnic because his superiors at work are not so competent as he in building a fire.

No conclusive evidence has been found to support any of these approaches alone. But, enough evidence has been accumulated to establish that each of them has some merit. It can be concluded that all must be considered in understanding and predicting effective leadership behavior. In other words, *effective leadership depends on the leader, his followers, the situation, and the interrelationships between them.*[6] Leadership is one element in *a social system.*

## Styles of Leadership

Over the years, writers and researchers have identified different "styles" of leadership. Three frequently mentioned ones are (1) autocratic or authoritarian, (2) democratic or consultive, and (3) free rein or laissez faire.[7] The autocratic leader mainly seeks obedience from his group by use of formal authority, rewards, and punishments. He deter-

[5]George C. Homans, *The Human Group* (New York: Harcourt, Brace & World, Inc., 1950), p. 426.

[6]Robert Tannenbaum and Warren H. Schmidt, "How to Choose a Leadership Pattern," *Harvard Business Review*, XXXVI, No. 2 (March–April, 1958), 95–101.

[7]For a more detailed discussion of these terms, see Auren Uris, *How to be a Successful Leader* (New York: McGraw-Hill Book Co., 1953), pp. 32–39; or Robert T. Golembiewski, "Three Styles of Leadership and Their Uses," *Personnel*, XXXVIII, No. 4 (July–August, 1961), 34–45. The "loaded terms" used in describing these styles should warn you to be cautious in making hasty evaluations of them.

mines policy and makes all decisions. The democratic leader draws ideas and suggestions from his followers and encourages them to participate in things that concern them. In some cases, he may let the group determine policy; in others, he may ask their advice but make the final decision himself. The free rein leader plays down his role in the group's activities and acts primarily to provide information, materials, and facilities for the group in accomplishing its objectives. He exercises a minimum of control.

Ask yourself which of these styles is most effective in today's setting. Your answer, after having read the preceding section, should be: It depends on the leader, the followers, and the situation. How a particular leader behaves will depend largely on his own assumptions, feelings, and perceptions in given situations. For example, he may think of himself as being dominant and therefore feel comfortable with an authoritarian style, or he might think of himself as a facilitator and feel more comfortable with a laissez faire style. In addition to himself, he also considers the nature of the task, the other people involved, and the setting in which they find themselves. The captain of an airplane about to crash is unlikely to consult with his subordinates about what course of action should be taken. In contrast, a man supervising a group of creative scientists may utilize a laissez faire approach even though he by nature prefers to be authoritarian. Another leader may prefer a democratic style of leadership but work in a company that expects its managers to behave more along the lines of the authoritarian style. We can conclude that the behavior of a particular leader will be his individual synthesis of his own assumptions, feelings, and perceptions about all of the factors mentioned.

You may be bothered by the fact that you know leaders who do not fit neatly into the categories just presented. You should be. The fact is that people do not fit into the neat boxes created by researchers and writers. Nevertheless, it does appear that many leaders *do* tend to approximate, much of the time, one style or another. The concepts, therefore, can be useful in understanding and describing the leadership behavior of specific persons; they can also enable us to evaluate different types of leadership in different situations.

## Style, Satisfaction, and Productivity

In 1945 researchers at Ohio State University began extensive research that ultimately identified two major dimensions of leadership.[8] These were termed *initiating structure* and *consideration*. Initiating structure included "the leader's behavior in delineating the relationship between himself and members of the work-group and in endeavoring to establish well-defined patterns of organization, channels of communica-

[8]Roger M. Stogdill and Alvin E. Coons, eds., "Leader Behavior: Its Description and Measurement," *Research Monograph* No. 88 (Columbus, Ohio: Bureau of Business Research, Ohio State University, 1957).

tion, and methods of procedure." This dimension is similar to delineating the required system. Consideration included "behavior indicative of friendship, mutual trust, respect, and warmth in the relationship between the leader and the members of his staff.[9] This closely translates to being attentive to members' personal systems and building and maintenance behavior. The Ohio State studies were helpful in pointing out the importance of both the task and human dimensions of leadership. Note that these two dimensions are not mutually exclusive.

At about the same time the foregoing research was being conducted, studies were being initiated at the University of Michigan to investigate the relationships between leadership style and worker satisfaction and productivity. This research continued for many years and a major summary of the findings presented by Rensis Likert indicated that there is indeed a discernible difference between the general pattern of leadership of the most successful and the less successful ones.[10]

One of the characteristics of the more successful managers was their orientation towards their workers. The successful managers were *employee-centered*, whereas the less successful ones were *production-centered*. The employee-centered supervisor is genuinely interested in and concerned about his individual employees. He develops a friendly supportive relationship and identifies with the employees, or the employees *and* the company, rather than primarily with the company. The production centered supervisor is primarily concerned with getting out production. He tends to emphasize authority and control, and assumes that people work primarily for economic reasons. He tends to identify much more strongly with the company than with his employees, and he expects his employees to do the same. The research findings indicated that the employee-centered supervisor tends to get better results, *both in productivity and employee satisfaction*.

Likert's summary found also that successful managers tended to supervise generally rather than closely. Although they made clear what the objectives were and what needed to be done to achieve them, they were then willing to give their employees considerable freedom in doing the job. This kind of behavior enables the subordinates to pace themselves and to use some of their own ideas and skills in performing their work. The less successful supervisors, on the other hand, tended to give much more frequent and specific directions for accomplishing the work. They tended to assume that if workers were given too much freedom they

[9]Andrew W. Halpin, *The Leadership Behavior of School Superintendents* (Chicago: Midwest Administration Center, University of Chicago, 1959), p. 4.

[10]Rensis Likert, *New Patterns of Management* (New York: McGraw-Hill Book Co., 1961), and *The Human Organization: Its Management and Value* (New York: McGraw-Hill Book Co., 1967). See also Saul W. Gellerman, *Motivation and Productivity* (New York: American Management Association, 1963); and Abraham Zaleznik, C. R. Christensen, and F. J. Roethlisberger, *The Motivation, Productivity, and Satisfaction of Workers: A Prediction Study* (Boston: Harvard University Division of Research, 1958).

would loaf. Research findings indicate that this is not necessarily so; the workers' behavior depends on the various factors and conditions accompanying the freedom. The more successful supervisors, who supervise more generally, seem to have employees who are more interested and involved in their work, who assume more responsibility for it, and who get better production results.

Although the Michigan studies found that most employee-centered supervisors tended to get best production results, not all did so. Further, some production-centered supervisors did get good results. Thus, the problem remained to find an improved explanation for why some supervisors get better results than others.

Fred Fiedler has conducted research on leadership for many years and has developed what he calls a "contingency theory of leadership."[11] It is designed to explain why task-oriented supervision works in some situations and human-oriented supervision works better in others. His theory attempts to identify critical variables in a given situation that make it favorable or unfavorable for the leader. The three main variables he identifies are the quality of a leader's relationships with his group members, the degree to which the task is structured, and the formal power position of the leader.

Situations are favorable to the leader if all three of the above variables are high, and vice versa. A highly favorable situation to a leader is one in which he is liked and well-accepted by his followers, the task is well-defined, and the leader has considerable authority and power attributed to him. Fiedler's theory is that task-oriented leadership is most appropriate when the situation is either very favorable or unfavorable to the leader, and that human-oriented leadership is most appropriate for intermediate situations. An example of a highly favorable situation would be a well-liked military officer commanding a group on a clearly defined mission. An example of a very unfavorable situation might be the disliked chairman of a voluntary civic committee that has a vague function. An intermediate situation would be the chairman of a group of professional personnel assigned the task of developing a planning procedure. In the latter situation the chairman might or might not be well-accepted by his peers, the task is somewhat vague, and it is likely that the chairman has rather limited authority.

Fiedler's theory has been researched by himself and others, and although the findings generally support the theory, many knotty questions remain.[12] The utility of the theory for practitioners is that it emphasizes the importance of analyzing a given situation to determine the appropriateness of leadership style required, and it suggests some of the situational variables to observe and assess. The theory is also useful in pushing forward our understanding of leadership.

[11]Fred E. Fiedler, *A Theory of Leadership Effectiveness* (New York: McGraw-Hill Book Co., 1967).

[12]Terence R. Mitchell et al., "The Contingency Model: Criticisms and Suggestions," *The Academy of Management Journal* (September, 1970), pp. 253–67.

Several other variables relating to supervisory style have been researched and discussed. It is not our purpose here to cover them completely; instead, we want only to point out that the style of supervision does appear to have considerable impact on both the productivity and satisfaction of employees. We have no formulas for prescribing successful supervisory behavior, but we can emphasize the impact supervisory style has on employee behavior and the importance one's assumptions about man have on his style of supervising. We must conclude that the style of leadership that contributes most to productivity and satisfaction is still a sufficiently open question to make it desirable for individuals to continue to look for their own answers, both in their own experience and in the observations of others.

STYLE FLEXIBILITY. One might also conclude from what has been said about effective leadership that a leader should vary his style with the followers and situation. Some such variation might be desirable at times but there is both a problem and a danger involved. The problem is that many leaders feel more comfortable with one style than another. For example, some people prefer to make decisions and give directions alone, while others feel much better if they consult with and invite the participation of their subordinates. This fact makes it difficult for many leaders to switch styles easily. The danger involved is that if people switch from styles that are natural and comfortable for them to those that are not, they may be less effective—at least in the short run—than if they remained more in their "typical," most natural pattern. No amount of prescription can aid leaders in making the lonely decision whether to switch or stick.

Leaders who know which style fits their own needs best can seek job roles and settings most suitable to it. They can increase their chances of both success and satisfaction by finding positions in which their leadership style is compatible with the needs and expectations of their followers in given situations. Those leaders who find themselves in positions in which this kind of compatibility does not exist are faced with the difficult decision whether they should try to change themselves, their followers, or the situation in which they find themselves. And if a man feels he needs to be able to choose among various leadership styles yet is currently comfortable and successful with only one style, he is faced with taking the risk of attempting growth, which may disrupt his present situation, or accepting the risk that his dependency upon one style may hurt him if phenomena outside him change.

## AUTHORITY AND POWER

Because the terms *authority* and *power* are central in understanding management and leadership, we will discuss them here in some detail.

*Formal authority* can be thought of as the *right* to command or compel another person to perform a certain act. *Power* is the *ability* to influence or to cause a person to perform an act. It is possible for a manager to have formal authority without power, just as it is possible for a subordinate to have power without formal authority. The distinction between these terms may be significant for the manager, who may assume that his formal authority automatically gives him power but overlook the fact that his subordinates also have power, at times greater than his own. The manager in such a situation can encounter difficult and frustrating experiences without knowing why.

An example may clarify the distinction between authority and power. Assume that a foreman orders one of his workers to lift a hundred-pound bag of cement and carry it twenty-five yards to a construction area. Assume that the supervisor is a small man weighing 125 pounds and that the worker is six-feet-three and weighs 250 pounds. The foreman has the formal authority (the right) to order the worker to lift and carry the cement, but what happens if the worker refuses to do it? Can the foreman *make* him do as he says? He can threaten him, tell him he will be disciplined, even fired. But if the worker refuses to carry the cement, there is little the supervisor can do besides trying to implement his threats. On the other hand, the worker may tell the supervisor to go stick his head in the water barrel. He has no authority to tell the supervisor to do this, but he may have the power to carry out his "suggestion."

In short, if formal authority were dependent upon physical power only, life would be even more difficult than it is. Ultimately, formal authority is dependent upon the law, but most frequently it results from a shared perception that those with formal authority have rights that *ought* to be acknowledged. This "ought" is so widely believed that those with formal authority may very frequently have real power as a result.

## Sources of Authority

FORMAL AUTHORITY. The source of formal authority is sometimes traced to society itself. Among the rights granted citizens by the Constitution that the people of the United States approved nearly two hundred years ago was the right to own property and to do with it as they wished within the law. One manifestation of property rights is the ownership of stock in corporations. The stockholders normally delegate authority to a board of directors to manage the corporation, and the board, in turn, delegates certain authority to the president and officers. Thus, authority is delegated down through the formal organizational channels. Different managers are given the right to command others in certain areas to achieve the formal organizational purposes.

ACCEPTANCE THEORY. A second way of looking at authority is to see its source as residing with the subordinate.[13] It is reasoned that unless the subordinate "accepts" the authority of the superior, there is no real authority. When subordinates obey the commands given them, they accept the formal authority of those giving orders, and thus, authority exists. However, if they refuse to obey, authority is not accepted and, thus, does not exist.

The usefulness of this theory is limited partially by the fact of life that those who have formal authority also usually have various sanctions that are a source of power in helping them enforce it. A manager usually has the right to discipline and fire or recommend the firing of his subordinates, who may, therefore, find it too expensive to reject the authority of their superior. But subordinates do in fact sometimes reject it, and so the acceptance of orders by subordinates is at least a part of the source of authority.

Most subordinates are willing to accept the authority of the superiors within certain limits that demarcate what has been called the *zone of acceptance.*[14] Even though they may not like what they are ordered to do, workers will follow directions—up to a certain point, which will vary from worker to worker and situation to situation. A subordinate may reject an order outside his zone of acceptance regardless of the sanctions imposed upon him. Most managers, intuitively aware of their workers' zones, avoid overstepping them.

Recall our distinction between a manager and a leader; it is relevant here. A subordinate may accept or reject either the authority of the *role* or the authority of the *man* in the role. A few students accept what any professor says simply because "Professors should know." Other students reject what a particular professor says in spite of his role; they discriminate between the man and the role in deciding whether to accept or reject the authority. The same thing is true in business organizations, and the challenge for the formal leader is to gain the acceptance of his subordinates *as a man* in a role, as well as their acceptance of the authority *of the role.*

Acceptance usually must be gained from more than just subordinates; it must be sought from peers as well. There are very few units of any size or consequence in most of our larger business organizations that are not dependent on the activities of other units. One of the tasks of the formal manager is to maintain working relations with these other units. If his peers do not accept him in his role, they can make the successful operation of his unit very difficult.

INFORMAL AUTHORITY. A third way of thinking about the source of au-

[13]For a thorough discussion of this concept, see Chester I. Barnard, *The Functions of the Executive* (Cambridge: Harvard University Press, 1960), Chapter 12; and Herbert A. Simon, *Administrative Behavior*, 2nd ed. (New York: The Macmillan Co., 1960).

[14]Simon, *Administrative Behavior*, p. 12.

thority is to see it as coming informally from the personal qualities, abilities, or charisma of the individual. An illustration of this is provided by the foreman who must repair a machine with which he is not very familiar. If one of his workers knows the machine well from his long experience in operating it, the foreman may defer to him and let him give instructions to the group repairing the machine. In this case, the worker's source of authority is his technical knowledge.

Suppose three chemists of equal rank are all trying to solve a technical problem. If one has more knowledge of the problem than the other two, they are likely to allow him to tell them how to proceed. Another common example is the exertion of authority in informal groups when no formal authority is a consideration.[15] The sources of informal authority are numerous and include such things as knowledge, ability, status, role, personality, age, seniority, sex, and skill. This way of thinking about authority is, of course, closely related to the acceptance theory. The sources of informal authority just mentioned are often the factors that cause people to accept the authority of others.

AUTHORITY OF THE SITUATION. Sometimes a situation dictates what people will do.[16] For example, assume that Jones and Smith arrive simultaneously to process a document at Swanson's desk. If Jones' document is clearly more urgent than Smith's, that fact of the situation is likely to determine who is served first. The urgency of Jones' document may even transcend what would, otherwise, be a determining factor, such as rank. Frequently, certain factors in a given situation determine who will do what in what order; i.e., the demands of the situation rule.

## Sources of Power

Power and authority often go hand in hand, even though at times they do not. The authority (right) to make certain decisions or to give certain orders often serves as a real source of power. Examples of power-laden decisions are those of hiring and firing, allocating funds, assigning duties, and administering rewards and punishments. People are often susceptible to influence and direction from those who have the right *and* power to make these decisions, which are a potential means of helping or hurting others.

Another source of power is information and communication. Those who have access to information and an ability to communicate effectively can often wield considerable influence in an organization. Think of the importance dictators attach to controlling the public information system.

[15]Tony Sarto, in The Slade Company case (pp. 508–520), provides an example.

[16]Mary Parker Follett, in Henry C. Metcalf and L. Urwick, eds., *Dynamic Administration: The Collected Papers of Mary Parker Follett* (New York: Harper & Brothers, Publishers, 1941), p. 58.

Another source of power is the ability to perform, to do what people in the organization (and outside it) expect and respect. People frequently admire excellent performance, and they will often allow themselves to be influenced by those whose performance they admire. Personality traits can also be an important source of personal power to influence others. An aggressive and dominant person may be followed willingly by more passive people simply in response to his personality. Charisma is a mysterious but very real source of power for some individuals.

## Use and Misuses of Authority

Most managers believe they must have authority to accomplish their jobs. They believe it is their superior's responsibility to see that they have adequate authority in the areas for which they are held responsible and accountable. But a manager who either misuses or overuses his authority to get his subordinates to carry out their tasks may be inviting trouble. This is why it is important for the manager to understand the various sources of authority and power and the differences among them.

Most people who have worked in the business world have seen a situation in which subordinates have "fired" their boss. By dragging their feet on assignments, by causing the organization to do a relatively poor job, and by directing criticisms to appropriate ears, a unified group of subordinates can cause such trouble that their boss's superiors may question his ability to handle his work group. Under these conditions the subordinates may sometimes be shown the door; but occasionally the boss is fired. That this can and does happen illustrates that managers are dependent, in part, on their work groups, just as their work groups are dependent, in part, on the managers. Although the manager has formal sanctions to back up his authority, the work group has informal sources of power it can utilize. The manager who relies only on his formal authority to direct the efforts of others may, therefore, not achieve the best results. It is desirable that he also be a leader; in short, he should be able to influence his subordinates as well as give them orders.

Managers, our illustration also suggests, are often "caught in the middle" between the values, orders, and expectations of their superiors and the values, needs, and expectations of their subordinates. The manager usually needs to retain the support of both his superior and his subordinates, and the dilemma he feels when there is conflict between the two can create intensely uncomfortable feelings. The pressure is compounded when the values and expectations of his peers are also involved, as they frequently are. Different managers resolve these internal dissonances in a variety of ways. Some ignore, or pay less attention to, either the subordinates or the superior, usually the former. Others try to find compromises that satisfy both, at least enough to avoid undue problems.

But however they handle them, most managers experience the discomfort of man-in-the-middle problems.

### The Functions of a Formal Leader

Effective leaders or managers in required systems take responsibility for adequate communications and help remove obstacles or omissions that stand in the way of performance. They see that goals are developed, clarified, communicated, and comprehended. Plans, policies, procedures, and methods are developed to help people collectively to achieve compatibly aligned group and organizational goals. Controls are established to insure that standards of performance are being met, and if not, that appropriate corrective action is taken. Relationships between people and their own groups as well as other groups are established, and actions are initiated to insure adequate coordination and cooperation of different individuals and groups. Fair, equitable, and appropriate incentives are established to motivate people to contribute to the achievement of group and organizational goals. All of these functions illustrate a leader's initiation of structure essential to effective group effort. Additionally, effective leaders usually demonstrate concern and consideration for individuals.

Frequently one of the more difficult functions of a formal leader is the integration of group or organizational goals with individual goals. Normally, the closer together these goals are, the more effective the performance will be. However, it is not unusual that differences exist, sometimes substantial ones. It is not always possible for a leader to reconcile and integrate the differences arising from personal systems, but he tries to do so when they continue to exist excessively. Alternative approaches often employed include persuasion, coercion, compromise, and changing the people or goals.

## MANAGEMENT BY OBJECTIVES

One increasingly used approach used by formal leaders to determine and integrate goals is a process called management by objectives (MBO).[17] It involves participation and sharing of important management functions. Generally, this approach involves the identification of goals for individuals, groups, and entire organizations. Subordinates and superiors jointly determine and agree upon the results they seek to achieve, along with the standards that will be used to measure those

[17]Peter F. Drucker, *The Practice of Management* (New York: Harper and Row, Inc., 1954); George S. Odiorne, *Management by Objectives* (New York: Pitman Publishing Corp., 1965); John W. Humble, *Management by Objectives in Action* (London: McGraw-Hill Publishing Co., Ltd., 1970).

results. Periodic reviews are made jointly by superiors and subordinates to evaluate progress and results against the previously set objectives. This process encourages several important steps, including the clear establishment and agreement of results sought, "ownership," acceptance of goals, and a basis for measurement of performance and contribution. A successful MBO process incorporates the development of plans necessary to achieve goals and appropriate adaptation of organizational structure to foster success, including necessary personnel, facilities, equipment, and other resources. Successful implementation of MBO can help achieve commitment and focus attention on essential functions of the managerial process.

Figure 1 illustrates some of the steps in the management by objectives process.

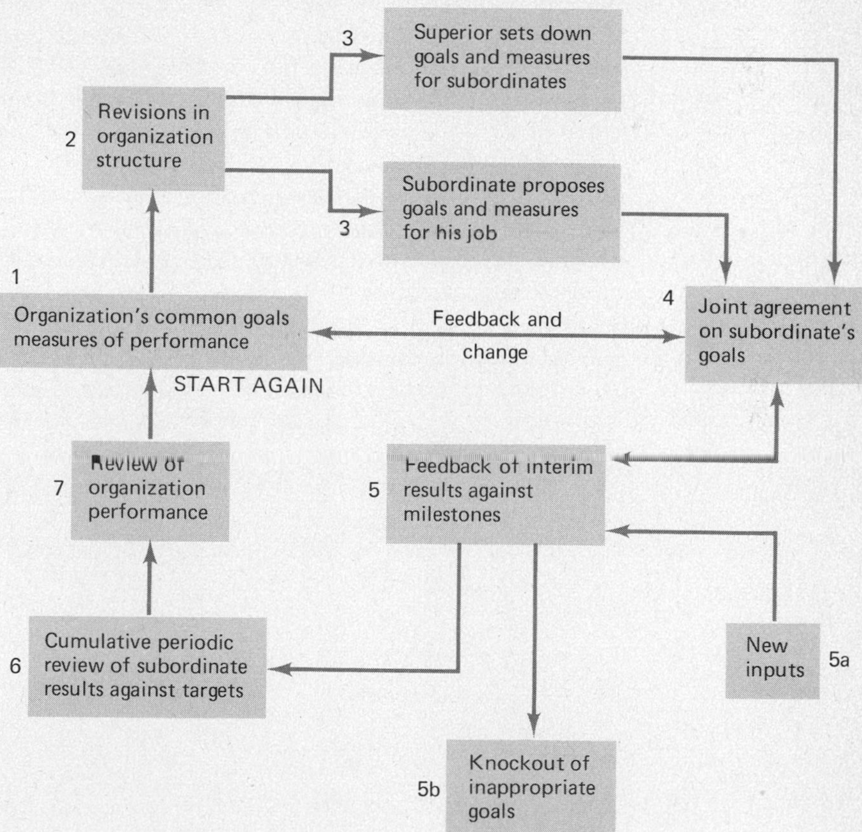


**Figure 1** The MBO Process[18]

[18]Taken from Paul Hersey and Kenneth H. Blanchard, *Management of Organizational Behavior*, 2nd ed. (Englewood Cliffs, N.J.: Prentice-Hall, Inc., 1972), p. 106. Used with permission.

Management by objectives is not a panacea. Many companies have implemented MBO programs with varying results. Some have been favorable, but some have not.[19] The latter have encountered problems such as excessive paperwork, inadequate participation and commitment, distortion of reported results, and overemphasis on production elements measured. Top management support appears to be an essential ingredient in the successful programs. Overall, MBO appears to be a useful approach that will be practiced for many years to come. An important effect of MBO is emphasis on sound management.

## SUMMARY

A leader, whether formal or informal, is one who influences his followers to achieve an objective in a given situation. He may or may not have formal authority (the right to command), but he normally has some source of power (the ability to influence) that enables him to lead. One style of leadership (authoritarian, democratic, laissez faire) is not better than another, per se; which is better depends on the nature of the leader, his followers, and their setting. What patterns can you see about your own leadership? What similarities are there in the persons you have led and in the situations you have been in while leading? What are your own sources of power in your present life? What style of leadership do you find most comfortable yourself? What style of leadership do you like in your superiors? Your answers to these questions are most likely to have significant meanings for your own life, and for your work in organizations, whether as manager or member. Finally, an increasingly used approach to leadership called M.B.O. was shown to be a method of identifying, clarifying, and integrating individual and organizational goals. This can be an effective way to influence behavior in organizations toward positive consequences.

[19]See Anthony P. Raia, "Goal Setting and Self Control," *Journal of Management Studies* (February, 1965), pp. 34–53.

# CHAPTER 9

# Assumptions about Man, Leadership, and Motivation

One important determinant of a leader's behavior toward his followers is the assumptions he makes about man, and particularly how he assumes man to be motivated. In this chapter we will explore some of the kinds of assumptions leaders make about man and about motivation.

Many factors influence a manager's or a leader's style of behavior. Two important ones—the nature of his subordinates and the setting—are mentioned in Chapter 8. Another is the nature and condition of the leader himself. His attitudes, values, psychological defenses, knowledge, and skills, all of which have been developing since birth, influence his feelings, assumptions, perceptions, and behavior. Although exploring the nature of man in depth is beyond the scope of this book, it should be pointed out as a centrally relevant factor in understanding the behavior of individuals.

Two other important influencing factors are the leadership style of the leader's superiors and the values of the organization. It is as difficult for a leader with a democratic style to survive well under an authoritarian superior as it is for one with an authoritarian style to survive under a democratic superior. It is equally difficult for a leader to survive well if his style is incongruent with the values of the larger organization. Those leaders tend to be promoted who best reflect the values of their superiors or the organization and whose leadership style is congruent with those values. Thus, organizational values and related leadership styles tend to be self-perpetuating and mutually reinforcing and to constitute pressure for conformity on the individual.

## Assumptions about Man

All of us, though we may not be aware of it explicitly, have developed theories about man, from observing the kinds of responses we get from people in various situations and from a complex variety of learning and folklore. This section will explore some of the kinds of assumptions sometimes made about man and show the effect that they can have on leadership style.

Keep in mind during the following discussion that frequently we will be talking about *generic* man, not any individual man. The difference is important. Also keep in mind that we will use two dichotomous sets of assumptions in order to emphasize the differences between these sets. The conceptual utility of such emphasis is at the expense of the sliding scale of reality.

One set of assumptions about man fits strikingly with the *rational, economic concept of man* fostered by writers like Adam Smith and Frederick Taylor. This set of assumptions would include the following:

1. Most men by nature resist work and are inherently lazy. Therefore, they must be motivated by external incentives.
2. The objectives of most men are in conflict with the objectives of the organization, and men must therefore be directed, motivated, coerced, and controlled in order to insure their conformity to the organizational needs.
3. Most men are motivated mainly by economic incentives. Because the economic resources of a firm are under the control of the managers, the managers have a powerful tool for motivating and controlling the employees, who must passively accept their fate if they expect to achieve economic rewards.
4. Most men seek security and want to avoid responsibility; therefore they are willing to accept the direction of managers.
5. Behavior based on feelings is irrational, and because many men behave according to their feelings, they cannot be trusted to direct their own behavior. However, some men are able to check their feelings and behave rationally. Because the organization must insure that feelings do not interfere with rational and economic decision making, these latter men must direct and control the majority, whose behavior is based on their feelings as well as their minds.[1]

[1]This set of assumptions and the one following are similar to those set forth by Douglas McGregor and classified under the terms "Theory X" and "Theory Y" in his

Do you agree with these assumptions? Although many readers will feel reluctant about accepting them as they are bluntly stated above, more than a few may believe they are close to being accurate.

If you accept them, the implications for the kind of leadership or management required in an organization are clear. For example, if it is assumed that people are by nature lazy, passive, uncooperative, resistant to change, irresponsible, uncreative, dull, and motivated only by money, it follows that managers should make all decisions about what employees will do, tell them how and when to do it, oversee them, and establish controls to insure that they do it as directed. In addition, the managers must motivate their subordinates to work by either rewarding or punishing them. In sum, the manager who makes these assumptions is likely to follow a highly authoritarian approach.

Unfortunately, he is likely to have problems. Most workers will find this kind of management unpalatable, and some will actively seek to resist and even sabotage it. Others will become passive and unproductive. Only a few will voluntarily and enthusiastically support their boss and the organization's objectives. But, as noted above, this is exactly what the assumptions anticipated, and thus they are self-fulfilling.

A second path open to managers accepting the kinds of assumptions mentioned is what has been termed "the soft approach." Following this approach, a manager may be permissive, try to satisfy his workers' demands, and work for harmony, expecting that if he can make the workers happy, they will be more productive. However, many managers fear that such an approach only enables workers to take advantage of the organization and to be unproductive as well as happy.

Although most of us know people who tend to substantiate many of the assumptions made above, there is some doubt whether the assumptions are true because of the *nature* of man or because of the way organizations have been designed and the subsequent impact such designs have upon men. For example, if work is designed so that it is unchallengingly simple and if controls are established so that no creativity is allowed, it is not surprising that many men find their work dull and, in turn, become dull themselves.[2]

Those doubting the rational, economic concept of man have developed quite a different set of assumptions, leading to a *social, self-actualizing concept of man*. Some of the assumptions of this view are:

1. Most men enjoy some kinds of work and will sometimes voluntarily exert mental and physical energy in performing the tasks.

---

*The Human Side of Enterprise* (New York: McGraw-Hill Book Co., 1960). See also Edgar H. Schein, *Organizational Psychology* (Englewood Cliffs, N.J.: Prentice-Hall, Inc., 1965), Chapter 5.

[2]For an elaboration of this thesis, see Chris Argyris, *Personality and Organization* (New York: Harper & Row, Publishers, 1957) and *Integrating the Individual and the Organization* (New York: John Wiley & Sons, Inc., 1964).

2. Most men have other reasons than money for working, and these reasons are at least as important to them as is money.

3. Most men are capable of directing and controlling their own work in achieving organizational objectives to which they are committed.

4. Most men are willing to accept and even will seek responsibility under certain conditions.

5. Most men are capable of demonstrating more of both creativity and intellectual ability than they do in many organizational settings.

6. Most men want, seek, and enjoy friendly, supportive relations with other people.[3]

It is clear that the two sets of assumptions have quite different implications for leadership. If it is assumed that man has the potential for development, the capacity for assuming responsibility, and the readiness to direct his own behavior toward organizational goals, it follows that the task of managers is to create opportunities for him to do so. The manager thus becomes a facilitator, supporter, and sympathizer rather than only a director and controller. Rather than establishing all organizational conditions and directing all work, the manager would arrange conditions only to the extent that they enable people to direct their own efforts in achieving organizational objectives.

One of the major differences between the two approaches is that those managers accepting the rational, economic concept of man place heavy or exclusive reliance upon *external control* of human behavior, whereas those accepting the social, self-actualizing view rely heavily on *self-control* and *self-direction*. Managers accepting the latter view are likely to have a democratic style, with an occasional touch of laissez faire, assuming that some of the other factors mentioned are neutral.

## Hierarchy of Human Needs

One assumption about man that fits the social, self-actualizing view of him is that he has a hierarchy of needs. This concept, developed by A. H. Maslow, is helpful in explaining both the variety and complexity of human motives.[4] It helps explain why one man may behave differently from another in a similar situation, and at the same time suggests some-

[3]These assumptions underly McGregor's "Theory Y."

[4]Abraham H. Maslow, *Motivation and Personality* (New York: Harper & Brothers, 1954). You will recall that Chapter 6 presented a view of man based upon his "internal frame of reference." This view, which states that a specific individual behaves so as to protect, maintain, and enhance his self-concept, is most useful for thinking about the people you associate with, listen to, and learn about. But for man in general, or for specific persons about whom you know little, it is useful to think in terms of a need-hierarchy view of behavior. You can use both views as you come to sense some of the specific needs of specific people and how these needs relate to their own unique self-concepts.

thing that all men have in common. Maslow assumes that all men have basic human needs, which he classifies as follows:

1. *Physiological Needs.* Food, shelter, rest, exercise, and protection from the elements.
2. *Safety Needs.* Protection against nature and against the threat of physical or psychological danger or deprivation.
3. *Love Needs.* Association, affection, and acceptance.
4. *Esteem Needs.* (a) One's own need for achievement, confidence, independence, freedom, and a feeling of adequacy; (b) one's need for recognition and appreciation from *others.*
5. *Self-Actualization Needs.* To fulfill one's full potentialities, to become what one is capable of being.

Maslow assumes that these needs exist in the form of a hierarchy, that some of them are more basic than others, and that man seeks to satisfy the more basic ones before directing his behavior toward satisfying the others. Thus, Maslow assumes that most men seek first to satisfy their physiological needs, then their safety needs, then their love needs, next their esteem needs, and finally their self-actualization needs. It is assumed that lower-order needs must be satisfied at least to a degree for man even to survive. Although it appears that a majority of people seek to satisfy their needs in an order that approximates Maslow's hierarchy, there are clearly some variations and exceptions.

An important point in the hierarchy of needs theory is that a satisfied need ceases to motivate. This means that as man's physical needs are satisfied, his other needs begin to create tensions that cause him to seek to satisfy them. The physiological needs continue to exist, but they become less important in motivating behavior. So long as a man has enough to eat, he will devote his time and energy to behavior aimed at satisfying some other need. But should he become really hungry, he will begin to spend his time trying to obtain food—a basic physiological need.

The concept that a satisfied need ceases to motivate has limitations. It clearly applies to certain physical and safety needs, but it seems clear that the needs for love, esteem, and self-actualization are close to insatiable and, therefore, continue to motivate behavior even after they have been in some degree satisfied. Most of the people in the United States have, to a quite large extent, satisfied their physiological and safety needs. If these needs, once satisfied, cease to motivate behavior, it becomes clear that the primarily economic incentives offered by most business organizations, which are designed to help people satisfy just these needs, do not appeal to the real or potential motivators of behavior—the needs for love, esteem, and self-actualization. Indeed, until the last two or three decades, little attention was devoted to helping people satisfy their higher-order needs.

The hierarchy of needs concept helps us to gain some insight into why man is complex, variable, and dynamic. He is complex because he has a variety of needs, and at any given time several of them may be motivating him all at once, even though one or a few may appear to dominate.

## HUMAN NEEDS AND MOTIVATION

Man is variable. Each person has his own set of needs, and there is no conclusive evidence that men feel their needs in the neat order suggested above. Quite the contrary, as Maslow himself points out. The variety with which each man feels his own needs is a major contributing factor to the uniqueness of man. It helps explain, in part, why it is dangerous to assume that all men will respond the same way to given stimuli.

Man is also dynamic. The hierarchy of importance of his personal needs changes with time, partly because certain needs cease to motivate as they are satisfied. Take a man whose behavior is not much directed to achieving his work goals because he feels an overwhelming need for achieving love and affection. Let him fall in love, and you may find that he works a lot harder than he did before. The needs hierarchy is dynamic, and it is dangerous to assume that a person's behavior can't change.

### Motivational Process[5]

Needs alone do not adequately explain behavior. In this section we will develop a more complete model of the motivational process, which can serve as a tool for analyzing specific situations. The model includes several variables that influence the behavior of specific individuals. Each variable needs to be assigned meaning when applied situationally.

INCENTIVES. We start building our model with the assumption that each individual surveys his world to find opportunities to satisfy his various needs. We will use the term *incentive* to mean much the same as opportunities, goals, and rewards. Thus, individuals direct their behavior toward reaching perceived incentives. These may be either positive and attracting incentives or negative ones to be avoided.

We make a further assumption that individuals are sometimes un-

[5]This section draws on the work of Lyman W. Porter and Edward E. Lawler, III, *Managerial Attitudes and Performance* (Homewood, Ill.: Richard D. Irwin, Inc., 1968); Victor H. Vroom, *Work and Motivation* (New York: John Wiley & Sons, Inc., 1964); J. G. Hunt and J. W. Hill, "The New Look in Motivation Theory of Organizational Research," *Human Organization* (Summer, 1969), pp. 100–109.

conscious of both some of their needs and some of the reasons for their behavior. Much remains unknown about men's unconscious needs, feelings, thoughts, and behavior, and although psychologists debate the relative importance of the unconscious, virtually none dispute its existence. Thus, it is essential that we remember that needs can only be inferred from behavior; they cannot be seen.

Incentives alone do not always stimulate behavior. Before an individual exerts the effort to reach an incentive, he makes, either consciously or unconsciously at least three evaluations. First, he evaluates how important the incentive is to him in terms of his own need priorities. Although one incentive may be important to one person, it may not be to another. Second, he estimates the probability of reaching the incentive. If he perceives the probability of achieving it as low, he may not be motivated to exert the effort toward reaching even a valued incentive. Third, he evaluates the cost in terms of effort and lost opportunity to satisfy other needs. An individual may perceive an incentive as desirable and obtainable, but if the perceived cost in effort is too great, he is unlikely to move toward it.

Incentives, or goals, as we have discussed in Chapter 7, can be categorized as *manifest* and *latent*, as well as extrinsic and intrinsic. To review, manifest goals are the apparent ones sought, and usually are organizational goals. They are instrumental in reaching latent goals, which are directly satisfying to personal needs. Thus, the rewards for achieving manifest goals have extrinsic value, and those for the achievement of latent goals have intrinsic value. For example, Joe may work hard to finish an assigned task early, even though he does not find the work interesting, challenging, or satisfying. What he really hopes to achieve is a promotion, which in turn would be instrumental in partially satisfying his need for status. Working hard is behavior-directed toward finishing the task early (first manifest goal), which in turn he hopes will lead to a promotion (second manifest goal), which in turn will satisfy some of his status needs (latent goal). If Joe does not perceive a relationship between hard work and a promotion, he is unlikely to be motivated to finish the task early. Further, if he lacked high status needs, the promise of a promotion would hold little attraction.

EFFECT AND PERFORMANCE. If an individual decides that a perceived incentive is important, achievable, and "profitable," he is likely to exert effort toward reaching it. Effort combined with ability leads to performance, or accomplishment; thus, even if an individual exerts effort, he may not perform adequately if he lacks either innate or learned ability. The relationship between performance and effort is mutually dependent. Poor performance may induce more effort for awhile, depending on the perceived value and achievability of the incentive, but continued poor performance often leads to reduced or withdrawn effort. On the other hand, high performance easily achieved might reduce effort. You can see, therefore, that effort depends on performance, just as performance depends on effort.

SATISFACTION. The motivational process continues during and after performance as the individual evaluates the rewards he does or does not receive. Satisfaction is a function of his expectations and how fully he actually achieves the rewards he has sought. The following formula describes the relationship:

$$\text{Satisfaction} = \frac{\text{Realization}}{\text{Expectations}} + \text{Equity}$$

If "one" represents a normal, or expected, degree of satisfaction, an individual will realize greater than normal satisfaction if he realizes more reward than he expected, and vice versa. How "just" or equitable an individual perceives his reward in relation to other "reference" people will also affect his satisfaction.

We might assume that an individual with satisfied needs will continue to exert effort to perform. This assumption might often be correct, but not always. Recall that needs are dynamic, and that satisfied needs cease to motivate. Thus, some individuals may achieve more than expected satisfaction, and, as a result, will diminish their effort to perform in the direction of the satisfying incentive. For some individuals, lack of satisfaction may increase the need to exert even more effort to perform. At this point the individual is beginning the motivation cycle at the starting point where he surveys and evaluates the opportunities to satisfy his needs.

MODEL OF THE MOTIVATIONAL PROCESS. The model illustrated in Figure 1 does not enable us to predict the behavior of any individual. However, it does provide a description of some of the important determinants to consider in understanding what might engage the motives of a specific individual. In making such an analysis try to answer these questions:

1. What are the latent goals an individual seeks? (What important needs is he trying to satisfy?)
2. What is the relationship between manifest goals and his latent goals as you perceive it and as he perceives it? (How he perceives it determines his behavior.)
3. What expectations does the individual have for reaching his latent goals by reaching the manifest goals?
4. How does the individual evaluate the potential profitability (reward less cost in effort or lost opportunity) of the incentive?
5. How effectively does the individual perform, and what relationship does this have to ability, effort, and satisfaction?

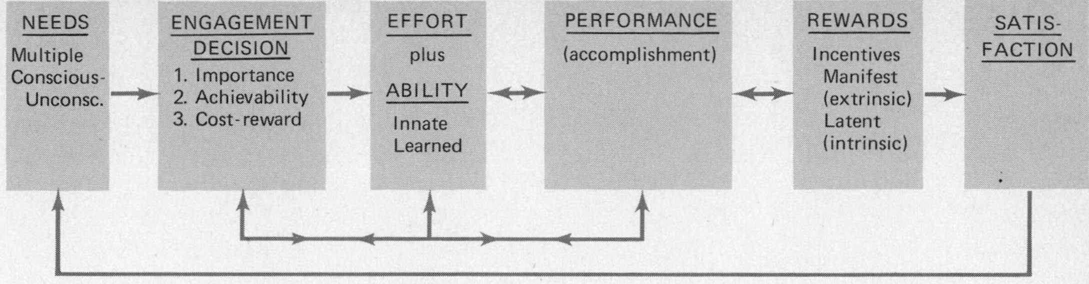


**Figure 1** Motivational Process

The model and its underlying assumptions suggests that no layman, and probably no professional, is ever fully equipped to understand another person. Most of us are not qualified as psychoanalysts, and to fully understand behavior requires an understanding of the unconscious and goal conflicts. But this does not mean we can do nothing. We can learn more about listening, empathizing, and understanding another. We can learn to be more aware of and sensitive to ourselves and others by observing how each sees himself and his world. Such observation includes listening and looking for behavior patterns, including what people discuss, how they use their time, and what they appear to seek and avoid. An individual's talk and behavior give many cues about what he values, fears, and seeks.

## Herzberg's Two-Factor Theory

Frederick Herzberg has developed a theory that has become popular with many managers. His two-factor theory is called the *hygiene-motivation theory*. He developed it first by researching a sample of accountants and engineers, but later extended his studies to various kinds and levels of people in organizations. He gave them these directions:[6]

> Think of a time when you felt exceptionally good or exceptionally bad about your job, either your present job or any other job you have had. This can be either the 'long-range' or the 'short-range' kind of situation, as I have just described it. Tell me what happened.

Herzberg divided the responses according to whether they represented good or bad feelings. He called the satisfiers "motivators" and the dissatisfiers "hygiene factors." He found that many of the motivators related to job content and job experiences, and that many of the dissatisfiers

[6]Frederick Herzberg, Bernard Mausner, and Barbara Block Snyderman, *The Motivation To Work*, 2nd ed. (New York: John Wiley & Sons, Inc., 1959), p. 141.

related to environmental conditions. Figure 2 shows some of the important factors in each category.

The concept of "dissatisfier" surprised some who thought of the items in that category as positive incentives for work. Herzberg reasoned that many people today consider less time, more money, and more security as "rights." If they are not in line with expectations, they cause dissatisfaction, but if they are in line, they are often taken for granted. In this respect they prevent dissatisfaction but do not induce positive motivation.

| Dissatisfiers | Motivators |
|---|---|
| (Job environment) | (Job content) |
| Work rules | Challenging job |
| Lighting | Feeling of achievement |
| Coffee breaks | Responsibility |
| Titles | Growth |
| Seniority rights | Advancement |
| Wages | Enjoyment of work |
| Fringe benefits | Earned recognition |

**Figure 2**

The logical application of Herzberg's findings and theory was *job enrichment*. Some possibilities for enriching a job include removing some of the controls while retaining accountability, increasing the accountability of individuals for their own work, providing a complete natural unit of work for the individual, introducing new and more difficult tasks not previously assigned, and providing opportunities for individuals to develop expertise. These steps all are intended to provide opportunities for satisfying what Maslow called the higher-level needs.

Many applications have been made of Herzberg's theory, and many successes have been reported. However, some failures have also been recorded, and considerable criticism has been directed at the theory, much of it relating to methodology. The hygiene-motivation theory is relatively simple, which explains partially both its appeal and its weakness. Even though the theory is not without fault, it has had significant impact on management behavior and has helped advance our understanding of motivation and work.

## Behavior Modification

Another applied approach to motivation is termed *behavior modification*. It is built on Edward L. Thorndike's "law of effect" and B. F.

Skinner's "operant conditioning." The law of effect states that if behavior is reinforced it will tend to be repeated. Skinner is the best-known contemporary proponent of operant conditioning, which calls for positive reinforcement of desired behavior. Unlike those who take a more psychoanalytic approach, Skinner's followers do not concern themselves with subconscious or deep causes of behavior. Instead, they analyze the work environment to determine what causes an individual to behave as he does. They then use reinforcing techniques such as praise, recognition, and rewards along with systematic feedback that tells an individual how he is doing.

The kind of reinforcement and its timing are important aspects of behavior modification. Reinforcement can be positive or negative. Positive reinforcement strengthens the association between a response and its reward. A negative reinforcement can take the form of either withholding a positive reward or administering a "painful" punishment. Generally, research indicates that positive reinforcement is more effective than negative in achieving lasting change, although negative reinforcement may be effective in causing short-term termination of an undesirable behavior.

The closer positive reinforcement follows the desired behavior, the more likely it will be repeated. This can cause some problems in an organizational setting. For example, money has the potential for being an extrinsic reinforcer, but money is usually paid at regular intervals, which may occur too long after the behavior being reinforced. For this reason reinforcers such as praise and recognition are easier to administer.

Some reinforcers are intrinsic in nature. This means that the desired behavior produces directly related need satisfactions. For example, many people feel a keen sense of satisfaction when they complete a difficult task. This feeling can serve as reinforcement to tackle another task in order to get the same good feeling. On the other hand, extrinsic reinforcers, such as money, praise, and attention, are not a natural result of most desired behaviors, but they are satisfying to individuals and are effective reinforcers if associated with the desired behavior.

Although behavior modification has been practiced with good results in schools and mental institutions, it has not been given much attention in business until the past few years. Now, increasing numbers of companies are beginning to investigate this approach and to apply some of its techniques.[7] Although it is useful to know about behavior modification and to apply it when appropriate, it clearly is only a part of the total process of motivation. As with all management techniques, it is not a panacea.

## Money as a Motivator

Money is a major incentive in our society. It has appeal as an incentive for managers because it is concrete and easily manipulable. How-

[7] "Where Skinner's Theories Work," *Business Week*, December 2, 1972, pp. 64–65.

ever, money is also a complex incentive, and for this reason is subject to being misused.

Money used to be considered the only important incentive, under the assumption that people worked primarily for economic reasons. Researchers like Elton Mayo and Fritz Roethlisberger demonstrated in the famous Hawthorne studies that money is by no means the only incentive, and in some respects may not be most important.[8] They demonstrated the importance of recognition and affiliation as motivating incentives. Research studies subsequently showed that workers frequently mentioned money in about the middle of various incentives. Some people have subsequently concluded that money is not very important as an incentive. They are probably quite wrong.

Money is a multifaceted incentive, having both economic and psychological meaning. It is symbolic and instrumental in nature. In addition to providing for physical and safety needs, it may also help to satisfy the needs for power, status, esteem, and achievement. It can even be instrumental in partially satisfying social needs. Having sufficient money may enable someone to join a particular club or group. For achievement-oriented people it serves as a measurement of accomplishment.

Evidence indicates that money, in itself, does not usually serve as a motivator to work harder or better. However, in the absence of what is perceived by the recipient as adequate or fair compensation, money is a source of dissatisfaction. How a recipient compares in compensation with those he perceives as equals may be more important than the amount he receives. Money, then, is frequently related to levels of satisfaction, even though additional amounts normally do not lead to harder work.

Appropriate uses of money and other incentives as part of a motivational plan should be related to the needs of the workers, the motivational requirements of the job, the motives of the managers, and the organizational climate.[9] For example, whether or not a worker has high needs for achievement, power, or affiliation will likely make a difference in how he responds to incentives. Similarly, jobs vary in their motivational requirements. Assembly-line jobs are hardly appropriate for people with high achievement needs, just as demanding jobs are not suitable for those with low achievement needs.

Assume you are in charge of a group of people who have high affiliation needs and enjoy being members of a group. If you assume that money motivates, and instigate a money incentive system that is meant to induce workers to produce more and socialize less, you may be introducing a dysfunctional element into the system. You might more appropriately try to develop a group incentive that would foster feelings of helping the group, thus increasing its cohesiveness.

[8]F. J. Roethlisberger and W. J. Dickson, *Management and the Worker* (Cambridge, Mass.: Harvard University Press, 1939).

[9]David C. McClelland, "Money as a Motivator: Some Research Insights," *The McKinsey Quarterly* (Fall, 1967), pp. 10–21.

A comprehensive discussion of money as an incentive is beyond our scope here. However, we want to emphasize the importance of careful situational analysis of a total system when attempting to design an incentive system.

## SUMMARY

Concepts of generic man can help sharpen and deepen our understanding. But because concepts are abstractions of reality, there is some danger that they oversimplify the complex realities that truly characterize an individual man. The more we tend to accept one concept as explaining all there is to know about all men, the greater the danger is likely to be. Both the rational, economic view of man and the social, self-actualizing view tend to highlight certain aspects of man's nature. The fact that research evidence and personal experience exists to support, at least partially, both of these views, as well as some others, only emphasizes that man is indeed a richly complex and fascinating (and sometimes frustrating) being.

The degree of satisfaction a man feels or the productivity he achieves depends on more than just the nature of his needs or his motivation. A man who is highly motivated to achieve a certain objective may lack the necessary skill, and thus experience feelings of dissatisfaction. Further, the very nature of the task may tend to stultify rather than satisfy his high motivation. Or he might find that he dislikes intensely the people with whom he is working, and even though highly motivated and able to do the work, may be both dissatisfied and ineffective. Thus we see that man's satisfaction, growth, and productivity are dependent upon a variety of psychological, social, and task factors—including both his ability and his social relationships.

Man is a highly complex, variable, and dynamic being. To understand him we do not need simple explanations or prescriptive formulas, but rather skills in sensitive observation, accurate diagnosis, and perceptive synthesis. These skills are neither easily nor cheaply achieved but must be acquired through practice.

CHAPTER 10

# Intergroup Relationships

Most large organizations are comprised of many small groups distinguishable from one another by their particular memberships, goal sets, tasks, space, and numerous other background characteristics. A major organizational problem is how group-member behaviors and outputs can be coordinated and integrated dynamically through time. An appreciation of how well this problem is being handled in an organization will be assisted by shifting our conceptual focus to some relatively enduring but sometimes abstract *relationships* between groups: connectedness, functionality, and climate.

[1]An excellent source of approaches to and research findings on intergroup behavior is in J. M. Thomas and W. G. Bennis, *Management of Change and Conflict* Middlesex, England: Penguin Books Ltd., 1972). See also Muzafer Sherif, ed., *Intergroup Relations and Leadership* (New York: John Wiley & Sons, Inc., 1962). See also Robert R. Blake, Herbert A. Shepard, and Jane S. Mouton, *Managing Intergroup Conflict in Industry* (Houston: Gulf Publishing Co., 1964); Harold J. Leavitt, *Managerial Psychology*, rev. ed. (Chicago: University of Chicago Press, 1964); and Edgar H. Schein, *Organizational Psychology* (Englewood Cliffs, N.J.: Prentice-Hall, Inc., 1965). See Amitai Etzioni, *A Comparative Analysis of Complex Organizations* (New York: The Free Press of Glencoe, 1961) for a comprehensive typology of organizations having considerably different intergroup implications.

## INTERGROUP CONNECTEDNESS

When diagnosing intergroup relations it is useful to determine the degree and type of connectedness between groups. Some are connected closely, some loosely, and some hardly at all. Some groups are relatively independent of one another, while others have some kind of dependent relationship. For example, three groups (call them A, B, C) may constitute an assembly line. A does its part and moves the product to B, which performs its function and moves it to C. This constitutes a sequential dependent relationship. However, the dependency varies. For example, A is dependent on B and C, B is dependent on A but independent of C, and C is dependent on both A and B.

Sometimes a relationship is mutually dependent, as for example the relationship between production and purchasing. The latter is dependent on production for direction, and production is dependent on purchasing for its supplies. These are only samples of the kinds of dependent relationships that can exist between groups. The important point is to look for the kinds of connections that exist.

In determining the type of connecting relationship, it is useful to note how the groups interact. The interactions are formal or informal and direct or indirect. Table 1 shows a classification scheme adapted from Paul E. Mott that helps to focus on some relevant variables.[2]

## FUNCTIONALITY AND DYSFUNCTIONALITY

The relationships between some groups are collaborative and harmonious, while between others they are competitive and conflicting. The important question, though, is whether the relationships are functional or dysfunctional for the organization, groups, and individuals concerned.

The question of functionality is critical in evaluating the behavioral consequences of intergroup relationships.[3] Behavior and results that are functional for one group may not be for another, and what is functional for one or more groups may not be for the total organization. For example, members of two groups may each want a particular machine, say a duplicator, and rather than share one decide that each should have its own. This decision avoids directly confronting conflicts that might

[2]Paul E. Mott, *The Characteristics of Effective Organizations* (Evanston, Ill.: Harper and Row, Publishers, 1972).

[3]See M. Deutsch, "Productive and Destructive Conflict," *Journal of Social Issues,* XXV, No. 1 (January, 1969), and L. Coser, *The Functions of Social Conflict* (Glencoe, Ill.: The Free Press, 1956).

**Table 1 Relevant Variables of Intergroup Connectedness**

| | *Degrees and Types of Connectedness* | | |
|---|---|---|---|
| | *Directly Connected* | *Indirectly Connected* | *Not Connected* |
| *Organized Relationships* | Formal interrelatedness, guided by informal norms | Informal use of third parties or a special exchange vehicle | Groups formally segmented by mutual agreement |
| *Unorganized Relationships* | Informal interrelatedness, guided by informal norms | Informal use of third parties or a special exchange vehicle (e.g. sociotechnical) | Circumstantial or coincidental lack of connectedness |

arise over where a single duplicator would be housed, how it would be charged, and who would maintain it. Although the decision to each have a single machine may be functional for each of the groups, it may *not* be for the total organization in terms of cost and efficiency. Such a decision would be an example of *suboptimization*, which means that what is good or optimal for a subunit of an organization is less than optimal for the larger organization.

Within the larger organization, there are often a number of subgroups that "ought" to collaborate to achieve the goals of the larger organization, yet they tend to compete—even fight—among themselves for resources, status, power, freedom, and rewards. Group-member behaviors like individuals', attempt to *protect, maintain, and enhance* their groups. They resist those other groups and factors which they perceive as threats to what they value and possess, and they seek those groups and factors which they see as enhancing their own situations.

## IMPACT OF ORGANIZATIONAL CLIMATE

The climate of the organization as a whole usually has significant impact both on the kinds of relationships that develop between groups and on how conflicts between them are resolved. Some organizations encourage competition and allow conflict-inducing elements to exist, others are quite the opposite and encourage collaboration and try to eliminate elements that stimulate conflict. For this reason it is useful to sense the overall organizational climate when diagnosing and assessing the relationships between specific groups.

Organizational climate often imposes a richly elaborated and detailed set of constraints upon behaviors by members of the groups within. These constraints are embodied concretely in the shared ideas implanted by present and past influential organization members. These ideas, though most often not explicitly stated, have potency. Here are some examples:

1. Ideas about what is appropriate and inappropriate behavior;
2. Ideas about how suborganizational units' members should behave and relate to one another;
3. Ideas about what are acceptable and unacceptable issues that may lead to constructive or destructive intergroup competitiveness;
4. Ideas about the range, quality, and degrees of acceptable competition between organizational units;
5. Ideas about how intergroup issues should be considered and resolved.

### Intergroup Climate

Similarly, the *intergroup* climate is an immediately relevant subenvironment embedded within the *organizational* climate and within which intergroup-related behaviors occur. Figure 1 portrays schematically the relationships between these entities and climates.

### Trust between Groups

Of particular importance in an organization's climate is the general degree of trust between groups. Low trust probably correlates with high levels of group goal suboptimization. Units successfully pursuing their own objectives end up producing dysfunctional behavioral consequences for other groups and the larger organization. Furthermore, low trust accelerates the likelihood of dsyfunctionally high intergroup conflict. In fact, a deterioration of mutual trust is thought to be a central trigger for a potential downward spiral into destructive intergroup conflict.

## ASSESSING INTERGROUP RELATIONSHIPS

Identifying the characteristics of intergroup relationships, especially negative ones, is usually easy. One symptom is lack of coordination or

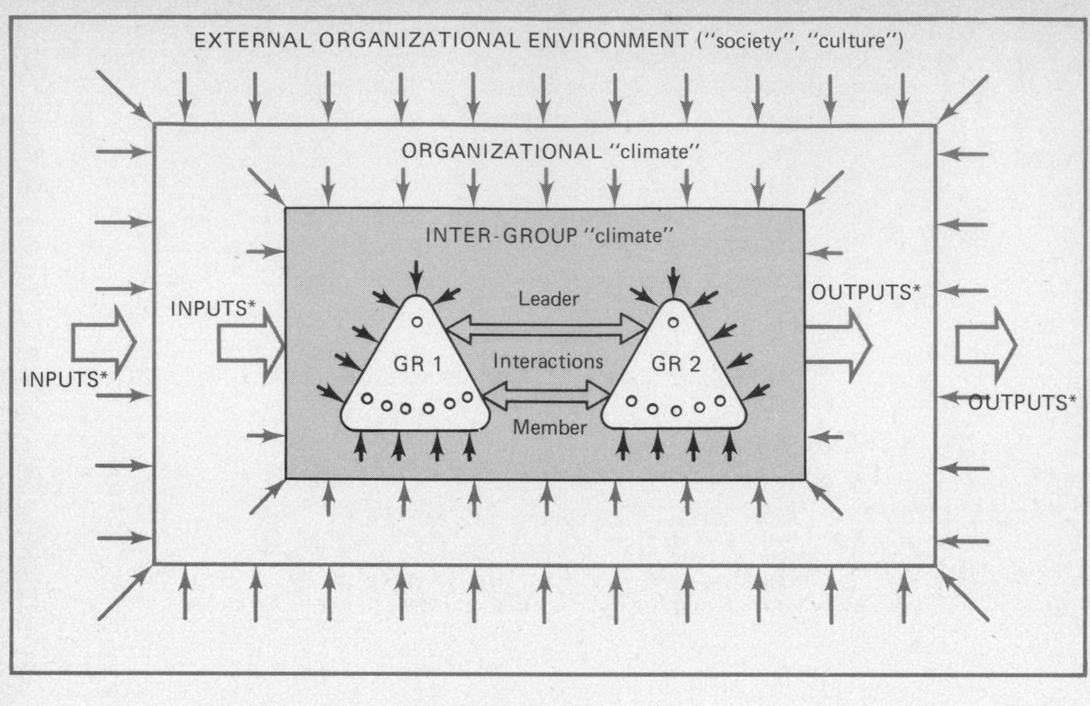


**Figure 1** Intergroup Behavior and Climate

breakdown in work-flows. Frequently concurrent with such breakdowns is another symptom—poor communications. (Groups that fail to exchange information adequately, whether in terms of content or timing, may relate poorly to each other; in any event, they are inefficient.) Delays and mistakes in interchanging work and communications essential to the operation of each group can be a cause as well as a symptom of poor relations. These factors often lead to tensions and negative sentiments. The more the groups depend on one another, the more this is likely to be so.

Another common symptom of intergroup relationships is what members of one group say about the other group. Words communicate feelings (sentiments), and these are crucial to the relationships between groups, just as they are between individuals. Criticisms, bickering, snide remarks, and intentional ignoring of others are clear indicators of difficult relations, just as the opposites indicate satisfying ones.

## Collaboration and Conflict

In addition to recognizing when difficult relationships exist, it is useful to assess the meaning of them. The central issue in making this assessment is whether collaboration is better than competition, or, more exactly, what degree of each is desirable. Americans have been raised on the "cultural ought" that competition is good. Most American boys and girls learn the virtues (and experience some of the pains) of competition in sports, schools, and social affairs. The advantages of "free competition" are extolled throughout their schooling. At the same time, they experience the advantages of collaboration. Girls and boys compete with others to make the team, but as members of the team have to cooperate to achieve desired results. Businesses do the same. One competes against the other, but they join together in associations to share information, deal with the government and public, and work for certain commonly beneficial goals.

Your education and your experience with collaboration and competition have made you aware of the advantages and disadvantages of each. You know that competition can stimulate some people to increased effort and improved results. At the same time, for some people, in some settings, competition can be destructive. Certain individuals, in some situations, experience it as personally threatening and upsetting and consequently quit or withdraw. Competition can also be cutthroat. In an effort to win, some competitors try to hurt others while also doing well for themselves. For some, the goal of winning justifies any means that help to reach it.

Collaboration, like competition, has both advantages and disadvantages. Collaboration frequently enables people and groups to achieve more than they could alone; it frequently creates "good feelings" among those cooperating. But it can also lead to rigidity, and stultification. Unlike contented cows, contented groups do not always achieve the best possible results.

In sum, the issue is to decide what degree of competition, with its constructive tension and incentive, and what degree of collaboration, with its pooling of talent and energies, is most functional for a particular group in a particular setting. Some collaboration and some competition can be functional; too much can be dysfunctional. The particular mix and value of each must be assessed situationally.

Once you have determined some of the important differences that exist between two groups the next question to ask is whether they are likely to result in intergroup friction. You can best answer this question by considering whether the members of either group are likely to think of the differences as functional or dysfunctional and feel them as enhancing or threatening to their welfare. Groups of people, like individuals, seek those relationships that they perceive as enhancing, are rather pas-

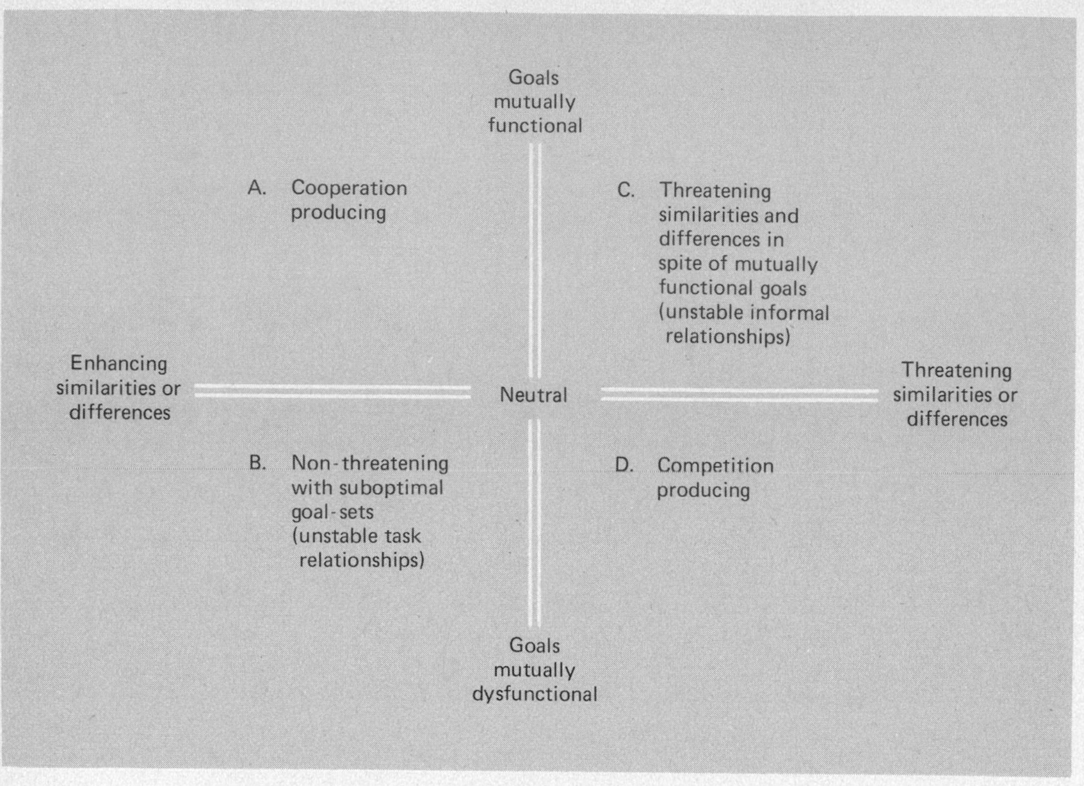


**Figure 2** Framework for Interpreting the Important Perceived Similarities and Differences of Group Characteristics in Intergroup Relations

sive about those that are neutral, and either avoid or attempt to change those that are threatening. Noting that there is a whole range of possibilities between "enhancing" and "threatening," we can see the relationships illustrated diagrammatically in Figure 2. Remember that the functional-dysfunctional dimension represents the members' analytical *judgment* about the utility of perceived similarities or differences in terms of achieving desired goals or maintaining desirable characteristics. The enhancing-threatening dimension represents their *feelings* about the similarities and differences they perceive.

To read Figure 2, consider two groups that have exclusive but complementary goals. If both groups work successfully toward achieving the goals, each will perceive the activity of the other as enhancing its own activity, and the situation will be viewed as functional for both. Such a situation would be plotted in the A section of the figure. If one group could only achieve optimum production results at the expense of the other but both wished to avoid trouble, they might agree, tacitly or otherwise, to avoid friction by not producing as much as possible. This behavior might be perceived as enhancing but dysfunctional, because results would be less than could otherwise be achieved. Such a situation would be plotted in B. Think of an example that might be plotted in C and D. For C you might use a characteristic such as high productivity norms; and for D, conflicting goals.

### Diagnosing the Causes of Conflict

We now examine some causes (or "*determinants*") of intergroup relationships through an adjunct to your Sherlock Process, *differential analysis,* which allows you to make your analysis systematic and as simple or elaborate as you desire. The main causes of intergroup conflict are often conflict between mutually exclusive goals; competition for limited resources, status, power, and similar benefits; differences in values, norms, and personal orientations; and the perception (whether "valid" or not) by one group that another group threatens it in relation to any of the above. Another frequent cause is mere "difference," which exceeds members' capacity to tolerate incongruity in the absence of connectedness by direct channels of communication.

DIFFERENTIAL ANALYSIS. Some of the potential conflict that exists between groups rises out of the nature of their *required task goals and activities.* For example, a prime aim of production frequently is to minimize costs. To do this may mean seeking standard parts and products and long production runs. Sales, on the other hand, has as a prime goal the satisfaction of customers with the company's product. To do this may require a variety of product lines, including specialized items that appeal to individual customers' particular needs.

Another source of potential conflict can stem from the personal backgrounds and orientations of the people making up the separate groups. For example, research scientists are likely to have considerable formal education, to value highly the scientific process, to dislike being concerned with mundane details unrelated to their research, to be familiar with highly permissive work atmospheres, and to be used to thinking of results in relatively long time periods ranging from weeks or months and even to years. Production people, on the other hand, frequently have had less education, value a pragmatic process of handling unusual problems, concern themselves with very immediate, tangible types of get-the-work-out problems, work in rather structured work atmospheres, and look for hourly, daily, and weekly results. Sales personnel often have backgrounds and orientations that differ to some extent from each of these.

Some intergroup conflict results as groups compete for their share of the organization pie, which consists of resources, authority, power and influence, status, rewards, favorable work assignments, and other related ingredients. One useful analytical approach is to apply what we have termed *differential analysis* in observing and interpreting intergroup behavior. This means looking for both the similarities and differences between groups. The answer to the question "Similarities and differences in what?" is suggested by Figure 3, which is an abbreviated restatement of some of the important variables we have already discussed in this book.

ASSESSING IMPORTANCE. After observing the similarities and differences, the next step is to assess their significance as either important or unimportant. Similarities might be important in competition for the same goals or collaboration built upon shared attitudes and values. How important

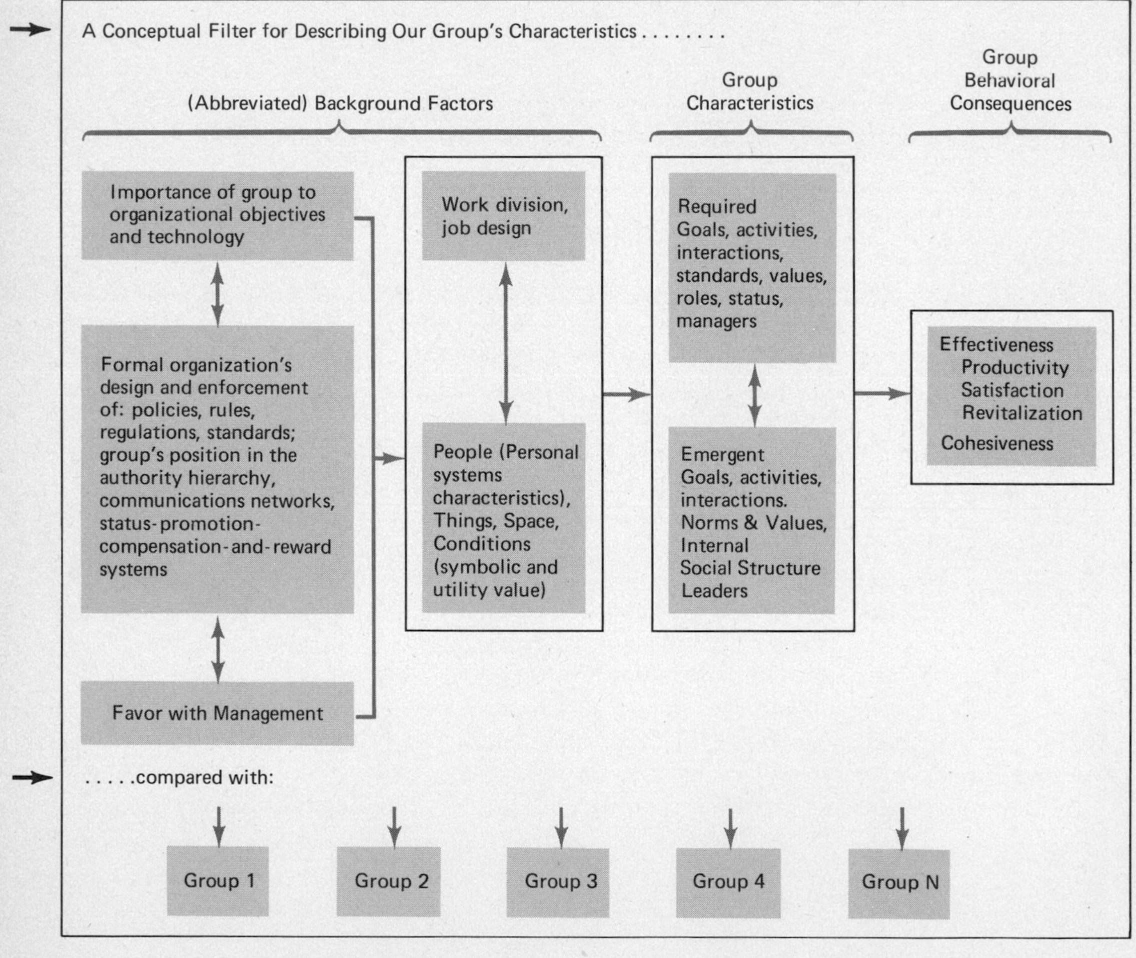


**Figure 3** Frequently Relevant Aspects for Detecting Intergroup Similarities and Differences

or unimportant a group judges a certain perceived similarity or difference will influence how it behaves toward the other group. It will matter very little whether it perceives a particular variable as very functional or dysfunctional or enhancing or threatening if it also perceives it as unimportant. Groups may virtually ignore threats they perceive as unimportant but behave very aggressively if they think even a mild threat extremely important to their maintenance or growth.

AN ILLUSTRATION. It is dangerous to think in terms of single variables when making comparisons between groups, because usually the relationships are influenced by a complex system of factors. For example, here is a simple illustration using just two variables, influence in decision making and perceived status. Assume that the two major departments in a small electronics company are production and research. Clearly, the work of each department is important to the other, but in any one company one of the departments might be viewed as more important than the other. If both departments share the same view about status, the result is likely to be quite different than if there is disagreement. If production appears to have more influence on decisions that affect both production and research (e.g., determination of what projects are undertaken; allocation of resources; determination of product line) and if at the same time research thinks of itself as more important to the company (because it perceives production as routine and technically simple compared with research), the behavioral result is likely to be friction. On the other hand, if the research department's perception of production's status is congruent with its apparent influence on decisions, friction is less likely to exist.

Table 2 represents an extension of the former case; you can see that friction might develop because of the incongruence of perceptions about status. And the very fact that both departments share perceptions about rank in "influence on key decisions" is likely to be a source of intensified

**Table 2 Comparison of Perceptions of Status and Influence**

| | *Perception of status (importance of function)* | | *Perception of influence on key decisions* | |
|---|---|---|---|---|
| *Viewed by* | *Production* | *Research* | *Production* | *Research* |
| Production | 1 | 2 | 1 | 2 |
| Research | 2 | 1 | 1 | 2 |

friction because of its incongruency with research's perceptions of status. Research perceives production as having more influence but believes it should not have more. Thus, a source of irritation exists.

Whether such differences in perceptions are judged as functional or dysfunctional or experienced as enhancing or threatening must be determined situationally. In the example above it might be that the discrepancy would be judged dysfunctional, because the two departments might be unwilling to share information, ideas, or problems, because each would like to "show up" the other department or at least "keep it down." But, can you see how it might be judged functional if different behavioral results occurred? Again, in this example, research might feel threatened because it perceives production as having disproportionate influence on decisions that affect research. Production might feel enhanced by this but simultaneously feel threatened by research's lack of agreement about production's status.

It does not require much imagination to see how easily this example could be expanded to greater complexity and yet simultaneously become more realistic. Just add sales, accounting, personnel, and purchasing departments. Although some consensus of perceptions is likely to exist about the two variables used in Table 2, some disagreement is certain. Then, for good measure, add some additional variables, such as allocation of space, equipment, and resources. Such complexity is enough to send us hustling back to the simplicity of our theoretical illustrations! The following list displays some of the signs and symptoms of such a downward spiral of increasing conflict.[4]

*Preliminary Stages of Intergroup Conflict*[5]

1. Beginnings of doubt and distrust appear. The intergroup climate deteriorates.
2. Viewpoints become distorted (stereotyped) and polarized ("We're only good; you're only bad").
3. Cohesiveness (close-knittedness, attractiveness, importance, friendliness, etc.) within each group *rises*.
4. Conformity and adherence to norms *rise* in each group.
5. Readiness for more authoritarian leadership *increases* in each group.
6. Hostile behaviors, signs of breakdowns in required intergroup behaviors and *reductions* in intergroup *interactions* accompany the negative sentiments.
7. Complete segregation is mutually *desired*, and positive emergent intergroup interactions virtually cease.

[4]M. Sherif and C. Sherif, *Groups in Harmony and Tension: An Integration of Studies on Inter-Group Relations* (New York: Harper Brothers, 1953).

[5]Adapted from Sherif and Sherif.

Intergroup conflict usually occurs when one or more of the groups feels either frustrated or potentially frustrated because it is being hindered from reaching its goals as it wants. Some groups look within for the source of the hindrance and, indeed, sometimes find it within. A group's own people, methods and procedures, equipment, interaction patterns, or similar factors might be preventing it from attaining its goals as well as its desires. But groups may also look outside for the source of the problem, just as individuals do, and again may find it there. One group can in fact present limitations and hurdles to other groups in attaining their goals. And again like individuals, groups may attribute more of the trouble to outside sources than is factual, often employing a process of *stereotyping*.

A related result of one group's finding the source of its problems and frustrations in an outside group is that it begins to stereotype the outsiders. For example, production people may begin to think and say "Sales is just that way; they have no understanding of what goes into getting this product out; they are out of touch with [our] reality." Or the manufacturing or assembly departments, or the inspectors, or the production control or quality control sections, all might stereotype the others. For stereotyping to take place, there must be a visible group to be stereotyped. The visibility is important; the group must be seen by, or be in some contact with, the stereotyping group and must have some characteristics or behavior patterns that enable the stereotyping group to perceive it as a source of the frustration. The stereotyping group will by definition think of all the members of the other group as similar; it will also perceive each of them as a source of frustration.

The stereotyped group perceived as the source of the stereotyping group's troubles need not necessarily be that source. For example, a less visible group or one with which the stereotyping group needs to be on good terms (e.g., an upper-level management group) may be a source of the trouble. But the stereotyping group may displace its hostility on the stereotyped group because it is either more visible or safer to react against.

There are other common patterns of behavior of groups competing with others, which, although they do not always hold, recur with sufficient frequency to make an awareness of them useful in observing and interpreting intergroup behavior. One aspect of what happens can be observed within each of the competing groups. If it perceives itself as competing with another group, or under attack in some way from it, it is likely to become *more cohesive*. The members are likely to minimize their own differences and to maximize their energy and loyalty to the group goals. As the threat or conflict with the other group increases in intensity, the group members become correspondingly more cohesive and pay increasing attention to the main group tasks and take steps to weaken the adversary (which actually take energy away from *required* and/or *personal* systems in exchange for *group maintenance behaviors*). As this happens, less attention and concern *is given to satisfying individual personal needs,* for the group goals tend to transcend them. Also, as the perceived threat or conflict increases, the internal structure of the group is likely to tend toward more rigidity, and the group leaders tend to become more authoritarian, especially when there isn't time for a *problem-solving* mode of functioning. This rigidity and leadership behavior tend to be accepted by the group members as essential to dealing with the external threat.

What happens between the competing groups is also relevant. As the conflict grows in intensity, they tend to see each other as the "enemy," even though they may not consciously think or talk about it. As this happens, the groups tend to form more stereotypes and to see only certain aspects, usually negative, of each other. Simultaneously, they tend to exaggerate their own strengths and virtues. As this is happening and each group is developing negative feelings about the other group and its members, interaction between the groups and members is often reduced until it reaches the point where only essential task interaction is taking place, as would be predicted by the general relationships between *interactions* and *sentiments*. This lack of interaction and communication tends to reinforce and perpetuate the negative stereotypes that each group has formed of the other. When members of the conflicting groups do have to interact—for example, in a meeting—they tend to distort the behavior and words they observe and hear in such a way that their negative perceptions are left intact. This *selective perception* is likely to be applied to their own words and behavior, also (but in a positive way), as they tend to recall and exaggerate the behavior and words that have maintained and enhanced their own positions and image.

As time moves along during the competition, the groups' perceptions of themselves tend to change if either one or the other is perceived as "doing better" or "winning" (assuming that there is a win-loss situation). The members of the "winning" group tend to feel good and more relaxed about how things are going, and their negative perceptions of their competitors may diminish and their positive perceptions of themselves may be reinforced. These feelings sometimes result in some complacency, which, in turn, may result in slightly less attention to task and slightly more attention to the satisfaction of certain individual needs.

The feelings of complacency and the lessened concern about task accomplishment are more likely to occur if the group perceives itself as having been successful over time and thus likely to continue that way than if it has just recently accomplished its ascendent position and perceives its competitor as still a potent threat. In any event, the group is likely to remain cohesive, and little attention will be devoted to assessing critically its methods and modes of behavior.

Naturally, the feelings and behavior in the losing group differ from those described above. The group members are likely to feel bad, to become even more tense than before, and to look for something or someone to blame. They are likely to look outside the group and to rationalize or blame, say, "circumstances" ("They weren't really better—luck was just against us!"), a higher level boss or manager, or the unethical behavior of the other group. If the reason for losing or having lost is clearly not "outside" the group, the group members may look inside. They may find "impersonal" sources such as their procedures, methods, or equipment; or they may fix the blame on certain members, most likely the leaders, deviants, or isolates. This kind of criticism, combined with the negative feelings and tensions resulting from the perceived loss, tends to make the group less satisfying to its members and, consequently, *less cohesive*. In an effort to improve its functioning, the group may change its leadership or some of its patterns of behavior. This kind of self-examination tends to bring unresolved conflicts out in the open, which may result in confrontation and angry feelings but which also serves the purpose of helping the group to deal with its problems and to find more effective ways of behaving. Thus it is that the losing group's mode of behavior is much more likely to change than is that of the winner, *assuming both groups continue to function*.

## APPROACHES TO MINIMIZING DYSFUNCTIONAL INTERGROUP CONFLICT

When confronting intergroup conflict remember that such conflict is not always dysfunctional, at least for the larger organization and even sometimes for the groups and individual members. Also keep in mind that some intergroup conflict is normal, if not inevitable, because the groups unavoidably have conflicting goals and compete for limited resources, status, positions, and other mutually sought-after factors. It is not always, therefore, either necessary or wise to try to reduce intergroup conflict.

Broadly speaking, there are three general strategies to consider in coping with intergroup conflict. They are: (1) win-lose; (2) compromise; and, (3) win-win. Of course, a fourth strategy is lose-lose—undesirable as it appears, this strategy is sometimes stubbornly or unwillingly (unconsciously) used by competing groups. The first of these strategies calls for competitive behavior designed to enable one group to win at the expense of the other group. A compromising strategy leads to each of the competing groups gaining some, and also giving up some of what it wants. The win-win strategy requires collaborative behavior designed to integrate the groups' goals and efforts in a mutually beneficial "synergistic" or "creative" way. Often the win-win strategy is the ideal to strive for. If it does not seem feasible, a compromise strategy may be appropriate and failing both of these, the win-lose approach may be the behaviorally appropriate last resort.

There are several specific approaches designed to reduce intergroup conflict and tension. One effective way is to find legitimate *superordinate goals* that appeal to both groups. This concept is illustrated by what happens occasionally when a company that has negative relationships with a strong union is faced with financial failure. If the union is aware of the company's position, it may change from being antagonistic and competitive in reaching its own goals (e.g., increased wages, shorter hours) to being cooperative in order that the company may survive. The goal of company survival is superordinate to the narrower goals of both management and the union, because failure would mean neither group would have any chance of obtaining its goals in any degree.[6] This is equivalent to shifting from a win-lose to a win-win strategy.

A somewhat related approach is to find a "common enemy" for the groups. You can think of many examples of groups which at one time were bitter rivals joining together in close collaborative effort to fight a common enemy. This happens both at an international level and within a country during time of war or catastrophe. It happens in sports when members of rival teams join together on all-star teams. It happens in the same way in the business world, both between and within companies.

Another approach is to have an outsider, often a common boss, serve as a judge or arbitrator and hand down either a win-lose or a compromise verdict. In either case, but especially in the first, the decision is likely to do little to eliminate or reduce the causes of the bad feelings that may exist between the groups. This approach is sometimes necessary because of the pressures of time or because the boss feels the decision must go a certain way. In addition to being quicker and more certain, it may appear easier because the complex and often uncomfortable processes of improving intergroup relationships are avoided. But these advantages are usually realized at the cost of genuinely improved relationships over the long haul, and frequently the causes of the conflict are not eliminated.

Another approach is to attempt to increase the amount of interaction and communications between groups. The assumption is that as groups interact and communicate more, they will come to understand and appreciate each other better, and there will be less likelihood of oversimplified stereotypes developing. There is probably some truth to this assumption in some settings, but it does not always hold. For example, when two conflicting groups are competing for scarce values or resources or when their goals are inherently conflicting, increased interaction is likely to do little in developing positive sentiments. Another complication is that if individual members are sent as "representatives" of their group, it is difficult for them to forget that they represent the group and its norms and values. Therefore, their behavior is somewhat restricted and they frequently do not feel free to change. They do not want to endanger their position within their own group. It is usually easier for a subgroup to allow itself to be influenced than for a single representative, but here again, of course, there are exceptions.

[6]Note, though, that survival does not always prevail as a superordinate goal. Witness the closing down of the New York *World Journal Tribune* in 1967.

Another approach that is used in a few companies is to bring the conflicting groups together in "confrontation meetings." The purpose of these sessions is to give the groups an opportunity to air their differences and complaints, express some of their negative and positive feelings, and hear those of the other group. An effort is then made to "work through" the differences. This kind of interchange does not guarantee harmonious relationships, but it does tend to expose the differences and therefore frequently brings about greater understanding, which, in turn, helps the intergroup relationships. A somewhat different approach calls for a more structured meeting in which, for example, each group will have one representative tell the other group, when all are assembled together, how its group sees both itself and the other. During each of these talks, the other group must remain quiet. The groups then part, discuss what they have heard, and analyze the differences (and distortions) in perceptions and attitudes apparent between the two groups. They may also attempt to understand the reasons for the differences. The groups then reassemble and each representative discusses the distortions and differences his group has analyzed. Finally, the discussion is thrown open to the assembled groups with the common goal of better understanding their intergroup relationships. Individuals can often influence improved intergroup relationships by informally initiating and maintaining a network of contacts with key members of interfacing groups. Such contacts increase awareness of pending changes, problems, and opportunities. The contacts can also serve to facilitate communications between the groups and help keep key people in tune with current conditions.

Often intergroup conflict results from an incomplete mutual knowledge of *required interactions* between the groups. The general strategy of getting together under a *problem-solving* frame of reference or a *brain-storming* atmosphere in which the groups have the task of working out their *required activities, interactions,* and *sentiments* in the interface between them can lead to a successful reduction in dysfunctional conflict. However, this is less likely to be successful when scarce resources, great status differences, or power imbalances exist. Then, "structural integration" may be employed; this consists of permanently installing an office or manager having authority to resolve differences.

## SUMMARY

Conflict between groups in an organization is common and sometimes unavoidable, yet not necessarily dysfunctional. Although groups have to collaborate to achieve certain mutual goals, they also compete to achieve conflicting goals and to obtain limited resources and benefits. This competition sometimes causes conflict. Differences between group characteristics, such as goals, activities, norms, and values, also produce friction. People in groups, like individuals, attempt to protect, maintain, and enhance their group in their situation as they perceive it. They tend to oppose groups that threaten their positions. Dysfunctional friction sometimes can be minimized by a variety of approaches, including establishing superordinate goals, finding a common enemy, choosing an arbitrator, fostering more intergroup interaction, and arranging confrontation meetings.

# CHAPTER 11

# Larger Organizational Structures

We now turn to a more elusive level of analysis, the total organization. In Chapter 1 we said that an organization's climate influences the tones and tempos of members' behaviors and contributes strong cumulative pressures toward conformity. These pressures are implicitly created and sustained by widely shared mutual expectations of members and enforced in much the same way as are norms in small groups. However, sensing the climate of an organization does not direct our attention toward understanding the explicitly required and observable operating details of how people and work are related. How is a highly intricate massive human effort put together? In this chapter, we delve more deeply into the alignment of goals among individuals, small groups, and larger organizational units. Second, we explore the key concept of "structure" as it is applied in organizational analysis. Last, a generalized "map" of the total organization is developed with a discussion of its relevance to goals and structures.

## ALIGNMENT OF GOAL SETS

Organizations of any size are made up of various groups. Over time these groups tend to become entities in and of themselves. They become cohesive, semiautonomous units. Thus, we can think of organizations as comprised of three types of entities: individuals, small groups, and larger organizational units.[1] To varying degrees each of these entities may be considered to have its own set of goals. These are the emergent product of required and personal systems through their histories within the context of the total organization and its climate through time. Often, these goal sets are interrelated in a complex way and contain internal inconsistencies that are conflict-prone.

The degree of alignment and compatibility of the goal sets between entities varies *vertically*, up levels of analysis from individuals to the total organization, and *laterally*, as in the case we have discussed of intergroup relationships. At any rate, there is generally some conflict between them that becomes manifest as noncooperation, impositions of inequities (e.g., compensation, privileges, etc.), and ultimately in the behavioral consequences of eroded productivity, satisfaction, and capacity for revitalization and change.

## THE NATURE OF ORGANIZATIONAL STRUCTURES

In ongoing organizations, structures are actually "maps"[2] abstracted from real situations and based upon observed behavioral patterns of how, when, and where people behave. Structures consist of intricate and reliably shared experiences that lead to the anticipation, readiness, and propensity of members to behave in predictable ways definable by their group and organizational roles and jobs.

You can think of the various types of structures we discuss in this chapter as sets of overlays, or filters, each of which focuses on and pulls together particular aspects or types of behavior in an organization. These structures actually serve as a sort of honeycomb or crude lattice-work consisting of highly repetitive behavioral patterns that literally hold organizations together and, hopefully, result in desired consequences, including productivity, satisfaction, and revitalization. Table 1 displays the most frequently found structures in organizations.

### Implications of Structural Changes

Introduction of change even requiring only minor modifications of an organizational structure usually results in disruption of other aspects

[1]Remember, groups and organizations are *not concrete behaving entities*. Only individuals within them behave. We should remember that, if and when we ascribe human characteristics to groups and organizations, we may be either consciously or unconsciously reifying or "making abstractions human," which they are not. Although groups and organizations acquire a "climate," they do not behave. Only people do. Furthermore, we can always expect that each "entity" will evoke behaviors tending to *protect, maintain*, and *enhance* the *entity as its membership perceives* it within its situation.

[2]See reading, "Maps, Territories and Cases," p. 131.

**Table 1 Types of Organization Structures**

*A. Basic Structures*

1. *Authority*—reflecting distributions of power, status, and influence.

2. *Task and Decision Centers*—reflecting clusters and divisions of work by type or specialization; and reflecting who is involved with what kinds of decision, under what circumstances or ground rules, and when.

*B. Ancillary Structures*

1. *Objectives*—producing organizational goals, plans, and budgets or projecting task performance in relation to time, cost and other specifications.

2. *Communications*—observable as interactive patterns and flows, both verbal and written.

3. *Policy*—manifest as policies, procedures, rules, regulations.

4. *Control*—measurement, reporting, auditing, and authorizing initial or corrective commitment of resources in relationship with planned task performance.

of the same structure plus disruptions of various aspects of other structures; often the initial change tends to become erased or neutralized. The change source is often subject to being punished for violating norms or standards of conduct. One manager described this phenomenon as "the norm of conserving the status quo." Another technical executive likened it to a spinning gyroscope—"you try to push it one way and it moves in another direction which often mashes your finger."

Keep in mind, nevertheless, that organizations are extremely dynamic, so that "structure," which connotes a static state, is a bit of a misnomer. It is useful to think of various elements—decisions, information, activities, goods, materials, authority, influence—as *flowing* into, through, and out of the structure. We might begin our visualization of organization by thinking in terms of groups or clusters of people separated either by what they do, where they do it, or both. For example, in a manufacturing organization, some people are clustered together making the product, some are out selling it to the customers, other people are sitting at desks "figuring," and others are in laboratories inventing new products.

Some people are "doing" and others are "thinking." Some are making decisions, and others are acting to carry out decisions already made.

## BASIC ORGANIZATIONAL STRUCTURES

The first basic structure is primarily concerned with the "people configuration" and the fundamental units that comprise the organization's authority structure. The second is the task and decision-center structure. In contrast to small groups, larger organizational units are not characterized by face-to-face day-to-day proximity of a majority of members at specified places and times. The authority structure and the task and decision-center structures often remove the *requirement* for interpersonal interaction in achieving coordinated task behavior.

### The Basic Authority Structure (or Hierarchy)

Many people think of an "organization's structure" as being synonymous with its authority structure. Although the latter is not the only structure that relates people and work, it is a key one. Some observers believe that its importance may be decreasing in our society because more emphasis is coming to be placed on cooperative effort focused around work and communications structures than on compulsory efforts resulting from orders. Furthermore, persons with formal authority and power are increasingly relying upon subordinates and peers having technical expertise. This expertise is also a source of power, making cooperation necessary, often after a good deal of bargaining and negotiating.

Formal authority in a business organization is frequently seen as a right to command others, which is thought to be delegated down through the organization. The ultimate source of authority is said to rest with the owners, who in turn get their authority from the Constitution and its provision for property rights. In our modern corporations, the owners (stockholders) often delegate almost complete authority to professional managers to direct the organization. The managers are thus responsible for seeing that the organization effectively achieves its objectives, and they are seen as accountable to the owners for results.

Several concepts relating to authority are part of the common knowledge and language of most managers. These concepts are commonly labeled "principles," and although frequently violated in practice, they have significant impact in shaping the structure of formal authority relationships in most organizations. Even if it is granted that the relative importance of this structure compared with some others is diminishing, the fact remains that it still has today for many managers the most impact of them all. Thus, we will discuss briefly some of the basic authority-structure concepts. They include *unity of command, span of authority, delegation, decentralization,* and *line staff*.

UNITY OF COMMAND. For many decades, managers have known about and generally accepted what is called the "principle of unity of command." This "principle" states that no man should have more than one superior. It is based on the belief that a man will be "pulled apart" if he has two or more superiors. If two bosses give a subordinate conflicting orders, which will he obey? In recent years, it has become apparent to many observers that although the logic of this principle is clear, it is not adhered to in practice. It is not at all uncommon for managers in business organizations to be subject to directives from more than one manager, particularly in larger organizations where functional specialists direct activities in their area throughout the organization. Frequently, this direction is not in the form of formal orders, but is given as "advice" and "recommendations." But the effect is often the same as though direct orders had been given.

SPAN OF AUTHORITY. The original statement of this concept was that no superior should have more than five or six subordinates reporting to him if their work interlocked,[3] the reason being that the number of relationships between manager and subordinates increases geometrically as more subordinates are added. Thus, some believe it becomes impossible for one man to keep all of the relationships sorted out in a way that enables him to operate effectively if he supervises "too many" people. The original statement of the concept is much debated, and, in practice, it is often violated. The concept is useful, because there are limits to the number of subordinates a specific manager can effectively supervise in a specific setting. However, the actual number depends on many factors, including the number of times the manager must see his subordinates, the time he must spend with each, the importance and uniqueness of the decisions to be made, the degree of experience and training of the subordinates, and the competence of the manager, to mention just a few. Thus, the concept can be a useful guide for thought but should not be applied rigidly in making judgments.

DELEGATION. In all except the smallest organizations, managers must delegate some of their authority in order that the work may be divided and organizational objectives achieved. The ultimate responsibility for the achievement of the objectives is the manager's alone; this he cannot delegate. But he can delegate some of his authority to his subordinates to

[3]Lyndell F. Urwick, "The Manager's Span of Control," *Harvard Business Review*, XXXIV, No. 3 (May–June, 1956), 39–47.

direct work that will contribute to the achievement of the objectives, and he can hold his subordinates responsible for these subtasks. The traditional principle of delegation has stated that managers should be given sufficient authority to command others in performing the necessary work. In practice, however, this principle is often not adhered to. Many managers find that they are held responsible for certain results when they do not have as much authority as they would like in commanding others. In practice, managers must utilize their persuasive and other motivational talents.

Although most managers pay lip service to the principle of delegation, many find it difficult to delegate well in practice. This is true because there are certain psychological barriers that make delegating uncomfortable. For example, some managers have an aversion to taking a chance, and delegating sometimes involves certain risks, particularly if the subordinate is in the process of gaining experience. Following along this line, some managers lack confidence in their subordinates. Others believe "I can do it better myself" and, therefore, reason that it takes more sense to do the job alone. Still others are sometimes jealous and fearful of the competition subordinates "on the rise" might give them if they are given too much opportunity. But some of the reasons managers hesitate to delegate are related to the subordinates, who, for example, may be reluctant to accept increased responsibility. In sum, there are barriers to effective delegation, although the advantages of it are great. Delegation is an art that many managers can improve.

DECENTRALIZATION. Both delegation and decentralization involve the transfer of authority. But delegation is usually thought of as being the person-to-person transfer of authority, whereas decentralization is thought of more frequently as the transfer of authority from one organizational body to another. Decentralization, furthermore, can refer to things other than authority. Both activity and geographical decentralization, for example, are possible. But it is the decentralization of authority that we will discuss here. Primarily a mental concept, a philosophy of organization, it is neither good nor bad per se, and it exists in organizations as a matter of degree rather than completely or not at all. It is a philosophy that cannot be imposed easily on an organization unwilling or unable to accept it. In a decentralized organization, each division is relatively independent, but it is brought together in a corporate system through centralized policies. Decentralization can be thought of as decentralized operations and responsibilities with centralized control and coordination.[4]

[4]For representative discussion of the much-discussed concept of decentralization, see Ralph J. Cordiner, *New Frontiers for Professional Managers* (New York: McGraw-Hill Book Co., 1956), and Harold Koontz and Cyril O'Donnell, *Principles of Management: An Analysis of Managerial Functions*, 5th ed. (New York: McGraw-Hill Book Co., 1972).

The degree to which an organization should be decentralized depends on various factors, including the importance and costliness of decisions to be made; the availability of trained managers; the uniformity and stability of policies; business dynamics; and the size of the organization. The advantages of decentralization include the following:

1. Faster decision making
2. Greater flexibility and tactical mobility
3. Valuable training for subordinates
4. Greater likelihood that subordinates will demonstrate initiative and incentive
5. Getting decisions made closer to the point of action
6. Recognition and preservation of human values

Some of the disadvantages include:

1. Possibility of duplication of work
2. Greater problems of control or loss of control
3. Greater problems of coordination and communication

Proponents of decentralization maintain that this kind of organization emphasizes and preserves the human dignity of men while still making possible the great advantages of mass production, marketing, and research that can be carried on only by large companies.

LINE-STAFF.[5] The terms *line* and *staff* are common in management circles, although their meaning has been vague and subject to debate. For quite some time, line and staff were distinguished by determining which functions were *essential to the operations of the business* (line function) and which *helped* the essential departments (staff function). Thus, in the traditional manufacturing firm, the production, sales, and finance departments were considered line; whereas personnel, purchasing, and engineering were considered staff departments. This distinction became increasingly meaningless, however, as managers became aware that some of the staff departments were as essential as the line departments in achieving the company's objectives. For example, the engineering department in an aerospace company may be "more" essential in producing airplanes than the production department.

Another distinction frequently made between the terms relates to authority relationships. Line indicates a superior-subordinate relationship;

[5]For representative discussions of line-staff, see Ernest Dale and Lyndall F. Urwick, *Staff in Organization* (New York: McGraw-Hill Book Co., 1960); Koontz and O'Donnell, *Principles of Management*; and Gerald G. Fisch, "Line-Staff Is Obsolete," *Harvard Business Review*, XXXIX, No. 5 (September–October, 1961), 67–79.

staff connotes an advisory relationship. It is possible for one man to have both line and staff status; the personnel manager, for example, has line authority over his subordinates in the personnel department but usually only an advisory (staff) relationship with the production manager.

Although many people think of line-staff as described above, the concept is necessarily made much more complex for use in actual practice. In fact, it has become so complex that some have suggested the terms are no longer useful. Nevertheless, they are frequently used, and thus it is helpful to have some understanding of them.

The reason line-staff concepts have become so complex is that in practice some so-called staff (advisory) departments and managers in effect direct and order line department personnel over whom they supposedly have no authority. For example, the purchasing manager in a corporation may tell the production manager what quantity of goods should be purchased or what supplier will be used. This will happen if the purchasing manager has functional authority in all matters pertaining to purchasing (or if he exerts informal authority, the source of which is his expertise). The personnel manager may prescribe what type of training program will be established for the production department, even though the personnel manager is usually thought of as being a staff manager with no direct authority over production. The engineering manager may have final authority to decide what kind of design will be utilized in building an airplane and tell the production department how the plane will be built.

It has become apparent that, in practice, there are several different concepts of staff, and there does not appear to be much uniformity between companies as to which concept is applied. In some companies "staff" refers to advisory departments, e.g., planning, market research, or training; in others it refers to service departments, e.g., personnel or purchasing; in still others it is a matter of function and refers to those departments that have authority over other departments in their functional area—e.g., some engineering departments.

There is much evidence that, in practice, considerable friction develops between some so-called line and staff departments. This friction often leads to delay and disagreement in decision making within the organization. Line people sometimes believe that staff people tend to assume line authority, that some of their advice is "ivory tower" in nature, that some of them fail to see the whole picture (because they are too specialized), and that some try to steal credit for results. On the other hand, some staff people believe that the line people tend to resist new ideas that they are distrustful of staff and do not accept staff advice, and that the line people do not give staff enough authority and opportunity to help the line achieve good results. These kinds of feelings and the resulting confusion that exists over formal authority lead many managers to believe that line-staff problems are among the most difficult organizational problems they face.

### The Basic Task and Decision Center Structure

If the organization's objectives have already been established (usually by the higher levels in the authority hierarchy), theoretically the next step is to determine what functions or activities need to be carried out to achieve them. The following is to divide the organization in such a way that the essential functions can be accomplished. In actual practice, organizations usually grow over time without going through this kind of neat and logical process, but usually an attempt is made to divide the work, people, and resources so that the purposes can be achieved efficiently and effectively. This division, which separates people and work in time and space, creates a structure of work and decision centers, each of which is occupied by one or more persons.

The organizational problem is to insure that what the people decide and do relates in some way to the achievement of the organization's objectives. Thus, the goal is to divide work according to some rational design and to order it in time so that efficient work-flows are established. Frequently the work of one activity and decision center depends on that of others, and thus the various centers are connected by flows of decisions and work.

Work can be divided in several different ways, and many of the larger companies use more than one. One common method is to divide it along *functional lines*. In the typical manufacturing company, this would mean dividing it into production, marketing, finance, accounting, personnel, and so on. Another way of dividing work is along *product* or *service* lines. Each unit is responsible for all work–including all the functions–relating to a certain product or group of products. Sometimes the units are called "divisions" of the larger organization. General Motors is an example of a divisionalized organization.

A third way of dividing work, used particularly in aerospace and research-oriented companies, is along *project* lines. In this approach, the necessary personnel, resources, and facilities are grouped according to a particular project that is to be carried out. The project may last only a few months or several years, and the work frequently requires personnel and resources from several regular departments. A project manager is assigned to coordinate all the planning and work connected with the project, and he may be "loaned" certain people to work on the project, either full- or part-time. One implication for behavior of this type of work division is that people are often brought together for relatively short periods and do not have as much time as they do under some other arrangements to develop norms, internal structures, and customary patterns of behavior.

Work is sometimes divided along other lines, such as space or customer type. For example, some large banks in California divide their work geographically, assigning similar work to different branches within the bank's area. Other companies might divide into divisions that serve particular customer groups, such as industrial, government, or consumer groups.[6]

Within these larger divisions, work is often divided into smaller units. For example, a production department might be subdivided by functions such as production planning and control, manufacturing, assembly, inspection, and quality control. The way a specific production unit is organized varies with several factors, including the type of product manufactured: some products are made in single units or small batches, others in large batches, and still others on a mass basis. Chemicals are manufactured by different processes than are machines. Thus, the type of function or product and the related required technology have much to do with how the work is divided.

Usually economic efficiency is a vital criterion considered in dividing work, and such approaches as specialization and utilization of special abilities and resources are followed in achieving this efficiency. In addition, noneconomic factors, some of which are not always either desirable or rational, influence how work is divided. An example, sometimes, is tradition. Some companies divide their work in certain ways because "We have always done it this way."

It is sometimes useful to conceptualize and observe a decision-center structure as distinct from the authority or task structures, although they often are identical or close to it. Identifying who makes decisions and how they are made can tell much about an organization. This diagnostic process helps further clarify who becomes involved in making and executing planned (and planning) tasks, by what process (e.g., in committee, alone, alone after consulting with subordinates and staff), in what sequence, and with what additional contingent approvals, if any. Except in very large organizations, which have formalized planning, research review, control review, and other procedures, the decision-center structure is rarely spelled out explicitly.

## VARIATIONS OF THE BASIC STRUCTURES

Organizational design is concerned with particular blendings of authority and task structure. Some frequently encountered variations include the following, in order of organizational size and complexity:

1. Simple Line Organizations: Functional, Product (or Purpose, e.g., Regional) (see Figures 1A and 1B).

[6]For a more detailed discussion of this subject, see Ernest Dale, *Planning and Developing the Company Organization Structure* (New York: American Management Association, 1952); and Ernest Dale, *Management Theory and Practice* (New York: McGraw-Hill Book Co., 1965).

2. Simple Line-Staff Organizations (see Figure 1C).

3. Mixed (Line-Staff, Functional, Purpose) Organizations (see Figure 1D).

4. Complex Matrix Organizations (see Figure 3).

5. Committee Superstructures (at top hierarchical levels above any of the simple or complex variations that have been mentioned).

6. Conglomerate or Holding Company Metastructures (at top hierarchical levels above modified multiple Committee Superstructures).

The way in which people and work are related through organizational design of structure has significant impact on behavior. Structural design influences such factors as freedom, dependence, and specialization, which in turn affect the degree to which people can determine and control their own behavior, exert their own initiative and creativity, and do significant work.

The structure of organizations can be described by a variety of terms, including these contrasting pairs: tall or flat; centralized or decentralized; specialized or general; independent or interdependent; tight or loose; mechanistic or organic. Any specific organization is usually characterized by more than one of these features, all of which have impact on the behavior of people.

## Tall or Flat

"Tall" organization structures are characterized by more levels of managers and supervisors than are comparably sized organizations having "flat" structures. The spans of authority are narrower in tall structures than in flat ones. From the organization's point of view, tall structures provide more control and direction than do flat ones; from the employee's point of view, they are more restrictive and offer fewer opportunities to make decisions and exert initiative. Tall organizations make it possible for managers to keep in touch with their area and people more closely, because they have fewer subordinates and a narrower area to supervise. Centralized or decentralized structures also influence the degree of freedom the managers and employees have in various organizational divisions. Some of the advantages and disadvantages of these two different structural approaches have already been discussed.

## Specialized or General

Some organizational structures are designed so that work is divided into minute, specialized parts; in some factories, in fact, the concept is carried to extremes in which people are required to stand in one position and tighten bolts all day. It used to be generally assumed that, in terms

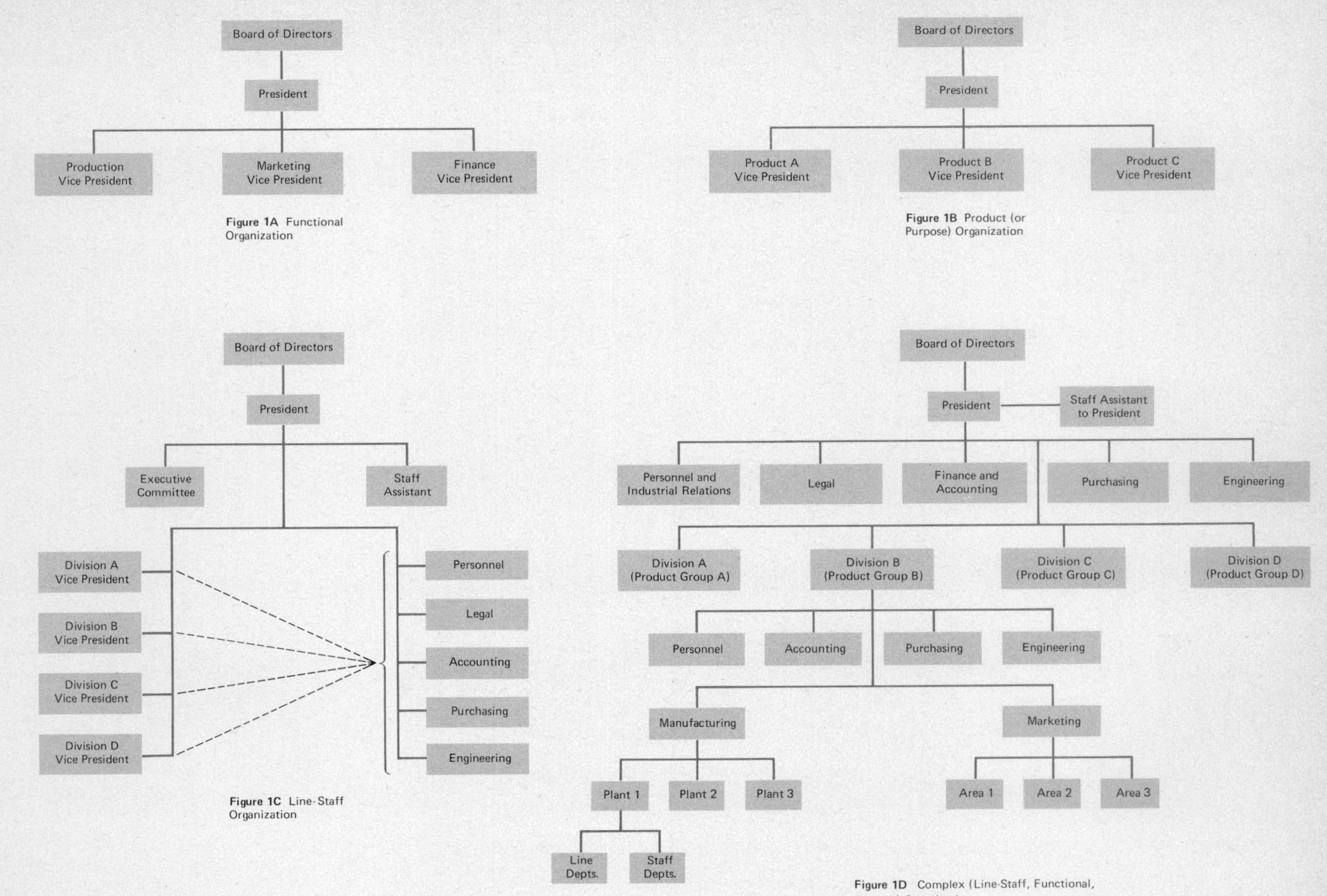


**Figure 1** Variations of Basic Organizational Structures

of output and efficiency, such specialization was useful. Today this assumption is frequently questioned, even if it is still sometimes accepted. The reason for the questioning is that although some people enjoy simple tasks, many more find them economically necessary but psychologically undesirable. People find that little is required of them, and they have little chance to demonstrate their full capabilities. They often see little relationship between what they do and the final product. Little room is left for individual initiative or creativity, and the psychological result is boredom, passivity, and sometimes hostility toward the system that treats them like automatons.

These feelings sometimes lead to unsatisfactory productivity, although such things as assembly lines and strict supervisors can help achieve high productivity in spite of the personal feelings of the workers. Nevertheless, the results from the individual's point of view are less than satisfactory, and so sometimes are the productivity results. Consequently, such techniques as job enlargement and job rotation are instituted in many organizations in order to give workers more opportunities to do significant work and to utilize their talents more fully.

### Independent or Interdependent

The degree of interdependence in a particular structure depends in part on how the work is divided and in part on the degree of freedom and specialization of the workers. For example, consider structures 1 and 2 in Figure 2.[7] Assume that A, B, and C are separate functions performed by different sections. Which of the two forms requires more coordination? What happens if there is a breakdown in A in structure 1? in structure 2? What are the advantages and disadvantages of the two forms?

### Tight (Mechanistic) or Loose (Organic)

Whether an organization is "tight" or "loose" depends largely on the detail of the policy and procedures structures and on the philosophy and styles of supervision of upper level managers. Those organizations in which an effort is made to spell out in detail the authority and other relationships and the work procedures and methods are often termed "mechanistic." Their opposites are referred to as "organic."[8]

The difference is described by Joan Woodward as follows:

[7]This illustration is taken from James C. Worthy, *Big Business and Free Men* (New York: Harper & Brothers, 1959), p. 91.

[8]This concept was developed by Tom Burns. See his *Management in the Electronics Industry: A Study of Eight English Companies* (Edinburgh: University of Edinburgh Social Science Research Center, 1958).

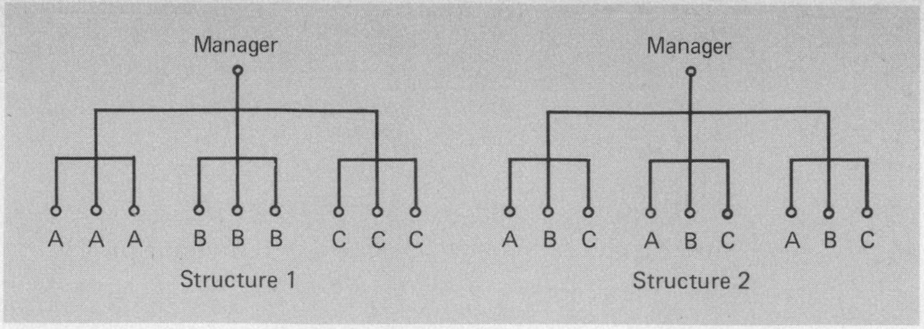


**Figure 2** Interdependence of Units

> "Mechanistic" systems are characterized by rigid breakdown into functional specialisms, precise definition of duties, responsibilities and power, and a well developed command hierarchy through which information filters up and decisions and instructions flow down. "Organic" systems are more adaptable, jobs lose much of their formal definition, and communications up and down the hierarchy are more in the nature of consultation than of the passing up of information and receiving of orders. In this type of situation, the chief executive is not regarded as omniscient.[9]

An example of another organic and also highly complex organizational structure is the "matrix" structure (see Figure 3). Here two hierarchical structures intersect one another. There may or may not be the addition of staffs and/or committees. One of the two hierarchical structures is often functionally oriented while the other is often product- or project-oriented. The former develops relevant expertise for the *long run* which is applied on specific *short-term* projects managed by members of the latter hierarchical structure. Large organizations, of course, usually have many projects underway simultaneously (e.g., aerospace, electronics). The matrix structure allows an organization to be responsive quickly to changes in the market environment through its project structures without getting out of balance or "burned out" by virtue of the longer-range perspective of the functional hierarchical structures.

Our purpose here is not to say which of these various organizational characteristics are "good" and which are not. The fact is that this is not known with certainty. All that is known is that what is good for organizations in one type of industry is not at all necessarily good for organizations in another. The crucial point is that the appropriate characteristics need to be determined situationally. But it is helpful to be able to distinguish the characteristics. It is also useful to keep in mind that whatever the design, various impacts are felt by individuals within the structures. Thus, the structures will affect both how well work is accomplished and how well people are satisfied and grow.

[9]Joan Woodward, *Industrial Organization: Theory and Practice* (London: Oxford University Press, 1965), p. 230.

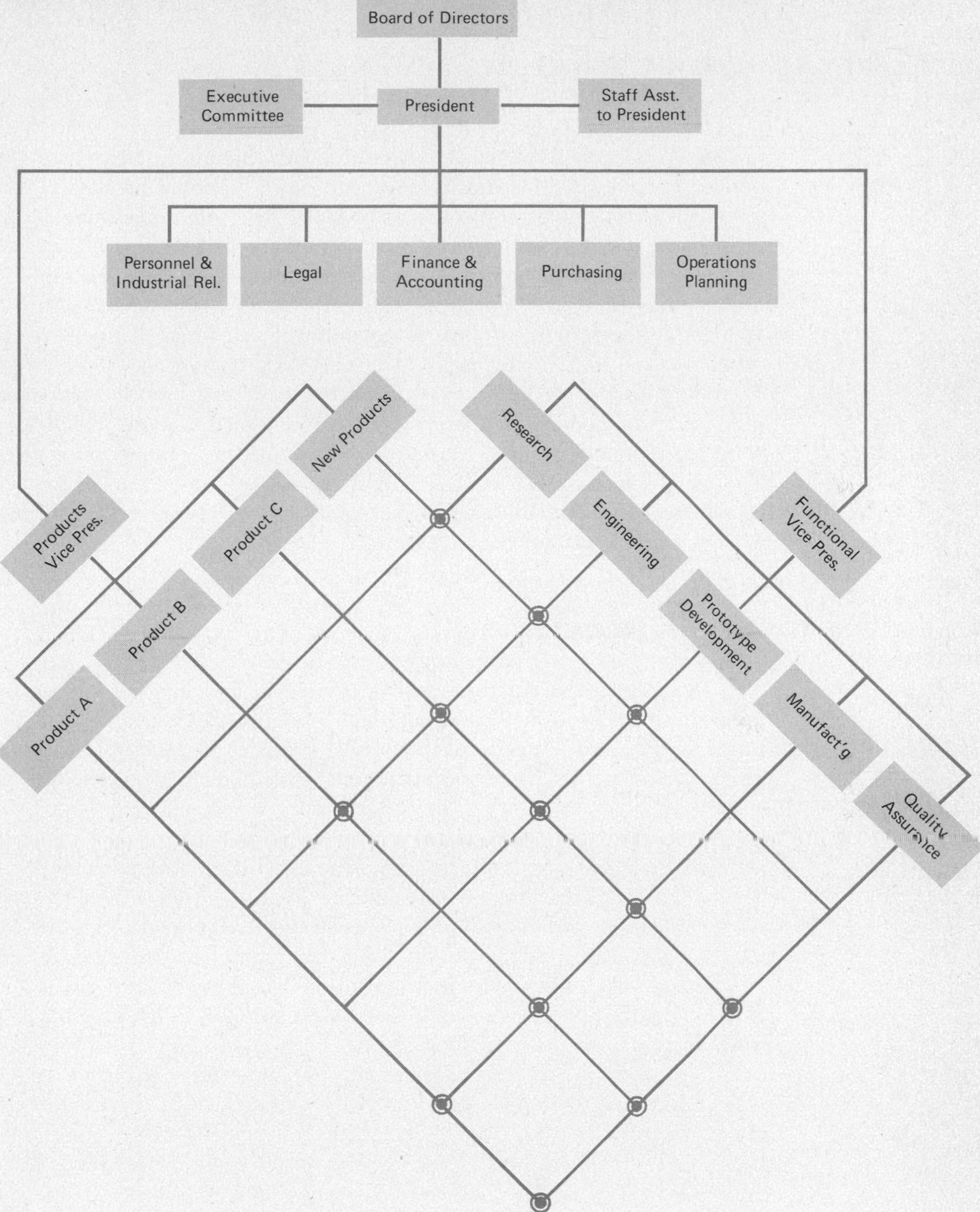


**Figure 3** Complex, Mixed Line-Staff Matrix Organization
(Circles denote task groups)

## ANCILLARY ORGANIZATION STRUCTURES

The concept of structure is abstract, and we have been arbitrary in what have been termed "basic" as opposed to "ancillary" structures. Although we have called authority and task "basic," it could be argued that any of the others (e.g., "objectives structures" or "communications structures") are just as "basic." The main point is that all the observable structures, basic and ancillary, are highly interrelated. For example, a foreman may be discussing a new tool with his men, and he sees that his behavior lies within the scope of an authority structure (superior-subordinate), task structure (impact of new tool upon division of work, scheduling and/or sequencing), objectives structure (group goals surrounding technological change issues, possibly affecting plans and threatening some members), and communications structure (interactions initiated by foreman; their content, their emotional tone, the degree of freedom experienced by workers to ask questions, vent feelings, etc.). We now turn to the ancillary structures.

### Objectives Structure

The objectives structure defines the short- and long-term goals of the overall organization. The detail plans, budgets, and allocations of personnel, plant, and equipment hopefully provide coordination for efficiently pursuing the overall organizational objectives throughout the organization.

The aim of the larger organization is that the work people do will contribute efficiently and effectively to the organization's goals. Thus, an essential step in organizing is to delineate clearly the objectives of both the organization and its subunits. These objectives serve as guides for planning, directing, and controlling the work required in the organization.

The objectives of the total organization, like those of individuals and groups, are multiple. Organizations strive to survive, to make profits, to grow, and to fulfill social responsibilities. The prime objectives for most firms is to make a profit for the owners, but some firms strive to "maximize" profit, while others only try to make a "satisfactory" profit. For example, because of regulations, most investor-owned utility companies traditionally have not been considered as profit conscious as have some other types of companies such as the automobile or electronics industries.

Most organizations have a hierarchy of objectives, but it is usually not very clearly set forth and so must be deduced somewhat intuitively. Different objectives may be more important than others in different companies. And like other aspects of organization, the hierarchy can change over time. Early in the life of an organization survival may be the prime objective; once the organization has become established, growth may become most important. Thus, the importance of different goals varies both between organizations and over time, within them.

One of the key problems in the objectives structure is that of achieving balance and unity. The goals of subunits are sometimes in conflict, and the people in those subunits usually are more concerned with achieving their subunit goals than the less clear (to them) objectives of the larger organization. This common occurrence is referred to by many as *suboptimization,* a term previously defined in Chapter 10. Thus, a common organization problem is that of balancing subunit goals in such a way that they contribute to the larger organization's objectives.

It can be seen that the basic task structure connects the currently approved *objectives* with the appropriately detailed plans of other *suborganizational units, small groups,* and *particular jobs,* which have been placed together into clusters having specialized task capabilities. Sometimes the "jobs" and "positions" involved are enduring enough to outlive their human occupants, in which case individuals are viewed as filling an organizational "role structure."

## Communications Structure

Task specialization and spatial separation make communication both essential and difficult. Different specialized groups must know what other groups are doing and what they, themselves, should be doing if the work of each group is to contribute to the achievement of the total organizational task. In addition, organizations need to communicate with their external environments. They need to monitor what is happening in their environment; they need to obtain information from and send information to certain of its segments.

Most organizations have channels of communication that connect both the organization with its environment and individuals and groups with each other in order that information may be transmitted and received. In addition, the emergent system of every organization has an informal network, commonly called the grapevine. It is sometimes faster than the formal network, and usually carries information that is relevant to the personal interests of the employees.

Symptoms of poor communication are usually easily identifiable. Work does not get completed correctly or on time. The quality, quantity, or timing of decisions is poor. People have hard feelings toward one another. Of course, poor communication is not the only cause of such problems, but frequently it is involved, and often in a major way.

Both the kind and the direction of information affect the quality of communications in an organization. Research has indicated that negative information is more likely to flow down the organization than up; and positive information is more likely to flow up. Some information gets distorted, either intentionally or unintentionally; some of it is omitted or repeated; and some of it arrives too early or too late to be useful. For example, subordinates who have made mistakes are sometimes reluctant to tell their bosses about them. Consequently, they sometimes "forget" to mention the mistakes, or they diminish the true extent of them in reporting. Sometimes one person may neglect to mention a bit of information to another person because he does not believe it is important when in fact the latter person may need or want it very much.

The communications structure reflects the patterning of information flows throughout the organization. It usually resembles the formal authority structure, although informal communications may depart significantly from it. As we have seen, the authority structure formally and informally *differentiates* jobs or positions (roles) and individuals. The differentiation is with respect to rank and status and delimits the degree and scope of discretion open to the office-holders (such as the dollar amount a given executive may authorize for expenditure without approval from higher authority). The authority structure is sometimes referred to as "the organization structure" and may be kept up-to-date in chart form. Thus, the charts also suggest who speaks to whom or through whom the distribution of memoranda should pass, always keeping a superior advised of messages addressed to his subordinates. So, we can see that communications structures are very closely linked with authority structure.

## Policy Structure

One of the major purposes of organization is to relate and coordinate individuals and groups separated by task and space. The authority structure helps accomplish this by defining, at least partially, who can tell whom to do what, and who has the authority to make what kinds of decisions and to take what actions. This authority structure is supplemented with a structure of explicit and implicit policies, procedures, methods, and rules, which channel and direct many decisions and actions.

A policy is a statement of intent that is made to guide others in their decision making without being so specific as to specify decisions. Theoretically, the top executives of any company, but especially the larger ones, necessarily determine policies that help guide the behavior of people within the organization. However, in fact, people at lower levels often have an important hand in fashioning policy. This happens in two ways. First, people at lower levels make recommendations to those at upper levels. Second, people in upper levels sometimes formalize policies to fit behavior patterns that have already emerged at lower levels. In the latter case, policy follows practice.

A frequent characteristic of policy statements is that they are vague enough to permit managers to select among specific decisions, depending upon the managers' view of the specific conditions surrounding the decision. An example might be a manager faced with a request from two employees for six months' leave of absence to travel in Europe. One employee has one year's seniority, an adequate but not better work record, and plans to marry within a year a serviceman with three years more to serve. The other has ten years' seniority, is a very good worker, and has roots in the company's areas and a demonstrated desire to continue working. The manager knows the policy states "It is the policy of the company to permit leaves of absence of reasonable length for personal purposes when employees are deserving and their absence will not impair their department's work seriously." Note the words "reasonable," "deserving," and "seriously." They require interpretation, and thus *permit* certain decisions but do not *require* them. The manager may know what he can do, but he may choose not to do it.

In addition to policies, certain procedures and methods are usually designed to facilitate work. For example, there may be eight discrete steps in a particular work process, and a sequence established for each step. Step three might involve notifying two departments that the first two steps are completed. Such a suggested process is called a procedure. It tells people *when* they should do something. *How* they do it is the method they use. The method is formally prescribed in some cases and is left to the operant's discretion in others. Anyone who fails to follow the prescribed procedures and methods is usually open to censure if problems result. Yet much of life in organizations involves evading required procedures and methods, or redesigning them, and again the reasons are usually people-problems rather than errors in the logic of the design of the procedures and methods.

Most organizations have rules and regulations to supplement policies, procedures, and methods. Rules and regulations say what one *must* do or not do and often specify penalties for infractions. "No one is to punch another's time card" is an example. There are no ifs, ands, or buts about it. It says "no one," period.

So there is a sliding scale from *guides* (policies) to *suggestions* (procedures) to *requirements* (rules and regulations). Nearly all organizations include the entire scale, but different companies may vary widely in their relative *emphasis* upon various parts of the scale. At the less specific end of the scale, there is more freedom but less certainty, and the reverse is true of the more specific end. Knowing where a particular organization stands on the scale is thus important in understanding how it functions.

Furthermore, there is wide variability between organizational units (e.g., research division versus accounting department) in the reliance placed upon or the attention paid to the policy structure.

### Control Structures

The control structures involve behaviors directed toward keeping running records upon key aspects of task performance versus planned cost, time, and other specifications (or milestones) and initiating corrective action when actual variances exceed preset standards. Another important subset of control structures monitor an organization's finances.

Auditing is a control function of a somewhat different kind, although the general control system elements in Figure 4 still apply. However, the "plan" and "standards" refer more to adherence and compliance with policies, procedures, rules, and regulations than with performance against the current plan. Thus, the variances from "standards" refer often to the validity of critically important financial and performance *reports*, which higher levels of management utilize in their decision making. How valid are the financial statements and operating reports (e.g., for various products, projects, profit centers: percent complete, accrued costs and manhours, costs per man-hour, goods in process valuation, resources committed for subcontracting, overhead ratios, etc.)? Organizational "slack"—actually budgeted by *un*needed funds, schedule, or manpower—are usually invisibly buried in reports.

The larger and more complex the organization, the farther top and middle managers are isolated from the concrete data as well as the implications and impact of their own behaviors. Their reliance is more highly upon summarizations that have been subject to various categorizations, aggregations, allocations, adjustments, and distributions. Even when the reporting *procedures* are "appropriate" and have been "validly" performed, the management information system (MIS) may inadequately reflect the present organizational status in a fashion that is necessary or timely enough for a planning basis.

Separate information systems may reflect the current situation in terms of different variables (e.g., different "cuts" at categorizing, aggregating, adjusting, allocating, and distributing and even acquiring the

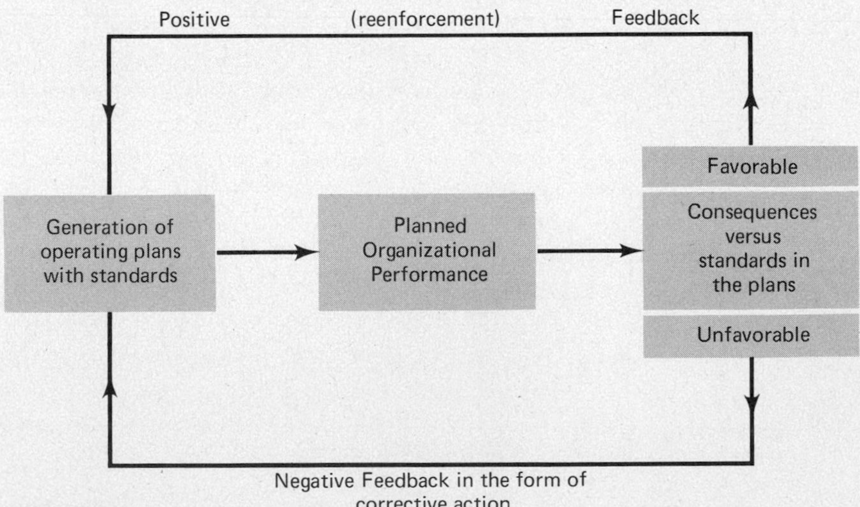


**Figure 4** Basic Elements of All Control Structures

basic data) or kinds of variables (e.g., various trends, ratios, and projected planning parameters).

An organizational system is influenced by the *manner* in which its members control, audit, and report its condition, because the organizational entities involved are affected by real or expected reactions and responses to information purported to represent their plans, condition, and performance. Distortions, obfuscations, and other "adaptations," both intentional and unintentional, are virtually inescapable to some degree. Those "Sherlocks" involved with control structures had better be unusually competent, skeptical, compassionate, and discreet, especially with regard to the psychological and social behavioral processes surrounding this sensitive area.

### Additional Ancillary Structures

In addition to or in place of the structures we have mentioned, some organizations may have different *types* of structures. For example, a committee structure may replace staffs in a way and may embody some of the aspects of decision centers, control, policy, and objectives structures. Additionally, they may strongly influence both formal and informal communications and authority structures. As another example, computerization of a management information system may unambiguously define an organization's formal authority and formal communications structures in terms of access to MIS; informal authority and communications structures are no doubt additionally affected.

## ORGANIZATIONAL SYSTEM AREAS AND LEVELS

This "map" identifies distinctly different system locales or domains of primary responsibility. It applies equally well, incidentally, to any of the three entities we have earlier mentioned; namely, individuals, groups, and organizational units. The fundamental idea is that any system or organizational entity can be viewed as existing in an *external* environment, which is one of the system *areas* of concern. The system has inputs from the environment that cross or "span" the system input *boundaries*, and it also sends outputs into the environment through a *boundary area* of a second, output, type. Finally, it has an *internal* area that is contained entirely within the system itself. This is often referred to as the throughput" or "processing" area. These three areas (external, boundary, and internal) comprise one dimension of the two-way map.

The second dimension of the map consists of the top, middle, and lower "levels" of a system or organizational unit. First, we can say that members functioning at top levels of an organization are generally held

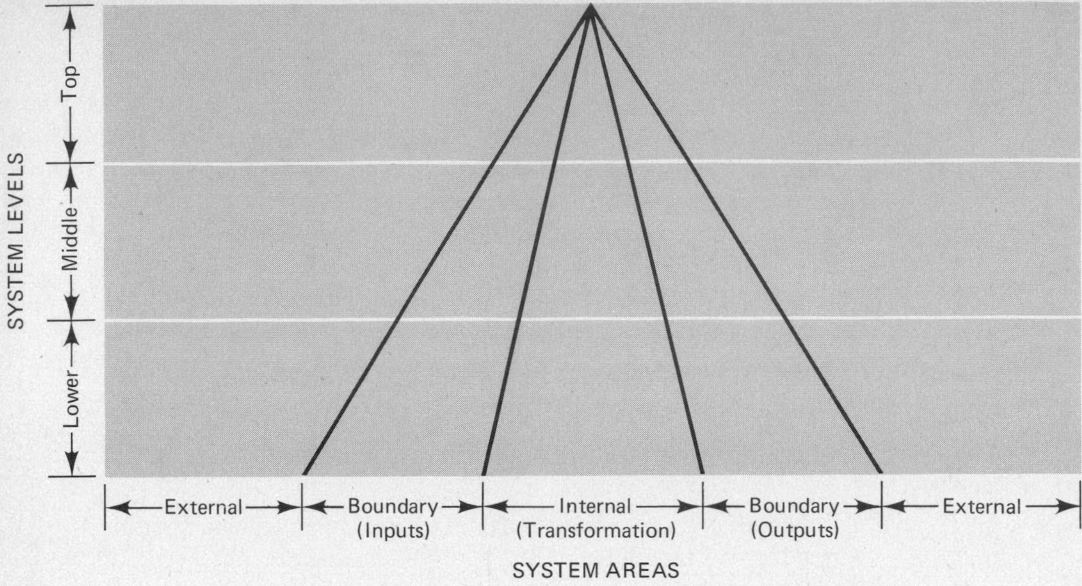


**Figure 5** Generalized Two-Way Map of System Areas and Levels

most responsible for keeping watch over the external environment, especially for longer-term implications of importance to the organization. Members at middle levels in the organization are concerned primarily with the system input and output boundary arrangements ultimately involving informational, financial, and physical flows. The initial arrangements are legal and informational for the most part (e.g., the creation of purchase orders for supplies and material, the arrangements for distributing, advertising, and marketing the products). Members at the lower levels in the organization are concerned with the internal processing that accepts and then converts inputs into marketable outputs.

In some organizations, of course, the inputs are primarily informational and the conversion process operates upon information and then sends it out in a different form. In small organizations, many of these system levels and areas are handled by the same persons or groups. See Figure 6 for some of the implications of the "levels" dimension in the typology.

## STRUCTURAL FORMS

Empirical research has indicated that organizational units often reach equilibrium states with respect to large numbers of observable

| System Focal Characteristics | System Levels Higher | Lower |
|---|---|---|
| Planning horizon | Longer-term | Shorter-term |
| Content of behaviors | More abstract | More concrete |
| Nature of inputs & outputs | More informational | More physical (matter/energy) |
| Organizational functions | Building & maintenance | Task performance |
| Critical assessments | Managerial decision-making | Technical problem-solving |
| System areas of concern | All, especially external & boundary | Especially internal & boundary |

**Figure 6** Focal Characteristics By System Level

variables.[10] These variables may be related to the various kinds of organizational structures that have been discussed early in this chapter. Table 2 summarizes many of these findings.

Of great importance is the fact that different organizations and/or organizational subunits at different areas and levels may vary with respect to the detailed configuration of interrelationships within a given structure. These configurations may take one of several structural forms (e.g., in a communications structure, information may flow primarily from the top downward, in contrast to another in which information flows omnidirectionally).

Stable or equilibrium forms have been identified for most of the basic and ancillary types of structures we have mentioned. Furthermore, a predominance of one form in one type of structure does often tend to spill over into the other basic and ancillary structures at the same system area and level as well. This provides us with a powerful additional method for checking out hypotheses through the Sherlock Process that were gained with respect to one structure (e.g., communications) and then can be cross-checked against another (e.g., authority).

It should be noted that the same structural form may not permeate an entire organization, however. Thus, we also mapped three major systems areas and levels. Together these few observable variables (structural form, location in the two-way map of system area and level) comprise a concise description of an organizational unit. We can locate it within the total organization and infer or hypothesize an immense amount of im-

[10]Rensis Likert, *The Human Organization* (New York: McGraw-Hill Book Co., 1967).

**Table 2 Characteristics of Structural Forms***

| *Pure Hierarchical Form* | *Complex or Mixed Form* | *Nonhierarchical or Participative Form* |
|---|---|---|
| *1. Kinds of attitudes developed toward organization and its goals:* | | |
| Attitudes usually are hostile and counter to organization's goals. | Attitudes are occasionally hostile and counter to organization's goals, but usually support the behavior necessary to achieve them. | Attitudes generally are strongly favorable and provide powerful stimulation to behavior implementing organization's goals. |
| *2. Amount of responsibility felt by each member of organization for achieving organization's goals:* | | |
| High levels of management feel responsibility; lower levels feel less; rank and file feel little and often welcome opportunity to behave in ways to defeat organization's goals. | Managerial personnel usually feel responsibility; rank and file feel relatively little responsibility and only sometimes behave in ways to achieve the organization's goals. | Personnel feel real responsibility for organization's goals and are motivated to behave in ways to implement them. |
| *3. Subordinates' feeling of responsibility for initiating accurate upward communication:* | | |
| None at all. | Relatively little to moderate. Usually communicates "filtered" information but only when requested. May "yes" the boss. | Considerable responsibility felt and much initiative. Group communicates all relevant information. |
| *4. Sideward communication, its adequacy and accuracy:* | | |
| Usually poor because of competition between peers and corresponding hostility. | Fairly poor when there is competition between peers. Otherwise, fair to good. | Good to excellent. |
| *5. Psychological closeness of superiors to subordinates (i.e., how well does superior know and understand problems faced by subordinates?): Accuracy of perceptions by superiors and subordinates:* | | |
| Often in error. | Sometimes moderately accurate, but with frequent error not unusual. | Usually quite accurate. |

**Table 2 Characteristics of Structural Forms (continued)**

| *Pure Hierarchical Form* | *Complex or Mixed Form* | *Nonhierarchical or Participative Form* |
|---|---|---|
| *6. Extent to which an adequate structure exists for the flow of information from one part of the organization to another, thereby enabling influence to be exerted:* | | |
| Downward only. | Almost entirely to very largely downward, but small to moderate capacity for upward and between peers. | Capacity for information to flow in all directions from all levels and for influence to be exerted by all units on all units. |
| *7. How adequate and accurate is the information available for decision making at the place where the decisions are made?:* | | |
| Partial and often inaccurate information only is available. | Reasonably adequate and accurate information available. | Relatively complete and accurate information available based both on measurements and efficient flow of information in organization. |
| *8. To what extent do the different hierarchical levels tend to strive for high performance goals?:* | | |
| High goals pressed by top, resisted by subordinates. | High goals sought by higher levels but with some resistance by lower levels. | High goals sought by all levels, with lower levels sometimes pressing for higher goals than top level. |
| *9. At what hierarchical levels in organization does major or primary concern exist with regard to the performance of the control function?:* | | |
| At the very top only. | Largely at the top, but some shared feeling of responsibility felt at middle and to a lesser extent at lower levels. | Concern for performance of control function likely to be felt throughout organization. |
| *10. Excessive absence and turnover:* | | |
| Tends to be high when people are free to move. | Moderately high when people are free to move. | Low. |

* Adapted from Rensis Likert, *The Human Organization.*

portant information about the unit in relatively brief and unambiguous terms. We now turn to the various structural forms.

For our purposes we will consider three basic structural forms. The first is a pure *hierarchical form*, the second is a *complex* or *mixed form*, and the third is a *nonhierarchical form* or, as it is sometimes called, a *participative group form*. These are illustrated in Figure 8.

In the pure hierarchical form, authority is absolutely delineated vertically such that there is strict adherence to the principle of unity of command (see p. 243); communications follow this same pattern, being mostly downward through the hierarchy; and the major organizational subunits are fairly independent of one another so that work-flow structures do not often involve crossing suborganizational boundaries. In the second structural form—the complex or mixed form—the hierarchy is still quite evident. However, there are staff units, advisory units, consultative units, and relationships; a great deal of liaison is required for coordination of the entire organization. In the third structural form—participative group—we see that within each group little hierarchy is apparent, communications are between all members of the group, and the leader of the group simultaneously belongs to another group and thereby provides linkage with task functions carried out by other working units. When carried to its logical extreme, this form of organization is considered to be highly "organic."

It is generally believed that structural forms of the pure hierarchical type are most efficient in situations requiring few and slight changes. The complex or mixed structural form and participative group structural form increasingly provide capability for rapid change internally to adapt to changing external and/or internal environments.[11]

Similarly, organizational system areas and levels most directly affected by more rapidly changing environments are more likely to take on mixed, complex, or participative group structural forms. On the other hand, organizational system areas and levels that are more protected from external change tend toward the hierarchical in their structural forms. The dimensions described in Table 2 can be employed as a guide for observation and discussion with organization members in the Sherlock Process of grasping and understanding the interrelated parts of an organizational unit.

By describing a concrete organizational unit in system areas and levels of the typology, one can anticipate and later "objectively" verify many of its situational or behavioral characteristics. Consider two firms A and B; firm A's administrative services department is *internal* and at a *lower* level while firm B's is *internal* and at a *middle* level in the total organization. We would expect the administration services department's

[11]Refer to F. E. Emery and E. L. Trist, "The Causal Texture of Organizational Environments," *Human Relations*, XVIII, No. 1 (1965), and William H. McWhinney, "Organizational Form, Decision Modalities and the Environment," *Human Relations*, XXI, No. 3 (1968) for detailed discussion of organization-environment relationships.

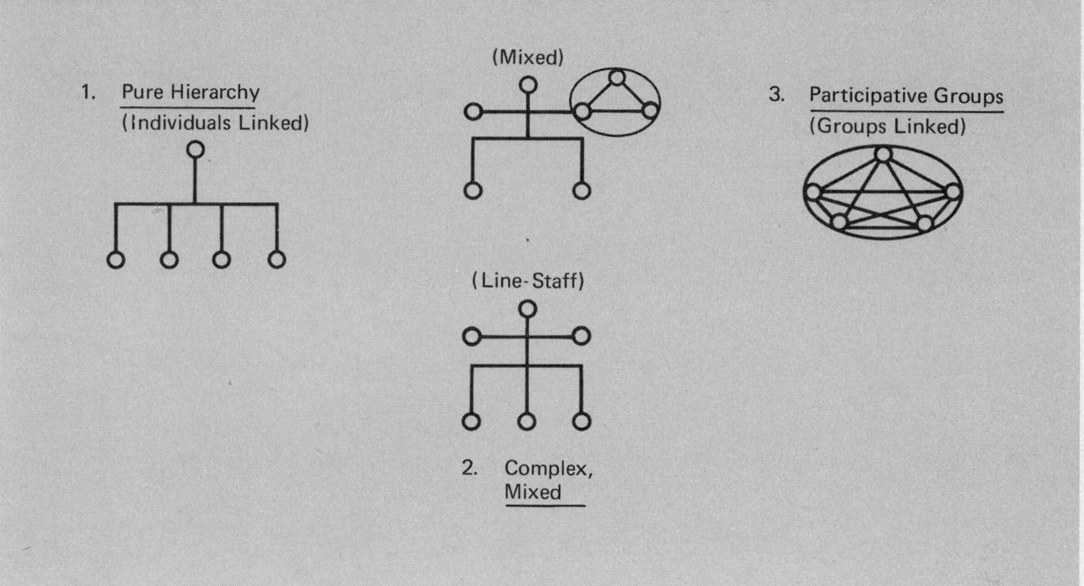


**Figure 8** Three "Structural Forms"

tasks in firm A to be relatively standardized and routinely carried out according to preset plans and policies. But, because of its "higher" level, we might wonder if administrative services in firm B might extend into managerial realms such as facilities planning; perhaps routine details may be left for operating divisions to handle *on their own*. Additionally, we know that both departments, being *internal*, are relatively more protected (sometimes termed "buffered") from frequent and direct contact with the organization's environment. Therefore, changes due to unpredictabilities and ambiguities in the environment are less likely to interfere directly with both of these internal department's activities than with departments in boundary areas; moreover firm A's department, in comparison with firm B's, would be more "buffered."

As you no doubt recognize, the structural form has a tremendous effect upon the kind of behaviors that occur within these richly ordered organizational fields. And, when considered in combination with the two-way map of system areas and levels, these structural forms provide a very comprehensive representation of an entire organization.

## SUMMARY

In this chapter we have gained a familiarity with the structural building blocks applicable to the organizational level of analysis. First, the *basic structures* (authority and task and decision-centers) and the *ancillary structures* (objectives, communications, policy, and control) were examined as alternative overlays or filters useful for highlighting important types of behavioral patternings. Additionally, a two-way generalized "mapping" of any organizational system's *areas* and *levels* along with their behavioral implications is provided as an integrative conceptual framework for understanding behavior in larger organizations. Finally, three basic *structural forms* (pure hierarchical, complex or mixed, and nonhierarchical or participative group) were suggested as guides for diagnosing current equilibrium states that include many variables. These summarized structural forms can apply to different organizational structures.

The next chapter addresses some of the dynamics of behaviors in organizations that repeatedly appear as observable major stages of initial formation, stabilization, and either adaptation or decline.

CHAPTER 12

# Social System Development and Change

This chapter discusses the creation and initial development of organizations through various stages as well as major changes demanded or offered by critical internal and/or external "environmental" conditions. All social system entities (e.g., individuals, groups, and larger organizational units) develop and change continuously. As some social system entities mature, others are already relatively stabilized, and still others are faced with either an impetus for change toward revitalization or disintegration. Each stage involves new problems to be resolved and opportunities for learning and growth.

When you enter any group or organization, it is useful to identify its current stages of development, and further, to understand how the related basic issues are being handled. Looking for such data will help you to recognize and diagnose the social system's problems and how explicitly and effectively they are being handled. This kind of diagnosis may also suggest actions you might wish to take to influence the system.

## FORMATION AND INITIAL DEVELOPMENT

Newly started social systems, whether small groups or complex organizations, face several simultaneous issues. Usually one of these is

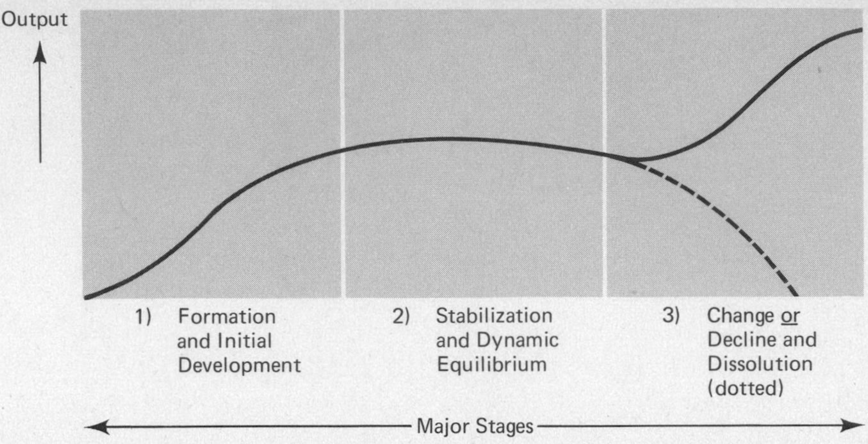


**Figure 1** Major States of Social Systems' Development and Change

*manifestly* prominent at any given time while the others are *latent* determinants of behavior.[1] How effectively these issues are resolved during formation and initial development greatly influences the later structuring, climate, and effectiveness of the social system. The four initially important issues confronting new social systems are: membership (inclusion), dominance, intimacy, and task.

MEMBERSHIP. The first issue deals with inclusion or membership. For an individual this means that he wants to start his own organization or he knows something about the larger system he is about to join. The latter case concerns his acceptability within it, and his ultimate decision of whether or not he wishes to be included. He wants to know how his contribution will fit and how he will benefit from participation. For a small group, this issue deals with the question of who shall and shall not be included as members. For the larger organizational units the issue is whether or not individual qualifications correspond to organizational needs, keeping in mind how to divide the members into potentially effective suborganizational units and groups.

DOMINANCE. The issue of dominance, control, and authority for the individual has to do with how dependent or independent he will be within a group and to what degree he wants and anticipates that he can influence other members. One aspect of this issue is that of formal and informal leadership, both of which are often weak or ambiguous at the outset. This issue is often never resolved thoroughly, and the maneuvering for leader-

[1]By "manifest" we refer to the content of human communications taken at face value; by "latent" we refer to simultaneous but hidden meanings or implications of the manifest communications, either consciously or unconsciously intended.

ship positions can be highly subtle and indirect. Sometimes these issues are easily resolved, while in other cases, the issue festers and impedes progress in the major and substages of development. For the group this issue involves the degrees of freedom or restriction, independence or dependence, that the group members will experience as part of a subunit of the larger organization. For the larger organization the issue takes a form of the development of the authority structure or hierarchy within the organization.

INTIMACY. The third issue, that of intimacy, interpersonal closeness, and trust, concerns the feeling tone of the system. Depending upon emotional and cognitive styles, some individuals will have strong likes and/or dislikes relating to this issue. They want to know how close others in the group may feel or appear to feel, how close they themselves feel, and whether or not that level is comfortable. For the small group this issue is dealt with by the individual members and results in the group's general atmosphere. For the larger organization the issue of intimacy goes into the creation of important aspects of organizational character or climate, especially of trust, which, in turn, influences the cooperativeness and competition between units. Resolutions of intimacy issues also extend to formality, protocol, and policies. For example, people in some organizations use first names regardless of level.

TASK. The fourth issue is that of required task. For the individual this involves whether or not the social system's task or objectives can be aligned with his interests and qualifications. For the small group the task reflects the goals for which its members are selected or initially join together to achieve. Also, the ability of a group to accomplish its tasks effectively influences its ability to cope with its environment and satisfy its own member needs. At the level of the organization the task dimension becomes complexly defined in a task structure, which includes the administration of changes, plans for the use and productivity of resources, and the ultimate ability of the organization to perform, with respect to productivity, satisfaction, and revitalization.

## Interaction of Task and Social Issues

The members of newly formed social-systems must cope with both the ultimate task and the building of new structures that bring order to key social process-related issues. The task issues include the definition of problems and approaches, the assessment of resources, and the determination of what work is to be done and who will do it. The social issues, which often are of more immediate but undisclosed or latent concern to the membership, include determining how they and others fit together, what formal hierarchical positions persons will be filling, who will be the

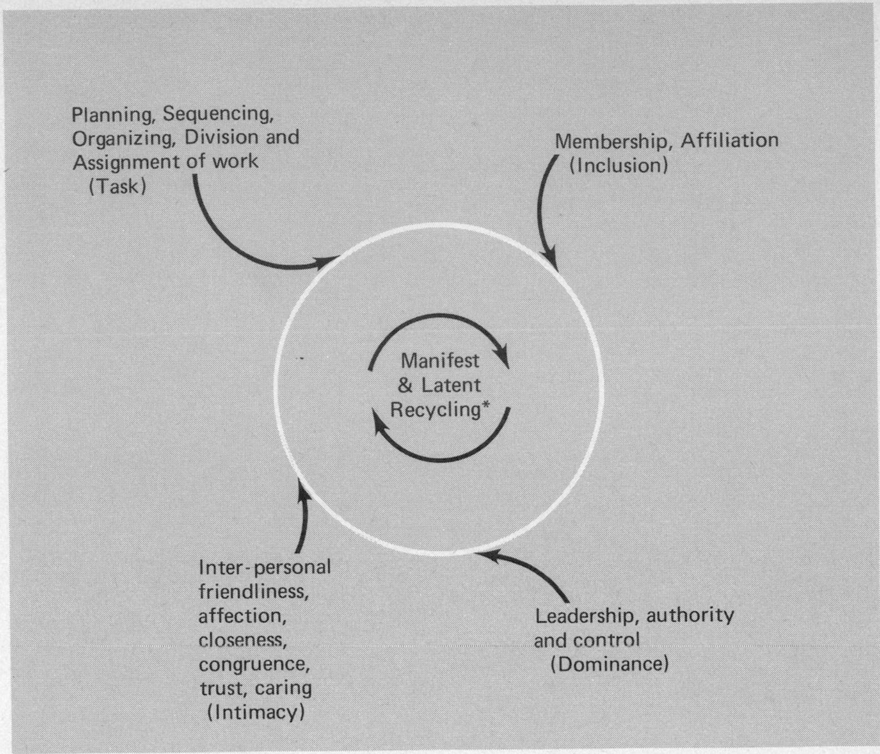


*"Manifest" refers to the literal content or subject of inter-personal communications. "Latent" refers to the simultaneous implicit process issues for which the manifest content always has some implications.

**Figure 2** Four Subphases of Formation and Initial Development

informal leaders, and a tentative assessment of the value of closeness, involvement, and participation for each member (see Figure 2).[2]

As this initial development progresses, there is continued clarification of member roles and the rapid emergence of norms, communications, and interaction patterns. Individuals continue to assess the psychological and interpersonal value of the social system to them. These assessments begin to take on more consistency as the possibilities are narrowed toward probabilities and predictabilities. In turn, they influence the attitudes and motivations of individual members.

Task performance usually receives rapidly increasing focus from system members. As they begin to understand how the initial ambiguities in the larger social system are becoming structuralized, they turn their attention more fully to the work to be done. Economic resources all flow

[2]For richly detailed theory and examples of the latent and manifest phases and counterphases of development, see W. G. Bennis and H. A. Shepard, "A Theory of Group Development," *Human Relations*, IX, No. 4 (1956), and W. R. Bion, *Experiences in Groups* (London: Tavistock Publications, 1961).

outward until some productive output has begun. Probably too little manifest consideration is afforded the social process issues of membership, dominance, and intimacy. The negative consequences, if such omissions occur, may be hidden for years. They remain hidden because substitute activities compensate for the omissions. For example, elaborate control procedures may be established in organizations in which issues of trust remain unsolved.

### Oversights in Social System Formation

The success of the system, of course, is largely a function of how well these task concerns are resolved. However, their resolution is dependent upon prior resolutions of the underlying social process issues. Common mistakes or oversights in this initial stage include the failure to acquire or utilize member sentiments concerning all four issues which ultimately becomes reflected in an inability to develop adequate plans or sufficient alternatives for accomplishing or revising objectives.

Plans often emerge in the form of indefinite verbal statements about things that must be considered. Systematic, detailed planning is often not done. Thus the social system encounters problems in later stages that might otherwise have been avoided. This is especially true about organizational planning itself. Organizations seldom begin or exist in the sequential order or with the neatness that theories about them might suggest. In fact, one piece of extensive research indicated that in many organizations little or no conscious planning of organizational structure was done in advance. Instead, they tended to formalize relationships that were emergent,[3] often creating unconscious norms which later constrained the groups. Yet some theoretical ways of thinking are useful because they help simplify the complex reality to which they apply, and this helps both in better understanding the whole and in knowing what factors can be altered in attempting to bring about change. Besides, many people believe that organizations *should be* as theory prescribes, and thus their behavior and thinking are affected accordingly. Thus, some familiarity with some of the conventional terms and theories relating to organization is useful in understanding and communicating with others.

A second common mistake is quickly developing an alternative without considering several others. Time and ambiguity pressures, expressed as member impatience, often cause the leader and/or members excessively to "satisfice"; i.e., accept a seemingly satisfactory but not optimal or maximized alternative that might have better been compared with several carefully considered alternatives. Once a social system has established procedures, they may be accepted by members too uncritically (or they

[3]Joan Woodward, *Industrial Organization: Theory and Practice* (London: Oxford University Press, 1965), p. 75.

may even be ignored). Established procedures do furnish comfort, but sometimes also lead to complacency without even a provision for periodic critical review.

## STABILITY

Social systems operating in the second major stage of development encounter continuing task- and social process-related problems. The former include problems of more efficient resource allocation, upgrading and balancing people qualifications, assignments, and commitment; suitable improvements in technology, management, organization; and constant environmental monitoring, assessment, and adjustment. Social patterns are normally well-established by this second major stage, but continuing residual and also newly emerging problems of inclusion (losing members through attrition, transfering members, absorbing new members), dominance (control, promotion), and intimacy (liking, friendliness, and trust) all continue.

Recall the feedback mechanisms that carry minor adjustments and changes back into the flow of the Social System Conceptual Scheme, (pp. 92–93) and also recall the dynamics of interpersonal relationships. Both of these tend to reach equilibrium conditions (interaction, sentiments, congruence). Thus in this second major stage, there is a continual process of minor changes feeding back into adjustments that become new requirements. There is an overall stabilization and/or consolidation consisting of many minor incremental changes and adjustments. These comprise a dynamic equilibrium both internally between units and externally with suppliers, competitors, markets, and various regulatory agencies of local, state, and federal governments. This stage may predominate during a period of gradual sales and/or profit growth and expansion, or a period of relative placidity or gradual erosion.

Because we are discussing dynamic equilibrium between social systems and their environments, we pause for a more thorough examination of social system definition and the characteristics of their environments.

### System Definition

It may still come as a surprise to some that all system definition is an abstract, arbitrary, and human endeavor, albeit of great usefulness. The systems of interest to us are *dynamic and changing*; they are usually referred to as open systems as opposed to closed systems. Open systems normally receive inputs from and give outputs to their environments. Thus, they both influence and are influenced by their environments in both predictable and unpredictable ways. For this reason it is very important that we regularly define, scan, and monitor the system, its boundaries, inputs, outputs, and environments. The definition of a system also denotes its *boundaries and environment*. The definition might include concepts of things, space, and degrees of relevance. Some environmental factors are immediate, others intermediate or remote; some are relevant and others are nonrelevant as indicated in Table 8, Chapter 1. Distinguishing between these different types of environmental elements and variables helps us to simplify and reduce the task involved in a systems analysis. Figure 3 illustrates the important fact that different levels of organizational entities become partial environments for lower-level entities, while Figure 4 illustrates some implications of alternative systems definitions.

These alternative types of systems definitions are primarily concerned with the different inputs and outputs involved, as well as the different vulnerabilities to system openness (see Figure 4). Of great importance in social systems is the fact that in addition to external openness they are subject to or vulnerable to an internal openness.

The purpose of this review and elaboration of the human act of systems definition has been to add clarity to alternative options available, and to their important implications. System parts, boundaries, inputs,

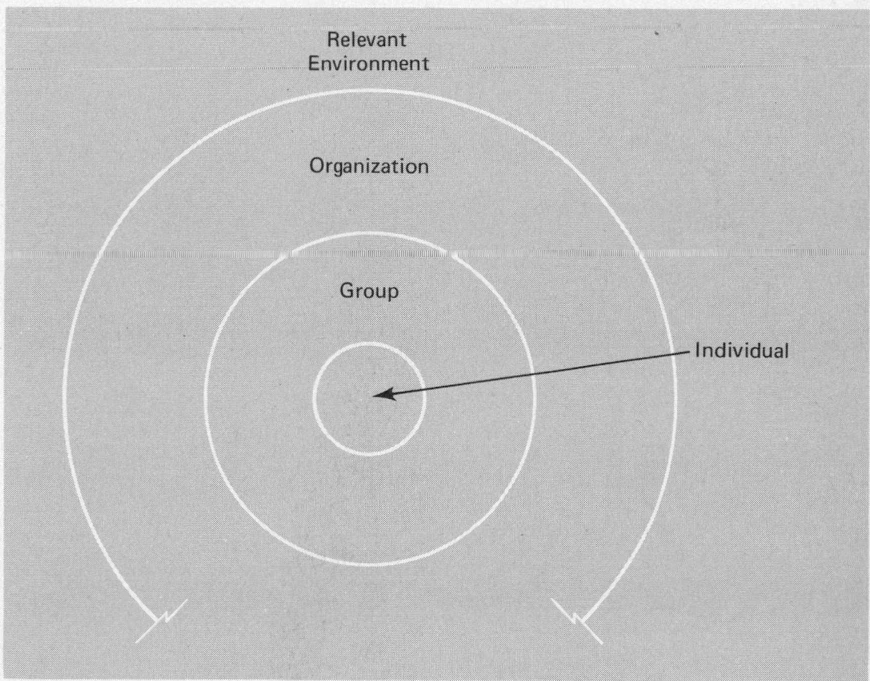


**Figure 3** Higher-Level Social System Entities Provide Partial Environments for Imbedded Lower-Level Social System Entities

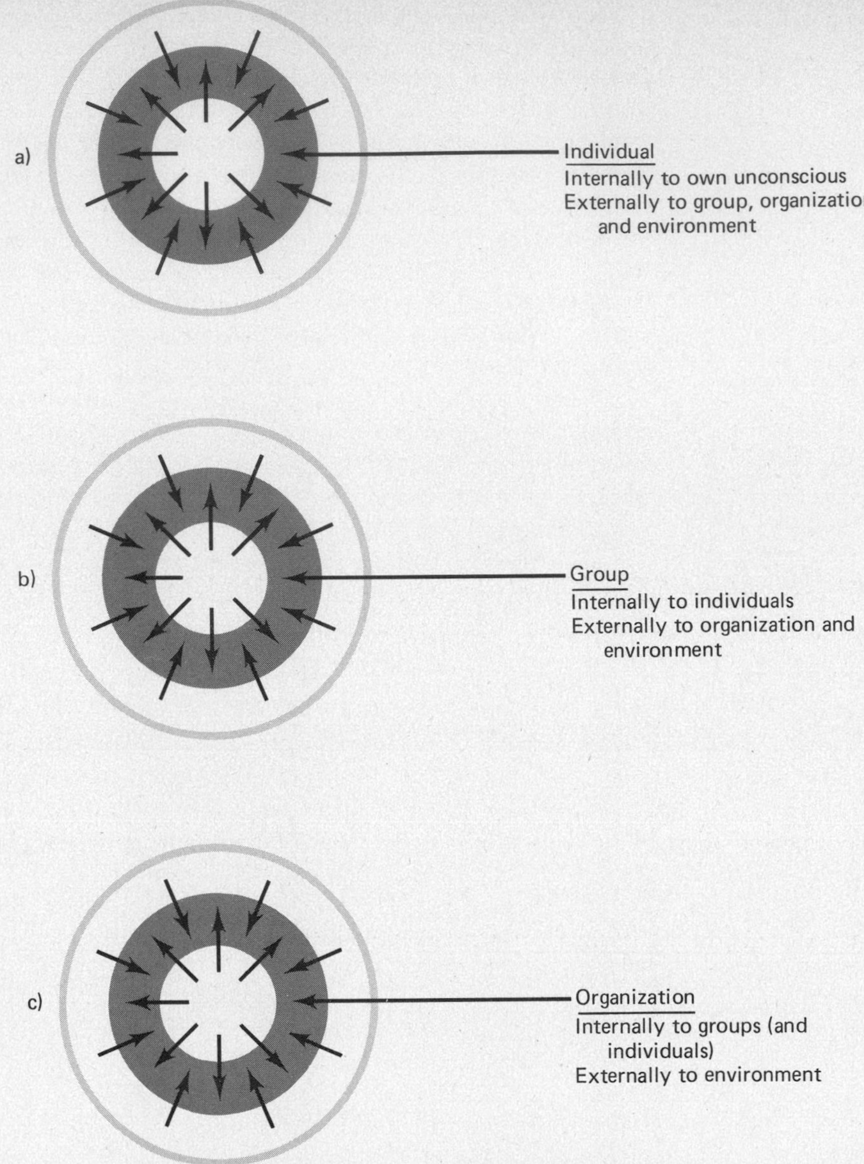


**Figure 4** System Openness, Internal and External

outputs, and internal and external environments are all affected by one's choices of systems definitions. In general, it appears best for managers to define their systems and subsystems such that authority can be most clearly delegated to persons accountable for their own performance. "Cost center" approaches in accounting and "points of strategic control" in management principles reflect this basic idea.

## Environmental Characteristics

Organizational and social environments can be characterized along a virtually unlimited number of dimensions. We have selected two important ones that are helpful in assessing the importance and impact of environments upon particular social systems. The first dimension ranges from "supportive" through "hostility" and the second, which we call *contingency-severity*, ranges from certainty through turbulence.

For the larger organization, elements of competition, consumer demand, technology, law, and social values all indicate aspects of the complexity making up the nature of the social systems environment along both of these dimensions.[4]

CONTINGENCY-SEVERITY. Social systems encounter different types of environments. Some are relatively calm and stable, others are turbulent. *Contingency-severity* is a concept that designates the level of ambiguity, unidentifiability, and volatility of elements in a system's *relevant* environment. The more unstable and uncertain the environment, the more quickly must an organization be able to respond and adapt to unanticipated events. The nature of the environment encountered by a particular organization influences the type of organization structure and processes appropriate for it in responding to unanticipated events.

Now we consider four levels of *contingency-severity*. They are certainty, risk, uncertainty, and turbulence. Level one describes environmental elements for which relevance to the social system is known and their presence or absence can be observed or measured and predicted with a high degree of certainty. If comprised overwhelmingly with elements of this type, this would be a placid, stable environment subject to little unexpected change. At an individual level of analysis, this might describe the environment facing a high school graduate pondering career decisions. He might know that a college education either would or would not help him, and that if he went through certain steps in education and experience it would be highly probable that he would be able to achieve certain career objectives. For an organization, a level one environment is one in which most or all of the important variables for success are known,

[4] Our first environmental dimension closely resembles the relatively subjective "enhancing-threatening" dimension employed in an intergroup differential analysis, while contingency-severity, the second dimension, deals primarily with ambiguity or unpredictability of elements in the environment. Contingency-severity has both objective and subjective aspects; the objective-subjective mix depends in part upon the knowledge and psychological makeup of the estimator. It has been popular to employ more objective characteristics for describing the environment such as technology or industry in the work of Joan Woodward, Lawrence and Lorsch, A. K. Rice, Eric L. Trist, and J. D. Thompson. Of course, *contingency-severity* may also be related to "technology" and to "industry" with any desired degree of precision.

the technology is known and stable, just as are the customers and competitors. Clearly, such an environment approaches an ideal seldom experienced by either individuals or organizations today.

Level two environments include many elements of risk. Although the relevant variables are known, they cannot be predicted with certainty. The individual facing a career decision can make an estimate of probability of certain events happening, but he knows that he runs certain risks in making his decision. For example, he might assume that society will probably need teachers when he graduates, but because of population trends, other people's decisions, economics, and social values, he cannot know this with certainty. However, he knows enough about each variable to make reasonable predictions. An organization can do likewise. Its members can assume that it will succeed, but they do not know with certainty what competitors or consumers will do. Thus it is possible to develop a product—say an automobile called the Edsel—that has a high probability of succeeding, but because of the vagaries of consumer tastes and competitor tactics and strategy, it may fail. The essence of level two is that one can only make reasonable statements of probability about the future, and some risk is encountered that the statements may be inaccurate.

Level three environments include large quantities of elements of uncertainty, which are more "severe" than mere risk. They are more severe because some of the relevant *probabilities* cannot be calculated with reasonable certainty—although the relevant variables are known, they are unpredictable. The individual making his career decision in such an environment may have no way of knowing or measuring how many people are likely to be competing for jobs in his area, even though he knows this is a relevant variable. Thus, he cannot calculate a very relevant probability. Similarly, a business organization may know that competition, product design, and consumer income are all important variables, but may not be able to calculate the relevant probabilities connected with each. Further, competitors will be developing new products, marketing approaches, and other strategies that make probability calculation hazardous, if not impossible. A key source of uncertainty in predominantly level three environments is the behavior of others, especially in response or reaction to one's own behaviors. The now highly developed field of mathematical gaming under conditions of cooperation and competition are useful in developing strategies at this level of contingency-severity. Bargaining and negotiating are also appropriate behaviors.[5]

Level four environments are the most difficult. They involve turbulence, which means that the relevant variables for your survival are not even known! For example, the career-deciding individual often has no way of knowing what will be relevant skills when he completes his edu-

[5]Paul E. Torgerson and Irwin T. Weinstock, *Management: An Integrated Approach* (Englewood Cliffs, N.J.: Prentice-Hall, Inc., 1972), Chapter 4.

cation and training (contingencies of war, political disruption, and technological obsolescence may intervene). The business organization may suddenly encounter a whole new and unforeseen technology that replaces its own, thus making its products and production approaches obsolete. Turbulence connotes such changes coming from the external environment itself, like a lightning bolt out of the blue. They tend to be inherently unpredictable from systems boundary or internal systems areas employing conventional means of organizational intelligence or market surveillance and research. It has been proposed that new informational relationships between organizations, universities, think tanks, and governments may be necessary eventually to reduce turbulence. The sources may be technological, legislative, or competitive, to mention a few. The impact can be shattering, and individuals and organizations that survive in such environments are able to adapt and change quickly and effectively.[6]

People and organizations in our society today seldom experience a predominantly level one environment. Most encounter predominantly either a level two or three contingency-severity. Some concerned practitioners and students of this question predict that there is a distinct trend in the world toward contingency-severity level four. Some individuals in organizations believe they have already encountered such environments.

## Behavior within Stable Organizations

Each group member continues to assess the relative benefits and costs of group membership to him personally, giving a certain amount of physical and psychic energy and commitment to the group, and in return expecting an appropriate amount of "income" or satisfaction. This concept is sometimes referred to as the *norm of reciprocity* or *social exchange.*

Furthermore, each member tends to evaluate his "return" not only in terms of his costs in the group but also in terms of a *social-comparison* process with other groups and activities. If the returns to some others appear too great, feelings of tension and discontent are likely to ensue. This reaction relates to what has been termed an expectation or "cultural ought" of *distributive justice.* It is not necessary that all returns be equal, but it is important that they be sufficiently fair in the perceptions of the group members. Those who contribute the most "should" receive proportionately the most.

If one (or more) member is dissatisfied with his return or the fairness of others' returns, he may seek to make an adjustment by varying his

[6]See Stanley Young, *Management: A Systems Analysis* (Glenview, Illinois: Scott, Foresman and Co., 1966), p. 52; P. A. Raynolds, "Developing Managerial Capabilities for Coping with Turbulent Environments," *Proceedings of the Academy of Management*, 31st Annual Meeting (1971); Harold L. Wilensky, *Organizational Intelligence: Knowledge and Policy in Government and Industry* (New York: Basic Books Inc., 1967).

own inputs, possibly after some negotiation. He may decrease them to correspond more closely with what he perceives as his return, or he may increase them even more with the expectation that the return will increase to a level more in line with his input. A common problem is to strive to maintain a reasonably equitable distribution of benefits and to help individual members achieve the satisfaction they seek. A measure of the degree of success the leadership of a social system has attained in achieving dynamic equilibrium with its internal environment would be reflected in goal alignments of type (A), Figure 5.

However, members behave manifestly so as to appear to be aligned in state A, while in reality (consciously and/or unconsciously) they are in one of the unaligned (B) states. Symptoms of the latter cases would include any structural breakdowns especially increasing departures of actual performance from plans, which trigger negative (corrective) *control* feedback adjustments in the system. However, impaired performance may also result from poorly detailed plans, perhaps because of an unrealistic, distorted, and/or inadequate understanding of the external environment's *contingency-severity* and/or *degree of hostility*.

## Contingency Theories

The external environment's contingency-severity and degree of supportiveness or hostility strongly influence the nature of the dynamic external equilibrium a social system may achieve. Furthermore, the social system's predominant internal structural forms and "climates" are crucially affected also. And these, in turn, strongly influence the social system's capacity for achieving a dynamic internal equilibrium.

Organizations confronting more severe external environmental pressures are more often found to employ mixed or complex structural forms along with nonhierarchical participative group structural forms. Organizations confronting less severe external contingencies are more likely to employ pure hierarchical forms or mixed structural forms that tend toward the pure hierarchical.

In summary, members of each social-system define, scan, monitor, and interpret their environment and proact and/or react, usually through a series of relatively minor adjustments. This process includes an assessment and understanding of how and to what degree the environment influences the system, and, in turn, can be determined by it. Such an understanding helps with the development of suitable short- and long-range strategies leading to objectives and policy structures that are in harmony with basic authority and task structure. When a dynamic equilibrium is achieved, the organization is usually a sort of mirror image of its immediate and relevant environment. If the leadership has been farsighted, the organization also incorporates provision for coping with its intermediate and remote but relevant environments without expending excessive resources upon the immediate but nonrelevant environment.

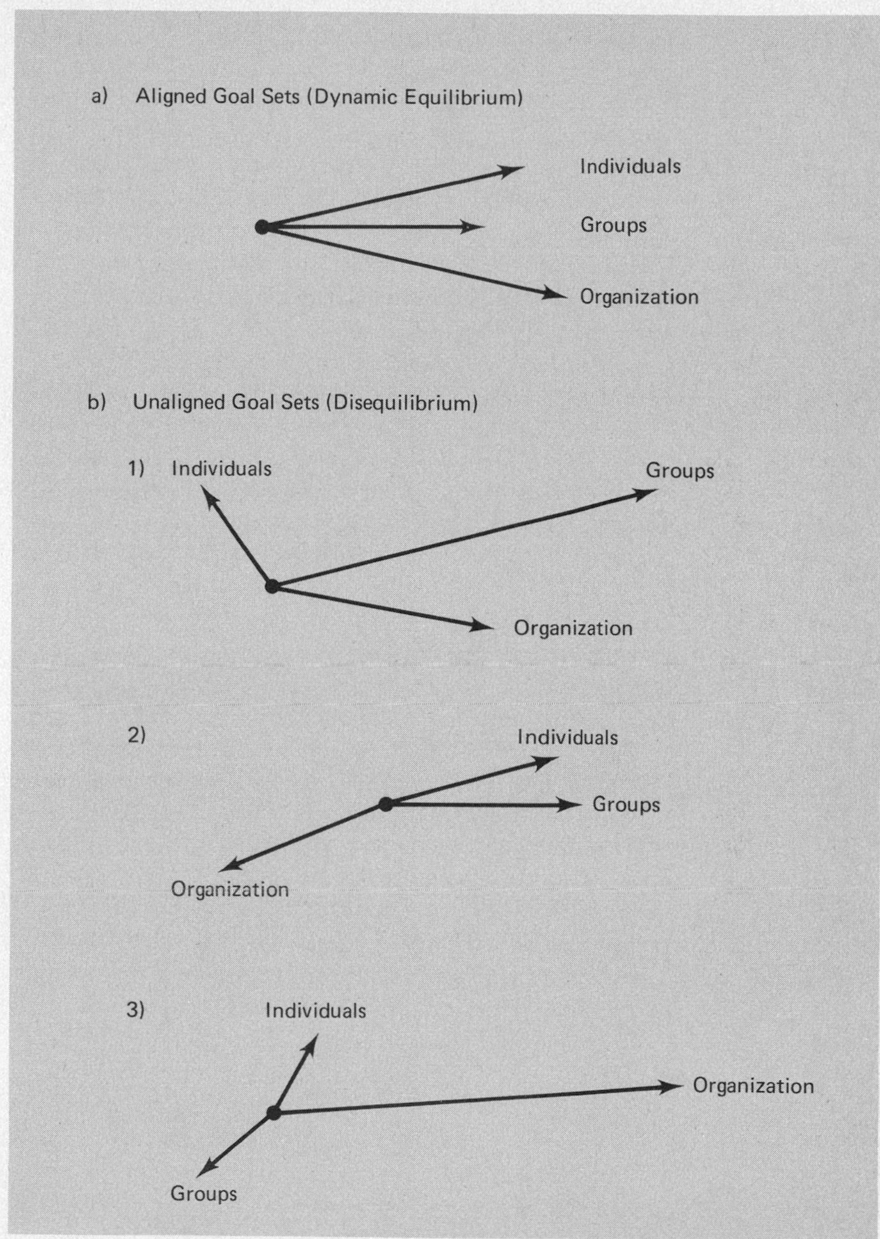


**Figure 5** Alignment of Entity Goal Sets

*Note:* Individuals, groups, and organizations are shown as sharing some "here and now" point in time, as well as vectors representing the direction and intensity of each entity's goals.

## MAJOR CHANGE OR DECLINE AND DISSOLUTION

Change is a fact of life, and all individuals and organizations are confronted by some impetus for change. We are distinguishing between relatively minor adjustments in the second major stage and substantial change in this third major stage. A social system is subject to change both from within and without. An organization may receive a strong impetus for change from the external environment (e.g., from the new class action suits filed by consumer groups, the ecology movement, the changes in international economics and trade, technological developments) and/or from the internal environment (e.g., through changes in the values, ideas, attitudes, and knowledge of its members). These two sources of vulnerability constitute the "openness" of "open systems." In this case of a major impetus for change, the response to which is always a matter of judgment, it is concluded that minor adjustments within the range of existing basic and ancillary structures are inadequate. Major change in structures and/or processes are deemed necessary.

### Responses to Change

Responses to a major impetus for change vary. Although some persons think that resistance to change is "natural," everyone seeks some change. The key is whether or not the change is perceived as being helpful, neutral, or hurtful. This is an important point, because it indicates that resistance to change is only a symptom. It only tells us that the individual or social system resisting the change perceives it as being, on balance, harmful rather than helpful. Thus, resistance *can* be viewed as a signal that further diagnosis is required rather than something automatically to be overcome. The conclusion is not shared regarding the need for a major change and all of the risks this entails.

### Resistance to Change

Resistance to change may develop for a variety of reasons. A common one is that people do not know how to change or do not understand why it is important to do so; they may perceive their relative social economic status endangered or diminished. Another reason is that an individual might feel psychologically threatened, his self-concept endangered. Another important but often overlooked reason for some resistance is that the change involved is not a good idea. Not all change is good, and some resistance can be considered as being intelligent. (Of course, the eye of the beholder determines what is good and intelligent, and it is likely that most who resist change perceive their resistance as appropriate and intelligent!)

Research and experience has indicated that resistance to change occurs often more for social process than for technical change reasons. Thus, it is important that change agents understand in depth the psychosocial aspects of a particular system so that they will know how people will be affected and perceive the contemplated change. People often resist any changes that alter their customary social and working relationships. For this reason, technical and staff personnel who are concerned with developing new approaches must be alert to considering more than just the technical or logical value of their proposed ideas. If they hope to gain successful implementation, they must also consider the important social relationship dimensions of the change.

Resistance can be countered by trying to remove the causes or reasons for it and/or by increasing the pressure for change. Which of these two general approaches to take must be determined situationally; there is no easy answer as to which is better, and a combined approach is probably to be preferred.

## Strategies to Cause Change

In developing a strategy for change, it is always useful to define clearly what is to be changed. Is it knowledge, attitudes, behavior, or entire group or organizational processes? Each of these is increasingly difficult to change, and each requires proportionately more time to consummate. In most instances, each of these four types of change requires that those preceding must be changed first.

Organizational change can be influenced by changing people, technology, or organization structure, processes, and conditions. A change in any one of these variables usually produces important changes in the others. Thus, any change should be considered from a system's viewpoint involving all structures and processes so that the *total* ramifications and impact of the desired change can be seen. Unanticipated consequences of shallowly conceived changes have wreaked havoc for many innocent organizational change agents.

The change process involves three general stages. The first is "unfreezing," or developing a willingness and readiness for change. The second is the change process itself, which involves new learning. The third is "refreezing," or the consolidating of the learning from stage two. Those trying to influence change must consider the steps to take in entering and successfully crossing each of these three stages (see Figure 6).

PARTICIPATION. One common approach of facilitating change is to encourage participation. Managers used to think it useful to invite partici-

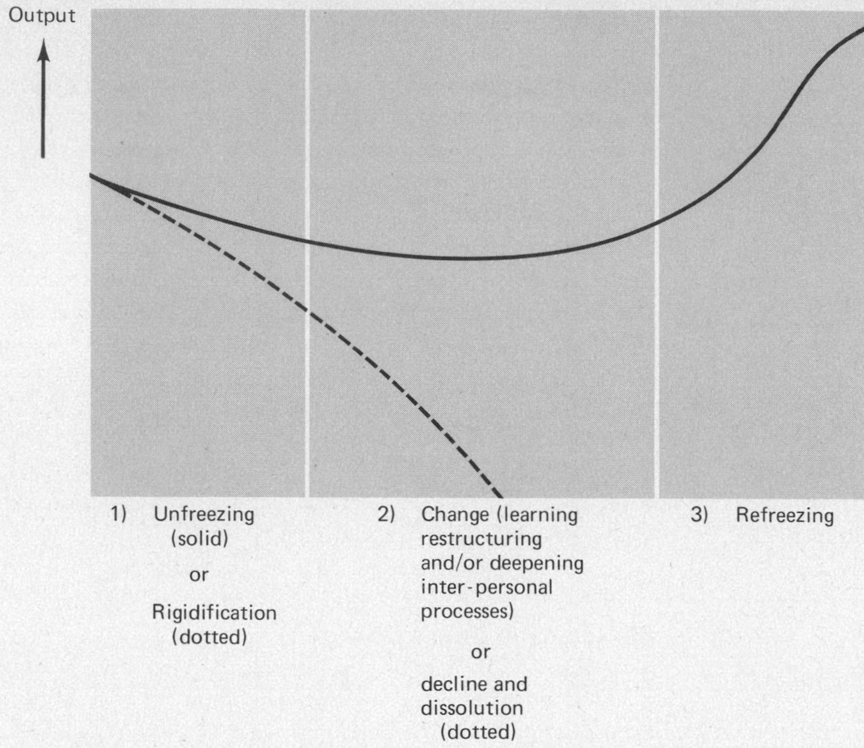


**Figure 6** Substages of the Major Change Stage (Schematic Diagram)

pation under the assumption that this would induce motivation and acceptance of change. Recently, however, managers have begun to view this differently. They invite participation to get quality ideas, and the ensuing motivation or commitment is seen as a valuable byproduct. Thus the switch has been from the emphasis on motivation to the emphasis on valuable inputs from those participating.

One risk involved in participation is that of inviting it and then rejecting the inputs of the participants. Of course, how the rejection is perceived varies with groups. For example, in a group that is used to participation and to having many of its suggested ideas accepted, it is unlikely that there will be negative feelings when one or a few ideas are not accepted. A group not used to participation, however, may feel annoyed and angry if its ideas are rejected. Thus, those inviting participation should consider carefully whether or not they really want inputs, how they would react to them, and what would be the consequences if suggested ideas are rejected. Participation can have dysfunctional as well as functional consequences for a particular group.

STRUCTURAL SURGERY. One common change strategy could be called *structural surgery*. This means the redesign of the authority, task, and other structures to accommodate changes in the external or internal environment. This approach is sometimes efficacious in localized difficulties, but it has limitations when the nature of the change requires adjusting to a deeper level of contingency-severity rather than just adapting to a configuration change in the external environment at the same contingency-severity level.

ORGANIZATIONAL DEVELOPMENT. This is a broad term that includes many approaches that are all aimed at improving organizational processes that occur within a structure. "OD," as it is frequently called, is directed toward improving interpersonal and intergroup skills, confronting conflict, developing openness and trust, improving communications, and improving those processes vital to the success and revitalization of the social system.

## SUMMARY

We see that social systems, through the structuring of member behaviors, have the property of partially closed systems especially when they have achieved "successful" (surplus-producing) dynamic equilibrium conditions internally and externally. In fact, managers can be seen to be attempting to close off their vulnerable open social systems from internal and external environmental contingencies.

We see further that present-day social system environments are changing faster and faster, often getting ahead of organizations. Occasionally, successful organizations are challenged by a major impetus for change, demanding a high capacity for revitalization that leads to a pervasive restructuring of the system and/or a deepening of the quality of its interpersonal relationships and social processes.

Readings

# The Coming Death of Bureaucracy

*Warren G. Bennis*

Not far from the new Government Center in downtown Boston, a foreign visitor walked up to a sailor and asked why American ships were built to last only a short time. According to the tourist, "The sailor answered without hesitation that the art of navigation is making such rapid progress that the finest ship would become obsolete if it lasted beyond a few years. In these words which fell accidentally from an uneducated man, I began to recognize the general and systematic idea upon which your great people direct all their concerns."

The foreign visitor was that shrewd observer of American morals and manners, Alexis de Tocqueville, and the year was 1835. He would not recognize Scollay Square today. But he had caught the central theme of our country: its preoccupation, its *obsession* with change. One thing is, however, new since de Tocqueville's time: the *acceleration* of newness, the changing scale and scope of change itself. As Dr. Robert Oppenheimer said, ". . . the world alters as we walk in it, so that the years of man's life measure not some small growth or rearrangement or moderation of what was learned in childhood, but a great upheaval."

How will these accelerating changes in our society influence human organizations?

A short while ago, I predicted that we would, in the next 25 to 50

• Reprinted by permission from *Think* Magazine (November–December, 1966), pp. 30–35, published by IBM. Copyright 1966 by International Business Machines Corporation.

years, participate in the end of bureaucracy as we know it and in the rise of new social systems better suited to the twentieth century demands of industrialization. This forecast was based on the evolutionary principle that every age develops an organizational form appropriate to its genius, and that the prevailing form, known by sociologists as bureaucracy and by most businessmen as "damn bureaucracy," was out of joint with contemporary realities. I realize now that my distant prophecy is already a distinct reality so that prediction is already foreshadowed by practice.

I should like to make clear that by bureaucracy I mean a chain of command structured on the lines of a pyramid—the typical structure which coordinates the business of almost every human organization we know of: industrial, governmental, of universities and research and development laboratories, military, religious, voluntary. I do *not* have in mind those fantasies so often dreamed up to describe complex organizations. These fantasies can be summarized in two grotesque stereotypes. The first I call "Organization as Inkblot"—an actor steals around an uncharted wasteland, growing more restive and paranoid by the hour, while he awaits orders that never come. The other specter is "Organization as Big Daddy" —the actors are square people plugged into square holes by some omniscient and omnipotent genius who can cradle in his arms the entire destiny of man by way of computer and TV. Whatever the first image owes to Kafka, the second owes to George Orwell's *Nineteen Eighty-four.*

Bureaucracy, as I refer to it here, is a useful social invention that was perfected during the industrial revolution to organize and direct the activities of a business firm. Most students of organizations would say that its anatomy consists of the following components:

- A well-defined chain of command.
- A system of procedures and rules for dealing with all contingencies relating to work activities.
- A division of labor based on specialization.
- Promotion and selection based on technical competence.
- Impersonality in human relations.

It is the pyramid arrangement we see on most organizational charts.

The bureaucratic "machine model" was developed as a reaction against the personal subjugation, nepotism, and cruelty, and the capricious and subjective judgments which passed for managerial practices during the early days of the industrial revolution. Bureaucracy emerged out of the organization's need for order and precision and the workers' demands for impartial treatment. It was an organization ideally suited to the values and demands of the Victorian era. And just as bureaucracy emerged as a creative response to a radically new age, so today new organizational shapes are surfacing before our eyes.

First I shall try to show why the conditions of our modern industrialized world will bring about the death of bureaucracy. In the second part of this article I will suggest a rough model of the organization of the future.

## Four Threats

There are at least four relevant threats to bureaucracy:

1. Rapid and unexpected change.
2. Growth in size where the volume of an organization's traditional activities is not enough to sustain growth. (A number of factors are included here, among them: bureaucratic overhead; tighter controls and impersonality due to bureaucratic sprawls; outmoded rules and organizational structures.)
3. Complexity of modern technology where integration between activities and persons of very diverse, highly specialized competence is required.
4. A basically psychological threat springing from a change in managerial behavior.

It might be useful to examine the extent to which these conditions exist *right now:*

1. *Rapid and unexpected change*—Bureaucracy's strength is its capacity to efficiently manage the routine and predictable in human affairs. It is almost enough to cite the knowledge and population explosion to raise doubts about its contemporary viability. More revealing, however, are the statistics which demonstrate these overworked phrases:

- Our productivity output per man hour may now be doubling almost every 20 years rather than every 40 years, as it did before World War II.
- The Federal Government alone spent $16 billion in research and development activities in 1965; it will spend $35 billion by 1980.
- The time lag between a technical discovery and recognition of its commercial uses was: 30 years before World War I, 16 years between the Wars, and only 9 years since World War II.
- In 1946, only 42 cities in the world had populations of more than one million. Today there are 90. In 1930, there were 40 people for each square mile of the earth's land surface. Today there are 63. By 2000, it is expected, the figure will have soared to 142.

Bureaucracy, with its nicely defined chain of command, its rules and its rigidities, is ill-adapted to the rapid change the environment now demands.

2. *Growth in size*—While, in theory, there may be no natural limit to the height of a bureaucratic pyramid, in practice the element of complexity is almost invariably introduced with great size. International operation, to cite one significant new element, is the rule rather than exception for most of our biggest corporations. Firms like Standard Oil Company (New Jersey) with over 100 foreign affiliates, Mobil Oil Corporation, The

National Cash Register Company, Singer Company, Burroughs Corporation, and Colgate-Palmolive Company derive more than half their income or earnings from foreign sales. Many others—such as Eastman Kodak Company, Chas. Pfizer & Company, Inc., Caterpillar Tractor Company, International Harvester Company, Corn Products Company, and Minnesota Mining & Manufacturing Company—make from 30 to 50 per cent of their sales abroad. General Motors Corporation sales are not only nine times those of Volkswagen, they are also bigger than the Gross National Product of the Netherlands and well over the GNP of a hundred other countries. If we have seen the sun set on the British Empire, we may never see it set on the empires of General Motors, ITT, Shell, and Unilever.

## Labor Boom

3. *Increasing diversity—Today's activities require persons of very diverse, highly specialized competence.* Numerous dramatic examples can be drawn from studies of labor markets and job mobility. At some point during the past decade, the U.S. became the first nation in the world ever to employ more people in service occupations than in the production of tangible goods. Examples of this trend:

- In the field of education, the *increase* in employment between 1950 and 1960 was greater than the total number employed in the steel, copper, and aluminum industries.
- In the field of health, the *increase* in employment between 1950 and 1960 was greater than the total number employed in automobile manufacturing in either year.
- In financial firms, the *increase* in employment between 1950 and 1960 was greater than total employment in mining in 1960.

These changes, plus many more that are harder to demonstrate statistically, break down the old, industrial trend toward more and more people doing either simple or undifferentiated chores.

Hurried growth, rapid change and increase in specialization—pit these three factors against the five components of the pyramid structure described above, and we should expect the pyramid of bureaucracy to begin crumbling.

4. *Change in managerial behavior*—There is, I believe, a subtle but perceptible change in the philosophy underlying management behavior. Its magnitude, nature, and antecedents, however, are shadowy because of the difficulty of assigning numbers. (Whatever else statistics do for us, they most certainly provide a welcome illusion of certainty.) Nevertheless, real change seems under way because of:

a. A new concept of *man*, based on increased knowledge of his complex and shifting needs, which replaces an oversimplified, innocent, push-button idea of man.

b. A new concept of *power*, based on collaboration and reason, which replaces a model of power based on coercion and threat.

c. A new concept of *organizational values*, based on humanistic–democratic ideals, which replaces the depersonalized mechanistic value system of bureaucracy.

The primary cause of this shift in management philosophy stems not from the bookshelf but from the manager himself. Many of the behavioral scientists, like Douglas McGregor or Rensis Likert, have clarified and articulated—even legitimized—what managers have only half registered to themselves. I am convinced, for example, that the popularity of McGregor's book, *The Human Side of Enterprise,* was based on his rare empathy for a vast audience of managers who are wistful for an alternative to the mechanistic concept of authority; i.e., that he outlined a vivid utopia of more authentic human relationships than most organizational practices today allow. Furthermore, I suspect that the desire for relationships in business has little to do with a profit motive per se, though it is often rationalized as doing so. The real push for these changes stems from the need, not only to humanize the organization, but to use it as a crucible of personal growth and the development of self-realization.[1]

The core problems confronting any organization fall, I believe, into five major categories. First, let us consider the problems, then let us see how our twentieth century conditions of constant change have made the bureaucratic approach to these problems obsolete.

1. *Integration.* The problem is how to integrate individual needs and management goals. In other words, it is the inescapable conflict between individual needs (like "spending time with the family") and organizational demands (like meeting deadlines).

Under twentieth century conditions of constant change there has been an emergence of human sciences and a deeper understanding of man's complexity. Today, integration encompasses the entire range of issues concerned with incentives, rewards and motivations of the individual, and how the organization succeeds or fails in adjusting to these issues. In our society, where personal attachments play an important role, the individual is appreciated, and there is genuine concern for his well-being, not just in a veterinary-hygiene sense but as a moral, integrated personality.

## Paradoxical Twins

The problem of integration, like most human problems, has a venerable past. The modern version goes back at least 160 years and was precipitated by an historical paradox: the twin births of modern individualism and modern industrialism. The former brought about a deep concern for

[1]Let me propose an hypothesis to explain this tendency. It rests on the assumption that man has a basic need for transcendental experiences, somewhat like the psychological rewards which William James claimed religion provided—"an assurance of safety and a temper of peace, and, in relation to others, a preponderance of loving affections." Can it be that as religion has become secularized, less transcendental, men search for substitutes such as close interpersonal relationships, psychoanalysis—even the release provided by drugs such as LSD?

and a passionate interest in the individual and his personal rights. The latter brought about increased mechanization of organized activity. Competition between the two has intensified as each decade promises more freedom and hope for man and more stunning achievements for technology. I believe that our society *has* opted for more humanistic and democratic values, however unfulfilled they may be in practice. It will "buy" these values even at loss in efficiency because it feels it can now afford the loss.

2. *Social Influence*. This problem is essentially one of power and how power is distributed. It is a complex issue and alive with controversy, partly because of an ethical component and partly because studies of leadership and power distribution can be interpreted in many ways, and almost always in ways which coincide with one's biases (including a cultural leaning toward democracy).

The problem of power has to be seriously reconsidered because of dramatic situational changes which make the possibility of one-man rule not necessarily "bad" but impractical. I refer to changes in top management's role.

Peter Drucker, over twelve years ago, listed 41 major responsibilities of the chief executive and declared that "90 per cent of the trouble we are having with the chief executive's job is rooted in our superstition of the one-man chief." Many factors make one-man control obsolete, among them: the broadening product base of industry; impact of new technology; the scope of international operation; the separation of management from ownership; the rise of trade unions and general education. The real power of the "chief" has been eroding in most organizations even though both he and the organization cling to the older concept.

3. *Collaboration*. This is the problem of managing and resolving conflicts. Bureaucratically, it grows out of the very same social process of conflict and stereotyping that has divided nations and communities. As organizations become more complex, they fragment and divide, building tribal patterns and symbolic codes which often work to exclude others (secrets and jargon, for example) and on occasion to exploit differences for inward (and always fragile) harmony.

Recent research is shedding new light on the problem of conflict. Psychologist Robert R. Blake in his stunning experiments has shown how simple it is to induce conflict, how difficult to arrest it. Take two groups of people who have never before been together, and give them a task which will be judged by an impartial jury. In less than an hour, each group devolves into a tightly-knit band with all the symptoms of an "in group." They regard their product as a "masterwork" and the other group's as "commonplace" at best. "Other" becomes "enemy." "We are good, they are bad; we are right, they are wrong."

## Rabbie's Reds and Greens

Jaap Rabbie, conducting experiments on intergroup conflict at the University of Utrecht, has been amazed by the ease with which conflict and stereotype develop. He brings into an experimental room two groups and distributes green name tags and pens to one group, red pens and tags to the other. The two groups do not compete; they do not even interact. They are only in sight of each other while they silently complete a questionnaire. Only 10 minutes are needed to activate defensiveness and fear, reflected in the hostile and irrational perceptions of both "reds" and "greens."

4. *Adaptation*. This problem is caused by our turbulent environment. The pyramid structure of bureaucracy, where power is concentrated at the top, seems the perfect way to "run a railroad." And for the routine tasks to the nineteenth and early twentieth centuries, bureaucracy was (in some respects it still is) a suitable social arrangement. However, rather than a placid and predictable environment, what predominates today is a dynamic and uncertain one where there is a deepening interdependence among economic, scientific, educational, social and political factors in the society.

5. *Revitalization*. This is the problem of growth and decay. As Alfred North Whitehead has said: "The art of free society consists first in the maintenance of the symbolic code, and secondly, in the fearlessness of revision. . . . Those societies which cannot combine reverence to their symbols with freedom of revision must ultimately decay. . . ."

Growth and decay emerge as the penultimate conditions of contemporary society. Organizations, as well as societies, must be concerned with those social structures that engender buoyancy, resilience and a "fearlessness of revision."

I introduce the term "revitalization" to embrace all the social mechanisms that stagnate and regenerate, as well as the process of this cycle. The elements of revitalization are:

1. An ability to learn from experience and to codify, store and retrieve the relevant knowledge.
2. An ability to "learn how to learn," that is, to develop methods of improving the learning process.
3. An ability to acquire and use feedback mechanisms on performance, in short, to be self-analytical.
4. An ability to direct one's own destiny.

These qualities have a good deal in common with what John Gardner calls "self-renewal." For the organization, it means conscious attention to its own evolution. Without a planned methodology and explicit direction, the enterprise will not realize its potential.

*Integration, distribution of power, collaboration, adaptation* and *revitalization*—these are the major human problems of the next 25 years. How organizations cope with and manage these tasks will undoubtedly determine the viability of the enterprise.

Against this background I should like to set forth some of the conditions that will dictate organizational life in the next two or three decades.

1. *The environment*. Rapid technological change and diversification will lead to more and more partnerships between government and business. It will be a truly mixed economy. Because of the immensity and expense of the projects, there will be fewer identical units competing in the same markets, and organizations will become more interdependent.

- Interdependence rather than competition.
- Turbulence and uncertainty rather than readiness and certainty.
- Large-scale rather than small-scale enterprises.
- Complex and multinational rather than simple national enterprises.

## "Nice"—and Necessary

2. *Population characteristics*. The most distinctive characteristic of our society is education. It will become even more so. Within 15 years, two-thirds of our population living in metropolitan areas will have attended college. Adult education is growing even faster, probably because of the rate of professional obsolescence. The Killian report showed that the average engineer required further education only 10 years after getting his degree. It will be almost routine for the experienced physician, engineer and executive to go back to school for advanced training every two or three years. All of this education is not just "nice." It is necessary.

One other characteristic of the population which will aid our understanding of organizations of the future is increasing job mobility. The ease of transportation, coupled with the needs of a dynamic environment, change drastically the idea of "owning" a job—or "having roots." Already 20 per cent of our population change their mailing address at least once a year.

3. *Work values*. The increased level of education and mobility will change the values we place on work. People will be more intellectually committed to their jobs and will probably require more involvement, participation and autonomy.

Also, people will be more "other oriented," taking cues for their norms and values from their immediate environment rather than tradition.

4. *Tasks and goals*. The tasks of the organization will be more technical, complicated, and unprogrammed. They will rely on intellect instead of muscle. And they will be too complicated for one person to comprehend, to say nothing of control. Essentially, they will call for the collaboration of specialists in a project or a team-form of organization.

There will be complication of goals. Business will increasingly concern itself with its adaptive or innovative-creative capacity. In addition, supragoals will have to be articulated, goals which shape and provide the foundation for the goal structure. For example, one might be a system for detecting new and changing goals; another could be a system for deciding priorities among goals.

Finally, there will be more conflict and contradiction among diverse standards for organizational effectiveness. This is because professionals tend to identify more with the goals of their profession than with those of their immediate employer. University professors can be used as a case in point. Their inside work may be a conflict between teaching and research, while more of their income is derived from outside sources, such as foundations and consultant work. They tend not to be good "company men" because they divide their loyalty between their professional values and organizational goals.

## Key Word: "Temporary"

5. *Organization*. The social structure of organizations of the future will have some unique characteristics. The key word will be "temporary." There will be adaptive, rapidly changing *temporary* systems. These will be task forces organized around problems-to-be-solved by groups of relative strangers with diverse professional skills. The group will be arranged on an organic rather than mechanical model; they will evolve in response to a problem rather than to programmed role expectations. The executive thus becomes a coordinator or "linking pin" between various task forces. He must be a man who can speak the polyglot jargon of research, with skills to relay information and to mediate between groups. People will be evaluated not vertically according to rank and status, but flexibly and functionally according to skill and professional training. Organizational charts will consist of project groups rather than stratified functional groups. (This trend is already visible in the aerospace and construction industries, as well as many professional and consulting firms.)

Adaptive, problem-solving, temporary systems of diverse specialists, linked together by coordinating and task-evaluating executive specialists in an organic flux—this is the organization form that will gradually replace bureaucracy as we know it. As no catchy phrase comes to mind, I call this an organic-adaptive structure. Organizational arrangements of this sort may not only reduce the intergroup conflicts mentioned earlier; they may also induce honest-to-goodness creative collaboration.

6. *Motivation*. The organic-adaptive structure should increase motivation and thereby effectiveness, because it enhances satisfactions intrinsic to the task. There is a harmony between the educated individual's need for tasks that are meaningful, satisfactory, and creative and a flexible organizational structure.

There will also be, however, reduced commitment to work groups, for these groups will be, as I have already mentioned, transient structures. I would predict that in the organic-adaptive system, people will learn to develop quick and intense relationships on the job, and learn to bear the loss of more enduring work relationships. Because of the added ambiguity of roles, time will have to be spent on continual rediscovery of the appropriate organizational mix.

I think that the future I describe is not necessarily a "happy" one.

Coping with rapid change, living in temporary work systems, developing meaningful relations and then breaking them—all augur social strains and psychological tensions. Teaching how to live with ambiguity, to identify with the adaptive process, to make a virtue out of contingency, and to be self-directing—these will be the tasks of education, the goals of maturity, and the achievement of the successful individual.

### No Delightful Marriages

In these new organizations of the future, participants will be called upon to use their minds more than at any other time in history. Fantasy, imagination, and creativity will be legitimate in ways that today seem strange. Social structures will no longer be instruments of psychic repression but will increasingly promote play and freedom on behalf of curiosity and thought.

One final word: While I forecast the structure and value coordinates for organizations of the future and contend that they are inevitable, this should not bar any of us from giving the inevitable a little push. The French moralist may be right in saying that there are no delightful marriages, just good ones; it is possible that if managers and scientists continue to get their heads together in organizational revitalization, they *might* develop delightful organizations—just possibly.

I started with a quote from de Tocqueville and I think it would be fitting to end with one: "I am tempted to believe that what we call necessary institutions are often no more than institutions to which we have grown accustomed. In matters of social constitution, the field of possibilities is much more extensive than men living in their various societies are ready to imagine."

# When Human Relations May Succeed and the Company Fail

*William M. Fox*

While the title of this article may sound facetious, it is meant in earnest. The concept of human relations in industry, like many other worthwhile movements, has been subjected to oversimplification and perversion.[1] Among the guilty are "human relationists" with an inadequate

• Reprinted from *California Management Review*, VIII, No. 3 (Spring, 1966), 19–24, by permission of the publisher.

[1] See, for example, James V. Clark, "Distortions of Behavioral Science," *California Management Review*, VI, No. 2 (Winter, 1963).

concept of human relations, who mistakenly preach participation, permissiveness, and democracy for all, and those employers who confuse popularity with managerial effectiveness and misinterpret the Golden Rule in dealing with their subordinates.

This article should not be construed as an attempt to discredit the findings of behavioral science. My purpose in writing is to demonstrate that a problem arises when the concept of human relations is misunderstood and misapplied in business organizations.

Part of the problem lies in lack of clarity as to the role "good human relations in an organization" should play. Many mistakenly regard it as an "end" toward which the organization should endeavor rather than as what it should be—a "means" for achieving the organization's primary service objectives. I define primary service objectives as the firm's chief objectives which not only specify how a firm hopes to create and distribute salable utilities profitably but also how it will justify its existence in a competitive milieu. Good human relations—along with policies, rules, plans, procedures, specifications, functions, organization structure, etc.—should serve as a tool, a means, for the achievement of these objectives. There are at least five rather common situations in industry when good human relations are regarded as an end rather than as a means.

1. *When elimination of conflict becomes a primary goal of the organization.* Few of us enjoy the prospect of unpleasantness with another human being—especially when we must initiate it. We hate to fire or discipline an ineffective employee who has an attractive family and tries hard to please us, and we find it most distasteful to face the possible rejection or disapproval of subordinates when we feel that duty demands that we fly in the face of their sentiments. Nor do we enjoy the anxiety generated by the prospect of able young men bringing new ideas and new skills into the organization which may threaten our status and feelings of competence.

There is strong temptation for peace of mind to settle for being popular rather than effective and for hiring only those who fit in with our scheme of things and offer little likelihood of ever "rocking the boat." A striving for complete harmony and absence of stress in a large company can be rationalized into respectability with the "custodial" philosophy of management. Under this philosophy, it is felt that the firm has completed its entrepreneurial-expansionist phase and that the major functions of the management team are to traditionalize and perpetuate the "winning combination," to instruct neophytes as to its mysteries, and to protect it at all costs against the subversive influences of change.

In the absence of control afforded by the vigilance of large stockholders, it is surprising how long a group of noncompetitive "custodians" can coast on the momentum of a formerly successful corporation, milking its assets via unwarranted bonuses for years before they are found out. This can be quite pleasant as long as it lasts, but the future failure of the company is virtually assured in the process.

It is instructive to observe how few of the most successful companies of 1900 are still extant and to hear of the misfortunes and close calls of those who momentarily thought they were competition proof. No—the function of human relations in an organization cannot be the elimination of conflict, for this will create a state of dormancy and lead to eventual disaster. The legitimate function of human relations in an organization is to facilitate the introduction of change with a minimum of conflict.

2. *When there is no "price of admission" (i.e., individual and group goals are permitted to conflict with company goals or be unrelated to them*). Employees can be quite happy and team minded as they do nothing or as they actively subvert an organization. There is no natural law which assures a relationship between high morale and the effective pursuit of an organization's primary service objectives. A number of researchers seemingly have been startled by this discovery. Actually, the absence of such a relationship is not too surprising. A source of misunderstanding has been the tendency to use the word "productivity" in one context only—the efficient creation of goods or services for the firm. Yet a widely accepted concept of high morale is that it exists to the extent that individual group members are willing to subordinate their immediate convenience or interest to the achievement of group goals. If we think of the productivity of a group as the efficiency with which it achieves its goals, then the relationship between high morale and productivity becomes apparent and tautological.

In other words, employees can be quite productive by striking well as a team, by withholding production well as a unit, and so on. The challenge to management is to create good group morale and concurrently to see to it that group goals are consistent with company goals. Or, to put it another way, to demonstrate to employees that the satisfaction of their diverse individual needs can and will take place to the extent that they discharge their obligations to the firm and to the extent that such activity does not detract from the achievement of company goals.

A good analogy, perhaps, is afforded by the Marine Corps. Its primary objective is, presumably, to fashion one of the finest fighting forces in the world, an organization prepared to tackle military assignments that impose personal hardships and risks greater than those which an average military organization could or would impose on its members. Is it likely that the typical Marine is looking for an improved opportunity to have his head blown off? Hardly! It seems much more plausible to argue that the Corps functions in such a way as to satisfy important personal needs of its members—for feelings of acceptance, worthwhileness, etc.—in the process of preparing to carry out, and in carrying out, its hazardous assignments. The "price of admission" for the Marines to stay in the Corps—and to continue to enjoy the satisfaction of needs that they believe only the Corps can satisfy so well—is to do the work of the Corps and identify with its objectives in a manner consistent with its high standards of excellence.[2]

3. *When certain "good works" need not be justified in terms of contribution to primary service objectives*. This can happen, for example, when the rehabilitation of personnel rather than the effective utilization of personnel becomes a primary goal. Sometimes the latter will encompass

[2]For further discussion of the relationship between individual needs and organizational goals, see William M. Fox, *The Management Process* (Homewood, Ill.: Richard D. Irwin, Inc., 1963), Chapter 8.

the former, but this is more the exception than the rule. Take the case of the dependent subordinate who has strong emotional needs for assignments well within his competence, close supervision, and personal acceptance. For many routine assignments he can become a productive, dependable, and loyal employee. It might be argued that such an individual would be better off if he could be weaned from his dependency needs through appropriate counseling and guidance, and this is probably true. However, normally, unless organizational needs warrant it, the company cannot justify the diversion of its resources to this type of therapy.

Or consider the maladjusted troublemaker who is so insecure and hostile that he will not respond to positive supervision. He is compelled by his neurotic needs to subvert and challenge the authority of the formal leader. In fact, he tends to perceive positive leadership behavior either as appeasement—the leader is afraid of him—or as an attempt to put something over on him. Though such individuals may be helped by professional counseling, supervisors do not have the time, skill, or justification for administering it. They must protect their own integrity with their groups and make every effort to eliminate disruptive influences in them. If a troublemaker does not respond to negative sanctions, he should be fired! For good human relations in an organization must pay its way through contribution to company goals. Any worthwhile undertaking, whether it has to do with the rehabilitation of personnel or some other desirable practice, must operate within this framework if the firm is to succeed.

Danger lies also in an overexpansion of benefits and services. This may result from an excessive desire to please—even competitors—or from a desire to dodge the responsibilities of leadership through "committeemanship" or undue reliance upon the opinions of specialists. Cameron Hawley reports some startling data brought back by American executives after visits to counterpart operations in Europe.[3] "Until I got on the inside," said one executive, "I thought they had us licked over here because of wage rates. I know differently now. For every penny they're saving in direct labor costs, they've got us whipped by three cents in general overhead and burden. Inside the plant it's about a stand-off . . . but when you get to the office, they make us look like fools." He pointed out that his company and the European firms are about the same size in terms of units produced. His company has about 1,200 hourly workers in the plant, the overseas firm 1,300. But the contrast in salaried employees is a different story: 912 in the United States *vs.* 221 overseas.

Hawley hypothesizes that a lot of the "organizational fat" which plagues some of our companies may have resulted from the whipped-boy role that American employers were cast in during the great depression. Many young executives determined then that when their turn at the wheel came they would win public approval by introducing real democracy into business. With time, this evolved into substituting group-thinking for one-man-rule and trying to keep everybody happy. And in the process of hiring ten men to make one man's decisions, needed discipline and internal surgery went by the board—and with them the possibility of adherence to high standards of performance.

[3]"The Quality of Leadership," *Personnel*, May–June, 1960.

As part of the problem, the number of staff specialists has been increased without adequate justification. In the area of selection, for example, much effort and money are expended each year on the administration of tests and interviews which have little if any validity (that is, no one has bothered to base their usage upon statistically demonstrated ability to predict success or failure on the job).[4] Elaborate counseling, training, and public relations programs have been established and expanded with little evidence as to ability to pay their way through contribution to company goals.

4. *When there is adherence to "the bubble-up theory" (good theory and practice at lower levels do not square with what is practiced at the top).* Sound human relations training can backfire. Or in medical terms it can be very iatrogenic, i.e., it can cause more harm than the difficulties it is designed to overcome. An organization cannot be reformed from the bottom up. Yet this is what is often attempted when lower level supervisors are instructed in philosophies and practices of management which are incompatible with the values and behavior of their superiors. Research has uncovered several cases wherein foremen have been less effective after good training in human relations than they were before—and in comparison with their colleagues who did not receive the training.[5]

This result is not too surprising. For when we move from training designed to impart information to that designed to alter basic behavior, we move toward the necessity of a preceptor system. There are several ways in which supervisory behavior may be altered. One is to structure the "compulsions" of the environment—formal sanctions, group pressures, role assignments, etc.—to produce the desired behavior. Another is to help the individual gain insight into his behavior and then to support and encourage him in experimenting with more productive modes. And closely related to the first two is the process of identification wherein a "junior" individual adopts the values and behavior of some "senior" individual whom he admires and wishes to emulate.

Harry Levinson of The Menninger Foundation goes so far as to hypothesize that "one of the significant differences between those who become executives and those who do not lies in the presence or absense of certain kinds of identification models."[6] He points out that every human being in later life tends to repeat unconsciously those modes of behavior which he learned in the family. Consequently, organizations of people tend to assume qualities like those of the family. In the same way that a boy grows and matures through identification with authority figures, a supervisor or junior executive will grow in stature and competence to the extent that his superiors provide models with which he can identify. It is interest-

[4]Among more than 100 companies interviewed by *Fortune*, only one noted any difference in ability between graduates hired over the counter and recruits painstakingly selected as the "cream of the crop." See Herrymon Maurer, "The Worst Shortage in Business," *Fortune*, April, 1956, or William M. Fox, ed., *Readings in Personnel Management from Fortune* (New York: Holt, Rinehart and Winston, Inc., 1963), p. 26.

[5]For an example, see Harold E. Burtt, "Why Most Supervisor Training," *Management Methods*, January, 1958, p. 28.

[6]"A Psychologist Looks at Executive Development," *Harvard Business Review*, September–October, 1962, p. 70.

ing that Levinson and his colleagues found support for this concept in their intensive study of a large utility company.[7]

Top management, far more by its action than its pronouncements, will establish a "climate" for supervisory behavior. Autocratic managers are better advised to prescribe standards of supervision for their organizations which both they and their subordinates can accept and practice than to risk the disruptive effects of a "double standard." They should not expose their subordinate managers to human relations training until they, personally, can understand, accept, and practice the substance of such training—or step aside to make room for others who will. The right theory is "the trickle-down theory."

5. *When "intelligent autocracy" would have been more productive for the organization.* Democratic, consultative leadership, based upon participation, effective two-way communication, and nondirective counseling, which we associate with the expression "good human relations," is superior for the majority of employees in a wide range of organizations and in most instances. But there are important exceptions. I have already discussed the need for more directive, unilateral supervision for the dependent employee and for the maladjusted troublemaker. There are two other situations which deserve our attention.

First, time is required for a supervisor to gain acceptance and build the kind of relationship with his subordinates which will ultimately lead to higher productivity and long-term individual growth. If a temporary work group or committee is composed of mature people who share and practice a positive philosophy of leadership, then it will probably function best under such leadership. However, in other temporary work group situations, positive leadership may well be less productive than intelligent authoritarianism. For example, consider a group of casual common laborers hired for a period of three months to do road work. Because of their lack of education and skill, they require close supervision. They perceive this particular job as a stopgap, offering little opportunity for growth, enhanced self-esteem, advancement, or lasting security. It seems likely that motivation of such a group in terms of negative sanctions would be superior to an attempt to develop positive values that are largely precluded by the character of the workers and the work environment.

Second, a situation which deserves our attention has to do with a firm, or part of a firm, which can operate more efficiently under centralized autocracy. When a company is operating in a relatively stable environment with little competition (e.g., a railroad during the years before the advent of good roads, busses, trucks, and planes), centralized management can reduce its load to manageable proportions through the extensive use of rules, procedures, and standard practices. This is feasible because centralized management will be confronted for the most part with predicta-

[7]See Harry Levinson, Charlton Price, Kenneth Munden, Harold Mandl, and Charles Solley, *Men, Management, and Mental Health* (Cambridge, Mass.: Harvard University Press, 1962), especially Chapter 4, "Interdependence." In his book *Personal Adjustment* (New York: The Macmillan Company, 1963), p. 140, Sidney Jourard asserts that "It is by means of *identification* that we acquire our most important values, and it is through identification that we change our values from time to time throughout life."

ble situations. The security-minded, dependent-type employee can be attracted, held, and effectively utilized in this environment because there is little need for fast, innovative local action to cope with unforeseen developments. In fact, given well-conceived goals by those at the top and a well-drilled and disciplined organization, centralized autocracy can spare top managers the problems of dealing with the centrifugal tendencies generated by decentralized, autonomous units staffed with creative and ambitious young men.

The cult of "excessive permissiveness" has been seen in progressive education and also among certain overzealous "human relationists." There are those who imply that sweetness and light will conquer all and that any form of negative motivation is self-defeating and outmoded. There is little question that positive motivation is superior to negative motivation when it is appropriate. But there are instances when it is not, and negative motivation—intelligently applied—is definitely superior to no motivation. Reference has been made to certain situations for which a positive permissive approach is inappropriate—with dependent or transient employees and maladjusted troublemakers, and for certain stable, predictable organizational environments. In addition, one must have the time, rapport, skill, or insight to make a positive approach productive.

Not only is time necessary for a supervisor to gain acceptance from his subordinates and to build useful relationships with them, but time can also be a major limiting factor in many specific situations. No one expects an infantry platoon leader caught with his unit in an ambush to confer with his subordinates as to the best course of action; it is his job to give the right orders and to give them quickly and concisely. Actually, any attempt on his part to be consultative on such an occasion might diminish the respect of his men and jeopardize his effectiveness with them in the future. In fact, unilateral leadership is the only appropriate mode for the occasion and—in this context—is positive leadership.

Positive motivation is based upon accurate perception of subordinate needs and upon effective interpersonal communications. It is difficult for a supervisor to perceive the needs of a subordinate or effectively to communicate with him if he cannot establish rapport with him—a relationship of mutual trust. Often this is not easy, even with the best of intentions, for if we find it difficult to "warm up" to a person, it is virtually impossible to establish such a relationship with him. Also, a supervisor will not perceive subordinate needs if he lacks the skill or insight required. It is not surprising that most of us lack this skill in dealing with those individuals who are themselves incapable of perceiving their own needs. And even when rapport, perception, and effective communication have been achieved, the supervisor must attempt satisfaction of the subordinate's needs within the framework of organizational constraints. At times, this will not permit the supervisor sufficient flexibility to deal in a positive manner with a particular case.

In real life situations, the use of negative motivation is inescapable. One of the significant differences between a good human relations environment and a poor one is that, in the former, negative motivation is used only when necessary and then in a goal-oriented, nonpunitive manner.

Five common situations in industry when human relations tends to be regarded as an end rather than a means for the achievement of company objectives were examined. These were:

1. When elimination of conflict becomes a primary goal of the organization.
2. When there is no "price of admission" (i.e., when individual and group goals are permitted to conflict with company goals or be unrelated to them).
3. When certain "good works" need not be justified in terms of contribution to primary service objectives.
4. When there is adherence to "the bubble-up theory" (when good theory and practice at lower levels do not square with what is practiced at the top).
5. When "intelligent autocracy" would have been more productive for the organization.

I have examined instances in which the application of sound human relations may lead to company failure. When will successful human relations lead to company success?

1. When the concept of human relations is seen as a tool, or means, for the achievement of the firm's goals.
2. When it is properly integrated with other key tools. Among these are well-defined goals and high standards of performance—arrived at whenever possible through consultation and enforced with the aid of a system of rewards and penalties which responds to every important facet of activity.

When top management can lead the organization to internalize high standards of performance and make them part of the organization's culture, its battle for excellence will be largely won. For it will have sown the seeds of continuous regeneration, founded in the basic psychological truth that "we value more those things we must strive for, and we value ourselves more for having made the effort."

# CHAPTER 13

# Learning and Ideals

How can I do it better? How can I behave more effectively? These are questions we frequently ask ourselves, at least implicitly. In seeking a satisfying, successful experience all of us try to learn about ourselves and our world, and how we can develop our full potential and live well in our environment. Thus it is that learning is one of the most central of human processes. The high degree to which human beings can learn distinguishes them from other animals, and this ability is one of man's most valuable traits. Man's ability to learn new knowledge, attitudes, and skills influences the kinds of success and satisfaction he experiences.

## LEARNING

People frequently associate learning with school and the classroom, but much personal learning occurs outside schools. Children and adults learn from their peers, from reading, watching TV, traveling, going to parties, playing, and working. Many important aspects of our self-concept, which influences perceptions and behavior, are developed informally (and often unconsciously) outside the classroom, just as are many of our values, attitudes, beliefs, assumptions, and skills.

Various aspects of the subject of learning can be conceptualized and theorized. For example, we can say that learning takes place when a stimulus exists, when there is a person with a need to learn and an ability to achieve new perceptions, when a response to the stimulus occurs, and when some feedback on the effectiveness of the behavior is received. People perceive situations in which they need to behave, decide on the best course of action to be taken given all they perceive in their environment (including their past experience), behave accordingly, perceive (see, feel, and interpret) the results, decide (often unconsciously) whether they are satisfactory, and either repeat the behavior or try a new form of it when they encounter a similar situation. Some learning takes place in this way. However, much learning is achieved when we are totally unaware that it is happening. Learning is a continuous, usually trial-and-error, process. The process and results are often uncertain at best.

## Perceptions, Concepts, and Territory

Learning can be distinguished conceptually in several ways. One can learn knowledge (facts, categories, principles, theories), attitudes, and skills, and the factors relevant for learning one are often different from those relevant for learning the others. Learning can also be distinguished as being physical or mental, simple or complex, conscious or unconscious, intended or unintended, extrinsic or intrinsic, to name just a few possibilities.

The brief discussion of learning in this chapter is based on the assumption that everyone behaves in ways that are most satisfying to him.[1] Learning takes place when we are able to distinguish new modes of behavior that lead to satisfying results. Thus, perception—the way we see and interpret our world, including ourselves—is a central factor in the learning process. We learn as we perceive new behavioral possibilities, try them, and assess the results.

Thus, "a learning" is a new perception that can lead to different behavior. Imagine a newborn child. His perceptual world is little more than a buzzing confusion, but as he develops, he is increasingly able to distinguish one thing from another about himself and his environment. As his perceptual field broadens and deepens, so do the behavioral possibilities available to him.

In sum, your ability to learn will depend on your ability to perceive things more fully and accurately, and then to use your perceptions to guide your behavior. The feedback you get about the effectiveness and satisfaction of your behavior influences whether you accept or reject the newly tried behavior as useful. Of course, the danger exists that you may

[1]Remember that a person with a negative self-concept may feel more satisfaction while failing than while succeeding.

misinterpret or inadequately interpret the results. A child might walk across a river turned to ice on a cold winter day and learn that it is safe to walk across an iced river. If he were to use this learning on another day when the temperature was just above thawing, though, he might fall through. His perceptual field may not be sufficiently discriminating to include the temperature, along with the iced condition of the river, as a relevant factor.

Words and concepts are fundamental tools used to enlarge perceptions and learning. Human beings can relate words and concepts to people, things, and ideas, and this ability facilitates both memory and the ability to think and predict. Assume that a native of the South Seas visits Alaska in winter. He steps off the plane and slips on the ice. His ability to relate ice to slipperiness may enable him to avoid slipping on any ice he might encounter in the future. The more people, things, and ideas a man encounters, the more experiences he has, and the more words and concepts he has to use in identifying and remembering what he has observed and experienced, the greater is likely to be his learning.

One of the major aids to man's ability to develop broad perceptual fields and a wide range of behavioral possibilities is his ability to relate concepts and the territory they represent. For example, think what the ultimate behavioral implications have been for mankind because some men related the concepts of water, heat, steam, energy, and work. Then man related the concepts of the sun with energy. Thus it is that man's ability to use and remember words and concepts and relate these concepts and the experiences they represent is a key to his learning.

Concepts are useful in discriminating and perceiving more fully and accurately. But note the importance of being able to relate the concepts to actual territory. A student might learn through words what the concept "lathe" means but fail to recognize a lathe when he sees one in a factory. How often have you seen something, or experienced something, and then exclaimed: "Oh, that's what that is!" or "That's what that means!"?

Experiencing certain things, ideas, or feelings is usually more conducive to learning than just hearing or thinking about them. We have all heard that the corporation president's job is often a lonely one, and that the responsibility of making final decisions is taxing. Most of us can understand these words readily enough, but for those of us who have not actually experienced the feelings being described, their meaning is undoubtedly much less than those who have experienced the territory.

A distinction should be made between knowing and behaving. You can learn in the sense of "knowing" but still not learn in the sense of altering behavior. You may "know about" playing golf (grip the club correctly, keep your head still, left arm straight . . . ) and not be able to play (behave) well. Or you may know about the advantages of expressing your thoughts and feelings openly and not be able to behave openly. Or you may know how to analyze a case but be unable to analyze as well the situations in which you are personally involved. In sum, cognition is a useful step, but not a guarantee, for improved behavior.

## Unintended and Unconscious Learning

Most of our learning is probably achieved while we are unaware of its taking place. Sometimes the learning is even unintended. For example, consider the young lad who has learned a few profane expressions from his peers and who one day repeats them in front of his parents, who, we will assume, do not approve of little children using profanity. The father may "teach" the son not to use profanity by giving a strong lecture on the subject. The son *may* learn that profanity is "bad" and that he should not use it. On the other hand, chances are equally good that he will learn that it is "dangerous" to use it around Dad and Mom but desirable to use it around his peers (in order to be "in"). He may also begin learning that what is acceptable behavior to some is not to others. He may even learn that he cannot be open with his Dad, at least on some things, a learning that Dad surely did not intend to occur.

Unconscious learning is sometimes very powerful and central to the development of our self-concepts. To illustrate this point, let us assume we can observe a fifteen-year-old boy approach a pretty girl he has been eyeing for some time in order to ask her for a date. Assume it is the first time he has ever asked a girl for a date and, in fact, the first time he has ever made such a direct approach to any girl. Can you imagine the feelings the boy might have if she rather coldly rejects his invitation? or if she accepts it eagerly? Assuming the first instance, it would not be surprising if the boy were cautious about asking for another date; but assuming he did, try to imagine his feelings. Some doubt, some fear, some hope, and some anticipation might all be felt in varying degrees. Again, think of his feelings if he is turned down—or if he is accepted. Assume he is rejected four or five times in a row. Can you predict some of the learnings he is developing, probably largely unconsciously, about himself and his ability to relate to girls? Can you see how his attitudes towards girls and dating are probably developing? Think how different the learning of the boy who easily gets his dates might be. And in both cases there might be what some would term "mislearning."

## The Intangibility and Measurement of Learning

Another important aspect of learning is its intangibility. Learning is nonobservable; it takes place within people and can only be inferred from actual behavior. For this reason, it is called an intervening variable. Because it must be inferred from behavior, it is often difficult to measure: Other factors influence behavior, and it is sometimes difficult to distinguish what part of the behavior is attributable to learning. Two men may be assigned a task and given instructions on how to accomplish it. One may achieve much better results than the other, but that does not necessarily mean he has learned more. He may have had more ability to begin with, or he may have had a greater motivation to succeed than the other.

Performance is the result of learning, ability, motivation, and a variety of external factors. One man may produce more even having learned less because his ability or motivation enables him to perform more effectively. A student who works hard in a course and learns a great amount may see another student work less hard, appear to learn less, but receive a higher grade. Such situations are common both in school and in the business world. The factor sometimes overlooked is the initial degree of skill or knowledge brought to the task, and the resultant effect on performance. Often it is performance that is observed, judged, and rewarded.

## Conditions for Learning

People learn most effectively when these factors are present: (1) a personal need that the learning can help satisfy; (2) an opportunity to experience some reward or to avoid punishment (psychological or material); and (3) some kind of feedback that helps the individual assess the value to him of the learning. For a moment imagine yourself in an extremely boring lecture class that you are taking because it is required. If you see little relationship between what you are hearing and your own experience, the chances of your learning anything of lasting value to you are quite remote. What might cause an exception? If you see yourself as an outstanding student, or if you see yourself as very conscientious, you may listen hard and seek to learn even if the subject matter seems irrelevant. The subject matter may be irrelevant, but earning a high grade is not. On the other hand, imagine yourself in a class dealing with something important to you, one that you feel is giving you insights or skills that will help you develop your own potential and be more successful in your world. Clearly your chances of learning are improved.

People also learn more effectively when they are actively, rather than passively, involved. A student can follow a lecture or book (someone else's learning) or a subject, say mathematics, and appear to understand it. Yet when confronted with a problem that requires him to apply what he has "learned," he may find he has not made the material his own at all. If he works through the problem and applies the material, he is much more likely to make it on his own. Active involvement and learning go together.

Assume yourself back in that dull class. Assume that you are only partially aware of what is being said until you hear the professor saying "The following material is important and will likely appear on the next examination." Look around. Students become alert, pencils begin to move, notes are taken. The payoff in the boring class is not the subject matter—it is the grade. Usually the grade results from doing well on exams, and so the bored student does what is needed to do well on exams, if he can do so without disproportionate discomfort.

People learn fastest and most effectively when what they are learning meets an immediate need and has high potential for reward—i.e., satisfying the felt need. The certainty, amount, timeliness, and importance of the reward are all factors that influence the degree of learning that will take place.

Our example of the dull class illustrates the difference between extrinsic and intrinsic learning. As we are using those terms here, "extrinsic" learning is learning for the sake of something else; "intrinsic" learning is learning for its own sake. A college sophomore may learn ancient history because he is required to (the grade in the required course is what he values, not the learning), whereas he may eagerly seek to learn more about how to do well in a subject that will help him meet his immediate or future goals and needs.

Distinguishing between extrinsic and intrinsic learning can be useful to those who are attempting to make the most of their own lives and who are developing some of their values. Doing things for the sake of something else, for example, can cause one to get on a never-ending treadmill.[2] Consider the student who only takes a course to get a passing grade, and only wants the grade to get a degree, which he only wants so that he can get a job, which he only wants so that he can earn money and achieve status, which he only wants so that he can impress others, which he only wants . . . Some people, we suspect, go through most of their lives doing things for the sake of something else rather than for the satisfaction the activities bring in and of themselves. On the other hand, some people seek and find those activities that are satisfying for their own sake. Most of us engage in activities that involve some of both, and it is difficult to distinguish between the two in some cases. It is also difficult, if not impossible, to choose those activities that have only intrinsic value for us; and when such choices are available, a price is usually attached.

Learning takes place with more certainty when clear feedback is available. Simple skills and concepts can be learned because a teacher or other agent can provide feedback on the rightness or wrongness of the previous behavior. The sooner the feedback is given in such situations, the more meaningful it is likely to be. The problem facing everyone in many learning situations, especially informal ones, is that such feedback is often unavailable. When it is, it often comes long after the behavior and may not even be related to the original event. For example, you may behave toward another person in a way that offends him. He may not tell you this fact, and consequently you do not get clear feedback about the appropriateness of your behavior, at least as the other person per-

[2]See Sidney Jourard's "Some Lethal Aspects of the Male Role," on pages 185–92, for an interesting elaboration of this point.

ceives it. Or he might "tell" you he is offended through symbolic "language" such as reducing or eliminating the interactions he has with you. You may or may not "hear" this indirect feedback.

It is common for people not to receive clear or timely feedback in complex behavioral situations. This, incidentally, has some relevance for students learning about behavior in formal courses. Equally competent and well-intentioned people, even professors (!), may disagree on what is or is not appropriate behavior in some cases. Thus, they are sometimes unable to give clear feedback on certain behavior or issues, and consequently an important element of learning is missing. This adds to the uncertainty (as well as the challenge and interest) of the learning process.

### Learning and Risk Taking

Significant learning usually involves taking some risks, and as Maslow has pointed out,[3] we are likely to feel opposing drives—one to learn, the other not to. This is because we simultaneously have needs to know and fears of knowing. Consider the young man in an earlier example. Assume that he attends his first party, and without any preparation tries to dance. If he feels awkward and uncomfortable, he is likely to withdraw to the sidelines. Depending on how strongly he feels uncomfortable, he may stay there quite a while. The longer he stays, the more difficult it is for him to try again, which clearly is the only way he will learn how to become a better dancer. The longer he postpones trying, the more likely it is that because of his anxiety or fear he will avoid those situations in which he might be expected to dance. Withdrawal leads to procrastination and postponement, which in turn strengthens the need to avoid the activity. As some of his peers become better dancers through their practice, he comparatively becomes worse and thus the need to avoid the activity increases. On the other hand, if after his initial attempt he tries again, and maybe again, he may find that he becomes more at ease in the activity, and his adeptness is likely to increase correspondingly.

The avoidance of taking risks in learning can be unnecessarily depriving. Our young man who was rejected when he asked for dates might likely have learned to be cautious and cool around girls and to avoid approaching them, in order to protect himself from the pain of rejection. If he one day met a girl who was very appealing to him, he would probably be cool toward her in order to protect himself from a possible rejection. The girl might feel attracted to him also, but his coolness might raise such a barrier for her that she would not dare commit herself openly but would wait for him to approach her. It is easy to see how these two might "miss" each other, because the boy has learned out of his past experience that being too open in expressing his fondness for someone can lead to pain. Because he is unwilling to risk incurring such pain again, he misses

[3]See his "The Need to Know and the Fear of Knowing," on pages 322–27.

what might be a very rich experience. We probably all miss rich experiences of one kind or another in our lives because of our unwillingness to take the risks often concomitant with learning. People who have experienced success more than failure are often more open to new experiences and even seek and enjoy the risks that go along with them. Openness to new experience and willingness to take risks are usually essential in learning.

Age and success sometimes are deterrents to willingness to take risks in learning. Older or successful people are usually slow to change certain fundamental values and beliefs. The point here is not to place a value on such reluctance but only to say that it exists. The reason is that every human being has some kind of "structure" of knowledge, beliefs, values, and skills that provides him with stability and enables him to behave with some sense of certainty and direction. The older and, particularly, the more successful people grow, the more they tend to be unwilling to relinquish some of the structures they see as having contributed to their present status. Thus a manager who has found a particular technique or way of handling his affairs to be successful is often very reluctant to try another that may or may not work. Such reluctance has value because it provides some sense of stability, security, and certainty, but at the same time it may in some instances block learning a new and better way. Learning often requires unlearning as a preliminary step. The problem confronting most people when faced with taking risks involved in new learning is that there is frequently no guarantee that the new learning will be better for them than the old.

Thus, courage is an essential ingredient in much learning. Uncertainty is common in a multidimensional world, and the ability to tolerate ambiguity is helpful in facing and living with uncertainty. Courage is required in testing out "reality" with all its ambiguities inherent in concrete behavior and phenomena. Particularly, courage is required to try again after failure.

## IDEALS

Ideals, or values, constitute one set of vitally important learnings. Values significantly influence perceptions and behavior, often in unconscious ways. They add a dimension of stability of behavior and often are a source of resistance to change.

### Individual Values and Society

We all learn values during our formative years from "important others," including parents, teachers, peers, and entertainment, athletic, historical, and other similar "models." We learn what is "good" and "bad" and what "ought to be" and "ought not to be" from these sources, largely at a preconscious or unconscious level. We tend to deeply internalize our ideals, and over time we come to accept them as "fact" or "truth" without realizing that they may be relative and learned. Consequently, we neglect to test them for validity against our perceptions of "reality" in specific situations; in fact, our perceptions are even colored by them.

Most importantly, values or ideals are widely shared in a specific culture. They emerge over time to meet specific needs in the society; i.e., they have a survival function for the society. For example, in early pioneer days in the United States rugged individualism was a value because the environmental and population conditions required it for the survival of both people and society. In heavily populated, maturely developed society, such a value might not be as functional as one of social sensitivity and collectivism. The important point is that values may have to change as society changes because of such factors as population, technology, resource availability, pollution, and economics.[4] It is undoubtedly true that some values are more universal and eternal than others, but individuals often do not discriminate in this way. Instead, values are accepted as "true" when they selectively come to mind even though the reasons for some of them may have altered. Thus, a value that once was functional for a society may either no longer be functional or even be dysfunctional.

This reasoning implies that we need some understanding of what our values are, what their sources are, what function they perform for us and for society, whether conditions have changed to alter their functionality, and whether they should be altered. The first step in this process is to become aware of our values. The next step is to explore their utility. This is a difficult and often threatening process.

## Reductive "Oughts"

It is possible for oughts to be reductive and binding, to diminish human experience. But they are not *necessarily* negative forces. Beliefs about what ought to be can serve as worthy goals, as helpful guides for behavior, and as useful boundaries. A fairly prosaic example might be the notion, which most of us accept, that a red light means we ought to stop our car. Without most of us behaving according to this ought, city driving would be even more dangerous than it already is, and so we recognize the general usefulness of conforming to the ought, even when it clearly has no immediate utility in a specific situation. How many of us have stopped and waited at a red light when it is clear that there is no traffic in any direction, and thus whether we wait or not has no value ex-

[4]See P. A. Raynolds' "Behavior in Future Organizations," pp. 357.

cept to stay within the law. The legal sanctions help us to conform so that people will not see such a situation as an opportunity for decision, on the probably correct assumption that too many such decisions would be made if any were approved. Yet the absurdity of waiting when there is no traffic and no threat of being apprehended is often amusingly accepted because we recognize the great usefulness of the rule, law, and *ought* in general.

Thus, beliefs that men ought not to kill or steal or what have you are useful as *general* goals, just as is the traffic signal. Yet there are situations in which men are asked to make decisions that involve conflicts in ideals. The submarine commander whose ship is being attacked and who has to choose between staying surfaced in the hope of rescuing a crewmate or submerging to protect his ship and the rest of his crew has no easy out. To leave a man behind or to risk the loss of everything are his options. The rules may say he ought to submerge, yet his cultural oughts may say he should try to rescue the crewmate, and his crew may believe that it is brave to try to save the man and cowardly to leave, and so on and on.

## Legalistic, Existential, and Situational "Oughts"

Even in less dramatic settings, say a student caught cheating in school, the situation is as complex. The resolution of such complexity is often accomplished by one of three ways that we will label legalistic, existential, and situational. The legalistic submarine captain might say to himself that the rule book tells him to submerge and therefore do so. The prevailing ought for such a man will be the letter of the law, no matter what. The existential[5] captain (if there ever was one) might, in reaction to the legalistic mode, assume that the rules in the book are of *no* use at all, and simply do what his impulse led him to do in the moment without reference to what others have said he ought to do or to the future consequences. The situational captain might try to take into account as many of the factors in the situation as he possibly could, including the rules and his own impulses. He would not think the rules useless or perfect, nor regard his own impulses as determining or of no import. He would try to assess the relevance of the past to his decision, and the implications of his decision for the future, to the extent he has knowledge of both. And he would weigh the probability of losing his ship and the missing crewman against the probability of losing his ship and crew if he tries. In short, he would make his decision in reference to the complexity

[5]We apologize to those who find our use of this label a smear on the philosophical movement, although we intend it as a commentary on some of the less useful aspects of it.

of the situation, as he is able to perceive it, and not by reducing the complexity either to adherence to rules or to indulgence of impulse.

Those who slavishly adhere to one source of oughts (whether governmental, religious, or organizational) at the expense of all the remaining factors can be described as imprisoned by them. It is in such instances that oughts can be reductive. By avoiding complexity by means of a reductive system, a man is diminished. All of us have known such people. Their rigidity is hard to accept.

Yet those who say that none of the oughts are of any use at all, and react against all of them because they are not always "right," make the error of thinking that anything that is not always right is never right. This "either-or" response is really the same as the legalist's. Both are attempts to avoid ambiguity; they are just at opposite ends of the spectrum. The legalist's response leads to rigidity; the existentialist's, to a valueless chaos.

The situationalist permits to come to awareness as many of the factors as he can deal with and chooses even though ambiguity remains. He knows there is no perfect option, that he will feel both good and bad no matter what he does. Reason can help him, but the choice remains his own, and he accepts the consequences.

The oughts we have been considering here are ones that men believe are relevant in all situations for all men. Exceptions are permitted only by national or organizational consensus. In wartime, killing becomes a necessary evil and sometimes even a "good." It's as if we say "What the culture giveth, only the culture can take away." Yet individuals do insist, from time to time, on making their own choices. And institutions also take stands that are unpopular because they challenge the cultural ought. To see the national stance as unquestionably "good" or assuredly "bad" is as naïve as to see opposing individuals or groups in the same way.

Think of the many ideas you have about how you and others ought to behave. Teachers ought to ______? Managers ought to ______? Ministers ought to ______? Try answering each of these questions both in terms of what they ought to *feel* and what they ought to *do*. And then try to hear yourself. What are your own oughts? Can you be so sure they are "all good" or "no good"? Try to see how your own beliefs are different from those of others and see whether you can begin to question, for yourself, your own *is-ought* relationships. To what extent do you get angry with others who do what you desire to do but believe is undesirable, bad, or wrong? To what extent do you try to solve the problem of is-ought conflict by acquiescence to the oughts or outright rejection of them rather than recognizing that the problem is one for living with, not solving? We know these are hard questions to deal with and that a more highly developed intellectual construction of the process might relieve your uncertainty. But we also *believe* that leaving it open for your own exploration can mean more for you (if you search) than closing it off by an intellectual construction. Listen for others' oughts; try to hear your own.[6] And out of the initial confusion some clarity may emerge that will be your own in a way that ideas alone cannot be.

## SUMMARY

Learning is a continuous and sometimes unconscious, trial-and-error process. It involves gaining new perceptions that lead to behavior changes. We learn most effectively when we have a possibility of satisfying our personal needs, when we expect to receive some reward or to avoid punishment, and when we can receive feedback that helps assess our learning. Important learning often involves some risk-taking; thus the importance of courage.

Ideals, or values, constitute some of our learnings that most influence our behavior. Thus, it is important that we are aware of our values and are able to assess their relevantness and functionality for effective behavior in specific situations. Values can serve either to hinder and harm or to free and protect.

[6]See "How Ethical Are Businessmen?" on pages 327–57 for the results of a comprehensive survey of ethical questions faced by businessmen.

# CHAPTER 14

# A Multidimensional View

We have explored a number of ways of thinking about the behavior of persons in organizations. Our major focus has been upon ways of thinking that were drawn from sociology and psychology. But because the behavior we have studied is so much more complex than the relatively simple ways of thinking we have used, and because the behavior is "whole" and our ways of thinking are such that they best illuminate certain "parts," it was necessary as we went along to consider concepts and ways of thinking that "pick up" still other parts. Mainly, we considered additional ways of thinking that relate to ideals, to purpose, and to learning.

These five "dimensions," if you will, are the major ones underlying the conception and structure of this book: social, psychological, ideals, purpose, and learning. Each dimension is studied by men at times virtually to the exclusion of the others. Some sociologists explore man's behavior within the confines of their discipline. Some psychologists do likewise. So too do other philosophers and theologians, engineers and managers, and even learning theorists. The value of a single focus is considerable; it is lessened mainly by the difficulty of relating what is thus illuminated to the complex realities of everyday living.

Many men, however, deal with one dimension as primary and another one or two as relevant but secondary. Some combine several dimensions into a "new" field for study. Social psychologists, for example, explicitly concern themselves with two dimensions. Some therapists focus upon psychology and learning. There are many ways to explore the complexity of the behavior of men.

We have emphasized the social and psychological dimensions, not because we think them necessarily more central than any of the other three, but rather because our experience is that they offer a means, which we understand best, of dealing eventually with all five dimensions. And we see *all five* dimensions as relevant for the kind of awareness and understanding that seems most likely to lead to more effective behavior.

In this chapter we will attempt to share with you our simplified way of thinking about each of the five dimensions and their interrelationships, as well as our view of the utility of this way of thinking.[1]

We proceed from a concern for what a man *experiences* of and from each of the dimensions. Ways of thinking about the dimensions that emphasize their "out-thereness" rather than their "in-hereness" seem less useful to us. And we will proceed in steps. First we will consider each dimension separately, then we will consider how conflict is experienced between the dimensions, within each dimension, and finally the suggested outcomes one experiences in using this way of thinking in the world.

## The Demand of Each Dimension

The social dimension of a man's experiencing has at its center *norms* that he feels as relevant in guiding his behavior. These norms relate to all the members of his group and "tell" him *what he ought to do in specific settings* and in *specific roles* (say as leader). These norms are often experienced by him as a powerfully stated directive: "Conform, or else."

The psychological dimension of a man's experiencing has at its center his own uniqueness. It directs him to be as he is, to become who *he* can be, and is most easily understood in terms of his self-concept and frame of reference. This uniqueness is often experienced as an injunction to "Be true to yourself, or else."

The ideals dimension has at its center the ultimate good things that a man believes in, and these beliefs relate to what he *ought to do in all settings, in any role.* Ideas such as freedom and equality, honesty and truth, sin and salvation are included here. A man experiences this dimension as demanding "Hold fast to the eternal verities, or else."

The purpose dimension has at its center the immediate task that a man is aware of what ought to be done. In managerial settings especially

[1]We are enormously indebted here to Professor Emeritus Fritz J. Roethlisberger of the Harvard Business School for the ideas underlying this formulation and to Professor Harold Spear of the University of Southern California for an initial structure of the formulation itself. Neither of them, of course, is responsible for our changed expression of his conceptions.

this dimension is seen as the explicit reason for the organization's existence, and thus it is often thought that it "ought" to be the central dimension of a manager's experiencing. It is often experienced as the warning "Be efficient, or else."

Finally, the learning dimension has at its core the knowledge that a man feels he ought to possess. It relates to a man's need to know, to understand, to apprehend, to see and experience, to be powerful in his environment. It is often experienced by a man as the demand "Learn, or else."

### Conflict across Dimensions

By now you will see some of man's problem. Each of the dimensions has its own "ought," its own demand, which is experienced by men as an exclusive directive. Take a student in a classroom setting. He may feel he *ought* to be learning and doing what he believes a student is supposed to do in any class, and yet he wants to go skiing and his group of friends have seemed insistent that he leave class early to meet them for the trip to the slopes, and yet the teacher is giving an assignment upon which much of his grade will depend. Can you see how in one moment, i.e., the *present,* this student might be experiencing the dimensions as mutually exclusive? How a *perfect* option that would satisfy all of them is not available to him? How he is being forced to choose among the *available* options?

Take another example. A teacher entering a classroom wants to discuss with his students an event that has occurred on the campus, but his teaching plan for the day includes material that needs to be covered if the next week's schedule is to be met. His fellow professors feel it is important to focus upon the material to be covered, and yet he wonders what he might learn with the students from examining the event, and believes it is important to be flexible in class design. He has to choose fast among the available options. The class is about to start.

Both the student and the teacher have choices to make in the present. And the choices available to them will be experienced by them as not satisfying some of the demands of all the dimensions. Thus, across the dimensions, a person experiences conflict.

You may have already sensed why this complexity is only part of it. For within each dimension there is conflict experienced. Let us examine briefly each one.

### Conflict within Dimensions

Within the social dimension, norms can exist for a group that are experienced by a member as mutually exclusive. A worker may experience two norms, say, "A man ought to help any fellow worker who asks for it" and "A man ought to produce 600 pieces a day." Say the man is behind in his work because he talked a lot earlier in the day and is trying hard to get his production up near the group's norm, when a fellow worker asks him to leave his work to give help. He has, again, a choice. Which norm should he obey? It may be that the group has insufficient experience with such a setting to have developed modes of resolution. He has to resolve the conflict, and may experience the situation as "either-or," which could be threatening because he has to break one norm or the other. If one of the norms, say the helping one, is more important to the group, the choice may be easier, but the production norm still will remain unmet.

Within the psychological dimension, internal conflict exists too. The student mentioned earlier wants the approval of the teacher at least as expressed in grades, as well as the approval of his peers who are waiting to go skiing. One is immediate, the other in the future. He may both want to go and to stay. A person experiences ambivalence often in life. "I want to ask her out, I'm afraid she will refuse." "I feel a need to know this, I'm afraid to learn this." Back and forth we go in the human condition. "I want to tell the boss just what I think of him, I'm afraid to express such strong feelings."

Within the ideals dimension, conflict often occurs. How can one be both honest and truthful and not hurt others? How can one be involved with others and yet be free? Consider this example: A young woman in a new dress asks you what you think of it. She obviously wants your approval and is uneasy about the judgments your friends may make of her at the party to which you are going. You don't like the dress, and think she doesn't look good in it. Do you tell her your truth, or do you "build her confidence" (lie?) by exclaiming how lovely she looks? Is it better to make her feel good in the present or to help her grow over the long run so that she is less frightened of others' judgments even if that makes her suffer at the party? If she is looking right at you for an answer, you hardly have time to consider the fine points intellectually, and even if you did it would result in an intellectual impasse because of all you cannot know.

The purpose dimension is no less complex. "Get the production out, have no scrap, and be sure there are no accidents and have no grievances and . . ." can drive a foreman to distraction. He may experience it as impossible. If he does this, he can't do that. More than one student has observed that if the "task" of college is personal learning, the getting of grades gets in the way. Yet survival demands grades. How can one get decent grades and still maximize one's learning? Compromise, that word that has become so ugly somehow, is the "way out," and some students become cynical as a result. The choices are often unclear, and yet the "oughts" of the purpose dimension are unyielding.

Finally, the learning dimension completes our exploration. One ought to know more. More about what? How can I know more about the wilds of the Sierras and the latest findings in archeology and the way my car works and the government of cities and the meanings of Zen while I learn more about how I relate to others and what I care about and want to do after schooling and yet study what my school requires? If I try to learn about people and myself by analytical methods with their seductive statistical significances, how can I study enough to know anything important? Yet if I proceed clinically, with the constant possibility of personal distortion, how can I ever be sure that what I learn is true? And if I go one way, how can I go the other? Besides, if I choose to learn either a lot about a little, or a little about a lot, no matter which way I choose to learn about it I may hear the residual fear that knowing is presumptuous, that *hubris* is dangerous, and therefore be afraid to learn.

So it should be clear that in addition to conflict *across* our five dimensions, man experiences conflict *within* them. Given this experiential complexity you may be sorely tempted to throw up your hands and, in effect, to say to hell with it all.

If you do, you certainly will not be alone. Retreat from the complexity of experiencing is a common reaction. Let us try to explain why we find the multidimensional view of experiencing useful even if it makes large demands upon its users. Before we do, perhaps a summary (Table 1) will be helpful, and a chart (Table 2) giving examples of the conflicts.

Given the conflict experienced within and across the dimensions, how can anyone ever keep track of what is going on, in the present, so as to be able to make better decisions; i.e., to *behave* "better?" Let us explore the alternatives first.

It is all too common to see people withdraw from the complexity of their experiencing to focus upon one or two of the dimensions to an extent that reduces the experienced reality of the others. The foreman whose one-dimensional resolution of his complex experiencing leads him to focus upon purpose, to see his world as a place in which he is safe only when he obeys the injunction "Be efficient or else," does not really escape the realities of the other dimensions. He simply tries to hide from them and thus lock out his experiencing of them. His fellow foremen's norms, his employees' norms, his bosses' expectations, his own needs for affection and approval, his church's teachings, his need for growth can be ignored only in part, and then only with great effort and anxiety that can eat out his stomach. As long as he can continue to focus upon just one dimension he is diminished as a man, and because of his foreman's role he may diminish other men. The constant threat that his "efficiency" may not prevail as a result of his dedication to it must be bitter irony to live with. If he urges speed on his employees and exceeds his output quota only to have one of them seriously injured when his boss wants more output but no accidents, what can he feel? Fury? Fear? There is no one-dimensional escape from the human condition, only the illusion of one, and it can be more costly for a man in the long run than the discomfort of dealing with all of what is experienced as real.

**Table 1 A Multidimensional Scheme**

| *Dimension* | *Refers to* | *Experienced conflict within dimension* | *Experienced demand of dimension* |
|---|---|---|---|
| *Social* | What one ought to do in specific settings or roles | Mutually exclusive experiencing of norms | Conform or else. |
| *Psychological* | What one ought to do to be as one is, as one can become | Mutually exclusive experiencing of desires and fears | Be true to yourself or else. |
| *Ideals* | What one ought to do in all settings and roles | Mutually exclusive experiencing of ideals | Hold fast to the eternal verities or else. |
| *Purpose* | What one ought to do to get tasks done | Mutually exclusive experiencing of task goals | Be efficient or else. |
| *Learning* | What one ought to do to know more about oneself and the world and the relationship between the two | Mutually exclusive experiencing of learning goals and means | Learn or else. |

Many persons, of course, do not seek such an extreme avoidance of experiencing more than one dimension. They focus on two or perhaps three to an extent that seriously reduces their experiencing of the others. The teacher who is greatly concerned with his own and his students' learning and personal experiencing may focus upon the psychological and learning dimensions to such an extent that the social, ideals, and purpose dimensions are avoided as much as possible. The advancing executive who focuses largely upon the purpose and social dimensions may do so at the diminishing of the others as he climbs higher in his organization by efficiently conforming. The minister who focuses upon ideals and purpose can become a sanctimonious executive whose major response to the impact of the other dimensions is righteous anger.

Most of us seem to have a recognizable preference for some of the dimensions and a somewhat stunted appreciation of the others. We function pretty well, and we seek to heighten our sensitivity to preferred dimensions as far as possible, while seeking at least adequate responsiveness to the others. The theoretical possibility of a person truly experiencing fully all five dimensions may be extremely rare in fact.

So our response to the multidimensionality of experiencing varies both in terms of the number of dimensions focused upon as well as the *extent* to which the focus is intense. The fewer the dimensions focused upon and the greater the intensity of that focus, the poorer the experiencing and the less effective the behavior of a man. To the extent that

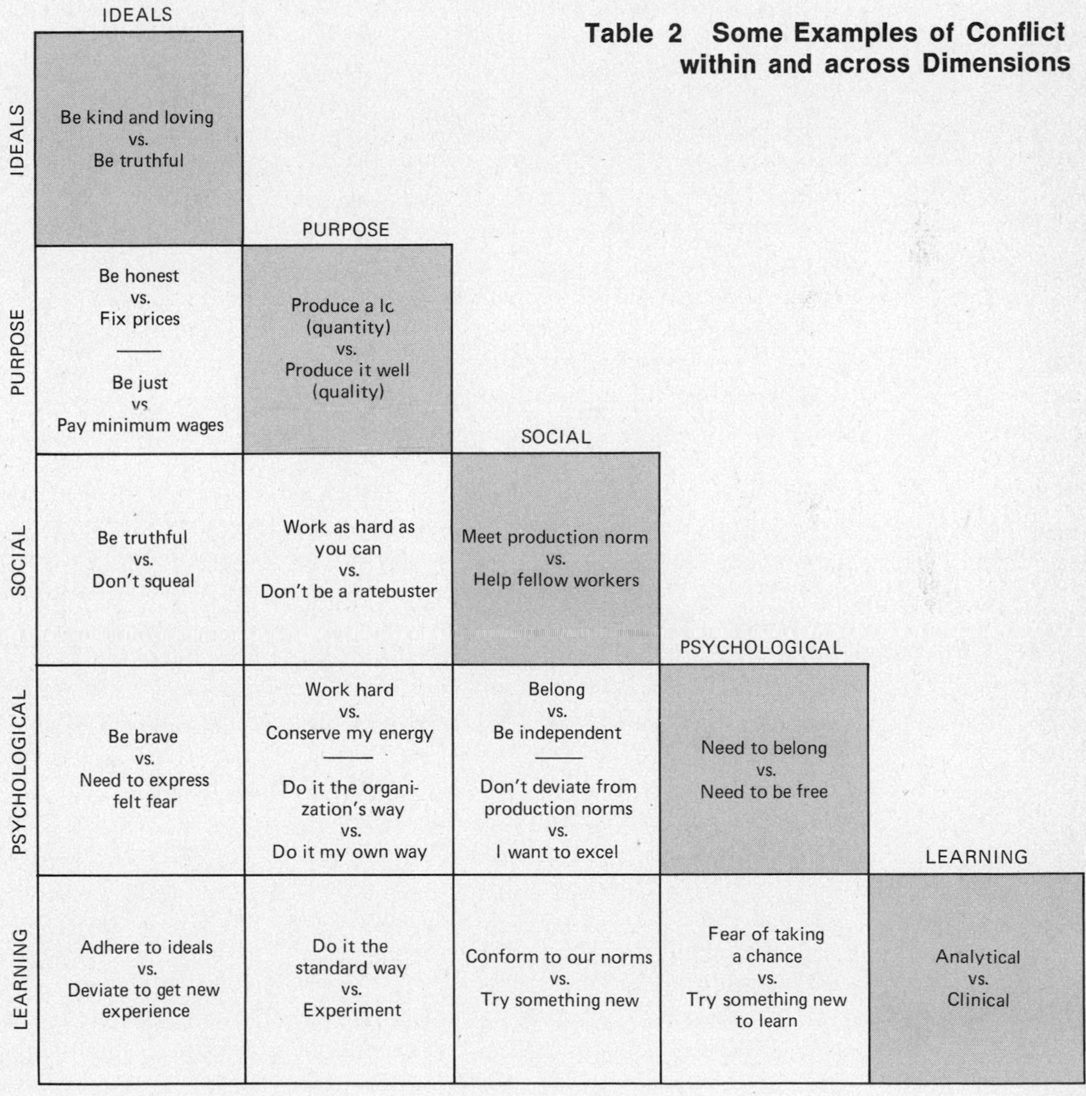

**Table 2 Some Examples of Conflict within and across Dimensions**

| | IDEALS | PURPOSE | SOCIAL | PSYCHOLOGICAL | LEARNING |
|---|---|---|---|---|---|
| IDEALS | Be kind and loving vs. Be truthful | | | | |
| PURPOSE | Be honest vs. Fix prices —— Be just vs Pay minimum wages | Produce a lc (quantity) vs. Produce it well (quality) | | | |
| SOCIAL | Be truthful vs. Don't squeal | Work as hard as you can vs. Don't be a ratebuster | Meet production norm vs. Help fellow workers | | |
| PSYCHOLOGICAL | Be brave vs. Need to express felt fear | Work hard vs. Conserve my energy —— Do it the organization's way vs. Do it my own way | Belong vs. Be independent —— Don't deviate from production norms vs. I want to excel | Need to belong vs. Need to be free | |
| LEARNING | Adhere to ideals vs. Deviate to get new experience | Do it the standard way vs. Experiment | Conform to our norms vs. Try something new | Fear of taking a chance vs. Try something new to learn | Analytical vs. Clinical |

any of the five dimensions is diminished in his experiencing and behavior, so too is he diminished.

But then how is one to open to greater experiencing of all the dimensions, in the present, instant to instant, when such experiencing often includes conflict within and between the dimensions? Isn't one simply immobilized by the experiencing of the lack of perfect options and the limited utility of the available options that are perceived? And if he decides and acts, isn't he at that moment forced to focus more on some dimensions than others? Let us try to answer these questions as best we can.

What a multidimensional focusing involves is an awareness in the present of as much of what is going on as your current capacity permits. It asks that you accept that you cannot at any one instant comprehend all of what is going on, any more than you could comprehend a total organization in Chapter 1 of this book. Thus, your own *imperfection* is a limiting factor, and although you can grow, and become able to see more of what is going on, some of it will continue to escape you.

What *is* available to you in your experiencing will often seem *ambiguous*. It will not be absolutely clear what things or events or persons mean, although you can grow and become able to understand more. You may experience, as a result of the imperfection and ambiguity, the *uncertainty* that surrounds your decisions for action. You may not feel sure what the outcomes will be. And yet you will feel the need to *do*, and not just *be*, to act and not just sit there experiencing.

These three features of our experiencing—imperfection, ambiguity, and uncertainty—should not make us either cynical or complacent; we should try to become as open to them as we can and accept them insofar as possible. Only in that way can we grow and thereby reduce our own imperfection, the ambiguity of our perceptions, and the uncertainty of our decisions. For only as we experience and accept them can we become more *flexible* in our responses to the various dimensions, dealing now with this and now with that one, reversing ourselves as we become aware of the need of a new direction, and picking up later what we left before.

In other words, we must deal with the stuff of living, not just with concepts about "life"; we must experience the present in terms of flows, not containers; as bits and pieces, not neat packages. And we must think of our "balance," in responding to the five dimensions, over time, not just in the present. All of us will, in any instant, be "out of balance" to some extent, but over time our balance in dealing with all the dimensions may be pretty good.

Your capacity to grow in human skill will be proportionate to the extent to which you can accept the experiencing of imperfection, ambiguity, and uncertainty in yourself and outside you and respond to this experiencing with flexible, reversible, and, over time, balanced behavior that seeks to work things *through* rather than out.

Once you have accepted the initial discomfort that inevitably comes with increased awareness, the growth that you will slowly achieve can do more than give you increased skill at dealing with yourself and the world. It can give you a feeling of well-being, an excitement for the fullness of life, a greater understanding of yourself, an increased capacity for joy as well as sorrow—in short, a more complete experiencing of yourself as the subject rather than the object of your life.

But you will recognize that your potential for this kind of living will be realized eventually only by accepting and working through the discomfort of your own learning now and tomorrow and the next day. It is not easy. There are no formulas. The outcomes cannot be sure. You may not make it.

We know that this view may seem less attractive than the illusions of perfection, clarity, and certainty that are often offered us. But we believe that any growth in us as human beings must proceed from what *is* for man, not from what we wish were or are afraid might be. We hope you will agree, and while balancing uneasily, will continue to grow over time in understanding, skill, effectiveness, and humanity.

# The Need to Know and the Fear of Knowing

*Abraham H. Maslow*

## Fear of Knowledge: Evasion of Knowledge: Pains and Dangers of Knowing

From our point of view, Freud's greatest discovery is that *the* great cause of much of psychological illness is the fear of knowledge of oneself—of one's emotions, impulses, memories, capacities, potentialities, of one's destiny. We have discovered that fear of knowledge of oneself is very often isomorphic with, and parallel with, fear of the outside world. That is, inner problems and outer problems tend to be deeply similar and to be related to each other. Therefore we speak simply of fear of knowledge in general, without discriminating too sharply fear-of-the-inner from fear-of-the-outer.

In general this kind of fear is defensive, in the sense that it is a protection of our self-esteem, of our love and respect for ourselves. We tend to be afraid of any knowledge that could cause us to despise ourselves or to make us feel inferior, weak, worthless, evil, shameful. We protect ourselves and our ideal image of ourselves by repression and similar defenses, which are essentially techniques by which we avoid becoming conscious of unpleasant or dangerous truths. And in psychotherapy the maneuvers by which we continue avoiding this consiousness of painful truth, the ways in which we fight the efforts of the therapist to help us see the truth, we call "resistance." All the techniques of the therapist are in one way or another truth-revealing, or are ways of strengthening the pa-

• Reprinted by permission from Abraham H. Maslow, *Toward a Psychology of Being* (Princeton, N.J.: D. Van Nostrand, Company, Inc., 1962), pp. 57–64.

tient so he can bear the truth. ("*To be completely honest with oneself is the very best effort a human being can make.*"—S. Freud)

But there is another kind of truth we tend to evade. Not only do we hang on to our psychopathology, but also we tend to evade personal growth because this, too, can bring another kind of fear, of awe, of feelings of weakness and inadequacy.[1] And so we find another kind of resistance, a denying of our best side, of our talents, of our finest impulses, of our highest potentialities, of our creativeness. In brief, this is the struggle against our own greatness, the fear of *hubris*.

Here we are reminded that our own Adam and Eve myth, with its dangerous Tree of Knowledge that mustn't be touched, is paralleled in many other cultures which also feel that ultimate knowledge is something reserved for the gods. Most religions have had a thread of antiintellectualism (along with other threads, of course), some trace of preference for faith or belief or piety rather than for knowledge, or the feeling that *some* forms of knowledge were too dangerous to meddle with and had best be forbidden or reserved to a few special people. In most cultures those revolutionaries who defied the gods by seeking out their secrets were punished heavily, like Adam and Eve, Prometheus and Oedipus, and have been remembered as warnings to all others not to try to be godlike.

And, if I may say it in a very condensed way, it is precisely the godlike in ourselves that we are ambivalent about, fascinated by and fearful of, motivated to and defensive against. This is one aspect of the basic human predicament, that we are simultaneously worms and gods. Every one of our great creators, our godlike people, has testified to the element of courage that is needed in the lonely moment of creation, affirming something new (contradictory to the old). This is a kind of daring, a going out in front all alone, a defiance, a challenge. The moment of fright is quite understandable but must nevertheless be overcome if creation is to be possible. Thus to discover in oneself a great talent can certainly bring exhilaration but it also brings a fear of the dangers and responsibilities and duties of being a leader and of being all alone. Responsibility can be seen as a heavy burden and evaded as long as possible. Think of the mixture of feelings of awe, humility, even of fright that have been reported to us, let us say, by people who have been elected President.

A few standard clinical examples can teach us much. First is the fairly common phenomenon encountered in therapy with women.[2] Many brilliant women are caught up in the problem of making an unconscious identification between intelligence and masculinity. To probe, to search, to be curious, to affirm, to discover, all these she may feel as defeminizing, especially if her husband, in his uncertain masculinity, is threatened thereby. Many cultures and many religions have kept women from knowing and studying, and I feel that one dynamic root of this action is the desire to keep them "feminine" (in a sadomasochistic sense); for instance, women cannot be priests or rabbis.[3]

[1]S. Cohen, "A Growth Theory of Neurotic Resistance to Psychotherapy," *Journal of Humanistic Psychology*, I (1961), 48–63.

[2]H. A. Overstreet, *The Mature Mind* (New York: W. W. Norton & Company, Inc., 1949).

[3]A. H. Maslow, H. Rand, and S. Newman, "Some Parallels Between the Dominance and Sexual Behavior of Monkeys and the Fantasies of Psychoanalytic Patients," *Journal of Nervous and Mental Disease*, CXXXI (1960), 202–12.

The timid man also may tend to identify probing curiosity as somehow challenging to others, as if somehow, by being intelligent and searching out the truth, he is being assertive and bold and manly in a way that he can't back up, and that such a pose will bring down upon him the wrath of the other, older, stronger men. So also may children identify curious probing as a trespass upon the prerogatives of their gods, the all-powerful adults. And of course it is even easier to find the complementary attitude in adults. For often they find the restless curiosity of their children at least a nuisance and sometimes even a threat and a danger, especially when it is about sexual matters. It is still the unusual parent who approves and enjoys curiosity in his children. Something similar can be seen in the exploited, the downtrodden, the weak minority or the slave. He may fear to know too much, to explore freely. This might arouse the wrath of his lords. A defensive attitude of pseudo-stupidity is common in such groups. In any case, the exploiter, or the tyrant, out of the dynamics of the situation, is not likely to encourage curiosity, learning, and knowledge in his underlings. People who know too much are likely to rebel. Both the exploited and the exploiter are impelled to regard knowledge as incompatible with being a good, nice, well-adjusted slave. In such a situation, knowledge is dangerous, quite dangerous. A status of weakness or subordination, or low self-esteem inhibits the need to know. The direct, uninhibited staring gaze is the main technique that an overlord monkey uses to establish dominance.[4] The subordinate animal characteristically drops his gaze.

This dynamic can sometimes be seen, unhappily, even in the classroom. The really bright student, the eager questioner, the probing searcher, especially if he is brighter than his teacher, is too often seen as a "wise guy," a threat to discipline, a challenger of his teacher's authority.

That "knowing" can unconsciously mean domination, mastery, control, and perhaps even contempt, can be seen also from the scoptophiliac, who can feel some sense of power over the naked women he peeps at, as if his eyes were an instrument of domination that he could use for raping. In this sense, most men are Peeping Toms and stare boldly at women, undressing them with their eyes. The biblical use of the word "knowing" as identical with sexual "knowing" is another use of the metaphor.

At an unconscious level, knowing as an intrusive penetrating into, as a kind of masculine sexual equivalent can help us to understand the archaic complex of conflicting emotions that may cluster around the child's peeping into secrets, into the unknown, some women's feeling of a contradiction between femininity and boldly knowing, of the underdog's feeling that knowing is a prerogative of the master, of the religious man's fear that knowing trespasses on the jurisdiction of the gods, is dangerous and will be resented. Knowing, like "knowing," can be an act of self-affirmation.

## Knowledge for Anxiety-Reduction and for Growth

So far I have been talking about the need to know for its own sake, for the sheer delight and primitive satisfaction of knowledge and understanding *per se*. It makes the person bigger, wiser, richer, stronger, more

[4] Ibid.

evolved, more mature. It represents the actualization of a human potentiality, the fulfillment of the human destiny foreshadowed by human possibilities. We then have a parallel to the unobstructed blooming of a flower or to the singing of birds. This is the way in which an apple tree bears apples, without striving or effort, simply as an expression of its own inherent nature.

But we know also that curiosity and exploration are "higher" needs than safety, which is to say that the need to feel safe, secure, unanxious, unafraid is prepotent, stronger than curiosity. Both in monkeys and in human children this can be openly observed. The young child in a strange environment will characteristically hang on to its mother and only then venture out little by little from her lap to probe into things, to explore and to probe. If she disappears and he becomes frightened, the curiosity disappears until safety is restored. He explores only out of a safe harbor. So also for Harlow's baby monkeys. Anything that frightens sends them fleeing back to the mother-surrogate. Clinging there, he can first observe and *then* venture out. If she is not there, he may simply curl up into a ball and whimper. Harlow's motion pictures show this very clearly.

The adult human being is far more subtle and concealed about his anxieties and fears. If they do not overwhelm him altogether, he is very apt to repress them, to deny even to himself that they exist. Frequently, he does not "know" that he is afraid.

There are many ways of coping with such anxieties and some of these are cognitive. To such a person, the unfamiliar, vaguely perceived, the mysterious, the hidden, the unexpected are all apt to be threatening. One way of rendering them familiar, predictable, manageable, controllable, i.e., unfrightening, and harmless, is to know them and to understand them. And so knowledge may have not only a growing-forward function, but also an anxiety-reducing function, a protective homeostatic function. The overt behavior may be very similar, but the motivations may be extremely different. And the subjective consequences are then also very different. On the one hand we have the sigh of relief and the feeling of lowered tension, let us say, of the worried householder exploring a mysterious and frightening noise downstairs in the middle of the night with a gun in his hand when he finds that it is nothing. This is quite different from the illumination and exhilaration, even the ecstacy, of a young student looking through a microscope who sees for the first time the minute structure of the kidney or who suddenly understands the structure of a symphony or the meaning of an intricate poem or political theory. In the latter instances, one feels bigger, smarter, stronger, fuller, more capable, successful, more perceptive. Supposing our sense organs were to become more efficient, our eyes suddenly keener, our ears unstopped. This is how we would feel. This is what can happen in education and in psychotherapy—and does happen often enough.

This motivational dialectic can be seen on the largest human canvases, the great philosophies, the religious structures, the political and legal systems, the various sciences, even the culture as a whole. To put it very simply, too simply, they can represent simultaneously the outcome of the need to understand and the need for safety in varying proportions. Sometimes the safety needs can almost entirely bend the cognitive needs to their own anxiety-allaying purposes. The anxiety-free person can be more bold and more courageous and can explore and theorize for the sake of knowledge itself. It is certainly reasonable to assume that the latter is more likely to approach the truth, the real nature of things. A safety-philosophy or religion or science is more apt to be blind than a growth-philosophy, religion, or science.

## The Avoidance of Knowledge as Avoidance of Responsibility

Anxiety and timidity not only bend curiosity and knowing and understanding to their own ends, using them, so to speak, as tools for allaying anxiety, but also the lack of curiosity can be an active or a passive expression of anxiety and fear. (This is not the same as the atrophy of curiosity through disuse.) That is, we can seek knowledge in order to reduce anxiety and we can also avoid knowing in order to reduce anxiety. To use Freudian language, incuriosity, learning difficulties, pseudo-stupidity can be a defense. Knowledge and action are very closely bound together, all agree. I go much further, and am convinced that knowledge and action are frequently synonymous, even identical in the Socratic fashion. Where we know fully and completely, suitable action follows automatically and reflexly. Choices are then made without conflict and with full spontaneity.[5]

This we see at a high level in the healthy person who seems to know what is right and wrong, good and bad, and shows this in his easy, full functioning. But we see this at another level altogether in the young child (or in the child hidden in the adult) for whom thinking about an action can be the same as having acted—"the omnipotence of thought," the psychoanalysts call it. That is, if he has had a wish for the death of his father, he may react unconsciously as if he had actually killed him. In fact, one function of adult psychotherapy is to de-fuse this childish identity so that the person need not feel guilty about childish thoughts as if they had been deeds.

In any case, this close relation between knowing and doing can help us to interpret one cause of the fear of knowing as deeply a fear of doing, a fear of the consequences that flow from knowing, a fear of its dangerous responsibilities. Often it is better not to know, because if you did know, then you would have to act and stick your neck out. This is a little involved, a little like the man who said, "I'm so glad I don't like oysters. Because if I liked oysters, I'd eat them, and I hate the darn things."

It was certainly safer for the Germans living near Dachau not to know what was going on, to be blind and pseudo-stupid. For if they knew, they would either have had to do something about it or else feel guilty about being cowards.

The child, too, can play this same trick, denying, refusing to see what is plain to anyone else: that his father is a contemptible weakling, or that his mother doesn't really love him. This kind of knowledge is a call for action which is impossible. Better not to know.

In any case, we now know enough about anxiety and cognition to reject the extreme position that many philosophers and psychological theo-

[5]But see S. Cohen, "Neurotic Ambiguity and Neurotic Hiatus Between Knowledge and Action," *Journal of Existential Psychiatry*, in press.

rists have held for centuries, that *all* cognitive needs are instigated by anxiety and are *only* efforts to reduce anxiety. For many years, this seemed plausible, but now our animal and child experiments contradict this theory in its pure form for they all show that, generally, anxiety kills curiosity and exploration, and that they are mutually incompatible, especially when anxiety is extreme. The cognitive needs show themselves most clearly in safe and nonanxious situations.

A recent book summarizes the situation nicely.

> The beautiful thing about a belief system is that it seems to be constructed to serve both masters at once: to understand the world insofar as possible, and to defend against it insofar as necessary. We do not agree with those who hold that people selectively distort their cognitive functioning so that they will see, remember and think only what they want to do. Instead, we hold to the view that people will do so only to the extent that they have to and no more. For we are all motivated by the desire which is sometimes strong and sometimes weak, to see reality as it actually is, even if it hurts.[6]

## SUMMARY

It seems quite clear that the need to know, if we are to understand it well, must be integrated with fear of knowing, with anxiety, with needs for safety and security. We wind up with a dialectical back and forth relationship which is simultaneously a struggle between fear and courage. All those psychological and social factors that increase fear will cut our impulse to know; all factors that permit courage, freedom and boldness will thereby also free our need to know.

# How Ethical Are Businessmen?

*Raymond C. Baumhart, S. J.*

What would you do if—

- as a director of a large corporation, you learned at a board meeting of an impending merger with a smaller company? Suppose this company has had an unprofitable year, and its stock is selling at a price so low that you are certain it will rise when news of the merger

[6]M. Rokeach, *The Open and Closed Mind* (New York: Basic Books, Inc., 1960), p. 400.

• Reprinted by permission from *Harvard Business Review*, XXXIX, No. 4 (July–August, 1961), 6–31. 

becomes public knowledge. Would you buy some stock? Or tell a friend? Or tell your broker?

• as president of a company in a highly competitive industry, you learned that a competitor had made an important scientific discovery which would give him a substantial advantage over you? If you had an opportunity to hire one of his employees who knew the details of the discovery, would you do it?

What do you think about—

• an executive earning $10,000 a year who has been padding his expense account by about $500 a year?

• an executive owning stock in a company with which his own company regularly does business?

• the idea that management should act in the interest of shareholders alone?

These problems were posed as part of a lengthy questionnaire on business ethics completed by some 1,700 HBR executive readers—34% of the 5,000 cross section polled. This high rate of return, and the hundreds of thoughtful essays written by these anonymous administrators on the margin of their questionnaires and on separate letterheads paint a picture of executives' deep concern over business behavior. (For a profile of these respondents, see Table 1.)

During the past decade, much has been written about ethics in business. Most of the books and articles are based on the experiences of one man, or on a priori reasoning. Few authors have approached business ethics empirically, surveying the ideas, problems, and attitudes of a large number of businessmen. This study employs such an empirical approach.

We hoped that in the process of securing and reporting the data, we would prompt top management to re-examine fruitfully its thinking and practices. In addition, we wished to give scholars the businessman's point of view, that is, what he regards as ethical problems and unethical behavior—though, of course, this is not meant to imply that ethics is a matter of statistics, or a majority response constitutes an ethical answer.

Here are some of the highlights of our study:

Executives are alert to the social responsibilities of business as these are expressed in general terms. They see the corporation as a human society, a microcosm of the larger society in which it functions. (See the section on "Business Responsibility?")

As for specific business practices, executives often disagree about what is the ethical thing to do. (See "I'm Ethical, But Is He?")

Though our respondents profess a lofty level of ethical aspiration for themselves, they reveal a lower opinion of the practices of the "average" businessman. (See "Cynicism.")

Executives say that the man most likely to act ethically is one with a well-defined personal code. If he also has a boss who is highly ethical, his behavior will be consistently upright. But watch out, say executives, for there are many pressures for unethical conduct. (See "Ethical Influences.")

Executives admit and point out the presence of numerous generally accepted practices in their industry which they consider unethical. Our respondents cite many daily problems in which the "economic" solution conflicts with the "ethical" solution. (See "Chapter & Verse.")

If unethical practices are to be reduced, executives say that top management must lead the way. The men at the top must be individuals of principle, who unmistakably reveal their ethical attitude, not only verbally, but also by forceful actions. (See "Pressure.")

As a help in correcting unethical practices, most executives would welcome a written code of ethics for their industry. But this code must have "teeth," be capable of enforcement, and embody specific guides for conduct if it is to do the job. (See "Code of Ethics.")

Most executives believe that organized religion and clergymen have been lax in providing guidance for the ethical problems of business. At the same time, the welcome which businessmen give to clerical advice is directly proportional to the amount of knowledge that the individual clergyman has about business. (See "Role of Religion.")

Now, for the details, let us turn to the specifics of our findings, so that you can compare your thinking and your views with those of the executives surveyed and interviewed in our study.

## Business Responsibility?

Polybius, the Greek historian, summarized a nation's decline in a single sentence: "At Carthage, nothing which results in profit is regarded as disgraceful."[1] Modern critics have leveled the same charge at U.S. business, and we wondered if executives still adhere to this Carthaginian creed. To find out, we asked respondents to comment on a recent statement by a student of business: ". . . the businessman exists for only one purpose, to create and deliver value satisfactions at a profit to himself. . . . If what is offered can be sold at a profit (not even necessarily a long-term profit), then it is legitimate. . . . The cultural, spiritual, social, and moral consequences of his actions are none of his occupational concern."[2]

From top to bottom of the corporate ladder, a convincing 94% say: "We disagree!" As one personnel director sees it: "This man lives in a vacuum, ignoring the society that gave him his opportunity, his responsibility to make it better rather than worse as a result of his existence." In twentieth century America, it seems, some things which result in profit *are* regarded as disgraceful—even by professional profit-makers.

In fact, our respondents indicate that they regard untempered profit maximization as immoral—agreeing with the thesis advanced in HBR recently by Professor Robert N. Anthony.[3] Five out of every six executives

[1] *The Histories of Polybius* (New York: G. P. Putnam's Sons, 1923), III, p. 393.

[2] Theodore Levitt, "Are Advertising and Marketing Corrupting Society? It's Not Your Worry, Levitt Tells Business," *Advertising Age*, October 6, 1958, p. 89.

[3] "The Trouble with Business," *Harvard Business Review*, November–December, 1960, p. 162.

in our survey reacted affirmatively to this paraphrase of his view: "For corporation executives to act in the interest of shareholders alone, and not also in the interest of employees and consumers, is unethical."

Further, the answers of our executive panel reveal attitudes far different from those of the legendary rugged individualist. For example, only one executive in five agrees with the traditional dictum, "Let the buyer beware." But don't conclude that the "ethical" attitude revealed by these answers stems solely from a desire to do what is right *because* it is right.

**Table 1 Profile of the Executives Responding**

*Management position*

| | |
|---|---|
| *Top management:* chairman of the board; board member; owner; partner; president; division or executive vice president; vice president; treasurer; secretary-treasurer; controller; secretary (to the corporation); general manager; general superintendent; editor; administrative director; dean; and assistants thereto. | 45% |
| *Upper middle management:* functional department head (e.g., advertising, sales, promotion, production, purchasing, personnel, engineering, public relations, brand manager, and the like). | 27 |
| *Lower middle management:* assistant to functional department head; district manager; branch manager; section manager; and the like. | 12 |
| *Nonmanagement personnel:* all others employed in the business. | 9 |
| *Professional:* doctor; practicing lawyer; practicing CPA; professor; consultant; military officer; government official; union official; clergyman; and the like. | 7 |

| *Formal education* | | *Income group* | |
|---|---|---|---|
| High school or less | 5% | Under $10,000 | 12% |
| Some college | 19 | $10,000–19,999 | 45 |
| Bachelor's degree | 36 | $20,000–29,999 | 23 |
| Graduate school | 40 | $30,000–39,999 | 8 |
| | | $40,000–49,999 | 4 |
| | | $50,000–74,999 | 4 |

This conclusion would ignore the belief of our respondents that "sound ethics is good business in the long run." Only one respondent in a hundred disagrees with this statement!

Apparently management does believe that shady or ruthless operations might make money for a time, but that a corporation cannot mistreat the public for long and still survive. Once stung, the public has a long memory. For the long run, say executives, sound ethics not only is good public relations but also is conducive to making money.

**Table 1 (continued)**

| *Formal education* | | *Income group* | |
|---|---|---|---|
| | | $75,000–99,999 | 2 |
| | | $100,000 and over | 2 |

| *Age* | | *Company size by number of employees* | |
|---|---|---|---|
| Under 30 years | 6% | 1–49 | 15% |
| 30–34 | 12 | 50–99 | 7 |
| 35–39 | 16 | 100–249 | 10 |
| 40–44 | 18 | 250–499 | 9 |
| 45–49 | 17 | 500–999 | 10 |
| 50–54 | 13 | 1,000–9,999 | 26 |
| 55–59 | 10 | 10,000–19,999 | 7 |
| 60–65 | 5 | 20,000 or more | 16 |
| Over 65 | 3 | | |

*Industry*

| | | | |
|---|---|---|---|
| Manufacturing consumer goods | 16% | Construction | 2% |
| Manufacturing industrial goods | 25 | Mining or extraction; oil | 2 |
| Engineering, research and development | 6 | Retail or wholesale trade | 7 |
| Management consulting and business services | 6 | Transportation, public utilities | 5 |
| Banking, investment, insurance | 10 | Advertising, media, publishing | 4 |
| | | Consumer services | 3 |
| | | Other | 14 |

*Note:* Of the 1,700 total returns, 1,531 were received in time for machine tabulation, and the balance inspected and found to have no significant demographic or opinion differences.

Are executives as socially responsible as these findings suggest? We wonder, especially in light of the fact that 15% of our panel agree with the statement that "whatever is good business is good ethics." This response prompts us to exercise caution in praising our panel's posture of social awareness. To say that "whatever is good business is good ethics" makes economic efficiency the norm of ethical behavior; in other words, the economic consequences of a business transaction determine whether it is right or wrong. This is the same as saying that if a thing makes money, it is good—and sounds pretty much like that Carthaginian creed that nothing resulting in profit is disgraceful. The small size of this group doesn't alter the fact of its existence.

However, looking at the sum of our information about the social consciousness of the executives responding, we gain the over-all impression that most businessmen have a definite awareness of their social responsibilities. They view the corporation as being more than a money-making producer of goods and services. Their level of ethical ideals appear to be high. There is even substantial agreement among them that a few specific practices are absolutely wrong. Thus:

- 88% regard providing a "call girl" as always unethical.[4]
- 86% say they regard padding expense accounts as always unethical.

Clearly, these executives see a business enterprise as a society of human beings—a society with obligations not only to the people who provide capital, but also to employees, customers, suppliers, government, and even, at times, competitors.

## I'm Ethical, But Is He?

Although our respondents profess a lofty level of ethical aspiration for themselves, they reveal a lower opinion of the practices of the "average" businessman. It is commonly observed that there is sometimes a discrepancy between what a man *says* he thinks or does, and what he *actually* thinks or does. Such a discrepancy is very likely to be present in answers to questions which require ethical choices, as in this study. Replies to such queries often correspond more closely to the image which the respondent would like others to have of him than to a realistic picture of himself. It is human to try to picture oneself in the most favorable way.

[4] [*Harvard Business Review* editors' note.] "That some of these practices are especially controversial is attested to by the fact that we received a number of letters from purchasing agents protesting our connecting purchasing agents with "call girls" in the questionnaire and requesting that we refrain from publishing our findings. The question was included for methodological reasons, with no evidence in the questionnaire itself that we believe this to be a prevalent practice by purchasing agents or that we were singling them out for attention. As was originally intended, the findings are reported above by Father Baumhart without explicit reference to purchasing agents; but, in the light of public editorializing about our asking the question, we feel that we must take some notice of it, if only to avoid the appearance of yielding to pressure tactics on the part of an important segment of American business."

We wanted to take this tendency into account in our study, and so we asked some of our case situation questions in two different ways. One half of our panel was asked: "What would *you* do?" The other half: "What would the *average* executive do?" These questions and their replies are shown in Figure 1. The differences in the answers of the two groups are striking.

Such differences certainly need closer scrutiny. Could they have been due to a flaw in our sampling? Apparently not. Our panel was split on a random basis. On checking, the two halves of our sample match demographically; in fact, the two halves of our sample are so very much alike in their opinions that the replies to the 25 questions which all executives were asked are, statistically, virtually identical. Hence, the differences in the replies of the two groups must clearly signal that our respondents did recognize the ethical content in the questions, and reacted accordingly.

Actual business practice, then, is probably closer to what respondents say "the average executive would do" in Figure 1 than it is to what they say "I would do." On this basis, the number of executives who apparently condone expense account padding and would use privy knowledge for personal financial gain is hardly reassuring.

## Cynicism

The possibility that general business behavior is quite different from the personal ethical attitudes reported by our respondents is increased by their cynicism about typical executive behavior. This cynicism is illustrated by our panel's reaction to this observation by a friendly critic of business, who said: "The American business executive tends to ignore the great ethical laws as they apply immediately to his work. He is preoccupied chiefly with gain."[5]

Almost half of our panel agree. This same cynicism is underscored in replies to a later question about adoption of industry-wide ethical practices codes. Four of every seven executives believe that businessmen "would violate a code of ethics whenever they thought they could avoid detection."

If our respondents possess the high ethic described earlier, and at the same time are cynical about the ethics of other executives, then undoubtedly they do not identify themselves with the "average" executive. Would such a lack of identification be true of doctors, lawyers, or professors? And does it not suggest that management still has a distance to go before it can truly be called a profession?

Coupled with this cynicism is the clear suggestion in our data that some executives have a "double ethic." This double ethic consists of applying one standard to friends and another standard to strangers. Some examples:

- Many executives who would tell a friend secret news of a forthcoming merger would not tell their broker.

[5]Rabbi Louis Finkelstein, "The Businessman's Moral Failure," *Fortune*, September, 1958, p. 116.

Case 1

Imagine that you are the president of a company in a highly competitive industry. You learn that a competitor has made an important scientific discovery which will give him an advantage that will substantially reduce, but not eliminate, the profits of your company for about a year. If there was some hope of hiring one of the competitor's employees who knew the details of the discovery, would you try to hire him?

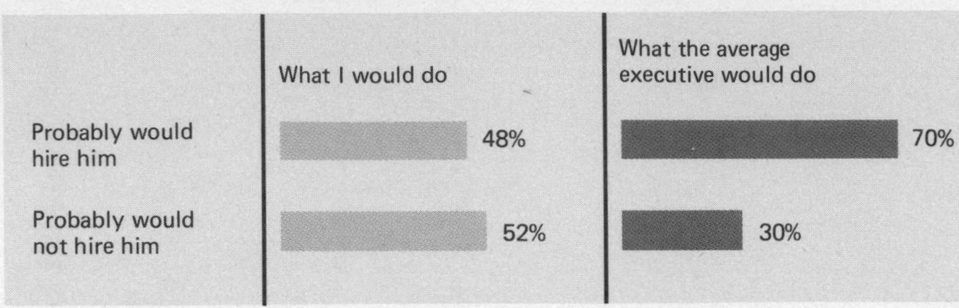


Case 2

Imagine that you are a member of the board of directors of a large corporation. At a board meeting you learn of an impending merger with a smaller company which has had an unprofitable year, and whose stock is presently selling at a price so low that you are certain it will rise when news of the merger becomes public knowledge.

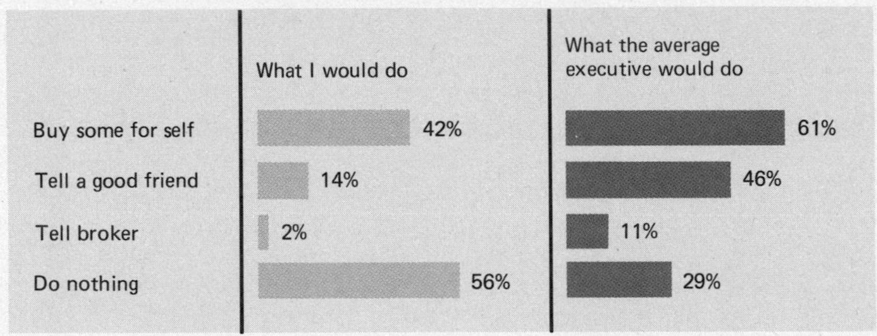


Case 3

As president of a company manufacturing consumer goods, you are considering new ideas for increasing sales. Your marketing department has presented two programs, each of which would achieve the desired increase in sales. One program employs an advertising theme portraying ownership of your product as a symbol of the purchaser's superiority, while the other program uses an advertising theme emphasizing the quality of your product.

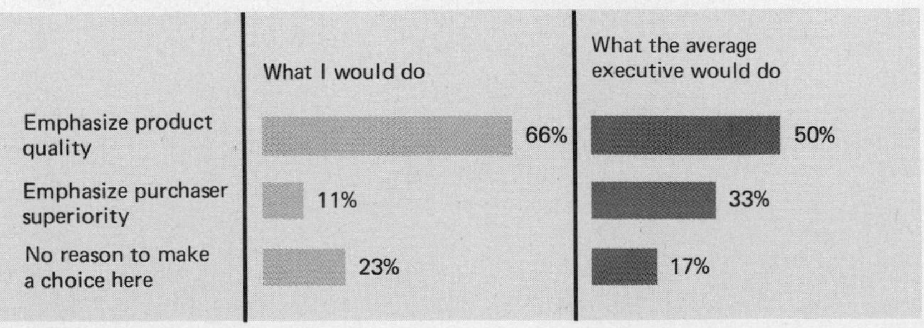


**Figure 1**

**Case 4**

An executive earning $10,000 a year has been padding his expense account by about $500 a year.

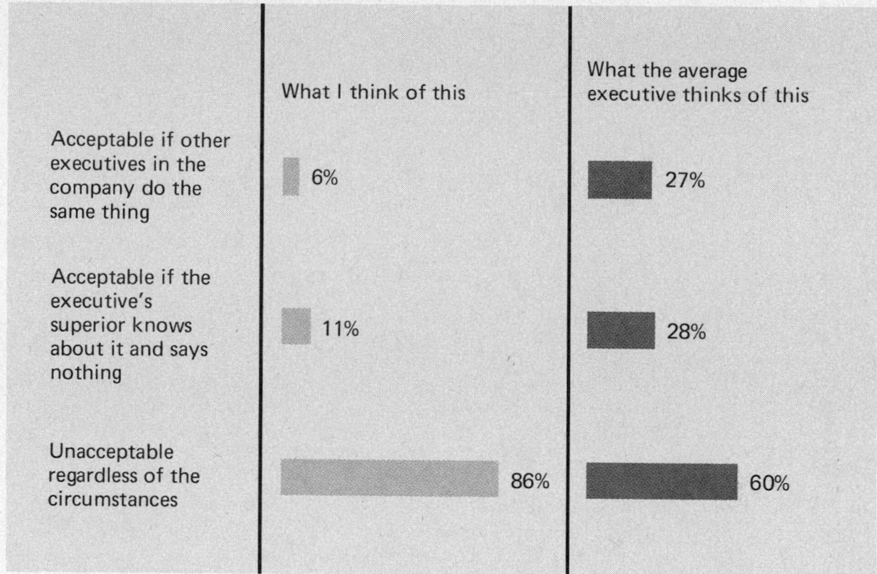


**Note:** Not all figures add up to 100 per cent, since some respondents gave more than one answer to some of the problems.

**Figure 1** *(Cont.)*

- Essay answers about practices of pricing, hiring, and rebidding on contracts reveal the existence of an ethic which has a special niche for friends.

Favoring friends can be an expression of gratitude, which is praiseworthy—unless the gratitude is displayed at the expense of justice.

## Ethical Influences

This cynicism, this double ethic, undermines—as we shall see later—the ability of an executive to believe that written codes of ethics will really work. Such cynicism must certainly be considered when trying to predict a man's behavior in a touchy situation, especially *if he believes that most others would behave unethically if they were in his position.* Which is going to influence him more—his ethic, or the behavior of others?

We asked a random one half of our respondents to rank five factors according to the influence they exert on an executive to make *ethical* decisions. The five factors are: company policy, industry climate, behavior of superiors, behavior of equals, and personal code of behavior. We asked the other random one half of our respondents to rank five similar factors according to the influence they exert for *unethical* decisions. The rather remarkable results can be found in Figure 2.

**A. WHAT INFLUENCES AN EXECUTIVE TO MAKE ETHICAL DECISIONS?**

| Possible influence | Importance as an ethical influence — Average rank |
|---|---|
| A man's personal code of behavior | 1.5 |
| The behavior of a man's superiors in the company | 2.8 |
| Formal company policy | 2.8 |
| Ethical climate of the industry | 3.8 |
| The behavior of a man's equals in the company | 4.0 |

**B. WHAT INFLUENCES AN EXECUTIVE TO MAKE UNETHICAL DECISIONS?**

| Possible influence | Importance as an unethical influence — Average rank |
|---|---|
| The behavior of a man's superiors in the company | 1.9 |
| Ethical climate of the industry | 2.6 |
| The behavior of a man's equals in the company | 3.1 |
| Lack of company policy | 3.3 |
| Personal financial needs | 4.1 |

**Figure 2**

**Note:** The average rankings given are derived from a ranking of each item in the five groups (1, 2, 3, 4, 5), with most influential = 1, least influential = 5.

What can we learn from the rankings? Here is one line of interpretation:

- If an executive acts *ethically* (Part A), this is attributable to his own set of values and his ability to resist pressure and temptation, with some credit due to his superiors and company policy.
- If an executive acts *unethically* (Part B), it is largely because of his superiors and the climate of industry ethics.

A wag might say that this sounds like the legendary playwright who blamed all his failures on inept casts and stupid audiences, and accepted the praise for his successful shows as his rightful due. On the other hand, a friend of business might say that it is a hopeful sign that many executives indicate they follow their own consciences in making decisions.

It is obvious that those around a man influence his behavior. But to what extent does this influence operate? Are executives "other-directed" rather than "inner-directed," as David Riesman suggested in *The Lonely Crowd?* Do executives look mainly to the company for their standards; are they the "organization men" described by William H. Whyte, Jr.? Or, more simply, what do our data say about the following item from the *Wall Street Journal*, commenting on the recent antitrust decisions in the electrical industry: "The simplest, if not the complete, answer [to why high-ranking executives had knowingly done wrong] goes back to the organization man"?[6]

[6]John Bridge, "Antitrust and Organization Man," *Wall Street Journal*, January 10, 1961, p. 10.

Close examination of our data reveals a tendency in every age group, company milieu, and management level for a man to accept the values of his superiors. This tendency, stemming from a respect for the talents of the superior as well as for his authoritative position, should be acknowledged by every administrator as a part of his power for good or evil. The larger the number of his subordinates, the greater is his power in this matter. And it is also natural for men to expect responsible action from someone with so much power.

Thus, Judge J. Cullen Ganey, in his statement on the electrical industry antitrust cases, despite the absence of probative evidence, felt compelled to say that "the real blame is to be laid at the doorstep of the corporate defendants and those who guide and direct their policy.[7] And the public has been reluctant to accept the idea that the electrical equipment companies top managements are blameless, for the public holds these men in a position analogous to the parents of a 21-year-old who has done serious wrong. Though the parents be liked and respected, they must endure the common opinion that they should somehow have prevented the son's mistake. Our data would indicate that this belief is based on the facts of executive behavior: men do look to their superiors for guidance.

Have the troubles of the electrical industry introduced bias into the answers given to our questions? Undoubtedly. A pilot study preparatory to the present survey was completed before Judge Ganey's January decision, and we can compare results from the two studies.[8] There is a noteworthy difference in the ranks assigned in the question discussed above.

In the pilot study, formal company policy was ranked as the second most important factor influencing ethical behavior; superiors were ranked as the third. In the present study, these two factors have changed places, presumably because of the ineffectuality of policy directives used by the defendant companies. Also, from the time of the pilot study to the present one, there has been a slight increase in the percentage of men who say that unfair pricing or price collusion is the source of a personal role conflict.

Also of interest is our finding that financial need is ranked as *least* important of the five factors influencing unethical behavior. We doubt that money is unimportant to our respondents. A partial answer undoubtedly lies in the fact that some 86% of the executives responding have five-figure incomes. At least the pressures of starvation are not at the door. What is important is to note that bad example, pressure from superiors or equals, and industry environment are seen by our respondents as more closely related to dishonest behavior than is the need for money.

We asked John J. Brennan, Jr., Vice President and Treasurer of Electronics Corporation of America, how he interpreted our findings. Here are the remarks he made in reply:

> The pattern and level of corporate ethical standards are determined predominantly by the code of behavior formulated and promulgated by top management. The rest of the organization, almost perforce, will follow these ethical operating precepts and examples; but in the absence of such norms,

[7] *New York Times*, February 7, 1961, p. 26.

[8] In conducting the pilot study, the author was ably assisted by the Reverend Alexander D. Stewart, William J. Gies, Roger L. Hall, Robert J. Russell, and Robert C. Valtz.

the same organization will be motivated by individual, and possibly inconsistent, codes of behavior.

The crucial matter, therefore, is whether or not each individual comprising top management has a *well-defined*, high-standard personal code of behavior. If each has this clear, objective, consistent concept of ethics—however acquired—he has the yardsticks, the guiding principles, against which to measure the ethical import of his decisions.

The executive whose concepts of ethics are vague, and whose principles or ethics are ill-defined—and possibly even vacillating and inconsistent—is in constant danger of yielding to expediency and even pursuing unethical practices; or, worse, providing an undesirable environment wherein his subordinates can make such decisions based solely on their own personal ethical principles, with no frame of ethical reference from the top.

Of course, a well-defined personal code, however high in standards, does not of itself ensure ethical conduct; courage is always necessary in order to assert what one knows to be right.

A Nestor of the business world once said that the best advice he could give to a young man embarking on a business career was: find a good boss. Our data suggest a corollary: *if you want to act ethically, find an ethical boss.*

Hearty approval of this notion came from James J. Valtz, Export Manager of the Allied Kid Company, who said:

> My advice to the young is: find an ethical boss. I was profoundly impressed as a young man by the example of our company's founder, Soloman Agoos. His behavior in the financial crisis of 1920, when the market for leather goods broke, was exemplary.
>
> All of his employees appreciated the level at which he wanted the business conducted. For example, no one would think of yielding to pressure from even the largest foreign customer for false invoices, which would enable the customer to evade customs duties.

The importance of this is underlined by looking at the differences in rankings that one's fellow executives have in influencing a man's behavior. These peers are said to have little influence for *ethical* behavior, but are relatively important in influencing *unethical* conduct. In other words, an executive's fellows are more likely to drag him down than to lift him up.

Clearly, then, the opportunity for any one administrator to influence ethical behavior effectively is immense, if only by refraining from encouraging unethical behavior. The importance of this influence increases if the belief of ethical businessmen—that they are not like the average executive—makes them reluctant to take responsibility for improving the behavior of others.

Such reluctance is characterized by statements like "if he wants to lie and cheat, that's his business." But such apparent indifference is meretricious. Lewis B. Ward, Professor of Business Research at the Harvard Business School, compares this reluctance to the "I won't squeal" attitude that students take about cheating by others—an attitude which has led to the downfall of academic "honor systems" in some colleges. Without the exercise of individual responsibility, how can group morality do other than deteriorate? If one's fellow executives encourage dishonesty—explicitly or by silence—how long will it be before men believe they "are suckers for being honest"?

Edmund Burke said, "All that is necessary for the forces of evil to win in the world is for enough good men to do nothing." This is a universal problem. It confronts us as bus passengers when we see a couple of toughs strong-arm another passenger. It confronts all of mankind when a strong nation tries to force its will on a small one. It confronts a business executive when he sees wrong being done in his industry. The responsibility is clear: *I am my brother's keeper.*

## Chapter & Verse

Every industry develops its own way of doing things, its generally accepted practices. Since industry climate is an important influence on unethical behavior, how does this influence manifest itself in specific practices that are generally accepted in the industry?

To find out, we asked: "In every industry, there are some generally accepted business practices. In your industry, are there any such practices which you regard as unethical?" The answers are shown in Figure 3.

Taking away those who "don't know," we have the startling finding that four out of five executives giving an opinion affirm the presence in their industry of *practices which are generally accepted and are also unethical!*

Surely a candid admission! And, just as surely, a clarion call for corrective action! Generally accepted practices are the sun and rain of an industry climate. When a goodly number of these practices are unethical, how can the climate be otherwise? And, as our respondents have said, an unethical climate is an important influence on decision makers.

If our respondents, and their fellow leaders in American industry, are

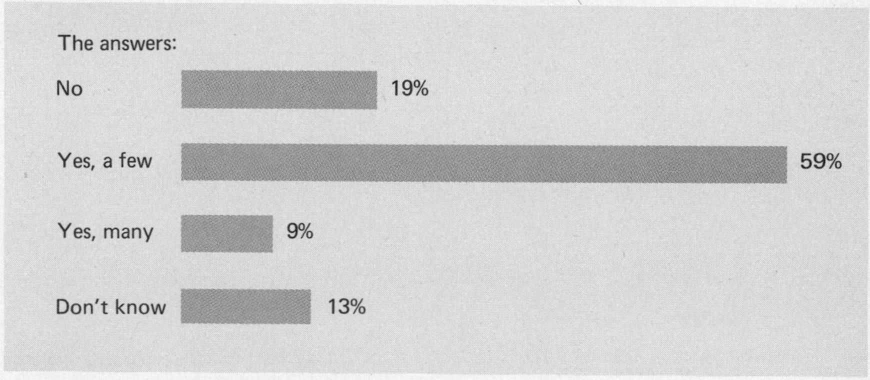


**Figure 3** "In your industry are there any generally accepted business practices which you regard as unethical?"

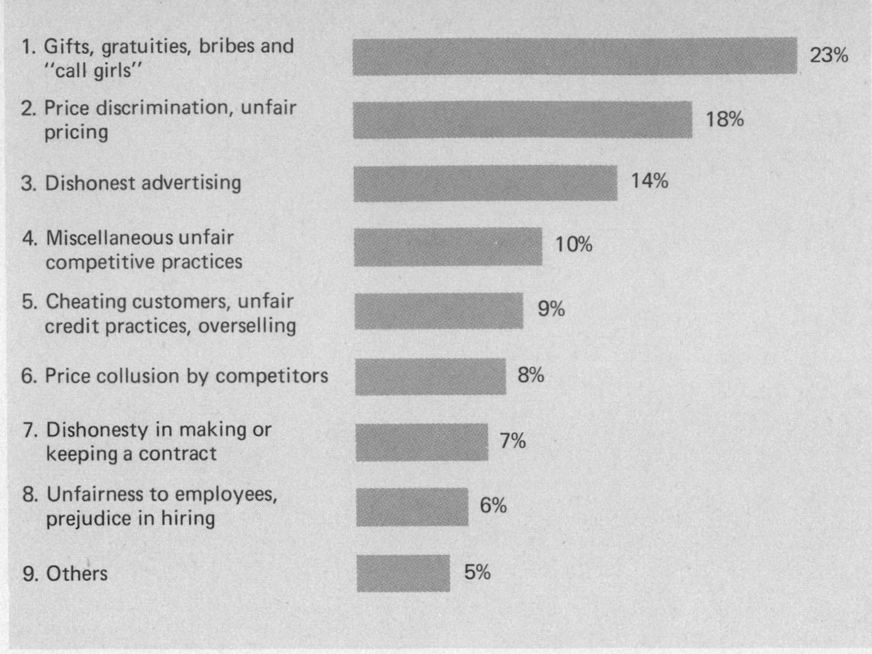


**Figure 4** The Unethical Practice Executives Most Want to Eliminate (percentage of executives specifying this practice)

in earnest in professing lofty ethics, industry practices are a logical starting place for putting their ideals into operation.

More than half of our respondents were willing to tell us the "one practice in their industry they would most like to see eliminated." We have analyzed and grouped the replies, and Figure 4 contains chapter and verse of the unethical practices that our executives want erased in their own industries.

Perhaps seeing some of their answers will give a sense of their sincerity and good will in reporting these practices. Thus:

- *Insurance Executive:* "Seeking preferential treatment through lavish entertainment."
- *Manager, Consumer Services Company:* "Kickback to purchasing department employees."
- *Financial Counsel:* "Payoffs to government officials."
- *Personnel Director, Western Manufacturing Firm:* "The idea that industry should have a few
- *Young Financier:* "Mutual fixing of rates of interest to be charged a borrower at two or more banks."
- *Top Executive, Mass Communications Firm:* "Deliberate distortion of facts."
- *Research and Design Expert:* "Ambiguous advertising intended to mislead consumers."
- *Sales Manager, Pharmaceu-*

women employees on the payroll for entertainment of prospective customers."

• *Secretary, Construction Firm:* "Price rigging between supplier and contractor."

• *President of Small Company:* "Accounts of similar size, purchasing ability, and credit rating are charged prices varying as much as 25% (by our competitors). So far, we have not deviated from our policy of charging the same price to everybody."

• *President, Consumer Services Company:* "Occasional exchanges of price information prior to contract bidding."

*ticals:* "Misleading ad claims."

• *Vice President, Manufacturing Company:* "Underbidding with the intention of substituting inferior workmanship or materials."

• *President, Consulting Firm:* "Selling a 'tremendous bill of goods' of which the buyer knows too little."

• *Manager, Midwestern Bank:* "Loaning customer *more* than he needs or more than is prudent for him to borrow."

• *Vice President, Company Making Industrial Products:* "The payment or large gifts to employees of other companies, customers, or competitors for 'favors' or information."

The place for correction to begin is with such "accepted" industry practices. They need not be tolerated and certainly provide a convenient place to begin the difficult job of self-regulation. And these activities are a practical place to begin, for each executive knows about them, and is able to do something about them directly.

## Drawing the Line

Of course, to decide exactly where to draw the line on many of these issues is not easy. For example, the majority of executives regard gift giving as an "unwise practice." Similarly, the majority think that "a company should have a written policy about gifts." But only 27% of these same executives are willing to stipulate a $100 maximum value for gifts. Presumably, the other 73% are of the opinion that there are situations where gifts of greater value are appropriate and acceptable.

With respect to gift giving, as well as to owning stock in a company which does business with one's own company, most HBR readers (and rightly, in this reporter's opinion) refuse to say that the practice is *always* unethical. The broad principle is clear: an executive must be loyal to his company. But not every gift promotes disloyalty or results in the recipient's favoring one supplier over another. Nor does every executive who owns stock in a company which does business with his own face a conflict of interest.

These are complex problems; often they involve, simultaneously, several ethical principles. The details of each particular case determine the application of the various principles and, consequently, make the difference between an ethical and an unethical practice. At the same time, this inability or unwillingness to draw immediate and fast lines raises two serious questions: (1) How do executives react to having to make decisions with strong ethical content? (2) Do executives need better guidelines to help them make the correct decision in such situations?

## Role Conflict

The first of these questions relates to what a social scientist calls "role conflict." A role conflict confronts an executive when he is required to fill simultaneously two roles (patterns of behavior) which present inconsistent or contradictory expectations. For example, the behavior expected of an executive as an "economic man" often differs from what is expected of him as an "ethical man." To investigate such situations, we posed the following question: "Probably there have been times when you have experienced a conflict between what was expected of you as an efficient, profit-conscious businessman and what was expected of you as an ethical person. Please describe the situation which has been for you the source of deepest concern because of such a conflict."

Nearly half of our respondents generously spent the time necessary to supply us with an essay answer. Surprisingly, one out of every four executives reporting says that he has *experienced no such conflict*!

It is difficult to believe that these men never experienced a situation in business where cheating, lying just a little, or using a minor shady practice could have brought them some advantage. All such situations contain role conflicts. In fact, even in the most reputable company, whose top management makes it relatively easy for executives to act ethically, it seems unlikely that all such temptations are absent. Perhaps some respondents believed they were being asked to reveal a conflict in which they had acted unethically, and replied "no such conflict" because, in the situation, they had acted ethically.

But it is hard to escape the conclusion that many executives who answered "no such conflict" have a deficient notion of ethics, or lack an awareness of the social implications of business decisions. One professor of business administration, commenting on these answers, said that they reminded him of some executives who identify as ethical problems only those situations involving large sums of money. He has now overcome his surprise at such statements as, "Our company has no ethical problems. The last one we had was five years ago when the treasurer absconded with $50,000."

## Specific Situations

What kinds of conflicts were mentioned by remaining 75%? They cover a wide range and make fascinating reading. Firing and layoffs were reported by 102 executives as being the problems over which they had experienced the deepest concern. Thus:

- In the words of one training supervisor: "When it is necessary to reduce the work force, the decision of separating the older, less efficient employees, or the younger employees with greater technical skills and vigor, is a real tough problem."
- An eastern plant manager sees a similar problem in a broader context: "No provision in our society for providing useful work for well-meaning, moral, hard-working individuals who just can't make the grade in the occupation they have chosen, and must be dismissed for efficiency reasons. This is a most serious problem for me, and I have fired *many* persons for this reason."
- The president of a small company has the same problem, but a different solution: "Discharge of ethical but incompetent employees. I can't do it."
- A well-paid vice president is anxious about "employees with long, good records, and whose work becomes inefficient. How long can I carry them on the payroll? What is the measure of my loyalty to a man who helped build my business?"
- The product supervisor in a large manufacturing company is especially aware of one facet of the layoff problem: "Treatment of clerical-level, salaried employees during periods of economic recession. This group seems always to take the brunt of any workforce reduction."
- Finally, a southern personnel director thoughtfully observes: "It has always concerned me that the industry's regular [periodic] reductions in work force should always bear so heavily on the 'little people'—particularly when adversity has not always been equally shared by stockholders and top management."

That final quotation deserves some reflection on our part. No doubt most discharges and layoffs are ethical, and probably the conflicts cited by some of the 102 are waged between their head and their heart, rather than between economic efficiency and ethical behavior. But justice can, at times, demand that the brunt of a recession be borne by stockholders and executives, rather than by the little people. Perhaps we should recall here that 73% of our respondents agree that "for corporation executives to act in the interest of shareholders alone, and not also in the interest of employees and consumers, is unethical." But it will take a secure and courageous administrator, indeed, to stand up and suggest reducing prices and dividends instead of reducing the number of wage earners.

## Communications

One in ten of our respondents has experienced deepest concern over a problem in honest communication—of telling the whole truth. Some examples:

- A vice president, industrial manufacturing, is disturbed by "requests by customers for false billings to avoid taxes or help in their depreciation schedules."

- A controller reports he had to decide how to handle "a good friend caught cheating on his expenses."
- A securities salesman finds that "my customers often approach me with an idea that would be profitable to me, but which I feel is unwise for them. At times, my best advice will cost me a sale and perhaps a customer."

## Collusion & Gifts

Opportunities for collusion and other sharp practices in pricing are the next most frequently mentioned conflict—by 79 executives. For instance:

- The president of a small southern company mentions "the use of extreme pressure by competition to force me to collude with them to fix prices."
- A sales manager is annoyed by "price differentials extended to 'price buyers,' but not to loyal customers—a rotten practice."
- And the treasurer of a small retailing firm puts a perennial problem in the form of a question: What is a *fair* profit at retail level for installment purchases?"

Gifts, entertainment, and kickbacks compose the fourth most prevalent conflict category for 56 men. Specifically:

- A top executive in one of our giant corporations deplores "attending industry 'junkets' in the name of promoting the welfare of the industry, which are actually only 'binges' at the expense of neglected stockholders for whom we are trustees and managers."
- A western sales manager is bothered by 'the excessive entertainment which some buyers seem to feel it is our duty to supply. I feel a buyer who can be bought for entertainment is not a moral person fundamentally, and I don't trust him."
- The head of a consulting firm notes a conflict with a happy ending: "As manager of a business, I was asked for a kickback by the buyer of an important customer; I refused the request and lost the customer. For months after, I was not sure I was right from a business angle. Now, years later, I know I was right, for the concern came to me for management counsel."

## Pressure

A number of executives, 40 to be exact, though they cite different kinds of conflicts, stress an important theme in their essays: pressure from superiors played a part in the situation in which they had experienced the deepest concern. For example:

• A controller resents "repeatedly having to act contrary to my sense of justice in order to 'please.' In upper middle management, apparently, one's own ethical will must be subordinated to that of interests 'at the top'—not only to advance, but even to be retained."

• A young supervisor is concerned with "pressure to get too much work out of too few people in too short a time."

• A division manager is unhappy over "strong pressures for superior results which lead to compromise of personal integrity in operations."

• The sales manager of a very large corporation phrases his views most bluntly: "The constant everyday pressure from top management to obtain profitable business; unwritten, but well understood, is the phrase 'at any cost.' To do this requires every conceivable dirty trick."

But many men voice more than these generalized anxieties, and cite specific practices toward which they are being pushed—and which they do not like. Thus:

• A high-salaried assistant manager is worried because "my management has, in effect, required that I go along with certain antitrust violations involving restraint of trade."

• Another executive says: "As controller, I prepared a P & L statement which showed a loss. An executive vice president tried to force me to falsify the statement to show a profit in order to present it to a bank for a line of credit. I refused, and was fired on the spot."

• A young engineer testifies that he was "asked to present 'edited' results of a reliability study; I refused, and nearly got fired. I refused to defraud the customer, so they had others do it."

• Still another engineer deplores "cheating in the makeup of reports caused by demanding improvement in index numbers."

Of course, the task of top management is to get results. And to do so every executive must apply some sort of pressure or sanction to subordinates in order to obtain excellent work. A good boss ought to have the ability to "stretch" his men. But it is important that he not "overstretch" them, physically, psychologically, or ethically.

How can a top executive guard against pushing his men too far? By knowing them. By taking the time to understand them. By reflecting on the kinds and amount of pressure he is applying to them. To gain such knowledge requires excellent two-way communication between the boss and his subordinates. Such clear communication is especially important in large, decentralized corporations.

Without careful observation of what is going on, a superior can unwittingly hand down impossible demands—even in a memo that, for example, insists on a certain share of market, or sets too large a sales or profit goal for the period. Perhaps the possible injustice of such demands can be seen by comparing this situation to the father who insists that his son, whose I.Q. is 100, get a straight-A report card.

Impossible demands, say our respondents, especially if accompanied by an implied "produce or get out" attitude, can quickly result in unethical behavior. One certainly wonders if the lonely subordinate, faced with demands like these, does not occasionally dream about a union for middle management, complete with seniority and grievance procedures.

A common retort—and defense—of top management on this issue maintains that "it is only fair that pressure be kept on subordinates. After all, stockholders and competitors keep the pressure on top management all the time."

Yet, few *top* executives in our survey specifically mention such pressures. Perhaps "pressure" is part of a self-induced image of how a president or vice president *should* act. This reporter doubts that widely disparate and anonymous stockholders exercise specific pressure on top management comparable to the pressure that top executives bring to bear on their subordinates. As for the pressure of competition, few industries operate under conditions of absolutely free competition. Perhaps the very fact that executives blame competitive pressure for widespread unethical behavior is a good sign that cutthroat competition exists in an industry and ought to be modified.

Though most of the 40 men say that pressure from superiors was for *unethical* behavior, several volunteered the information that their particular bosses had helped them to act ethically:

- According to one vice president, "I am fortunate in that my top management has never countenanced any deviation from ethical procedures. In our company we are expected to base decisions on what is right, without regard for possible loss."
- This influence is echoed by a California sales manager: "The company I work for, the largest of its kind, was founded by a Christian gentleman. Policies are ethical in the strictest sense. For twenty years I have needed only to follow policy."

## Code of Ethics?

This brings us to the second question posed earlier in the article: Do executives need better guidelines to help them make the best decision in situations with an ethical dimension? Will they welcome such guidelines? To put it another way, granting the presence of many unethical practices in American industry (and we have presented ample evidence that executives believe this is so), what can be done to improve matters?

It is true that a number of industries already have ethical codes. In fact, in 1958 the National Association of Manufacturers issued a Code of Moral and Ethical Standards. The NAM code was designed in part to answer criticism of big business for not having a norm for measuring corporate morality that was comparable to the 1957 AFL-CIO Ethical Practices Code. But the NAM code, like so many industry codes, has been ineffectual. Perhaps this is because such codes have no enforcement provisions and are filled with generalities and platitudes that signify little but good will.

To find out what executives think of ethical codes, and what kind of a code they might want, we posed a number of questions. The first was: "How do you feel about an effort to develop a code of ethical practices for your industry? How would you react if a group of experienced executives in your industry tried to draw up such a code?" The answer is a resounding "*good idea*!" Only one man in ten opposes such an effort. Indeed, the pattern (as shown in Figure 5) is overwhelming.

To get a deeper understanding of their reply, let us look at some of the spontaneous comments written in the questionnaire margins:

- A management consultant feels he "would regret the necessity of a code, but would favor one strongly."
- A Kansas engineer favors the code, which he sees as "written to control the minority."
- A public utilities executive not only favors a code, but thinks it would be "easy to enforce if management wants it enforced."
- A California Rotarian adds that "after 26 years in business, I think a code would be a triumph of optimism over experience."
- A labor relations director adopts a similar tone: "I have seen the AFL-CIO code operate—codes don't solve any problems."
- Opposition to codes comes from a Pennsylvania marketer who "thinks the stimulus to act ethically should come from outside business, social, or trade organizations."

## What a Code Can Do

We wanted to probe the reasons why executives favor or oppose an ethical code, and thereby find out not only how a code could operate, but

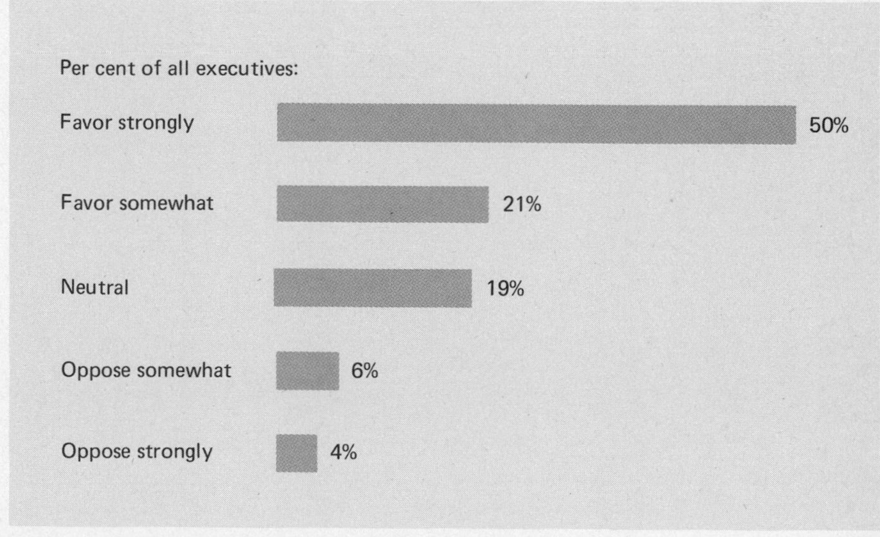


**Figure 5** "How do you feel about an effort to develop a code of ethical practices for your industry?"

also whether it could be made to work at all. To find out, we posed the following hypothetical situation: "Assume, for the moment, that an ethical practices code has been drawn up for your industry by experienced executives. What do you think such a code and its reasonable enforcement would accomplish?" We asked for comments on seven ideas. These themes with the opinions of executives are summarized in Figure 6. Looking for a pattern, we see the following:

- 71% believe a code would raise the ethical level of their industry.
- 87% believe that a code would not be easy to enforce.
- Executives split pretty evenly over the problem of whether a code would reduce sharp practices in tough, competitive situations.
- 88% would welcome a code as a useful aid when they wanted to refuse an unethical request impersonally.
- 81% disagree with the idea that codes protect inefficient firms.
- 81% agree that a code would help executives by defining clearly the limits of acceptable conduct.
- Finally, executives split again (this time 57% agree) over the thorny problem of whether people would violate the code whenever they thought they could avoid detection.

Summing up, their replies indicate a moderate optimism about the potentialities of a code, coupled with a strong belief that enforcement and adherence would be difficult jobs.

| | Per cent of all executives giving this rating to each consequence | | | | |
|---|---|---|---|---|---|
| POSSIBLE CONSEQUENCES OF A CODE | Agree | Partially agree | Neutral | Partially disagree | Disagree |
| The code would raise the ethical level of the industry | 36% | 35% | 12% | 7% | 10% |
| The code would be easy to enforce | 2 | 7 | 4 | 23 | 64 |
| In situations of severe competition, the code would reduce sharp practices | 13 | 38 | 9 | 19 | 21 |
| Executives would welcome the code as a useful aid when they wanted to refuse an unethical request impersonally | 59 | 28 | 5 | 4 | 4 |
| The code would protect inefficient firms and retard the dynamic growth of industry | 3 | 8 | 8 | 11 | 70 |
| The code would help executives by defining clearly the limits of acceptable conduct | 48 | 33 | 7 | 5 | 7 |
| People would violate the code whenever they thought they could avoid detection | 13 | 44 | 8 | 20 | 15 |

**Figure 6**

The near-unanimous agreement on the idea that a code would help executives in making decisions deserves additional discussion. Why would a code help? After all, a code is a form of restriction on business behavior. Perhaps the following illustration best portrays why men are sometimes willing to impose restrictions on themselves:

> Suppose that you and your family live on a high hill, with a lovely, large back yard. The yard's only drawback is that it ends in a long, sheer drop on three sides. You have two obvious choices: (1) You can caution all who enter the yard about the danger of falling over the edge; consequently, no one will go closer than six or eight feet, and you yourself will often be anxious about how close you are to it. Or (2) you can build a fence six inches from the edge, and eliminate anxiety at the same time that you gain more space for playing and gardening.

There are many businessmen who are willing to "fence themselves in" with an ethical practices code, provided that experienced executives in their industry have a hand in formulating it, because the fence will increase the area in which they can securely and ethically do business.

A code of ethics can help in other ways, say executives. For example, take situations in which it is difficult to refuse an unethical request—such as when it comes from a friend or associate. A direct refusal gives a holier-than-thou impression—and seriously jeopardizes what otherwise may be very pleasant interpersonal relationships. Faced with such a request, one looks for a way to refuse without offending. A specific code of ethics, say seven out of eight of our respondents, would provide an impersonal and welcome way of refusing such a request.

What about opposition to industry codes? Some of it is undoubtedly rooted in the belief that "you can't legislate virtue." In the words of a young manager of personnel relations for a large corporation, "I feel that this cannot be legislated, and that an attempt to draw up a code would be a sham."

Such an objection appears to confuse what is internal to a person with what is external. Presumably, most men acknowledge that a written rule can't change a man's heart. However, our respondents favor a written code not because it can change men internally, but because it can make it easier for good men to conform their external behavior to their internal ideals. At the same time, a code can discourage wrongdoers by making it easier to detect and punish unethical behavior.

## Will a Code Work?

All these things are what a code can do. But will a code actually work? As noted, our executives have mixed feelings on this subject. They agree that a code would be difficult to enforce; they don't know whether it would help reduce sharp practices in really competitive situations. Also, they are cynical (as mentioned earlier) about the behavior of other businessmen, with four out of every seven agreeing that "people would violate the code whenever they thought they could avoid detection."

Realistically, our panel sees enforcement as a major problem, and backs this up with marginal comments of "I would not think an enforcement agency is feasible," or "A code is impossible to police."

In order to discover the most acceptable form of enforcement, we posed the following question: "Assume that an ethical practices code has been drawn up for your industry. Which of the following groups would you choose to enforce the code?" The answers are shown in Figure 7.

## Self-Enforcement?

How realistic is this seeming preference for self-enforcement? Note that 60% of the executives prefer some form of outside regulation. One element is clear: executives want to keep for themselves the greater share of responsibility for enforcement. Only 4% would use a government agency.

Much of our other evidence questions the current effectiveness of self-enforcement. We have seen, for example, that internal company pressures (by superiors and fellow executives) are important influences on ethical behavior. We have also seen that executives believe that such internal enforcement has failed to reach its potential for creating ethical behavior and has been effective in those firms where top management has taken a strongly ethical stand. It is not, then, that self-enforcement cannot work, but rather that it has not been made to work. Perhaps this is the very reason why so many (60% to be exact) would prefer a form of business regulation which is largely external to the company.

But even such external forms of enforcement have many difficulties.

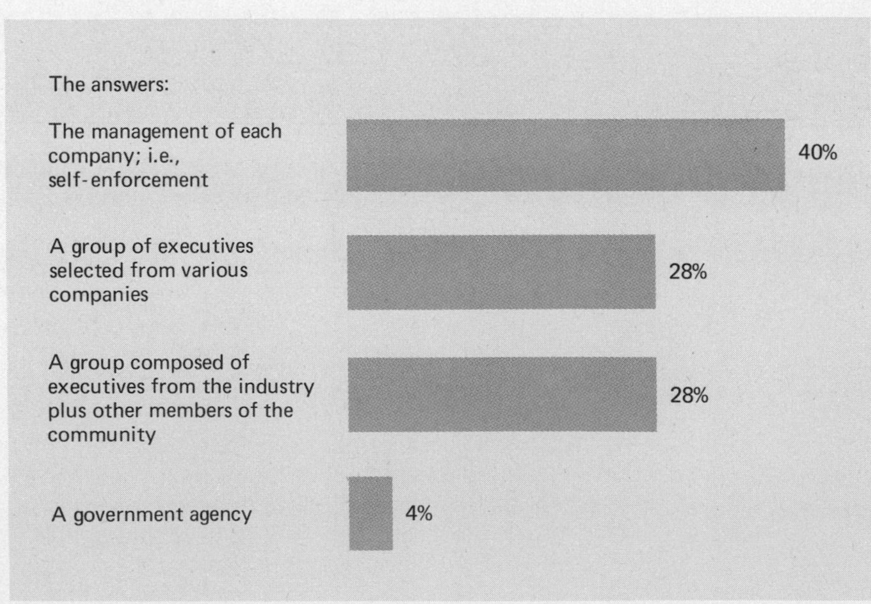


**Figure 7** "Which of these groups would you choose to enforce the code?"

To illustrate, let us consider the "Standards of Practice" of the American Association of Advertising Agencies. It is clear from our data that a good number of HBR executives identify dishonest advertising as the one unethical practice they would most like to see eliminated from their industry. Yet no one can deny that the broad standards put forth by the AAAA are carefully worded. From such evidence, one can hardly escape the assumption that the Committee for Improvement of Advertising Content is not enforcing the Standards of Practice as rigorously as executives (and probably the public) would like.

Perhaps one flaw in the AAAA code is a reluctance to believe that an ounce of prevention is worth a pound of cure. The fact that all regulation takes place *after* an advertisement has done its work, in effect, means that one can get around the code. If, as the executives responding in this survey indicate, most executives would violate a code when given the chance, then it is logical to conclude that specific norms, spelling out in advance what the committee regards as wrong, would be more effective as preventive regulation than such general statements as "misleading exaggerations" and "misleading price claims."

After seven years of operation and some 300 decisions, the AAAA committee ought to be able to formulate more detailed directives than the two quoted above, directives which will make it more difficult for corner-cutters to plead that they didn't intend to mislead consumers. The AAAA problem is presented here not because it is unique or egregious, but simply because it aptly exemplifies the flaw in many industries and in many existing codes: the absence of specific, detailed statements of what industry members regard as unethical, and the teeth to put these statements into action.

Which industry would care to lead the way?

More specifically, *how* can an industry begin to lead the way? How can the detailed norms needed for an effective code be formulated? Here the achievement of the American Psychological Association in formulating its *Ethical Standards of Psychologists* is a good model. The APA used an empirical approach, gathering data about the ethical problems confronting psychologists. Members of the APA were asked to "describe a situation they knew of firsthand, in which a psychologist made a decision having ethical implications, and to indicate what the correspondents perceived as being the ethical issues involved."[9]

These reports were examined to discover patterns in the problems and thereby to provide a plan for organizing the information supplied. After the reports were categorized into six ethical areas, they were analyzed to obtain a number of specific problems in each area. Following this analysis, six committees were appointed, each concentrating on the specific ethical problems of a single area. After much discussion and thoughtful study, these committees hammered out the *Ethical Standards of Psychologists*. With adaptation to its own circumstances, any industry could produce its own code in the same way. The issue is not whether it can be done, but whether top management wants it done.

[9]*Ethical Standards of Psychologists* (Washington, D.C.: The American Psychological Association, 1953), p. vi.

## Top Management

With this in mind, there remains one fundamental question: Should the difficulties of enforcement or the likelihood of limited success deter efforts to construct industry codes? This answer can only come from top management which, as Adolf A. Berle, Jr., wrote, "has substantially absolute power. Thus the only real control which guides or limits their economic and social action is the real, though undefined and tacit, philosophy of the men who compose them."[10] That this power operates, for good or evil, is attested to by our executives when they indicate that "if you want to be ethical, find an ethical boss." The time for each member of top management to make more explicit his philosophy, his ethic, is right now.

Henry Ford II, speaking in Minneapolis on April 20, 1961, concurred with this view: "It is up to us in our various companies and industries to see to the establishment of our own formal principles of ethical practice, plus the effective means of self-policing those principles."[11]

Among the administrators most optimistic about a code of ethics for businessmen is John B. Shallenberger, President of the Connellsville Corporation. Mr. Shallenberger, in his capacity as Research Officer of the Comité Internation de l'Organisation Scientifique, recently had the unique opportunity of interviewing some 7,500 managers in 109 different countries. Here is his opinion, based on his globe-circling research:

> In about 40% of these confidential interviews, I detected a desire to talk about ethics in business. This was not the subject of the interview, and any mention of the subject was spontaneous on the part of the manager being interviewed. Thus, it became evident that there lies deep-seated in the minds of managers a desire to do good, a kind of noble aspiration which seeks expression. Many managers indicated a latent desire to do greater good than they felt they could in the role they were expected to play as managers.
>
> In my opinion, based on wide and intimate exposure to top managers, they are potentially a great force for good. All that is needed is a code, a delineation of parameters of performance, or a set of guidelines by which to steer one's course of management behavior, plus a general recognition by boards of directors and stockholders that managers desire to perform their duties on a high ethical plane and for the benefit of mankind.
>
> Managers are shy to speak openly of ethics, just as most people blush to mention God in daily conversation. But when the way is opened for free and socially accepted discussion of ethics and morals, managers will be the first to reveal deep-seated desires that, in their fulfilling, would bring powerful forces to bear on the improvement of the lot of multitudes of people.
>
> Two effective steps would go a long way toward unleashing this latent force, and I submit them as a proposal for action:
>
> 1. Codification of ethical standards of manager performance.
> 2. Establishment of a 'Hippocratic Oath' to be administered by a suitable body of authority to all persons admitted to top-management levels.

[10] *20th Century Capitalist Revolution* (New York: Harcourt, Brace and Company, 1954), p. 180.

[11] *New York Times*, April 21, 1961, p. 16.

## Role of Religion

But what about the more traditional institutions for improving human behavior? We wondered what HBR subscribers thought of the efforts of organized religion to assist the businessman. Our interest stemmed from the discussion initiated last year by J. Howard Pew, a director of the Sun Oil Company. Mr. Pew, speaking as President of the United Presbyterian Foundation, charged the Church with meddling in secular affairs.[12] To look into this issue, we asked: "In your opinion, how much guidance did your church and clergymen provide for the ethical problems you and your business acquaintances faced in the last five years?" The answers are shown in Figure 8.

Why did 23% refuse an opinion? Some of the 23% were men in our sample who have no religious affiliation, and therefore felt that the question was not addressed to them. Perhaps others prefer not to criticize the clergy. But probably the principal reason is the lack of communication between businessmen and the clergy. The arresting conclusion is, in any case, that for those who gave an opinion, 4 out of every 5 were dissatisfied with what organized religion had or had not done.

It would be erroneous to conclude that all those who are dissatisfied would be willing and ready to accept help from the clergy for business problems. For nearly 20% of this group indicate both that their church has been of no help to them in the past five years and that they want no help. And for many different reasons:

- A young New York stockbroker: "The average clergyman has such a scant understanding of the U.S. economy that his intervention in this area would be a mistake."
- A Louisiana insurance broker: "I don't believe the clergy should be permitted to preach to businessmen."
- The president of a small financial institution: "If the clergy would stick to their business of preaching the gospel, they and business would be better off. The clergy admits the weakness of their faith when they turn from the gospel and try to get into other fields of influence and preach a doctrine of social gospel."
- Or, as another president writes: "The writer's religious convictions are not in need of assistance." But, curiously enough, he states elsewhere in his reply that "it is more difficult to know what is right than to do it."

Though the view that the Church should make no effort to help businessmen as businessmen is clearly present in our survey, and its presence will disturb many clergy, it is a minority view. In fact, a minority of comparable size thinks that the Church's recent efforts to assist business ethics

[12]In a speech in Chicago on March 19, 1960, before the National Council of Presbyterian Men.

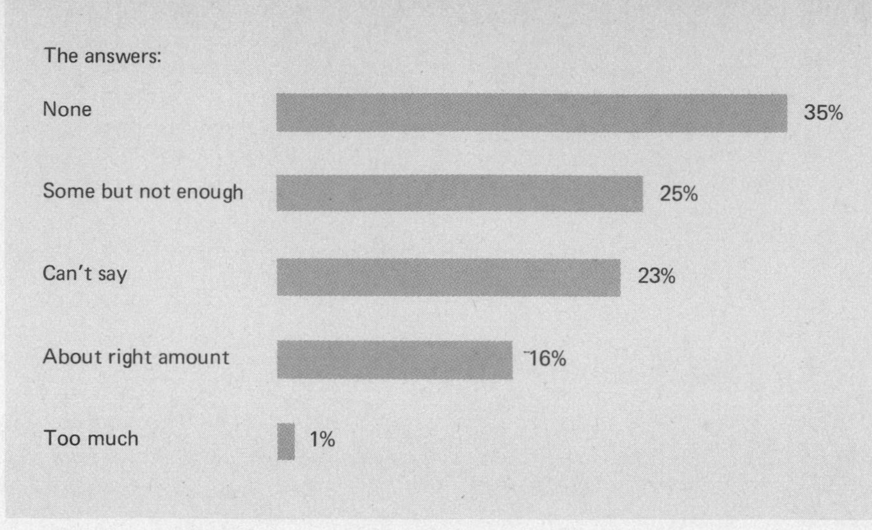


**Figure 8** "How much guidance did your church and clergymen provide for the ethical problems you and your business acquaintances faced in the last five years?"

have been adequate. The top executive of one of the country's giant corporations blames businessmen for not hearing the Church's message: "Too few men understand or listen."

Most executives who criticize organized religion's current lack of guidance in business ethics hope for religious help in the future. And they give some clear indications of their preference for Church practice:

- Executives strongly favor traditional forms of guidance (sermons, writing) over recent innovations (such as the presence of a clergyman at the office or factory).
- Executives prefer the explanation of ethical principles over (a) the application of these principles to typical business situations, and (b) the motivation to do good rather than evil.
- Executives like the idea of a clergyman meeting regularly with small groups of businessmen to discuss management problems.

The preference for "explanation of ethical principles" over "applications" deserves study. Here are some of the comments:

- A personnel director: "I don't think the average clergyman knows enough about business to be specific."
- A president: "The question of competency enters here. The personality and ability of the preacher or padre makes all the difference."

Such reservations about the level of business knowledge possessed by the average clergyman are common in our replies. Presumably, they were born during a sermon when an ill-informed cleric ventured into economic waters well over his head.

On the other hand, our data intimate that most businessmen welcome the assistance of clergymen who are well educated in business, economics, and the social sciences. Indeed, many of our respondents favor the idea of regular meetings, attended by a small group of businessmen and a clergyman, for the purpose of discussing problems in business ethics. The idea is receiving a thorough trial from a number of Catholic Employers and Managers Study Groups.

A Louisiana vice president likes the idea because it will help the clergy to understand the complexity and pressures of businessmen's problems, for "too many clergymen are 'ivory tower' fellows."

Similarly, as Vincent P. Stanton, Investment Analyst for Loomis-Sayles & Company, points out: "This is an encouraging sign, for it indicates an active, rather than merely a passive, interest in improving business ethics."

## Medial Norms

Businessmen, trying to cope with the prickly problem of writing specific industry codes, could use the assistance of competent moral philosophers and theologians. One form which this aid might profitably take is the construction of *medial norms* to provide guidance for the solution of everyday problems in business.

Such medial norms are needed. In America, there is widespread acceptance among businessmen of the handful of general ethical principles which are the foundation of Judaeo-Christian civilization. But between these general principles (such as "Thou shalt not steal") and the concrete problems of the businessman (such as whether or not price-fixing is stealing from customers) a wide gap appears.

If scholars cooperate with businessmen, this gap can be filled with medial norms, refinements, and applications of the general principles. These norms would shed light not only on daily business decisions but also on the content of industry codes. Naturally, because specific business problems change, ample provision would have to be made for altering the medial norms when advisable.

## Plant Pastors

Several companies, including Le Tourneau Incorporated, Texas Aluminum, Reynolds Tobacco Co., and D-X Sunray Oil, have employed "plant pastors," i.e., clergymen available at the plant or office for individual consultation by employees. We asked our executives for their opinion on using chaplains in industry. Their response does not encourage this practice. Most men prefer such consultation to take place at the synagogue, parsonage, or rectory.

Why the lack of interest in plant pastors? Mr. Stanton suggested:

Perhaps administrators are wary of the many practical problems which appear to be involved. For example, it may be difficult to find a clergyman with the understanding of complex business relationships necessary to apply ethical principles to specific problems successfully. Will the clergyman be forced into the role of a judge rather than a guide? Will he seem to represent either a management or labor viewpoint, and hence lose some of his effectiveness? What denomination should he come from, and will this be acceptable to all? Will he be heard by those who should hear him, if contact is purely voluntary, as it should be?

## What of the Future?

Anyone who is pessimistic about U.S. business ethics would qualify his views after reading a sample of our completed questionnaires. They contain many heartening examples of courageous decisions made for ethical reasons. Thus:

- A sales manager refused to give a "payoff required to secure distribution of a consumer product in a grocery chain. Have been tempted but have not gone along with this 'under-the-counter' dealing. Our sales are hurt as a result."
- The president of a company engaged in mass communication faced the choice of "giving up a valued client of long standing and great profitability, and having to resort to laying off hard-to-replace employees; or yielding to the client's demand to do something I didn't believe in. I chose the former course."

With men like these holding some of the reins of industry, surely there is reason for hope. Of course, the continuing good influence of organizations like Better Business Bureaus and the Federal Trade Commission affords additional reason for optimism.

Someone has defined a leader as a man who raises his own standards above the ordinary and is willing to let other people judge him by these raised standards. Here are several signs that ethical leadership is present in business today: (1) The forthright speech delivered recently by Henry Ford II not only reproved the actions of some of his acquaintances, but also promised that the Ford Motor Company would maintain the highest standards of business integrity. (2) The Gillette Company, in its 1960 Annual Report, introduced a section specifying company practice with respect to gift taking and conflicts of interest. Perhaps shareholders in other firms would like to see this idea adopted, and even extended. (3) The Association of National Advertisers and the American Association of Advertising Agencies recently invited all advertising media to criticize advertisements considered offensive, and have developed a procedure of evaluating the criticisms.

This survey provides useful empirical knowledge about the problems and views of executives concerning business ethics. Some of the findings are not complimentary to businessmen. They are reported, not to chastise, but to reveal specific areas for improvement.

Only the candor of our respondents made this report possible. Presumably, they chose to reveal these business shortcomings in the hope of remedying them. Our recommendations for action are based on the confidential opinions generously supplied by HBR readers. It is their hope, and ours, that industry will act on these candid sentiments by rectifying behavior from within, rather than delaying until regulation comes from without.

It is noteworthy that, in our responses, there were no major differences of opinion among the various levels of management. The same is true of analysis by industry, business activity, and income levels. (We are, however, still examining our data for differences in opinion by age, education, and religious affiliation and hope to have some interesting information for you at a future date.)

Further, the desire for *change* permeates executive belief from the top to the bottom of the corporate structure. But this change will not come about, say executives, merely by hoping for it, instituting half-measures, or issuing platitudes. The time has come for courageous top-management leadership to implement executives' desires to raise the level of business ethics.

# Behavior in Future Organizations: A Glimpse at Rising Awareness

*Peter A. Raynolds*

In recent years we have been deluged with dire predictions about future events. In aggregate, these predictions seem enough to cause us to wonder if man should be officially declared an endangered species, possibly before the year 2000.[1]

## Simple-Cause Concern

There has been lively debate over the "true" or "basic" cause of "the problem." Some appear to believe that the primary culprit is pollution

[1]Rachel Carson's *Silent Spring* (Greenwich, Conn.: Fawcett, 1962) was one of the earliest books to arouse national concern over insecticides as pollutants. Paul Ehrlich's *The Population Bomb* (New York: Ballantine Books, 1968) contains a popularization of the vast data supporting population concerns and no really positive scenarios about probable future world population resolutions. Alvin Toffler's comprehensive *Future Shock* (New York: Random House, 1970) warns us about both man's inability to adapt to rapid change and the technological and population dilemmas.

from an exploitative technology, and that we should "return to the land." Others maintain the world population explosion is the real problem leading to exhaustion of energy and food supplies.

Often persons tend to regress toward overly simplistic thinking when confronted with situations perceived to contain threats having crisis proportions. This is a very common ego-defense mechanism. In a way, the very presence of this controversy is reassuring even with its polarization of opinion, because it indicates a rising awareness of the magnitude and urgency of the problems that confront mankind in the next couple of decades. The controversy itself will attract further attention and hopefully attract much creative, deliberate, and constructive action.

## Are We "Advanced?"

There appears to be a lack of concern about how the institutionally solidified behavioral *structures* of "economically advanced" societies may be contributing to the many world-wide ecological and social-stress problems. Of course, these problems are certainly determined largely by deeply imbedded learned qualities (values, beliefs, attitudes, and knowledge) in the individuals who are behaving within *authority hierarchies* responsible for conduct of planning, organizing, and control within institutions and organizations in the typical *task structures* they employ, and the social role-sets they retain (e.g., as consumers, family members, etc.)

Do the "advanced" industrial societies, with their members' seeming compulsions toward achieving personal riches or "contributing" to societal GNP growth actually frequently also obscure other "lower," unsatisfied physical or psychological needs? Might such hidden needs (for dominance, affiliation, achievement, affection, attention, etc., combine into an inevitable pattern of grossly unstable and undesirable social-system characteristics?

If so, it is unfortunate that members of many developing nations appear to be seeking to be like the economically advanced nations. They sometimes seem almost mesmerized into laying the behavioral patternings for inevitably the same mistakes, even though these mistakes seem now to confront us with dire consequences. There may be alternative paths that the advanced as well as the developing nations could take to avoid such catastrophe.

## Multiple-Cause Concern

Fortunately, there do appear to be some who are concerned with future problems who are not subject to overly simplistic thinking. One such body is the prestigious National Industrial Conference Board (NICB),[2]

[2]"Perspectives for the '70s and '80s: Tomorrow's Problems Confronting Today's Management," *NICB, Special Report* (1970); see also Charles E. Silberman, "The U.S. Economy in an Age of Uncertainty," *Fortune*, January, 1971. In another approach, Dennis Gabor, in *Innovations: Scientific, Technological and Social* (New York: Oxford University Press, 1970)

which has attempted to display multiple prospects for the future, to estimate the impact of these prospects upon the society as well as the probabilities of changing or reversing the undesirable to desirable trends and outcomes.

The NICB approach essentially starts with the basic question, "what indications are there that any unusually difficult national problems are in fact emerging?" Their conclusion, based upon painstaking research are that the United States is presently in a complex *major* national, political, economic, and social *transition* (see Table 1 for some of the predominant characteristics uncovered).

Secondly, the NICB study goes on to identify a set of more specific problems (see Table 2) that are logical outgrowths of the features comprising major transitions presently underway in the nation.

In an independent inter-disciplinary in-depth analysis, Eric L. Trist summarizes important social-psychological trends in the nation's present movement from an industrial to a post-industrial era (see Table 3).

These careful researchers and analyses are largely consistent with the findings of an increasing number of later studies. The Trist set, in particular, avails itself to analyses of individuals and organizations with respect to the changing times of the '70s and '80s.

## Is the United States in Major Transition?

Some very basic facts support the view that the NICB's and Eric Trist's diagnoses and analysis of major transition are mutually consistent in general:

First, we *are* undergoing rapid multiple technological revolutions involving knowledge explosions never before experienced on the face of the earth. Many of the fruits of these discoveries and developments have relatively fast applications in an economic sense, thereby amplifying the rate of and problems of transition. Furthermore, specific organizations have uneven capacities for keeping up with the new developments.

Second, accompanying our relatively great economic abundance is a shift away from the "lower-level" individual needs, considered in Maslow's framework; in addition, there is a greater mobility and fluidity of movement among virtually all workers, students, and the public in general. In other words, economic abundance removes constraints upon individuals who formally were tied to their jobs, education limit and geographic location.

Third, world mass media communications of economic abundance as it exists in the economically advanced nations tends to emphasize the increasing gap between the so-called have and have-not nations. This information creates stresses in the aspirations and expectations among

---

offers a very concise, fact-filled, readable treatment of many of the major innovations creating and hopefully solving some of the more likely problems that confront us. *The Futurist* (Washington, D.C.: World Future Society), *World* ed. Norman Cousins (New York: World Magazine, Inc.), and *Futures Conditional* ed. Robert Theobald (New York: Futures Conditional), are three periodicals devoted to keeping abreast with what needs to be done and what is actually being done.

**Table 1 Adapted from the *Major Themes Presented in the NICB Forecast* (conducted '68–'69), *ibid.***

*1. The United States is in a period of* major transition *from an* industrial *post*-industrial *society; in more detail:*

| *From* | *To* |
|---|---|
| A. Pluralistically directed nation | More centrally (or techno-cratically) directed |
| B. Unified nation | Divided nation |
| C. Rural America | Urban America |
| D. Smaller organizations | Larger and more powerful organizations |
| E. Two party system | Three or Four party system |
| F. A majority of older people | A majority of the young |
| G. A quest for quantity | A quest for quality & equality |
| H. Production economy | Service Economy |
| I. Three class society | Two class society |
| J. Second Automation Revolution | Third Automation Revolution |
| K. Private control of higher education | Public control of higher education |
| L. Serious obsolescence in existing institutions | Need for newly designed institutions |
| M. Old ways of perceiving roles and responsibilities (See Table 2 for NICB's enumeration of problems associated with these major transitions) | New ways of perceiving roles and responsibilities |

**Table 1 (continued)**

2. *Obsolescence is attacking and in some instances weakening key institutions in the United States' infrastructure:*

   A. Education B. Political Institutions

   C. Legal and Criminal Justice Systems D. Food Production

3. *Shifts in the U.S. power structure are occurring rapidly and largely unpredictable, with some exceptions:*

   A. Information itself is becoming a source of power,

   B. In the short run, holders of seemingly relevant information will receive power from national leaders,

   C. In the longer run, holders of knowledge, influence, and/or control over complex information systems will acquire considerable power.

   D. Today's leaders are vulnerable to challenge from new power holders within their own organizations and from without, especially in view of the lack of foresightedness becoming evident in the increasing appearance of the noxious and unstable world eco-systems.

4. *Confusion of identity, roles, responsibilities is appearing in the U.S.*

   (A) Both centralization and decentralization of institutions and power, (B) More "instant" communications between individuals, yet a feeling of isolation and loss of identity among an increasing number of urban dwellers, (C) More options and opportunities for education, work, and life styles, yet the portent of less personal freedom and sense of relevance, (D) A recognition that change is accelerating and adaptation is necessary, yet a reluctance (especially an institutional lag) to adapt to and manage change in a timely and economical way.

**Table 2** ***Problems Associated with Society's Major Transition,* (NICB), *ibid.***

1. The rate of change which is shrinking research and planning time;
2. outdated criteria used to examine new problems and opportunities;
3. micro and piecemeal ways of dealing with problems at macro scale;
4. public insistence on "instant" solutions and leader impatience with problems that demand attention over longer periods of time;
5. inexperience in bringing about large-scale collaboration on the part of leaders in and between the private and public sectors;
6. the pushing and pulling on the part of those who, through fear or selfish interests, resist change, and those who want to lead and accelerate it;
7. competing demands for scarce talents and resources, and the increasingly frequent absence of needed skills;
8. uncertainty on the part of decision makers and institutions as to the nature of their new roles and responsibilities in a changing society;
9. the temporary inability of our systems of checks and balances, of regulations and controls, to function effectively during the transition; and
10. the question of how to regularize the irregular.

numbers of the economically developing nations in the form of motivation to acquire abundance.

Fourth, there *is* a population worldwide explosion occurring primarily in the economically less-developed nations. Considering the rate of world population growth (including the slowing rate appearing in the most technologically advanced societies), all possible sources of food supplies and energy appear to be inadequate to sustain conservatively

**Table 3** ***Changes in Emphasis of Social Patterns in the Transition to Post-Industrialism***

| *Type* | *From* | *Towards* |
|---|---|---|
| Cultural Values | achievement | self-actualization |
| | self-control | self-expression |
| | independence | inter-dependence |
| | endurance of distress | capacity for joy |
| Organizational Forms and Characteristics | mechanistic forms | organic forms |
| | competitive relations | collaborative relations |
| | separate objectives | linked objectives |
| | own resources regarded as owned absolutely | own resources regarded also as society's resources |
| | responsive to crisis | anticipative of crisis |
| | specific measures | comprehensive measures |
| | requiring consent | requiring participation |
| | short planning horizon | long planning horizon |
| | damping conflict | confronting conflict |
| | detailed central control | generalized central control |
| | small local government units | enlarged local government units |
| | standardized administration | innovative administration |
| | separate services | co-ordinated services |

Adapted from E. L. Trist, "Urban North America: The Challenge of the Next Thirty Years (A Social Psychological Viewpoint)," a presentation at the Town Planning Institute of Canada, June, 1968, Minaki, Ontario.

forecast future population. Needless to say, population pressures are running counter to motivations for material abundance especially in the economically underdeveloped nations, adding to international stresses. Such stresses often seem to have inevitable military implications that further endanger the possibilities of world abundance. Military expenditures seem repeatedly to take precedence without necessarily contributing to a nation's wealth.

Considered altogether, these underlying factors, with their technological, social, and individual psychological ramifications, point to increasingly widespread basic U.S. organizational problems resulting from a rapid, pervasive, complex, and disorderly transition. The upheavals associated with this sort of transition have been described as "turbulent" by some writers.

## EFFECTS UPON BEHAVIOR IN ORGANIZATIONS

Under "turbulent" conditions, managers are constantly confronted by surprises and shocks that break through the conventional organizational buffers (e.g., the energy crisis, unpredictable cost changes, interruptions in deliveries of raw materials, etc.).

It is reasonable to expect reactive effects, almost reflexes on the parts of individuals involved, in some of the initial organizational decision making in response to changes that will have origins primarily external to the organization. These will hopefully be followed by longer-term, more thoughtful and proactive responses to both internal and external complexes of organizational contingencies.

### Initial Short-Term Effects

We are already seeing a rush of concern over motivating workers (consider management by objectives, positive feedback, behavior modification, job enrichment or enlargement, etc.). Many managers and theoreticians seem to believe that motivation is manipulable and that higher intrinsic motivation through participation in one's own job design will inevitably lead to higher productivity. Much good may come from these initial efforts, but a couple generations experiencing relative satiation of "basic" needs has lead to changes in the realm of individual values and their impact upon the shaping of specific "higher" needs.

Values held by members of the culture appear to be fragmenting, which implies that changes in individual psychological needs are also occurring. Some of these value changes appear to have to do with the greater social concern over such relevant matters as interpersonal relationships, sexual and racial job equality, and, of course, the maintenance or enhancement of our ecological world environment. It is difficult to imagine a "motivational program" that would effectively suspend the ultimate effects of such fundamental value changes. If, for example, an organization were obviously contributing to a major irreversible deterioration of the local ecology, "job enrichment" would be unlikely to achieve the intended consequences.

We can also expect structural "surgery" in efforts to "take care of" problems, often before they come to the attention of top management or the general public. An example of this might be seen in some of the organizational responses that have occurred with respect to the Equal Opportunities Act. Creation of a token training program or suborganizational unit to deal with this problem is largely cosmetic.

*Longer-Term Effects*. Organizations responding to the impetus to change with revitalization are likely to undertake both basic structural and developmental strategies in the long run.

*Scanning and Sensing.* Relevant information which might bear upon the future becomes crucially important under turbulent conditions surrounding a major transition. The creation of various external environmental scanning units for entirely new kinds of information will increasingly appear in the boundary areas of an organization. Besides scanning, another function that organizations may undertake with increasing intensity and on a larger scale will be the sensing (or monitoring) of changes, variables, and indicators known to have relevance in the external and internal organizational environment.

The main difference between scanning and sensing is that scanning is primarily a search for major qualitative changes leading to discontinuities that might provide opportunities or dangers to the organization (e.g., new technologies that might leap-frog the organization's current in-plant [or even planned] new technology). Sensing, on the other hand, involves monitoring of continuous gradual changes and shifts in indicators. Minor adjustments in supply and demand, in markets, in the competition, and perceptions of and within the organization are already known to be highly relevant to social systems. This sensing would be an ongoing or periodic monitoring undertaken by members of boundary units in the organization as well as members of units buried deeply within it, and even by external observers of the organization who are lodged in various important vantage points (e.g., customers, competitors, distributors, regulatory agencies, and the general public).

*Training.* The major transition confronting the United States at the present time will increase drastically the incidences of aborted plans, major projects and products, some of which will have not even reached the market. Personnel within organizations, being less protected (or buffered) from the major surprises originating in both the external and internal environments of the organization, will have to cope with increasing ambiguity and inconsistency.

Thus in the long term run, training of personnel in organizations, especially administrative and managerial personnel, should be expected to emphasize behavioral flexibility, capacity for handling incongruities, ambiguities, and rapid changes. These personal qualities may accompany changes in the general climate of the organization, particularly increasing the "depth" or congruence of prevalent interpersonal relationships. Consequently, the impetus for organizational development strategies that have increasing interpersonal skills as major objectives will very likely result in changing the *structural forms* of organizational units away from the purely hierarchic.

## SUMMARY

In the somewhat longer run, then, we anticipate the evolution of major structural innovations in the design and integrated functioning of new units that conduct external environmental scanning. Furthermore, we anticipate an even more rapid adoption of organizational sensing activity directed toward and undertaken by semipermanent panels or samplings of completely external, boundary unit, and internal personnel. Finally, managerial personnel will increasingly develop capabilities for coping with turbulent conditions in both task and interpersonal aspects of their responsibilities.

# Interpersonal Relationships: U.S.A. 2000

*Carl R. Rogers*[1]

*Man's greatest problem, at this point in our swiftly changing technological progress, concerns our ability to assimilate change. With the population doubling during the next generation, can we humanize crowded living? The intensive group experience, perhaps the most significant social invention of this century, may help. The magnetism of the new openness and intimacy may prove more powerful than the trend toward treating man as a role or as a mere mechanism. By the year 2000 we shall probably change from the present pattern of action required to prevent conception to one in which infertility is standard and positive action is required to conceive. Parents may increasingly become not the authorities directing youth, but changing persons living in ever-changing interactions with their children. Institutionalized religion is likely to fade out, but the mysteries of life will acquire fresh challenge.*

*Educators seem to show greater resistance to change than do any other institutional group. A revolution in our schools is long overdue. It is ironic that alert industry now does more than do schools to free up communication among persons. But the most tragic trend is the increasing breakdown of communication between the privileged and the ghetto.*

I want to make it very clear at the outset that I am not making predictions about the year 2000. I am going to sketch possibilities, alternative routes which we may travel.

One important reason for refusing to make predictions is that for the first time in history man is not only taking his future seriously, but he also has adequate technology and power to shape and form that future. He is endeavoring to *choose* his future rather than simply living out some inevitable trend. And we do not know what he will choose. So we do not

• Reproduced by special permission from *The Journal of Applied Behavioral Science*, "Interpersonal Relationships: U.S.A. 2000," Carl R. Rogers, July, August, September, Vol. 4, No. 3, 1968, NTL Institute.

[1] Carl R. Rogers is a resident fellow, Western Behavioral Sciences Institute, La Jolla, California.

know what man's relation to man will be in this country 32 years from now. But we can see certain possibilities.

## Man's Greatest Problem

Before I try to sketch some of those possibilities I should like to point to the greatest problem which man faces in the years to come. It is not the hydrogen bomb, fearful as that may be. It is not the population explosion, though the consequences of that are awful to contemplate. It is instead a problem which is rarely mentioned or discussed. It is the question of how much change the human being can accept, absorb, and assimilate, and the rate at which he can take it. Can he keep up with the ever-increasing rate of technological change, or is there some point at which the human organism goes to pieces? Can he leave the static ways and static guidelines which have dominated all of his history and adopt the process ways, the continual changingness which must be his if he is to survive?

There is much to make us pessimistic about this. If we consider the incredible difficulties in bringing about change in our great bureaucracies of government, education, and religion, we become hopeless. When we see how frequently the people take action which is clearly against their long-range welfare—such as the resolute refusal to face up to the problem of the urban ghettos—we become discouraged.

But I see two elements on the other side of the balance. The first is the ability of the Western democratic cultures to respond appropriately—at the very last cliff-hanging moment—to those trends which challenge their survival.

The second element I have observed in individuals in therapy, in intensive encounter groups, and in organizations. It is the magnetic attraction of the experience of change, growth, fulfillment. Even though growth may involve intense pain and suffering, once the individual or group has tasted the excitement of this changingness, persons are drawn to it as to a magnet. Once a degree of actualization has been savored, the individual or the group is willing to take the frightening risk of launching out into a world of process, with few fixed landmarks, where the direction is guided from within. So, in this field of interpersonal relations, though there is much reason for despair, I believe that if our citizens experience something of the pain and risk of a growth toward personal enrichment they will grasp for more.

With this context of uncertainty about our ability or willingness to assimilate change, let us look at some specific areas of interpersonal relationships as they may be.

## Urban Crowding and Its Possible Effects

The world population will more than double in the next 32 years, a ghastly trend which will affect us in unknown ways. The population of the United States, which was comfortably remembered in my grammar school days in 1915 as 100 million, 52 years later reached 200 million, 22 years from now is predicted to reach 300 million, and in the year 2000 will be between 320 and 340 million, though hopefully it will be starting to stabilize itself at about that time. The great bulk of these millions will reside in a great megalopolis, of which there will probably be three. One trend which we may follow is to crowd more and more closely together, as we are now crowded in our ghettos. I understand that Philip Hauser, the noted demographer, has stated that if all of us were crowded together as closely as the residents of Harlem all of the people in the entire United States could be contained in the five boroughs of New York City. The future may resemble this, if we choose to push in more and more closely together.

Such crowding has consequences. Even in rats, as Calhoun[2] has so vividly shown, overcrowding results in poor mothering, poor nest building, bizarre sexual behavior, cannibalism, and complete alienation, with some rats behaving like zombies, paying no attention to others, coming out of their solitary sorrows only for food. The resemblance to human behavior in crowded rooming house areas, the complete lack of involvement which permits people to watch a long-drawn-out murder without so much as calling the police, the poor family relationships—this could be a trend which will be carried even further by the year 2000.

On the other hand, we could learn to decentralize our great urban areas, to make them manageable, to provide not only for more efficiency but for warmer and more human interpersonal relationships. We could use more space, build smaller cities with great park and garden areas, devise plans for neighborhood building which would promote *humanization*, not dehumanization. What will the choice be?

## Closeness and Intimacy in the Year 2000

In my estimation, one of the most rapidly growing social phenomena in the United States is the spread of the intensive group experience—sensitivity training, basic encounter groups, T-groups (the labels are unimportant). The growth of this phenomenon is rendered more striking when one realizes that it is a "grass roots" movement. There is not a university nor a foundation nor a government agency which has given it any significant approval or support until the last five or six years. Yet it has permeated industry, is coming into education, is reaching families, professionals in the helping fields, and many other individuals. Why? I believe it is because people—ordinary people—have discovered that it alleviates their loneliness and permits them to grow, to risk, to change. It brings persons into real relationships with persons.

In our affluent society the individual's survival needs are satisfied. For the first time, he is freed to become aware of his isolation, aware of his alienation, aware of the fact that he is, during most of his life, a role interacting with other roles, a mask meeting other masks. And for the

[2]J. B. Calhoun, "Population density and social pathology," Sci. American, CCVI, No. 2 (1962), 139–50.

first time he is aware that this is not a *necessary* tragedy of life, that he does not have to live out his days in this fashion. So he is seeking, with great determination and inventiveness, ways of modifying this existential loneliness. The intensive group experience, perhaps the most significant social invention of this century, is an important one of these ways.

What will grow out of the current use of basic encounter groups, marathons, "labs," and the like? I have no idea what *forms* will proliferate out of these roots during the coming decades, but I believe men will discover new bases of intimacy which will be highly fulfilling. I believe there will be possibilities for the *rapid* development of closeness between and among persons, a closeness which is not artificial, but is real and deep, and which will be well suited to our increasing mobility of living. Temporary relationships will be able to achieve the richness and meaning which heretofore have been associated only with lifelong attachments.

There will be awareness of what is going on within the person, an openness to all of one's experience—the sensory input of sound and taste and hearing and sight and smell, the richness of kaleidoscopically changing ideas and concepts, the wealth of feelings—positive, negative, and ambivalent, intense and moderate—toward oneself and toward others.

There will be the development of a whole new style of communication in which the person can, in effect, say, "I'm telling you the way it *is*, in me—my ideas, my desires, my feelings, my hopes, my angers, my fears, my despairs," and where the response will be equally open. We shall be experimenting with ways in which a whole person can communicate himself to another whole person. We shall discover that security resides not in hiding oneself but in being more fully known, and consequently in coming to know the other more fully. Aloneness will be something one chooses out of a desire for privacy, not an isolation into which one is forced.

In all of this I believe we shall be experimenting with a new ideal of what man may become, a model very *sharply* different from the historical view of man as a creature playing various appropriate roles. We seem to be aiming for a new *reality* in relationships, a new openness in communication, a love for one another which grows not out of a romantic blindness but out of the profound respect which is nearly always engendered by reality in relationships.

I recognize that many individuals in our culture are frightened in the depths of their being by this new picture of man—this flowing, changing, open, expressive, creative person. They may be able to stop the trend or even to reverse it. It is conceivable that we shall go in for the manufactured "image," as on TV, or may insist more strongly than ever that teachers are *teachers*, parents are *parents*, bosses are *manipulators*—that we may rigidify every role and stereotype in new and more armor-plated ways. We may insist with new force that the only significant aspect of man is his rational and intellectual being and that nothing else matters. We may assert that he is a machine and no more. Yet I do not believe this will happen. The magnetism of the new man, toward which we are groping, is too great. Much of what I say in the remainder of this paper is based on the conviction that we are, for better or for worse, in labor pains and growth pains—turning toward this new view of man as becoming and being—a continuing, growing *process*.

## Man-Woman Relationships

What do the coming decades hold for us in the realm of intimacy between boy and girl, man and woman? Here too enormous forces are at work, and choices are being made which will not, I believe, be reversed by the year 2000.

In the first place the trend toward greater freedom in sexual relationships, in adolescents and adults, is likely to continue, whether this direction frightens us or not. Many elements have conspired together to bring about a change in such behavior, and the advent of "the Pill" is only one of these. It seems probable that sexual intimacy will be a part of "going steady" or of any continuing special interest in a member of the opposite sex. The attitude of prurience is fast dying out, and sexual activity is seen as a potentially joyful and enriching part of a relationship. The attitude of possessiveness—of owning another person, which historically has dominated sexual unions—is likely to be greatly diminished. It is certain that there will be enormous variations in the quality of these sexual relationships—from those where sex is a purely physical contact which has almost the same solitary quality as masturbation to those in which the sexual aspect is an expression of an increasing sharing of feelings, of experiences, of interests, of each other.

By the year 2000 it will be quite feasible to ensure that there will be no children in a union. By one of the several means currently under study, each individual will be assured of lasting infertility in early adolescence. It will take positive action, permissible only after a thoughtful decision, to reestablish fertility. This will reverse the present situation where only by positive action can one *prevent* conception. Also, by that time, computerized matching of prospective partners will be far more sophisticated than it is today and will be of great help to an individual in finding a congenial companion of the opposite sex.

Some of the temporary unions thus formed may be legalized as a type of marriage—with no permanent commitment, with no children (by mutual agreement), and, if the union breaks up, no legal accusations, no necessity for showing legal cause, and no alimony.

It is becoming increasingly clear that a man-woman relationship will have *permanence* only in the degree in which it satisfies the emotional, psychological, intellectual, and physical needs of the partners. This means that the *permanent* marriage of the future will be even better than marriage in the present, because the ideals and goals for that marriage will be of a higher order. The partners will be demanding more of the relationship than they do today.

If a couple feel deeply committed to each other and mutually wish to remain together to raise a family, then this will be a new and more binding type of marriage. Each will accept the obligations involved in having and rearing children. There may be a mutual agreement as to whether or not the marriage includes sexual faithfulness to one's mate. Perhaps by the year 2000 we shall have reached the point where, through education and social pressure, a couple will decide to have children only when they have shown evidence of a mature commitment to each other, of a sort which is likely to have permanence.

What I am describing is a whole continuum of man-woman relationships, from the most casual dating and casual sex relationship to a rich and fulfilling partnership in which communication is open and real, where each is concerned with promoting the personal growth of the partner, and where there is a long-range commitment to each other which will form a sound basis for having and rearing children in an environment of love. Some parts of this continuum will exist within a legal framework; some will not.

One may say, with a large measure of truth, that much of this continuum already exists. But an awareness of, and an open acceptance of, this continuum by society will change its whole quality. Suppose it were openly accepted that some "marriages" are no more than ill-mated and transitory unions and that they will be broken. If children are not permitted in such marriages, then one divorce in every two marriages (the current rate in California) is no longer seen as a tragedy. The dissolving of the union may be painful, but it is not a *social* catastrophe, and the experience may be a necessary step in the personal growth of the two individuals toward greater maturity.

## Parents and Children

What of the relationships between parents and their children? Here it is terribly difficult to foresee the future. If parents in general hold to the static views which have served reasonably well through the centuries of little change—"I know the values that are important in life," "I am wiser than my child in knowing the direction his life should take"—then the generation gap will grow so large that our culture will literally be split wide open. This may be the course of future events.

But there are straws in the wind which point in another way. Some parents wish to be *persons*—growing, changing persons—living in person-to-person relationships with the youngsters in their families. So we see the development of family encounter groups (still in their infancy) in which parents learn about themselves from their own and others' children, and children learn about themselves from their own and others' parents. Here the self-insights, the awareness of how one comes across to the other generation, bring changes in behavior and new ways of relating based on an open respect for oneself, out of which can grow a genuine respect for the other.

A new type of parent education is also developing in which there is respect for the parent as a person with feelings and rights as well as for the child and his feelings and rights. We find family groups where parent and child each *listen* to the other, where honest, open expression is also mutual. Parental authority and childhood submission give way before a realness which confronts realness. Such family relationships are not necessarily smooth, and the problems of process living are as perplexing as the problems brought on by static views; but there is communication and there is respect, and the generation gap becomes simply the communication gap which in some degree separates all individuals.

It may be hard for us to realize that some help for this new type of family relationship may come from industry. Some corporations, realizing that to start to educate a child at six is much too late, are beginning to dream up learning activities, learning "packages," which will not only be fun for the children but which will involve the whole family in mutually pleasurable and communicative activities. Everyone will have a good time learning—together.

Let me turn to quite a different facet of the relations of parents and children. What will the future hold for children from broken homes—who will continue to exist even if my most optimistic speculations come true? I trust there will be widespread experimentation in dealing with these youngsters. Perhaps we should take a lesson from the *kibbutzim*, where the child is cared for and gains his security from workers who love children and are trained to care for them, and where the contacts with parents, though relatively brief, tend to be full of love and fun. Perhaps some of the "hippie" groups are showing the way in their small, close communities where the child is, ideally at least, cared for by all. We are in desperate need of creative approaches to this problem. Almost anything would be better than the present situation. Now the child is often fought over in court. He learns that one parent is bad, the other good. He is often exposed to the attempts of each parent to win him away, emotionally, from the other. He is often experienced as a burden by the mother, who is attempting to reestablish herself in a job and a new life. Or he is the sole focus of the mother's affection, which may be even worse. *He* is the one who suffers from divorce, and we have been most unimaginative in trying to promote his welfare. Hence my hope is that there will be many types of experimentation three decades from now, in helping the child of divorced parents to grow in the most favorable possible environment.

## Learning in Interpersonal Relationships

What of education in the year 2000, especially as it involves interpersonal relationships?

It is possible that education will continue much as it is—concerned only with words, symbols, rational concepts based on the authoritative role of the teacher, further dehumanized by teaching machines, computerized knowledge, and increased use of tests and examinations. This is possible, because educators are showing greater resistance to change than any other institutional group. Yet I regard it as unlikely, because a revolution in education is long overdue, and the unrest of students is only one sign of this. So that I am going to speculate on some of the other possibilities.

It seems likely that schools will be greatly deemphasized in favor of a much broader, thoughtfully devised *environment for learning*, where the experiences of the student will be challenging, rewarding, affirmative, and pleasurable.

The teacher or professor will have largely disappeared. His place will be taken by a facilitator of learning, chosen for his facilitative attitudes as much as for his knowledge. He will be skilled in stimulating individual and group initiative in learning, skilled in facilitating discussions-in-depth of the *meaning* to the student of what is being learned, skilled in fostering creativity, skilled in providing the resources for learning. Among these resources will be much in the way of programmed learning, to be used as the student finds these learnings appropriate; much in the way of audio-visual aids such as filmed lectures and demonstrations by experts in each field; much in the way of computerized knowledge on which the student can draw. But these "hardware" possibilities are not my main concern.

We shall, I believe, see the facilitator focusing his major attention on the prime period for learning—from infancy to age six to eight. Among the most important learnings will be the personal and interpersonal. Every child will develop confidence in his own ability to learn, since he will be rewarded for learning at his own pace. Each child will learn that he is a person of worth, because he has unique and worthwhile capacities. He will learn how to be himself in a group—to listen, but also to speak, to learn about himself, but also to confront and give feedback to others. He will learn to be an individual, not a faceless conformist. He will learn, through simulations and computerized games, to meet many of the life problems he will face. He will find it permissible to engage in fantasy and daydreams, to think creative thoughts, to capture these in words or paints or constructions. He will find that learning, even difficult learning, is fun, both as an individual activity and in cooperation with others. His discipline will be self-discipline.

His learning will not be confined to the ancient intellectual concepts and specializations. It will not be a *preparation* for living. It will be, in itself, an *experience* in living. Feelings of inadequacy, hatred, a desire for power, feelings of love and awe and respect, feelings of fear and dread, unhappiness with parents or with other children—all these will be an open part of his curriculum, as worthy of exploration as history or mathematics. In fact this openness to feelings will enable him to learn content material more readily. His will be an education in becoming a whole human being, and the learnings will involve him deeply, openly, exploringly, in an awareness of his relationship to himself, an awareness of his relationships to the world of others, as well as in an awareness of the world of abstract knowledge.

Because learning has been exciting, because he has participated heavily and responsibly in choosing the directions of his learning, because he has discovered the world to be a fantastically changing place, he will wish to continue his learning into adult life. Thus communities will set up centers which are rich environments for learning, and the student will *never be graduated*. He will always be a part of a "commencement."

## Persons in Industry

In view of my past prejudices I find it somewhat difficult but necessary to say that of all of the institutions of present-day American life, industry is perhaps best prepared to meet the year 2000. I am not speaking of its technical ability. I am speaking of the vision it is acquiring in regard to the importance of persons, of interpersonal relationships, and of open communication. That vision, to be sure, is often unrealized but it does exist.

Let me speculate briefly on the interpersonal aspect of industrial functioning. It is becoming increasingly clear to the leaders of any complex modern industry that the old hierarchical system of boss and employees is obsolete. If a factory is turning out one simple product, such a system may still work. But if it is in the business of producing vehicles for space or elaborate electronic devices, it is definitely inadequate. What takes its place? The only road to true efficiency seems to be that of persons communicating freely with persons—from below to above, from peer to peer, from above to below, from a member of one division to a member of another division. It is only through this elaborate, individually initiated network of open human communication that the essential information and know-how can pervade the organization. No one individual can possibly "direct" such complexity.

Thus if I were to hazard a guess in regard to industry in the year 2000 it would be something different from the predictions about increasing technical skill, increasing automation, increasing management by computers, and the like. All of those predictions will doubtless come true but the interpersonal aspect is less often discussed. I see many industries, by the year 2000, giving as much attention to the quality of interpersonal relationships and the quality of communication as they currently do to the technological aspects of their business. They will come to value persons as persons, and to recognize that only out of the *communicated* knowledge of all members of the organization can innovation and progress come. They will pay more attention to breakdowns in personal communication than to breakdowns of the circuitry in their computers. They will be forced to recognize that only as they are promoting the growth and fulfillment of the individuals on the payroll will they be promoting the growth and development of the organization.

What I have said will apply, I believe, not only to persons in management but to persons classed as "labor." The distinction grows less with every technological advance. It also applies, obviously, to the increasingly direct and personal communication between persons in management and persons in the labor force, if an industry is to become and remain healthily productive.

## Religion as Interpersonal Living

Historically, much of man's life has revolved around his relationship to his God or gods and around his relationship to others who share his religious views. What will be the situation three decades from now?

It is definitely conceivable that out of a deep fear of the rapidly changing world he is creating, man may seek refuge in a sure dogma, a simplistic answer to life's complexities, a religion which will serve him as a security blanket. This seems unlikely, but I can imagine the circumstances under which it might occur.

The more likely possibility—or so it appears to me—is that by the year 2000, *institutionalized* religion, already on the wane as a significant factor in everyday life, will have faded to a point where it is of only slight importance in the community. Theology may still exist as a scholastic exercise, but in reality the God of authoritative answers will be not only dead but buried.

This does not mean at all that the concerns which have been the basis of religion will have vanished. The mysterious process of life, the mystery of the universe and how it came to be, the tragedy of man's alienation from himself and from others, the puzzle of the meaning of individual life—these mysteries will all be very much present. There may, indeed, be a *greater appreciation* of mystery as our knowledge increases (just as theoretical physicists now marvel at the true *mystery* of what they have discovered).

But religion, to the extent that the term is used, will consist of tentatively held hypotheses which are lived out and corrected in the interpersonal world. Groups, probably much smaller than present-day congregations, will wrestle with the ethical and moral and philosophical questions which are posed by the rapidly changing world. The individual will forge, with the support of the group, the stance he will take in the universe—a stance which he cannot regard as final because more data will continually be coming in.

In the open questioning and honest struggle to face reality which exist in such a group, it is likely that a sense of true community will develop—a community based not on a common creed nor an unchanging ritual but on the personal ties of individuals who have become deeply related to one another as they attempt to comprehend and to face, as living men, the mysteries of existence. The religion of the future will be man's existential choice of his way of living in an unknown tomorrow, a choice made more bearable because formed in a community of individuals who are like-minded, but like-minded only in their searching.

In line with the thread which runs through all of my remarks, it may well be that out of these many searching groups there may emerge a more unitary view of man, a view which might bind us together. Man as a creature with ability to remember the past and foresee the future, a creature with the capacity for choosing among alternatives, a creature whose deepest urges are for harmonious and loving relationships with his fellows, a creature with the capacity to understand the reasons for his destructive behaviors, man as a person who has at least limited powers to form himself and to shape his future in the way he desires—this might be a crude sketch of the unifying view which could give up hope in a universe we cannot understand.

## The Relationship with the Slum Dweller

I have left until the last the most difficult area: the relationship between the persons in the urban ghettos (Negroes and other minority groups) and the persons outside the ghetto.

Our inability to accept the changing nature of this anguished struggle is one of the deepest reasons for pessimism regarding the future. The more favored community seems, thus far, unwilling and unable to understand the effects upon individuals of a lifetime of defeat, frustration, and rejection. It seems, thus far, unable to comprehend that rebellion is *most* likely, not least likely, to occur in the very cities and situations in which there is, at last, some hope. We seem reluctant to give the ghetto dweller responsibility, the one thing which might restore his human dignity—because he will make mistakes. We seem to have no recognition that learning from mistakes is the only true way to independence. And, most tragically of all, we appear—on both sides—to have lost the belief that communication is possible. Thus I cannot deny the possibility that the next decades will see a growing rebellion, a bloody guerrilla warfare in our cities, with concentration camps, with military government, with fear and hatred in the heart of every citizen. It took a century for the hatreds between the North and the South to diminish to manageable proportions. How many centuries will it take for the hatreds of the new war to die down, a war which may be too late to prevent?

What makes it, from my point of view, incredibly tragic is that the deepest, most basic issues revolve around communication. Distrust, suspicion, disillusionment have grown to such mammoth proportions on both sides—though perhaps especially on the part of the ghetto dweller—that it is taken for granted that communication is no longer possible. Yet funds, however great, and vocational retraining and housing projects and all the rest can do little without free, direct, honest communication between persons.

Is it impossible? It is my contention that if we mounted a massive effort to reestablish communication, in groups ranging from militant blacks through liberals of both colors to conservative whites; if we drew into this effort dedicated individuals, from the ghetto and outside, who were desirous of improving relationships; if we drew on the expert knowledge available in the social and behavioral sciences; if we backed this effort with a sum at least equivalent to the cost of all our B-52 bombers—then there might be a chance of preventing the bloody tragedy which faces us.

I should not want to be understood as saying that improved communication, improved interpersonal relationships, would *resolve* the situation. What I am saying is that if, in small groups or large, the hatreds and the disillusionments could be accepted and *understood*; if suspicion and despair could be fully voiced and met with respect; then out of such groups might slowly grow a mutual respect in which responsible decisions could be taken and realistic solutions worked out. In these decisions the ghetto dweller would be a fully involved participant, as would the person from outside. Leadership in the ghetto would meet on a fully equal basis with leadership in the "establishment." Both would bear responsibility, through black power and white power, for seeing that the decisions were *carried out*. Idealistic, you say? But we have the knowledge and the wealth which would make such a massive effort possible. And if we choose to follow the present trend, we have in South Vietnam a full color picture of how guerrilla warfare not only sacrifices lives but brutalizes the minds and hearts of the living. Shall we permit it to happen here? Or shall we choose to make a great and concerted effort to behave as persons with persons? On this issue I dare not even speculate.

## Conclusion

Perhaps it is just as well that I conclude on this somberly precarious note. I hope I have made it clear that the potentialities for change and enrichment in the interpersonal world of the year 2000 most assuredly exist. There can be more of intimacy, less of loneliness, an infusion of emotional and intellectual learning in our relationships, better ways of resolving conflicts openly, man-woman relationships which are enriching, family relationships which are real, a sense of community which enables us to face the unknown. All of this is possible if as a people we choose to move into the new mode of living openly as a continually changing process.

# Cases

## Acting Out of Character

"We've just had a real fight in my group. I think I've got things straightened out now. But for a time I was worried."

The speaker was Mike Mayo, a section head in the Sounds System Laboratory of Rolands, Horn & Oliver, a medium-sized producer of electronic signaling systems. Mike went on to explain to the casewriter how the conflict had arisen.

MIKE: "My group got this project. Potentially it had a huge payoff—20 million or more. My boss, Dr. Spoke, considered it top priority and it looked to both of us like an outstanding opportunity to make a breakthrough. We put three of our senior associates on the project, and right away they were fighting.

"I won't confuse you with technical details but we were working with transducers which had to have very low breakdown voltages. I called together the three

•  Prepared by Mr. Charles Hampden-Turner, Research Associate, under the direction of Assistant Dean Charles D. Orth. The collection and writing of this case were made possible by a grant from the Industrial Research Institute. This case was prepared as the basis for class discussion rather than to illustrate either effective or ineffective handling of administrative situations.

associates, Don Steiger, Jo Arnes, and Kurt Kalcheck. Almost right away Don Steiger objected to the project on grounds that it was theoretically doubtful, if not impossible. Don is only about twenty-six. He received his Ph.D. last year and demonstrated his first device three years ago. Frankly, I think he's brilliant. He's going to shoot up in this organization.

"The rest of us were rather taken aback by the speed and certainty with which Don responded. I'm not sure what Jo Arnes would have said if Don hadn't been so positive. At any rate Jo was lukewarm at best. However I received immediate support from Kurt Kalcheck. Kurt is much older than the other two, who are close friends. Kurt must be in his fifties. He has very little advanced math and a background in engineering. He's one of the very few senior associates without a doctoral degree. But Kurt is very loyal, diligent, practical, and reliable and he'll work tremendously hard. We get along very well. Kurt said he would set up an experiment and see what happened.

"It was agreed that the three of them should get together and plan a preliminary investigation to decide whether the project should proceed. I remember thinking at the time that Don Steiger wasn't going to do any collaborating with anyone and I was right.

"At 9:30 the next morning, Dr. Spoke received an elaborate theoretical report, which demonstrated the mathematical impossibility of the project's objective. There was a forceful summary to the effect that we would be wasting our time proceeding any further. Don must have stayed up half the night to complete it. Both Dr. Spoke and I were impressed by Don's speed and thoroughness. It was typical of him.

"It was going to take time for us to evaluate the report and Dr. Spoke was very busy that week. I was wondering whether to call Kurt Kalcheck off the project when some five days after Don's report had been submitted, Kurt came to see me. He had assembled the transducers and they worked. He'd done it! I was tremendously excited and so was Dr. Spoke. Many people were congratulating Kurt. Don and Jo were called in and told the news. Don said nothing about having been wrong but began to examine Kurt's setup minutely.

"A couple of hours later I received a call from Dr. Spoke. Don was in his office complaining that Kurt refused to share information with him. I said I would handle it and I called Don, Jo, and Kurt into my office. I said that this was Kurt's discovery and that no one must deprive him of the full credit for it. Probably Don could write a better article for the professional journals but Kurt must be permitted to exploit his work. I sympathized with Kurt's fear that his ideas would be taken over.

"Don shrugged this off. He denied that he had the smallest intention of depriving Kurt of any credit. He merely wished to build on Kurt's work, for which he required information. Shared information was the basis of science.

"That fight was two weeks ago and I think I resolved it. In a way Kurt was acting out of character. He isn't *expected* to discover new things. In fact Jo has announced that Kurt was only following my orders, which isn't true. Kurt is expected to be the practical one.

"But you know something, I think Kurt has a lot of talent, if only he and others would start to believe it."

The casewriter asked to speak to Kurt Kalcheck. Kurt was a thin, balding man with glasses. He had a polite but earnest style of speaking and a distinct Polish accent. He was asked about his background and his life up to the present.

KURT KALCHECK: "I was born in Poland and educated in Munich, Germany. In 1939 I won a scholarship in engineering to Michigan University where I studied for my master's. A few years later America entered the war and I came to work here at Rolands. It didn't seem so important to have a doctor's degree in those days. I had only been here a few months when I was fired as a security risk. It was my Munich background and the fact that Poland was occupied.

"It was a pretty bad time to be a security risk or to speak with any sort of mid-European accent. I couldn't afford to return to the University and had to take temporary jobs. In 1945 Rolands took me back again and I did some really important work on vacuum tubes. Thousands of systems used the miniature tubes I had developed. Then, quite suddenly the technology changed over to solid state devices and I was given only routine assignments on tubes. The creative work was no longer coming my way and hundreds of young Ph.D.s fresh out of the University were way ahead of me.

"Have you ever stopped to think what happens to people in these technical upheavals? I often wonder what it must have been like to be an expert on propeller-driven airplanes and then suddenly find oneself at the bottom, nobody wanting all your knowledge. Industry makes these studies on how to use waste products and it never stops to think of the human beings it consigns to the scrap heap. Management says it's 'up to the individual.' There's all these orientation programs for newcomers but what about *reorientation* for some of us?

"Sometimes I think of all the brilliant people we have here and yet most of us are alone. Just a few yards away behind a wall there are probably a dozen men from whom we could learn so much. And yet there are high walls everywhere with many noncommunicating people duplicating each other's efforts. Oh, we *emphasize* 'teamwork' but our individual noses are so close to our individual grindstones that we just don't notice each other. People here are strongly opinionated and individualistic. They like to work by themselves. Maybe they fear others will steal their ideas.

"I'll give an example of the quite needless rivalry that goes on here. One of the production division's development groups has been sent over here—to the research laboratory. The idea is to 'facilitate' the production of our ideas. They'll come in and seize your idea and five days later they'll be developing it in a half-cocked state before we've even evaluated it ourselves. And since this new pressure on us to do application work is intensifying—we are converging with this fiercely competitive marketing-oriented group, who seem intent on hustling everything through. This is duplication and it's hurting the company. Why doesn't management give us clearer assignments, which don't overlap? We're doing some work on missile defense systems as you may know. Now what happens when the government gets competitive bids from different parts of this company? Because that's going to happen any day now.

"I've complained several times about this. The other day the marketing manager of this manufacturing division which has invaded us was in here. He told me, 'Don't cry about it. Get in quickly—that's life!' He wants all our information. I must confess I've always found it difficult to push in front of people. We spend hours laying down a list of priorities, then all of a sudden it turns into a game of how to get around them. It seems so destructive to me. Beyond a certain point competition becomes detrimental to the organization. While I'm waiting my turn—as I promised to do—someone else comes barging in and grabs the needed equipment. It gets so that my civilized behavior is just exploited. There has to be a better way!

"It's bad enough when this fighting goes on between departments but when it's *inside* the very group you are working with, when you cannot even trust your closest associates, then things are really falling apart."

CASEWRITER: "I understand that there has recently been a dispute between you and Don Steiger. Is that what you were referring to?"

KURT KALCHECK: "Well, that was typical, although more unpleasant than usual because it was so close to us all. We were called into Dr. Spoke's office to discuss the development of very low frequency transducers. There was a definite application in mind. We all agreed to explore it but after the meeting Don walked off by himself and began writing a paper. He likes to show how quickly he can respond. He didn't consult us, of course, and the memo virtually told us, 'That's my conclusion, and that settles it.'

"Well, Don's got a good brain—but it doesn't matter how brilliant you are, it's always dangerous to say that something can't be done and even more dangerous to put it into writing. I couldn't follow Don's theoretical arguments very closely and he didn't seem inclined to explain them to me. Mike Mayo had told me to go ahead and so I did. I went to the manufacturing division and succeeded in getting some low-frequency devices from them, which they had recently developed. It was difficult getting them and they made me promise not to let anyone else use them. That's the sort of suspicion we have around here! I set up some experiments and within eight days I'd achieved 20 percent efficiency, which Don had argued couldn't be done.

"Well, you never saw a faster change of attitude from anyone than Don's. Instead of offering to work with me he began taking notes and a couple of hours after my first demonstration he was setting up a duplicate experiment on his own. Every few minutes he would come down from his lab and look at what I had done. It was quite clear that he was imitating my setup.

"I didn't protest until his lab technician came into the room, went over to my setup and without asking me picked up a couple of filters. I said, 'Hey—I'm using those!' He said, 'You're not. They were on the table.' I explained that I borrowed the equipment from many different people. I'd waited my turn until it was ready and that I would need all the filters I had. 'Why can't you wait your turn,' I said, 'and why duplicate this setup? Aren't we supposed to be working together?' 'That's what *I* thought,' he said. 'All right, keep your filters!' and he threw them down hard onto the table and walked out. Why did he have to do that? We've been friends for ten years. We used to sit together at lunch—now he won't speak to me. And it's all so silly and unnecessary. I'm really ashamed to discuss it.

"Well, a few moments later Don comes into the room. He says, 'I understand you obtained some special devices from the product division. Can I have some of them or at least their specifications?' I said I was sorry but the information was confidential. If he went to the product division they might help him, but I had been made to promise that I would keep the devices to myself. He didn't argue but went straight to Mike Mayo, who followed him back into this room. He said, 'Mike, tell Kurt that he must share information or I'll go straight to Dr. Spoke.' I said, 'The information is confidential.' As Mike hesitated for a moment Don left the room, heading straight for Dr. Spoke's office.

"I repeated my story to Dr. Spoke who said that if the information was confidential that was that. A promise was a promise. I told Don he could have all my measurements but not the product division's specifications. I said, 'Don, we can go on fighting but people get hurt in these fights. No one really comes out ahead.' He said he could do nothing without the specifications and I knew it. Last I heard, he was trying to order a duplicate set of devices from the division. And I've got all we need already!

"People like Don don't realize that one *has* to work with other people. The equipment we use is expensive and we have to borrow back and forth all the time. No one can afford to be an island in this place. If you don't cooperate with other people then they are not going to help you when you're in a jam and need equipment. There's no point appealing upstairs to Dr. Spoke. He can't tell us how to cooperate. We have to learn."

The casewriter next tried to meet Don Steiger. After a series of delays he eventually managed to speak to him. Don was very cautious, would pause some time before answering, and chose his words carefully. Of the many persons interviewed in this company he expressed the most concern that his opinions could get him into trouble.

DON STEIGER: "Yes, I'd say I was satisfied with my job. Very satisfied on the whole, although there are always exceptions. I've sought employment elsewhere from time to time. Complaints? Well, it's a loose organization—too loose in my opinion. We don't always get cooperation from the other divisions and from each other. I feel we should be appraised of what other people are doing and have access to their work. People upstairs should take the reins more firmly in their hands, insure better cooperation and that we get the equipment we need. It's a false economy being as short of equipment as we are. My technician takes a week to get equipment together. It shouldn't take that long. There isn't enough attention to doing what is best for the company. That has been my chief objective."

CASEWRITER: "I've been talking with Kurt Kalcheck. That's his chief objective, too."

DON STEIGER: "Well, of course you have to have some trust of people and he hasn't. It is in his makeup, his personality. He thinks someone is going to take something away from him. He's an extreme case as far as I'm concerned. I've never come across such distrust. . . . But I don't see how you're going to disguise all this I'm saying. It's bound to get out, isn't it? As far as I'm concerned this incident is closed. Who's going to read this case?"

CASEWRITER: "Well, I'm not sure how to reassure you. My experience has been that by the time these cases are typed up, disguised, and presented to the company for clearance, the incidents described are all water under the bridge. I've talked to about a dozen people. They have all expressed several opinions which were more negative than any expressed by you."

DON STEIGER: "Hm . . . all right. Well, I assured Kurt that my motives were entirely honorable. I had no intention at all of depriving him of credit. All I wanted was to set up some more advanced experiments. There was a good opportunity for collaboration between us. He made an interesting discovery. I could have come up with a model and proposed a further series of experiments.

"Of course I do move a great deal faster than most other people. I realize, even if they don't, that a relatively small laboratory like this has some running to do. I attend professional conferences and I know what's going on. RCA has ten people on a project similar to ours. I suspect that Bell has thirty. We have the advantage of flexibility and concentration on one area provided we react fast. Kurt doesn't realize that I chose him to work with us. I'm all for cooperation. When you're working by yourself, just one small mistake can put you weeks behind. Kurt is thorough and he checks things. I've been a loner here for five years and I felt the need for collaboration. That's the only way we're going to beat RCA. Everytime I work on a project I think, will they beat me to it? We're up against keen competition, make no mistake about it.

"I've got a good record so far. A number of awards from the company and a couple from the industry. I'm after a reputation as an inventor and an original theorist. Most of my friends are professionals and the people I want to impress are fellow theoreticians and people at home. There was an article about me in the local paper last week."

CASEWRITER: "Mike Mayo feels that he helped to resolve the dispute between you and Kurt."

DON STEIGER: "Mike didn't solve anything. I solved it. I solved it by keeping right away from Kurt. It's the only thing to do. I can work with Jo Arnes but not with Kurt. He wants to keep everything under wraps. Mike gets very enthusiastic and so does Kurt, but we need to inject some realism into our work. But I'd rather not say anything more. . . ."

# Bellefonte Rubber Works

Works manager Bill Dalton looked pensively at the heavy raindrops as they beat against the glass sections of the window in his corner office at the Bellefonte Rubber plant. It suddenly occurred to Bill that in his four years as manager at the plant, he had never before allowed himself the luxury of watching the raindrops splash against the plant windows. He had been too busy with internal plant problems.

He thought to himself: "When it rains, it really pours at Bellefonte." Then he turned his back on the July cloudburst and looked at the letter of resignation on his desk. It was signed by Jack Fletcher, one of the day foremen. Jack had worked at the plant seven years—the last four years as a foreman of the belt department. Because of his apparent progress, Jack was promoted to a day foreman about a year ago on Bill's recommendation. Jack seemed to appreciate the prestige of his new position and the straight day shift, even though he was on call at the plant twenty-four hours a day if trouble developed in the belt department. However, Jack's attitude had changed considerably the last few months. Jack's problems on the floor had become more serious as well as more frequent.

The first sign of serious trouble in the belt department after Jack became day foreman developed in the weeks preceding December 31, 1962. The inventory at the end of the year showed a terrific shortage in the belt department where Jack assumed a consistent profit was being made. Jack became very antagonistic toward the accounting department head whose records showed that the materials and labor input in the belt department, when balanced against the value of the belt department output, left a shortage of over $45,000 for 1962.

Jack refused to believe that the accounting department's monthly book inventory of work in process gave a true picture of his operation (see Figure 1). Even though he was no statistician, Jack could see where the materials drawn and the labor cost had deviated from the desired norm. He had tightened down on his crew's use of rubber and fabric drawn for belt making after July, and, as a result, the department approached the norm of a full accounting of the raw materials requisitioned

• Bellefonte Rubber Works was prepared by Edward L. Christensen of Brigham Young University. It is intended as a basis for classroom discussion and is not designed to present either correct or incorrect handling of administrative problems. Used by permission of the author.

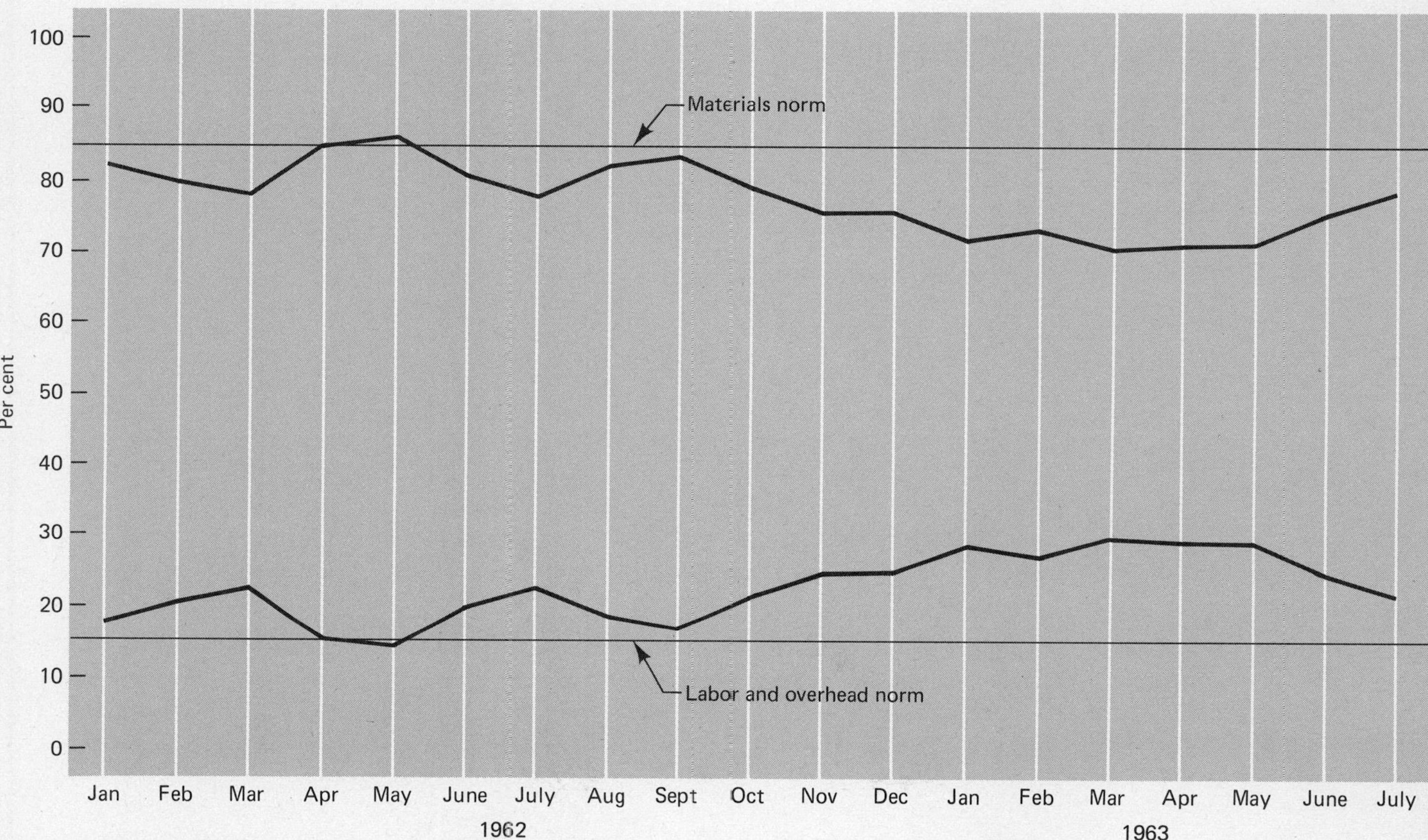


**Figure 1** Percentage Relationship of Materials to Labor and Overhead for Work-in Process Book inventory (norm developed from physical inventories April 30, 1963 and September 30, 1962)

in August and September. The chart did indicate this all right. He had also checked carefully the direct and indirect labor time card reports of his men during the same period. The chart reflected a favorable trend toward the desired norm during August and September. Then, after September, the amount of materials actually accounted for in belts produced dropped off, and the labor time going into the belts increased even though the actual belt footage produced did not increase.

It was the first week in January, 1963 that Bill Dalton had a long talk with Jack about the need for operating the belt department as if it were a separate business in downtown Bellefonte. Bill pointed out the difficulty of staying in business very long with raw materials being drawn for work in process only to have large amounts ending up as waste in the city dump. Didn't Jack think a foreman ought to hold his crew responsible for unusual and increasing material wastage?

Perhaps a bigger drain on the profit anticipated in the belt department was due to the way Jack was failing to control the time reported by his crew. Bill had insisted there was no point in arguing with the accounting department about the reliability of its reports on the belt operation. Jack was told that if he approved unreliable, inaccurate information on the time cards, he was likely to get back an unreliable, inaccurate summary of the month's operation. It was clear enough to Jack what Bill was trying to tell him.

Jack's men were paid a base rate plus an incentive for so many items produced above a minimum set by a time-and-motion study. Time spent on directly producing belts was charged and paid as "direct labor." In case of a breakdown or other direct work stoppage, the men would go to work cleaning up, getting supplies, or doing other maintenance chores. Time spent in such "nonproductive" work was charged and paid as "indirect labor."

The record of so much direct or indirect labor time was submitted to the foreman at the end of the shift by each man. The foreman, who supposedly was aware of any direct labor interruptions which occurred during the shift, would verify the time card claim by initialing it. The reporting of time appeared to operate on the honor system, especially if the foreman gave the impression of blinking at or being oblivious to a "doctored" time card.

It was simple enough for a man to claim two hours of indirect labor, and claim—if questioned by the foreman—that he had trouble for that long. Yet during that two hours he could have been turning out belt footage for which he would receive incentive pay also. It didn't take long for a workman to accumulate an hour of indirect labor through an ordinary day by reporting material shortages or work stoppages for a few short intervals.

Jack understood clearly what Bill meant, because Jack had passed out some pretty fat pay checks to members of his crew on pay day. He had seen some of the men on a base pay of $40 a week come out with a

$45 bonus! If a belt department had sixty employees doing this, the labor cost charged against the belt footage produced mounted up fast.

Actually, Jack had not given too much thought to the fudging on time cards which he signed daily. He didn't think of this practice as really cheating anybody, and he was sure most of his men didn't look at it as a dishonest practice. It was "just one of those things."

At the conclusion of their talk, Jack told Bill that the belt department would push both the materials and labor charges back into normal operating position. During the month of January, Jack made good on his promise of improvement, although the department still had a long pull ahead. Then suddenly, at the end of February, the belt department made its poorest production record in fourteen months.

Bill, who had been anxiously watching this plant trouble spot, maneuvered Jack into his office for a chat. The foreman half anticipated what was coming. In fact, he didn't wait for Bill to ask him about his family or about Jack's plans for a trip to Pittsburgh to see his son, who was a freshman at Carnegie Tech. Jack came right to the point of issue by saying: "I know what's on your mind, Bill, but before you start boring into me about competition and profits, I want to tell you something."

"Good enough, Jack," Bill agreed. "Why don't you tell me what's on your mind?"

A deep sigh escaped Jack as he settled down in his chair and wondered momentarily where he should begin. "Have you ever seriously considered the pressures that I face every day out on that floor?" Jack began. Bill nodded understandingly and Jack, feeling encouraged, continued. "You know, I'm the fall guy for everything that goes wrong in the belt department. Not one man in my crew is faced with taking initiative to improve our operation. Not one of them will make the most trivial decision. I guess the union won't let them. Brother, when I was working on the line years ago—before the union came along—we felt responsible. Where is the pressure today? On the worker? Oh no! Right on the back of a foreman whose hands are tied more often than they are free to clean house out there.

"At our foremen's training sessions on Wednesdays, Bill, you have stressed the importance of the service departments [see Figure 2] to production. Without doubt you are right or you wouldn't keep them on the payroll. But they never have produced a single foot of belt that ever went out of this plant. Am I right?"

Bill nodded in partial agreement. "Yes, in a way. But, I think you will agree that if, for example, the planning department failed to provide you with specifications; if the laboratory didn't test and control the quality of your product; if Purchasing didn't supply you with needed materials; and if Selling didn't find an outlet for your belts—you just wouldn't be able to go it alone, Jack. Isn't that right?"

"Well, yes, in a way; but that isn't what I meant," Jack replied. "These services, like accounting, which is always making reports on our

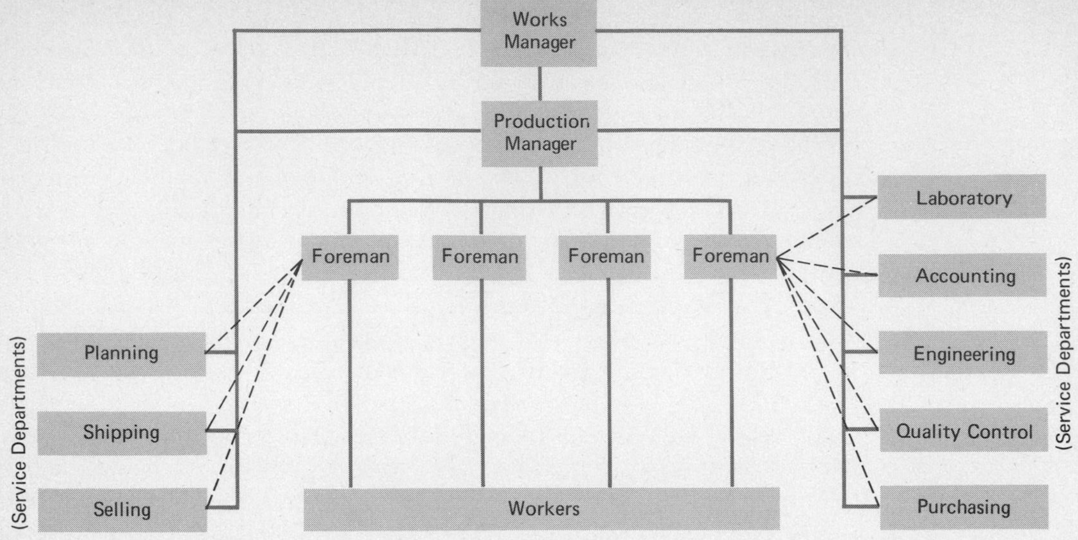


**Figure 2** Partial Organization Chart

costs and output, are never under pressure. Their work—I guess they work—is specialized. Every contact I have with them turns out to be pressure on me, not on them. For example, the engineer is much better paid than I am, yet he has fewer problems. He works mostly with things, not people. If he has any headaches, I fail to see them. Most of these service people have quiet, clean, unhurried jobs. Don't they?"

Bill shook his head. "Sometimes we don't see all the pressures that are focused on the other fellow. They do wear different clothes than the men on the production line. However, I'm sure you wouldn't want them to try to do their work in a noisy place or on a greasy table. What are you suggesting that I do about this, Jack?"

"Well, I'm not suggesting anything. I'm only saying that a foreman has the toughest job in this plant. From the time I get a production order until I meet the time schedule that comes with it, I'm on the spot. I must keep a variety of belts moving along those lines. I'm responsible for costs, waste, supplies, quality control, stoppages, breakdowns, maintenance. You name it; I seem to have it. Then I can't step on anyone's toes. I'm supposed to maintain discipline and yet I have to be a good guy. My time schedules stay the same even though some joker doesn't show up for work. All the time I have quality control, the inspector, the shop steward, and the accounting guy with the sharp pencil on my back. How about my morale? Who gives a damn about Jack Fletcher or how he feels?"

"You're right in general, Jack," Bill responded, "but you are an important person in this whole operation. If this were not so, you wouldn't be the focal point of these pressures. You are the catalyst in this process. Although you are in the middle of it all, you have to keep everything under control. In fact, Jack, if we didn't feel these pressures in this competitive industry, we wouldn't be around long. These pressures aren't mean, or vindictive, or intended by anyone. They are a sign that we are sensitive to potential trouble and that we ought to recognize them for what they are worth in our productive efforts."

Jack looked thoughtfully out the window for a moment. Then he ventured: "You make this sound better than I feel about it. I don't know what a catalyst is, unless he is a guy with a thick skin and a thick head. Now you take last week. My pay check was $437.50 for the month. I put in about ten hours a day, five days a week, not to mention three Saturdays, for that check. When I handed out the checks to the crew that works for me, I noticed that about a dozen of the men made something over $500. A foreman must have a thick skull all right to stay here after every shift for an hour or two signing time cards, checking other things, and helping the next foreman get under way. I can't leave the minute the whistle blows like the hourly men do. In fact, if they have serious trouble in the belt department on the next shift, I might be called out here in the middle of the night, just because I'm day foreman. Do you think this setup is fair to a foreman, Bill?"

Bill shifted uneasily in his chair. He knew this was a tough one to explain. "I can honestly say I think you are worth more to this operation than one of those men who got a bigger pay check than you did last month. But I also believe that your envelope didn't contain something you get in addition—something which goes only to a man in your position. If you should become sick, Jack, as you were two years ago, we carry you on the payroll, and we are glad to do it. We are not able to do that for your crew. If you need an afternoon off to take your family to Lewistown or your wife to a doctor, you need only suggest this to me. Moreover, you have been recognized by your men as a leader. I know they have confidence in you. People in Bellefonte respect you because of your position here at the plant. This prestige means something to your family, believe me. I might ask you, Jack, how many of those twelve who had a larger pay check than you, fully earned it? We can't account for their excess time in the inventory. I'm not so sure many of them were entitled to a larger check than you received."

Jack sat studying his safety helmet for a brief time. Then he stood up. "Thanks anyway, Bill," he said. "If it's all right with you, I'll give this thing another try. I better get back on the floor."

"Thanks for the chat, Jack. I know you can put the belt department back in the black if anyone can," Bill said as he opened the door and gave Jack a parting pat on the back.

Bill had been pleased to observe that during June and July the belt department made obvious improvement in its operation (see Figure 1). Jack was apparently getting on top of all those pressures that had laid him low a couple of months ago. Then, out of the clear blue sky came Jack's letter of resignation. The letter was brief:

Dear Bill:

This thing isn't getting any better. It may be even worse. I guess I want out. Can you use me in the maintenance department where they were short-handed this week?

Jack

Here was a chance to move someone else into the position of day foreman in the belt department. Bill wasn't certain whom he could confidently move into that position. He wasn't at all sure he wanted to let Jack step down, although he knew Jack was having a struggle. But this could be said about nearly every one of the other ten foremen at Bellefonte Rubber Works.

Bill felt he understood the situation faced by his foremen—especially the day foreman on the lead-off shift. He had followed a policy of placing the night-shift foremen on the day shift. This gave them some experience with the larger crews, the ringing telephones, and the full impact of contacts with the service departments as well as customers. After two weeks of this, the foremen were usually happy to get back on the night shifts. There was good reason for Bill's paying the day foreman a little more money each month, which he did.

No one knew better than Bill that good foremen were scarce. A good foreman had to be many things. He had to be a diplomat, a disciplinarian, a counselor, an instructor, an example to his men, an engineer, a repairman, a lawyer, an inspector, a judge, a manager, a psychologist. While wearing all these hats, he had better arrange to be making a profit in his department. Bill just didn't keep this kind of man on reserve. In fact, if a foreman possessed a fair capability in these desirable areas, he was usually promoted to a higher position in management.

As Bill mentally scanned his roster of eleven foremen and those he considered potential foremen, he was not inspired. Yet he would argue with anyone that his eleven foremen compared favorably with those in any other plant in his company. Still, each of his foremen had specific weaknesses and certain strengths. At the moment he could think of three men who had indicated an interest in becoming day foremen at the Bellefonte plant. They were Sam Craven, Chuck Weatherby, and George Maitland.

Sam Craven had been a foreman twenty years ago for Sharon Rubber Products in Sharon, Pennsylvania. Although he had been fairly young at the time, Sam had established himself at the Sharon plant as a foreman who made things move. His crews turned out the items on schedule or else. He didn't spare himself and he developed a reputation for not sparing his men. One of Bill's older friends told him that he had worked for Sam at Sharon. This friend confirmed the fact that Sam had an enviable record for output, but he had no friends among his crew. Bill was reminded, too, that Sam worked in a place where the plant was not unionized.

When Sam came to see Bill about possible openings at the Bellefonte plant, he had expressed an interest in working as foreman. This meeting had taken place last December. Sam had recently been retired from the U.S. Army as a master sergeant. According to his discharge, Sam had entered the Army soon after leaving his job as foreman at Sharon Rubber Products. The earlier part of his army career had been spent in the infantry. The last twelve years Sam had been attached to a number of different finance disbursing units.

Chuck Weatherby had been working for the past eleven years at the Bellefonte Rubber Works. During the last six years he had been a foreman on the night shift. Bill felt that Chuck leaned rather heavily on the day foreman whenever a problem of any consequence came along in his department. Moreover, he had only thirty-five men on his shift whereas the belt department typically had over seventy-five men on a day crew.

The men on Chuck's shift seemed to like him all right. At times Bill felt he had to practically force Chuck to use the tools and techniques available to a foreman. During the years, Chuck had attended all the training sessions that had been sponsored for the plant foremen on Wednesday afternoons. It was debatable how effective these sessions had been in upgrading his performance.

Bill recalled that it was on Chuck's shift that a costly mistake had been made on a large ore-conveyor belt. The specifications had called for a belt 48 inches wide, 3/4 of an inch thick, 1000′ long, six plies of cotton-nylon fabric, and a heavy rubber compound all around. The belt, which had to be out in three weeks, was contracted for $14,000. By mistake, Chuck had started the belt through with five, instead of six, plies of fabric. By the time the error was picked up, valuable time had been lost and an enormous waste had occurred. Chuck had blamed the error on "scheduling in" the custom order when his shift had a four-week backlog of other belts.

About two months ago, Chuck had mentioned that he was interested in the day shift and asked Bill to keep him in mind. Chuck said he could use the money that went with handling the larger crew on the day shift.

The third person who had expressed an interest in becoming a day foreman was a college graduate by the name of George Maitland. George, who was married and about twenty-five years of age, had majored in psychology at Pennsylvania State University. He had worked at the Bellefonte plant for the past three years. In fact, it was the only job he had ever held other than part-time summer work in a grocery chain store.

The foremen under whom George had worked were unanimous in classifying him as a very reliable and effective employee. However, this opinion was qualified in each instance by some reference to the fact that George was good in spite of his college education.

George had taken an interest in problems of the foreman. Occasionally, he had asked them questions about their work. Some of the foremen answered his questions; others let him feel he was getting a bit too "nosey." George did appear to show a great deal of insight into the forces that constantly impinged upon the individual foreman. They didn't know, however, that George was taking courses in foreman training in an extension program at Penn State.

Bill knew that George was taking classes in production control, labor law, and human relations. One of the professors at Penn State had mentioned the fact to Bill during a Rotary luncheon some time ago. Later Bill had asked George about his evening courses and his plans for the future. It was during the ensuing conversation that George expressed a desire to get into management—the sooner the better. George had some ready answers, too, for plant problems that had bothered Bill and his foreman for a long time. It was clear that this young man didn't lack confidence.

Could it be that Jack Fletcher, whose resignation Bill held in his hand, would want to reconsider? Bill looked again at the promising record of the last two months. Then his eyes settled upon the dismal record of the preceding months. Whatever he did, Bill would have to act promptly. He needed a day foreman to manage the belt department, the basic producing unit at Bellefonte Rubber Works.

# Blackman-Dodds

This case consists of an interchange between a superior and subordinate in a research laboratory. The subordinate, a newly hired professional research worker, made an appointment to see the director. The following interview took place.

Dr. Richard Dodds, a physics research worker, entered the office and showed his superior, Blackman, a letter. This letter was from Prof. Wilkin of another research institution, offering Dodds a position; Blackman read the letter.

DODDS: What do you think of that?

BLACKMAN: I knew it was coming. He asked me if it would be all right if he sent it. I told him to go ahead, if he wanted to.

DODDS: I didn't expect it, particularly after what you said to me last time. . . . I'm really quite happy here. I don't want you to get the idea that I am thinking of leaving. But I thought I should go and visit him—I think he expects it—and I wanted to let you know that just because I was thinking of going down, that didn't mean I was thinking of leaving here, unless of course, he offers me something extraordinary.

BLACKMAN: Why are you telling me all this?

DODDS: Because I didn't want you hearing from somebody else that I was thinking of leaving here because I was going for a visit to another institution. I really have no intention of leaving you know, unless he offers me something really extraordinary that I can't afford to turn down. I think I'll tell him that; that I am willing to look at his laboratory, but unless there is something unusual there for me, I have no intention of leaving here.

BLACKMAN: It's up to you.

DODDS: What do you think?

BLACKMAN: Well, what? About what? You've got to make up your mind.

DODDS: I don't consider this job too seriously. He is not offering anything really extraordinary. But I *am* interested in what he had to say, and I would like to look around his lab.

BLACKMAN: Sooner or later you are going to have to make up your mind where you want to stay.

DODDS [*sharply*]: That depends on the offers, doesn't it?

BLACKMAN: No, not really; a good man always gets offers. You get a good offer and you move, and as soon as you have moved, you get other good offers. It would throw you into confusion to consider all the good offers you will receive. Isn't there a factor of how stable you want to be?

DODDS: But I'm not shopping around. I already told you that. He sent me this letter, I didn't ask him to. All I said was I think I should visit him, and to you that's shopping around!

BLACKMAN: Well, you may choose to set aside your commitment here if he offers you something better. All I am saying is that you will still be left with the question of you've got to stay some place, and where is that going to be?

DODDS: You really don't think that I could find a better job than the one you have offered me here?

BLACKMAN: I don't know. I'm not thinking about that.

DODDS: How would it look if I were to leave?

BLACKMAN: To me, if you wanted to go, I'd say fine, if that's what you want. But frankly I think there would be a few raised eyebrows if you were to leave now.

DODDS: But I'm not shopping around, I want you to understand that.

BLACKMAN: You've got the problem of all young men who are sought after, you've got to decide what you will accept and what you won't accept.

DODDS: Look, I came in here, and I want to be honest with you, but you go and make me feel all guilty, and I don't like that.

BLACKMAN: You are being honest as can be.

DODDS: I didn't come in here to fight. I don't want to disturb you.

BLACKMAN: I'm not disturbed. If you think it is best for you to go somewhere else, that is O.K. with me. We can get another plasma physicist any day, just as good as you. They are standing in line to get in here. What bothers me is how restless you want to appear to me and Wilkin. For one thing, you've got everything analyzed out in terms of what you want; tenure, appointment, and space. Things like that.

DODDS: That's obvious. I can't understand you. You really think that no one will ever be able to make me an offer that will make me want to leave this place.

BLACKMAN: All I am saying is that it looks funny. You asked me how it would look, and I'm telling you it would look funny so soon after you getting fixed up here.

DODDS: Well, I was just trying to be honest, and . . .

BLACKMAN [*interrupting*]: All the jobs you get offered at this stage in your career are the same. They are all the same. One may give you a little more salary, but it will have a lousy lab. Another may offer you tenure and a higher title, but you would be dead in ten years if you went there. What you should be looking for is an opportunity to do work and to develop in an environment. Your colleagues, the really important ones, don't give a damn whether you are a Junior or Associate research worker. Don't get me wrong. I don't want to hold you back. If you feel it's best for you to go, I wouldn't want to hold you here under any circumstances. I just want to give you some advice.

DODDS: But I don't see what this has to do with me. All I said was I would consider his offer if it was so good I couldn't afford to turn it down. Do you think I should turn it down even if it is a better job?

BLACKMAN: All I'm saying is maybe it's too fast.

DODDS: What of it? Are you telling me that a young person coming up shouldn't take the best job offered to him?

BLACKMAN: What should they take?

DODDS: Young people should take the best jobs they can get, and go where they want.

BLACKMAN: Yes, but not too fast.

DODDS: How fast?

BLACKMAN: I don't know. Enough time to settle in and do a job of work.

DODDS: One, two, three years?

BLACKMAN: It depends.

DODDS: When should I be thinking of leaving this laboratory, then? When do you think would be the best time for me to go?

BLACKMAN: I can't answer that. It's up to you to decide.

DODDS: If I were to leave this year what would it look like?

BLACKMAN: I think it would look like Dodds had a lot of opportunism and self-interest. You know what I mean? Like he was restless. It would not look good.

DODDS: I don't understand you. I came in here to be honest with you, and you make me feel guilty. All I wanted was to show you this letter, and let you know what I was going to do. What should I have told you?

BLACKMAN: That you had read the letter, and felt that under the circumstances it was necessary for you to pay a visit to Wilkin, but that you were happy here, and wanted to stay at least until you had got a job of work done.

DODDS: I can't get over it. You think there isn't a place in the world I'd rather be than here in this lab. . . .

# The Case of the Changing Cage

## Part I

The voucher-check filing unit was a work unit in the home office of the Atlantic Insurance Company. The assigned task of the unit was to file checks and vouchers written by the company as they were cashed and returned. This filing was the necessary foundation for the main function of the unit: locating any particular check for examination upon demand. There were usually eight to ten requests for specific checks from as many different departments during the day. One of the most frequent reasons checks were requested from the unit was to determine whether checks in payment of claims against the company had been cashed. Thus efficiency in the unit directly affected customer satisfaction with the company. Complaints or inquiries about payments could not be answered with the accuracy and speed conducive to client satisfaction unless the unit could supply the necessary document immediately.

Toward the end of 1952, nine workers manned this unit. There was an assistant (equivalent to a foreman in a factory) named Miss Dunn, five other full-time employees, and three part-time workers.

• The Case of the Changing Cage, by C. E. Richards and H. F. Dobyns, was published as "Topography and Culture: The Case of the Changing Cage" in *Human Organization*, Volume XVI, No. 1. It is reprinted by permission of the publisher and the authors. This case was prepared as the basis for class discussion rather than to illustrate either effective or ineffective handling of administrative situations.

The work area of the unit was well defined. Walls bounded the unit on three sides. The one exterior wall was pierced by light-admitting north windows. The west interior partition was blank. A door opening into a corridor pierced the south interior partition. The east side of the work area was enclosed by a steel mesh reaching from wall to wall and floor to ceiling. This open metal barrier gave rise to the customary name of the unit—"The Voucher Cage." A sliding door through this mesh gave access from the unit's territory to the work area of the rest of the company's agency audit division, of which it was a part, located on the same floor.

The unit's territory was kept inviolate by locks on both doors, fastened at all times. No one not working within the cage was permitted inside unless his name appeared on a special list in the custody of Miss Dunn. The door through the steel mesh was used generally for departmental business. Messengers and runners from other departments usually came to the corridor door and pressed a buzzer for service.

The steel mesh front was reinforced by a rank of metal filing cases where checks were filed. Lined up just inside the barrier, they hid the unit's workers from the view of workers outside their territory, including the section head responsible for overall supervision of this unit according to the company's formal plan of operation.

## Part II

On top of the cabinets which were backed against the steel mesh, one of the male employees in the unit neatly stacked pasteboard boxes in which checks were transported to the cage. They were later reused to hold older checks sent into storage. His intention was less getting these boxes out of the way than increasing the effective height of the sight barrier so the section head could not see into the cage "even when he stood up."

The girls stood at the door of the cage which led into the corridor and talked to the messenger boys. Out this door also the workers slipped unnoticed to bring in their customary afternoon snack. Inside the cage, the workers sometimes engaged in a good-natured game of rubber band "sniping."

Workers in the cage possessed good capacity to work together consistently and workers outside the cage often expressed envy of those in it because of the "nice people" and friendly atmosphere there. The unit had no apparent difficulty keeping up with its work load.

## Part III

For some time prior to 1952 the controller's department of the company had not been able to meet its own standards of efficient service to clients. Company officials felt the primary cause to be spatial. Various divisions of the controller's department were scattered over the entire twenty-two-story company building. Communication between them required phone calls, messengers, or personal visits, all costing time. The spatial separation had not seemed very important when the company's business volume was smaller prior to World War II. But business had grown tremendously since then and spatial separation appeared increasingly inefficient.

Finally in November of 1952 company officials began to consolidate the controller's department by relocating two divisions together on one floor. One was the agency audit division, which included the voucher-check filing unit. As soon as the decision to move was made, lower level supervisors were called in to help with planning. Line workers were not consulted, but were kept informed by the assistants of planning progress. Company officials were concerned about the problem of transporting many tons of equipment and some two hundred workers from two locations to another single location without disrupting work-flow. So the move was planned to occur over a single weekend, using the most efficient resources available. Assistants were kept busy planning positions for files and desks in the new location.

Desks, files, chairs, and even wastebaskets were numbered prior to the move, and relocated according to a master chart checked on the spot by the assistant. Employees were briefed as to where the new location was and which elevators they should take to reach it. The company successfully transported the paraphernalia of the voucher-check filing unit from one floor to another over one weekend. Workers in the cage quit Friday afternoon at the old stand, reported back Monday at the new.

The exterior boundaries of the new cage were still three building walls and the steel mesh, but the new cage possessed only one door—the sliding door through the steel mesh into the work area of the rest of the agency audit division. The territory of the cage had also been reduced in size. An entire bank of filing cabinets had to be left behind in the old location to be taken over by the unit moving there. The new cage was arranged so that there was no longer a row of metal filing cabinets lined up inside the steel mesh obstructing the view into the cage.

## Part IV

When the workers in the cage inquired about the removal of the filing cabinets from along the steel mesh fencing, they found that Mr. Burke had insisted that these cabinets be rearranged so his view into the cage would not be obstructed by them. Miss Dunn had tried to retain the cabinets in their prior position, but her efforts had been overridden.

Mr. Burke disapproved of conversation. Because he could see workers conversing in the cage, he "requested" Miss Dunn to put a stop to all unnecessary talk. Attempts by female clerks to talk to messenger boys brought the wrath of her superior down on Miss Dunn, who was then forced to reprimand the girls.

Mr. Burke also disapproved of an untidy working area, and any boxes or papers which were in sight were a source of annoyance to him. He did not exert supervision directly, but would "request" Miss Dunn to "do something about these boxes." In the new cage, desks had to be completely cleared at the end of the day, in contrast to the work-in-progress piles left out in the old cage. Boxes could not accumulate on top of filing cases.

The custom of afternoon snacking also ran into trouble. Lacking a corridor door, the food bringers had to venture forth and pack back their snack tray through the work area of the rest of their section, bringing this hitherto unique custom to the attention of workers outside the cage. The latter promptly recognized the desirability of afternoon snacks and began agitation for the same privilege. This annoyed the section head, who forbade workers in the cage from continuing this custom.

## Part V

Mr. Burke later made a rule which permitted one worker to leave the new cage at a set time every afternoon to bring up food for the rest. This rigidity irked cage personnel, accustomed to a snack when the mood struck, or none at all. Having made his concession to the cage force, Mr. Burke was unable to prevent workers outside the cage from doing the same thing. What had once been unique to the workers in the cage was now common practice in the section.

Although Miss Dunn never outwardly expressed anything but compliance and approval of superior directives, she exhibited definite signs of anxiety. All the cage workers reacted against Burke's increased domination. When he imposed his decisions upon the voucher-check filing unit, he became "Old Grandma" to its personnel. The cage workers sneered at him and ridiculed him behind his back. Workers who formerly had obeyed company policy as a matter of course began to find reasons for loafing and obstructing work in the new cage. One of the changes that took place in the behavior of the workers had to do with their game of rubber band sniping. All knew Mr. Burke would disapprove of this game. It became highly clandestine and fraught with dangers. Yet shooting rubber bands *increased.*

Newly arrived checks were put out of sight as soon as possible, filed or not. Workers hid unfiled checks, generally stuffing them into desk drawers or unused file drawers. Because boxes were forbidden, there were fewer unused file drawers than there had been in the old cage. So the day's work was sometimes undone when several clerks hastily shoved vouchers and checks indiscriminately into the same file drawer at the end of the day.

Before a worker in the cage filed incoming checks, she measured with her ruler the thickness in inches of each bundle she filed. At the end of each day she totaled her input and reported it to Miss Dunn. All incoming checks were measured upon arrival. Thus Miss Dunn had a rough estimate of unit intake compared with file input. Theoretically she was able to tell at any time how much unfiled material she had on hand and how well the unit was keeping up with its task. Despite this running check, when the annual inventory of unfiled checks on hand in the cage was taken at the beginning of the calendar year 1953, a seriously large backlog of unfiled checks was found. To the surprise and dismay of Miss Dunn, the inventory showed the unit to be far behind schedule, filing much more slowly than before the relocation of the cage.

# Castleton Metals Company

The Castleton Metals Company of Boston was a large refiner and fabricator of platinum-group metals, silver, and gold. Its products were nationally distributed to widely different markets, thereby leading to complexity and diversity in methods of selling. For example, platinum laboratory-ware was widely used by research groups in universities and in the chemical industry; experimental quantities of precious metal chemicals were also supplied to these customers. Wire and sheet forms of platinum were employed extensively by electrical concerns. Platinum catalysts were important materials in petroleum and pharmaceutical processing. Silver solder was utilized by steel companies. In addition, Castleton was a major supplier of metals to the decorative arts: jewelers and silversmiths.

Many of the company's products were sold directly to customers without benefit of middlemen, because the personal contact was considered so essential in view of the strong competition in the industry. This condition was especially true in connection with sales to decorative users, most of whom were located in New England, New York, and Pennsylvania. Other items might be sold directly because of their technical application

 This case was prepared as the basis for class discussion rather than to illustrate either effective or ineffective handling of administrative situations.

in industry. For example, silver solder, a highly competitive item, was being used in a method of brazing which frequently necessitated technical advice from Castleton. Direct selling and servicing were here done on a national scale. In other items where the company had found competition to be not quite so keen, middlemen were used for national distribution.

As of November 1961, responsibility for the marketing function in this company fell upon Mr. Austin, the general manager, who apart from his general administrative duties devoted a considerable amount of time to sales planning and, on occasions, to selling. (See Figure 1 for an abbreviated organization chart.) Reporting to him were two sales managers and one metallurgist, respectively: Mr. Okum of silver sales, Mr. Cloud of precious metals, and Mr. Finder. The sales managers were charged with the responsibility for sales and salesmen in their separate areas. The metallurgist busied himself with such technical problems as might come from customers, as well as with departmental research and development; the office force at large considered this staff position to be inferior to that of sales manager, possible because much of Mr. Finder's work originated from the managers. In addition, each sales manager had a male assistant reporting to him. Each of the six men had a personal secretary.

The securing of a high caliber of office personnel was most important for this company because of the complicated nature of its sales function. The situation was one which demanded competent, experienced and long-term employees, both male and female. In the words of Mr. Austin, "We need men who will stay with us for many years because it takes so long to train them." He added that the average person would have only a surface knowledge of precious metals after about five years with the company. Also of importance was the complete cooperation which was needed among all members of the office force. This was required especially on those occasions when the general manager, or the sales managers, and at times their assistants, had to leave on business trips. Under the circumstances, it was necessary for the remaining men in the department to

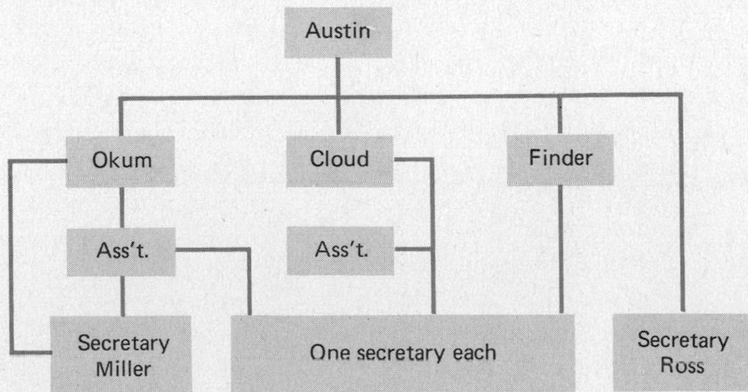


**Figure 1** Abbreviated Organization Chart

handle the more pressing matters and to share the burden of work even though this might mean crossing the line of supervision between silver and precious metals.

The women, too, had to be adaptable and cooperative under these conditions. They were needed particularly when the men returned to the office to find a considerable amount of correspondence and other matters held over for their immediate attention. The girls were expected to pitch in, and customarily did so without protest. If anything, it was most uncommon for them to fail to volunteer their services under such circumstances. In speaking of this situation, Mr. Austin stated that he was proud of the way in which the individuals in his office were able to work together as a group.

Exemplary of the compatibility and congenialty of the secretaries were the numerous social activities which they shared together after office hours, such as at dinner and theater parties. Also, even though there were known inequities in salaries paid, with these attributable to differences in age, experience, length of service, and the degree of tightness of the labor market, the girls had never complained about the matter.

The securing of satisfactory office personnel was made additionally difficult because the company plant in which the sales division was housed was approximately fifty years old, unattractive, and located in a waterfront area. Therefore, as a means of securing and retaining employees, Castleton paid above average salaries, had completely air conditioned and otherwise modernized its office, and leaned over backward in an effort to satisfy the wishes of its workers. Furthermore, the office was very spacious, with more than enough room for individual desks, plus two extra ones for such company salesmen as might drop in, an infrequent occurrence. Illustrative of the ample space provided was that a telephone conversation spoken in normal tones by one person could not be overheard by his neighbor.

The following situation developed against this background. In April of 1962, sales of some of the company's lines declined measurably —primarily, it was believed, due to general economic conditions. Consequently, the volume of correspondence and detailed work dropped. In an effort to stimulate sales, the general manager, and the sales managers in particular, adopted the policy of making frequent trips into the field for the purpose of contacting customers and salesmen; this, too, resulted in less work for the secretaries during these absences. In net effect, the work loads were reduced to such an extent that the girls often had little or nothing to do. The general manager, as well as the president of the company, felt no concern over this inactivity, for he believed that sales would increase. He was also aware that Mr. Finder's secretary was planning to resign in May in order to accompany her husband, whose business was taking him to another state. Hence, from his point of view the situation was entirely temporary.

However, in June the general manager realized that the volume of work was still inadequate. So, after having given some thought to the matter, and not wishing to lay off any of the girls, he concluded that the situation might be bettered were he to reorganize the sales group to the extent of requiring all the girls to report directly to the men who spent more time at the office than did some others. He felt that a better distribution of work might result. Therefore, he requested his own secretary, Miss Ross, to devote as much time to sales work as she possibly could during his absences; prior to this time, Miss Ross had not been expected to work for the department except in connection with Mr. Austin's own endeavors, although she had voluntarily done so on many occasions. Furthermore, Mr. Okum's secretary, Miss Miller, was told that she would be under the direct supervision of the metallurgist. No other action was contemplated at this time.

When telling the two women of the changes which were to become effective immediately, Mr. Austin remarked about the advantages of direct supervision and concluded his explanation with a request for continued cooperation. Neither girl questioned his decision.

Within a few days after the reorganization, an air of tension developed within the department. This was manifested by a soberness of demeanor in contrast to the friendliness and humor which had previously characterized the work scene. Also, whereas formerly, before work started and during lunch hour, the girls had circulated about the office chatting with everybody, they now segregated themselves by congregating in a corner of the room.

Over a period of several weeks the situation worsened. The secretaries appeared obviously unwilling to give their services to other than their immediate superiors; even here they were slow to respond, despite having plenty of free time at their disposal.

The men in the office did not express any concern over the problem except among themselves. They decided, as did Mr. Austin, that what they were seeing amounted to nothing more than a display of feminine temperament coupled with a short-lived maladjustment attributable to the organizational change. They thought that the situation would iron itself out in time.

However, over the ensuing weeks matters grew worse. Miss Ross, for example, spoke to Mr. Austin and the other men only when spoken to. Miss Miller advised Mr. Okum rather than Mr. Finder that she was resigning from her position. Furthermore, the other girls were often absent from work due to illness, and when on the job performed their duties with indifference.

During the last two weeks of her employ, all the men took a hand in attempts to induce Miss Miller to remain with the company. They proposed a salary increase as well as a revision of the department's organizational structure. All these efforts failed. Miss Miller was adamant in declaring that she was leaving for personal reasons, that her mind was made up, and that no compromise would cause her to remain.

After her departure from the company, considerable difficulty was encountered in finding a suitable replacement. A new girl was finally hired early in October of 1962, but she submitted her resignation three weeks later without stating her reasons for leaving. In the middle of November, the general manager was able to secure another substitute who this time remained with the company.

At about this time, sales began to pick up and work loads increased. However, the attitude of the girls did not improve correspondingly. Therefore, Mr. Austin issued orders calculated to reduce disciplinary infractions and improve the quality and quantity of the work which was being turned out. He was partially successful, but recognized that relationships in the department remained far from harmonious.

# Center City Engineering Department

The Center City Engineering Department employed approximately 1,000 people, all of whom worked under the provisions of the Civil Service System. Of these employees, about 100 worked in the Design Division. Parker Nolton, an associate engineer, had been employed in the design division for nineteen years and was known personally by virtually everyone in the division, if not in Center City itself. Nolton had held the position of associate engineer for seven years on a provisional basis only, for he had never been able to pass the required civil service examinations to gain permanent appointment to this grade, although he had taken them often. Many of his co-workers felt that his lack of formal engineering education prevented him from passing the examinations, but Nolton felt that his failures were the result of his tendency to "tighten up" when taking an examination. Off the job, Nolton was extremely active in civic affairs and city-sponsored recreational programs. During the past year, for example, he had been president of the high school PTA, captain of the bowling team sponsored by the engineering department in the municipal bowling league, and a member of the managing committee of the Center City Little League.

• Reprinted from *Human Elements of Administration: Cases, Readings, Simulation Exercises*, by Harry R. Knudson, Jr. Copyright © 1963 and reprinted by permission of Holt, Rinehart and Winston, Inc. This case was prepared as the basis for class discussion rather than to illustrate either effective or ineffective handling of administrative situations.

As Center City grew and the activities of the engineering department expanded to keep pace with this growth, younger men were hired into the department in relatively large numbers. Among those hired were Ralph Boyer and Doug Worth. Both of these young men were graduate engineers, and had accepted the positions with the engineering department after fulfilling their military obligations. Ralph Boyer had been an officer in the Army Corps of Engineers. In order to give the new men opportunities to achieve permanent status in the Civil Service System, examinations were scheduled with greater frequency than they had been in the past. Nolton's performance on the examinations continued to be unsatisfactory. The new men, however, passed the exams for successively higher positions with flying colors. Ralph Boyer in particular experienced marked success in these examinations and advanced rapidly. Three years after his initial employment he was in charge of a design group within the design division. Parker Nolton, in the meantime, had been shifted from the position of a project engineer to that of the purchase-order coordinator. The position of purchase-order coordinator was more limited in scope than that of a project engineer, although the responsibilities of the position were great. He continued to be classified as an associate engineer, however.

Ralph Boyer continued his successful career and soon qualified for the position of senior engineer. A new administrative group that had been created to meet the problems that arose in the design division because of the expanding activities of the engineering department was placed under his direction. Doug Worth, too, was successful in his examinations and was shortly promoted to the grade of associate engineer and transferred into the administrative group headed by Ralph Boyer.

One of the functions under the new administrative group was that of purchase-order coordination. This relationship required that Parker Nolton report to Ralph Boyer. Nolton, however, chose to ignore the new organizational structure and dealt directly with the chief engineer, an arrangement which received the latter's tacit approval. Nolton was given a semiprivate office and the services of a junior engineer to assist him in his activities. His assistant, John Palmer, soon requested a transfer on the grounds that he had nothing to do and there was no need for anyone in this position. Nolton, on the other hand, always appeared to be extremely busy and was continually requesting additional manpower and assistance to help him with the coordination of purchase orders.

Some four months after the organizational changes noted above had taken place, the chief engineer left the company and his replacement, Stan Matson, was appointed from within the division. Matson was the logical successor to the position; his appointment came as no surprise and was well received by all the employees. His appointment was shortly followed by the assignment of Ralph Boyer to a special position which took him completely out of the design division. Doug Worth was assigned to the position thus vacated, supervisor of the administrative group, and consequently inherited the supervision of Parker Nolton's activities. This assignment, initially made on a provisional basis, was soon made permanent when Worth passed the required examinations and was awarded the grade of senior engineer. Doug Worth had never worked closely with Parker Nolton but had been on cordial terms with him since his arrival in the engineering department. He had had contact with Nolton in several recreational activities in which they both had participated.

During the months that followed, Parker Nolton continued his direct reporting relationship with the chief engineer, now in the person of Stan Matson, and never consulted or advised Doug Worth regarding the progress of his activities as purchase-order coordinator. His former assistant, John Palmer, had been transferred and had been replaced by an engineering aide. Both the aide and Nolton appeared to be busy most of the time, and Nolton was still requesting more manpower for his activity through formal channels. When occasions arose which required that Doug Worth check on Nolton's activities, he was always forced to go to Nolton's office for information. Nolton always claimed to be too busy to leave his own office. During the conversations which occurred when Worth visited Nolton, Nolton frequently gave the impression that he regarded Worth's activities and interest as superfluous. Several times he suggested that in future situations Worth just send the inquiring party directly to him if questions arose about his activities. He often made the comment that he knew everyone in the department and often it was better to handle many situations informally rather than through channels.

Doug Worth was concerned with Nolton's attitude, for he did not feel that he could effectively carry out his responsibilities as supervisor of the administrative group if he did not know the current status of activities in all of the functions under his control. Consequently, he attempted to gain more cooperation from Nolton by approaching the subject at times when the two men were engaged in common off-hours recreational activities. These attempts were uniformly unsuccessful. Nolton always quickly brought the conversation around to the standing of the bowling team, the progress of the PTA, or any other unrelated subject at hand.

After several attempts to talk with Nolton in a friendly way off the job, Worth concluded that the situation as it currently stood was intolerable. While he realized he must do something, Worth felt he understood Nolton's attitude and reactions and was sympathetic. After all, Nolton has been in the department for years and had been relatively successful. He knew all the ropes and had many friends. Worth reflected that it must be a blow to a man like Nolton to have to report to young, relatively inexperienced men. Worth had faced similar problems during his military career, when he had had more experienced men (many years his senior) under his command. After much thought, he decided his best approach would be to appeal to Nolton in a very direct manner for a greater degree of cooperation. Thus, Worth approached Nolton on the job and suggested that they have a talk in his private office where they would not be disturbed by all the activity in Nolton's office. Nolton protested that he could not take time away from his duties. Worth was firm, however, and Nolton reluctantly agreed to come to Worth's office, protesting all the way that he really could not spare the time.

During his opening remarks to what Worth had planned as a sympathetic discussion of the situation, Worth referred to "the normal relationship between a man and his supervisor." Nolton's reaction was violent. He stated that he didn't regard any young upstart as a "superior," especially his. He told Worth to run his own office and to let him, Nolton, run his. He concluded by stating: "If you haven't anything more to say, I would like to get back to my office where important work is being neglected." Worth, realizing that nothing more could be accomplished in the atmosphere that prevailed, watched in silence as Nolton left.

Doug Worth subsequently reported his latest conversation with Nolton to Stan Matson, the chief engineer. He also related the events which had led to this conversation. In concluding his remarks he stated that he could no longer take responsibility for Nolton's actions because Nolton would neither accept his guidance nor advise him of the state of his work. Matson's reply to this last statement was "Yes, I know." This was the only comment Matson made during the interview, although he listened intently to Worth's analysis of the situation.

At the next meeting of the supervisory staff (of which Worth was a member but Nolton was not), Worth proposed that Nolton be transferred to the position of design drafting engineer, in effect a demotion. As Worth was explaining the reasons for his proposed action regarding Nolton, one of the other members of the supervisory staff interrupted to proclaim very heatedly that Nolton was "one of the pillars of the entire engineering department" and that he would be violently opposed to the demotion of "so fine a man." Following this interruption, a very heated, emotional discussion ensued concerning the desirability of demoting Nolton.

During this discussion Stan Matson remained silent; yet he reflected that he should probably take some action during the meeting regarding the Nolton situation.

# Claremont Instrument Company

One of the problems facing the supervisory staff of the Claremont Instrument Company in the summer of 1948 was that of horseplay among employees in the glass department. For some time this question had troubled the management of the company. Efforts had been made to discourage employees from throwing water-soaked waste at each other and from engaging in water fights with buckets or fire hoses. Efforts to tighten up shop discipline had also resulted in orders to cut down on "visiting" with other employees. These efforts were made on the grounds that whatever took an employee away from his regular job would interfere with production or might cause injury to the employees or the plant machinery.

Production was a matter of some concern to the officials of the company, particularly since the war. In spite of a large backlog of unfilled orders, there were indications that domestic and foreign competition in the relatively near future might begin to cut into the company's business. Anything which could help to increase the salable output of the company was welcomed by the officers; at the same time, anything which might cut down overhead operating expenses, or improve the quality of the product, or cut down on manufacturing wastage was equally encouraged.

The Claremont Instrument Company had been located for many years in a community in western Massachusetts with a population of approximately 18,000. The company employed approximately 500 people. None of these people were organized in a union for collective bargaining purposes. The company produced a varied line of laboratory equipment and supplies. Many of its products were fabricated principally from glass, and over the years the company had built up a reputation for producing products of the highest quality. To a considerable extent this reputation for quality rested upon the company's ability to produce very delicate glass components to exacting quality standards. These glass components were produced from molten glass in the glass department. Figure 1 presents a partial organization chart of the company.

The entire glass department was located in one wing of the company's main factory. In this department the glass components such as tubes, bottles, decanters, and glass-measuring devices were made from

 This case was prepared as the basis for class discussion rather than to illustrate either effective or ineffective handling of administrative situations.

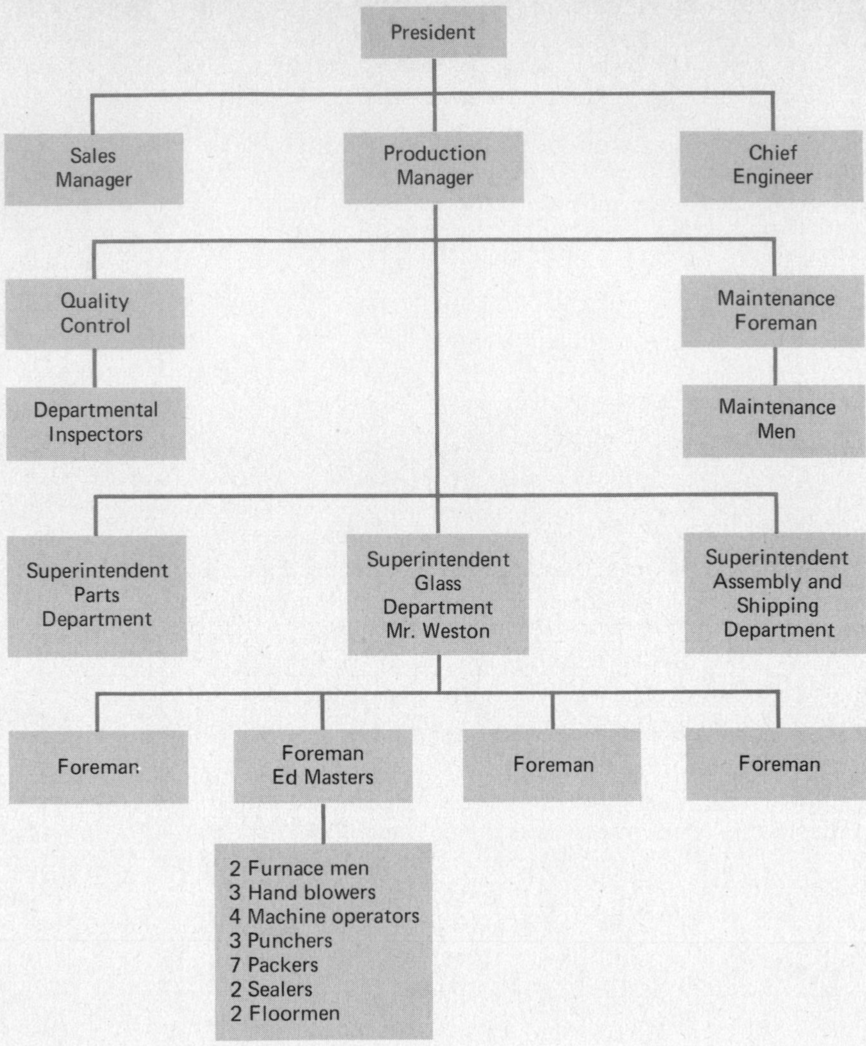


**Figure 1** Partial Organization Chart

molten glass. Some of these glass parts were produced by hand-blowing operations, but most of them were produced on bottle-making machinery which in effect blew the molten glass into a mold. This operation of blowing the glass by hand or by machine was the most critical operation in the department and required a high degree of skill. Immediately following the blowing operation some of the parts were "punched." The "puncher" was a mechanical apparatus into which the glass components were placed; as the machine revolved, a small gas flame melted the glass in a small area and blew a hole in the glass component. Next the parts were placed on a mechanical conveyor where they were annealed by an air-cooling process.

Then the parts were picked off the conveyor by women known as packers whose duty was to inspect them for defects of many kinds and to give them temporary packaging in cardboard cartons for transit to other parts of the factory. The final operation in the department was performed by sealers whose job it was to seal these cardboard cartons and place them in stacks for temporary storage. Figure 2 is a floorplan of the glass department.

The glass department was operated on a continuous, twenty-four-hour, seven-day-a-week basis, because of the necessity of keeping the tanks of molten glass hot and operating all the time. Four complete shifts worked in the department. The different shifts rotated as to the hours of the day they worked. Roughly each shift spent two weeks at a time on the day shift, on the evening shift, and on the night shift. Each shift worked on the average five days a week, but their days off came at varying times throughout the week. The glass department was located in a separate wing of the plant and the employees of the department used a special entrance and a special time clock.

Each of the four shifts employed about twenty-three people. Each shift had its own foreman and assistant foreman and hourly workers as indicated in Figure 1. All these workers were men with the exception of the packers. The foreman was a full-time supervisor, but the assistant foreman usually operated a glass machine and only substituted for the foreman in his absence. The furnace men prepared the molten glass for the glass blowers while the floormen cleaned up broken glass and other waste and filled in on odd jobs.

An inspector from the quality control department and a maintenance man from the maintenance department were assigned on a full-time basis to each of the four shifts. The inspector worked with the packers and was responsible for the quality of all glass components. The maintenance man was responsible for the maintenance and satisfactory operation of all machinery in the department.

Several physical conditions made work in the glass department unique in the plant. The fact that the glass furnaces were located in this department meant that the department was always unusually hot. The glass-blowing machines were run principally by compressed air, and each movement of a machine part was accompanied by the hiss of escaping air. This noise combined with the occasional sound of breaking glass made it impossible for the members of the department to converse in a normal tone. An oil vapor was used to coat the inside of the molds on the glass machines, and when the hot glass poured into the mold, a smoke was given off that circulated throughout the department.

In the summer of 1948, Ralph Boynton, a student at the Harvard Business School, took a summer job as one of the floormen on one of the shifts working in the glass department. While on this job, he made the above observations about the Claremont Instrument Company in general and the glass department in particular. In the course of the summer Ralph

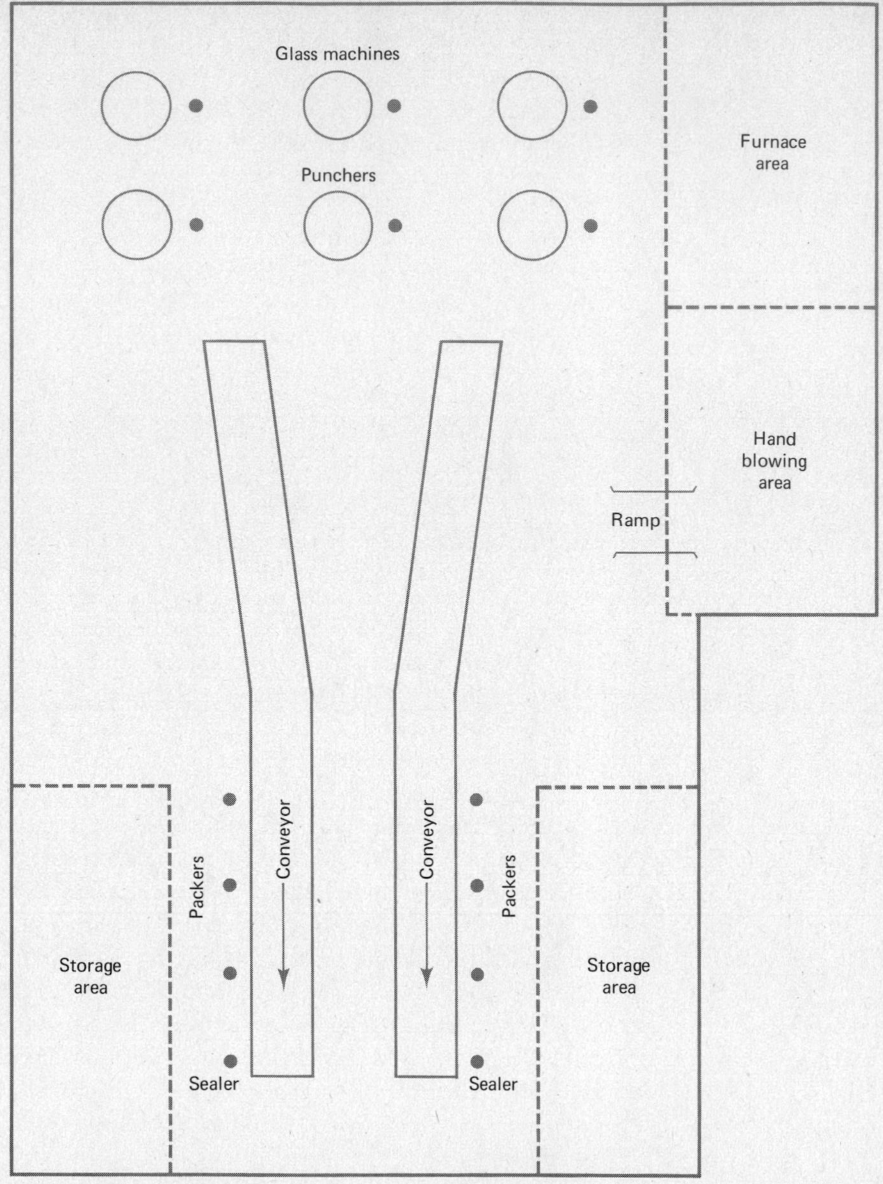


**Figure 2** Floorplan of Glass Department

became particularly interested in the practice of engaging in horseplay, and the description that follows was based on his observations.

The foreman of Boynton's shift, Ed Masters, had worked a number of years in the glass department and had been promoted to foreman from the position of operator of one of the glass machines. In Ralph's opinion the foreman was generally liked by the shift employees. One of them commented to Ralph, "If everything is going okay, you don't see Ed around. If anything goes wrong, he's right there to try and fix it up." Another one of them commented, "He pitches right in—gives us a hand—but he never says much." Frequently when a glass machine was producing glass components of unacceptable quality, Ralph noticed the foreman and the maintenance man working with a machine operator to get the machine in proper adjustment. On one occasion Ralph was assigned the job of substituting for one of the sealers. Shortly after Ralph had started his work Ed Masters came around and asked how he was doing. Ralph replied that he was doing fine and that it was quite a trick to toss the cartons into the proper positions on the stack. Ed replied, "You keep at it and it won't be long before you get the hang of it. You'll be tired for a while but you'll get used to it. I found I could do it and I am a 97-pound weakling."

Ralph also picked up a variety of comments from the employees about one another. The shift maintenance man, Bert, referred to the men on the shift as "a good bunch of guys." One of the packers referred with pride to one of the machine operators: "That guy can get out more good bottles than anybody else." On one occasion when the glass components were coming off the end of the conveyor at a very slow rate, one of the packers went around to the glass machines to find out what the trouble was. When she came back she reported to the rest of the packers, "Ollie is having trouble with his machine. It's out of adjustment, but he will get it fixed in a few minutes." Ralph noticed that a record was kept of the total daily output of each shift of packers. These women seemed anxious to reach a certain minimum output on each shift. When the components were coming through slowly, he heard such comments as, "This is a bad night." If the work had been coming slowly, the packers regularly started "robbing the conveyor" toward the end of the shift. This was the practice of reaching up along the conveyor and picking off components for packaging before they reached the packer's usual work position.

A short time after Ralph started to work, the company employed another new floorman for the shift. This new man quickly picked up the nickname of Windy. The following were some of Windy's typical comments: "My objective is the paycheck and quitting time." "I love work so much I could lay down and go to sleep right beside it." "These guys are all dopes. If we had a union in here, we would get more money." "I hate this night work. I am quitting as soon as I get another job." Most of the other employees paid little attention to Windy. One of the sealers commented about him. "If bull were snow, Windy would be a blizzard." One night Windy commented to three of the men, "This is a lousy place. They wouldn't get away with this stuff if we had a union. Why don't the four of us start one right here?" None of the group replied to this comment.

Ralph had a number of opportunities to witness the horseplay that concerned the management. At least one horseplay episode seemed to occur on every eight-hour shift. For example, one night while Ralph stood watching Ollie, one of the machine operators, at his work, Ollie called Ralph's attention to the fact that Sam, the operator of the adjacent machine, was about to get soaked.

"Watch him now," Ollie said with a grin, "last night he got Bert and now Bert is laying for him. You watch now." Ralph caught sight of Bert warily circling behind the machines with an oil can in his hand. Sam had been sitting and quietly watching the bottles come off his machine. Suddenly Bert sprang out and fired six or seven shots of water at Sam. When the water hit him, Sam immediately jumped up and fired a ball of wet waste which he had concealed for this occasion. He threw it at Bert and hit him in the chest with it. It left a large wet patch on his shirt. Bert stood his ground, squirting his can until Sam started to chase him. Then he ran off. Sam wiped his face and sat down again. Then he got up and came over to Ollie and Ralph. Sam shouted, "By Jesus, I am going to give him a good soaking." Ollie and Ralph nodded in agreement. Later Ollie commented to Ralph, "It may take as long as three hours for Sam to work up a good plan to get even, but Bert is going to get it good."

Sam was ready to get back at Bert as soon as he could be lured close enough to the machine. Sam pretended to watch his machine but kept his eye out for Bert. In a little while Bert walked jauntily by Sam's machine. They grinned at each other and shouted insults and challenges. Bert went over to a bench to fix something and Sam slipped around behind his machine, pulled down the fire hose and let Bert have a full blast, chasing him up along the conveyor as Bert retreated. Sam then turned off the hose, reeled it back up and went back to his machine.

All the other employees on the scene had stopped to watch this episode and seemed to enjoy it. They commented that it was a good soaking. Bert came back to the machines after a while, grinning, and hurling insults while he stood by Sam's machine to dry off from the heat of the machine. The other operators kidded him some and then everyone went back to work seriously.

A little later the foreman came through the department and noticed the large puddle of water on the floor. He instructed Bert to put some sawdust on the puddle to soak up the water. Ralph was told later that Ed Masters had told Bert, "I want more work and less of this horsing around." A few minutes later Ed Masters and Bert were discussing a small repair job that had to be done that evening.

On another occasion Ralph asked Ollie what he thought of the horseplay. Ollie commented, "It's something each guy has to make up his own mind about. Personally I don't go in for it. I have got all the raises and merit increases that have come along, and I know Bert hasn't had a raise in over a year. Whenever something starts I always look back at my machine so that I can be sure that nothing goes wrong while I am looking away. Personally, I just don't care—you have to have some fun, but personally I don't go for it."

Just at this point Al, one of the punchers, came down from the men's lavatory ready to take his turn on one of the punch machines. He was a moment or two early and stood talking to Sam. Ollie got up from where he had been talking to Ralph and started to holler, "Hey, Al—hey, Al." The other operators took up the chant and all of them picked up pieces of wood or pipe and started drumming on the waste barrels near their machines. Al took up a long piece of pipe and joined in. After a minute or two, one of the operators stopped and the drumming ended quickly. Al lit a cigarette and stepped up to take the machine for his turn.

Ralph later had an opportunity to ask Bert what he thought of the horseplay. Bert said, "You have to have some horseplay or you get rusty. You have to keep your hand in." Ralph noted that Bert's work kept him busy less than anyone else since his duties were primarily to act as an emergency repairman and maintenance man. Ralph asked, "Why doesn't Ollie get into the horseplay?" Bert replied, "Ollie can't take it. He likes to get other people, but he can't take it when he gets it. You have got to be fair about this. If you get some guy, you are surer than hell you will get it back yourself. Now you take Sam and me. We've been playing like that for a long time. He don't lose his temper, and I don't lose mine. I knew I was going to get that hose the other night; that was why I was baiting him with a squirt gun." Ralph asked, "Does Ed Masters mind it very much?" Bert answered, "Hell, he's just like the rest of us. He knows you've got to have some of that stuff only he gets bawled out by the superintendent if they see anything going on like that. That's why we don't play around much on the day shift. But on the night shift that's when we have fun. The only reason we don't squirt the foreman is because he's the foreman. As far as we're concerned, he is no different from us. Besides, he ain't my boss anyway. I'm maintenance. I don't care what he says."

About the middle of the summer the superintendent of the glass department returned from his vacation and immediately thereafter an effort was made by him through the foremen to tighten up on shop discipline. The men on the machines and the punchers were forbidden to walk up to the other end of the conveyor to talk to the packers and sealers and vice versa. The foreman started making occasional comments like "Keep moving" when he saw a small group together in conversation. On one occasion a small group stood watching some activity outside the plant. Ed came by and quite curtly said, "Break it up." Everyone seemed quite shocked at how abrupt he was.

About this same time, the word was passed around among the employees that a big push was on to step up the output of a certain product in order to make a tight delivery schedule. Everyone seemed to be putting a little extra effort into getting this job done. Ralph thought he noticed that the foreman was getting more and more "jumpy" at this time. On one occasion Ed commented to some of the employees, "I am bitter today." One of the machine operators asked him what the trouble was and Ed made some comment about a foremen's meeting where the superintendent was telling them that the playing around and visiting would have to stop.

One night a short time later Ralph saw that preparations were being made for an unusually elaborate trap for soaking Jim, one of the sealers who had recently begun to take part in the water fights. A full bucket of water was tied to the ceiling with a trip rope at the bottom in such a way that the entire contents would be emptied on Jim when he least suspected it. Many of the employees made a point of being on hand when the trap was sprung. It worked perfectly, and Jim was given a complete soaking. Ralph thought Jim took it in good spirit because he turned quickly to counterattack the people who had soaked him. Shortly after the crew had gone back to work, Ruth, one of the packers, was coming down the ramp from the area where the hand-blowing operations were performed. She was carrying some of the glass components. Ruth slipped on some of the water that had been spilled during the recent fight and fell down. She was slightly burned by some of the hot glass she was carrying. Those who saw this happen rushed to her help. The burn, while not serious, required first-aid attention, and the assistant foreman went with Ruth to the company dispensary for treatment. Ralph thought that the employees all felt rather sheepish about the accident. Ruth was one of the more popular girls in the department. The word went around among the employees that a report on the nature and cause of the accident would have to be made out and sent to higher management. Everyone wondered what would happen.

# Daniels Computer Company

## Part I

Daniels Computer Company's memory engineering department was composed of four sections: magnetic, electronic, mechanical, and electrochemical. The customary development work undertaken by the department involved well-known principles of memory design. Each section carried on its phase of development in logical sequence, using the results of the previous section as a starting point. The members of each section were expert in their own fields. The sections were close-knit socially. The manager of the department left technical direction to section supervisors, reserving for his own responsibility the securing of essential services and

 Prepared from a student report by J. Barkev M. Kassarjian under the supervision of John A. Seiler. This case was prepared as the basis for class discussion rather than to illustrate either effective or ineffective handling of administrative situations.

maintenance of the development schedule. The department rarely failed to meet its schedule or technical requisites.

In July 1962, the memory department was assigned the development of a memory incorporating several new design concepts which had never been experimentally evaluated. The functioning of the special computer which was to incorporate the new memory depended upon the most advanced memory device possible within the limits of the new concepts. Development time was one-half the length of more routine developments.

The memory department manager selected the four most competent project engineers from the four sections to work on the special project. Each project engineer was directed to select five engineers and five technicians to work with him on the project. Because of time limitations and the unknown aspects of the new memory concepts, the four groups were to work on their own aspects of design simultaneously. Each team, remaining in the geographic confines of its home section, but independent of its former supervision, commenced immediately to test design schemes and components relevant to its own division of the technology. The project group members quickly became enthusiastic about their new assignment. The department manager left technical supervision to the project engineers of each group.

### Prediction Worksheet

From what I know of the special project operation described in Part I, I would predict that:

1. The four project engineers (would) (would not) work well together to coordinate the work of their separate sections. (Note the reasons for your prediction.)
2. Enthusiasm among the members of the four special groups would (increase) (stabilize) (wane) as the project developed. (Explain why.)
3. Work on the special project would (progress smoothly) (be uneven, though satisfactory) as time went on. (Explain why.)
4. Social relationships will tend to be (project-wide) (special-group oriented). (Explain why.)

## Part II

In late August 1962, the project engineers of the four special groups met for the first time to explore the technical prerequisites each had discovered. The goal of the meeting was to establish parameters for each group's subsequent design effort. It quickly became apparent that each group had discovered concept limitations within its own area which were considered by that group to be controlling. Inevitably, the position of any one group required considerable extra work by one or more of the others. The meeting concluded without compromise of original positions.

In the ensuing weeks all four groups worked desperately to complete certain design segments before complementary segments were completed in other groups. Haste was believed necessary so that the tardy group would have to reformulate its designs, basing them upon that which was already completed. Development of the new memory proceeded in this fashion until the project engineer of the slowest group proved experimentally and theoretically that several designs completed by other groups imposed technologically impossible conditions upon his area of design. A number of personal frictions developed between the groups at this time, with aspersions cast concerning the competence of out-group members. Even department members not formally involved in the special project became involved, siding with their section mates. Enthusiasm for the project on the part of group members waned.

**Postprediction Worksheet**

On the form below, check the degree of accuracy of your predictions from Part I of the case and note the major reasons for accuracy or inaccuracy.

| Question | Degree of Accuracy* | | | Reasons |
|---|---|---|---|---|
| | A | P | I | |
| 1. | | | | |
| 2. | | | | |
| 3. | | | | |
| 4. | | | | |

*A = accurate; P = partly accurate; I = inaccurate.

## Part III

On November 1, 1962, an engineer with considerable memory design experience was hired from outside the Daniels Company to become chief engineer for the special project. The four project engineers were directed to report to the new man. After examining the work of each group, the chief engineer indicated the basic approach to be taken in designing the new memory. Outstanding technical conflicts between groups were summarily dismissed by reference to the new approach. Each group was given a clear set of design instructions within the overall design plan. Firm design time schedules, based on project group interdependence, were set. Frequent progress reports were required of each project engineer.

### Prediction Worksheet

From what I know of the special project operation and the changes in that operation described in Part III, I would predict that:

1. The four project engineers (would) (would not) work well together to coordinate the work of their separate sections. (Note the reasons for your prediction.)
2. Enthusiasm among the members of the four special groups would (increase) (stabilize) (continue to decrease). (Explain why.)
3. Progress of the special project would be (ahead of) (level with) (behind) the planned development time schedule. (Explain why.)
4. The leadership style displayed by the chief engineer would be (functional) (dysfunctional) for total work group performance. (Explain why.)
5. Social relationships will tend to be (project-wide) (special-group oriented). (Explain why.)

## Part IV

For several weeks after the chief engineer set the direction of the project, the project engineers vied with each other to see who could catch the chief engineer in error. Considerable time was spent in experimentation designed to find a weakness in the new design plan. Few problems in the plan could be found. The chief engineer defended his theoretical positions vigorously and continued to demand that schedules be met.

Schedules were met and the four groups worked simultaneously on related design aspects. Communication with the chief engineer grew in frequency. Communication directly between groups at all levels became common. Design limits were quickly discovered before the effort of other groups was needlessly expended.

The cohesion within technical groups became less pronounced, particularly among lower status engineers and technicians. Several lunch groups comprising members of several technical groups began to appear. Enthusiasm for the project was again expressed by the team members.

**Postprediction Worksheet**

On the form below, check the degree of accuracy of your predictions from Part III of the case and note the major reasons for accuracy or inaccuracy.

| Question | Degree of Accuracy* | | | Reasons |
|---|---|---|---|---|
| | A | P | I | |
| 1. | | | | |
| 2. | | | | |
| 3. | | | | |
| 4. | | | | |
| 5. | | | | |

*A = accurate; P = partly accurate; I = inaccurate.

# The Delinquent Store

Harper Stores, Inc., a small chain of discount stores, retails health and beauty aid products. Its founder, Don Harper, had worked several years for a large pharmaceutical company, but, becoming increasingly frustrated by "the big company atmosphere, where promotion is proportional to length of service, and innovation is discouraged," he had, at age twenty-five, resigned to attend the Harvard Business School, where he planned to prepare himself to manage his own concern. While a student, Harper worked as a marketing consultant to a health and beauty aid rack jobber[1] who had formerly been one of his customers. He also managed a

 This case was prepared by Charles Hampden-Turner and Patricia Deeter under the direction of Professor John A. Seiler as the basis for class discussion rather than to illustrate either effective or ineffective handling of an administrative situation.

[1]A rack jobber is a middleman between manufacturer and retailer, performing buying, warehousing, and delivery services. Rack jobbers typically specialize in fast-moving, heavily promoted items such as health and beauty aids, phonograph records, and housewares. The rack jobber physically stocks the racks or shelves allocated by his customers to the products he carries, and often supplies the racks themselves, as well as other in-store displays and selling aids, billing the retailer at a discount off retail.

magazine subscription service, designed and taught an evening course in general management for small merchants in a local, depressed area, and organized an effort to establish a metropolitan psychiatric evening clinic. With a classmate, he wrote a play about the electrical industry price-fixing scandals then current.

Harper liked to try things out "just to see what would happen." As a result, he evolved a number of marketing and management strategies which were thought to be unique, especially to health and beauty aid retailing. He felt that people needed a "legitimizing factor beyond price to explain to their friends why they patronized a discount store." Accordingly, he strove to create a pleasant, open, orderly atmosphere in his stores, yet had customers serve themselves, even to the point of "bagging" their own purchases to give them the feeling that they had "earned" their discount. Harper successively tried two philosophies for drawing customers to his stores, one relying on advertising, the other on prime location. When it turned out that his customer potential lay essentially in the middle class which refused to go far out of its way for specialized discount shopping, he chose exclusively to "out-store" his competitors.

About his role Harper said, "The company must be able to get along without me. I am not really interested in the day-to-day routine of Harper Stores. I enjoy setting up an organization and getting it started, but then I want to be able to leave it running of its own motivation and momentum, while I look for suitable additions in the way of new product lines, market areas, or entirely different kinds of opportunities."

In order to develop the kind of management which was capable of acting on its own, hiring criteria were based largely on eagerness, personality, and intelligence, rather than experience. "Without that," said one of the first men to join Harper, "I would never have got the job, because I certainly didn't have any experience. I'd worked in a grocery store as a kid one time, but that was as far as my knowledge of retailing went."

Harper had begun operations with the establishment of two stores in May of 1963. He hired a store manager who, in turn, hired a cashier. The store manager and cashier served as full-time staff for each store, with additional part-time help as needed. The decision to staff stores in this manner was based on observation of current practice in similar stores. However, personal observation and financial considerations soon led Harper to believe that the operation of a small discount store did not require both a full-time manager and a cashier. Consequently, as he added new stores, he promoted one manager to regional supervisor and the other to advertising manager. The cashiers assumed all of the former managers' duties except for advertising. Under the supervision of the regional manager, the cashier processed customer purchases, opened and closed the store, withdrew and deposited cash daily with the local bank, kept a petty cash account for small operational expenses, controlled decisions over contract cleaning arrangements and designed, purchased and installed window decorations. Cashiers chose their own part-time help and set up work schedules within allotted budgets. They were encouraged to recommend new items to the rack jobber, based on customer inquiries, and to suggest advertising ideas, based on their knowledge of local conditions.

In hiring girls to be cashiers for Harper Stores, the regional supervisor looked for those who showed an interest in people and who were intelligent, but not so intelligent that they might become bored with the job. Previous job experience as a clerk or cashier was thought desirable, since the Harper Stores cashier job offered such girls a significant advancement in responsibility.

Harper's philsosphy of giving cashiers maximum responsibility with minimum supervision had remarkable results. After a year's experience with cashier store managers, there had been no turnover, and not even any absenteeism. The cashiers were proud of "their" stores and treated them as such. Harper was extremely pleased that his philosophy of giving responsibility to workers who were not usually thought to have the desire or capacity for it was working so well. His executives also seemed to respond positively to the freedom they were given. One said, "I quickly began to feel both independent and responsible." Another commented, "Don suggested rather than directed, and I liked that."

During the year and a half after Harper had installed cashiers as store managers, the company grew rapidly. The number of stores reached twenty, and a second regional supervisor was hired to develop and supervise stores in an adjoining state. The executive position of controller was also established.When it appeared that one of the first stores to be started in the new region was having some difficulty, Don Harper decided to use this excuse to encourage his management staff toward further independence of his direct supervision. He suggested that the regional supervisors and company executives (each of whom, though a specialist, was supposed to be able to do any job, particularly that of opening a new store), try to act together to solve the new store's problems.

The "delinquent" store, which was consistently operating at a sales level below the necessary break-even, was located next to the top-rated department store in a semi-industrial city of 70,000 population. It was almost identical to Harper's other stores, each of which had been financially successful. The management "task force" set out to find out why this store, ostensibly so like the others, had such a poor record. At the rate which new stores were being established, it was considered essential to apply the answer to this question to the location, staffing, and other policies of the rapidly spreading organization.

Harper invited a case writer who had been researching other aspects of the company to observe the task force at work. The case writer accepted gratefully and was offered a ride by Lee Perkins, the company's first regional supervisor and a member of the new task force. Lee presided over almost twenty highly successful stores. As they rode together, Lee talked about the company. On the subject of Don Harper, Lee was very talkative:

"I don't know what it is with Don—but he's confident, and somehow when you're with him, you get confident too. There's a sort of sense of trust between us. He believes in letting me get on with the job and yet somehow I know he's back of me . . . not telling me what to do, but believing I can do it. Know what I mean?

"I don't know how to put this . . . but I used to be quite a timid sort of guy. I lost a number of repair jobs (Lee had been running a typewriter repair service when Harper hired him), and it used to bother me to make a decision. Once I fired a guy and couldn't sleep nights. I used to have to invent some wild excuse as much for my sake as his. Well, now I can make that sort of decision. Hell, I don't *like* to fire a guy, but sometimes it has to be done, and I've quit worrying so much about being right or wrong.

"See, here we have a system in this company. We trust each other. We believe that the other guy will do a good and honest job. We can run it this way because we choose our people carefully, using psychological tests[2] and interviews. In this way a girl will be given responsibilities that other companies just wouldn't dream of giving her. But the people we choose have independence and self-respect and initiative, and we know it and they know it and we get on fine. You ought to come around and see the girls in my area. We have a great relationship of mutual respect, and they get some really good merchandising ideas. I let them experiment because I respect their judgment.

"Now there *are* people who take advantage of trust. We have an advertising manager [the second of the two original store managers] who called Don on the telephone to say he didn't make a conference because he was going to the hospital with an ulcer. Well, when you tell Don a thing like that he gets concerned. He wanted to send this guy a 'get well' present—that's typical of Don. So he rings several hospitals near this fellow's home, and somehow he discovers he's not ill at all. He's in New York on a family emergency. So he invites this fellow over to dinner the next week, and very nicely fires him. Tells him exactly why, and how a company like this can't work if people cheat on each other. That guy's wife is still working for us and the fellow doesn't bear us a grudge. He reckoned he deserved it. So you see we can trust our employees but we expect *them* to be trustworthy as well."

"Has this policy landed you in trouble?" the researcher wanted to know. "Surely there must be times when you worry a great deal about some subordinate who might take advantage of you?"

"No, we haven't had trouble. We've spotted the unreliable people early in the game. For instance, I had a very pretty young girl, hard-working, clean, grateful to get the job. She said she'd been a model and was tired of fellows mauling her. Well, I wasn't too sure. As I saw it this job might be a step down, a sort of *rest* for her. She asked me about sick-

[2]Mr. Perkins was referring to the application form which Don Harper had designed to screen job applicants (see Figure 1).

ness benefits and that made me suspicious. Well, she'd been working three weeks when I decided to check. I found out something she hadn't stated on her application. She'd been working for a local electrical company, so I fired her."

"This was reprehensible?"

"Well, you see, she wanted to disguise her attendance record, so I checked on it."

"And it was poor?"

"Well, it was 'fair,' actually, but what with the other things, it all added up!" He nodded and paused. "Of course, she burst into tears when I fired her. Couldn't believe it had happened to her. In fact she called up Don Harper and said a lot about working hard and loving her job. 'If Lee Perkins has fired you, you stay fired,' Don said. So that didn't do her any good. In another location we had to make a completely clean sweep of the whole staff, the girl and her two assistants. Once you get a bad one they affect their assistants and replacements, and the whole social system has to go. But I wouldn't want you to think this is usual. I've never had such pleasant and smooth-working relations as I have with most of the staff, and they are extremely enthusiastic about their work.

"Why, with one girl, I had to say, 'we won't *pay* you unless you take some time off!" She'd worked fourteen months without any time off. I think you can say that in this organization people are important. I like to treat people as Don treats me. You know, I can call him and say I can't make a meeting, I've had one too many. He'll understand. He'll know I'm sorry. The important thing is that I don't pretend. If I had my way, Don's manner of behaving towards people would go right on down through the organization."

The researcher asked about the investigation they were going to make at the problem store. "What is your guess about the trouble?"

"Well, it's been a most unfortunate area. As you know we discount drug store items, and the state pharmacist's association is sore as hell. Ed Sharp has only two stores to supervise so far and a lot of red tape to cut through. Neither of the stores is doing as well as expected and I guess he's feeling pretty frustrated. We'd hoped he'd have a dozen stores by now and soon have an area like me, but this new state hasn't been a lucky one for us."

"What precisely is Ed Sharp's job?"

"Well, he's on his way to being a regional supervisor, but it's not much of a region yet. He's also helping to locate stores and negotiate leases. That's the beauty of this organization, we make our own jobs. Don hires us and says, 'See what you can carve out for yourself.' That's the kind of freedom and initiative we have. Ed will gradually concentrate on what he's doing best. A lot is up to him. For instance, there's a new fellow joining this task force, Sean something—Cassidy, I think. Well, he doesn't have a specific job at all. He's an old friend of Don Harper's from the company he worked for before and he's just been told to join us and find himself something to do. If he's any good, he'll make his own job. We're expanding rapidly and there's plenty of room. It'll be interesting to see what he's like. My guess is that he'll have a lot to learn about the way we operate. Yes, I think it'll take him several months to settle down."

An hour or so later Perkins and the researcher arrived at a hotel and waited in the bar for the rest of the task force to assemble. Over a drink Lee confided to the researcher:

"Look, when this Sean arrives, why don't you arrange to share a room with him tonight? We'll all be sharing. I'm very interested to know about him, what he thinks and how well he knows Don. I'd be very interested in having a fellow like you size him up."

At that moment, Ed Sharp arrived, in company with Jeff Harris, the company's advertising manager. Ed was tall, somewhat older than the others, with a deep voice and a face which in repose was serious.

Jeff Harris was quiet and retiring, and only occasionally interjected a short statement or judgment on the matters discussed. He had been a classmate of Harper's at Harvard.

As they waited for the others, Ed told jokes. When Sam Shrieber, who was a partner in the rack-jobbing company, working exclusively with Harper Stores, joined the meeting it was decided to start discussion without the remaining two members, who had been delayed. The meeting adjourned to one of the bedrooms.

Ed opened the meeting in a businesslike way by handing around a report which minutely described local training conditions in the town. He then described a heated exchange between himself and the local pharmacist's association from which he had apparently emerged creditably. Ed turned to the delinquent store itself.

ED: I think everyone ought to take a good look at her, that's Miss Evans. Our policy is to concentrate on people, and that's where at least some of this trouble must lie.

LEE: You think we should all talk to her? Won't that be a bit too much? We could get her views on everything, on the town, competition after all, she's in the best position. . . .

ED: You'll find she's guarded. I think we ought to *observe* her.

SAM: I'll tell you what. Lee, she doesn't know you, so don't you shave tomorrow, put on some old clothes and come in like a slob off the street. Pick up some little thing and complain!

LEE: Well . . . O.K.

SAM: See, I reckon she's two-faced. She's nice as pie to our people when they're stacking up the racks. But when Julie, my secretary, called up from New York, she said Miss Evans sounded kind of "funny" on the telephone, as if she was trying to keep Julie in her place. Maybe this Evans woman is just ingratiating to people *above* her. She's charming to me but I'm not sure its natural.

ED: Yeah, she keeps telling me how much work she has to do. Says she works six days a week and dares not take a lunch hour because the assistant cashier doesn't have a sharp enough eye for pilferage. I also suspect she's closing up at 6:30, not 7:00. [To the researcher] You might go around at about five minutes before closing time, stay in there until after 7:00 and see if she throws you out. She hasn't seen you, has she?

RESEARCHER: No.

ED: Of course I know she's trying to impress me. I'm not sure she's reliable. Still we must keep her happy until we're ready to replace her.

At that moment a call came through for Ed. He had been trying to get the whole group into a motel outside town, and a crisp interchange followed between Ed and the reservation desk. When Ed had succeeded in getting the group reservations for the night following, he excused himself and went down to the bar to check on the arrival of the others. As soon as the door closed behind him, Sam chuckled.

SAM: Ed is a tough guy! Did you hear the way he pinned that guy down?

LEE: Trouble is he only has two stores—maybe he thinks about them too much. He's had a tough time with his staff. One girl fired and that colored girl just left.

JEFF: Have you read this survey of Ed's? Pretty thorough! Why he's even gone down to the local girl's college and asked them about beauty aids. He sews things up.

There followed a long discussion of how much money could be made with some recent items on the drug market. When Ed returned without the missing members, the group began to parcel out the work for the next day. Jeff was told to take notes and draw up a work roster.

Jeff, it was decided, would talk to local newspapers and the chamber of commerce, and review rival advertising, since this was his field. Sam Shrieber would examine local competition and check the products that were being supplied by his company. Lee Perkins would pose as a customer, make himself disagreeable, and later help check the foot traffic passing the store front. Ed Sharp would check over the store and count the number of people actually entering the store, and how many left without buying. Sean Cassidy and Kurt Marslow, the controller, were still to arrive. They would ask passersby what they knew about the shop, help with the traffic check, and pose as customers.

Shortly after the divisions of labor had been decided, Sean Cassidy and Kurt Marslow arrived. They both expressed ideas about how they would like to operate the next day, after glancing at Jeff Harris' roster of duties. Since it was now after midnight, however, the task force retired to bed. Since Sean and Kurt had checked in together, they had been placed in the same room. The researcher was with Lee Perkins for the same reason.

Lee seemed worried about imitating a customer in order to test Miss Evans.

"I don't think it will work. She knows we're all coming and she's very suspicious of strangers."

"Why is that, d'you think?"

"Well, she told Ed Sharp that someone had been snooping around the shop at night and had moved her account book. She was afraid it might be thieves. But of course it wasn't. It was Ed himself, checking on her books."

"Did he admit it?"

"Hell no! He said perhaps it was me! I can tell you I'm pretty mad. I don't know what to say if she asks me. Better she should know it's us than some prowler. She's alone in that shop some of the time, especially in the evening, not that there's enough money to be worth taking."

At breakfast the next morning Sean Cassidy and Kurt Marslow talked to the researcher. Sean was a tall, slim, and good-looking man with an interest in sports. He smiled a lot and seemed completely at ease. Kurt talked mostly about the difference between the financial performance of the store they were to visit and that of the other Harper stores.

After breakfast four members of the task force went to the store, giving Lee enough time to pose as a disagreeable customer. By the time the force arrived Lee was talking amiably with Mary Evans.

Between 9:10 A.M. and 10:30 A.M. only three female customers entered the shop. During most of this period there were at least three task-force members in the store. Mary Evans was dusting hard at dusted shelves and straightening the rows of products. As the researcher approached her she said over her shoulder, "This is the cleanest shop in town. Every morning I do this, every morning!"

At 11:00 A.M., the researcher, Sean Cassidy, and Sam Shrieber adjourned to the local drug store for coffee. Sam had been checking on the competition and he regaled his listeners with the various disguises he had assumed in local stores. A discussion ensued as to whether it was better to pretend to be a retail audit clerk, a representative of the licensing authority, or a member of a retail association. Kurt Marslow joined them and explained the subtlety of asking questions to passersby so that they did not know one's intention. "What toothpaste do you buy?" was a most effective disguise for finding out where they bought it. Jeff Harris complained that since everyone was asking different questions, the results would not be comparable.

Back at the store, Lee Perkins was of the same mind as Jeff.

"You know, we've really got to get some direction and organization. That is, without stifling freedom. This is chaos. No one has been making a traffic count and its mid-day. Sean just walked off the job. He's going to have to learn our ways."

The whole group met for lunch and Lee was asked about his disagreeable customer episode.

LEE: Well, she didn't lose her temper. In fact, she was most apologetic. The floor had just been polished so I slipped and cursed. She said how sorry she was.

ED: Hmm . . . well, she was ready of course.

LEE: Have you checked her application for any lies? I found in my area. . . .

KURT: You know the trouble with that shop? It's too tidy! Too antiseptic! All those items in a dead straight line like soldiers, and the green walls, and Mary. It's not *friendly*!

ED: But the shop is standard. It's the same everywhere. Only Miss Evans is different. I think she's too tense, too anxious. She doesn't relax and that puts customers off. Have you noticed how stiff she is in her behavior, and how she's always tidying things, and there's never a thing out of place? Those eyeglasses on a chain around her neck! I mean, it's forbidding!

SEAN: Of course there were a lot of us there and none of us really talked to her.

JEFF: But I don't feel we *should*. That's undermining Ed's authority over her. All our proposals should go through him.

KURT: I agree. We mustn't undermine Ed.

It was arranged to meet again at six o'clock at the motel outside town, and to compare notes on the day's researches. Each person should be ready to present the area he'd researched. Lee suggested that Mary should be given some sort of present, in case she was anxious. Jeff said that Ed should be the one to give it, as Mary's boss. Ed made a notation in his book.

Five hours later the task force met in the bar just across from the motel. Jeff Harris began by explaining that advertising had followed the same procedure as with other store openings, and that as many people had presented coupons as was usual. The conclusion he drew was that people were entering the store once, but not again. Clearly, Jeff felt the advertising was not at fault.

Sam Shrieber assured the task force that the racks were filled as frequently and with the same products as the other stores. He had looked at the local competition, and he would make a few price changes, but there was no reason to suppose that the local demand pattern was different from elsewhere.

There followed some discordant discussion of the market research. It seemed that while the usual number of people were passing the shop, a lower proportion than usual were coming in. A number of questions had been asked about toothpaste and the answers seemed to show that people standing opposite the store had never heard of Harper Stores and, furthermore, had false teeth.

A survey revealed that there were three competitors of long standing within a block. However, their stores were all dirty, and their products had dusty, hand-lettered price tags. In comparing it with other Harper Stores members of the task force felt that this one did not have an effective window display.

Kurt voiced the opinion that Harper Stores was losing a chance to capitalize on the comparability of its various units. He suggested window display experiments. If one store's display seemed to pull better, then photograph it and circulate the picture so the display could be duplicated in all stores. He felt that the operation should be run with such "built-in" market research.

Ed thought they were straying from the point. "What should be done in this store now? Why are you so quiet, Charles? What do you think?"

The researcher, pressed to answer, said that from a marketing point of view, it seemed that people were passing the shop but not going in. He wondered what failed to attract them.

"It's that woman, she puts them off," Jeff pronounced, suddenly.

The next half hour was spent in a discussion of animated signs which lasted right through dinner until cigars were ordered at which point Kurt commented:

"I only talked to Mary for about 30 seconds—but I could tell. That woman's a phoney—no doubt about it. She's nervous—doesn't look you straight in the eye."

This comment was followed by a brief discussion of Harper Stores' prospects, after when the task force decided to continue their discussion in one of the motel rooms.

SAM: I think we've narrowed down the problem to two things: location and people. And from what we've heard, it can't be location, so it must be people, and that's her.

KURT: Look, let's not talk about people. Let's talk about *facts*—that's how you run a business.

SAM: Surely it's a fact that this woman is so busy fussing and dusting shelves that she doesn't see a customer waiting to buy something for over 10 seconds. And look at that notice—the first thing you see as you enter the shop: "Sorry, no checks"—well, it's negative.

KURT: It's company policy. We told her to do it.

SEAN: But people aren't coming in. . . .

SAM: Look, don't talk when other people. . . .

KURT: Frankly, I'm playing devil's advocate. Give me facts! Convince me!

ED: Look, this isn't a game. We don't want people playing at the devil or anything and everyone can't talk at once. No one's accusing anyone of failing to do anything. There's nothing wrong with the store location—that's established. It seems to be a question of attracting customers into the store and keeping them, and that's to do with people and that's where our trouble lies.

At this point several discussions started up simultaneously. Kurt was saying that you could not deal with one store in a vacuum. Sean said that this store was an exception and should be dealt with as singular. Suddenly Jeff said, "People don't change. You can't change her. You can't *tell* her to be more friendly. You can't order people to relax. You have to set them an example."

"Are you suggesting that we haven't helped her?" Ed was incredulous.

"I think we should get her a young girl, one of our best, and have her *show* Mary how to relax."

There was hubbub, and Ed held up his hand for silence.

"No one is listening to anyone in this room. I propose that we split into two groups. Sam, you take Lee and Sean into your room. We'll stay here, and after half an hour we'll meet and compare our final set of proposals."

This idea was readily accepted. The researcher followed the three last mentioned into Sam's room and they all collapsed onto the bed and into armchairs with some relief.

SAM: Phew! That's better. That fellow Kurt doesn't listen, doesn't let you get a word in edgewise. This is much better. You can hear yourself think! Now as I see it, Mary is not receptive to the way she's supervised. If Kurt wants to do some standardizing, let's analyze how we train and supervise personnel.

SEAN: But do we really know what we want her to be? Has she got the message? I thought the girls were supposed to be free, but Ed is in that shop supervising her three or four days a week from what I hear.

LEE: Well, I don't know if that's accurate. After all, you've just got here. I'd check that with Ed, if I were you.

SAM: It's a funny thing with this outfit. Everything goes swimmingly until we run into a hitch. We're accelerating and accelerating, and then suddenly it's like the gears are locked and we're going in reverse. Everyone gets riled up and the staff gets nervous and anxious. Even the day goes slower.

LEE: Don't you think we ought to draw up these proposals? I'm not going to say a thing when we go back to the others unless they rile us. Let's keep quiet and let Sam do the talking. Sam, you stand up to Kurt. He's really sharp.

(The researcher returned to the first group.)

ED: Right, Item 3: Mary must be told that customers can't be kept waiting. She must leave her dusting. The customer is God!—well king,—anyway. And she must be friendly. She can give away rain-bonnets and we can get her a badge, "My name is Mary, hi!" And we need laughter in the store—maybe a radio. Ease, laughter, friendliness! That's what sells.

KURT: We have three alternatives. Leave her as she is, change her, fire her. Let's concentrate on changing her. Tell her she's free! Tell her to use initiative. You know, there's seven people come to look at her store this week. I guess she doesn't feel so alone now. She feels impressed. And another thing, we should have a standard manual so that all our girls know the sort of people we want them to be. Let's give her a chance to accept constructive criticism.

ED: If she can't accept constructive criticism—for her own good—if she's insulted—then that's it, she's not our type.

JEFF: We'll have to get rid of her!

KURT: Well, remember we have an investment in that woman, time and money, and people develop if you know how to do it. Can't we tell her, "You don't have to look so businesslike?" You know, she's really trying.

ED: I could try and change her over the next few weeks.

KURT: Have you noticed how she bosses that assistant cashier? That girl has to do *exactly* what Mary says. I think that cashier might blossom if it wasn't for Mary. You know, if that cashier was supervised with understanding. . . .

JEFF: It's like goods on the shelf! Now some goods are bright and new. Some are dusty. Mary's dusty!

KURT: Hey, what's the time? We must finish these proposals.

JEFF: Don't let's get back with that other group until we can help it. This is much better.

ED: Well, obviously, I'm going to have to spend two or three days with this girl. Our sales operation has to be aggressive. I may have to take off the kid gloves.

JEFF: Look, why not send just one guy to talk with the other bunch. It would save going over all this. Whatever happens, everything must be channeled through Ed, so does it really matter what they come up with—I mean if we don't like it. . . .

KURT: Let's lay some ground rules. Each side has five minutes to fire off. Then we take ten minutes to synthesize. No one interrupts me and no one interrupts Sam. O.K.?

ED: O.K.

The researcher returned to Sam's group, which had just finished its agenda, and had come up with very similar ground rules. Lee was worried about Ed's suggestion that they give Mary a badge.

LEE: Maybe we ought to leave it to her, I mean, we shouldn't press her too much. I wonder if Ed's remembered the candy.

SEAN: You know, with all those people in the shop and Ed watching her so closely . . . I mean how d'you think she behaves when we're not here?

LEE: Things aren't going well for Ed. Maybe he worries too much. . . .

SAM: Look, let's stick to our agenda. After all it's Ed's responsibility. He'd really take offense if we didn't leave things to him. We give people freedom in this outfit.

LEE: Yeah, I say let's get with the other group and wind all this up!

The groups met. Sam and Kurt each read out their proposals and they were formally added together with little discussion. The complete list included the following:

1. More loss-leader activity, with five or six selected items each month.
2. Show more relaxed and friendly atmosphere with music, friendly badges, an animated furry animal in the window, and stop Mary's standing with her back to the door.
3. Build some imaginative window displays.
4. Get Mary to relax, take those eyeglasses off that chain. Bring an experienced girl in to teach her how to relax.
5. Ed should spend at least three days a week supervising Mary, and install some initiative in her, persuading her that she's free to use it.
6. In addition, any members of the task force should visit in the store when in the area. But Ed mustn't be undermined, since he is over her.
7. More joint advertising with manufacturers.
8. Explore in-store give-away premiums.
9. More tumbled displays and less straight lines on the shelves.

The task force then retired to bed.

Next morning the task force stopped off briefly at the store so Ed could give Mary the box of candy.

"That's for you from all of us," he said.

Mary showed her embarrassment. "Well, aren't you dolls! Thanks a lot—how sweet of you. But I wish I could help you gentlemen. I'd be very glad to do anything you propose. You've all taken a lot of trouble . . . I know . . . so if there's anything I could do."

"Mr. Sharp has our proposals and will be discussing them with you," said Sam. He shook hands with her and departed. The researcher waited until last, then explained hurriedly to Mary.

"Look, I have a ride back with the others, so I've only got a minute. But I'd be very interested to know how you feel about all this."

"Well, I'd very much like to tell you. I've been wanting to talk to

APPLICATION for EMPLOYMENT

Name ______________________ Address: ______________________

Telephone: ______________________ ______________________

Marital Status __________ Number of Children: __________ Social Security No. __________

Date you can start work: __________ Starting Salary Desired: __________

Are you currently employed? __________ Employer __________

Name of last school attended __________ When attended __________

FORMER EMPLOYERS (List last 3 employers)

| DATE (From-To) | NAME & ADDRESS OF EMPLOYER | SALARY | REASON LEFT |
|---|---|---|---|
| | | | |
| | | | |
| | | | |
| | | | |

Do you have any physical defects? __________ If so, list __________

There are no correct answers to the following questions — their purpose is to get to know you a little better.

If you felt an employer was underestimating your abilities, what would you do? __________

People who join clubs and organizations are __________

When I have a problem with another person, I __________

I am most happy when I __________

I am saddest when I __________

The greatest success in my life was __________

The biggest disappointment in my life was __________

When passengers argue with bus drivers, the bus driver should __________

Waiters in restaurants should be __________

I am most particular about __________

If I go to the supermarket at night and the car next to mine has left its lights on, I should __________

If I see two young children fighting, I should __________

The most important thing about me is __________

I think the above questions are __________

**Figure 1** The Delinquent Store

all these kind gentlemen, but there hasn't been a minute when I could relax. It's been rather confusing, because I'd like to help, really I would."

"Could I come down in a couple of weeks and talk to you—get things from your angle?"

"Oh please! That would be fine. I've got a lot of suggestions."

"Really? Well I have to run in literally 60 seconds. Could you tell me some of your ideas?"

Mary suggested in whole or part items, 1, 2, 4, 5, 7, 8, and 9 of the task force's agenda. In addition, she wanted to analyze the turnover of different lines and the profit accruing to different racks within the shop. She thought she could design a beautiful window design for Christmas. Did the researcher know what had been decided? But the researcher had to run. The car had been waiting nearly two minutes.

On the way home with Lee Perkins and Jeff Harris, the atmosphere was a little depressed and morose. Lee said he didn't think Sean had the right attitude. Had the researcher discovered how well Sean knew Don Harper? Jeff said that in some ways the time had been wasted because the task force found what they had expected all along. Was it worthwhile? Lee wasn't sure.

"I guess we're all pretty independent guys. We tend to frustrate each other. But I didn't like all that snooping around. You remember about that pretending to be a disagreeable customer? Well, I couldn't really do it. Hell, how can you talk to someone after doing that? I thought Mary was O.K. And if she was sharp with Julie on the phone, well who wouldn't be? That cheeky little kid wants paddling. Mary's old enough to be her mother.

"I'm not sure Don Harper would have handled the task force the way we did. Things are different in my area. I hope you won't think this is typical of us. It really isn't."

Some weeks later as the researcher was planning to visit Mary Evans to complete his investigations, he was told that Mary had been fired.

# Excelsior Bakeries, Inc.

Upon completing my junior year in college in early June, I returned to my home town, Pottersville, New York. The next day I went to see Mr. Roger Farnum, the plant superintendent of the local branch of Excelsior Bakeries, Inc., to find out when I should report for work. I had worked at the Excelsior plant the previous summer as a general helper on the slicing and wrapping crew for hamburger and hot dog rolls. Because I was a union member and had spoken to Mr. Farnum during spring vacation about a job for this summer, I was positive of being rehired.

When I walked into the office, Mr. Farnum said jokingly, "Hi, George, ready to go to work for a change after all that book learning?" I was rather surprised to see Mr. Farnum so jovial and cordial. I remembered him as always having a long face and never saying more than two words at a time. I finally answered, "Yes, sir, anytime you say and as soon as possible."

"Well, on the recommendation of Murphy, you're going to run the hamburger and hot dog machine this summer. Murphy wants to work on the ovens; and seeing as how we don't want to change a regular worker over to the wrapper just for a couple of months, we figured you would accept the added responsibility and could handle the job!"

Murphy, a regular employee of the plant, had run the wrapping machine last summer and had been leader over a crew of three other summer workers and me. I had visited Murphy at the plant during spring vacation, and he had told me he was going to work on the ovens this year because it was day work and paid more. I had casually mentioned to him at that time to try to get me the wrapping machine job, but I hadn't thought of it again, because it had always been assigned to a regular worker.

I was extremely pleased to accept the job, for I knew it meant six cents more an hour, and it would entail some leadership responsibility. I thought to myself, "Now I will be part of management and not just another worker."

Mr. Farnum told me to report for work that following Sunday, a week earlier than I had expected, so I could familiarize myself with the machine before the "rush season" started.

Excelsior Bakeries, Inc., was a large firm with many plants spread across the entire United States. The Pottersville branch produced mainly white, rye, whole wheat, and French bread, but supplemented these major lines with hamburger and hot dog rolls, dinner rolls, donuts, and other bakery products. It also distributed in its area of operation pies, cakes, crackers, and other specialties produced in the Boston plant.

Pottersville was located in a region which is noted for its many summer resorts, camps, and hotels, which are open from June until September. During the summer season, production and sales of the local Excelsior plant increased tremendously, as the summer population swelled the normal demand. This seasonal rise was especially significant in hot dog and hamburger rolls, whose sales increased over the winter months by approximately 100 to 150 percent in June; 150 to 250 percent in July; and 250 to 300 percent in August. Because of this great seasonal increase, the company had to hire about fifteen employees just for the three summer months. Five of these "extra help" were needed on the wrapping crew for hot dog and hamburger rolls. This "extra help" was usually drawn from college students on vacation, employment agencies, and transient workers. In the past several years the "extra help" had been predominantly college students, because they were more dependable and willing to remain on the job right up to Labor Day.

After I reported to work, I spent the first week with the regular employees. Ed Dugan, a past operator of the wrapping machine, worked with me, teaching me all the techniques of operating the machine efficiently. The machine was rather old and had to be tended carefully at all times, so that the cellophane wrapping paper would not jump off the rollers. The wrapping paper was expensive, and Joe McGuire, the night foreman, "blew his top" whenever a lot of paper was wasted.

Figure 1 shows the working area and the positions of each operator on the slicing and wrapping crew. Worker No. 1 took the pans of rolls from the racks and fed the rolls out on a conveyor, which carried them into the slicing machine. Worker No. 2 stacked the sliced rolls into two rows, one on top of the other, making groups of eight or one dozen. Worker No. 3 slid the groups of rolls down the table to worker No. 4, who fed them into the wrapping machine. Worker No. 5, the wrapping machine operator and crew leader, placed the wrapped packages in a box, keeping count of the actual number packaged. The work was rather routine and extremely monotonous and boring. Workers No. 1 through No. 4 continually exchanged positions in order to break the monotony.

The plant employees worked on a five-day week—working on Sunday and Monday; off on Tuesday; working Wednesday, Thursday, and Friday; and off again on Saturday. Production was on daily orders from the various sales routes. The salesmen left the plant early in the morning with their loaded trucks and, after making their deliveries, returned in

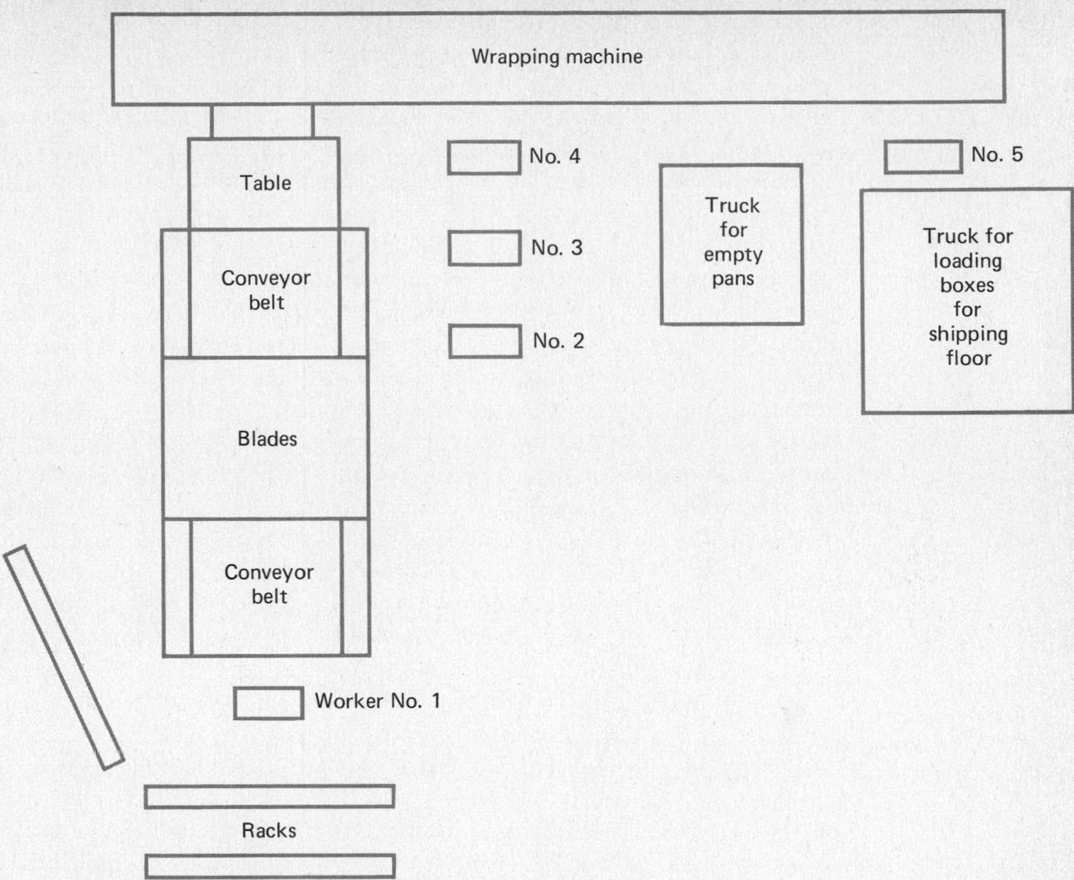


**Figure 1** Wrapping Machine Layout

the afternoon with the orders for the next day. The volume varied from day to day, and the wrapping crew did not begin work until all the rolls were baked. Therefore, the wrappers generally reported for work at a different time each day, being notified by the plant superintendent. Usually the crew began about 6:00 to 8:00 P.M. and worked until all the orders were filled for that night. The number of hours worked ranged from seven to fifteen or even more. All time over eight hours was overtime and paid for as time and a half. If a worker was a union member, the company had to guarantee him seven hours pay for any night on which they called him in. If there were not seven hours of slicing and wrapping, the foreman found something else for the men to do, such as thoroughly cleaning the machines, greasing the pans or other odd jobs. If a man wished, though, he could ask to "punch out" before seven hours was up, thereby forfeiting the guaranteed seven hours pay for that night and receiving pay only for the hours he had worked.

Four different types of packages were wrapped on the machine: hamburger and hot dog dozen-roll packages; and hamburger and hot dog packages of eight rolls. A different size and type of paper was used for each package. Different-sized plates had to be used in the machine also. On an average night a complete changeover of the machine had to be made about six times, each alteration taking about ten minutes. In addition, it took about five minutes to replace a roll of paper when it ran out and two to three minutes to replace the labels and seals. During these changeovers and replacements, which were made by the machine operator, the rest of the crew smoked cigarettes out on the shipping dock or else folded boxes for the operator if he needed them. I never asked anyone to make boxes, if he wanted to have a cigarette or wanted to get a drink of water. But if a man was just sitting around or "goofing off," I would ask him to fold boxes, as the crew is supposed to do during these breaks. Joe McGuire hated to see anyone sit around, but he never begrudged anyone a cigarette.

With the start of my second week, orders rose, and the rest of the summer help was called in. I was very pleased when three of my close friends were assigned to my crew. Art Dunn, a student at Williams, had worked on the wrapping crew with me the previous summer, as had Jack Dorsey, a student at the University of Vermont. Both Bill and Art had graduated from high school with me. Bill Regan, a Fordham student, had not worked for Excelsior the previous summer, but he had lived next door to me, and we had grown up together. The four of us had been close friends during high school days and since graduation, even though we went to different colleges. Harry Hart, the fourth man, was also new to the wrapping crew. Hart had graduated from high school a year before the rest of us and was attending the University of Massachusetts.

With the help of Art and Jack, I was able to train Bill and Harry quickly, and within a couple of nights they were thoroughly proficient in all four positions. During these first nights, Art and Jack thoroughly indoctrinated Bill and Harry into the "code" of the wrapping crew.

Excelsior Bakeries offered college students an excellent opportunity to make a considerable amount of money during the summer, paying an hourly rate of $1.03 and providing plenty of overtime. The "code" of the wrapping crew was a concerted group action to set the number of hours to be worked on a certain night. At the beginning of the night's work, the crew could fairly well estimate from the production orders just how long it should take to put the work out. If it was estimated to take about eight hours, the crew would purposely slow down to stretch it to nine or nine and one-half hours, so they could get overtime pay. On practically any night the work could be stretched out by an hour or so. Only on big nights of twelve or more hours did the crew work at normal speed. As an indication of the effectiveness of this slowdown, there were several occasions when a seven or eight hour night was estimated, but the crew "pushed the stuff through" and finished in six hours in order to have a few beers before the local bar closed at 3:00 A.M.

As a member of this crew the previous summer, I was one of the strong advocates of this code. If a new worker or a temporary replacement from somewhere else in the plant appeared on the crew, he had to conform, or the group gave him much verbal abuse or the even worse "silent treatment." These were unbearable conditions and the new man always accepted the "code."

Phil Murphy, the previous year's leader, although a regular employee of the plant, had cooperated with the group and never complained. He used to say, "After all, I want the overtime, too!"

After the first few nights of work, I noticed the "code" had begun to operate. I had never stopped to think of the effects this slowdown had on management and the operations of the plant. It raised labor production costs, delayed the salesmen in leaving for their routes, and raised other problems as well. At first, I was rather confused as to whether I should allow this practice to continue or "as part of management" put my foot down and take action to stop it. Because I could not think of any satisfactory course of action which would satisfy everyone, I allowed the code to operate. I rationalized myself into believing, "Well, if management isn't going to do anything about it, why the hell should I worry about it?"

The first couple of weeks went smoothly. The only problems I had to face were minor arguments among the crew and the usual horseplay and "goofing off" in the middle hours of the morning.

Joe McGuire, the night foreman, occasionally would say to me, smiling, "Took you guys a pretty long time to get those rolls out tonight, didn't it?" or on a really short night, "You can really shove those rolls through when you feel like having a few brews!" Joe could not see us working from his office, as the line of racks blocked his view, but he regularly walked over to check on us. When Joe appeared, the man feeding the slicing machine would place the rolls on the conveyor belt "back to back" with no space in between, the maximum rate at which the crew could operate. When Joe was in his office or "up front," a space of about six to twelve inches was allowed between rolls, thereby reducing the speed of production by ten to fifteen percent.

Occasionally a "little war" would break out between the wrapping crew and two donut men across the aisle from the wrapping machine; the members of each group would throw donuts or hot dog and hamburger rolls at the others. One night one of these battles was beginning to get out of hand to the point where the boys had stopped work. I reprimanded them and told them to "knock it off" and get back to work. Bill called me a "company man" and Art said something about the "lieutenant with the gold-plated bars." I was trying to ignore the comments when suddenly I heard the paper snap. I stopped the machine and adjusted it, but even after the machine had been adjusted package after package kept coming through unwrapped or "crippled." I tried everything I knew to find the cause of the trouble; but just when I thought I had the machine running properly, something else would go wrong. By this time I was ready to give up and call Joe for his advice. Then I noticed the four crew men having a good laugh for themselves. I had been so concerned about trying to change the adjustments on the machine that I had not noticed Bill tinkering with the machine at the other end. He was also feeding the hot dog rolls improperly, breaking them before putting them in the machine so they would slide off and get caught, thereby drawing unevenly on the paper. I lost my temper completely and was in the process of a real argument with Bill and the rest of the crew when Joe came down to see why the machine was shut down. When he asked, I stuttered, "Jesus, Joe, these—ah—this damn machine isn't drawing right. I've tried everything, but I think I've finally found the real reason. Let's try it now, fellas!"

That night when I was making my final count with Joe and the shipping foreman, I was considerably short on hot dog rolls, because of the many losses caused by Bill's tampering with the machine. Joe gave me quite a reprimand and said I'd better "watch it."

The next night when I came to work, Mr. Farnum stopped me and asked why I had lost so much paper the night before. I told him it was a breakdown in the machine. He gave me orders to weigh each roll of paper before we started wrapping each night and to weigh it again when we finished. I was to record the weights on tabulation control sheets kept in his office.

That night before starting work, I told the crew what had happened and what Joe and Mr. Farnum had said to me. I told them that I was being held responsible for paper and production control and that I would tolerate no more horsing around, especially tampering with the machine. I emphasized that I would not go "on the carpet" again for *anyone*.

Relations between me and the crew, with the exception of Harry, were rather strained for a couple of nights. None of them said very much to me. I also did not go swimming or play golf with them for a couple of days, which we usually did every afternoon. However, I did not have any more incidents of this sort, and the crew continued to meet the output schedule as they had before. Gradually the incident was forgotten, and relations among us became what they had been before the incident.

During the latter part of August, the annual Excelsior clambake was held. During the latter part of the afternoon, Joe McGuire called me over to the bar to have a drink. Mr. Farnum and Mr. Sommers, the plant manager, were with him. McGuire threw his arm around me and said to Mr. Farnum, "George did a great job this summer on the wrapper, didn't he, Rog?"

"Best season we've had so far, Joe."

# The Gage Company

In November of 1967 Russell Alger, executive vice-president of the Gage Company, began to wonder whether the only solution to the communication impasse which he and his boss had reached might have to be Alger's resignation.

Alger had come to Gage shortly after completing a Master's degree in engineering, rising through various departments and subsidiaries of the firm to his present position over a twelve-year period. Due to the simultaneous retirement of men two levels beneath Malcolm King, the president, Alger's latest promotion was a two-step jump. He had never worked closely with King before. King had promoted Alger on the basis of his past performance and the strong recommendation of his recently retired executive vice-president. Although King and Alger had no previous personal relationship, they shared a mutual respect.

After working closely with King for several months, Alger's view of his boss had changed. He sensed, too, that King may have come to regret his choice of Alger as executive vice-president.

The tariff barrier issue had marked the beginning of the rift between them. King believed that the basic industry in which Gage competed had to be protected from foreign competition in order to survive. To this end he invested much of his time as part of an industry group which kept in close touch with sympathetic legislators in Washington, urging the establishment of protective tariffs.

Alger, however, was convinced that by technical innovation, the Gage Company could beat competition, both foreign and domestic. He firmly believed that if Gage clearly understood the needs of the many separate markets which it could potentially serve and developed the capacity to deliver goods rapidly and in desired form, the company could assume a position of leadership.

King's response to Alger's point of view took the younger man back. King contended that Alger's ideas were impractical, that Alger was naïve in espousing them, that these matters were properly the province of the president and the Board, and if Alger wished to question his—King's—competence, he should say so directly instead of beating around the bush.

Alger decided, based on the vehemence of King's response, to avoid any further discussion with King where his and the president's opinion differed significantly. He found argument of this kind distasteful and began to restrict his activities to the execution of existing company policy. Because King was highly absorbed by activities in Washington and by his relationship with the Board, Alger exercised considerable latitude in his interpretation of policy. Wherever possible he took unobtrusive action to shape the organization to fit his thinking.

Little by little, for example, he had modified the company's pyramidal organization structure, inducing a "flatter" form by eliminating some levels in the hierarchy, as their occupants had retired or resigned. He had also worked to improve the company's competitive position by changing the sales organization from its traditional product orientation toward a greater concern for the customer's changing and proliferating needs.

From time to time, however, King questioned his second-in-command about one or another of these changes, and Alger, to avoid involvement in what seemed to him to be bombastic disagreements, typically retreated and sought other avenues of less interest to the president in which to improve corporate performance.

Finally, it seemed to Alger that the differences in philosophy between himself and the president were too pervasive to remain concealed. He was distressed that he could not speak freely to King and that communication had virtually ceased between them. For one thing, Alger felt he at least needed clarification of his area of authority. Although he anticipated that such a discussion might lead to a repetition of such arguments as that which had arisen over the tariff issue, he made the suggestion to King that they make it a point to sit down and discuss their respective areas of authority and responsibility. King agreed to this proposal, saying that as soon as time permitted he would arrange for a thorough review of the situation. However, Alger had yet to hear anything more on the subject.

. . . . .

From his point of view, Malcolm King was troubled by Russell Alger's behavior since the latter's appointment as executive vice-president. The first sign of trouble arose when Alger suggested that the company invest vast sums in new equipment, whose payout seemed to King to be questionable, indeed. Alger's judgment seemed intemperate to King, to suggest abandoning all the spade work which had been done in Washington and to jettison the relationship which had developed in the industry, in favor of a gamble with a fickle market at a very high cost. Apparently Alger was not prepared to support his contention in any event, since he quickly backed down when King challenged him.

King was disturbed, too, by some of the changes Alger had made in the organization. Alger seemed to want to throw out all of the established ways of doing business. King had largely avoided interceding in these matters until he could decide for himself what needed to be done. He would have liked to think over these changes out loud with Alger, but he never could pin Alger down to a position. Alger's request for a meeting to discuss delineation of authority was troublesome to King, since his recent doubts about Alger's judgment left King wondering just how much authority he could safely leave in Alger's hands.

King felt especially annoyed by Alger's tactics of gaining support for an idea among other executives of the firm behind King's back and carrying out a virtually irreversible change without coming to King first with a straightforward proposal. He felt that his own directness should be matched by a similar willingness on the part of his executive vice-president. King enjoyed an old-fashioned, knock-down disagreement. How else could you test the strength of a man's conviction? But Alger was perhaps too smooth, he thought, too well-educated, to be able to operate in this way. He seemed to take these issues personally and to react to King on a personal level as well. How the hell can you work with a man who won't stand up for what he thinks?

# Mr. Hart and Bing

The shop situation reported in this case occurred in a work group of four men and three women who were engaged in testing and inspecting panels for electronic equipment. The employees were paid on a piecework incentive basis. The personnel organization of the company included a counselor whose duty it was to become acquainted with the workers and talk over any problems which they wished to discuss with him. The summarized statements of "Bing," the employee, and Mr. Hart, the supervisor, are excerpts from five interviews the counselor had with each of them within a period of about two weeks.

*A summarized statement of how "Bing" felt*: "According to the system 'round here, as I understand it, I am allowed so much 'set-up' time to get these panels from the racks, carry them over here to the bench and place them in this jig here, which holds them in position while I inspect them. For convenience sake and also to save time, I sometimes manage to carry two or three over at the same time and inspect them all the same

 This case was prepared as the basis for class discussion rather than to illustrate either effective or ineffective handling of administrative situations.

time. This is a perfectly legal thing to do. We've always been doing it. Mr. Hart, the supervisor has other ideas about it, though; he claims it's cheating the company. He came over to the bench a day or two ago and let me know just how he felt about the matter. Boy, did we go at it! It wasn't so much the fact that he called me down on it, but more the way in which he did it. He's a sarcastic bastard. I've never seen anyone like him. He's not content just to say in a manlike way what's on his mind, but he prefers to do it in a way that makes you want to crawl inside a crack in the floor. What a guy! I don't mind being called down by a supervisor, but I like to be treated like a man, and not humiliated like a schoolteacher does a naughty kid. He's been pullin' this stuff ever since he's been a supervisor. I knew him when he was just one of us, but since he's been promoted he's lost his friendly way and seems to be havin' some difficulty in knowin' how to manage us employees. In fact, I've noticed that he's been more this way with us fellows since he's gotten married. I dunno whether there's any connection there, but I do know he's a changed man over what he used to be like when he was a worker on the bench with us several years ago.

"When he pulled this kind of stuff on me the other day, I got so damn mad I called in the union representative. I knew that the thing I was doing was permitted by the contract, but I was just intent on making some trouble for Mr. Hart, just because he persists in this sarcastic way of handling me. I'm about fed up with the whole damn situation. I'm tryin' every means I can to get myself transferred out of his group. If I don't succeed and I'm forced to stay on here, I'm going to screw him every way I can. He's not gonna pull this kind of kid stuff any longer on me. When the union representative questioned him on the case, he finally had to back down, 'cause according to the contract an employee can use any timesaving method or device in order to speed up the process as long as the quality standards of the job are met. During the discussion with me and the union representative, Mr. Hart charged that it was a dishonest practice and threatened to 'take it up the line' unless the union would curb me on this practice. But this was just an idle threat, 'cause the most he can do is get me transferred out of here, which is actually what I want anyway.

"You see, he knows that I do professional singing on the outside. He hears me singin' here on the job, and he hears the people talkin' about my career in music. I guess he figures I can be so cocky because I have another means of some money. Actually, the employees here enjoy havin' me sing while we work, but he thinks I'm disturbing them and causing them to 'goof off' from their work. It's funny, but for some reason I think he's partial to the three female employees in our group. He's the same with all us guys as he is to me, but with the girls he acts more decent. I don't know what his object is. Occasionally, I leave the job a few minutes early and go down to the washroom to wash up before lunch. Sometimes several others in the group will accompany me, and so Mr. Hart automatically thinks I'm the leader and usually bawls me out for the whole thing.

"So, you can see, I'm a marked man around here. He keeps watchin' me like a hawk. Naturally this makes me very uncomfortable. That's why I'm sure a transfer would be the best thing. I've asked him for it, but he didn't give me any satisfaction at the time. While I remain here I'm gonna keep my nose clean, but whenever I get the chance I'm gonna slip it to him, but good."

*A summarized statement of how Mr. Hart felt*: "Say, I think you should be in on this. My dear little friend 'Bing' is heading himself into a showdown with me. Recently it was brought to my attention by the quality control checker that 'Bing' has been taking double and triple setup time for panels which he is actually inspecting at one time. In effect, that's cheatin', and I've called him down on it several times before. A few days ago it was brought to my attention again, and so this time I really let him have it in no uncertain terms. He's been getting away with this for too long and I'm gonna put an end to it once and for all. I know he didn't like my calling him on it because a few hours later he had the union representative breathin' down my back. But you know what talkin' to those people is like; they'll sometimes defend an employee, even though they think he's takin' advantage of the company. Well, anyway, I let them both know I'll not tolerate the practice any longer, and I let 'Bing' know that if he continues to do this kind of thing, I'm gonna take official action with my boss to have the guy fired or penalized somehow. This kind of thing has to be curbed. Actually, I'm inclined to think the guy's mentally deficient, because talking to him has actually no meaning to him whatsoever. I've tried just about every approach to jar some sense into that guy's head, and I've just about given it up as a bad deal. I just can't seem to make any kind of an impression upon him. It's an unpleasant situation for everyone concerned, but I'm at a loss to know what more I can do about it.

"I don't know what it is about the guy, but I think he's harboring some deep feelings against me. For what, I don't know, 'cause I've tried to handle that bird with kid gloves. But his whole attitude around here on the job is one of indifference, and he certainly isn't a good influence on the rest of my group. Frankly, I think he purposely tries to agitate them against me at times, too. It seems to me he may be suffering from illusions of grandeur, 'cause all he does all day long is sit over there and croon his fool head off. Thinks he's a Frank Sinatra! No kidding! I understand he takes singin' lessons and he's working with some of the local bands in the city. All of which is O.K. by me; but when his outside interests start interfering with his efficiency on the job, then I've gotta start paying closer attention to the situation. For this reason I've been keepin' my eye on that bird and if he steps out of line any more, he and I are gonna part ways.

"I feel quite safe in saying that I've done all I can rightfully be expected to do by way of trying to show him what's expected of him. You know there's an old saying, 'You can't make a purse out of a sow's ear.' The guy is simply unscrupulous. He feels no obligation to do a real day's work. Yet I know the guy can do a good job, because for a long time he did. But in recent months, he's slipped for some reason and his whole attitude on the job has changed. Why, it's even getting to the point now where I think he's inducing other employees to 'goof off' a few minutes before the lunch whistle and go down to the washrooms and clean up on company time. I've called him on it several times, but words just don't seem to make any lasting impression on him. Well, if he keeps it up much longer, he's gonna find himself on the way out. He's asked me for a transfer, so I know he wants to go. But I didn't give him an answer when he asked me, 'cause I was steamin' mad at the time, and I may have told him to go somewhere else.

"I think it would be good for you to talk with him frequently. It'll give him a chance to think the matter through a little more carefully. There may be something that's troubling him in his personal life, although I've made every effort to find out if there was such a thing, and I've been unsuccessful. Maybe you'll have better luck."

# The Man without a Desk

Harlow Reid had been acting general manager for the audio division of the Prescott Equipment Company for over a year when Bill Holloway returned to Prescott after spending several months at a management school. Bill was told to report to Prentiss Seaver, vice-president for electronic and audio products, for a new assignment. When Prentiss told Bill he was to take over as general manager of the audio division, with Harlow Reid reporting to Bill as a product group manager, Bill was somewhat taken back. Harlow Reid had been Bill's boss twenty years ago when Bill started with Prescott Equipment.

Harlow Reid was an excellent engineer who had progressed through the company until, two years ago, a reorganization left him reporting to a younger man. After a year, Harlow stated that he could not get along with his new boss and requested a transfer. At that time the audio division general manager had fallen seriously ill and Harlow was given temporary charge of the division, a step up in responsibility. While he performed adequately in his new job, it was well known that he would eventually be replaced. To complicate matters further, the old general manager recovered sufficiently to act as a part-time consultant to Harlow. The old manager and Prentiss Seaver were close friends and Seaver relied heavily on his friend for counsel on division operations.

Bill Holloway confided in Prentiss Seaver some misgivings about taking the reins from Harlow Reid and becoming the latter's superior. Seaver was sympathetic, expressing his confidence in Holloway and yet offering to ask the executive vice-president to reassign Bill if the latter felt he could not handle the problem. Bill said he thought he could manage in time.

When Bill went to division headquarters, he was welcomed cordially by Harlow Reid and his staff, who seemed intensely busy and preoccupied by the rush of business. When Bill asked to be shown to his office, Harlow apologized, saying that he had just heard the day before that Bill was coming and he had not had time to arrange suitable space for Bill. He pointed out, too, that the office was extremely crowded and space was at a premium. He suggested that Bill make himself at home at the conference table in Harlow's office until something more permanent could be arranged. Harlow made no mention of Bill's former relation to him and Bill made no reference to it, either. Harlow then excused himself to go to a meeting and made plans to talk with Bill later in the day.

In later discussion with Bill, Harlow said that it had not been made clear just when Bill was to take over and, since Bill was relatively unfamiliar with the audio division, it would probably be some time before Bill could assume command. Meanwhile, Harlow offered Bill the use of any one of the staff members to orient Bill to the work of the division. In the course of the discussion, Harlow intimated that the product group management job he was supposed to assume when Bill took charge was really quite unnecessary, given the division's present volume of business.

The next day Bill and Harlow talked again, Harlow reporting that he had discussed Bill's situation with Prentiss Seaver who had agreed that Bill would want to "get read in" in the audio division and there was no hurry in making the switch in command. Harlow again became extremely busy and, although Bill tried to observe and listen in on the business of the day, he felt distinctly excluded. He still had no desk and again made his headquarters at the conference table. He busied himself with accounting records and reports and took a tour through the factory, but he got the distinct impression that he was being treated like a visitor, not the new general manager.

Over the next several days, Bill tried to get Harlow to give him some orientation on current problems. However, while Harlow seemed agreeable enough, he was constantly interrupted, finally saying that there was really no way to get properly oriented than to do the job. He seemed to indicate that he was waiting for Prentiss Seaver to give the word to turn over command but no word was forthcoming. Seaver visited the division several times to discuss specific problems with Reid and the former general manager, upon whom he seemed to rely greatly. When Bill attempted to engage Seaver in a conversation leading to a decision about when Bill would take over, Seaver was jovial and told Bill there was no hurry and Bill should take his time getting his footing.

For several days when the ex-general manager was away from the division, Bill used his office. Upon his return, Bill was reduced again to the conference table. Business was going on as usual. No one took any steps to brief Bill. Everyone seemed in close touch with Harlow, although Bill thought he detected some uneasiness in these working relationships. As he sat at Harlow's conference table, he wondered what he should do next.

# Markham Instrument Company (A)

In May 1959, Roger Finlay, president, and Frank Roberts, executive vice-president, of the Markham Instrument Company were faced with the problem of selecting a new factory superintendent to replace Edward Greene, whom they had asked to retire at the end of the summer. Greene, factory superintendent since 1945, had been offered the opportunity to remain as a production consultant, but had decided to retire fully. Although Markham had no mandatory retirement age, Greene was asked to retire at sixty-six because Finlay and Roberts believed the increasing difficulties between the production and engineering and production and sales departments were the result of Greene's personality and his inability to work with executives in the other divisions.

Finlay explained his thinking as follows:

> Our internal problems are primarily the result of personalities. Some people just irk other people. Ed Greene is most true of this. He's been a thorn in Robbie's [Roberts'] and my side for years. The personality problems are the reason for the difficulty between divisions. Ed is the worst, but there are other examples. He is tough but his output is very high and so is the satisfaction of the men who work under him. My most trusted engineer, who is the most loyal man I know, has been talking to me about this. He asks, 'Why do most of the designs find difficulty in production? Why should we work so hard when they deliberately foul things up?' Of course he is talking about production in general and not

 The fieldwork for these cases was conducted by Professors John A. Seiler and Robert L. Katz, and the cases were written by Mr. Jay W. Lorsch, Research Assistant, under the direction of Professor Seiler. This case was prepared as the basis for class discussion rather than to illustrate either effective or ineffective handling of administrative situations.

> just Ed, but I see it as a reflection on Ed. I know the men below are not as irascible as Ed is.
>
> I think a basic lack of confidence, which must have come from his childhood, has made Ed so vindictive. You know he hadn't been here three months when he insulted me publicly. I was going to fire him right away, but decided to give him another chance. I called him in and I called in the man I had been with and I demanded an apology from Ed. Well, it worked, because we've never had a row since, but maybe I should have fired him. Of course, I never would have kept him if he had been both ineffective and irascible, but he is a good production manager. The way I hope to improve these personality problems is through retirement. Ed and I have an understanding about this. The excuse I am using is to give the youngsters a chance to get ahead, so he will have to step down.

Frank Roberts had a similar view of the situation:

> I think the cause of these difficulties is, at least partly, from personalities and any company has this difficulty. Greene has the know-how. It's just awfully hard to change his disposition. He and I get along all right, but if he had a better disposition it would help a lot. The engineers would welcome his participation during the design stage, but he won't go in there and do it. I've never seen him in the engineering department. He says he knows it all, so why should he go in there, but he could give them a few tips on the problems that would be coming up.

### Production Department and Markham History

Markham was founded as a job shop manufacturer of mechanical measuring instruments for scientific laboratories by Henry Markham in 1917. Markham, a former professor, who was directly involved in the production process, treated his employees more as students and younger members of his family than as employees. For this reason he was known as "Pop" or "Doc" to the early Markhamites. Like "Doc" Markham, the early employees were concerned with technical skill, ingenuity, and quality work, at the same time placing great emphasis on being friendly and warm to fellow Markhamites.

In spite of company growth, in 1959, many of the older employees still clung to these early "Markhamite" values, especially "Pop" Markham's desire to create a family atmosphere. The typical "Markhamite" was also expected to be loyal to the company, as personified by top management, and to subordinate to that loyalty all departmental or personal interests.

While Markham grew during its first decade, the production division maintained its preeminence. In 1924, however, Pop Markham agreed to allow Roger Finlay and Frank Roberts to expand the company's sales activities, which up until this time had consisted of little more than mail order advertising. Thus began a continuing expansion of sales activities, as the market for the company's measuring devices grew and as competition became more active. As the company expanded, its instruments evolved from mechanical to electrical and electronic devices and required more scientific ability for design. Both of these trends caused Production, although expanded in size and technological specialization, to lose its dominant position to Sales and Engineering. To some extent this change in Production's status was offset by the fact that Roger Finlay, when he became president in 1942, allied himself with Production by placing the department directly under his supervision. As a result Production people developed a strong loyalty to Finlay.

Up until the beginning of World War II, Markham relied on its own internally developed and informal production methods. The emphasis continued to be on individual technical skill, ingenuity, and close personal ties. The war, however, brought a rapid expansion in the division's size, and an influx of "victory" workers who did not share the Markham "family spirit." These newcomers included a group of trained and experienced production specialists, who were particularly distressed by Markham's production methods. The new personnel coupled with the extraordinary wartime demands for output created continual crises which verged on chaos. A Production supervisor recalled the war period as follows: "We were hiring warm bodies as fast as we could get them. Piano tuners were running lathes; handbag salesmen were assembling gun mounts. It was a crazy, hectic time. I don't know how we got through it. We just held on as best we could until the war would end and we could get rid of all those people who just didn't belong. It was like trying to control a runaway horse with a toy whip."

In late 1945 Ed Greene, who had joined the company a few months earlier as a methods man, discovered that several executives were involved in malpractices and collusion which were eventually found to be so extensive that they cost the company much of its wartime profit and threatened its solvency. Greene alerted Finlay to this situation, and the result was a reorganization of the top and middle management in the production and controller divisions. Greene was made plant superintendent, although the materials control, purchasing, and inspection units were removed from his jurisdiction. This latter change, done to improve internal control, was interpreted by Greene and the other production supervisors as an attempt "to remove temptation," and in 1959 they still discussed the possibility of regaining their lost jurisdiction.

Greene immediately began filling the vacancies in production division management with production "hot shots" who had training or considerable experience in methods analysis, production scheduling and control, etc. One of these was Pat Mulcahey, who was hired as production planning manager, a position he still occupied in 1959.

These were Pat's early impressions:

> When I got here they had just hired a consulting firm to the tune of $15,000 for a study of production controls, and, as far as I could see,

> things were worse than they had been before. When Greene told Robbie [Roberts] and Finlay I could install a production system that would work I was hired. At first it seemed hopeless. There was no semblance of centralized control. I had to start from scratch and educate people on the basics of scheduling systems, spoilage controls, and so on.

The new production team, which did not share the Markhamite emphasis on friendly personal relationships, labored long and hard to install more systematic production methods and procedures. Formalized procedures were written, production schedules were formalized, the stacks of obsolete parts and scrap were cleaned up, and regular housekeeping regulations were implemented, so that the plant soon appeared neat and trim, and former production bottlenecks were eliminated. In looking back on this period production executives were satisfied that they had saved Markham from technological medievalism and insolvency. All of these changes did result in higher productivity and lower costs, and top management was generally satisfied with the performance of the production staff during the postwar period.

Production personnel, on the other hand, were unhappy at several of management's actions, which they felt failed to reward their efforts. In 1947 a jurisdictional trade was made between Finlay and Roberts, transferring Production from Finlay's responsibility to Roberts'. Production personnel felt that Finlay had symbolically turned his back on them. Again in 1951 they were disappointed when the controller and the sales manager were made vice-presidents and Greene was not.

Production management, however, continued to perform its task efficiently. Between 1947 and 1959 the division expanded from 100 to 600 employees. To adapt to this growth production management continued to place emphasis on systematization and specialization. Productivity remained high, but Finlay and Roberts received an increasing number of reports of disputes between production personnel, especially Greene, and executives in sales and engineering. Management began to feel that these disputes were having an adverse effect on the company's ability to meet the demands of a changing market and technology.

## Production Division in 1959

In 1959 the 600 persons in the production division were involved in planning and scheduling, machining and finishing parts, and assembling the finished product (Figure 1). Production employees were not unionized and were paid on an hourly basis in addition to a liberal profit-sharing program. Many of them also owned Markham stock under the company's stock ownership plan. Markham had a reputation for high employee morale, which was borne out by the low turnover among production workers.

As factory superintendent, Ed Greene reported to Frank Roberts

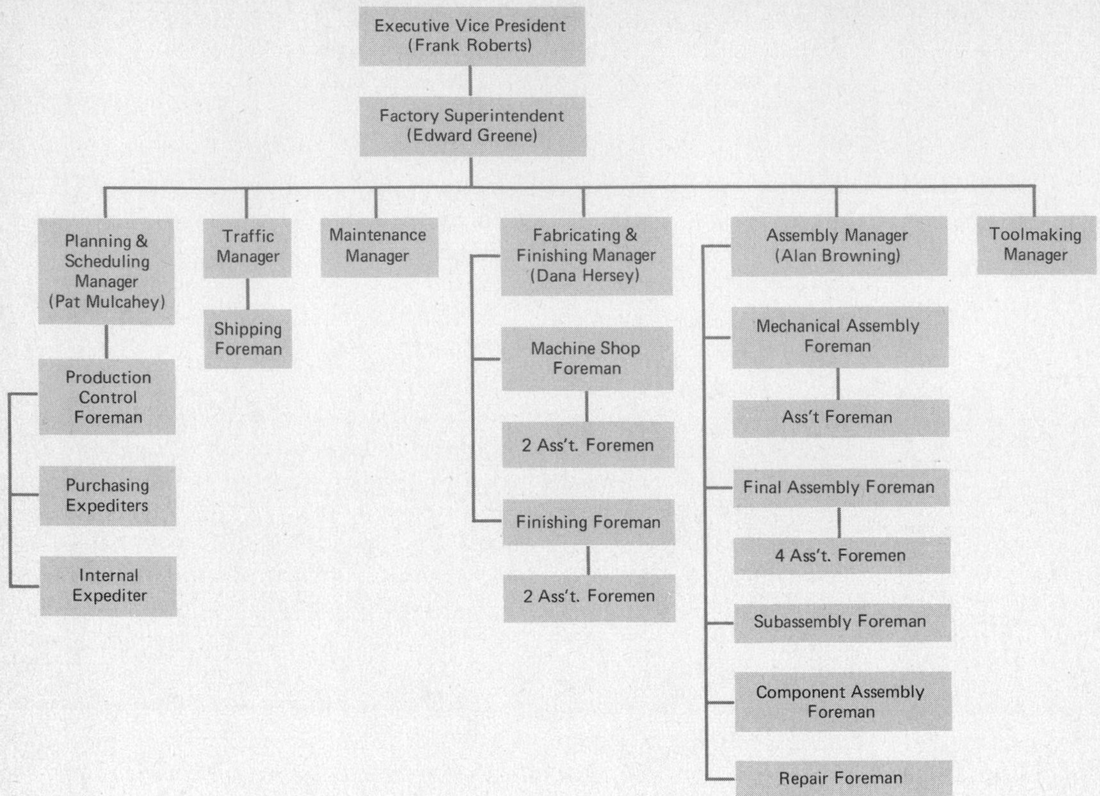


**Figure 1** Organization Chart, Production Division

(Figure 2). In addition to supervising all the activities of the production division, Greene was responsible for building and equipment maintenance, make or buy decisions, and recommendations for purchasing new equipment. One unusual aspect of the production division at Markham was that all methods work was performed by supervisors, rather than by a separate group. Greene and his subordinates, especially Alan Browning, assembly manager, spent considerable time improving and simplifying methods and work flows.

Ed could usually be found in his office with his coat off and his shirtsleeves rolled up, either working on these problems, examining blueprints of new products, or studying ideas for new machinery and equipment. He examined all engineering drawings for consistency and to make certain that they met production capabilities. If they did not, they were returned to Engineering for modification. The principal feature in Ed's office, in addition to the usual desk, chairs, etc., was about forty feet of shelving loaded with a carefree scrambling of blueprints, magazines, pieces of equipment, old memos, and notebooks.

Prior to joining Markham, Greene, a high school graduate, had worked in the production and methods departments of two large manufacturing companies for a total of over twenty years. Shortly before he was asked to retire, Greene described his position at Markham.

> Well, my job is really honest-to-God planning. I plan things out with Dana [fabricating and finishing manager], Pat [planning and scheduling manager], and Al [assembly manager]; we discuss the problems together, talk them over. We feel each other out—you know that is the way I run this place; it is not a one-man outfit. This isn't the first place where I have behaved this way. I've preached it everywhere I've ever worked. My motto is, "No one can do as much as all of us." I certainly get irritated with anyone who is I, I, I, and not we, we, we. I think the ideas have to come up from the people who work with me and they can't just be generated from the top and pushed down.

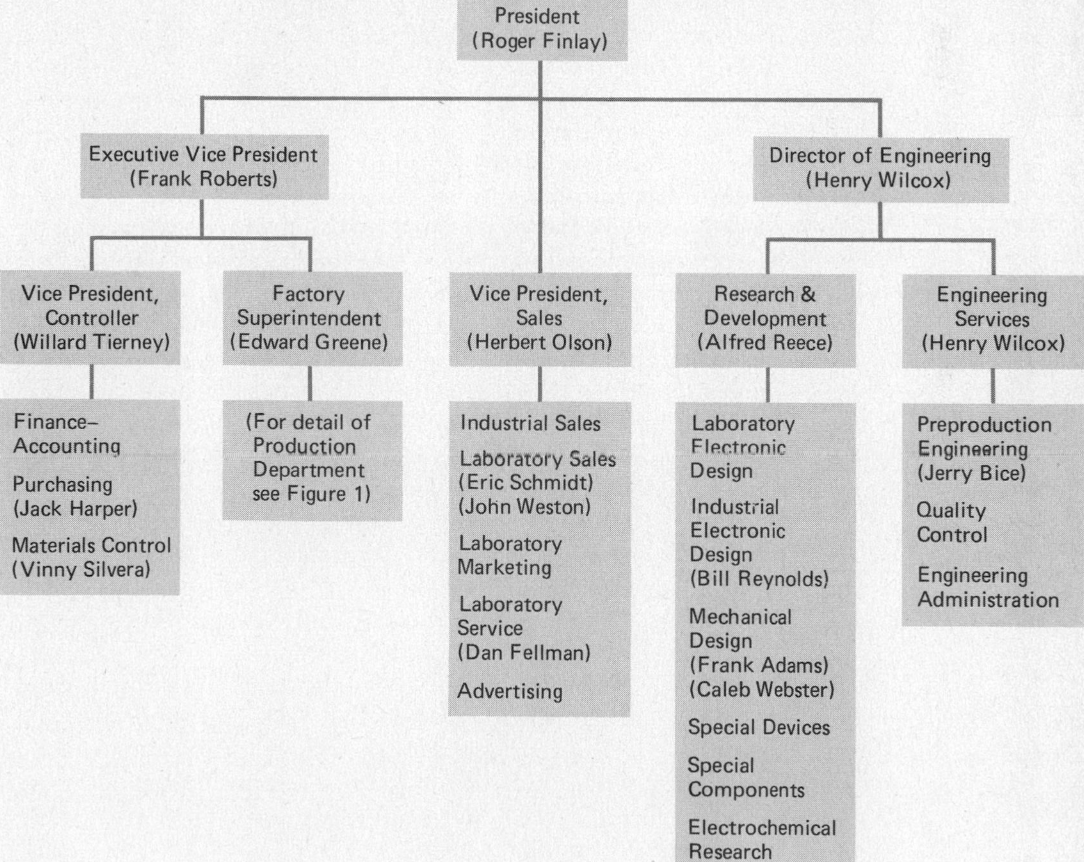


**Figure 2** Organization Chart, 1959

Note: Names have been included for persons mentioned in this case and in Markham Instrument Company (B), which follows.

I know the boys have their troubles, but I believe in developing managers and the way to do it is to let them manage. If anything goes wrong and they need help, they know whom to come to. If they don't they know all hell will break loose. This gives me time to get on with the big things, like planning for new products, or looking for new methods and equipment.

Alan Browning, assembly manager, was a large, heavy-set native of Vermont. He completed high school there, and held jobs in construction and as a garage mechanic before coming to work for Markham in 1944 as a drill press operator. By applying his mechanical aptitude to assembly problems, and developing some unique innovations, he advanced rapidly through several positions and at thirty-nine was the youngest member of the high echelon of production management. Browning, who shared an office with the final assembly foreman, was usually at his desk (which doubled as a workbench) with his sleeves rolled up tinkering with an assembly problem. His office was also frequently the scene of conferences with his foremen and assistant foremen aimed at simplifying assembling methods and solving layout problems. He still spent much of his free time working with his own or other employees' cars because of the enjoyment he got from it.

As assembly manager, Browning supervised about four hundred employees, mostly women, through five foremen. Most of these employees were involved in assembling many small parts into various subassemblies (modules), which were then combined into the finished instrument. Each worker was usually responsible for completing one module, although modules for several different instruments would normally be in production at the same time. Although these units contained electronic components, the assembly operations were mechanical ones, which were constantly being simplified and required little skill. Any problems with electronic components were handled by the engineers, so that production supervisors needed only a limited knowledge of electronics.

Each time a different instrument was introduced or reintroduced into the production flow, or whenever a parts shortage occurred, it was necessary to make some rearrangement of the work assignments and to orient the workers. Outside of these occasional changes, the work was routine and the women worked in a relaxed atmosphere.

The assembly department was physically quite pleasant, because of its cleanliness and the brightly colored decorative panels on the wall. Even though there was a shortage of space and women worked side-by-side at workbenches, there was no appearance of crowding. A low noise level enabled them to converse with each other and still hear the music played over the public address system. Twice each day work was stopped for coffee breaks with most of the workers congregating around various benches.

Alan Browning described his job as assembly manager in this manner:

I coordinate my various foremen on their work loads. I work with planning and scheduling to get the best way of getting the work done. I have quite a bit of contact with the tool room, machine shop, and engineering, particularly the latter on the question of parts which won't function properly and so on. One of my big jobs is product engineering; we do it every day, Ed Greene, my foremen, and I. Then too, I get personnel work; that comes up around deciding what policy we should have. Our personnel policy manual is obsolete, so I have to decide on some problems my foremen bring to me as to policy.

I don't get as much contact with the people on the floor as I used to when I was foreman. They will pretty much follow the organization chart, but I do get some of it if it can't be worked out on the foreman level. My idea is that you use a tack hammer for a tack hammer's job and you use a sledge hammer where a sledge hammer is needed, but you don't use a sledge hammer when all that is needed is a tack hammer.

Dana Hersey, manager of finishing and fabricating, began work at Markham in 1942 by helping to organize the machine shop on the night shift. Hersey, who was fifty, began his career as a machinist's apprentice for a national manufacturing concern after graduating from high school in New Haven. Before joining Markham he had had fifteen years' experience working for several large manufacturers as a machinist and machine shop foreman. Dana, who always wore his suit coat, spent most of his time in his office, which in contrast to the disarray of other production offices was neat and clean. He did, in spite of a pronounced limp, get out into the shop at least twice a day to talk with his foremen and some of the one hundred fifty workers, most of whom called him by his first name.

The fabricating and finishing department converted raw stock and castings into finished parts ready for assembly into the final product. Most of the men in the department were skilled machinists who had begun their careers as machinists' apprentices and who aspired to be toolmakers or model makers. Although they were capable of operating several types of machine tools, each man normally operated one type of machine working on lots of parts which could take from three days to two weeks to complete. The parts completed in Fabricating and Finishing did not go immediately to the assembly department, but instead were returned to the stock room to be reissued to assembly at the request of production scheduling, often two to four months later.

Because of the established methods of operating machine tools, Hersey did not become as involved in methods improvement as the other production managers. Although he and his foremen occasionally worked out improved jigs and tools, most of his time was devoted to scheduling and related problems. He described his job:

I think I can say that my job is really to answer questions in our area. My assistants are perfectly capable of running the department without me, except that I handle all personal relationship problems. I keep that

> work away from my assistants and, of course, I do make the final decisions. I do know more about the schedule and so on, so I am usually the arbiter as far as that goes. I also get involved with Ed Greene on buying new equipment.
>
> I made up my mind as I was growing up and going from one company to another about the things that I would put up with and the things that I wouldn't if I had authority. I have come up with certain ideals that I believe strongly in about the way employees should be handled. For example, I never think I can handle the job alone. When I started out I had to tread on a lot of toes to get people to think my way, but now I play very little part in the activities that go on in the department. I know my presence has some value, but I am not sure what. Things work very smoothly here really. I have no fear that anybody will ask my men what their opinion of me is. I'm sure that it wouldn't be uncomplimentary. You know, I am very reluctant to fire anyone. I always think that perhaps the reason I have to fire a man is really my fault. What we always do is find a spot for them; move them around as many times as it is necessary until they get a job they can do to be happy.

The fourth major executive in the production division was Pat Mulcahey, manager of production planning and scheduling. Pat, a native of New York City, was within one year of getting a bachelor's degree when he was forced for financial reasons to leave a local business college and go to work for a large rubber company. He spent sixteen years with this concern and three years with a major electrical manufacturer involved in production planning. When he joined Markham in 1946, he stepped into his present job and devised a systematic production-scheduling procedure.

Pat, who was always very neatly dressed, spent much of his time conferring with sales and engineering and other production personnel about scheduling problems. Although he did not have as detailed a knowledge of technical production matters as the other production managers, he did have a broad understanding of the entire division and the problems involved in meeting the demands placed on it by other divisions. There were about twenty-five men and women working under him as clerks and expediters maintaining production records and coordinating between production and the other divisions.

Pat described his job as follows:

> It's a combination. One of the biggest assets is a good memory, another is personality—you get work done by putting a little sugar on it. Control man is one job you can't fake your way through. You always have to be looking ahead. There is no such thing as this job being over.
>
> Start at one end, that's Sales; the other Engineering. You have to work with both and be a mediator between all the other departments. You have to make the decisions, get things done, regardless of who is to blame. You have to watch the inventory. That's a tough spot; management says hold it down, Production and Sales want it to be big; and you're in the middle, a glorified fall guy.

> In our production control department, we train our people and then don't stand over their shoulders. They make mistakes, but they know to check with me when they are not sure. They become more confident and relaxed.

As Figure 3 indicates, there was considerable social distance between the Fabricating and Finishing department supervisors and the other supervisors. (see Appendix 1). This distinction was also evident from their behavior and values. The majority of the production managers (excluding those in Fabricating and Finishing) did not engage in nonwork activity together. They devoted most of their efforts to planning the long-range

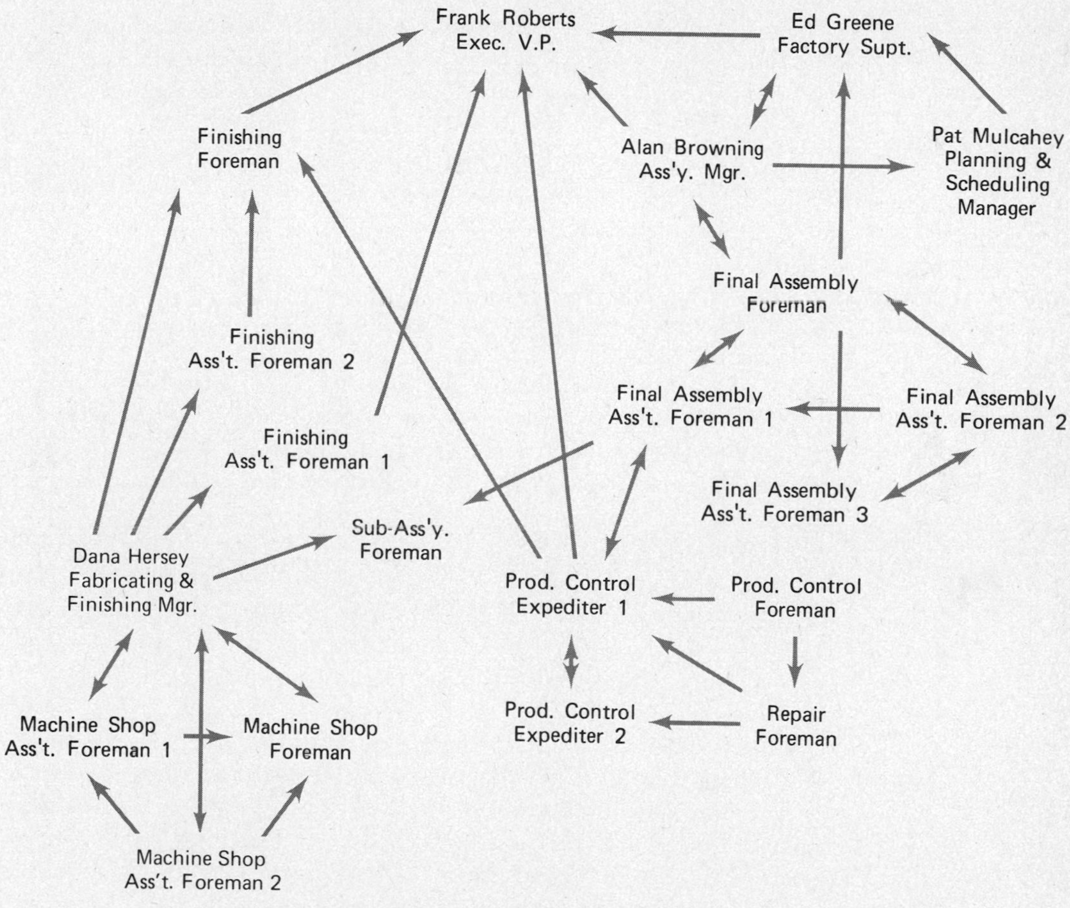


**Figure 3** Sociometric Membership Choices, Production Division

Note: For simplicity, minor members of the department who were either isolates or underchosen have been omitted. These choices are based on responses to interview questions and observations of nonwork interactions.

operations of the division, and valued highly those contributions which were novel and creative. They were always quite willing to "stick their necks out" to criticize ideas which they believed were contrary to the company's interest and in general were willing to take considerable personal risk to promote the good of the company. They wanted to be allowed autonomy to run the division as they saw fit and insisted that formal channels be followed. Finally, they were reluctant to accept newcomers who did not agree with them on these matters.

On the other hand, the group in Fabricating and Finishing did see each other frequently off the job, visiting each others' homes, and summer camps. However, there was general agreement that these contacts should not be allowed to influence their work evaluations.

Though they were interested in the welfare of the company they were equally concerned with the interests of their own unit. They routinized the work of their department in order to improve quality and quantity. At the same time they were intent upon doing their own work well and promptly and agreed that they shouldn't become involved in those matters which did not directly concern them.

Although there was this disparity between the two subgroups, there was agreement about certain other patterns of behavior. Production managers tended to avoid open conflict with each other. They were all willing to go the "extra step" in producing a high-quality product in large volume. For the most part they all believed a man should be able to work his way up the organizational ladder based on his professional expertise. This included a responsibility for bringing along younger members of the division. There was also agreement that each manager should be given jurisdiction in his own particular area of competence. They judged competence based on having skill in routine production operations, and experience in supervision. There was also a prevalent feeling that top management didn't appreciate their contributions in saving the company during the postwar period.

As Pat Mulcahey said, "When the place was near collapse we were the fair-haired boys, but once things got set up they ignored us altogether. The place was practically bankrupt after the war. You'd think when you've got some men who saved the thing they would leave you alone to run your division."

Ed Greene also had strong feelings about it. "Every time I think of what things were like when I came here in 1945 and the company was nearly bankrupt and all these people were stealing the company blind I get mad at the old-timers and how good they think they are. Then I ask myself, 'Where were the old-timers? Where was management? How come they had to wait for somebody like me to come along and straighten things out for them?' "

Figure 4 represents the physical layout of the plant, while Figure 5 indicates the observed interaction and influence patterns among Production executives (see Appendix 1).

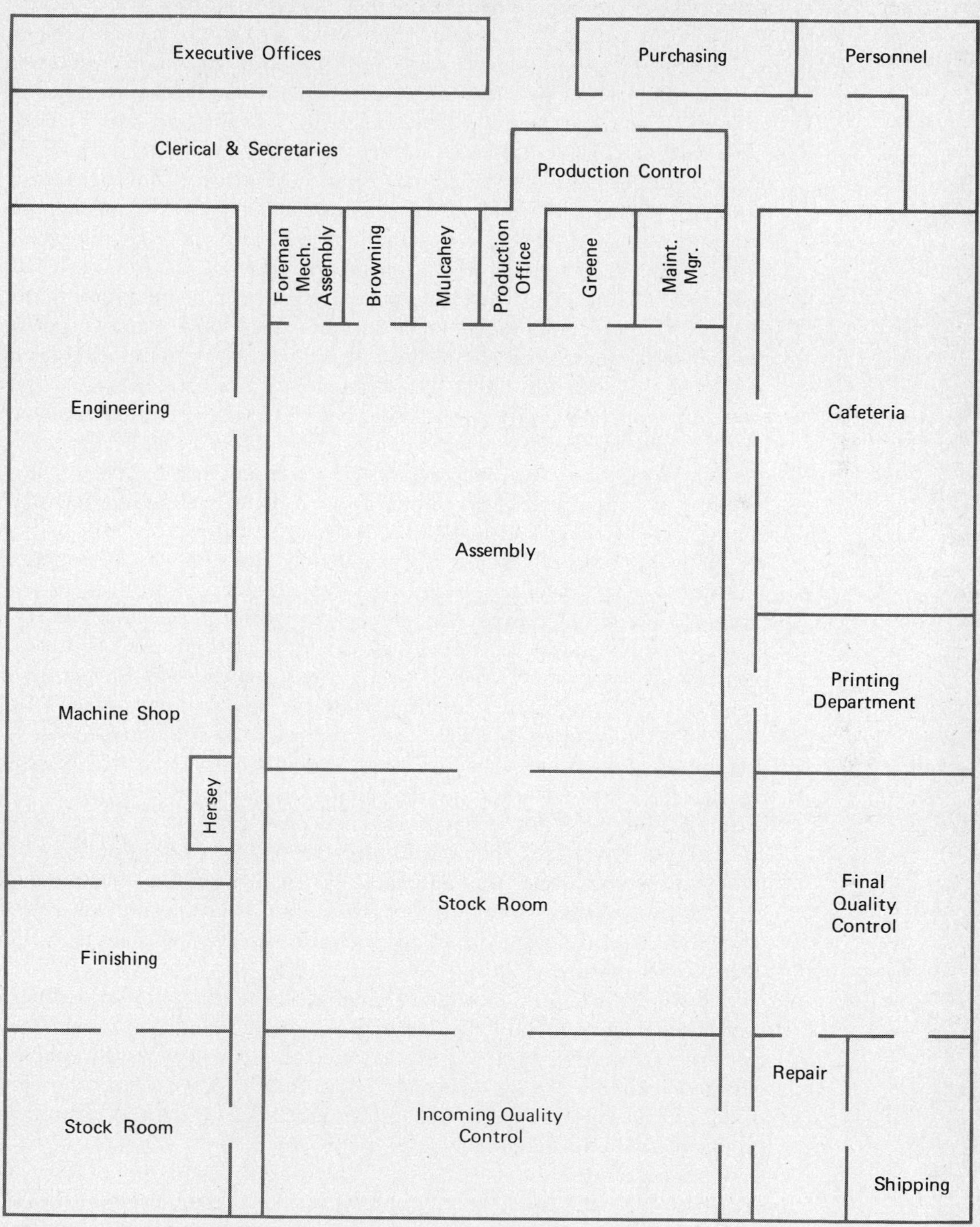


**Figure 4** Layout of Production Division and Adjoining Areas

## Relationship between Production and Other Divisions

The production division was largely dependent upon Sales and Engineering for determining the design, volume, and delivery dates of products. Top management, Sales, and R&D jointly decided on new methods or changes in existing products to meet the constantly changing demand for scientific and industrial measuring devices. The engineering services department developed the designs created by R&D, passing the drawings and specifications on to Production, which theoretically would follow these in producing the instruments. Sales was responsible for making forecasts of demand, from which production schedules were formulated. Beyond these initial contacts there was need for constant coordination between Production and the other two departments about changes in schedules and designs to meet the requirements of each department. Although the engineers were supposed to be able to anticipate manufacturing problems in designing instruments, it was often necessary to make changes after the design was submitted to Production to meet manufacturing requirements. It was around these changes that differences of opinion between Engineering and Production often arose.

The problem of scheduling production was complex. Production manufactured for inventory based on Sales' estimates. The finishing and fabrication department produced about eight months ahead of sales dates, while Assembly produced for sales two months in the future. The complexity of being able to forecast several months ahead was further complicated by management's predisposition toward small inventories because of the financial problems large inventories created and because of space limitations for storing inventory. Forecasting had also been complicated by a rapid increase in the number of products and by the uncertainties about the future demand for new products.

Figure 6 provides an indication of the pattern of relationships between production executives and those in Engineering and Sales which occurred around these problems (see Appendix 1). The production executives primarily involved in these interactions were, at the high level, Ed Greene, and, at the middle level, Pat Mulcahey.

In addition to these two divisions, production personnel worked with several other units, notably purchasing, accounting, and personnel. Contact with Purchasing centered around matters dealing with the quality, delivery, and cost of raw materials. In addition to Purchasing, the controller's division worked with production personnel on matters related to product cost and inventory controls.

The nature of the relationships which existed between production and these other divisions was described by the executives from the divisions involved (see Table 1 for list of executives mentioned in this case).

Ed Greene explained the Production viewpoint:

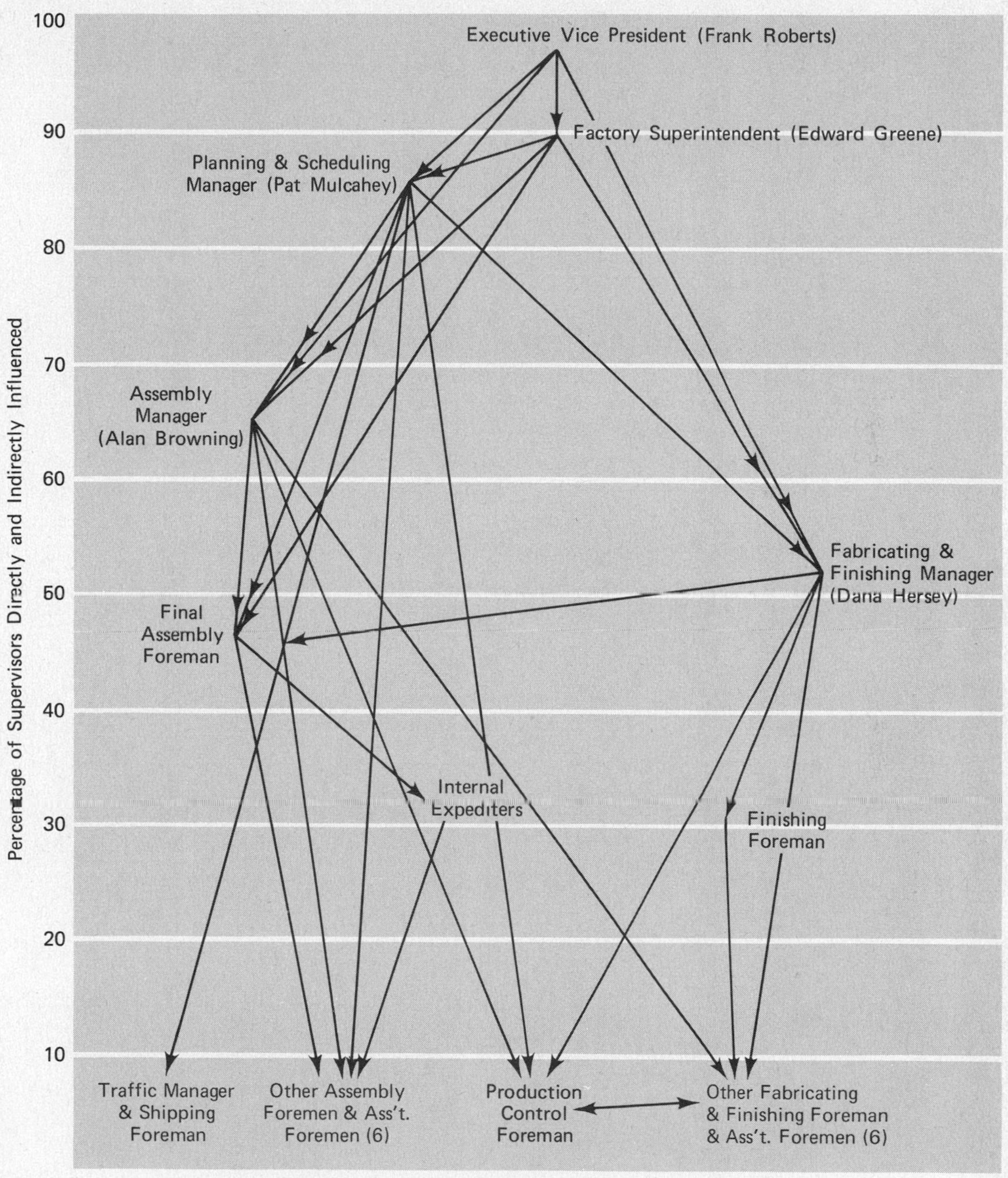


**Figure 5** Observed Interaction and Influence Chart, Production Division

Note: For simplicity, tool room manager, repair foreman, and maintenance foreman have been omitted. Arrows indicate direction on influence.

**Table 1 Executives Named in This Case**

| *Name* | *Present position* | *Age* | *Yrs. in co.* | *Yrs. in present position* | *Prior experience* |
|---|---|---|---|---|---|
| *Top Management* | | | | | |
| Roger Finlay | President | 63 | 34 | 17 | Assistant to President<br>Research Engineer<br>Sales Engineer |
| Frank Roberts | Executive VP | 65 | 37 | 17 | Sales Engineer |
| *Production Dept.* | | | | | |
| Edward Greene | Factory Superintendent | 66 | 14 | 14 | Methods Manager<br>Production Supervisor—Mechanic |
| Alan Browning | Assembly Manager | 39 | 15 | 10 | Drill Press Operator—Machinist |
| Dana Hersey | Fabricating Mgr. | 50 | 17 | 12 | Production Supervisor |
| Pat Mulcahey | Prod. Planning Manager | 48 | 14 | 14 | Production Planning & Scheduling |
| *Sales Department* | | | | | |
| Herb Olson | Vice President, Sales | 49 | 12 | 5 | Sales Manager<br>Sales Engineer |

**Table 1 (continued)**

| *Name* | *Present position* | *Age* | *Yrs. in co.* | *Yrs. in present position* | *Prior experience* |
|---|---|---|---|---|---|
| Eric Schmidt | Laboratory Sales Manager | 43 | 5 | 5 | Branch Manager<br>Sales Engineer |
| Dan Fellman | Order & Pricing Coordinator, Laboratory Sales | 51 | 18 | 13 | Repair Foreman<br>Repairman |
| *Engineering Dept.* | | | | | |
| Frank Adams | Assist. Head Mechanical Eng. | 47 | 7 | 7 | Mechanical & Project Engineer |
| Jerry Bice | Preproduction Engineering Manager | 40 | 10 | 5 | Technician<br>Production Foreman |
| *Controller's Dept.* | | | | | |
| Jack Harper | Purchasing Director | 51 | 7 | 7 | Purchasing<br>General & Cost Acctg. |
| Vincent Silvera | Manager, Materials Control | 58 | 38 | 3 | Building Superintendent<br>Machinist—Production Worker |

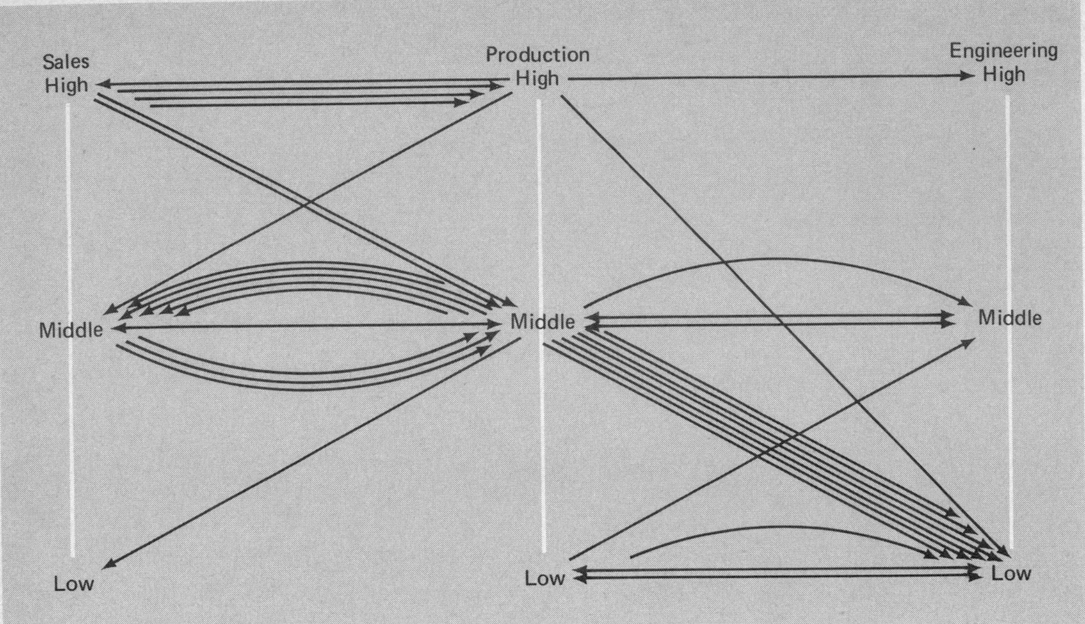


**Figure 6** Observed Interaction-Influence Pairs: Sales, Production, Engineering

Note: Each line represents a pair of individuals in two departments. One individual may be the member of several pairs with individuals in the other departments. Arrows represent direction of influence. *High, middle,* and *low* refer to formal job status as follows:

| | *Sales* | *Production* | *Engineering* |
|---|---|---|---|
| *High* | Sales VP<br>Industrial Sales Mgr.<br>Lab. Sales Mgr. | Executive VP<br>Factory Supt. | Dir. R&D<br>Dir. Engineering Sales |
| *Middle* | Sr. Sales Engineers | Dept. Mgrs. | Dept. Mgrs.<br>Sr. Engineers |
| *Low* | Jr. Sales Engineers<br>Clerks | Foremen<br>Asst. Foremen | Jr. Engineers |

Well, as far as our relationship with the engineer goes, I have a lot of hope for this new kind of system where we sit together and go over the detailed drawings. On this Beta recorder, we had considerable success sitting down with Hal Jones and some of the other engineers. Of course the engineers are always concerned about tolerances. I guess it is true of engineers everywhere, they are tolerance crazy. They want everything down to a millionth of an inch. Yet, I'm the only one in the company who's actually had any experience machining things to a millionth of an inch. You know if you really don't need it, it costs more.

Then we have a problem with their checker [of drawings], who never checks for consistency between drawings. As far as I'm concerned this means that their checker doesn't check. Finally, they have to listen to us because we can always figure out how to get things done. When the engineers say it can't be done our way, then we go right ahead and do it anyway, but we don't tell them how we do it, we just leave them in the dark. Of course they get sore at us for being smarter than they are, but they ought to be as smart as we out here in Production.

We get along pretty well with Sales, but of course there is some friction. They make promises to customers on equipment which hasn't been fully developed and that gets us into a lot of trouble. We insist that they give us a copy of every sales contract, because you really can't rely on them to tell you everything that is important to know. There isn't much you can do about it. You get into a fight and nothing happens. Finlay always backs Sales up even when they are wrong; he always favors them over us.

Eric Schmidt, laboratory sales manager, exemplified the attitude of sales executives:

When I have to go to production, I go to Pat Mulcahey instead of Ed Greene. Ed delegates the practical answers to what I need to know to Pat. However, Ed expects me to clear with him and I have to keep learning that, because it is so much easier to go through Pat. For example, I went to see Pat a few days ago, about the availability of some instruments, and Ed let me know I should have seen him first. I didn't get the instruments I wanted and Ed told me that if I had come up to see him instead of Pat, I'd have gotten them.

There are more tensions and deep-seated problems here than anywhere else in the company. Greene is put in the impossible position of constantly accommodating to changes in schedules and designs. This is a two-way street. We need a better recognition of the responsibility of sales toward the factory.

Dan Fellman, order and pricing coordinator for laboratory sales, expressed this point of view:

The trouble is that nobody will tell Production what to do. When everybody else is told to do something, they do it and quick, but nobody tells Production what to do. Everybody is afraid to make them mad, because if they walked out there would be nobody to replace them. This gives them lots of power, it's like one man running his own business—he's indispensable.

I don't know what it is with Production. I get along well enough with them, but I would just get along better if they were more cooperative. Those guys always say, 'It's my bat, and my ball, and we'll just play the game my way.'

Vince Silvera, supervisor of the materials control unit of the controller's department, described the situation:

> There are some men here who disrupt the applecart, but managem hands are tied. They are good men and they can't be replaced, so have to get along with them. I hate to say it, because it sounds management is weak, but they do have problems here. This is in tion to the superintendent, Greene. He's done a wonderful job an won't take any of his credit away, but his rough manner, his tactics, sh he is no Markhamite. He doesn't belong here. I believe sugar and hon are better than his methods. People cooperate with him because they fe the loss of their jobs and they have no security.

Jack Harper, director of purchasing, which along with the materials control unit had been shifted from the jurisdiction of production to the controller at the time of the crisis in 1945, spoke of his relations with production executives:

> Greene and Mulcahey are two characters of their own type. You could fight with them easily but I try to get along with them. I had it out with Mulcahey five years ago, and we haven't had much trouble since. I can't understand that man; he is smart and knows his job, but he wants to be the big shot. He could be a much bigger shot if he had the knack of getting along with people. You solve the problem by selling your idea to either Greene or Mulcahey and let them sell it back to you as their own idea. Doing it that way—back doors—you avoid arguments.

Frank Adams, who was assistant head of mechanical design, was one of the Engineers who had the most frequent contact with Production. He described his efforts to improve the relationship with Production:

> I am now able to sit down with Greene and his boys. I've been pushing on getting this kind of system for years. I finally got some consultation going with them and the purchasing people. We go over all the drawings item by item. This is the best way I know to get intercompany cooperation and a good exchange of information. What I am talking about is this great grey area between Engineering and Production. It's a very bad situation. I used to be told by Greene to just give them the design and they in Production would figure how to make it. It took me five years to break this down. You see Greene is a very strong character. He's got a good head, but he is a typical executive type—he stands up for his own people but he is tough to deal with.
>
> In the past all the engineering people have been afraid of Greene. Anything Greene said was O.K. This was known by management. But you can't design for production purposes alone, any designer knows that. I was called on the carpet many, many times for bucking Greene and it used to make me plenty sore, but I kept trying and now the bars are beginning to come down. It used to be we weren't allowed to talk to anyone in Production without Greene's permission. This has cleared up some, but we still have a long way to go.

Jerry Bice was another engineer who was involved in getting designs into production. He was responsible for combining mechanical and electronic designs and insuring that they met production requirements.

He was able to carry out this task with only a minimum of personal contact with production personnel, because of his own familiarity with production processes. He provided this opinion about the relationship between the two departments:

> The company is big enough now to require a product engineering department. Production should take their problems to this kind of group and not bother the project engineer. As it goes now, we find out from Production what they want in the way of assembling drawings. We don't do any scheduling of when parts should be assembled, Production does this. I personally want more exact controls on what is required by everybody. I don't want to keep being overridden from above and I don't want a lot of these second-guessers from Sales overriding me. For example, I was working with Pat on ordering some parts for a project, then Sales stepped in and changed their minds on producing it and we had a lot of leftover stock that was never used. Pat and I were really teed off. A product engineering group could decide what is to be made, and eliminate these problems.

Finlay and Roberts, being aware of these sentiments, held informal discussions with the vice-presidents and the director of research and development and reached the decision that Greene should be asked to step down. Herb Olson, sales vice-president, reflected the opinion of the senior executives when he said, "Greene is just too difficult to get along with. He is too rigid, unnecessarily so. All he ever worries about is his own division. Whenever problems arise, it is because we haven't got proper market research or the engineers have made design errors. Production never makes any mistakes, according to him, but I'm not sure he is always right. The way things are, nobody else knows what is going on down there. He is his own little king."

In considering candidates to replace Greene, Finlay and Roberts were aware of the strong company tradition that executive positions be filled from within the company, and they decided not to deviate from it. It therefore appeared that the new superintendent would have to be selected from the top production executives, Alan Browning, Dana Hersey, and Pat Mulcahey. In looking at these candidates Finlay and Roberts were concerned about the nature of the plant superintendent's job and what qualifications a person needed to fill it. They recognized that the production department had operated with high productivity, low costs, low labor turnover, and high morale, and they wanted to maintain this good record while improving relations between Production and the other divisions.

## Appendix 1

The material for this case was derived from a research project. In order to emphasize certain issues, the researchers have interpreted and summarized some of the historical and other data. The data for the various exhibits were gathered in the manner described below:

FIGURE 3. The researchers in gathering this data made their decisions on sociometric choices from answers to the question "Whom do you most like to be with?" and by observation of recurrent nonwork relationships.

FIGURE 5. The researchers developed the chart of interaction-influence relations by protracted observations of the individuals involved in interactions. Each interaction was recorded and a judgment made concerning the balance of influence between the individual involved on the basis of whose points of view tended to be dominant most frequently.

FIGURE. 6. The data for this figure were gathered in the same manner as those in Figure 5, except that the individuals involved in interaction were from different departments.

# Markham Instrument Company (B)

In the spring of 1959 the management of the Markham Instrument Company was confronted with an impasse in pricing the latest addition to its line of scientific measuring instruments. Markham had two basic product groups, instruments for use in scientific laboratories (Laboratory Products) and industrial instruments for use in manufacturing processes (Industrial Products). The present problem centered around the Dual Sensitivity Level Instrument (DSL) which was intended for the more specialized scientific laboratory market.*

## History of Development of the Laboratory Product Line

The line of scientific measuring devices, which the Markham Company introduced in 1924, was adversely affected by the business decline

 The fieldwork for these cases was conducted by Professors John A. Seiler and Robert L. Katz, and the cases were written by Mr. Jay W. Lorsch, Research Assistant, under the direction of Professor Seiler. This case was prepared as the basis for class discussion rather than to illustrate either effective or ineffective handling of administrative situations.

* An organization chart of Markham Instrument Company can be found on page 453.

of the 1930s. In 1935, however, the potential for reversing this trend appeared in the form of a major product innovation. A company salesman discovered a young inventor who had developed an electronically controlled measuring device. Markham officials found from comparative tests with their own instrument that the "shoe box" (a name derived from the new instrument's dramatically reduced size) was superior in performance, and they purchased the rights to develop it.

No one at Markham understood the new machine sufficiently to complete its development. Just at this time, however, Alfred Reece (Markham's director of research in 1959) approached the company seeking part-time employment to support his doctoral studies. When he demonstrated a thorough understanding of vacuum-tube technology, he was immediately hired. Working with Roger Finlay (representing Sales and Engineering) and Caleb Webster (Mechanical Engineering) he redesigned the "shoe box" until it met scientific and commercial standards.

Several competitors had already introduced comparable electronic devices to the scientific market, but they met considerable customer resistance. Dr. Markham pointed out in retrospect, "The change from electrical controls to a vacuum-tube amplifier was a big one for Markham. Scientists and technicians were against it. We had advertised the electrically controlled version as the only reliable standard regulator, and this had become the general consensus among our customers. Radio types on the market had been widely criticized and we needed strong evidence to justify our change in attitude."

Although Markham management believed their "shoe box" to be superior to competitors' electronic machines, they did not rely on this to overcome customer resistance. Instead they appealed to the customers' conservatism, which had been the major factor in blocking acceptance of competitors' machines. The new machine was designed to look and operate as much like the old machine as possible, even to the extent of compromising a few of the advantages of the electronic design. As Finlay said later, "Our customers distrusted the electronic devices which were already on the market, so there was nothing else to do but make ours look and act like the electrical one they were familiar with."

This strategy was successful. Dollar sales volume in 1936 doubled that of 1935, while the number of units actually tripled. Consistent with its past success, however, Markham continued to rely heavily on conscientious customer service to enhance its position in the scientific measurement field. Field sales offices and branch service agencies were set up throughout the country. Company salesmen, continuing their traditional practices, carried customer service to the extremes of repairing competitors' equipment, extending liberal credit and trade-in terms, and offering rapid emergency replacement service.

The next major change in these products occurred in 1946 when the company developed a chemical-sensitive paper, which, among other improvements, eliminated the inconvenient use of recording inks. This development gave Markham a competitive advantage and simultaneously, due to sole control of the paper supply, provided an increase in profit margins. During this period a portable measuring device, long sought by scientific field workers, was also developed. Although these innovations gave Markham a technical lead, the company still depended on customer service for the basic maintenance of its market position.

During the early 1950s competitors began work on a machine that gave the scientist the option of measuring either of two sensitivity levels simply by throwing a switch. In 1957, the competitors' development work reached fruition and these Dual Sensitivity Level (DSL) machines were introduced commercially. Markham was not disturbed by this new feature on competitive instruments, because potential applications for the additional sensitivity level were extremely limited. Furthermore, management's attention was diverted from this development by the addition to its own line of a transistorized portable, 40 percent lighter than any then available. This machine's compactness was expected to attract scientists engaged in field experiments, while its price, flexibility, and reliability were expected to make it also a replacement for most applications of the standard model.

Markham elected to push the transistorized model at the expense of the older, larger instrument, basing its decision on a prediction that customers would prefer the smaller machine. In adopting this strategy management was confident that its ability to take the customers' viewpoint, a company strength over the years, still enabled them to judge what the scientists wanted. Markham had historically been able to lag in technological innovation with little risk, because when their new products were finally introduced, they surpassed competition in meeting customer needs. Markham managers believed that this intimate relationship with the market was as strong as ever.

Company executives were quite pleased when sales of the transistorized model surpassed expectations. They were surprised, however, by two trends. First, sales of the older machine did not decline as had been expected. Second, Markham salesmen began asking for DSL instruments such as competition was offering.

To determine the feasibility of producing a DSL while maintaining the basic strategy of promoting the transistor instrument, exploration was begun on the redesign of the transistorized model. By the end of 1957 a tentative DSL design was developed, although two stubborn technical problems peculiar to a transistorized DSL remained unresolved. Before devoting more time to the solution of these difficulties top management decided to review the entire issue of producing a DSL machine. After some deliberation the DSL was dropped as being a short-lived fad rather than a long-term trend. It was felt that the difficulties in overcoming the remaining technical problems would not be worth the effort in view of the limited applications the customers had for the DSL feature.

During 1958, requests from the field for a DSL became more frequent, and Herb Olson (sales vice-president) began pressing for a reversal of the decision not to produce such a device. He pointed out that salesmen were becoming increasingly embarrassed by customer insistence on DSL features. In view of these increasing requests, Roger Finlay (president) became convinced in the fall of 1958 that Markham should add a DSL to its line, if only to satisfy the "gadget" appeal of such an innovation. Because the older standard machines were continuing to sell, and because the development of a transistorized DSL was still problematical, it was decided to proceed with a DSL redesign of the older machine.

Shortly after making the decision to go ahead with a DSL, Roger Finlay met with Herb Olson (sales vice-president), Alfred "Doc" Reece (director of R&D), Caleb Webster (in charge of mechanical design of the DSL), and Bill Reynolds (responsible for electronic design). Finlay told the three R&D men that though he was anxious to get the new machine into production as quickly as possible, the company's reputation was also involved, so that it would be necessary to do the usual careful job. Reece asked if all the same features that were in the standard would be included in the DSL. Finlay replied that while the DSL was to be patterned after the standard model, he wanted all the latest features included. Herb Olson explained that although the DSL was to be offered at approximately the same price as the standard model, they would still have to maintain the traditional external appearance and features of the DSL. In response to a question from Doc Reece, Olson pointed out that they were not too concerned with the weight of the DSL, because it was not to be a portable. As the meeting ended Reece indicated that they would have to do some careful planning to keep costs down, but he was sure it could be done. Webster and Reynolds agreed, stating that they thought the design could be completed by the end of the year.

In spite of this optimistic appraisal, the members of the research and development department did not greet the decision to redesign the older machine with unrestrained enthusiasm. In the first place, they felt that completing the redesign of the transistorized machine would be ultimately feasible and would be more technically stimulating. Second, they had several other challenging ideas which they believed would place the company in the growth space and missile field. The redesign of the standard machine would cause them to put aside these more exciting projects for several months.

In spite of these reservations, design work went ahead on the DSL. Meanwhile, inquiries and complaints from the field about the delay in offering a DSL continued to come into the home office. Although many sales personnel blamed R&D for the delay, Herb Olson explained the problem differently. "All these problems that the laboratory salesmen are having aren't just the fault of engineering. Top management simply didn't think the DSL was important. Well, this was a mistake. Of course, when this happens the people out in the field get to feeling sore and they come ask us why we don't have the equipment."

Ed Greene expressed a similar view. "Sollie [a formerly influential but now deceased member of R&D] was screaming four years ago for a DSL, but top management could see no need for it. Now all the machines on the market have this feature and we are breaking our necks trying to catch up."

## Pricing Meeting, March 6, 1959

The development work on the DSL machine was completed by the end of 1958, and late in January 1959 Production received the information it needed to establish production methods and estimate costs. By early March, cost estimates had been completed by the production department, and a meeting was arranged for the morning of March 6 to discuss the DSL selling price. The ten executives named in the seating chart, Figure 1, were all present when the meeting started, except Mr. Webster, who arrived later.

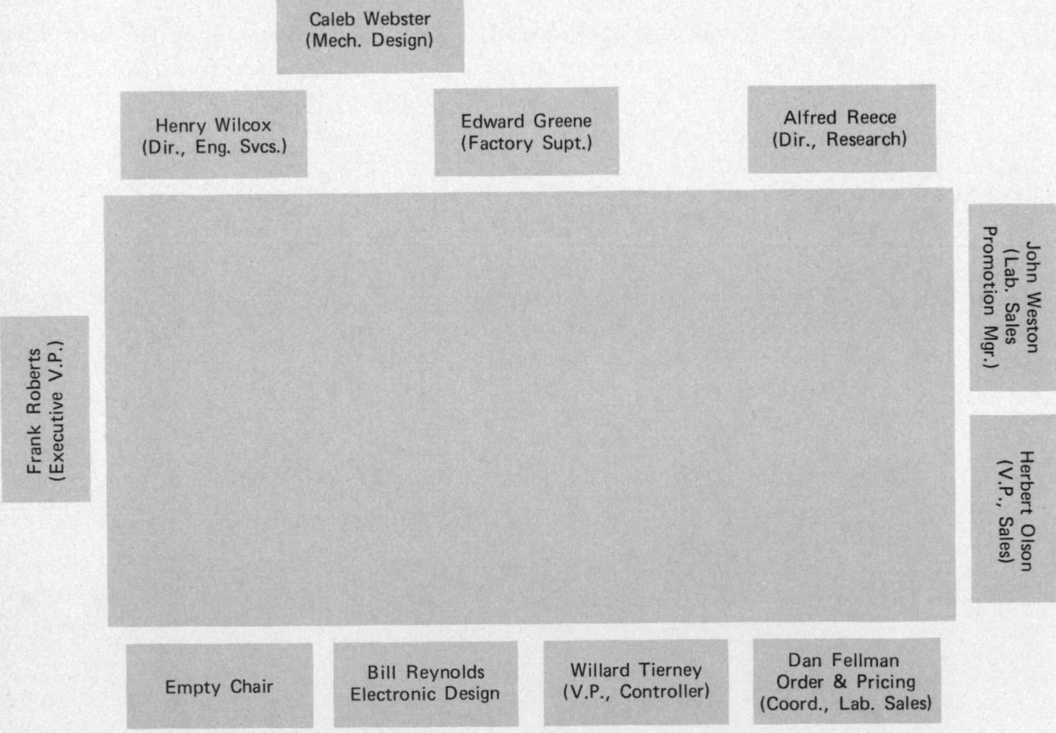


**Figure 1** Seating Arrangement, Pricing Meeting, March 6, 1959

Willard Tierney, acting as chairman, opened the meeting by asking Ed Greene to present his cost estimates. Greene's initial position (which he maintained throughout the meeting) was that the DSL was more expensive than had been expected. He concluded his presentation by saying, "You are going to have to sell this machine for a lot more than you thought. I think these figures are sound. If anything, we have been too loose in our estimates and the figures are too low. We can't lower them any more."

Herb Olson took a different position, maintaining that something had to be done to lower costs so the new machine could be sold at a realistic price. Representative of his remarks is the following statement: "The fact that the figures are sound isn't going to help us meet competition. The way you [others at the meeting] are talking we would have to sell this machine for $1,000. If we did that our volume would go to hell in a hand basket."

Olson was not alone in finding the costs higher than expected. Caleb Webster remarked, "I am really surprised at these estimates. I didn't think they would be that high." Doc Reece also felt the estimates were higher than he had thought they would be. Bill Reynolds, on the other hand, found the estimates realistic as far as the electronic parts were concerned. "I'm not at all surprised at Ed's figures, because I knew what they would be from my design work."

Confronted with this impasse Tierney summarized the situation at the end of the meeting: "I didn't think we could arrive at a decision today, and it doesn't look like we will, so why don't we adjourn and meet again next week? In the meanwhile Ed [Greene], Dan [Fellman], and Doc [Reece] can check over these costs to see if we can reduce them."

As the meeting broke up, Olson remarked, "If we can't do something about these costs, you guys can take it [the DSL] out in the field and give it to the salesmen yourselves. I won't do it."

## Pricing Meeting, March 13, 1959

During the next week Reece, Greene, and Fellman reviewed the cost estimates, and on March 13 a second meeting was held. The participants arranged themselves around the conference table as shown in Figure 2. Willard Tierney again served as chairman and opened the meeting by explaining that Doc Reece, Ed Greene, and Dan Fellman had agreed to certain minor changes in the DSL and that they now felt that it could be produced at $110 more than the standard. (This figure represented a decrease of $35 from the highest figure quoted at the previous meeting.) On this basis Tierney proposed that the DSL be priced at $875, $90 more than the standard. After he completed his remarks there was a full minute of silence, which Caleb Webster interrupted:

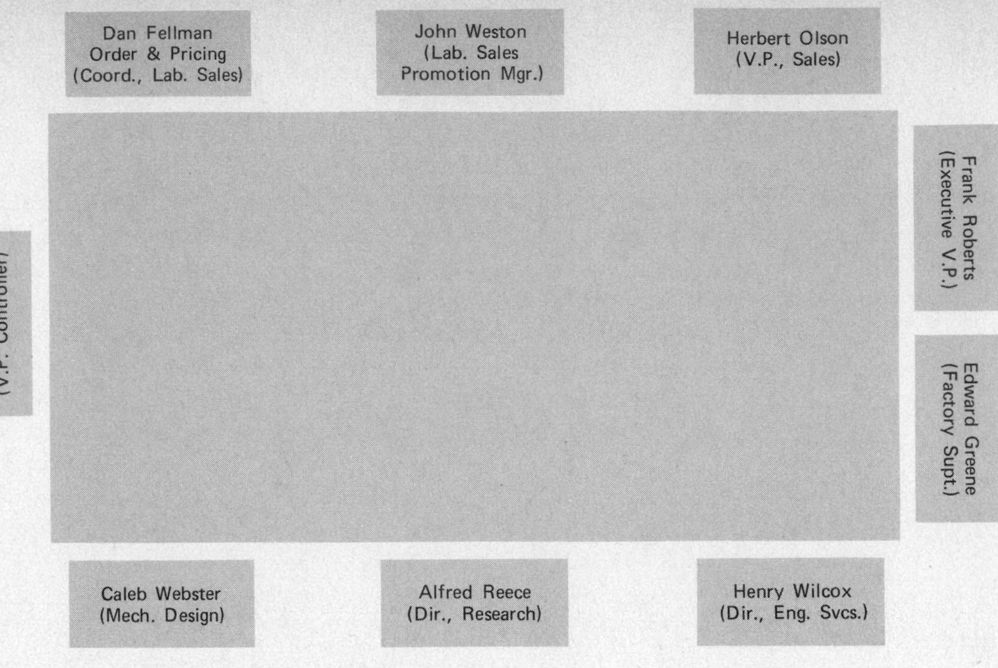


**Figure 2** Seating Arrangement, Pricing Meeting, March 13, 1959

MR. WEBSTER: I still don't understand it. I'd like to know where the big differences lie because I didn't think it would be that much.

MR. TIERNEY: Doc [Reece], can you itemize these so we will all know what they are in detail?

Reece and Greene then spent several minutes explaining the costs of various components, as well as the basis for their estimate of assembly costs. Webster, however, remained unconvinced. Tierney suggested that he and Greene work together to discover if further cost savings were possible. Greene replied:

MR. GREENE: I don't think there are many big changes we can make. It has been cut to the bone already.

MR. OLSON: Well, for example, look at that little trap door. It costs a lot of money.

Several minutes were devoted to the costs of the door which Roger Finlay had suggested to improve appearance and operating access. No one suggested changing the door, and the discussion then centered on the differences between the two models. Doc Reece concluded his explanation of the major causes for the difference:

DR. REECE: Look, there is twice as much shop time for parts on the DSL as there is on the old one. That is a big part of the difference. [*Pauses.*] Sitting around the table here we aren't going to remove Caleb's [Webster] doubts about the reasons for this big difference. He thought it would be less than $25 and it turns out to be between $90 and $120.

The meeting then divided into several conversations. Herb Olson and Frank Roberts talked together with John Weston listening; Doc Reece and Ed Greene carried on a conversation with Henry Wilcox listening. The others waited. After several minutes Roberts addressed the entire group.

MR. ROBERTS: It appears to me that you aren't going to change the spots on the leopard. We have to fix a realistic price. You have all the estimates you can get.

In spite of this statement, discussion about cost differences continued with Reece and Greene furnishing more details to Webster about the costs of subassemblies. Roberts interrupted this discussion.

MR. ROBERTS: We haven't heard from Herb [Olson]. He's probably got a lot to say.

Mr. Olson joked with the group, and then began to discuss the competitive aspects of the situation.

MR. OLSON: We have to consider the selling price of this machine in comparison to competition. Competitors are selling their machines at between $440 and $460 to the dealers, which means they are about $800 at retail. Measuretech [a competitor] retails at $785, and their machine does everything ours does. Of course, they, like everyone else, offer discounts. Whatever we do, we have to be in the ballpark on the initial list price. Perhaps controlling trade-ins will help some.

MR. ROBERTS: What do you think this price should be?

MR. OLSON: Oh, I suppose about $795, that's only $10 above the standard model.

Roberts, Wilcox, and Tierney then discussed the minimum DSL selling price. They agreed that using estimated costs, it would be necessary to price it at $875 to obtain the normal margin. Wilcox proposed that they set a target for cutting costs through redesigning the machine, because he thought cabinet and purchase part costs could be reduced in this manner. Olson supported this proposal, but Tierney disagreed.

Mr. Tierney: I don't know what we can find. Ed [Greene] has made a careful estimate and there is still a $110 difference.

Mr. Roberts: Well, maybe it is just being hopeful, but I think we should do what Henry [Wilcox] suggests.

Dr. Reece: All Ed can control is the shop costs, shop time, and assembly time. I don't think there is much fat in any of these figures.

Mr. Webster: I still can't see why the machine should be that high. The mechanical costs should be much less.

Mr. Greene: Let him [Webster] go somewhere to figure and add them up. Then he'll see. Damned if I'll give him any of my figures.

Mr. Tierney: You know, I still would feel more comfortable pricing it at $875. Otherwise I think we might be cutting it too close.

Mr. Olson: Competition is rough in this line, Will. $850 sounds much better than $875. Even at $850 we will have to work like hell to beat Asprey and some of the others.

Mr. Greene: I'll tell you this, I'd rather build that Asprey machine than ours.

The relative merits of competitors' machines were then discussed. The consensus was that competition was making the same machine, selling it at about $75 less than the $875 figure which had been suggested for the DSL. Olson suggested that Webster be allowed to restudy the design to see if he could reduce the cost so that the DSL could be priced at $850. Tierney replied.

Mr. Tierney: All right, maybe we should call this meeting off, and give Caleb [Webster] a chance to satisfy himself.

Mr. Roberts: That's just a waste of time. Let's get this settled.

Greene and Wilcox also objected to further study and Tierney withdrew his proposal.

Mr. Tierney: You're right. After all we have never priced any instrument with as much information as we have on this one.

Mr. Olson: That really doesn't make any difference. We still have to get the price down where we can sell it.

Tierney then continued the discussion of competitors' machines and prices. There was general agreement that the Simpson Company had, at $785, the best DSL on the market. Olson expressed particular concern about the advantage competitors had because of the light weight of their machines.

MR. OLSON: Look at these competitors' weights. Simpson's only weighs twenty pounds, while ours will be thirty-four. Even Asprey's is ten pounds less than ours. This is an important selling point and we can't ignore it.

DR. REECE: Damn it, don't start talking weights at this point. We were told from the start that they weren't important.

MR. TIERNEY: Herb [Olson], what do you think the end user pays for an Asprey?

MR. OLSON: Anywhere from $650 up. It depends entirely upon the deal and the trade-in. I was just wondering, though, if maybe we haven't got too many features on this machine. After all it is supposed to be sold as a general purpose machine.

DR. REECE: We designed it according to what Sales wanted. We have to go by what you fellows need. The trouble is that around here everybody wants eveything with frosting on it.

MR. OLSON: Right, and then we price ourselves out of the market.

MR. TIERNEY: It seems to me that we had better change our whole official attitude if this is the way our market and our competition are acting.

MR. GREENE: O.K. Then we ought to start with an estimate of the market and the price and then design within that.

MR. OLSON: That's exactly what got us into this mess. The district managers are really going to be unhappy about this one. Finlay told them the DSL would be available at $800, and now you are talking about a minimum of $50 or $75 more than this. They aren't going to be happy about pushing this one. I still would like to see Caleb [Webster] take another crack at cutting the cost.

MR. ROBERTS: Doc, can you and the mechanic [Webster] take another shot at redesign after we get it into production? Maybe we can reduce costs then.

MR. TIERNEY: I think that is wishful thinking. We have to resolve this on the basis of the information we have.

# Maynard Aircraft

## Part I

The instrumentation department of Maynard Aircraft played an important role in the development of new aircraft. The department at Plant 7 consisted of ten engineers and eighty technicians who worked on individual airplanes. Thus, a particular aircraft might have from one to four instrumentation engineers working on it and from one to six technicians who carried out orders issued by the engineers.

Before a job could be started, the engineers had to submit a written work order to the instrumentation foreman, who approved it and passed it on to the lead man. The lead man, in turn, assigned the work to one or more of the technicians who happened to be available from the eighty-man group and gave each of these technicians a written order with the technician's name on it. At the end of the job an inspector examined the work and put his approval stamp on the back of the work order. The order was then returned to the foreman, and was stamped and logged by the foreman in a workbook. The engineers officially had no direct control over the technicians, but because their written work orders were seldom blocked by the instrumentation foreman, the engineer had little trouble obtaining his work requests.

The nature of the work was such that skill and knowledge in working with electrical parts was definitely desirable. Most technicians had previously been in electronics companies as assembly workers, so that operations such as soldering wires and plugs presented no difficulty for them. However, more often than not, the particular job to be done involved working inside the airplane itself, which was full of test equipment and very limited in free space. Because several crews of men were working on the same plane, often it was necessary to work in a cramped, poorly lit section of the plane where other workers were engaged in a job. Thus, what would ordinarily be an easy and routine operation might take much longer than normal to carry out due to the inaccessibility of the location or the fact that other men were in the technician's way. Another drawback of the technician's job was the unevenness of the work flow.

Often one man would be given a number of work orders which he could not possibly complete in the specified time. When this happened the engineers had to wait for the work to be done. At other times, however, a technician might go for one or two days without receiving a work order and consequently have nothing to do. This would happen when most of the planes were out on test flights, or when the lead man was particularly concerned with some other job and had not had the time to make his usual rounds.

The technicians were paid on an hourly basis, and periodically were given small raises, so that wages were determined on the basis of seniority. The starting rates were about $2.25 per hour, while the highest rate paid to a technician was $3.50. The majority of technicians worked the eight-hour normal day shift, but several men would always be assigned to work on the night shift. Every two months this assignment would be shifted to others in the department so that the benefits or inconvenience of this night work were equally distributed to all of the technicians. (Some men enjoyed "working nights" as there were very few other workers around and no instrumentation foremen or lead men.)

During the day, the men could take smoking breaks outside in the halls whenever they wished and were, for the most part, loosely supervised. The lead man was a very easygoing person who walked from plane to plane handing out new work orders and collecting those which had been stamped by the inspector. He always spent extra time chatting with the men and was well liked by everyone.

## Prediction Worksheet

From what I know of the operations of the instrumentation department described in Part I, I would predict that:

1. Productivity of the technicians in terms of (a) quantity and (b) quality would be (high) (standard) (below standard). (Note the reasons for your prediction.)

2. Technicians would be (highly) (moderately) (dis-) satisfied with their job. (Explain why.)

3. Social interaction between technicians would be (high) (medium) (low) (a) during working hours, (b) outside the plant. (Explain why.)

4. Relations between technicians and engineers would be (cordial) (neutral) (strained). (Explain why.)

## Part II

Many of the technicians saw much of each other off the job, either through company-sponsored sports such as bowling or through activities of their own arranging. A typical technician also spent considerable time talking to other technicians during the day. He might go into the halls between the hangars and enter into a group conversation with four or five other technicians (this was especially prevalent during coffee breaks) or might seek out a friend working on another plane and coax him into taking a "break." During lunch periods the technicians usually ate in their cars, either by themselves or in pairs. Those who had tool benches in the hangar ate there, but there was little communication on the whole, at this time. The men either ate, read their newspapers, or attempted to sleep.

The engineers rarely spent any free time with the technicians, and had their own office where they remained whenever they were not working on a plane.

The technicians felt that the engineers were no smarter than they, and that much of the work they assigned was needless and poorly thought out. They were reluctant to do a job quickly and efficiently since they felt that they would only be presented with harder work that much faster. They employed many stalling techniques, such as taking a long "break" while they were supposed to be procuring a part from the stockroom, or going to borrow a tool which they claimed not to own.

The engineers, in an effort to expedite matters, would stand close by during a particular job, hoping to speed up the work, but rarely if at all did this achieve their purpose.

The friction between the engineers and technicians had, over the last few years, steadily increased to the point where work assigned by the engineers to the technicians rarely was completed in a manner satisfactory to the engineers, either in terms of time spent on the job or the quality of the work performed. The technicians felt that their opinion on matters relating to jobs at hand was rarely given any weight. The work had lost all interest for them and every day was only another eight hours.

The foreman of the instrumentation department was somewhat sympathetic to the problems of his men but felt relatively powerless, as far as changing the orders given to him by the engineers.

The plant superintendent had recently become very concerned with the situation existing in the instrumentation department as it was greatly hampering flight-testing operations which were crucial in the development of new aircraft. He felt immediate action had to be taken to clear up this situation.

On the form below, check the degree of accuracy of your predictions from Part I of the case and note the major reasons for accuracy or inaccuracy.

| Questior | Degree of Accuracy* | | | Reasons |
|---|---|---|---|---|
| | A | P | I | |
| 1. (a) | | | | |
| (b) | | | | |
| | | | | |
| 3. (a) | | | | |
| (b) | | | | |
| | | | | |

* A=accurate; P=partly accurate; I=inaccurate.

# Midville Beverage Bottling Company (A)

Jim Jackson is manager of the Midville Beverage Bottling Company. The city of Midville is a growing and progessive community of almost 225,000 people. Besides Midville, this soft drink bottling company owns and operates three small branch plants in Riverdale, Elmgrove and Lake City. The combined population of the entire territory is close to 350,000. Last year the company sold nearly 2.5 million cases of all products.

The manager, Jim Jackson, started out before World War II as a route salesman; worked his way up through the ranks; and has been general manager now for eight years. Midville is a family-owned business.

Mr. Smith was owner-manager when Jim joined the company in 1937. When Mr. Smith passed on in 1959, the widow and Dr. Smith, the only son, promoted Jim from sales manager to general manager.

Soon after he took over, Jackson appointed Harry Jones as general sales manager. Harry started on the routes and worked his way up. Harry is well-liked in the organization and by the trade. Under Harry's direction, sales have increased every year; so has the company's share of market. In fact, last year was by far the best in the plant's fifty-seven-year history. Sales of the plant's major soft drink were up 14 percent and the rapid growth of the new products and one-way packages added extra volume on top of that.

Even so, Jim is worried. He's due to retire in six years and has given a lot of thought to the problem of who will be his successor. The general sales manager would normally be the logical man; but Jim is not at all sure that Harry is capable of assuming top management responsibilities. As Jim put it to Mrs. Smith, "There isn't a better sales manager in the business. But as general manager, I just don't think Harry would be successful. He's very good at handling people, but when it comes to budgets and other administrative jobs, Harry's lost." Mrs. Smith asked Jim what he planned to do.

# Midville Beverage Bottling Plant (B)

Jim's first step was to hire a young man, Bill Shelby, as his staff assistant. Bill had a good background in marketing consumer products and was well-known by supermarket operators and buyers throughout the entire area. Bill had graduated from the state university six years before. He was very personable in manner and dress, and had all the latent attributes of an up-to-date, fast-thinking, forward-minded manager. For the first time, the company developed sales forecasts, case sales, budgets, operating budgets, and so on. Organization charts were instituted and a continuing educational program was started throughout the entire organization.

As Jim Jackson said, however, "It was all great, but I guess it was too much, too soon. This, I presume, was faulty timing on my part. But I felt we had so much to do and so little time to do it. Small but telling noncompliance began to show up in every department. The 'old-timers' just wouldn't accept Bill. One of the route supervisors, for example, told Harry to keep that 'smartaleck out of my territory before he gets it all messed up. If he thinks he can change everything around after I've had it running smoothly for fifteen years, he's got another think coming.' The older supervisors especially seemed to resent the 'young upstart.' So finally I figured it would be best to find Bill another job before the fire burst into flames."

Shortly before Bill Shelby left, Jim hired another staff assistant, Frank Farnsworth. Frank, too, was well-educated and, what was more important to Jim, had experience in the soft drink business.

"Maybe the reason the others wouldn't accept Bill Shelby was because he hadn't grown up in the business." said Jim to Mrs. Smith. "Frank Farnsworth, on the other hand, has worked for a progressive competitive bottling plant in another section of the country and has risen to assistant sales manager. He should work out just fine."

Frank Farnsworth proved to be an "eager beaver" and would work with his hands and heart, as well as his head. Sales contests were initiated and advertising beefed up for the first time in years. New products and new packages were added to the line. Beverage department studies were undertaken and the company's products received more shelf space, greater dominance, and increased sales in almost all larger supermarkets and other food stores as a result.

But as Jim reported to Mrs. Smith several months later, "While sales are up and business is humming, these new activities seem to focus attention on our previous inadequacies and opposition to Frank Farnsworth has begun to grow just as it did against Bill Shelby."

"I don't quite understand," said Mrs. Smith. "Well," said Jim, "just the other day one of our best route managers went over Harry's head to tell me that, 'These new fangled ideas about rearranging beverage departments just won't work. My stores are different. Tell that guy to keep out of my territory.' "

What are you going to do now?" asked Mrs. Smith. "If you let Frank Farnsworth go, you'll be right back where you started." Jim agreed. But the resistance and antagonism to Frank Farnsworth continued to grow. Jim finally found him a good job in another soft drink bottling plant in the part of the country from which he had come originally.

After these unfortunate experiences with the first two young men, Jim hired a third "trainee." But, as Jim said, "He was the most over-recommended man I ever knew. So when after a few months he did not work out, I let him find another job.

"We still need a bright young man not steeped in the one-product, one-package, one-price philosophy, well-grounded in the general refreshment business, who will look *forward* to developing our sales, profits, and people. But, I have great doubts that the old-timers will accept anyone of this caliber. They seem to be resisting any change for the better and regard all outsiders as a threat. Frankly, I just don't know what steps to take next."

# Midville Beverage Bottling Plant (C)

After the third young "trainee" left, Jim talked with several other bottlers and found many with somewhat similar problems. Briefly, he found that most of today's plant managers had come up through the ranks; from route salesman to route manager to plant manager. And, like Jim, many plant managers were concerned about the whole problem of management succession.

The first bottler Jim talked to pointed out that it's almost impossible to find talented, well-educated young men today who are willing to start at the bottom and work up. Also, starting salaries for college men are too high by comparison with current wage structures in most bottling plants.

The second plant manager with whom Jim talked felt that present middle management in most bottling plants, his own included, are generally not qualified by education to take over top jobs. Yet, if a top man is brought in from outside, the rest of the organization rebels. They resent the outsider, the man who "leap-frogs" over them. What's more, morale of the route managers suffers when outsiders are brought in over them. They see no future for themselves.

The third bottler told Jim that he had hired a sales manager away from a used-car dealer to take over as assistant sales manager. One of his route managers had asked, "Why wasn't I considered for the job?" This plant manager had offered various training courses and night school programs to his route managers but none of them had shown much aptitude or interest. He therefore, felt that he made the only move possible. "You can't expect cream to rise to the top if all you pour in is skim milk. So I just felt obliged to bring in a top-flight man from the outside," he told Jim.

The fourth bottler asked Jim why Harry couldn't be groomed to take over. Jim answered by saying, "As I told Mrs. Smith, Harry Jones is the best sales manager in the business. His record proves that. But he's never had much experience with fiscal matters, production schedules, taxes, purchasing and all the hundred and one other administrative jobs required of a general manager."

"Has Harry ever shown an interest in general management? Have you ever given him the opportunity to learn?" this bottler asked. "Well, some maybe," replied Jim. "But I figure a man ought to stick to what he does best. And for Harry, that's selling, sales promotion, advertising, sales training and trade relations; not fiscal and administrative activities."

The last plant manager Jim talked to said, "Jim, as you know, we don't want to 'raid' or 'pirate' from other bottlers. There has always been an unwritten agreement among us bottlers not to hire top men away from another plant. But maybe the time has come when we ought to join together in some way to find an answer to this problem." Jim agreed but didn't quite know how this might be done.

Jim Jackson thought over carefully what his fellow bottlers had said. "It still boils down to the fact that there's no one in my plant capable of taking over," he reflected. "Suppose I had a bad accident or became seriously ill—who'd run Midville? Hindsight says I should have been developing my replacement over the last five or ten years. But I haven't. So, what do I do next?"

# The Onondaga Metals Company

## The Hiring of William Taylor

In an attempt to secure employment since a recent layoff, William Taylor made an appointment to visit one of his father's friends, Mr. Norman Schermerhorn, president of Copper Works Company, Inc. During the course of the interview between the two, the president—who was most cordial—told Taylor that at present there were no openings in the company for men with his particular talents; rather, he was looking for individuals with engineering backgrounds who would be familiar with the technical work performed by the company.

As Taylor was about to leave Schermerhorn's office, the latter asked him if he knew Mr. Ralph Lea, president of Onondaga Metals. In response to Taylor's negative reply, the president asked his secretary to get

 This case was prepared as the basis for class discussion rather than to illustrate either effective or ineffective handling of administrative situations.

Lea on the telephone for him. There followed a few minutes of conversation between the two presidents, after which Taylor was directed to the Onondaga plant for an immediate interview with Lea.

During the ensuing meeting, Taylor was questioned quite thoroughly concerning his educational and business backgrounds. He was twenty-six years old and unmarried. He had had no experience in manufacturing, but had been fully employed as an accountant (except for the past few weeks) during the four years since graduation from college, where his major had been industrial management. He had worked his way through his last two years of college. He was now unemployed because the company in which he had been working had been in deep financial difficulty which brought about a large number of layoffs; in fact, the firm was now in bankruptcy.

His grades in college and high school had been high enough to bring him a number of honors. During these eight years of schooling he had been an active member in two honorary scholastic societies and a fraternity, and had been engaged in such activities as debating, drama, music, social and church affairs, and Boy Scouts; currently, his major interest lay in church affairs. He had come from a middle-class family, and his father had been well known in certain business circles. Lea's impression of Taylor was that this was a young man who was personable, intelligent, able to get along with people, and with enough ego and drive to make a name for himself.

Lea paused in his questioning, studied Taylor in silence for a few moments, and then turned to gaze out the window.

LEA [*turning back to Taylor*]: It's peculiar that you should happen to come along at this time . . . [*speaking hesitantly and carefully*] . . . because I have been looking for someone to assist me in. . . . Well, tell me Taylor, if you were a manufacturer who produced an assembled product, and one of the parts of that assembly was expendable in the sense that it necessarily and unavoidably wore out quickly, and if the customer knew that this costly part had to be replaced occasionally, what would you do if you realized that despite the top quality of your product—a fact recognized by customers—sales of that assembled product were declining because of the cost and inconvenience to them of that expendable part?

TAYLOR [*without hesitation*]: What is the profit on the product?

LEA [*giving Taylor a sharp glance*]: High. We are leaders in the field.

TAYLOR: If as you say, the product is of recognizable top quality, the part wears unavoidably, and the profit is high, I would reduce the replacement cost of the part, even to the extent of taking a loss on it, and absorb the loss.

LEA: Why would you do that?

TAYLOR: Mostly out of fear of competition cutting into my market.

LEA [*after a prolonged visual examination of Taylor*]: All right. This is what I have in mind. I have the need here for a man who can study this type of problem, and many related ones, and come up with the correct answer. The general manager on whom I depend for this type of thing now has too much to do, particularly in purchasing. The man for this job I have in mind should be one who is willing to stick and grow with the business and who could plan on taking over some of the manager's functions, perhaps in about a year's time. He would have to be a man upon whom I could depend implicitly. Would you be interested in such work, Taylor?

TAYLOR: Definitely, yes!

LEA [*shaking his head as if he were not quite sure he was doing the right thing*]: Good. You're hired. My initial directions are these. First, that you say nothing to the general manager about taking over any of his duties; if he should ask you about your job, tell him that you are slated for the assistant production control manager's post. Second, I want you to learn our manner of production by observing the men on their jobs: I want you to watch them carefully so as to learn everything they do, so that you will become thoroughly familiar with operations. Should they ask what your job is, tell them the same thing you'd tell the general manager.

I would suggest in this matter that you be careful with the operators because of an unfortunate incident caused last year by an efficiency expert I hired from a New York firm. Now, as to your salary. I'm willing to pay you $125 a week. Is this satisfactory? Good, then report to me on Monday morning at 8:30.

## Company Organization

An abbreviated organization chart is shown in Figure 1. Ralph Lea, president and secretary, and majority stockholder of Onondaga, was approximately fifty years old. His company, which he had bought into a number of years before, was small in that it employed only 150 people at the plant and 25 in its sales office in New York City. The company was nonunionized, although the AFL-CIO had previously and recently made attempts to organize the workers. Mr. Lea was proud of the fact that his people had rejected unionization, but he was fearful that this might come about in the long run because the company, being small, could not afford to pay wages equal to those of larger concerns.

Reporting to Lea was a treasurer-auditor who had charge of corpo-

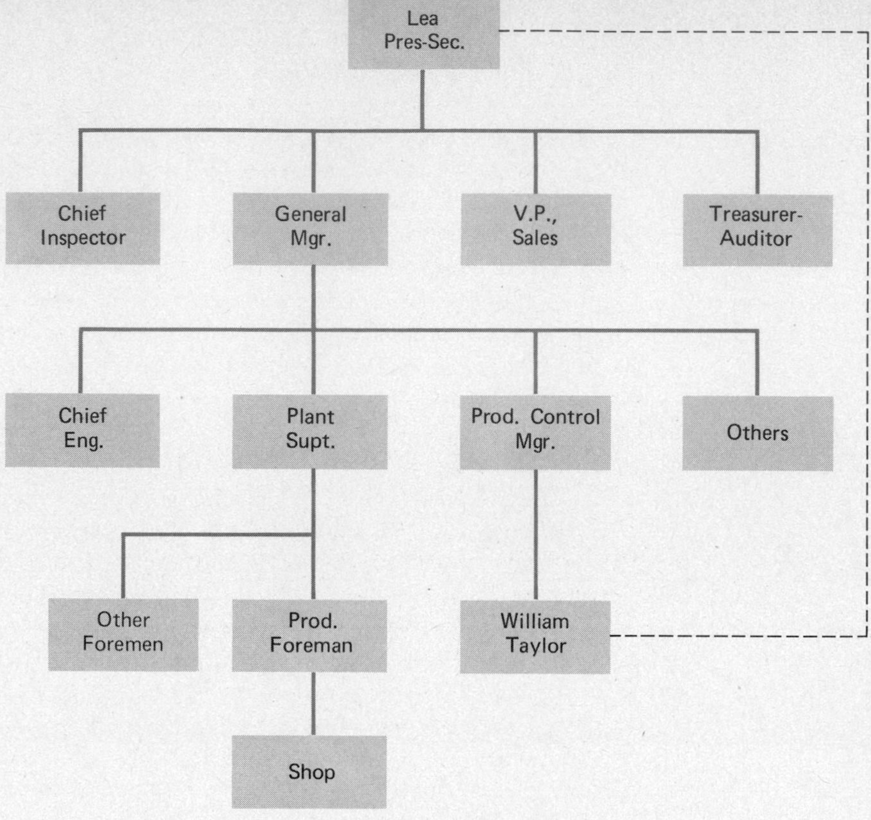


**Figure 1** Abbreviated Organization Chart

ration as well as accounting activities, a vice-president and minority stockholder who was in charge of sales, a general manager who also performed the purchasing function, and a chief inspector who had been elevated in this hierarchy because of Lea's desire to stress quality control. Reporting to the general manager were the plant superintendent, a chief engineer, and a production-control manager, among others. The superintendent's jurisdiction extended over a number of foremen, including the production foreman. The latter had direct charge of the shop.

At the time, 1959, the company was experiencing great demand for its products and was working at full capacity on a one-shift basis. Its operations were somewhat hand-to-mouth because of a lack of storage space for raw materials in the warehouse. Often, shipments to customers went out late owing to the raw material not having arrived in time for processing, or because of production or scheduling difficulties in the shop. A new warehouse was completed about six months after Taylor's being hired.

## Taylor's First Three Months

William Taylor reported to Mr. Lea on the following Monday morning, whereupon the latter requested him to repeat the directions he had received previously. Satisfied, Lea then called in the production-control manager, Hank Drake, who had been briefed to the effect that he was to have a man to help him in his work, but a fellow who was unfamiliar with manufacturing and who would have to spend several months studying plant operations. Hank was asked to introduce Taylor to the various department heads and then to let him be on his own. The desk to which Bill Taylor was assigned was butt-to-butt with Hank's, so arranged that they faced each other; these were located just about twenty feet from Mr. Lea's office.

Thereafter, for the first three months, Bill followed the president's instructions by occupying himself solely with studying the company's mode of operation. He followed the various products from their receipt as raw materials, into process, and through to their shipment as finished products. He complemented this study by close observation of the employees on their jobs, by questioning them as to what they were doing and why, by questioning supervisors, by lending a hand at various jobs, and by assembling products on his own time. During this learning period, Taylor was closely observed by Lea, who would either stop by at his desk to ask how things were getting along or who would request Taylor to report to his office, this latter about once a week.

During this three-month period, Bill tried his best to win the friendship of the supervisors and workers by chatting with them and explaining that he was new to manufacturing and had to learn what was going on before he undertook production-control work. Despite this effort, he realized that he was not being fully accepted by the supervisors, and was being rebuffed by the workers. The latter, for example, were evasive, terse, and would speak in undertones. On one occasion as Bill walked past a machinist, he thought he heard the expression "stool pigeon."

Inasmuch as he was disturbed by this entire situation, he had often sought the advice of the shop foreman, whom he particularly liked, with the hope that this man with twenty-five years experience with the company could give him some clue as to why the employees seemed to resent his presence. Invariably, the foreman said that he knew of no reason and attributed the problem to Bill's imagination. On several occasions, Taylor also spoke to the president about the matter, and was assured that the reaction was probably the result of the workers' experience with the efficiency expert of the previous year, and would iron itself out in time. Because it was rumored that Lea had men in the shop who were willing to pass on information concerning worker attitudes (by phone at night),

Taylor felt reassured by Lea's statements. Employees did not know for certain who these men were, but judged them to be from among the oldtimers, some of whom the company was obviously carrying.

## The Following Six Months

During the six months following the learning period, Taylor found that most of his assignments came directly from the president and occasionally from the general manager, rather than from the production-control manager. For example, the president requested him to make a complete study of economic lot sizes for all the company's products and, thereafter, to construct a production-control schedule based on a Gantt chart so as to enable control of the job lots put into production by the control manager and the shop foreman. In effect, this meant a production-control system which would be more complicated than the one currently in use.

The present method, which had been devised and operated by the production control manager, was this, in general. Each lot size was arbitrarily set at 1,000 units; the operations to be performed thereon and the time these would take were available from a card file supplied by engineering. Combining these data, the control manager would prepare two production orders for each lot to go into production. The original order would go to the timekeeper, an accountant whose desk was located in the office next to a small dispensing window facing into the shop, who, upon request of a worker or a foreman, would clock the orders when passing them out to either. When the orders were returned after completion of the operations, he would clock them in. These originals would then be picked up in batches periodically throughout the day by the control manager who would then again initiate the cycle, as necessary.

The duplicate production order was retained by the control manager, and would be filed by him in a due date box. If the original was not returned in accordance with that file, the manager would then go into the shop for the purpose of locating and expediting the lot in question.

In the final analysis, Taylor's dual assignment would result in changes in quantities, sequence, timing, etc.

Other jobs assigned to Taylor by the president were these: (1) a study of toolroom operations, and the installation of a system designed to control the time and money spent on each task by the tool and die makers; (2) an analysis of the tool crib, and the establishing of a control procedure to reduce tool theft; (3) inventory taking; (4) statistical work not connected directly with production; and (5) numerous special studies involving report writing with recommendations. During the period of doing this work, Taylor would be approached at his desk by Mr. Lea at least once a week, and would be invited into the latter's office to give a progress report.

In almost all of his work, Taylor was obliged to maintain an intimate and inquiring contact with the workers, supervisors, and executives. For example, on one occasion in the assembly room he approached one of the more friendly oldtimers to ask why he, and others, always mixed screws, nuts, bolts, springs, and washers all together in one pile on the bench, whereas were they kept separate so that they could be more easily picked up, the assemblers could turn out many more units of product per day. The worker remarked that he was well aware of that fact, but if his output rose too high, management would think of some way to cut the rate on the job.

Bill then asked the assembler whether he would be willing to change his methods if management would agree not to change the rate, to which the employee replied that he would give the matter serious consideration based on such a promise. Bill, to pursue the issue further, then went to the general manager who enthusiastically endorsed Bill's proposal, but who stated just as Bill, somewhat gratified, was about to leave his office, "We'll let it ride for about a year, then we'll find some reason for cutting the rate." Bill let the matter drop. On the whole, the general manager was somewhat brusque with Taylor and on one occasion accused him of being arrogant.

Bill's relationship with the production-control manager was fairly amicable, although Hank was often noncommittal, was seemingly upset by the nature of Bill's desk work, and sometimes became quite angry when Bill necessarily had to refuse to obey instructions about some phase of production control because of pressure from Mr. Lea to complete a special assignment quickly.

Bill's contacts with the plant superintendent were infrequent but seemingly pleasant. As to the foremen, he had had a few run-ins with them because of the inquiring nature of his work. These were usually terminated with words from Taylor that Mr. Lea wanted the information, so what was he supposed to do? One of the run-ins was quite serious, with Taylor and one of the assembly foremen in angry disagreement which resulted, however, in a mutual understanding and respect when the supervisor finally said after wagging his head hopelessly, "My God, Bill, I'm glad that I don't have your job!" Undoubtedly, a number of these conflicts were brought to Mr. Lea's attention during the weekly executive-supervisory meetings which he chaired, and to which Taylor was not invited.

The production foreman was the friendliest of them all, although Bill was aware that some of the workers disliked him intensely: the rumor was that he played favorites. True, the foreman did look askance at a production-control, Gantt-type schedule which Bill had hung in the former's office, stating that it was a prettily colored chart containing nothing that he did not already know; nevertheless, Bill spotted him studying lot progress on it many times. This supervisor, as everybody knew, had a colossal memory concerning tools, dies, and parts which the company had made over the years and for which blueprints had long ago been destroyed. He was invaluable in recreating those items with his own hands, but had a very poor memory when it came to assisting the engineering department in reestablishing specifications for them.

The attitude of the workers had changed somewhat for the worse, much to Taylor's regret. For instance, when the tool and die makers learned that he had been asked to time them for the purpose of establishing standards, they would often not reply to questions asked of them, feigning not to hear, or they would tell him to find out for himself. As stated previously, when he brought such worker reaction to the attention of the president and the shop foreman, he was always assuaged.

Toward the end of Taylor's ninth month with the company, Mr. Lea asked him to come to his office. There, the president spoke of a customer who had complained to him personally because Onondaga was often failing to meet delivery dates; he had threatened to cancel his orders unless the situation improved. Lea wanted to know why the new production-control schedule had not bettered what had been a previously prevailing situation before erection of the new warehouse. In reply, Taylor said that he had frequently heard from the sales department on a similar score, had pushed material through process as much as he could, and had often recommended the relatively expensive procedure of shipping rush orders parcel post. As to the schedule, however, it had helped to improve conditions and there was nothing wrong with it, for it was geared to operating times established by engineering and to existing machine capacities. He added that production could not be increased without purchasing newer or additional machinery, by working overtime, or by adding a second shift.

In further defense of the schedule, Taylor stated that he had personally been following many of the various lots through process. On a number of occasions he had experienced difficulty in locating them even after several tours of the shop, either because there was no production order with them for identification purposes, or because they would be buried under a pallet, or elsewhere. This same type of situation had happened so many times that he had begun to wonder what was going on. By observation as he went through the plant, and by examination of returned production orders, he had come to realize that the lots were being deliberately hidden by the operators. Furthermore, he had concluded that the men who hid their work were often in possession of two production-order cards at the same time, both of which were either clocked out at the end of the day, or one of which was clocked out then with the other being punched out at the start of work the next morning.

For example, Taylor continued, at 8 A.M. a machinist would pick up an order card from the timekeeper for a job scheduled to be finished at 4:30 that afternoon. Presumably, because the rate on the job was loose he could complete it earlier, say, at 2:30, thereby saving two hours. Then, at 2:30 he would hide the finished lot and would get another card without returning the first. Apparently, the second job for which he would ask was one which was scheduled for two hours and which could be completed by 4:30. He would then return his cards as previously indicated. Taylor added that he had actually observed an operator turn in one card at 4:30 and then go to the end of the line of machinists to return the other; obviously, the worker did this so as to make himself less conspicuous to the busy timekeeper.

Taylor went on to say that he had heard rumors about some kind of a schedule which the men had improvised which covered a two-week span; in his interest to find out what it was all about, he had inquired of the men who claimed they did not know what he was talking about. Clearly, however, the men were playing loose rates against fair or tight ones; furthermore, they were attempting to hide the loose rates by returning order cards in accordance with scheduled rather than actual times and, hence, this disguised overlapping could result in a greater take-home pay.

Taylor concluded by saying that if the workers would turn in their completed work instead of hiding it, a number of accumulated hours could be saved, especially on scheduled long runs. In turn, this would lead to earlier painting, assembling, and shipping.

Very much disturbed by Taylor's observations, the president consulted with the timekeeper who disclaimed knowledge of the problem, but who was able to substantiate Taylor's comments after study of his payroll records. Thereupon, Lea issued an order, signed by himself, which was to be posted throughout the shop: (1) Production order cards had to remain with the jobs for identification purposes; (2) the production foreman had to sign each card upon completion of a job; (3) no worker could receive a new production card without first having returned the signed one already in his possession, except by a written note from the foreman; and (4) any employee found to have two or more order cards in his possession at the same time would be subject to disciplinary action, including discharge for continued malconduct. The foreman was still allowed to withdraw cards at his discretion.

## Taylor's Discharge

Approximately ten days after the regulation was posted, Taylor was endeavoring to find a lot in process in order to expedite it as quickly as possible. He had made three tours of the shop without success when his attention was aroused by the close way in which a drill press operator was glancing at him. The machinist had previously claimed ignorance concerning the material, even though he should have been working on it at this time. Suspicious, Taylor decided to examine more closely a punch press located nearby which had been ripped down for repairs and whose parts were alongside covered by a tarpaulin. Removing some tools from the top of the canvas and examining beneath it, he found the lot of material which he had been seeking. He noticed that it lacked identification and had gone through the drilling operation.

Therefore, he returned to the operator once again in order to question him regarding the job; the latter still disclaimed knowing about it. However, Taylor had noted when on his way over to the man that he had made an involuntary gesture toward his left-hand shirt pocket and, in fact, there was now protruding from it a card which resembled a production order. Knowing that the operator already had an order in the card rack on the machine, and suspecting this to be a second, Taylor grimly reached out and snatched the card from the worker's shirt pocket. It proved to be the card for which he had been looking. Taylor asked, "You have two cards in your possession?" and when the man admitted his guilt, Taylor returned the card to him and left without further comment. The production order had not been signed by the foreman.

Taylor returned to his desk to explain the situation to the production-control manager, Hank. In concluding his comments, he said that he hesitated to tell the plant superintendent about the matter because he would get the employee into trouble and would be called a squealer for having done so. His relationships with the workers, he felt, were already too poor, but the practice had to be stopped. The foreman was apparently not watching his men, so what did the control manager think should be done? Whereupon, the manager jumped up from his chair, saying "I'll damn well fix it!" and left the office to report the matter to the plant superintendent.

The following morning, the plant superintendent told Mr. Lea that Taylor had snatched the production order card from the worker's shirt pocket and that something should be done to prevent further invasion of one's privacy and violation of one's person. Based on the superintendent's story and others which had been brought to his attention, Lea wondered whether he should ask Taylor to submit his resignation.

At 5 P.M. the day after the snatching episode occurred, Taylor was called into the president's office where he was asked to recapitulate the event of the previous day. This Taylor did in its entirety. Lea remarked that the superintendent had stated, after discussion with the drill press operator, that Taylor had ripped the card from the worker's pocket. This Taylor agreed he had done; he had snatched it, yes, because he had felt that the worker would have refused to give it to him.

Mr. Ralph Lea, with a decision obviously previously arrived at, reached into his desk and withdrew a check for two weeks' termination pay; this he handed to Bill Taylor, with his discharge effective immediately. The president then said that Taylor had been causing a considerable amount of labor unrest because of his mode of prying and his arrogant attitude, and that this was dangerous in an open shop such as existed at Onondaga. Also, he felt it to have been his own fault for having hired a young man rather than another more experienced in shop conditions. He suggested that Taylor seek a job in some industrial engineering firm, possibly in New York City. His parting words were: "Someday, Taylor, you will thank me for this."

As Taylor, shocked by the suddenness of it all, was packing his belongings, Lea's secretary came over to his desk and stated that she had known that he was to be discharged because she had prepared the separation check. She added that neither she nor the others in the office, when they heard about it the next day, would ever believe that the fault had been his; rather, that several people in management's ranks had been out to get him. She urged that he not lose contact with the friends he had made in the company.

Later, through one of these friends, Taylor heard scuttlebutt to the effect that subsequent investigation by the president indicated that the production foreman had been deeply involved in supplying workers—his favorites, so it was suggested—with second production order cards. This he had done by getting the cards himself from the timekeeper, or by authorizing their distribution through signed notes presented by the workers. When confronted with the evidence leading up to Taylor's discharge, he admitted his guilt, but pleaded that the men he had helped were those in financial difficulties requiring assistance. Also, the practice had previously been going on for so long a time, even without his help, that it was now a matter of shop routine which could not be broken without great friction. In fact, the men were now thinking more than ever of inviting the union into the shop.

At the time of this writing, some months later, Taylor's informant had been unable to discover what action had been taken against the foreman, but he did know that the drill press operator had been largely exonerated because of the foreman's involvement. Also, both were still working in their former jobs.

As of one year later, Bill Taylor was most interested to read in the newspaper that the Onondaga Metals Company had gone AFL-CIO.

# The Paul White Young Co.

The Paul White Young Co., a large advertising agency, was heavily involved in bringing out a new line of automobiles for its biggest client, Universal Motors.

In addition to its advertising duties, the Young company assumed a heavy share of the responsibility for preparing merchandising and marketing plans, not only for the new line, but for Universal Motors' regular makes of automobiles as well.

Because of the complexity of the account and the amount of billings involved (over $50 million per year), the Young company departed somewhat from normal advertising practice in its organization. Marketing and advertising plans were prepared by a small group of four or five men reporting directly to the account head, Mr. Thomas Jackson, who was about forty-nine years old.

The members of this planning group had considerable prestige in the company. Several hundred people who worked on various aspects of the account in research, copy, media, etc., drew their cues from them and followed the plans laid down by this group. This was true for a number of executives at Universal Motors as well.

From time to time the group was asked to lend a hand on other accounts which were in trouble, or which for one reason or another encountered specific problems they were unable to solve. In other words, people came to the Universal group for help, not the other way around. These requests for help tended to reflect the fact that prestige in advertising, and frequently salary, was directly related to size of account. The larger the account, the larger the agency's commission, and the better the people the agency assigned to it. In this particular case, only a handful of agencies in the country billed more than the Universal account alone.

Although the planning group members had responsibilities involving direct contact with the executives of Universal Motors, the major responsibility for "selling" the Young company's recommendations fell upon Mr. Jackson. He was assisted in this function by Alec Hughes, a thirty-six-year-old promotion expert who had risen to this position by successfully de-

veloping a number of special promotions which had substantially increased Universal Motors' sales volume.

Mr. Hughes was a bachelor and a native of a small Midwestern city. He had let it be known early that he was determined to succeed in the advertising business and was highly successful at Universal in implementing projects in which he believed. Given Universal's complex organization and the uncertainties and risks of automotive marketing decisions, Hughes' success was considered "amazing" in the eyes of other group members on the Universal account. They ascribed his success partly to "sheer drive and lung power" and partly to "the willingness of Universal executives to listen to a man who *says* he knows what to do and has the push to fight about it."

In contrast to the Universal organization, the management of the Young company deliberately maintained a philosophy of "informal organization." One executive noted that: "A man can go as high and as fast as his ideas, talent, and ability to command support and assume responsibility will take him regardless of age, status, salary, etc. Company executives have no doors on their offices, the idea being that they are always free to talk. There are no organization charts. A man can work in almost any area in which someone will give him something to do or ask his advice. This works both upward and downward. When people stop asking for his help, a man might just as well be fired around here."

In addition to Hughes, the other members of the planning group, as described by its youngest member, Peter Morton, were:

TIM JEFFRIES. Forty-three years old, ten years with Universal and ten years with the Young company. "A nice, decent, very competent man who spent the first fifteen years of his career in Detroit. Not high pressure enough to rise into top management in New York. He realizes that it was a mistake for him to move here, but he will stick it out because he's an old pro, a master sergeant type."

CHUCK HAMILTON. Forty-two years old, two and one-half years with Young. "Very competent professionally but somehow immature personally. Nevertheless, he's a top flight advertising executive who held responsible positions with several agencies before he went to Florida to start his own business. That business had not done as well as Hamilton hoped, so he sold out and joined Young."

GENE RUSSELL. Twenty-nine years old, seven years with Young. "Smooth, brilliant, savvy, and seven years on the Universal account. The boy wonder of the company."

PETER MORTON. Twenty-five years old, three years with Young. "I've

been with the group for a little more than a year, having been brought up by Mr. Jackson during a minor reorganization of the account."

At about this time, Alec Hughes was promoted to vice-president along with a large salary increase and a big office next to Mr. Jackson. Members of the planning group continued to report to Mr. Jackson.

Hughes' promotion caused some comment within the planning group. Its members felt that the promotion was as much due to Hughes' influence at Universal as to his potential within the agency. Hughes, a forceful and ebullient man, had worked well with the planning group in the past according to some observers in the agency. Some professed to admire the verve and skill with which he conceived and organized promotional efforts, most of which required a good deal of legwork. At the same time, other members felt that Hughes' personality had been the cause of minor tensions.

As a vice-president, Mr. Hughes caused considerable resentment among the group by beginning to issue orders, call meetings, and make assignments. Disposition of the workload had previously been handled on a casual basis, with the group working together on some projects, in pairs or groups on others, and with individuals having continuing responsibility for certain areas, such as parts and service problems, fleet sales, and so on. Authority was not assigned. It was assumed. Changes, revisions, and new projects were either phoned in directly from Universal Motors in Detroit, whose vice-president for marketing worked closely with the group, or were distributed by Mr. Jackson.

Mr. Jackson, although spending much of his time in Detroit, also noted these increasing objections among some Universal executives to Mr. Hughes' forceful presentations, although others appeared fully satisfied. Not long afterwards Mr. Hughes was offered an assignment as head of the new business department of the company. After thinking it over, Mr. Hughes declined the position on the grounds that he was an expert on Universal Motors and preferred to stay on the account, expressing appreciation for the offer.

Shortly thereafter Mr. Sterling Bell was introduced to the planning group and was installed in an office near Mr. Hughes and Mr. Jackson. In introducing Mr. Bell, Mr. Jackson merely noted that he "has joined us" but made no reference to his responsibilities.

Mr. Bell, a tall, distinguished-looking man who had formerly been in charge of a major liquor account at another agency, subsequently told one member of the planning group that he had been told he would be the "equivalent" of a group head, but would be working directly for Mr. Jackson.

Neither Mr. Bell nor Mr. Hughes was introduced to the other, nor did they take it upon themselves to do so. Both, however, continued to work with other members of the group. Both attended meetings in Mr. Jackson's office. Both made occasional trips to Detroit, and both contrib-

uted to the work going forward on the new line and on the new yearly models which were in the final stage.

During this period Mr. Bell seemed to be friendly and cooperative with the other members of the group, working with them as equals, and demonstrating unusual competence. In so doing, he won both the group's support and respect, emerging as a kind of natural leader in opposition to Mr. Hughes. As a result various members of the group made it clear that they preferred Mr. Bell to Mr. Hughes and even went so far as to tell Mr. Bell this. Despite these assurances, Mr. Bell at one point asked Mr. Jackson to give him the new business assignment which had been offered previously to Mr. Hughes. This request was refused.

About a month after Mr. Bell's appearance on the scene, Mr. Hughes called a meeting in his office to discuss various business matters. The meeting was called for 3 P.M.

The four members of the planning group discussed this meeting with each other, although never when all four were present. Individually they were inclined not to attend. At 3:10 P.M. Mr. Jackson's secretary notified the group's respective secretaries that the meeting was canceled.

# Phoenix or Ephemera?

Harry Moss was a group head in the Radar Detection Laboratory of Gideon and Trumpet, Inc., a large electronics producer. Harry's present concern was with one of the older employees in his group, Jo Enright. Harry's attempt to motivate Jo into productive work had seemed spectacularly, if briefly, successful. However, more recent events had given him pause. He recounted the following experience to the casewriter.

HARRY MOSS: "I became Jo's supervisor about three and a half years ago. Actually I had heard about him even before that. Jo was an enigma. He'd been with the company for twenty-five years, and there were legends about what he had accomplished years ago. But nearly everyone agreed that he had shot his wad sometime early in his career. At any rate he was one of the most notoriously unproductive employees we had. That was three years ago.

"I joined this group as a supervisor when I returned from our subsidiary in Belgium. We had a project that was top priority, and the high hopes of our laboratory director were riding with us, which is not always an advantage. It was important to assemble a top-flight creative group. I forget how Jo came to be among them. I do remember the director objecting that he wasn't right for it. He hadn't received a 'star rating' for eight years. His last significant contribution award was eighteen years ago. He was referred to as a 'has been.' All this was discussed along with the possibility of transferring him to a product division. I argued that we should give him a chance. I promised to support a decision to transfer him if things didn't work out.

"I'd heard from other old-timers in the company that Jo's good work had mostly been done in collaboration with a senior man called Horrocks. He's dead now. Jo never did anything again after Horrocks retired. Somewhere in the back of my mind I was thinking that Jo might respond to a good working relationship. He had a long string of patents and awards when he was working with Horrocks. I got to thinking we might recapture it.

"When you meet Jo, you'll see what I mean. He's kind of lethargic but very gracious and quite profound. You can't help feeling he has considerable potential. He's also very composed and reassuring—so much that I just can't get mad at him. He's older than me and sometimes I feel he's wiser. He's a very good judge of people and I used to consult him on a lot of human problems—home, lab, social, all kinds. His advice was remarkably insightful and sort of *effortless.* That's the strongest impression I have about him. He's coasting along on a fraction of his potential power.

"For years now there have been complaints about Jo's stock market dealings. You used to walk into the lab and as likely as not Jo would be talking to his broker on the telephone. Rumor has it that he's made himself rich and isn't scared of being fired. People have frequently made sarcastic remarks in his presence about his hobby—and all his superiors have heard about it. Jo doesn't give the smallest sign that he even hears criticism. I was told to crack down on his practice of issuing long instructions to Wall Street but I've refused. I'm not going to treat him like a baby. Anyway, threatening him would not work and I wouldn't feel right doing it.

"I decided to put Jo on the extremely important and central part of our project, which was to obtain very high frequency operation with diodes. We had not been able to use them at such high frequencies before and it was a challenge. During the next few days he would drop in to talk to me about this and that and quite soon he would start to talk about his work. I thought that this was an encouraging sign because generally speaking he eats lunch and talks informally to people outside the group whom he has known for a long time, and he doesn't discuss his work very much informally.

"The more he talked to me about his ideas for the project the more excited he became, and there was an animation in his voice which I had not heard before. When I told other people about his change of attitude they were rather dampening. 'Oh, he's had good ideas for a long time—only they never get implemented!' However, it was quite clear to me that he was implementing his ideas. He worked long hours with most intense concentration and every now and then he would burst into my office and tell me about it. We never heard from his broker during *that* time!

"To make a long story short, in the weeks that followed he made a number of breakthroughs which have put us literally years ahead of the rest of the industry. It took everyone by surprise. People stopped and asked me, 'What have you done with Jo? He's a changed man!' By the end of the year he'd got a pay raise, an achievement award from the company, and had been presented with a prize by the industry at a banquet in Washington. That's the story."

CASEWRITER: "Assuming that Jo's sudden creativity had something to do with your supervision, how do you behave differently from other supervisors?"

HARRY MOSS: "Well, I have always had a respect for Jo that others lack. I admire his mind, his judgment of people, and his ideas. I've always found him conversationally stimulating. For that reason I don't have to use any self-conscious supervisory techniques on him. I appreciate him and he knows it. I've always felt, though, that I have had to get the ball rolling between us. If we haven't seen each other for some time, it's I who will have to initiate and then he'll respond and keep coming back. But it's almost as if he needs winding up from time to time.

"And then, unlike some supervisors, I come right out into the open and say what I think. I'm not afraid to ask him to help me and to admit that I need results. I'm a lot franker than most people and this sometimes gets me into trouble. Jo, I think, appreciates it. I like to think that I have empathy and rapport with people."

CASEWRITER: "And how long did Jo's period of creativity last? Is he still a top-notch performer?"

HARRY MOSS: "That's another story in itself. I'm afraid we may have killed the spark. I shouldn't have let it happen. What with the Vietnam War, basic research is being cut back and we are getting more and more of these 'bluechip' projects. You know, development work, deadlines, guaranteed payoff, close scheduling—the sort of thing product divisions should be doing. One of these came up and Jo had just the experience needed for it. Moreover, the less creative people find it harder to avoid these assignments. Although Jo had improved out of all recognition in the last few months, there were many with better overall records who could be trusted to do basic research which would eventually pay off. You have to be *really* good to be left alone in this business.

"I asked that Jo be left with my group. I was afraid his productiveness would not survive transfer to routine, highly supervised work. 'It's only for a few months,' I was told. 'It's top priority.' I hoped that if Jo, too, complained vigorously we might prevail. But Jo didn't complain. He just shrugged, smiled, and joined John Blair's group without a murmur of protest. I didn't see him for about three weeks, when I happened to pass through the room in which he was supposed to be working. There he was, hard at it, dictating instructions to his broker.

"About eight months later my group was making disappointing progress on the work Jo had left and I began pulling strings to get him back. I was concerned about annoying John Blair. I needn't have worried. 'You want him back—you can have him!' said John. 'He's done nothing for me except make a killing on the market. Why don't they send him to the financial division?'

"I went to Jo and told him he was to rejoin my group. He nodded and smiled and moved again. I asked him to come and see me and really laid it on the line. 'You've got the most fertile brain in this lab,' I said. 'I'm going to try and get you another raise—but that's only a fraction of what you can be making. You've got the potential—we both know that.'

"He thanked me and left. He never said it was good to be back or that he enjoyed working with me, but he was his kind, obliging self. You know when people ask for his help, he will drop what he is doing and oblige them at once. No favor is too much trouble and he'll never complain. Perhaps that is why he gets moved around. We know there will be no unpleasantness. Lately I've been wondering whether at some level he doesn't resent it and if in the end we don't pay for it.

"I wish I could say that now everything is rosy again and that we'd recaptured our former productive relationship, but I'm not at all sure we have. It's been three months now since he came back. He's full of ideas when I talk to him but the results have not appeared. Perhaps he's storing them up. He does that sometimes. He did come up with some interesting results, but they weren't related to our objectives and I had to tell him so. Perhaps I never had the rapport with him that I thought I had. Perhaps I had it and I lost it, or perhaps it isn't connected with me at all. I wish I knew. I'm only sorry I let him be transferred."

The casewriter was later introduced to Jo Enright, a tall, white-haired man of about fifty years. He sat down in a chair opposite the casewriter. In contrast to several other people interviewed he seemed completely at ease from the first moment and never expressed any fears that his opinions could be used against him. Jo was asked about his recent creative resurgence after years in which he had been less active.

Jo Enright: "Well, it sometimes happens that by luck one finds oneself working in virgin territory, and it suddenly comes to you that what you are doing will affect millions of people. That's when I get excited. It's like opening up a frontier. Sometimes this will last for months or years and then it will dry up."

Casewriter: "But can't you convince your supervisors to let you advance on a frontier for years on end?"

Jo Enright: "Yes and no. Sooner or later the administration will tend to get into a rut. They frequently fall into the error of thinking they can organize the process of discovery. They seem to think that if you repeat some motions that were successful in the past, then this will guarantee productiveness in the future. But that isn't usually true. If you know exactly what you are going to discover and how long it will take—then you are not really doing research at all. It's the unexpected things—and having the time to follow up the unexpected things—that lead to really creative work.

"But it's when you start following the unexpected that other people are likely to lose interest in you. I can't do creative work without some cross-fertilization of ideas. Your group has to care about your ideas and it must be flexible enough to turn aside from what was originally defined as the best procedure. But many groups go dead the moment anything gets complex or ambiguous. When I can't get people interested in the unusual results I feel like I'm banging my head against a wall. It's useless and it hurts.

"In some ways it's like an aircraft trying to take off. When I first get an unusual idea I'm not always confident that I'm talking sense. Sometimes there is a key person who can give you that *early* understanding. If you get it, this gives you momentum and you can 'take off.' The trouble is of course that you have to *earn* other people's attention. This means that if you get into a rut with uncongenial people or poor administrators, it can become harder and harder to win people's attention. They say 'Oh, he's shot his wad!' Then they give you all the routine assignments and the bluechip stuff—and it's harder than ever to produce."

CASEWRITER: "When you were transferred from Harry's group to John Blair's, was that bad?"

JO ENRIGHT: "It was worse. It was worse. It was a bluechip project. Your work is paced. There are a lot of little segments—all with deadlines for completion, and no time to follow up the interesting results. It wasn't John's fault."

CASEWRITER: "Did you complain about being transferred?"

JO ENRIGHT: "I didn't have very much information on what the transfer entailed. Had I known—I *might* have complained. [*Laughs.*] I'm learning! For me, working is pushing unless you're discovering virgin territory. Then it's exciting and you get carried along."

CASEWRITER: "How would you rate Harry Moss as a supervisor?"

JO ENRIGHT: "The best thing about Harry is his flexibility. You can set goals jointly with him but if another lead appears, you can follow that. Harry's sound professionally, which means that when he understands an idea that comprehension is significant for me. Some supervisors treat you as if you were babbling to yourself, and then you think, 'Hell, forget it!' But when Harry reacts he's enthusiastic and he means it. He doesn't pretend to understand."

CASEWRITER: "How often do these opportunities to work in virgin territory arise? For instance, prior to last year how long had it been since you were working in virgin territory?"

JO ENRIGHT: "Oh, a long time. Fifteen years at least. Sometimes all the chips fall just right but more often they don't. In fact my recent work with high frequency diodes was a development of the direction I was working in twenty years ago. Some of my best early work was similar to this. It was like rediscovering an old trail."

CASEWRITER: "And where are you as of now? Back on the trail?"

JO ENRIGHT [*shrugs*]: "Perhaps. Who knows? You can't force these things. I'm looking around. I have a number of interesting leads. These slack, interim periods come and go. The system gets hard and then suddenly shakes loose."

CASEWRITER: "Can one struggle to get out of these interim periods?"

JO ENRIGHT: "Maybe. Perhaps I don't struggle enough."

# Relocation

## Background

Justice protects rights. In a seeming conflict of rights, justice may not know what right to protect. While there is never any real conflict for one right always precedes another—this precedence may not be immediately apparent. In a "conflict" of rights and duties, what are the relative rights and obligations of the counterclaimants?

## Facts

Early tomorrow, John Paul Grady, president of Grady Oils, will meet Spring Hill's mayor and town council to present a prepared statement. The statement is to the effect that Grady Oils will shortly shut down and move its refinery from Spring Hill to a more central location. Since the present location is the cause of high freight costs, making local operations unprofitable, J. P. Grady deems the company justified in moving to a more central location.

Over the years, J. P. Grady has been proud of his good relationship with the Spring Hill community. His company paid top wages to its employees, bought whatever supplies it could from the local merchants, saw that his company was a "good citizen" doing more than its part toward

• Copyright © 1968 by Perry Roets. Reprinted by permission. This case was prepared by Perry J. Roets, S.J., Associate Professor, Marquette University, as a basis for class discussion rather than to illustrate either effective or ineffective handling of administrative situations.

**Exhibit 1 (Grady Oils) Freight Out as a Percent of Sales 1955–1964**

| | | | |
|---|---|---|---|
| 1955 | 6% | 1960 | 3.8% |
| 1956 | 2.2% | 1961 | 4.7% |
| 1957 | 1.5% | 1962 | 5.1% |
| 1958 | 3.1% | 1963 | 5.4% |
| 1959 | 3.7% | 1964 | 6.5% |

the town's growth and development. He looks back with satisfaction at a company policy that has been more than fair, demonstrating leadership in all ways in this town. With regret he realizes that this era is over.

He knows that he is justified in moving the company. High freight costs have diminished the company's managerial profits. If this is allowed to continue, he reasons, soon Grady Oils will be in no position to fulfill any of its obligations. It will be forced out of business, and a business as everyone knows had both right and obligation to survive, grow, and develop, so that all connected with it may prosper too.

Grady hopes to make the decision more palatable and to soften the blow of leaving Spring Hill by gradually withdrawing operations over an eighteen-month period before ceasing refining altogether. By this time, the new refinery at a more central location will have been completed. Furthermore, he is prepared to donate the company's water pumping equipment to the town and write it off as tax loss. The equipment is rapidly becoming obsolete and is of insufficient capacity for use at the new refinery.

Mayor Meyer and his officials are not happy with the contemplated move. They have heard the inevitable whispers and persistent rumors

**Exhibit 2 (Grady Oils) Net Profits as a Percent of Sales 1955–1964**

| | | | |
|---|---|---|---|
| 1955 | 6.9% | 1960 | 1.3% |
| 1956 | 5.5% | 1961 | 0.9% |
| 1957 | 4.2% | 1962 | 0.3% |
| 1958 | 3.1% | 1963 | 1.2% |
| 1959 | 1.1% | 1964 | 1.8% |

**Exhibit 3 Spring Hill Population; Grady Oils Employment 1955–1964**

| *Spring Hill Population* | | *Grady Oils Employees* | |
|---|---|---|---|
| 1955 | 3,845 | 1955 | 965 |
| 1956 | 4,175 | 1956 | 1,312 |
| 1957 | 4,790 | 1957 | 1,546 |
| 1958 | 5,365 | 1958 | 1,944 |
| 1959 | 5,781 | 1959 | 2,133 |
| 1960 | 6,122 | 1960 | 2,401 |
| 1961 | 6,914 | 1961 | 2,888 |
| 1962 | 7,311 | 1962 | 3,121 |
| 1963 | 7,490 | 1963 | 3,344 |
| 1964 | 7,500 | 1964 | 3,305 |

of the probable move but did not wish to believe or face up to them. Now they can think of no other reason why J. P. Grady wishes to meet with them on the morrow. They fear the worst.

For twenty-five years, Grady Oils has made this town. Grady Oils, as the town's only real industry, directly employed more than one-half of the town's work force. The base of the town's growth and prosperity had been Grady Oils. Recently, on the strength of this relationship, the town "invested in its future" by building a new high school costing $2,000,000 and an elementary school costing well over $400,000. A new town hall had risen, a fire department had been established, water and sewage facilities expanded. To pay for these, the town and district were bonded; that is, they pledged themselves to pay town and district taxes based on yearly assessments until all debts are paid. For a town of 7,500 inhabitants, the present outstanding town debt of $2,400,000 is indeed staggering.

Mayor Meyer is indignant at what he regards as Grady Oils' apparent failure to fulfill its clear obligations. Certainly, given its predominant role in the community, he tells his fellow town officials, Grady Oils has failed to protect or shield the community from the adverse effects of its action. Waxing more eloquent, he ringingly accuses Grady Oils of a failure to contribute to the very institutions which in retrospect they now must realize were irresponsibly created. Nor has the company warned the community that in an expensive high school and elementary school now not needed, in expanded water and sewerage facilities as yet unpaid for, it could not be counted upon for any real support. Nor does the mayor think that Grady can justify his action by giving a year or so warning;

the warning is too late; the damage has been done. Spring Hill is about to become a ghost town. And in the mayor's angry opinion, Grady Oils is alone responsible.

# The Slade Company

Ralph Porter, production manager of The Slade Company, was concerned by reports of dishonesty among some employees in the plating department. From reliable sources, he had learned that a few men were punching the timecards of a number of their workmates who had left early. Mr. Porter had only recently joined the Slade organization. He judged from the conversations with the previous production manager and other fellow managers that they were, in general, pleased with the overall performance of the plating department.

The Slade Company was a prosperous manufacturer of metal products designed for industrial application. Its manufacturing plant, located in central Michigan, employed nearly 500 workers, who were engaged in producing a large variety of clamps, inserts, knobs, and similar items. Orders for these products were usually large and on a recurrent basis. The volume of orders fluctuated in response to business conditions in the primary industries which the company served. At the time of this case, sales volume had been high for over a year. The bases upon which The Slade Company secured orders, in rank of importance, were quality, delivery, and reasonable price.

The organization of manufacturing operations at the Slade plant is shown in Figure 1. The departments listed there are, from left to right, approximately in the order in which material flowed through the plant. The diemaking and setup operations required the greatest degree of skill, supplied by highly paid, long-service craftsmen. The finishing departments, divided operationally and geographically between plating and painting, attracted less highly trained but relatively skilled workers, some of whom had been employed by the company for many years. The remaining operations were largely unskilled in nature and were characterized by relatively low pay and high turnover of personnel.

The plating room was the sole occupant of the top floor of the plant. Figure 2 shows the floorplan, the disposition of workers, and the flow of

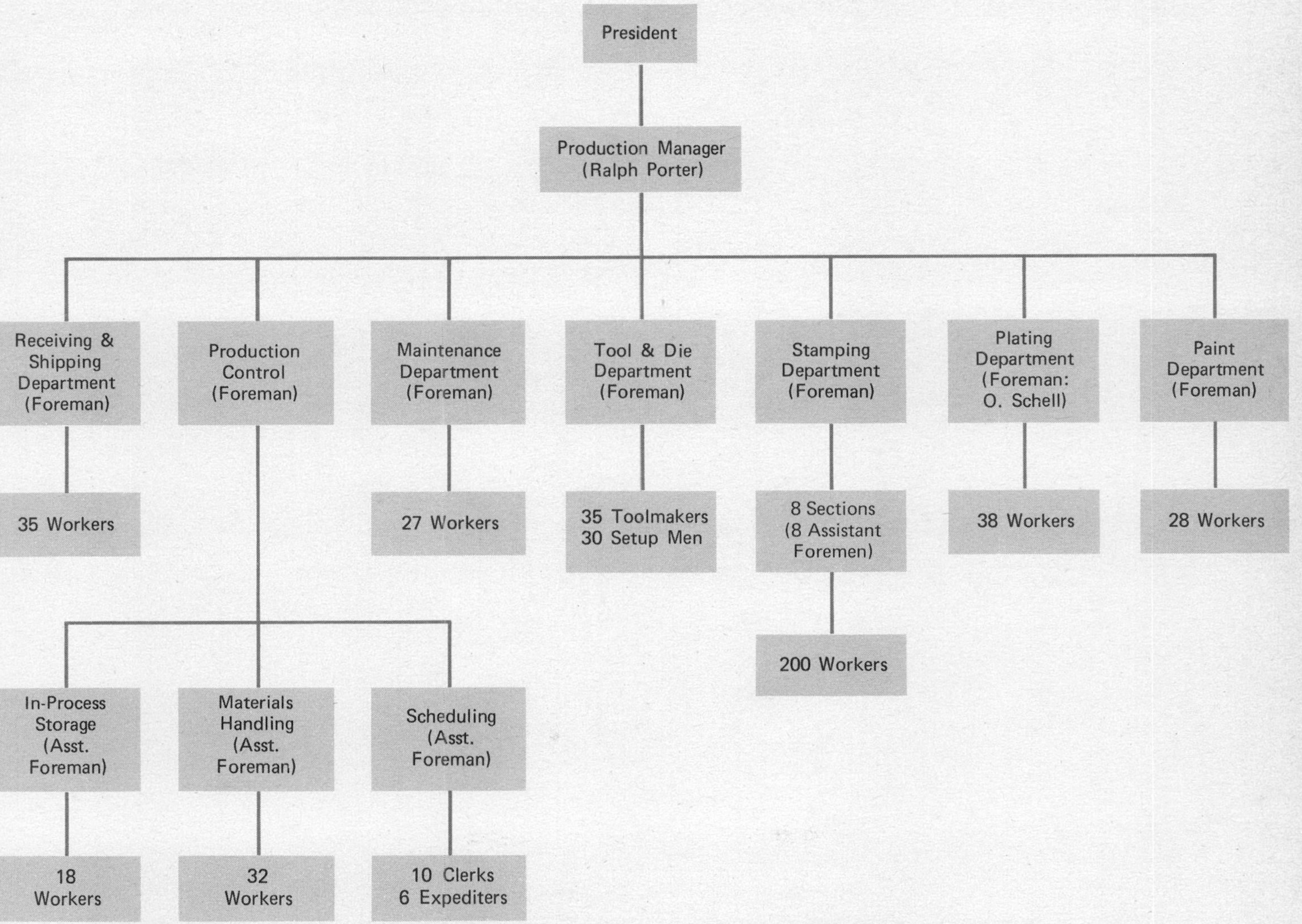


**Figure 1** Manufacturing Organization

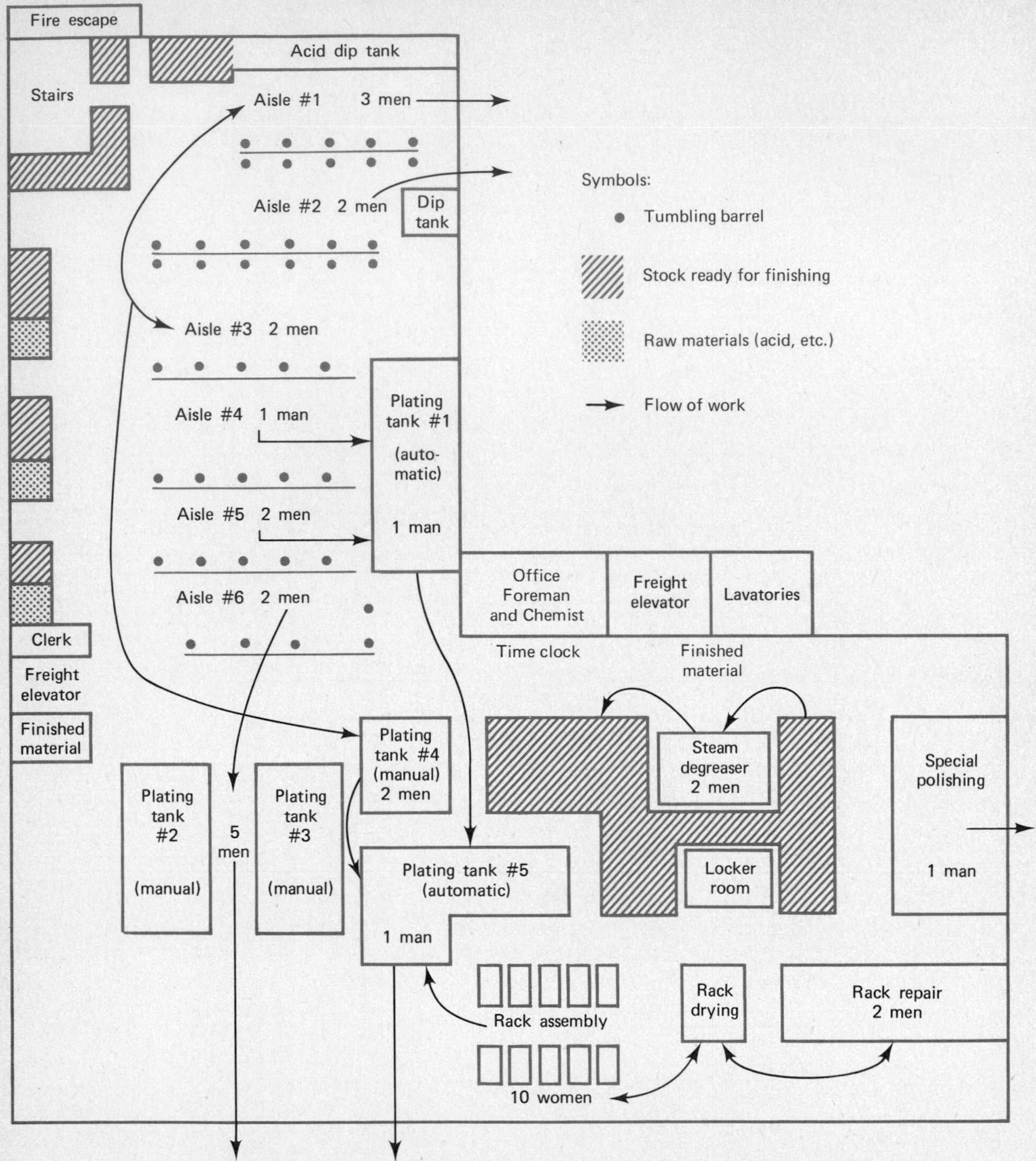


**Figure 2** Plating Room Layout

work throughout the department. Thirty-eight men and women worked in the department, plating or oxidizing the metal parts or preparing parts for the application of paint at another location in the plant. The department's work occurred in response to orders communicated by production schedules, which were revised daily. Schedule revisions, caused by last-minute order increases or rush requests from customers, resulted in short-term volume fluctuations, particularly in the plating, painting, and shipping departments. Table 1 outlines the activities of the various jobs, their interrelationships, and the type of work in which each specialized. Table 2 rates the various types of jobs in terms of the technical skill, physical effort, discomfort, and training time associated with their performance.

The activities that took place in the plating room were of three main types:

1. Acid dipping, in which parts were etched by being placed in baskets which were manually immersed and agitated in an acid solution.
2. Barrel tumbling, in which parts were roughened or smoothed by being loaded into machine-powered revolving drums containing abrasive, caustic, or corrosive solutions.
3. Plating—either manual, in which parts were loaded on racks and were immersed by hand through the plating sequence; or automatic, in which racks or baskets were manually loaded with parts which were then carried by a conveyor system through the plating sequence.

Within these main divisions, there were a number of variables, such as cycle times, chemical formulas, abrasive mixtures, and so forth, which distinguished particular jobs as they have been categorized in Table 1.

The work of the plating room was received in batch lots whose size averaged a thousand pieces. The clerk moved each batch, which was accompanied by a routing slip, to its first operation. This routing slip indicated the operations to be performed and when each major operation on the batch was scheduled to be completed, so that the finished product could be shipped on time. From the accumulation of orders before him, each man was to organize his own work schedule so as to make optimal use of equipment, materials, and time. Upon completion of an order, each man moved the lot to its next work position or to the finished material location near the freight elevator.

The plating room was under the direct supervision of the foreman, Otto Schell, who worked a regular 8:00-to-5:00 day, five days a week. The foreman spent a good deal of his working time attending to maintenance and repair of equipment, procuring supplies, handling late schedule changes, and seeing that his people were at their proper work locations.

Working conditions in the plating room varied considerably. That part of the department containing the tumbling barrels and the plating machines was constantly awash, alternately with cold water, steaming acid, or caustic soda. Men working in this part of the room wore knee boots, long rubber aprons, and high-gauntlet rubber gloves. This uniform, consistent with the general atmosphere of the "wet" part of the room, was hot in the summer, cold in winter. In contrast, the remainder of the room was dry, relatively odor-free, and provided reasonably stable temperature and humidity conditions for those who worked there.

The men and women employed in the plating room are listed in Table 3. This exhibit provides certain personal data on each department member, including a productivity skill rating (based on subjective and objective appraisals of potential performance), as reported by the members of the department.

The pay scale implied by Table 3 was low for the central Michigan area. The average starting wage for factory work in the community was about $1.25. However, working hours for the plating room were long (from sixty hours to a possible and frequently available seventy-six hours per week). The first sixty hours (the normal five-day week were paid for on straight-time rates. Saturday work was paid for at time and a half; Sunday pay was calculated on a double-time basis.

**Table 1 Outline of Work Flow, Plating Room***

*Aisle 1:* Worked closely with Aisle 3 in preparation of parts by barrel tumbling and acid dipping for high-quality plating in Tanks 4 and 5. Also did a considerable quantity of highly specialized, high-quality acid-etching work not requiring further processing.

*Aisle 2:* Tumbled items of regular quality and design in preparation for painting. Less frequently, did oxidation dipping work of regular quality, but sometimes of special design, not requiring further processing.

*Aisle 3:* Worked closely with Aisle 1 on high-quality tumbling work for Tanks 4 and 5.

*Aisles 4 and 5:* Produced regular tumbling work for Tank 1.

*Aisle 6:* Did high-quality tumbling work for special products plated in Tanks 2 and 3.

*Tank 1:* Worked on standard, automated plating of regular quality not further processed in plating room, and regular work further processed in Tank 5.

As Table 3 indicates, Philip Kirk, a worker in Aisle 2, provided the data for this case. After he had been a member of the department for several months, Kirk noted that certain members of the department tended to seek each other out during free time on and off the job. He then observed that these informal associations were enduring, built upon common activities and shared ideas about what was and what was not legitimate behavior in the department. His estimate of the pattern of these associations is diagrammed in Figure 3.

The Sarto group, so named because Tony Sarto was its most respected member and the one who acted as arbiter between the other members, was the largest in the department. The group, except for Louis Patrici, Al Bartolo, and Frank Bonzani (who spelled each other during break periods), invariably ate lunch together on the fire escape near Aisle 1. On those Saturdays and Sundays when overtime work was required, the Sarto group operated as a team, regardless of weekday work assignments, to get overtime work completed as quickly as possible. (Few department members not affiliated with either the Sarto or the Clark groups

**Table 1 Outline of Work Flows, Plating Room (continued)**

*Tanks 2 and 3:* Produced special, high-quality plating work not requiring further processing.

*Tank 4:* Did special, high-quality plating work further plated in Tank 5.

*Tank 5:* Automated production of high- and regular-quality, special- and regular-design plated parts sent directly to shipping.

*Rack assembly:* Placed parts to be plated in Tank 5 on racks.

*Rack repair:* Performed routine replacement and repair of racks used in Tank 5.

*Polishing:* Processed, by manual or semimanual methods, odd-lot special orders which were sent directly to shipping. Also, sorted and reclaimed parts rejected by inspectors in the shipping department.

*Degreasing:* Took incoming raw stock, processed it through caustic solution, and placed clean stock in storage ready for processing elsewhere in the plating room.

*Definition of terms: *High or regular quality:* The quality of finishes could broadly be distinguished by the thickness of plate and/or care in preparation. *Regular or special work:* The complexity of work depended on the routine or special character of design and finish specifications.

**Table 2 Skill Indices by Job Group***

| Jobs | Technical skill required | Physical effort required | Degree of discomfort involved | Degree of training required† |
|---|---|---|---|---|
| Aisle 1 | 1 | 1 | 1 | 1 |
| Tanks 2–4 | 3 | 2 | 1 | 2 |
| Aisles 2–6 | 5 | 1 | 1 | 5 |
| Tank 5 | 1 | 5 | 7 | 2 |
| Tank 1 | 8 | 5 | 5 | 7 |
| Degreasing | 9 | 3 | 7 | 10 |
| Polishing | 6 | 9 | 9 | 7 |
| Rack assembly and repair | 10 | 10 | 10 | 10 |

*Rated on scales of 1 (the greatest) to 10 (the least) in each category.
†Amount of experience required to assume complete responsibility for the job.

worked on weekends.) Off the job, Sarto group members often joined in parties or weekend trips. Sarto's summer camp was a frequent rendezvous.

Sarto's group was also the most cohesive one in the department in terms of its organized punch-in and punch-out system. Because the men were regularly scheduled to work from 7:00 A.M. to 7:00 P.M. weekdays, and since all supervision was removed at 5:00 P.M., it was possible almost every day to finish a "day's work" by 5:30 and leave the plant. What is more, if one man were to stay until 7:00 P.M., he could punch the time cards of a number of men and help them gain free time without pay loss. (This system operated on weekends also; at which times members of supervision were present, if at all, only for short periods.) In Sarto's group the duty of staying late rotated, so that no man did so more than once a week. In addition, the group members would punch a man in in the morning if he were unavoidably delayed. However, such a practice never occurred without prior notice from the man who expected to be late and never if the tardiness was expected to last beyond 8:00 A.M., the start of the day for the foreman.

Sarto explained the logic behind the system to Kirk:

"You know that our hourly pay rate is quite low, compared to other companies. What makes this the best place to work is the feeling of security you get. No one ever gets laid off in this department. With all the hours in the week, all the company ever has to do is shorten the work week when orders fall off. We have to tighten our belts, but we can get along.

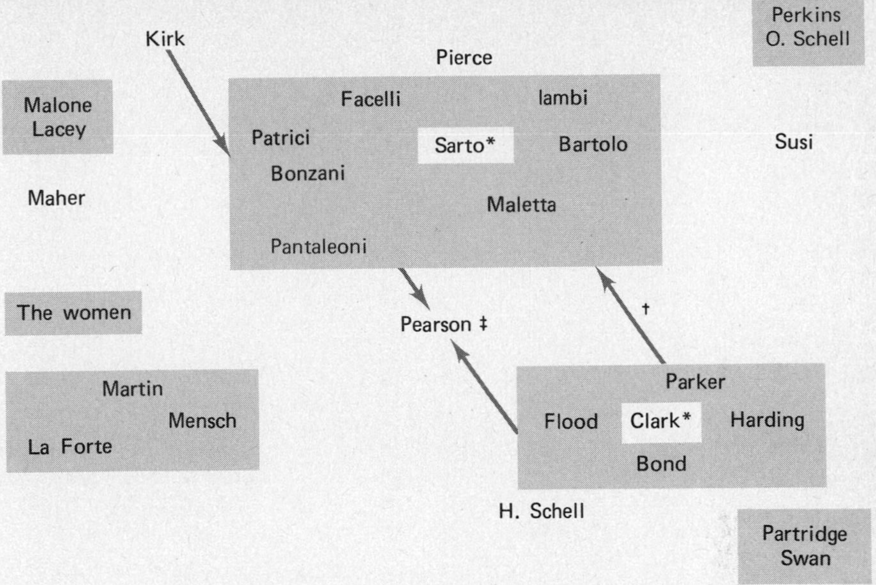


**Figure 3** Informal Groupings in the Plating Room

*The starred boxes indicate those men who clearly demonstrated leadership behavior (most clearly personified the values shared by their groups, were most often sought for help and arbitration, and so forth).
†While the two- and three-man groupings had little informal contact outside their own boundaries, the five-man group did seek to join the largest group in extraplant social affairs. These were relatively infrequent.
‡Though not an active member of any group, Bob Pearson was regarded with affection by the two large groups.

When things are going well, as they are now, the company is only interested in getting out the work. It doesn't help to get it out faster than it's really needed—so we go home a little early whenever we can. Of course, some guys abuse this sort of thing—like Herman—but others work even harder, and it averages out.

"Whenever an extra order has to be pushed through, naturally I work until 7:00. So do a lot of the others. I believe that if I stay until my work is caught up and my equipment is in good shape, that's all the company wants of me. They leave us alone and expect us to produce—and we do."

When Kirk asked Sarto if he would not rather work shorter hours at higher pay in a union shop (Slade employees were not organized), he just laughed and said: "It wouldn't come close to an even trade."

The members of Sarto's group were explicit about what constituted a fair day's work. Customarily, they cited Herman Schell, Kirk's work partner and the foreman's brother, as a man who consistently produced below

## Table 3 Plating Room Personnel

| *Location* | *Name* | *Age* | *Marital status* | *Company seniority (in years)* | *Department seniority (in years)* | *Pay per hour* | *Education** | *Familial relationships* | *Productivity-skill rating†* |
|---|---|---|---|---|---|---|---|---|---|
| Aisle 1 | Tony Sarto | 30 | M | 13 | 13 | $1.50 | HS | Louis Patrici, uncle<br>Pete Facelli, cousin | 1 |
| | Pete Facelli | 26 | M | 8 | 8 | 1.30 | HS | Louis Patrici, uncle<br>Tony Sarto, cousin | 2 |
| | Joe Iambi | 31 | M | 5 | 5 | 1.20 | 2 yrs. HS | | 2 |
| Aisle 2 | Herman Schell | 48 | S | 26 | 26 | 1.45 | GS | Otto Schell, brother | 8 |
| | Philip Kirk | 23 | M | 1 | 1 | 0.90 | College | | —‡ |
| Aisle 3 | Dom Pantaleoni | 31 | M | 10 | 10 | 1.30 | 1 yr. HS | | 2 |
| | Sal Maletta | 32 | M | 12 | 12 | 1.30 | 3 yrs. HS | | 3 |
| Aisle 4 | Bob Pearson | 22 | S | 4 | 4 | 1.15 | HS | Father in tool and die dept. | 1 |
| Aisle 5 | Charlie Malone | 44 | M | 22 | 8 | 1.25 | GS | | 7 |
| | John Lacey | 41 | S | 9 | 5 | 1.20 | 1 yr. HS | Brother in paint dept. | 7 |
| Aisle 6 | Jim Martin | 30 | S | 7 | 7 | 1.25 | HS | | 4 |
| | Bill Mensch | 41 | M | 6 | 2 | 1.10 | GS | | 4 |
| Tank 1 | Henry LaForte | 38 | M | 14 | 6 | 1.25 | HS | | 6 |
| Tanks 2 & 3 | Ralph Parker | 25 | S | 7 | 7 | 1.20 | HS | | 4 |
| | Ed Harding | 27 | S | 8 | 8 | 1.20 | HS | | 4 |
| | George Flood | 22 | S | 5 | 5 | 1.15 | HS | | 5 |
| | Harry Clark | 29 | M | 8 | 8 | 1.20 | HS | | 3 |
| | Tom Bond | 25 | S | 6 | 6 | 1.20 | HS | | 4 |

**Table 3 Plating Room Personnel (continued)**

| Location | Name | Age | Marital status | Company seniority (in years) | Department seniority (in years) | Pay per hour | Education* | Familial relationships | Productivity-skill rating† |
|---|---|---|---|---|---|---|---|---|---|
| Tank 4 | Frank Bonzani | 27 | M | 9 | 9 | 1.25 | HS | | 2 |
| | Al Bartolo | 24 | M | 6 | 6 | 1.25 | HS | | 3 |
| Tank 5 | Louis Patrici | 47 | S | 14 | 14 | 1.45 | 2 yrs. college | Tony Sarto, nephew<br>Pete Facelli, nephew | 1 |
| Rack assembly | 10 women | 30–40 | 9M, 1S | 10 (av.) | [10 (av.)] | 1.05 | GS (av.) | 6 with husbands in company | 4 (av.) |
| Rack maintenance | Will Partridge | 57 | M | 14 | 2 | 1.20 | GS | | 7 |
| | Lloyd Swan | 62 | M | 3 | 3 | 1.10 | GS | | 7 |
| Degreasing | Dave Susi | 45 | S | 1 | 1 | 1.05 | HS | | 5 |
| | Mike Maher | 41 | M | 4 | 4 | 1.05 | GS | | 6 |
| Polishing | Russ Perkins | 49 | M | 12 | 2 | 1.20 | HS | | 4 |
| Foreman | Otto Schell | 56 | M | 35 | 35 | n.a. | HS | Herman Schell, brother | 3 |
| Clerk | Bill Pierce | 32 | M | 10 | 4 | 1.15 | HS | | 4 |
| Chemist | Frank Rutlage | 24 | S | 2 | 2 | n.a. | 2 yrs. college | | 6 |

*HS = high school; GS = grade school.
†On a potential scale of 1 (top) to 10 (bottom), as evaluated by the men in the department.
‡Kirk was the source of data for this case and therefore in a biased position to report accurately perceptions about himself.

that level. Kirk received an informal orientation from Herman during his first days on the job. As Herman put it:

"I've worked at this job for a good many years, and I expect to stay here a good many more. You're just starting out, and you don't know which end is up yet. We spend a lot of time in here; and no matter how hard we work, the pile of work never goes down. There's always more to take its place. And I think you've found out by now that this isn't light work. You can wear yourself out fast if you're not smart. Look at Pearson up in Aisle 4. There's a kid who's just going to burn himself out. He won't last long. If he thinks he's going to get somewhere working like that, he's nuts. They'll give him all the work he can take. He makes it tough on everybody else and on himself, too."

Kirk reported further on his observations of the department:

"As nearly as I could tell, two things seemed to determine whether or not Sarto's group or any others came in for weekend work on Saturday or Sunday. It seemed usually to be caused by rush orders that were received late in the week, although I suspect it was sometimes caused by the men having spent insufficient time on the job during the previous week.

"Tony and his group couldn't understand Herman. While Herman arrived late, Tony was always half an hour early. If there was a push to get out an extra amount of work, almost everyone but Herman would work that much harder. Herman never worked overtime on week ends, while Tony's group and the men on the manual tanks almost always did. When the first exploratory time study of the department was made, no one in the aisles slowed down, except Herman, with the possible exception, to a lesser degree, of Charlie Malone. I did hear that the men in the dry end of the room slowed down so much you could hardly see them move; but we had little to do with them anyway. While the men I knew best seemed to find a rather full life in their work, Herman never really got involved. No wonder they couldn't understand each other.

"There was quite a different feeling about Bobby Pearson. Without the slightest doubt, Bob worked harder than anyone else in the room. Because of the tremendous variety of work produced, it was hard to make output comparisons, but I'm sure I wouldn't be far wrong in saying that Bob put out twice as much as Herman and 50 percent more than almost anyone else in the aisles. No one but Herman and a few old-timers at the dry end ever criticized Bobby for his efforts. Tony and his group seemed to feel a distant affection for Bob, but the only contact they or anyone else had with him consisted of brief greetings.

"To the men in Tony's group the most severe penalty that could be inflicted on a man was exclusion. This they did to both Pearson and Herman. Pearson, however, was tolerated; Herman was not. Evidently, Herman felt his exclusion keenly, though he answered it with derision and aggression. Herman kept up a steady stream of stories concerning his attempts to gain acceptance outside the company. He wrote popular music which was always rejected by publishers. He attempted to join several social and athletic clubs, mostly without success. His favorite pastime was fishing. He told me that fishermen were friendly, and he enjoyed meeting new people whenever he went fishing. But he was particularly quick to explain that he preferred to keep his distance from the men in the department.

"Tony's group emphasized more than just quantity in judging a man's work. Among them had grown a confidence that they could master and even improve upon any known finishing technique. Tony himself symbolized this skill. Before him, Tony's father had operated Aisle 1 and had trained Tony to take his place. Tony in his turn was training his cousin Pete. When a new finishing problem arose from a change in customer specifications, the foreman, the department chemist, or any of the men directly involved would come to Tony for help, and Tony would give it willingly. For example, when a part with a special plastic embossing was designed, Tony was the only one who could discover how to treat the metal without damaging the plastic. To a lesser degree, the other members of the group were also inventive about the problems which arose in their own sections.

"Herman, for his part, talked incessantly about his feats in design and finish creations. As far as I could tell during the year I worked in the department, the objects of these stories were obsolete or of minor importance. What's more, I never saw any department member seek Herman's help.

"Willingness to be of help was a trait Sarto's group prized. The most valued help of all was of a personal kind, though work help was also important. The members of Sarto's group were constantly lending and borrowing money, cars, clothing, and tools among themselves and, less frequently, with other members of the department. Their daily lunch bag procedure typified the common property feeling among them. Everyone's lunch was opened and added to a common pile, from which each member of the group chose his meal.

"On the other hand, Herman refused to help others in any way. He never left his aisle to aid those near him who were in the midst of a rush of work or a machine failure, though this was customary throughout most of the department. I can distinctly recall the picture of Herman leaning on the hot and cold water faucets which were located directly above each tumbling barrel. He would stand gazing into the tumbling pieces for hours. To the passing, casual visitor, he looked busy; and as he told me, that's just what he wanted. He, of course, expected me to act this same way, and it was this enforced boredom that I found virtually intolerable.

"More than this, Herman took no responsibility for breaking in his assigned helpers as they first entered the department, or thereafter. He had had four helpers in the space of little more than a year. Each had asked for a transfer to another department, publicly citing the work as cause, privately blaming Herman. Tony was the one who taught me the ropes when I first entered the department.

"The men who congregated around Harry Clark tended to talk like and copy the behavior of the Sarto group, though they never approached the degree of inventive skill or the amount of helping activities that Tony's group did. They sought outside social contact with the Sarto group; and several times a year, the two groups went 'on the town' together. Clark's group did maintain a high level of performance in the volume of work they turned out.

"The remainder of the people in the department stayed pretty much to themselves or associated in pairs or triplets. None of these people were as inventive, as helpful, or as productive as Sarto's or Clark's groups, but most of them gave verbal support to the same values as those groups held.

"The distinction between the two organized groups and the rest of the department was clearest in the punching-out routine. The women could not work past 3:00 P.M., so they were not involved. Malone and Lacey, Partridge and Swan, and Martin, La Forte, and Mensch arranged within their small groups for punch-outs, or they remained beyond 5:00 and slept or read when they finished their work. Perkins and Pierce went home when the foreman did. Herman Schell, Susi, and Maher had no punch-out organization to rely upon. Susi and Maher invariably stayed in the department until 7:00 P.M. Herman was reported to have established an arrangement with Partridge whereby the latter punched Herman out for a fee. Such a practice was unthinkable from the point of view of Sarto's group. It evidently did not occur often because Herman usually went to sleep behind piles of work when his brother left or, particularly during the fishing season, punched himself out early. He constantly railed against the dishonesty of other men in the department, yet urged me to punch him out on several emergency occasions.

"Just before I left The Slade Company to return to school after fourteen months on the job, I had a casual conversation with Mr. Porter, the production manager, in which he asked me how I had enjoyed my experience with the organization. During the conversation, I learned that he knew of the punch-out system in the plating department. What's more, he told me, he was wondering if he ought to 'blow the lid off the whole mess.' "

# Spearman Plastics, Inc.

In February 1967, John Spearman, president of Spearman Plastics, Inc., and a graduate of the Harvard Business School, was considering reorganization for his company. Spearman Plastics, Inc. (SPI) had just embarked on an expansion and diversification program designed primarily to reduce its dependence on its thermal plastics line, which in 1966 accounted for 43 percent of sales. The company had also set a goal to expand sales from the present $98 million level to the $300 million level in the succeeding five years. "To achieve these objectives," the president said, "it seems clear that we should begin to move away from our present functional structure towards some kind of divisional or product organization."

SPI manufactured a specialty line of plastic products in the United States and abroad. Most of the company's products had one characteristic in common: They were high-strength, light-weight plastic material designed for use under high temperature conditions. SPI's basic product, "Thermalite," was a highly versatile plastic that could be modified for various uses. The most sophisticated application of this product was to form the destructible outer coating of the "heat shields" of re-entry vehicles in the space program. The company's major customers were the aircraft and aerospace industries, although SPI's products were also adapted for various other industrial uses.

A sales force of one hundred men called on the company's various customers throughout the United States. Abroad SPI used a combination of independent distributors, company sales branches, and manufacturing subsidiaries. Its foreign subsidiaries were typically wholly owned, although three manufacturing subsidiaries in Europe were in the form of joint ventures with European nationals. Domestic sales accounted for 75 percent of sales in 1966. The remaining 25 percent was distributed in varying proportions among Canada, Europe, Latin America, and Asia.

## A Family Firm

SPI had been under the control of the Spearman family since its founding in 1926 by Jonathan Spearman, the company's namesake and

 This case was prepared by Raphael Rodriguez under the direction of Professor Jay W. Lorsch as the basis for class discussion rather than to illustrate either effective or ineffective handling of an administrative situation.

grandfather of John Spearman. Upon the founder's death in 1939, his son, Franklin Spearman, John's father, succeeded to the presidency of SPI. In 1965 John Spearman became president while his father retained the position of chairman of the board of directors.

Two other members of the Spearman family were active in the management of the company: Robert Spearman, younger brother of the president, was currently vice-president of marketing, and James Weston, brother-in-law of the president, was vice-president in charge of international operations (see Figure 1. All Figures at end of case.)

### Postwar Growth

The company's sustained and rapid growth in the past fifteen years (see Figure 3) had been founded on a strategy, originated by Franklin Spearman, of marketing a specialty line of plastics products designed for the most exotic and demanding applications of plastic materials. SPI's research organization had come up with a series of scientific breakthroughs in plastics technology which gave the company a continuing competitive edge in the market. The most significant of these, and the one on which SPI's sales growth in the past seven years had largely been built, was in the area of thermal plastics. The company began to market its "Thermalite" products in 1960.

### The Present Organization

Figure 1 shows a chart of the company's present top management organization. Not shown in the chart is the Operations Committee, established since John Spearman became president of the company. All members of SPI's top management organization participated in the proceedings of this committee. The president described its function as being a medium of communications to keep the company's executives informed of the various facets of the company's operations. Company executives also used the committee to make individual presentations of projects which were initiated by them or assigned to them.

## EXPANSION AND THE NEED FOR A NEW ORGANIZATION

In explaining the company's plans for a new organization, the president turned to the underlying shift in corporate strategy that had given rise to the issue of reorganization for SPI. Shortly after becoming president of the company in July 1965, John Spearman had launched an expansion and diversification program that envisaged the growth of sales to the $300 million level within the succeeding five years. Two acquisitions had already been made by SPI under this program. The first acquisition in October 1965 was NETOL, a small concern that had been conducting pioneering research in resins and in the plastic adhesives area. The second acquisition, made in March 1966, was Reschild-Bauer, Inc., a pharmaceuticals company with sales of $14 million in 1966.

John Spearman explained why, despite the continued increase of the company's plastic sales, he believed that the plastics business was no longer "an adequate solution" to SPI's long-term requirements:

> To begin with, history has demonstrated for us that the plastics industry generates more cash than you would want to reinvest into that business. Right now we have close to $35 million in cash and securities in this company (see Figure 4). We are already paying out 70 percent of earnings in dividends and the facts show that a higher payout ratio has little impact on the price of a stock. But having that much cash lying around means we get poor solutions to our problems. Instead, for example, of devising a more efficient scheduling system for the company, we would tend to say, "Well, let's just build more inventories of everything. Anyway we have the cash to do it." This is clearly uneconomic.
>
> In the second place, having all your eggs in one basket is always problematic in the plastics business. The rate of technological innovation and obsolescence is dramatically high in this industry. The legal life of our "Thermalite" patents may not be a good measure of how long this product will serve us. There are developments in the industry that could completely obsolete this line in a very short time. So this is the time to have some other flowers growing.
>
> Finally, the nature of our research in basic chemistry is such that there is fallout into other fields; biochemistry for one. We aren't going to make use of this fallout unless we organize ourselves to do so.

"All these factors argue for diversification," the president said. He wanted to maintain the company's growth record and the price of the company's stock (which was believed to depend upon it). To continue to justify the price-earnings ratio[1] enjoyed by SPI stock, the president believed that the company had to maintain a growth rate of about 15 percent annually. Diversification, besides protecting the company from the possible obsolescence of its current products, would enlarge the number of avenues for expansion open to the company in meeting its growth objectives.

"Given that we have to diversify, how do we go about planning and investigating the various alternatives open to us in order to determine which ones we follow?" the president asked.

> Well, first of all, the company's recent growth has greatly increased the pressures on my job under the present organization. I no longer feel that

[1]Currently about thirty times earnings per share.

I can manage our existing businesses and at the same time do a good job of looking for opportunities that will allow us to meet our growth objectives. I'm already spread too thin.

The implication of this is that I have to give up operating responsibility so that I can spend more time in planning for growth outside the plastics area. Setting up the plastics business as a division with a man having profit responsibility for it will free me of much of my current load and allow me to concentrate on the planning and implementation of our growth and diversification programs.

There is also the question of how you generate not only good ideas, but adequate follow-up down the line in the organization. There is a tendency on the part of managers who are functional specialists to solve problems on the basis of "let's spend more now so we can make more in the future." If this approach is not carefully controlled, growth in earnings per share is slowed down because it is obviously impossible to always continue to spend more now with the hope of making more in the future.

The divisional organization offers the possibility of two significant advantages. First of all, a divisional general manager has to develop a considerably broader view of the overall operations under his direction than is the case with a functional manager. Secondly, a divisional manager knows that sooner or later he will face the day of reckoning if he carries the "spend more now to earn more later" approach to his problems too far.

The president cited the case of Thermo-Ban, the company's newest product, to illustrate the need for more generalists at SPI.

## Thermo-Ban

Thermo-Ban was SPI's entry into the fabrication materials market. The new product was an inexpensive and highly durable plastic sheet designed for use in home and building construction in tropical climates. Thermo-Ban was a product of SPI research, an extension of the company's knowledge in the thermal plastics area. The difficulties that followed its introduction into the market were described by Mr. Solomon, Assistant Treasurer of SPI:

Thermo-Ban was a disaster when it was originally introduced in the Middle East. Before it was introduced, there had been a debate as to whether the product should be test marketed on a limited scale, or launched full scale in the Middle East market. Somewhere between the head office and the people in our English subsidiary (who were running the project), the decision was made to market it in all the major cities in the Middle East. A sales force was assembled and the product was launched.

Several serious bugs in the product were immediately discovered. The sheet cracked because of the continued dryness and construction workers

> didn't know how to work with the material. The product had to be withdrawn from the market. They tried it again in Central America with the same disappointing results.
>
> There was a new product committee in charge of the project. From the start, however, part of the committee was in the Middle East, part of it in England, and part of it here in Philadelphia. There were so many people involved, they haven't really decided who was responsible for the problem. The story is still a very confused one to me.

The president of SPI felt that he himself should have foreseen the problems that beset Thermo-Ban's introduction into the market. He felt that, had the product been in the hands of a division general manager, much of Thermo-Ban's problems in the market would have been avoided.

## THE ACQUISITION PROGRAM

In designing a new organization structure for SPI, John Spearman considered the need for an organizational unit which would identify and examine acquisition opportunities for the company—an activity which was expected to play an important part in the realization of SPI's $300 million growth objective. In 1966, SPI hired William Goodman, formerly of the IBM company, to conduct the search for preliminary investigation of acquisition opportunities for SPI. Mr. Goodman was currently being aided in this activity by Dr. Thomas, vice-president of the research department. The latter possessed extensive contracts with companies in the plastics and pharmaceuticals industries.

A more pressing issue, however, and one that had been raised by the company's recent acquisitions, was the question of how the actual acquisition and transitional management of new enterprises would be handled organizationally at SPI. The company was currently discussing with the California Research Institute, a well-known consulting firm, the creation of a separate organizational unit, perhaps a "Ventures and Acquisitions Department," to manage newly acquired companies until these became established as separate divisions themselves. As far as the two past acquisitions of the company were concerned, each case had been handled differently from the other. The following paragraphs describe the NETOL and the Reschild-Bauer acquisitions.

## NETOL, INC.

The first acquisition made under SPI's expansion and diversification program was NETOL, Inc., a Philadelphia-based concern which did highly specialized research in resins and in the use of plastics for high strength glues and adhesive materials. The company had been purchased by SPI primarily for its research knowledge, although NETOL had also achieved limited sales for its products.

NETOL was currently under the direction of Dr. Thomas. It was felt that at this stage, NETOL was still primarily a research operation which tied in closely with the research concerns of Dr. Thomas. It was felt that a close association between NETOL and the SPI research organization would facilitate "cross-fertilization" among the research personnel of both organizations—a key concept in SPI's strategy for expansion and diversification into related fields. NETOL's products were presently sold by a small number of SPI salesmen under a temporary arrangement agreed upon by Dr. Thomas and the vice-president of Marketing.

There was a feeling, nevertheless, that NETOL's assignment to Dr. Thomas was not the best use of the research director's talents. Mr. Solomon commented:

> The past success of this company had been built primarily on the outstanding productivity of the SPI research organization. Two years before Dr. Meyer (former research director) was due to retire in 1966, Jack (Spearman) and I agreed that finding a replacement for him was the most important and pressing problem facing the company at that time. Now that we have a man like Dr. Thomas, I'm not sure that getting him involved with NETOL's commercial operations is the best use of his talents. This problem again relates to the shortage of management talent in this company. Somehow, we have never worried about training new managers to back up our expanded activities until the need for such managers is upon us.

## RESCHILD-BAUER, INC.

Reschild-Bauer, Inc. manufactured a specialty line of ethical pharmaceuticals designed for the treatment of degenerative diseases in man. (Examples of degenerative diseases are peptic ulcers, arthritis, heart diseases, etc.). Its products were promoted to the medical profession throughout the United States by a force of sixty detail men, and distributed through several drug wholesalers in the United States. The company had one foreign subsidiary, Reschild-Europa, but it also licensed its products to other foreign pharmaceutical companies abroad. The company owned a research subsidiary, California Laboratories, Inc., where the company's basic research in human pharmacology was conducted.

Since its acquisition in March 1966, Reschild-Bauer, Inc. had been managed as a separate company. Although this company had looked like a very good acquisition prospect, SPI management had been disappointed to discover, after acquiring the firm, that Reschild-Bauer's asset values had been grossly overstated and that its executive organization was chaotic and inefficient. Mr. Thomas Copes, who was hired to manage Reschild-Bauer for SPI, reconstructed the events in the acquisition of the company:

> Reschild apparently had begun to slip in all the classic ways at the time it was acquired by SPI. There was great imbalance in its executive organization. Its sales manager, a very effective salesman, got all the allocation of company funds while the manufacturing manager, less effective as a salesman, got nothing. Financial control was loose and the manufacturing department was a mess. There were no formal procedures for production scheduling and control, and nobody had any data on costs.
>
> When Jack dismissed some top people, including the former president of the company, some others resigned. This created a vacuum in the executive organization of Reschild. As a result, Jack was forced to spend two days each week actually running this company. This arrangement lasted for six months until I was brought in last December. We have now filled in the other positions with new people.

Some SPI executives remarked that a "confidence gap," as they termed it, seemed to be reflected in the president's handling of some aspects of the Reschild-Bauer acquisition. According to Mr. Solomon:

> Before we acquired Reschild, Fred Kelly, vice-president of finance, practically begged Jack to be allowed to examine some of the assets of Reschild. But for some reason, Jack refused and instead handled the whole deal very much by himself. . . . Perhaps he was afraid that if we started to turn Reschild upside down, the way International Chemicals did with us on that abortive merger attempt years ago, we might lose what looked like a very good acquisition opportunity.[2] Still, we can't help wondering whether Jack really thinks we can do our jobs.

In February 1967, Reschild-Bauer, Inc. showed a modest profit for the first time since it was acquired by SPI. Despite its problems, Mr. Solomon felt that it had been a "good buy" for SPI, one that served as the company's entry into the biochemicals market.

## G. B. PEARSON COMPANY

In February 1967, SPI was seriously considering the acquisition of G. B. Pearson Company of Palo Alto, California, which had sales of over $300,000. The company manufactured a specialized plastic material used to form the protective package of various devices implanted into the human body, particularly electronic heart pacers. SPI management saw in

[2]International Chemicals had attempted to acquire Spearman several years earlier, but negotiations failed for a variety of reasons.

this company a unique opportunity to apply its plastics know-how to the medical field.

## RESEARCH AND DEVELOPMENT

SPI's expansion program also entailed a widening of the scope of the company's research in plastic chemistry. New areas of basic research were added to the company's research effort and new emphasis had been placed on broadening the applications of the company's products to include the wider industrial markets for plastics, particularly the industrial coating and fabrication materials areas. SPI had also decided to undertake Research and Development activities in two of its overseas subsidiaries. This was considered desirable in order to enable these subsidiaries to adapt their products to the requirements of their markets. Finally, the addition of NETOL had given SPI advanced research know-how in resins and in the plastic adhesives area.

The president of SPI was at this time concerned about the productivity of the SPI research organization. The "Thermalite" product had been considerably improved and developed since its introduction in 1960, but since that time, SPI had successfully introduced only two new products. Both these products were developed by a German plastics firm, and SPI sold these products in the United States under license from the foreign company. SPI itself had not produced a significant new product for the American market in the last seven years. "You have to conclude that something has happened to Research to get such a dry spell," the president of the company said.

> One thing that happened is that we were so concerned about our exposure in the high temperature plastics area that we wanted a better "Thermalite." It may be that we have spent far too much of our research time on this instead of trying new things. Today, we're still spending some time in this area. Another thing that happened is that the research organization grew greatly in size. This created many problems in research administration that Ernie Thomas has been able to solve.

Dr. Ernest Thomas (vice-president of research and development) joined the SPI organization in 1965. He commented on the performance of SPI's research organization:

> The company's research productivity has not been very good in recent years. To give you an indication of this, about 80 percent of our current plastics sales volume is accounted for by products developed at least eight years ago. Another 10 percent represent sales of plastic products

> developed outside the SPI laboratories, primarily by foreign companies. Only 10 percent of sales have been contributed by products developed at SPI in the last eight years. Putting the problem in another way, by 1974 we will lose our patent protection on 70 percent of all our existing products.

Dr. Thomas attributed the decline in research productivity at SPI to increased concentration of SPI's research resources into what he termed as "defensive research," i.e., efforts to extend and improve the company's current products, particularly the "Thermalite" product.

> When I first joined this organization, 55 percent of the company's research activities had no new product potential, these activities being concerned primarily with further testing and improving of the "Thermalite" plastic. Of the other 45 percent that had new product potential, only 25 percent represented research in *new* fields. I would like to bring the research organization to the point where at least 75 percent of research time has new product possibilities. By and large, this will be achieved through the hiring of more research personnel, although some redirection of our current research to new fields would also be involved.

In view of the greatly increased size of the research staff and the expanded scope of its activities, Dr. Thomas considered the establishment of a control system for the company's research activities to be one of his more important and immediate concerns. He explained that the California Research Institute consultants were working with the company to devise and implement a system of control for the research organization that would enable the company to maintain some direction in research without inhibiting the creative potential of research personnel.

He believed that to implement this program, various service staffs had to be established, staffs which the research organization could do without in the past because of the smaller size of the organization, but which nevertheless were now essential to the effective functioning of the research department. He believed that more research personnel with administrative interest and talent would have to be identified and trained to shoulder the burdens of administration and direction of SPI's enlarged research effort.

Although Dr. Thomas had spent his first year at SPI working with Dr. Meyer (his predecessor) and "being careful not to rock the boat," according to the president, signs of change were evident in the research department. The president believed that the SPI research organization had begun to adapt to Dr. Thomas' approach to research administration. "This is one area in which delegation of authority has taken hold," the president said, "But research being what it is, I'm scared to death that I have no way of being sure that our research activities today will give us the new products we will need to survive in the future in this industry."

## INTERNATIONAL OPERATIONS

Figure 5 shows the geographic extent of SPI's international activities. In recent years the rate of growth in international sales had begun to outstrip the growth of domestic sales of plastics. This trend was expected to continue in the future as the company increased its penetration of its existing foreign markets and as it entered new foreign markets for its products. Some SPI executives believed that the international market for SPI's products was the most promising avenue for growth in the future.

SPI had a policy of direct distribution in foreign markets because the standard royalty rates that could be obtained on licensing agreements were not considered satisfactory. As a particular foreign market for its products expanded, SPI replaced its independent distributors in that market with a sales branch, or a manufacturing subsidiary. All the company's foreign subsidiaries were controlled by means of annual operating budgets. These budgets were submitted at the beginning of the year to Mr. James Weston, vice-president of international operations, who reviewed them quarterly, in consultation with Alfred Kelly, the finance vice-president, and with Christopher Duncan, the production vice-president. Two of the more recently established subsidiaries of SPI, one in India and another in Spain, were managed directly by SPI's English subsidiary.

According to James Weston, the key problems of his position lay in assessing the desirability of making investments in particular foreign countries. When a decision had been made regarding the desirability of investing in a foreign country, there was a further question of how much investment the company would make and what form the company's investment would take, e.g., sales branch, manufacturing subsidiary, and so forth. These problems required him to be intimately familiar with the conditions in the company's markets in various countries.

Commenting on the trends in the foreign plastics markets, Mr. Weston said:

> We expect greater competition and more government control in almost all the chemicals and plastics markets abroad. In Latin America, for example, most of the countries there already regulate chemicals and plastics prices in one form or another. This, of course, increases our risk. For instance, following a recent devaluation of the Brazilian currency, we had to absorb large inventory losses because we have yet to negotiate with the Brazilian government for an increase in our prices in order to catch up with the inflation. The sales we had built up over the years in that country were, of course, wiped out. . . .
>
> We are newcomers in the international market and our limited product line is a weakness in these markets. We have a difficult time covering our overhead, with only a limited number of products to sell. Interna-

> tional Chemicals, by contrast, has been, in the international market longer and has a wider line of products to sell. This enables it to support stronger marketing programs and larger sales forces.
>
> Recently, we've decided to expand our product line in these foreign markets by buying domestic companies with an established line of plastics and chemical products to add to our own. We have recently bought one such company in Japan. In other countries, we may have to settle for joint venture arrangements with established companies there.
>
> Some of our products that have sold well here in the United States have had to be modified to meet the particular requirements of users in the various foreign markets. We also have problems in pricing. A number of our products have excellent potential abroad if we could only price them at a sufficiently low level to be within the means of users abroad. In short, we have most of the problems that firms operating internationally encounter.

Although the company enjoyed what was considered a satisfactory market share in most of its foreign markets, some SPI executives believed that not enough was being done to realize the full potential of the overseas markets. Some concern was also expressed over the fact that the company's English subsidiary was managing more and more of SPI's subsidiaries in foreign countries, instead of the head office. There seemed to be a general feeling, however, that the small size of Mr. Weston's staff had made it difficult for him to run the far-flung interests of SPI with greater effectiveness.

## THE NEW ORGANIZATION

The need for change in the company's organization and the general nature of this change was the subject of continuing discussion among the SPI executives in the Operations Committee in February 1967. Although no specific detailed proposal for a new organization had yet been mentioned in these discussions. Figure 2 shows John Spearman's tentative proposal for a new organization for SPI.

### Problems of Implementation

The president of Spearman Plastics, Inc. conceded that he was "flying on totally new ground" with regard to the reorganization of his company. He was concerned with the question of how to judge that the proposed new organization was "right," not only in terms acceptable to him, but also in terms that were understandable to the company's other executives. The question he had been asking himself was, "Who do I have to sell on this new organization?"

I've discussed the need for a new organization with the members of the Operations Committee. They all seem agreeable to it in principle. Nevertheless, I feel sure that when I draw boxes and begin to put names in them, I'll begin to hear some noise from these men. The big question will be, "Who'll get domestic plastics?"

The problem of implementation is people. I don't think for example, that Bob Spearman would accept the position of divisional vice-president of marketing for the domestic plastics division. We have played enough with boxes so he has made it clear to me he won't accept it. He feels we will be investing money in areas outside of plastics and as a major stockholder of this company, he deserves a greater say in these decisions than he would get if he were handling solely domestic plastics sales.

The possibility I've given the most thought to in this regard is the establishment of a development division. This will be the division that would assume operating responsibility for a new acquisition or a new area of internal development, and nurse these along until they logically fit the existing divisions or become divisions themselves. NETOL will probably be transferred to this division. . . . Whether Bob Spearman has the talent or the interest to run such a division, I don't know.

The president explained that broader managerial experience on the part of SPI managers was a widespread need in the company, one that was present "up and down the line" in the SPI organization.

There is a lot of bitching here that people don't have enough authority. But I know that there are areas here where people won't make decisions. Last week, for example, there were two items on my desk:

One had to do with the question of which kind of a wrist watch we should give as a twenty-five-year award to one of our scientists. The man to receive the award already had a good wrist watch for himself and wondered if we could give him one for his wife instead. . . . Now this matter should never have come up to me—although I am not surprised that it did. The man in charge of the award had spent twenty years in this company learning *not* to make decisions.

The other item was a question of who could use the reserved seats in the dining room. . . . It really strikes me as funny that this kind of question should come from people who just said, "I wish you would delegate more. . . .

John Spearman was particularly concerned about his father's reaction to the proposed new organization for the company.

I have to sell this plan to Dad, and to the board of directors. The members of our Board have been with Dad in this company for a long time, and they have great respect for his views. Dad is a genius for operating "from the seat of his pants" and he has built this company by making almost all the key decisions all by himself. . . . But he can't seem to see the need for change. He can't see why we have to move away from the organization that has served this company so well in the past.

John Spearman compared his style of management with that of his father, emphasizing the danger that his involvement in the situation might prevent him from making an objective observation and cause him to "misread" what had happened.

> Dad was a truly accomplished master of detail. I never understood how he did it, but he did. His technique was to get as many of the details on any problem and to deal with each of these problems in all their detail. He didn't like to deal with problems at an abstract or conceptual level. He did it detail by detail. On the question of a general salary increase for the company, for example, he would want to be involved not only with the general decision on the problem, but he would go right through and figure out who gets raises, when, and how much they got. . . . He didn't want to run the risk of someone else's judgment, the possibility of someone else making a mistake.
>
> I would prefer to have my subordinates make the detailed decisions for me. I feel that, now, people here are getting to exercise more and more autonomy, although I can't say that it is to a desirable enough degree. People still come to me to settle questions that nobody else will make a decision on. The long-range planning process that we are involved in, plus the greater emphasis on the use of budgets should lead to a different control climate throughout this company.

Some organizational issues also remained unsolved. The president could foresee problems in establishing a workable division of responsibilities between staffs at the corporate level and the division managers under the proposed organization. He was concerned that the first occupants of the new corporate staff positions would come from among the present functional specialists at SPI, people who, in his view, might have difficulty "letting go" of their accustomed areas of jurisdiction.

With regard to the research function, the president also pondered the question of corporate versus divisional research. "If your divisions depend upon a high technology input for growth, but this input comes from corporate research, how can you truly hold the divisional manager responsible for profit performance?" the president asked. "I haven't begun to see the answer to this question."

## THE EXPERIENCE AND VIEWS OF COMPANY EXECUTIVES

### Dr. Ernest Thomas

Dr. Ernest Thomas joined SPI to succeed Dr. Meyer, who retired in 1965, as director of research and development for the company. Dr. Thomas left his position of vice-president of research and development at Dawson Chemicals Company, where he had been a key figure in that company's successful diversification into the plastics and pharmaceuticals fields. His management interests at Dawson transcended the purely research aspects of the chemicals business, as he had actively participated in the various marketing and sales development programs that were necessary for Dawson's entry into the plastics and biochemicals markets.

Dr. Thomas defined his job at SPI as being primarily the director of research and development. However, he also took an active part in SPI's long-range planning and acquisition programs. Dr. Thomas was responsible for NETOL, and more recently, for directing the establishment of SPI's overseas research activities in its British and Japanese subsidiaries. Over all, Dr. Thomas was directly responsible for the activities of 400 people, 25 percent of whom possessed postgraduate degrees.

Under the new organization for SPI, Dr. Thomas envisioned separate product divisions that performed their own research activities. There would always be a central research organization for the whole company, he said, performing only the most fundamental kind of research. But to be real profit centers, as the SPI divisions were envisioned to be in the new organization, Dr. Thomas believed that these divisions should perform and shoulder the cost of their own research activities.

Commenting on the top management team at SPI, Dr. Thomas said:

> We have a highly motivated group of people here, and I think the tasks ahead of us will provide a challenge that we can meet. A strong point of this company is the absence of the kinds of company politics and personality conflicts that I have seen in other organizations I've worked with. This is a family corporation, and this fact moderates any excessive ambitions and rivalries for positions among the executive group. . . .
>
> Nor is it difficult to work with the members of the Spearman family. I am very happy to work for an enthusiastic and highly competent young man like John Spearman. Jim Weston is another very capable man, and I am sure that he will be of further great benefit to this organization. . . .
>
> I see no formidable difficulties in the realization of the new organization. John has done a good job of indoctrinating this group, of preparing his executives for that kind of change.

Asked what his own ambitions were, Dr. Thomas replied that he wanted to do the best job possible as vice-president of research for the company. He also entertained the possibility, he said, of someday becoming a group or product vice-president operating at the corporate level. For the moment, however, Dr. Thomas believed that he could do the company the most good in his present position.

## Mr. Alfred Kelly

Mr. Alfred Kelly, treasurer and vice-president of finance, joined the SPI organization in 1950, when the former president, Franklin Spearman, hired him with the title of assistant treasurer. He became vice-president of finance in 1959.

Asked to describe what his current responsibilities were, Mr. Kelly replied, "I don't know":

> Upon being accepted for the position, I was told my job was to handle accounting and taxes. No further attempt was ever made to define my position even though it has taken on and dropped off several major responsibilities over the years.
>
> John Spearman, since becoming president, has assumed some of the functions of a financial vice-president without discussing our relative roles and, I suspect, without even realizing this. For example, in the case of the Reschild acquisition, the financial section was not involved in any capacity so far as financial matters were concerned. The acquisition was headed up personally by John Spearman who apparently decided that an adequate purchase investigation was not necessary. On two or three occasions we brought to his attention that inventories in such an industry could be a very tricky thing and that they should be thoroughly investigated. Nothing was done and, as it turned out, the inventories were considerably overstated.
>
> Another matter concerns our expansion and diversification program. This organization had no long-range financial planning under Franklin Spearman. But our expansion and diversification program now requires the preparation of long-range financial plans. Yet John Spearman has effectively excluded the finance organization from participating in the acquisition program except as it relates to its own role in long-range plan.
>
> There is a young man by the name of Ed Solomon in our organization who was hired by me to work on treasurer and secretary assignments. He began to be used by both Franklin and John Spearman and ended up working for the three of us. His work has suffered a great deal because of this divided role and lack of job definition. On occasion he has received contradictory orders. This has all resulted in a very confused and unhappy Ed Solomon.

It appeared that Mr. Kelly was currently responsible for tax and budget matters, in addition to the accounting and treasurership functions. He was also responsible for SPI's computer facilities and from time to time handled legal, public relations, personnel, employee benefit and other widely assorted duties. A large part of his time was also spent on administrative duties in the international division.

Mr. Kelly expressed concern that a company with SPI's growth objectives did not have a viable staff to perform an effective job of financial management for the company. He pointed out that the company had no treasurer, tax expert, systems competence, and no internal audit staff. According to Mr. Kelly the small size of SPI's present financial organization was the result of the former president's cost consciousness and lack of understanding of the role of financial management in a modern corporation. He explained that the former president has no interest in such techniques as return on investment, stock turnover, etc. This lack of top-management interest, which came at a time when the company enjoyed an extremely liquid position and high profitability, meant that many widely accepted techniques of accounting and financial control were not used in the SPI.

Mr. Kelly felt the change to John Spearman and his dedication to growth and diversification had meant "a new ball game." An operating budget, installed in 1960, but largely ignored by both Franklin Spearman and John Spearman, was now in use at SPI. Rate-of-return concepts were employed in the company's recent acquisitions and in 1966 a capital budgeting procedure was established. The capital budget nevertheless had been largely ignored by top management because, in Mr. Kelly's view, of "lack of time and adequate personnel to deal adequately with all the problems and new techniques being put to use throughout our organization."

The objectives of SPI, as Mr. Kelly saw them, were to realize an annual growth rate that would enable the company to reach the $300 million sales level within the next ten years. The company, he said, wanted to maintain its reputation as a growth company and to expand its scope as a worldwide corporation. Not everyone shared these objectives, however. "Frank Spearman has been unable to accept with any interest and enthusiasm any diversification outside of the United States and outside of our present type of business," Mr. Kelly explained. "He is more concerned with protecting what he has built and achieved."

In Mr. Kelly's opinion the SPI organization suffered a major weakness in the lack of management capabilities to handle new businesses in new fields. He cited the case of Thermo-Ban. He was not sure, he said, that creation of a separate ventures and acquisitions department would overcome this weakness. He could foresee many problems in the transitional management of new acquisitions under the contemplated organization. Who was to decide when a new acquisition was ready to be transferred to another division? What if the existing divisions did not want the new business? Should division managers participate in acquisition decisions? These were some of the questions that were raised by Mr. Kelly as he discussed the company's reorganization plans.

When Mr. Kelly was asked what he enjoyed about his job, he replied:

> What I like most about my job at SPI is the personal freedom that I have to do my job. Under Franklin Spearman this company had never had a tradition for fixed and well-defined areas of responsibility. We had wide latitude in pursuing our interests in this organization. Now this is going or gone.
>
> In a way this is not all bad. The company is now at a stage where more systematic procedures for decision making and control are needed. The kind of "seat-of-the-pants" management we had in the past has to give

> way to more formal controls, such as the capital budget. I am not at all sure, however, that top management is willing to pay the price, to provide adequate staff, and to spend the personal time required to make these controls effective working tools.

Finally, Mr. Kelly expressed the hope that the trend towards a more systematic management climate would be accompanied by a more clear definition of organizational relationships and the removal of many of the ambiguities in the SPI organization, particularly with regard to the finance function.

## Dr. Christopher Duncan

Dr. Christopher Duncan joined SPI as a research chemist in 1945, shortly after receiving his Ph.D. in organic chemistry. Having shown interest outside the purely research aspect of chemistry, he was assigned to head a pilot operation of one of SPI's early projects in plastics. From this beginning, he moved up the SPI production organization until he became manager of the chemicals department of the production and engineering division. In 1950, he was sent on a special assignment to Brazil to investigate and make recommendations on SPI's ailing chemicals subsidiary there. His recommendations to close down this plant and to integrate its operation with a larger and more efficient SPI subsidiary in Canada was received favorably by SPI management. In 1963, he became president of Spearman Chemicals International, a subsidiary that ran all of SPI's chemicals operations abroad. Since 1963 he had also been vice-president of engineering and production. In both of these capacities, he was responsible for a total of some 900 people in the United States and abroad.

In addition to his ongoing responsibilities in the SPI production and engineering department and in Spearman Chemicals International, Dr. Duncan was responsible for setting up production facilities in the growing number of SPI plastics subsidiaries throughout the world. Dr. Duncan also aided Mr. Weston in evaluating production and cost performance and the annual plans of these subsidiaries.

Asked to comment on what type of organization SPI should move towards, Dr. Duncan replied:

> Is a functional organization really self-limiting? The scope and complexity of the plastics production operation has increased considerably as we achieved backward integration and added more products in our production operations. Yet, the technology of plastics production is basically a stable one. I think the present production organization can rather easily be modified to handle any increase in SPI's production activities which might reasonably be anticipated here and abroad, now and in the future. We do have problems in that we lack middle management personnel to

meet SPI's expansion requirements. Indeed, our management as a whole is too weak to handle our present volume in the face of increasing competition much less more business. But I am not sure that divisionalization is the way to solve this.

Dr. Duncan believed that the major growth opportunities facing SPI in the future lay in the international market. He did not feel, however, that SPI had done enough to exploit the full potential of the international market. He pointed out that with so many foreign subsidiaries to control and direct, Mr. Weston had practically no staff to support him in his work. Dr. Duncan was also concerned because administrative responsibility for Thermo-Ban and two of SPI's most recently established subsidiaries in India and Spain, had been assigned to the company's British subsidiary.

## Mr. Thomas Copes

Mr. Thomas Copes joined the SPI organization in December 1966 as president and chief executive officer of the Reschild-Bauer subsidiary. Before Mr. Copes' appointment at SPI, John Spearman had been managing Reschild-Bauer directly since June 1966. Mr. Copes left his position of vice-president and general manager of the Pharmaceuticals Division of Consolidated Chemicals, Inc. to join SPI, and had extensive experience in the pharmaceuticals business prior to his association with Consolidated.

Because the pharmaceuticals market and technology was unfamiliar to most SPI executives, Mr. Copes believed that Reschild would continue to be managed as a separate division from SPI's main plastics business. Reschild was currently set up as a profit center and Mr. Copes reported directly to John Spearman.

Mr. Copes reviewed the two major problems he had faced since taking over the management of Reschild-Bauer, Inc. The first problem involved Reschild's production organization. Mr. Copes explained that Reschild's production operations were inefficient and disorganized. There were no procedures for scheduling operations in a systematic way, and cost data on products were not available. The problem of installing a more efficient system of production was complicated by the fact that the company's production supervisors and foremen were unfamiliar with even the most rudimentary techniques of production planning and control. A consulting firm had been engaged to design and install a more efficient production system for Reschild.

The second problem had to do with Reschild's research subsidiary, California Laboratories, Inc. This subsidiary was run by Dr. Alfred Martin, one of the founders of Reschild. Although Mr. Copes acknowledged the high quality of the research performed by Dr. Martin and his group, Mr. Copes was concerned that Dr. Martin tended to run California Laboratories as an "independent research operation, pursuing his own research interests without much reference to the needs of Reschild." "It is a common problem with scientific personnel that their values are not always profit-oriented," Mr. Copes said. Mr. Copes did not see any easy solution to this problem.

Concerning SPI's expansion program, Mr. Copes had reservations about SPI's plan to diversify further into the pharmaceuticals business. In view of pending legislation concerning profits and practices in the pharmaceuticals industry, he wondered whether SPI might not be well advised to channel the bulk of its investments within the plastics industry—the business which it knew best and at which it had been very successful. Mr. Copes also expressed skepticism regarding SPI's hope of obtaining most of its new management requirements through its acquisition program. In his view:

> Usually, you can only acquire companies that are in the failure mode. And you can't expect to find good managers there. The Reschild-Bauer acquisition is an example of this, although now they say they've got a really great guy running this G. B. Pearson deal. . . . I think Mr. Goodman (director of planning and acquisitions) is being expected to do too much, considering his training and experience. . . . Frankly, I think he's just running around not really knowing where to go.

Asked why he came to join SPI, Mr. Copes replied:

> I left my job at Consolidated Chemicals because, after meeting John and seeing what he was trying to do, I felt it a great challenge to participate in his efforts to build up SPI. I can feel a greater sense of contribution in the future and success of this company than I could in an established giant like Consolidated.
>
> I think that to achieve the objectives that this company has set for itself, there is no substitute for down-to-earth and disciplined business thinking. . . . I can't see this business of calling people "presidents" of their divisions. It only causes them to lose their business perspectives and leads them to encase themselves in ostentatious offices such as this one (pointing to the red-carpeted and well-furnished executive offices built by the former managers of Reschild-Bauer).
>
> I view my job as being a general manager of a plant, a plant that has been losing money and has to be put back in shape. . . . John is a young and enthusiastic manager. . . . But I think he has the right instincts.

### Mr. Robert Spearman

Mr. Robert Spearman originally became involved in the operation of the SPI company as a salesman of its plastics products. In 1964, he became vice-president of marketing for SPI. Mr. Spearman organized his department into four major subdivisions: sales, advertising, marketing research, and distribution. There was a sales administration group which consisted of product managers who developed and supervised the execution of the company's sales programs for the company's various customer groups. Recently, some of the department's salesmen spent part of their time soliciting for NETOL's products, but Mr. Robert Spearman believed that his was a temporary arrangement and that eventually, NETOL's sales activities would be handled by a separate NETOL sales force. The Spearman marketing department did not include sales activities for Reschild-Bauer, Inc.

Asked to describe how his job had changed in recent years, Mr. Robert Spearman replied:

> The whole approach to my job here has changed since John took over as president from Dad. Dad tended to exercise a greater degree of personal supervision and control over the activities of this department. He often came around asking detailed questions about almost all phases of marketing. John hardly ever does this. He tends to be concerned primarily with overall results, and makes me responsible for marketing in these terms. I must say I like this better. I have a greater sense of autonomy in the operation of my department and I can discuss the marketing function in terms of overall results rather than in terms of day-to-day details.
>
> I wear two hats in this organization. As marketing VP I am accountable to John for the results of my department's operations. However, as a major stockholder of the company, I must have a voice in the overall management of this company. The Operations Committee is "show and tell" for John, and we are told about decisions that have already been made. In a sense, this is as it should be, because there are decisions which John must make as president and he can't let his subordinates make these decisions for him. But wearing my other hat as a major stockholder of this company, I feel I have an obligation to participate in the major policy decisions in this company. . . . You'll see me as two persons in this company. But I am careful to know when I am wearing one hat rather than the other, and I behave appropriate to each.

When Robert Spearman was asked to comment on the company's marketing philosophy, he replied that SPI had always gone by his father's philosophy, viz., "assume nothing we make is perfect; assume always that it can be improved."

> This philosophy has been a potent guiding principle and source of motivation for me. Many people would be skeptical and say that a business is run primarily for profit. But in my case what is another $10,000 a year in income? I already have and have always had most of the material things I want. Only when I can believe in the principle behind what we are doing, when I know that we are performing a unique and important service, is there any meaning in what I'm doing in this company. And as long as I know that the man running the company shares this code, as I know John does, then it doesn't make too much difference to me what title I have.

Robert Spearman considered the job of president of the company a "lonely" one. He said he enjoyed "people problems," and he liked to associate with bright individuals in his department, some of whom may someday rise to become "presidents" of SPI's divisions. He believed he would enjoy working on corporate personnel and organizational planning in the new SPI organization. He was afraid, he said, that his job in marketing might become routine and dull once he succeeded in organizing it and setting up the proper procedures for it.

## Mr. Paul Donalds

Mr. Paul Donalds came to SPI from Commercial Industries, Inc., where he held the position of Industrial and Public Relations Manager. Since he joined SPI in November 1966, he had spent his time familiarizing himself with SPI's operations and organization by interviewing all of the key executives of the company. He saw the planning of the company's new organization and the creation of a personnel department at the corporate level as the key problems facing him in the near future. Presently, SPI had separate personnel offices in the various functional departments, and a corporate personnel function, as such, did not exist.

Mr. Donalds observed that the major weakness of SPI was the absence of middle-management talent. He attributed this to the lack of any systematic executive training and compensation programs under what he characterized as the "highly cost-conscious" management of the company under Franklin Spearman. He pointed out that the company's present middle managers received salaries which were substantially lower than those paid for comparable positions within and outside the plastics industry. This, combined with a highly centralized pattern of management and a "paternalistic" outlook towards employees, he felt was not conducive to the development of aggressive and responsible middle managers. Those middle managers who remained with the company were likely to be weak and lacking in talent or else would have become so accustomed to operating under close and detailed supervision as to lose much of their sense of initiative.

Commenting further on the organizational strengths and weaknesses of SPI, Mr. Donalds said:

> This company has an aggressive and highly motivated management group whose members have grown up with the company and know the business very well. But this can also be a disadvantage. Some executives are not always completely capable of expanding the scope of their responsibilities beyond those matters which they have learned and come to know very well.
>
> There is some degree of provincialism with regard to new concepts of management, and the executives who have learned to manage the "hard way" tend to have rigid notions about how to manage the operations of

> the company. Moreover, there is currently a lack of effective communications among departments, this being due, I think, to the fact that the present company executives have not been accustomed to group decision making under the previous centralized management pattern. However, this is a temporary deficiency which will be overcome as they now begin to operate more as a top management team under John's more participative methods of management.

Mr. Donalds believed that the SPI company would have to search for managers from the outside to build up most of the middle management staff required to meet the expanded size and scope of SPI's operations in the next five years. He believed that some of this management talent could be found in Reschild, although for the most part he hoped that the company would be able to obtain good managers through the new businesses that it would acquire in the future. Simultaneously with the building up of the company's middle management, Mr. Donalds believed that the company should move away from the paternalistic pattern towards more formalized management, particularly in programs for recruitment and evaluation of managers. An informal management atmosphere would not work in a $300 million firm, Mr. Donalds said.

Finally, in moving towards more formalized management control and procedures, Mr. Donalds expressed a need for caution with regard to the SPI research department. He believed that, to some extent, the informal atmosphere and personalized approach taken by the former president with regard to the company's research activities, may have accounted for the research department's prolific record of creativity and innovation.

## Mr. William Goodman

Mr. William Goodman joined the SPI organization in December 1965. Among his initial assignments with the company was acting as controller for Reschild-Bauer, Inc., shortly after its acquisition by SPI. Having done a good job in this assignment, he was brought back to SPI to head a staff for planning and acquisitions. Currently, he assisted the president in corporate long-range planning and was also responsible for the investigation of acquisition prospects for the company. He had under his supervision an assistant statistician and an investment expert.

Mr. Goodman placed great emphasis on the acquisition program in the plans for reorganizing SPI. Too often, he said, companies that undertake programs of diversification through acquisitions fail because they are poorly organized for this purpose. With regard to SPI in particular, he explained:

> We are looking for small concerns in our acquisition program. These are the small opportunities that often fall through the crack in the floor

and are missed by big companies. We have to be systematic and careful if we are going to catch these.

He outlined what he believed to be the essential components of the organization structure of a growth company such as SPI. This organization, he believed, could be conceptually divided into three main parts: One part, composed of the various operating divisions (plastics, pharmaceuticals, etc.), would "continue" the company's present businesses; a second part, made up of the various research organizations at SPI, would attempt to "create" new business for and further develop the present business of the conglomerate company; finally, the third essential component of the organization, the ventures and acquisitions department, would "find" new businesses for the company to undertake. The chart below illustrates these concepts.

He believed, however, that this organization represented a long-run "ideal." For one thing, he said, SPI did not now possess the management talent to make such an organization a workable one. Much further training of present managers would be required and new executives from the outside would have to be brought in. He also anticipated that "ego problems" would arise in changing the organization because the company's present executives might be reluctant to make the necessary organization and responsibility changes.

A problem with regard to the company's acquisition program, according to Mr. Goodman, was the absence of long-range strategic plans on which diversification and expansion activities should be based. He noted the lack of any long-range financial projections, facilities, planning, and personnel and organizational development plans. He attributed this failure to the former president's one-man domination of the SPI operations.

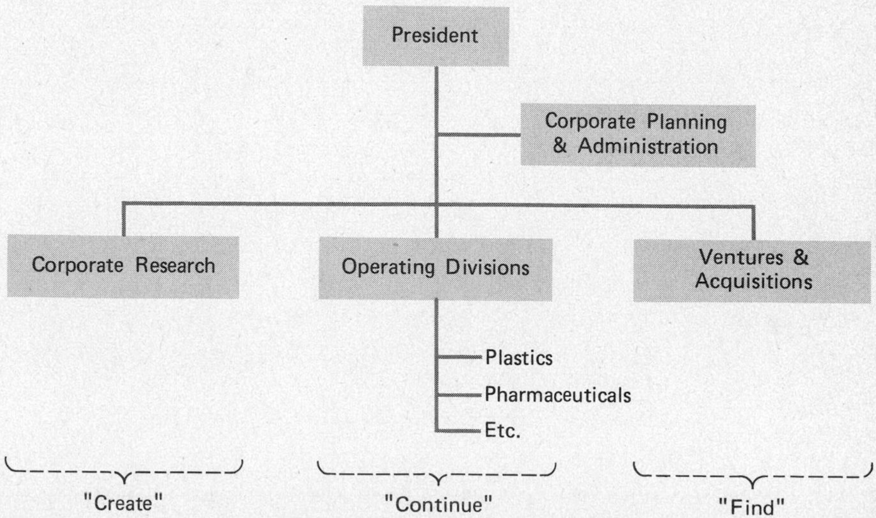

But the difficulty did not end with Franklin Spearman, Mr. Goodman explained. Even the present president was too enmeshed in operational matters, particularly in the domestic plastics business, to be able to devote much time to long-range planning. Mr. Goodman saw it as one of his most important functions to assist the president in the corporate long-range planning activities of the firm. He hoped that through the development of better plans and through the establishment of more systematic control procedures, the president would begin to be able to spend a greater proportion of his time at the planning and conceptual level instead of at the current operational level.

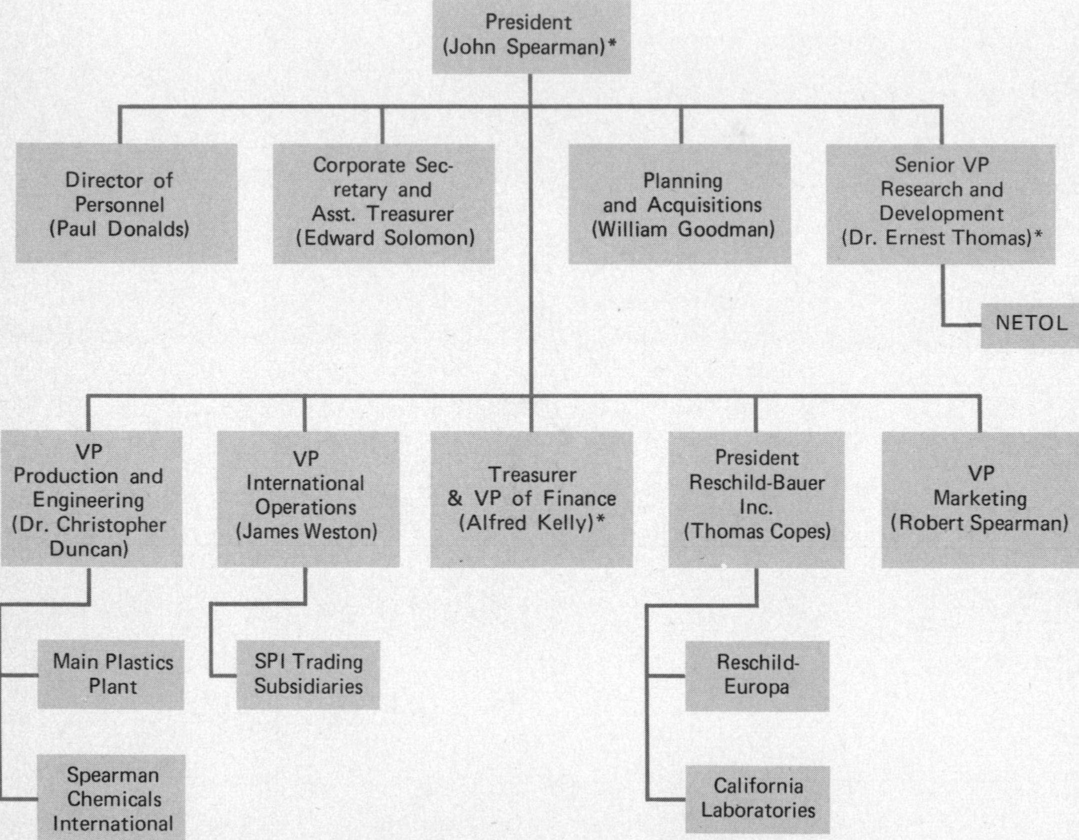


**Figure 1** Spearman Plastics, Inc., Present Organization Structure, February 1967

*Signifies membership in SPI Board of Directors.

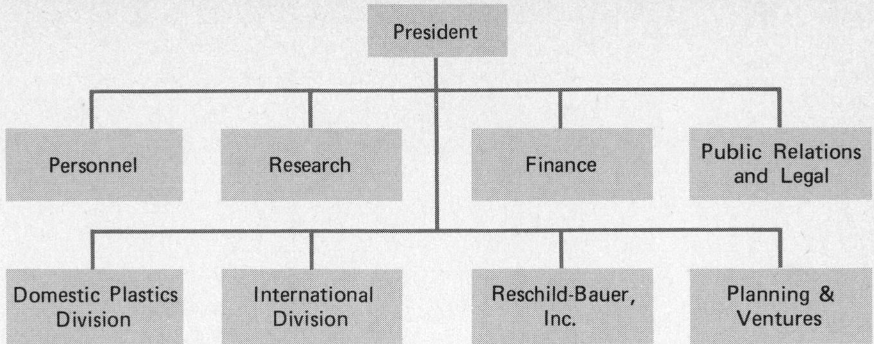


**Figure 2** Spearman Plastics, Inc., Proposed Organization Structure

## Mr. Edward Solomon

Mr. Edward Solomon, a graduate of the Harvard Business School, joined the SPI organization in 1958, as assistant treasurer for the company. Currently Mr. Solomon carried the designation of corporate sec-

**Figure 3 Spearman Plastics, Inc. and Subsidiaries**
*Annual Sales and Net Income After Taxes*

| *Year* | *Sales (000)* | *Net Income (000)* |
|---|---|---|
| 1953 | $20,830 | $ 4,908 |
| 1954 | 22,543 | 5,265 |
| 1955 | 24,463 | 5,537 |
| 1956 | 26,132 | 5,576 |
| 1957 | 27,607 | 5,837 |
| 1958 | 29,525 | 5,964 |
| 1959 | 35,821 | 7,956 |
| 1960 | 45,300 | 11,032 |
| 1961 | 57,132 | 14,825 |
| 1962 | 69,220 | 19,388 |
| 1963 | 71,171 | 18,560 |
| 1964 | 79,651 | 19,240 |
| 1965* | 84,771 | 18,283 |
| 1966* | 97,600 | 19,160 |

*Figures for 1965 and 1966 are consolidated figures.

retary and assistant treasurer. He was assistant to the vice-president of finance, and also to the president of the company.

Mr. Solomon's position had been described as a "catch-all" position, one which included such matters as insurance, real estate, public relations, pension plans, etc. Mr. Solomon considered his job to be one of the most ill-defined positions in the SPI organization. On the other hand, however, he found his job interesting in that it gave him the opportunity to be involved in almost all activities of the firm in all functional areas.

In describing the company's expansion and diversification program, Mr. Solomon stressed the need to relate the criteria for diversification and acquisitions to the strengths and weaknesses of SPI. He characterized SPI at present to be essentially a "specialty-line manufacturer of plastics."

**Figure 4 Spearman Plastics, Inc. and Subsidiaries Consolidated Balance Sheets As of Dec. 31, 1966 and 1965**

| *Assets* | | | *1966* | *1965* |
|---|---|---|---|---|
| Current Assets | | | | |
| Cash | | | $ 3,619,218 | $ 3,811,807 |
| Certificates of Deposit | | | 2,929,156 | 5,441,184 |
| U.S. Government Securities | | | 28,073,397 | 27,713,243 |
| Receivables less reserve | | | 19,136,017 | 18,956,146 |
| Inventories, at lower of cost (first-in first-out basis) or market: | | | | |
| | *1966* | *1965* | | |
| Finished Goods | 3,849,373 | 3,287,351 | | |
| Work in Process | 8,959,227 | 7,760,911 | | |
| Raw materials and supplies | 8,441,283 | 7,104,530 | 21,249,883 | 18,152,791 |
| Total Current Assets | | | 75,007,671 | 74,075,171 |
| Other Assets | | | | |
| Prepaid expenses and sundry other assets | | | 1,901,803 | 1,231,557 |
| Cash value of life insurance | | | 198,319 | 193,539 |
| Common Stock for Employees' Saving and Profit Sharing Plan | | | 1,984,565 | 2,380,159 |
| Investments in and advances to subsidiaries not consolidated | | | 586,494 | 389,091 |
| Patents, at cost less amortization | | | 435,588 | — |
| | | | 5,106,769 | 4,194,346 |
| Plant and Equipment: | | | | |

He identified the company's strengths as its research productivity, its manufacturing efficiency, and its financial resources, and untapped debt capacity.

He saw many important weaknesses in the company as well. Foremost among these, in his view, was the almost total lack of trained and functioning middle management talent in the company. He attributed this to the lack of systematic long-range planning under Frank Spearman, as well as to the "emphasis on expense control to avoid carrying excess personnel."

Mr. Solomon also had reservations regarding the breadth of competence of the present top managers at SPI. He was not certain whether the company's present functional executives were prepared to manage

**Figure 4 Spearman Plastics, Inc. and Subsidiaries Consolidated Balance Sheets As of Dec. 31, 1966 and 1965 (continued)**

| *Assets* | *Cost* | *Reserve for Depreciation* | *1966* | *1965* |
|---|---|---|---|---|
| Land | 3,766,346 | — | 3,766,346 | 3,144,325 |
| Buildings | 26,800,255 | 6,970,942 | 19,829,314 | 17,261,561 |
| Machinery and Equipment | 14,988,477 | 7,807,627 | 7,180,849 | 5,954,013 |
| | 45,555,078 | 14,778,569 | 30,776,509 | 26,359,899 |
| | | | 110,890,949 | 104,629,416 |
| *Liabilities* | | | | |
| Current Liabilities: | | | | |
| Accounts payable and accrued liabilities | | | 5,977,129 | 6,063,043 |
| Accrued taxes on income | | | 10,124,015 | 10,226,141 |
| Current maturity of note payable | | | 294,150 | — |
| Total Current Liabilities | | | 16,395,294 | 16,289,184 |
| Note Payable maturing serially to 1981 | | | 4,323,000 | 4,029,300 |
| Reserve | | | 2,564,000 | 1,600,000 |
| Shareowners' investment: | | | | |
| Cumulative convertible preferred stock | | | 1,750,685 | 1,525,000 |
| Common Stock | | | 15,235,982 | 15,235,982 |
| Paid-in surplus | | | 2,295,235 | 1,800,525 |
| Earnings retained | | | 68,326,753 | 64,149,425 |
| Total Shareowners' Investment | | | 87,608,655 | 82,710,932 |
| | | | $110,890,949 | $104,629,416 |

in new areas outside of the company's traditional business. This was a factor, he said, which could slow down the company's ability to carry out its expansion and diversification program.

The strain on the company's top management resources, according to Mr. Solomon, was well-illustrated in the Reschild-Bauer acquisition.

> We had no one here who could manage Reschild after the former managers there were fired or quit. So we had to bring in somebody from the outside—Tom Copes. I hope Tom is the man who'll straighten up that company. . . . But it's too early to tell. . . I hope he can do the job because we really have no one here who will.

In view of such problems, Mr. Solomon believed that SPI should endeavor to acquire only companies with good management people, or failing this, "at least know where to get them" before making the acquisition.

. . . . .

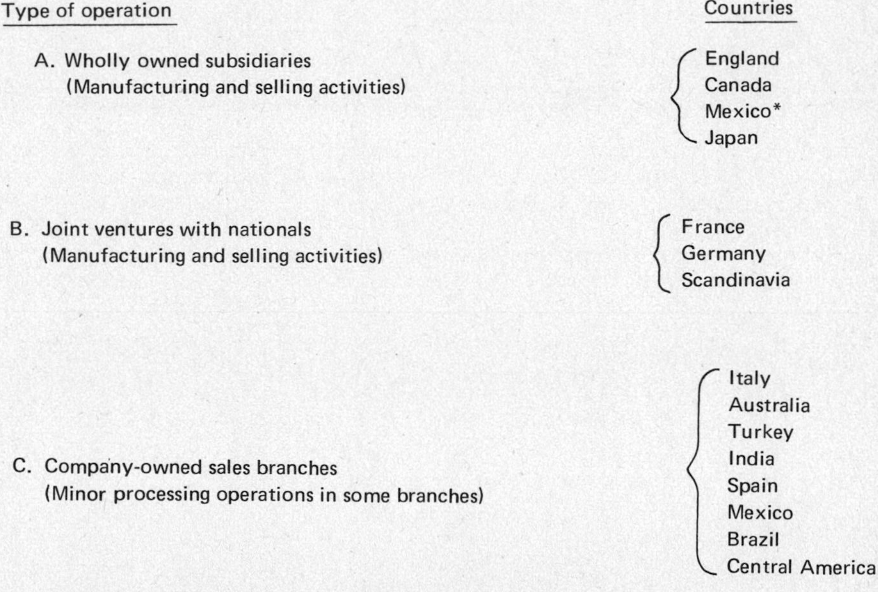


**Figure 5** Spearman Plastics, Inc., International Operations

Note: The company sells its products in twenty-seven other countries through independent distributors.

John Spearman wondered what assignments he should make under the new organization, given the company's executive resources. He also felt that he had to move quickly and effect the transition to a new organization within a year or two. Only in this way, he believed, would his company be in a position to realize the high goals he had set for it for the following five years.

# Specialty Chemical Company

## Part I

The Specialty Chemical Company employed approximately 2,200 hourly personnel to operate its plant on a three-shift basis. The plant was divided into several operating departments, and each department contained several process units. Department A's organization chart is shown in Figure 1.

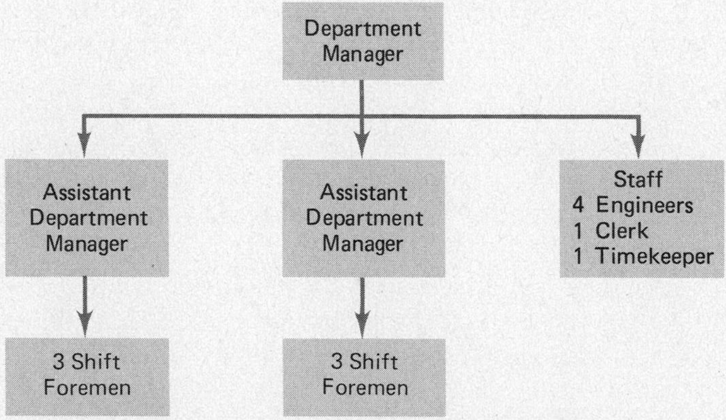


**Figure 1** Organization Chart, Department A

The operating departments' offices were located in the plant close to the units under their supervision. The main office building was just outside the plant's main gate.

The department manager was responsible for all phases of the department's operation and reported to the process superintendent in the main office building. He worked closely with other department managers in helping to plan the entire plant's operation.

The assistant department managers were responsible for the day-to-day operation of the unit within the department. They reported directly to the department manager.

The engineers were assigned to the operating department by the main office technical department. One engineer specialized in solving maintenance problems and worked closely with the assistant department managers and the hourly personnel who performed routine maintenance in the department. The other engineers worked on technical problems connected with the day-to-day operations and when time allowed worked on long-range technical studies (e.g., development of mathematical correlations to describe the operation of the units).

The work day followed a routine pattern. The assistant department managers looked over the previous day's records that were sent to the office from the individual operating units. They noted any changes that had occurred during the night and made mental notes of items to check. One of the engineers usually calculated miscellaneous operating information such as the change in quantity of available raw material and the excess capacity left in the final product storage tanks. Any special problems that came up were discussed and one of the engineers followed up on any details needing further investigation.

The office atmosphere was very relaxed. Coffee was available at all times. The department manager usually drank a cup of coffee and read the *Wall Street Journal* while the assistants reviewed the previous day's operation. He then checked with the assistants for a brief review and discussed any general future events which might have bearing on the department.

At the time these observations were made the department manager had just been promoted to his present position. He had been with the company for fifteen years and had once worked as an engineer for one of the present assistant department managers. He was an excellent technical man and was highly regarded by all who had worked with him. His management philosophy, which he openly stated, was based on his belief that a good engineer will find his own problems and should require little supervision.

When the main office requested a special technical survey, he would mention the problem to one of the engineers and specify the deadline, if one had been set.

## Prediction Worksheet

From what I know of the operation of Department A I would predict that:

1. Productivity of the department in terms of (a) quantity and (b) quality would be (high) (standard) (below standard). (Note the reasons for your prediction.)

2. Department members would be (highly) (moderately) (dis-) satisfied with their job. (Explain why.)

3. Projects would be completed (ahead of) (on) (behind) schedule. (Explain why.)

## Part II

Morale in the department was high. The engineers worked overtime (without pay) to complete projects ahead of schedule. They were careful to check and recheck every detail because the department manager seldom rechecked the work that was sent out of the department. During off hours, the engineers joked, drank beer, and went bowling with the department manager.

The production of the department increased 15 percent under the new department manager. The hourly men, many of whom had regarded the previous manager as a sneak, were glad to see the new department manager when he made his "rounds." He had told them that operating the plant was their job and they took pride in doing their work well.

### Postprediction Worksheet

On the form below, check the degree of accuracy of your predictions from Part I of the case and note the major reasons for accuracy or inaccuracy.

| Question | Degree of Accuracy* | | | Reasons |
|---|---|---|---|---|
| | A | P | I | |
| 1. (a) | | | | |
| (b) | | | | |
| 2. | | | | |
| 3. | | | | |

*A=accurate; P=partly accurate; I=inaccurate.

## Part III

During a personnel reshuffle, a new man was brought in as department manager for Department A. He had held similar managerial positions in the company's two other plants. He, too, had served in Department A as an engineer under the same assistant department manager.

Under the new regime, Tuesday afternoon became "meeting" time. The entire department staff met to report on the various active projects. Originally the meeting was designed to keep everyone up-to-date, but it soon turned into a briefing session during which time each engineer was told his duties for the next week.

In the mornings the department manager would arrive five minutes early to go over the previous day's "log sheets." When the assistants had gone over the sheets, he would question them regarding various details. Then he would visit each engineer's desk, checking on the man's progress.

A detailed account was now kept on all supply items, e.g., pencils, flashlights, padlocks, note pads. Hourly personnel were required to sign for such items. They were also required to call the office for permission to bring maintenance equipment into the operating area.

### Prediction Worksheet

From what I know of the operation of Department A and the changes described in Part III, I would predict that:

1. Productivity of the department in terms of (a) quantity and (b) quality would (increase) (remain at the same level) (decrease). (Note the reasons for your prediction.)

2. Department members would be (highly) (moderately) (dis-) satisfied with their job. (Explain why.)

3. Projects would be completed (ahead of) (on) (behind) schedule. (Explain why.)

## Part IV

Morale in the department dropped to a very low level. The new manager soon had the "behind the back" nickname of Captain Queeg. The engineers carried ball bearings which they banged together imitating the manager's habit of clanging his loose change.

The technical work issued by the department became progressively less complete. The engineers cared less and less about the accuracy of their work. Two months later one engineer requested a transfer to another department. Production on the operating unit dropped 10 percent from its previous level.

**Postprediction Worksheet**

On the form below, check the degree of accuracy of your predictions from Part III of the case and note the major reasons for accuracy or inaccuracy.

| | Degree of Accuracy* | | | Reasons |
|---|---|---|---|---|
| | A | P | I | |
| 1. (a) | | | | |
| (b) | | | | |
| 2. | | | | |
| 3. | | | | |

*A=accurate; P=partly accurate; I=inaccurate.

# Talking with George

THE SCENE: The controller's office in a large corporation on a Monday morning. George, director of economic planning, has just submitted a report to his immediate superior, the controller.

CONTROLLER: Sit down, George, while I look this over.

GEORGE: (virtually collapsing into a chair before the desk) This is the first chance I've had to sit down for a week.

CONTROLLER: (after examining major aspects of the report carefully but briefly) This is fine, George, just what we need. But why couldn't it have been ready for the treasurer on Friday, as we had agreed?

 This case was prepared as the basis for class discussion rather than to illustrate either effective or ineffective handling of an administrative situation.

GEORGE: Frank fell ill on Monday, that new girl's husband decided to accept a job in Des Moines—that makes three good girls I've lost in as many weeks—and by the time I had a look at the first draft it was already late and the draft was absolutely incomprehensible. Irving could have worked on it with me but he has been scheduled for months to go on vacation to California as of last Wednesday, and all his plans were made and I couldn't ask him to delay leaving. So, hard as we tried, and God knows we slaved over this report, it was just impossible to finish it by Friday. As it was, I finished it up on Saturday and Sunday. I've worked like a dog on this project and all I get are questions about why it wasn't ready sooner. There is very little appreciation around here for what goes into a report like that. The treasurer wants something, probably minor to him, and the word filters down to us until it is a major project. We go all out on it, then no one gives a damn what we put into it. You can ask Phil, I was here until six o'clock Saturday working on that damn thing.

CONTROLLER: I know you work hard, George. I have never suggested that you don't. This report is an excellent job, just what I wanted—but *you* shouldn't have done it. We have had this assignment for two weeks. We discussed it again ten days ago at my initiative. You never at any time during that period said it wouldn't be ready—until you came in here Friday morning asking me to phone the treasurer to ask for an extension.

GEORGE: He didn't really need it until tomorrow, anyhow. The board meeting isn't until then.

CONTROLLER: But he asked us to have it ready by Friday and we had plenty of time to do it. Why can't we schedule jobs and be sure they come out on time?

GEORGE: (Repeats his previous explanation for the delay, putting added emphasis on his own hard work and on the amount of overtime he had devoted to the report [for which he received no extra compensation].)

CONTROLLER: George, I don't want you to work harder. I don't want you to work overtime. I want you to organize your department so that jobs come out when they are scheduled.

GEORGE: I don't know *what* you want. I work harder than anyone around here. (Again repeats explanation for the report's delay, with some elaborations and additions.)

CONTROLLER: Let's go to lunch and talk some more about this.

GEORGE: I can't go out for lunch. I don't have time. My desk is piled high with papers. I'll probably be here until eight o'clock tonight. You don't have any idea how much work goes through my office. I've got to get back to work. (Gets up and moves toward the door, muttering that he works harder than anyone else in the company and no one gives a damn. "Those people in investment go home right on the dot of five o'clock. . . .")

# Technical Products, Inc.

The applied products division of Technical Products, Inc. was recently spun off from a research segment of the company to develop and produce a new highly advanced line of equipment. Charles Robinson, the new division manager, had continued the organization of functions which existed before the spin-off took place but he felt that some major organizational readjustment would soon have to be made to deal with already apparent inefficiencies.

The work of the division was carried out by three departments: engineering, which designed products to customer specifications; manufacturing, which produced to customer order and schedule; and process design, which integrated engineering designs and manufacturing processes through modification of each. All three departments were extremely cohesive, jealous of their prerogatives and proud of what each referred to as its "art."

The managers of all three departments were outstanding men in their respective fields. The engineering director devoted most of his time to the most advanced work, leaving his project engineers to deal with more routine products. He was outspoken, however, in desiring to keep his project engineers on engineering rather than administrative tasks and to maintain their allegiance to the engineering department. The manufacturing director and his staff were somewhat contemptuous of both product and process design personnel, feeling that the technical expertise possessed by manufacturing was more than sufficient to deal with problems which arose after the design stage. Process design, though ingenious in its contribution to design modifications and manufacturing technology, was constantly blamed by the other two departments for technical, cost, and schedule difficulties. In general, costs were not in line with other production organizations in the company and interdepartmental friction seemed to be at the bottom of frequent production bottlenecks.

As Charles Robinson contemplated these problems, three options occurred to him:

1. Leave the organization unchanged but mediate between the three departments on a continuing basis, trusting that the engineering director would strike a better balance between long- and short-range opportunities.
2. Establish a project management office reporting to Robinson, in which project managers would take responsibility for gaining interdepartmental support for their groups of products or projects.
3. Abandon the functional departments and reorganize vertically by product lines.

Before carrying his thinking further, he decided to talk with some of his management friends whom he knew to have faced in their companies problems similar to his.

Manager 1 described his disappointment with a project management system which had been established in his company. He said that the idea was logically sound but difficult to implement. Functional managers, he said, are loath to see their people responding to two sources of control, resent the budgets of the project management office, assert that many projects are so routine as to require no special liaison work, and basically see such a reorganization as chopping away the foundation of functional groups. He said the result was that these functional managers very effectively sabotaged the project concept's effectiveness by passive foot-dragging.

Manager 2 reported that his top management had long resisted any kind of project organization because they basically distrusted complex organization, saying that if an organization chart were a wiring diagram, it would blow the main fuse. These men saw in formal organization a loss of all the fun they remembered having in building their organization from scratch. However, to please customers who wanted some central contact point within the company, two program management offices had been established. Customers were pleased as a result, but the two offices began to empire-build, duplicating functions in the regular departments and creating confusion among employees by issuing orders in conflict with those from functional managers. His company, still as dedicated as ever to functional control, was now trying a centralization of program management and a forced reduction of program management staffs to reverse the trend of inefficiency and confusion which he attributed to the new organization.

Manager 3 suggested that Robinson consider establishing a new management role in the company to mediate and, if necessary, cast the deciding vote in conflicts between departments. He reported that such a strategy had worked well in his company so long as the manager was constantly on the scene and fully informed about what was going on. However, departments tended to revert to old patterns as soon as they were left untended, he warned.

Several managers alerted Robinson to a problem with reorganization in general which he had not previously considered. They pointed out that most organizations have accommodated through present structures certain idiosyncracies in particular managers and these accommodations may be badly upset by organizational change. One reported hiring a consultant who recommended sweeping changes, which required abolishment of a top-level job which had been created to use the talents of an ailing but still contributive executive. Another pointed out that promises made to junior managers concerning future job openings may turn out to be impossible to keep if basic organizational changes are made.

All of the other managers whom Robinson spoke with, instead of suggesting a solution to Robinson's problem, simply contributed their own staff-line duplications, their interregional jurisdictional disputes, their inability to secure competent managers from old divisions to staff new ones, and so on. Robinson was left feeling that there were a number of pitfalls in each of his three options but he was no closer to a solution than when he began his survey.

# Texana Petroleum Corporation

During the summer of 1966, George Prentice, the newly designated executive vice-president for domestic operations of the Texana Petroleum Corporation, was devoting much of his time to thinking about improving the combined performance of the five product divisions reporting to him (see Figure 1). His principal concern was that corporate profits were not reflecting the full potential contribution which could result from the close technological interdependence of the raw materials utilized and produced by these divisions. The principal difficulty, as Prentice saw it, was that

 This case was made possible by the cooperation of a firm that remains anonymous. It was prepared by Associate Professor Jay W. Lorsch from data collected by Professor Paul R. Lawrence, Mr. James A. Garrison, and himself. Case material of the Harvard Graduate School of Business Administration is intended as a basis for class discussion rather than to illustrate either effective or ineffective handling of an administrative situation.

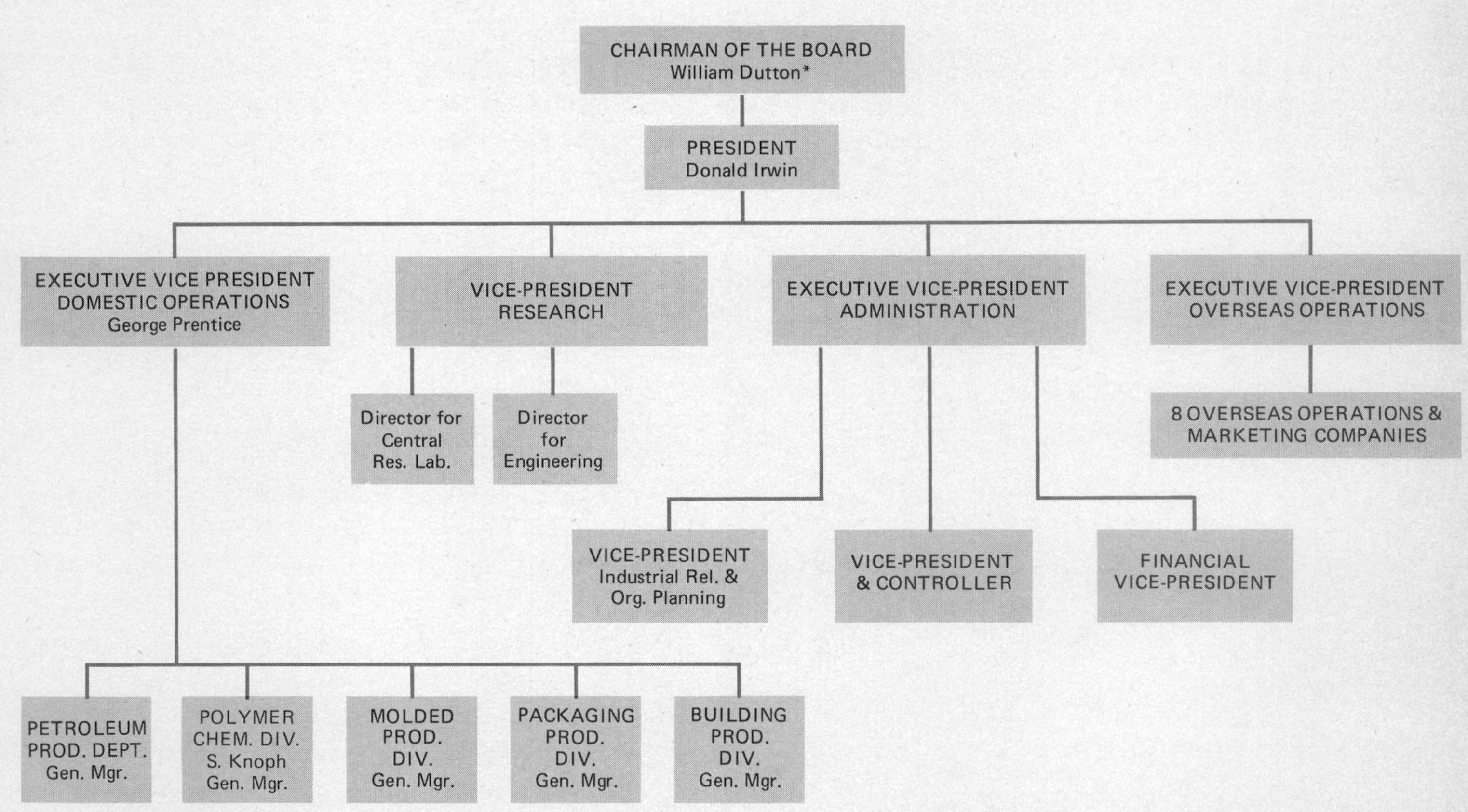


**Figure 1** Texana Petroleum Company—Partial Organization Chart, 1966

the division general managers reporting to him were not working well together:

> As far as I see it, the issue is where do we make the money for the corporation? Not how do we beat the other guy. Nobody is communicating with anybody else at the general manager level. In fact they are telling a bunch of secrets around here.

## RECENT CORPORATE HISTORY

The Texana Petroleum Corporation was one of the early major producers and marketers of petroleum products in the southwest United States. Up until the early 1950s, Texana had been almost exclusively in the business of processing and refining crude oil and in selling petroleum products through a chain of company-operated service stations in the southwestern United States and in Central and South America. By 1950 company sales had risen to approximately $500 million with accompanying growth in profits. About 1950, however, Texana faced increasingly stiff competition at the retail service station level from several larger national petroleum companies. As a result sales volume declined sharply during the early 1950s and by 1955 sales had fallen to only $300 million and the company was operating at just above the breakeven point.

At this time, because of his age, Roger Holmes, who had been a dominant force in the company since its founding, retired as President and chief executive officer. He was replaced by Donald Irwin, forty-nine, who had been a senior executive with a major chemical company. William Dutton, fifty-five, was appointed chairman of the board to replace the retiring board chairman. Dutton had spent his entire career with Texana. Prior to his appointment as chairman he had been senior vice-president for Petroleum Products, reporting to Holmes.

Irwin and Dutton, along with other senior executives, moved quickly to solve the problems facing Texana. They gradually divested the company's retail outlets and abandoned the domestic consumer petroleum markets. Through both internal development and acquisition they expanded and rapidly increased the company's involvement in the business of processing petroleum for chemical and plactic products. In moving in this direction they were rapidly expanding on initial moves made by Texana in 1949, when the company built its first chemical processing plant and began marketing these products. To speed the company's growth in these areas, Irwin and Dutton selected aggressive general managers for each division and gave them a wide degree of freedom in decision making. Top management's major requirement was that each division general manager create a growing division with a satisfactory return on investment capital. By 1966 top management had reshaped the company so that in both the domestic and foreign market it was an integrated producer of chemicals and plastics materials. In foreign operations the company continued to operate service stations in Latin America and in Europe. This change in direction was successful and by 1966 company sales had risen to $750 million, with a healthy rise in profit.

In spite of this success, management believed that there was a need for an increase in return on invested capital. The financial and trade press, which had been generous in its praise of the company's recovery, was still critical of the present return on investment, and top management shared this concern. Dutton, Irwin, and Prentice were in agreement that one important method of increasing profits was to take further advantage of the potential cost savings which could come from increased coordination between the domestic operating divisions, as they developed new products, processes, and markets.

## DOMESTIC ORGANIZATION 1966

The product division's reports to Mr. Prentice represented a continuum of producing and marketing activities from production and refining of crude oil to the marketing of several types of plastics products to industrial consumers. Each division was headed by a general manager. While there was some variation in the internal organizational structure of the several divisions, they were generally set up along functional lines (manufacturing, sales, research and development). Each division also had its own controller and engineering activities, although these were supported and augmented by the corporate staff. While divisions had their own research effort, there was also a central research laboratory at the corporate level, which carried on a longer range research of a more fundamental nature, and outside the scope of the activities of any of the product divisions.

The *petroleum products division* was the remaining nucleus of the company's original producing and refining activities. It supplied raw materials to the polymer and chemicals division and also sold refining products under long term contracts to other petroleum companies. In the early and mid-1950s this division's management had generated much of the company's revenue and profits through its skill of negotiating these agreements. In 1966 top corporate management felt that this division's management had accepted its role as a supplier to the rest of the corporation, and felt that there were harmonious relations between it and its sister divisions.

The *polymer and chemicals division* was developed internally during the late 1940s and early 1950s as management saw its share of the consumer petroleum market declining. Under the leadership of Seymour Knoph (who had been general manager for several years) and his predecessor (who was in 1966 executive vice-president of administration) the division had rapidly developed a line of chemical and polymer compounds derived from petroleum raw materials. Most of the products of this division were manufactured under licensing agreement or were materials the formulation of which was well understood. Nevertheless, technical personnel in the division had developed an industrywide reputation for their ability to develop new and improved processes. Top management of the division took particular pride in this ability. From the beginning, the decisions of what products to manufacture was based to a large extent upon the requirements of the molded and packaging products divisions. However, polymer and chemicals division executives had always attempted to market these same products to external customers, and had been highly successful. These external sales were extremely important to Texana since they assured a large enough volume of operation to process a broad product line of polymer chemicals profitably. As the other divisions had grown, they had required a larger proportion of the division's capacity, which meant that polymer and chemical division managers had to reduce their commitment to external customers.

The *molded products division* was also an internally developed division, which had been formed in 1951. Its products were a variety of molded plastic products ranging from toys and household items to automotive and electronic parts. This division's major strengths were its knowledge of molding technology and particularly its marketing ability. While it depended upon the polymer and chemicals division for its raw materials, its operations were largely independent of those of the packaging products and building products divisions.

The *packaging products division* was acquired in 1952. Its products were plastic packaging materials, including films, cartons, bottles, etc. All of these products were marketed to industrial customers. Like the molded products division, the packaging division depended on the polymer and chemical division as a source of raw materials, but was largely independent of other end product divisions.

The *building product division* was acquired in 1963 to give Texana a position in the construction materials market. The division produced and marketed a variety of insulation roofing materials, and similar products to the building trade. It was a particularly attractive acquisition for Texana, because prior to the acquisition it had achieved some success with plastic products for insulation and roofing materials. Although the plastic products accounted for less than 20 percent of the total division sales in 1965, plans called for these products to account for over 50 percent of division sales in the next five years. Its affiliation with Texana gave this division a stronger position in plastic raw materials through the polymer and chemicals division.

## Selection and Recruitment of Management Personnel

The rapid expansion of the corporation into these new areas had created the need for much additional management talent, and top management had not hesitated to bring new men in from outside the corporation, as well as advancing promising younger men inside Texana. In both the internally developed and acquired divisions most managers had spent their career inside the division, although some top division managers were moved between divisions or into corporate positions.

In speaking about the type of men he had sought for management positions, Donald Irwin described his criterion in a financial publication:

> We don't want people around who are afraid to move. The attraction of Texana is that it gives the individual responsibilities which aren't diluted. It attracts the fellow who wants a challenge.

Another corporate executive described Texana managers:

> It's a group of very tough-minded, but considerate gentlemen with an enormous drive to get things done.

Another manager, who had been with Texana for his entire career, and who considered himself to be different from most Texana managers, described the typical Texana manager as follows:

> Texana attracts a particular type of person. Most of these characteristics are personal characteristics rather than professional ones. I would use terms such as cold, unfeeling, aggressive, and extremely competitive, but not particularly loyal to the organization. He is loyal to dollars, his own personal dollars. I think this is part of the communication problem. I think this is done on purpose. The selection procedures lead in this direction. I think this is so because of contrast with the way the company operated ten years ago. Of course I was at the plant level at that time. But today the attitude I have described is also in the plants. Ten years ago the organization was composed of people who worked together for the good of the organization, because they wanted to. I don't think this is so today.

## Location of Division Facilities

The petroleum products, chemical and polymer divisions and the packaging products division had their executive offices on separate floors of the Texana headquarters building in the Chicago "loop." The plants and research and development facilities of these divisions were spread out across Oklahoma, Texas, and Louisiana. The molded products division had its headquarters, research and development facilities, and a major plant in an industrial suburb of Chicago. This division's other plants were at several locations in the middle west and east coast. The building products division's headquarters and major production and technical facilities were located in Fort Worth, Texas. All four divisions shared sales offices in major cities from coast to coast.

## Evaluation and Control of Division Performance

The principal method of controlling and evaluating the operations of these divisions was the semiannual review of division plans and the approval of major capital expenditures by the executive committee.[1] In reviewing performance against plans members of the executive committee placed almost sole emphasis on the division's actual return on investment against budget. Corporate executives felt that this practice together with the technological interdependence of the divisions created many disputes about transfer pricing.

In addition to these regular reviews corporate executives had frequent discussions with division executives about their strategies, plans, and operations. It had been difficult for corporate management to strike the proper balance in guiding the operations for the divisions. This problem was particularly acute with regard to the polymer and chemicals division, because of its central place in the corporation's product line. One corporate staff member explained his view of the problem:

> This whole matter of communications between the corporate staff and the polymer and chemical division has been a fairly difficult problem. Corporate management used to contribute immensely to this by trying to get into the nuts and bolts area within the chemical and polymer organization, and this created serious criticisms; however, I think they have backed off in this matter.

A second corporate executive in discussing this matter for a trade publication report put the problem this way:

> We're trying to find the middle ground. We don't want to be a holding company, and with our diversity we can't be a highly centralized corporation.

## Executive Vice President—Domestic Operations

In an effort to find this middle ground the position of executive vice-president of domestic operations was created in early 1966, and George Prentice was its first occupant. Prior to this change, there had been two senior domestic vice-presidents—one in charge of the petroleum and poly-

[1]The executive committee consisted of Messrs. Dutton, Irwin, and Prentice, as well as the vice president of research, executive vice-president of administration, and the executive vice-president of foreign operations.

mer and chemicals divisions and the other in charge of the end-use divisions. Mr. Prentice had been senior vice-president in charge of the end-use divisions before the new position was created. He had held that position for only two years, having come to it from a highly successful marketing career with a competitor.

At the time of his appointment one press account described Mr. Prentice as "hard-driving, aggressive, and ambitious—an archetype of the self-actuated dynamo—Irwin has sought out."

Shortly after taking his new position Prentice described the task before him:

> I think the corporation wants to integrate its parts better and I am here because I reflect this feeling. We can't be a bunch of entrepreneurs around here. We have got to balance discipline with entrepreneurial motivation. This is what we were in the past, just a bunch of entrepreneurs and if they came in with ideas we would get the money, but now our dollars are limited, and especially the polymer and chemical boys haven't been able to discipline themselves to select from within ten good projects. They just don't seem to be able to do this, and so they come running in here with all ten good projects which they say we have to buy, and they get upset when we can't buy them all.
>
> This was the tone of my predecessors (senior vice-presidents). All of them were very strong on being entrepreneurs. I am going to run it differently. I am going to take a marketing and capital orientation. As far as I can see, there is a time to compete and a time to collaborate, and I think right now there has been a lack of recognition in the polymer and chemicals executive suite that this thing has changed.

## Other Views of Domestic Interdivisional Relations

Executives within the polymer and chemicals divisions in the end-use divisions, and at the corporate level, shared Prentice's view that the major breakdown in interdivisional relations was between the polymer and chemicals division and the end-use divisions. Executives in the end-use divisions made these typical comments about the problem:

> I think the thing we have got to realize is that we are wedded to the polymer and chemicals division whether we like it or not. We are really tied up with them. And just as we would with any outside supplier or with any of our customers, we will do things to maintain their business. But because they feel they have our business wrapped up they do not reciprocate in turn. Now let me emphasize that they have not arbitrarily refused to do the things that we are requiring, but there is a pressure on them for investment projects and we are low man on the pole. And I think this could heavily jeopardize our chances for growth.
>
> . . . . .
>
> I would say our relationships are sticky, and I think this is primarily because we think our reason for being is to make money, so we try to keep

Polymer and Chemicals as an arm's length supplier. For example, I cannot see just because it is a polymer and chemicals product, accepting millions of pounds of very questionable material. It takes dollars out of our pocket, and we are very profit-centered.

. . . . .

The big frustration, I guess, and one of our major problems, is that you can't get help from them [Polymer and Chemicals]. You feel they are not interested in what you are doing, particularly if it doesn't have a large return for them. But as far as I am concerned this has to become a joint venture relationship, and this is getting to be real sweat with us. We are the guys down below yelling for help. And they have got to give us some relief.

. . . . .

My experience with the polymer and chemicals division is that you cannot trust what they say at all, and even when they put it in writing you can't be absolutely sure that they are going to live up to it.

. . . . .

Managers within the polymer and chemicals division expressed similar sentiments:

Personally, right now I have the feeling that the divisions' interests are growing further apart. It seems that the divisions are going their own way. For example, we are a polymer producer but the molding division wants to be in a special area, so that means they are going to be less of a customer to us, and there is a whole family of plastics being left out that nobody's touching, and this is bearing on our program. . . . We don't mess with the building products division at all, either. They deal in small volumes. Those that we are already making we sell to them, those that we don't make we can't justify making because of the kinds of things we are working with. What I am saying is that I don't think the corporation is integrating, but I think we ought to be, and this is one of the problems of delegated divisions. What happens is that an executive heads this up and goes for the place that makes the most money for the division, *but* this is not necessarily the best place from a corporate standpoint.

. . . . .

We don't have as much contact with sister divisions as I think we should. I have been trying to get a liaison with guys in my function but it has been a complete flop. One of the problems is that I don't know who to call on in these other divisions. There is no table of organization, nor is there any encouragement to try and get anything going. My experience has been that all of these operating divisions are very closed organizations. I know guys up the line will say that I am nuts about this. They say to just call over and I will get an answer. But this always has to be a big deal, and it doesn't happen automatically, and hurts us.

The comments of corporate staff members describe these relationships and the factors they saw contributing to the problem:

Right now I would say there is an iron curtain between the polymer and chemicals division and the rest of the corporation. You know, we tell our divisions they are responsible, autonomous groups, and the polymer and chemicals division took it very seriously. However, when you are a three quarter billion dollar company, you've got to be coordinated, or the whole thing is going to fall apart—it can be no other way. The domestic executive vice-president thing has been a big step forward to improve this, but I would say it hasn't worked out yet.

. . . . .

The big thing that is really bothering [the polymer and chemicals division] is that they think they have to go develop all new markets on their own. They are going to do it alone independently, and this is the problem they are faced with. They have got this big thing, that they want to prove that they are a company all by themselves and not rely upon packaging or anybody else.

. . . . .

Polymer and chemicals division executives talked about the effect of this drive for independence of the divisional operating heads on their own planning efforts:

The polymer and chemicals division doesn't like to communicate with the corporate staff. This seems hard for us, and I think the [a recent major proposal] was a classic example of this. That plan, as it was whipped up by the polymer and chemicals division had massive implications for the corporation both in expertise and in capital. In fact, I think we did this to be a competitive one-up on the rest of our sister divisions. We wanted to be the best-looking division in the system, but we carried it to an extreme. In this effort, we wanted to show that we had developed this concept completely on our own. . . . Now I think a lot of our problems with it stemmed from this intense desire we have to be the best in this organization.

. . . . .

Boy, a big doldrum around here was shortly after Christmas (1965) when they dropped out a new plant, right out of our central plan, without any appreciation of the importance of this plant to the whole polymer and chemicals division's growth. . . . Now we have a windfall and we are back in business on this new plant. But for a while things were very black and everything we had planned and everything we had built our patterns on were out. In fact, when we put this plan together, it never really occurred to us that we were going to get it turned down, and I'll bet we didn't even put the plans together in such a way as to really reflect the importance of this plant to the rest of the corporation.

A number of executives in the end use divisions attributed the interdivisional problems to different management practices and assumptions within the polymer and chemicals division. An executive in the packaging division made this point:

We make decisions quickly and at the lowest possible level, and this is tremendously different from the rest of Texana. I don't know another division like this in the rest of the corporation.

> Look at what Sy Knoph has superfluous to his operation compared to ours. These are the reasons for our success. You've got to turn your guys loose and not breathe down their necks all the time. We don't slow our people down with staff. Sure, you may work with a staff, the wheels may grind, but they sure grind slow.
>
> Also, we don't work on detail like the other divisions do. Our management doesn't feel they need the detail stuff. Therefore, they're [Polymer and Chemical] always asking us for detail which we can't supply, our process doesn't generate it and their process requires it, and this always creates problems with the polymer and chemicals division. But I'll be damned if I am going to have a group of people running between me and the plant, and I'll be goddamned if I am going to clutter up my organization with all the people that Knoph has got working for him. I don't want this staff, but they are sure pushing it on me.

This comment from a molding division manager is typical of many about the technical concerns of the polymer and chemicals division management:

> Historically, even up to the not too distant past, the polymer and chemicals division was considered a snake pit as far as the corporate people were concerned. This was because the corporate people were market-oriented and polymer and chemicals division was technically run and very much a manufacturing effort. These two factors created a communication barrier and to really understand the polymer and chemicals division problems, they felt that you have to have a basic appreciation of the technology and all the interrelationships.
>
> Building on this strong belief, the polymer and chemicals division executives in the past have tried to communicate in technical terms, and this just further hurt the relationship, and it just did not work. Now they are coming up with a little bit more business or commercial orientation, and they are beginning to appreciate that they have got to justify the things they want to do in a business or commercial orientation, and they are beginning to appreciate that they have got to justify the things they want to do in a business sense rather than just a technical sense. This also helps the problem of maintaining their relationships with the corporation as most of the staff is nontechnical; however, this has changed a little bit in that more and more technical people have been coming on and this has helped from the other side.
>
> They work on the assumption in the polymer and chemicals division that you have to know the territory before you can be an effective manager. You have got to be an operating guy to contribute meaningfully to their problems. However, their biggest problem is this concentration on technical solutions to their problems. This is a thing that has boxed them in the most trouble with corporation and the other sister divisions.

These and other executives also pointed to another source of conflict between the polymer and chemicals division and other divisions. This was the question of whether the polymer and chemicals division should develop into a more independent marketer, or whether it should rely more heavily on the end-use divisions to "push" its products to the market.

Typical views of this conflict are the following comments by end-use division executives:

> The big question I have about Polymer and Chemicals is what is their strategy going to be? I can understand them completely from a technical standpoint, this is no problem. I wonder what is the role of this company? How is it going to fit into what we and others are doing? Right now, judging from the behavior I've seen, Polymer and Chemicals could care less about what we are doing in terms of integration of our markets or a joint approach to them.
>
> . . . . .
>
> I think it is debatable whether the polymer and chemicals division should be a new product company or not. Right now we have an almost inexhaustible appetite for what they do and do well. As I see it, the present charter is fine. However, that group is very impatient, aggressive, and they want to grow, but you have got to grow within guidelines. Possibly the polymer and chemicals division is just going to have to learn to hang on the coattails of the other divisions, and do just what they are doing now, only better.
>
> . . . . .
>
> I think the future roles of the polymer and chemicals division is going to be, at any one point in time for the corporation, that if it looks like a product is needed, they will make it. . . . They are going to be suppliers because I will guarantee you that if the moment comes and we can't buy it elsewhere, for example, then I darn well know they are going to make it for us regardless of what their other commitments are. They are just going to have to supply us. If you were to put the polymer and chemicals division off from the corporation, I don't think they would last a year. Without their huge captive requirements, they would not be able to compete economically in the commercial areas they are in.

A number of other executives indicated that the primary emphasis within the corporation on return on investment by divisions tended to induce, among other things, a narrow, competitive concern on the part of the various divisional managements. The comment of this division executive was typical:

> As far as I can see it, we [his division and Polymer and Chemicals] are 180 degrees off on our respective charters. Therefore, when Sy Knoph talks about this big project we listen nicely and then we say, "God bless you, lots of luck," but I am sure we are not going to get involved in it. I don't see any money in it for us. It may be a gold mine for Sy but it is not for our company; and as long as we are held to the high profit standards we are, we just cannot afford to get involved. I can certainly see it might make good corporate sense for us to get it, but it doesn't make any sense in terms of our particular company. We have got to be able to show the returns in order to get continuing capital and I just can't on that kind of project. I guess what I am saying is that under the right conditions we could certainly go in but not under the present framework; we would just be dead in terms of dealing with the corporate financial

structure. We just cannot get the kinds of returns on our capital that the corporation has set to get new capital. In terms of the long run, I'd like very much to see what the corporation has envisioned in terms of a hook-up between us, but right now I don't see any sense in going on. You know my career is at stake here too.

Another divisional executive made this point more succinctly:

Personally I think that a lot more could be done from a corporate point of view and this is frustrating. Right now all these various divisions seem to be viewed strictly as an investment by the corporate people. They only look at us as a banker might look at us. This hurts us in terms of evolving some of these programs because we have relationships which are beyond financial relationships.

The remarks of a corporate executive seemed to support this concern:

One of the things I worry about is where is the end of the rope on this interdivisional thing. I'm wondering if action really has to come from just the division. You know in this organization when they decide to do something new it always has been a divisional proposal—they were coming to us for review and approval. The executive committee ends up a review board; not us, working downward. With this kind of pattern the talent of the corporate people is pretty well seduced into asking questions and determining whether a thing needs guidelines. But I think we ought to be the idea people as well, thinking about where we are going in the future, and if we think we ought to be getting into some new area, then we tell the divisions to do it. The stream has got to work both ways. Now it is not.

# Ward Metal Products Ltd.[1]

Ward Metal Products Ltd. was a large manufacturer of light- and medium-weight metal products such as metal frames, vestibule intercom panels, assorted metal containers, boxes, and cabinets. Its primary cus-

• Prepared by Professor P. E. Pitsiladis, April 1968, Sir George Williams University, Montreal. Use or reproduction of any portion of this case is prohibited, except with written permission. Reprinted by permission. This case was prepared as the basis for class discussion rather than to illustrate either effective or ineffective handling of administrative situations.

[1] All names and certain other data have been changed for the purpose of disguise.

tomers were contractors and hardware wholesalers. From rather modest beginnings in 1925, the company had steadily expanded, with few exceptions, and by 1966 it enjoyed a large volume of sales in eastern Canada. The company was located in Montreal, Quebec where a total of approximately three-hundred persons were employed.

## The Ward Family and Employee Relations

Over the years the ownership and senior managerial control of the company had remained in the hands of the Ward family. Dexter Ward, the founder and president, had become wealthy as a result of his activity and investment in this company and elsewhere. Largely through their aggressive support of and involvement in civic projects and welfare drives, Dexter Ward and other members of the family had become well known to both the French- and English-speaking segments of Montreal's population. The company itself had always enjoyed an excellent reputation for the treatment of its employees. For the type of industry, working conditions were good and wage levels throughout the company were unusually high. Applications for employment had always far exceeded the number of vacancies available, especially in the plant jobs. Although the company had a formal association of employees, numerous attempts by outside labour unions to further organize the production and maintenance employees of the firm had all failed; the main resistance to integration with unions had apparently come from the employees themselves.

The members of the Ward family were primarily oriented to production activities, each of them having served an apprenticeship in the production department during the early days of the company when production was, in fact, the only formally established function. Apprenticeship in the production department had become a training tradition with the family, and it was fully expected that this tradition would be maintained in the years ahead by younger members of the family, if and when they joined the company. While the Ward family members occupied the most senior corporate positions, they continued to display a rather keen interest in the day-to-day activities of the production department. For example, it was common practice for Dick Ward, senior vice-president of the firm, to make periodic visits to the production department to inquire into current problems and to chat informally among the rank-and-file employees. The employees, in turn, seemed to be proud of the "shirt-sleeve" relations they had with Dick Ward and other family members.

Nearly two-thirds of the company's personnel worked in the production department. A large majority of the jobs in this area were held by French Canadians, many of whom had considerable seniority with the company. Service history records of fifteen and twenty years were quite common. The French Canadian employees in the production department seemed especially to cherish the freedom they enjoyed under their supervisors—most of whom were also French Canadians. There appeared to be no special work problems between the supervisors and their men. Grievances were infrequent, and it was not unusual for some of the foremen to be seen with their subordinates after hours in the local tavern. Most of the nonsupervisory jobs in the production area were unskilled or semiskilled, necessitating only a couple of weeks of on-the-job training for new employees. It was common knowledge, however, that the employees (supervisors and subordinates) in this area were among the highest paid in the company. Salaries were a frequent topic of conversation among members of the accounting department, some of whom estimated that the salaries of their counterparts in production were at least a fifth higher than their own.

## Study of Operations

In 1966 Mr. Donald Chapman, general manager of the Ward company, conducted a review of all the firm's operations. The company had been facing keener price competition since 1963; although sales had continued at their higher level, profits had begun to drop off noticeably because of reduced margins. The president and other senior company officials had become most anxious to improve the profitability of the company, but they were unsure as to how this might be done. Mr. Chapman, who had joined the company some ten years earlier, concluded as a result of the study that cost and procedural controls throughout the organization were lacking. He believed, as well, that the rapid growth of the company since the end of the Second World War had created a need for additional specialized staff personnel in accounting, marketing, and related area. This need in his opinion had not been satisfied. Accordingly, he made it generally known that if the company was to maintain its market position and improve its profits, some of the organizational "vacuums" would have to be filled.

## Organization and Procedural Changes

In the early part of 1967, Mr. Chapman appointed Jack Sillman as the first comptroller and manager of the company's new administrative services department. As a chartered accountant, Sillman had previously served as a chief officer in the revenue department of the provincial government. According to organizational plans, the administrative services department was to include, as a start, all the existing accounting functions such as accounts payable and accounts receivable. In the months subsequent to the appointment, Sillman and Chapman held private, regular meetings to hammer out a long-term program for the services department. The primary function of the department was to tighten up controls throughout the company, but more particularly in "those areas where the potential for new economies was greatest."

In addition to the accounting functions, two new sections would eventually be established within the administrative services department. *First*, a budgeting section would be needed to install and administer a more sophisticated companywide budgeting program. Budgeting, as it had existed up until that time, was informal and for the most part consisted simply of each department manager submitting an annual estimate of expenditures for the coming year to the company treasurer for approval. *Secondly*, a systems section would be needed to conduct a procedures program involving the study and write-up of the more important of the interdepartmental administrative practices. Chapman regarded this function (of the systems section) as a particularly important means of outlining the responsibilities of various departments and of encouraging uniformity in recurring day-to-day practices. The heads of the sections in question would be hired as soon as possible, with additional staff being added gradually as the direction of the work became clearer and as the volume began to increase (see organization chart in Figure 1).

## Implementation of New Program

By the summer of 1967 both section heads had been appointed. George Finch, the new supervisor of the budgeting section, was to devote his time to developing the framework and details of the budgetary control program. Charles Bond, formerly a branch manager of a systems service organization, was to begin, as supervisor of the systems section, the study and write-up of interdepartmental procedures. In his discussions with the two men, Jack Sillman outlined the philosophy and the long-term program of the administrative services department, and he continuously emphasized the importance of diplomacy and a "go-softly" approach in dealing with other departments. He candidly pointed out that all of them were "green" to the company and that they should make every effort to avoid antagonizing anyone. All of the men were enthusiastic about the nature of their assignment and saw in it an opportunity to make a substantial contribution to the company.

Although the work of the systems section for the first six months was largely confined to the accounting area, the volume of work was such, and the progress sufficient, as to warrant the addition of two staff members, both of them graduates of local universities. With the advantage of a larger staff, Bond was advised by Sillman to begin working in the "direction" of the production department. George Finch in the meantime had worked out what he thought would be an acceptable budgetary control program. After Sillman had examined and approved the new program, Finch suggested that a meeting be arranged with the other department managers at which time they could outline the new program.

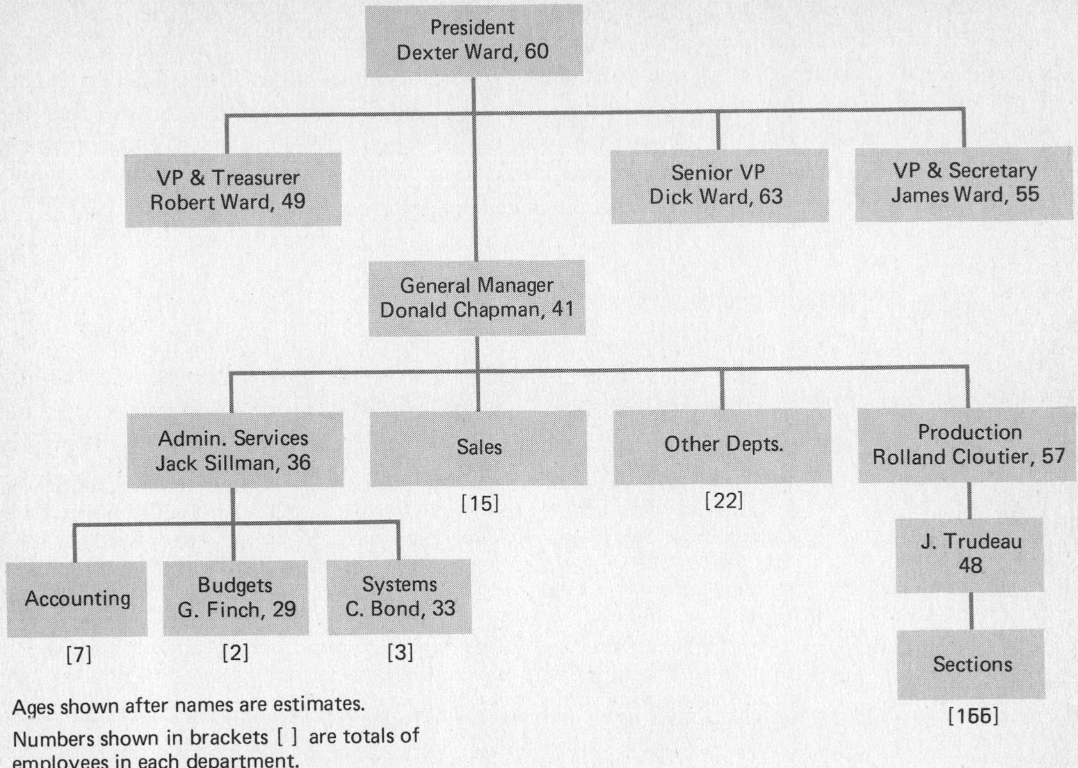


**Figure 1** Ward Metal Products Ltd. (Partial Organization Chart) Summer 1967

Ages shown after names are estimates.
Numbers shown in brackets [ ] are totals of employees in each department.

The meeting that followed was attended by the staff of the administrative services department and all of the departmental managers except "Rollie" Cloutier, manager of production. Chapman and other senior management officials had previously declined to attend, indicating that they preferred not to "interfere." Sillman was surprised by Cloutier's absence, however, inasmuch as he had been assured by Cloutier that the date and time of the meeting were perfectly acceptable. Finch described the new budgetary program to those present; no major objections were raised, but the reception was hardly more than lukewarm. Nonetheless, the department managers did agree to Sillman's suggestion that a task force be established to assist Finch in implementing the program and working out any of the problems that might arise. The task force was to consist of department representatives to be appointed by each of the managers.

After the meeting had been adjourned, Sillman called Cloutier by phone to express regrets at the latter's absence from the meeting. Cloutier explained that a last-minute problem on the plant floor had prevented him from attending. Sillman suggested that the two of them get together to discuss the new budgeting proposal, but Cloutier indicated that he did not think that a meeting would be necessary since he was sure that the new proposal would be acceptable. When told of the task force arrangement, Cloutier said he would assign Jacques Trudeau, an administrative assistant, to work with Nevil on the program.

## Interdepartmental Difficulties

In the months that followed, Sillman kept receiving unfavorable progress reports from both Finch and Bond. Bond complained:

> My boys can't seem to make any headway in their procedure work; the biggest problem is the production department; those people never have the time for us. Whenever we do manage to nail them down to a time and a place, they don't bother to show up anyway. We are generally left standing around sucking our thumbs. To top it all off, we've found that those procedure instructions which we have managed to issue over your signature are being ignored by the production people altogether. I'm fed up with the whole thing. So are the boys. We're not getting the support of the management and the people we are supposed to be working with won't cooperate.

Finch's complaints to Sillman were of the same nature. He reiterated his support for the idea of the task force arrangement but decried the lack of cooperation. Nobody seemed particularly enthusiastic about the idea of the new budgetary program. The decisions made in the task force meetings were not being followed-up. Jacques Trudeau, he said, was totally indifferent and couldn't be relied upon to look after his end of things.

From the reports he received and from his own personal feelings on the matter, Sillman believed that the situation had become acute. However, as a start, he thought that a heart-to-heart talk with Rollie Cloutier might be helpful. Early one morning Sillman called Cloutier and suggested they get together to discuss the situation. "There is no point in it, Jack," Cloutier replied, "I may just as well be sincere. We are busy people here in production and we do not have a lot of time to play around. Our problems are a helluva lot more complicated than anything you'll find in bookkeeping. We'll work with you but it will have to be in our spare time."

Sillman was taken aback by Cloutier's reaction and he decided to refer the entire matter to Chapman, the general manager.

# XXX Company

The XXX Company is a large (approximately 35,000 employees) East Coast manufacturing, research, development, and engineering firm specializing in aerospace systems, notably aircraft, spacecraft, and boosters. The organization of the company is primarily on a line-staff basis; however, when large programs are begun, a "project" organization is formed. The project office "borrows" its technical people from the technical departments for the duration of the program. During the early years of the U.S. space effort the engineering division of XXX Company was organized as illustrated in Figure 1.

The efforts of the advanced design group were to research and propose for new business programs. Study contracts leading to the larger system-design contracts also fell to the advanced design group. Figure 2 shows the organization breakdown of the advanced design group.

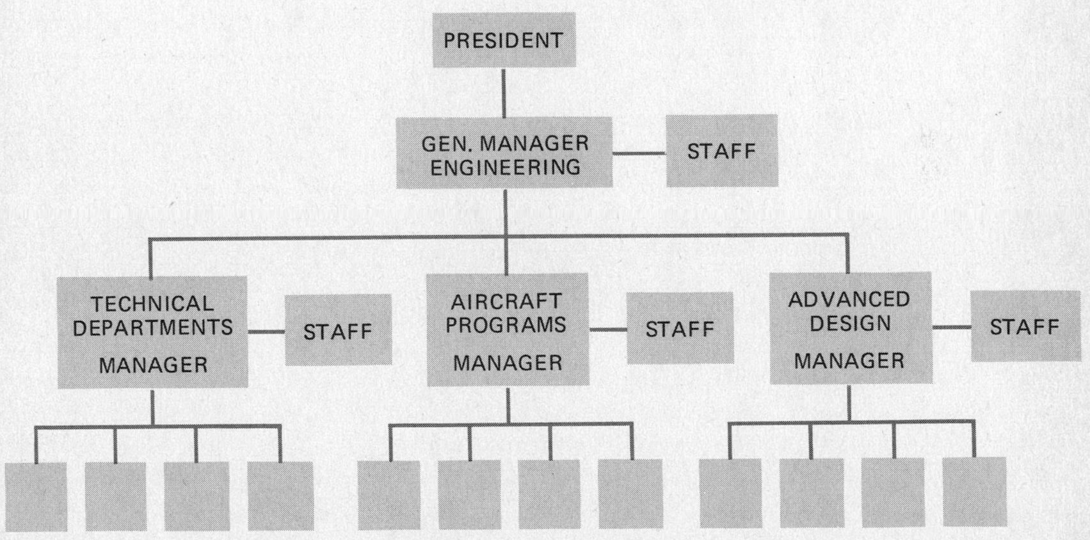


**Figure 1** XXX Company—Engineering Division Organization Chart

• This case was prepared by Mr. David L. Glazer under the direction of Mr. Robert C. Gronbach for the University of Connecticut's Masters in Business Administration program as a basis for class discussion rather than to illustrate either effective or ineffective handling of administrative situations. Reprinted by permission.

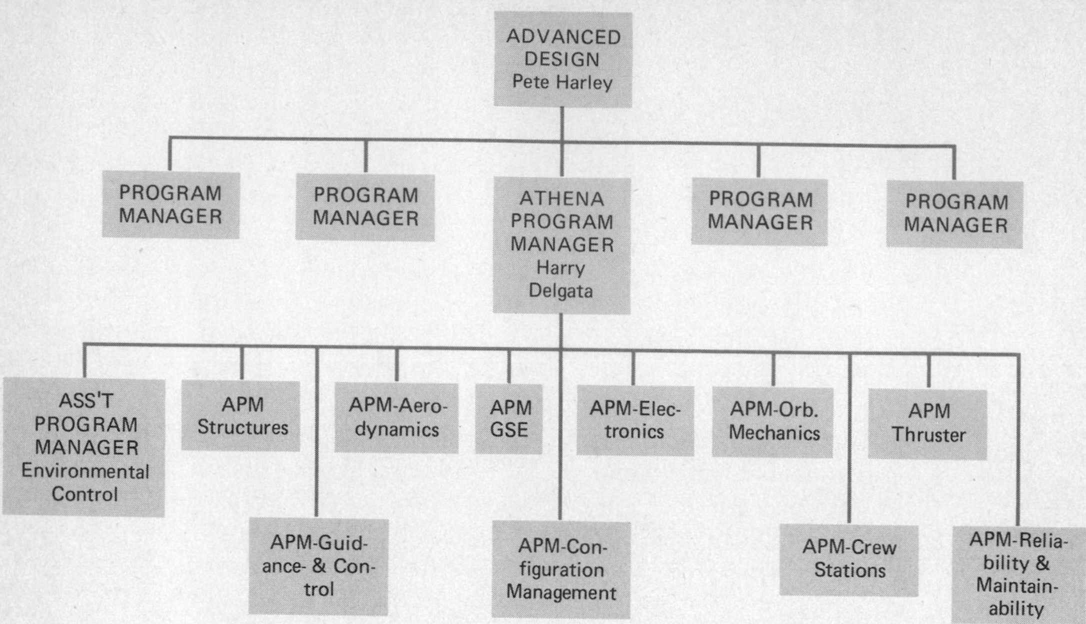


**Figure 2** XXX Company—Advanced Design Group Organization

In the late 1950s, as a result of Sputnik, the U.S. decided to accelerate the manned-space effort. The XXX Company believed they were in a position to provide a significant contribution to that effort. Thus, the advanced design group became the largest and technically strongest of the engineering division. The more notable program in the group was "Athena" (see Figure 2). Athena was to be the most ambitious space effort yet attempted. By the time of its completion, the Athena project was expected to cost in excess of $1 billion. Consequently, XXX Company had assembled approximately four hundred of its key technical talent for the proposal effort. The initial proposal effort had been successful and the XXX Company had been selected as one of three study contractors. The study contract was for $250,000 and would result in a final report, which the government would then use as the major criterion for prime contractor selection. The study contract was to last 120 days, and XXX Company decided to do a first-class effort, partially at their own expense. (The final cost to XXX for the study contract was in excess of $2 million.)

And so began a concerted effort to make XXX Company Number One in the newly expanding space technology business. The technical Athena project staff within the advanced design group worked an average of twelve to fourteen hours per day, seven days a week, with no overtime pay. Although there was considerable griping, by and large the personnel were committed to the program. After about one and a half months, the project became an effective, cohesive, productive group. The personnel began to eat lunch together instead of with friends from their technical departments. They were considered the "elite" of the engineering division, and this attitude tended to enhance their ego-involvement with "Athena."

This development did not go unnoticed by management. After about two months, optimistic feedback began to filter in from the customer and XXX Company management decided that plans must be made in the event of contract award.

Pete Harley was the head of Advanced Design. He was forty-one years old and had been with the XXX Company for fifteen years. His climb up the organizational ladder had been meteoric. He possessed the unique qualities of being a good businessman, manager, and engineer. He had the reputation of being "hard-nosed" yet fair. His approach seemed to result in good performance. For example, people rarely went into "dry-run" presentations without adequate preparedness because it was well known that Harley had the ability to seek out the critical aspects and ask pointed questions even though outside his specialty area. Once satisfied that a technical assistant program manager was effective, Harley would support him in all administrative matters. He was frequently heard to say, "I trust you. If I can't trust you, I get rid of you."

Because of the expansiveness of the Athena program, Harley took personal management control working jointly with Harry Delgata, program manager.

Harley presented a persuasive argument to management for keeping the team intact in the event of contract award to XXX Company. His most cogent argument was that each individual area would require significant expansion, and, because of knowledge obtained and commitment to the program, the present project people were certainly the most likely to manage each of their specific areas.

Management accepted Harley's arguments and a new group was formed reporting to the general manager of engineering, with Harley as Athena program manager. The result of this reorganization was that each project individual severed ties with his technical department, and there were now two groups for each specialty within the XXX Company.

Mike Turner was a twenty-six-year-old physiologist with a Ph.D. He was the youngest assistant program manager in the company's history and was responsible for the crew stations department. This department numbered twenty-two engineers, mathematicians, psychologists, bio-physicists, physicians, and physiologists. His "home" technical department, "life support," had been manned largely by theoreticians interested in the pursuit of the nature of man. Mike had been constantly at odds with his technical management because he was so much more interested in direct application of his specialty to hardware problems.

The result of the reorganization meant that each assistant program manager was elevated one notch to department manager. Mike's original department manager argued effectively that Mike did not possess the experience to manage at that level and, finally, it was agreed that Mike would be "acting" manager until a more senior man could be hired.

Two weeks later Dr. Carl Masters was hired. Mike's group knew little about Dr. Masters. He was a fifty-three-year-old chemist who had done considerable laboratory research in biochemistry, and had a good, though limited, reputation in his field. He had never managed more than three people.

Masters joined the company on a Friday. The Thursday before, Mike's group had worked from 8:00 A.M. to 3:00 A.M. Friday. In order to publish a critical section on target, it was expected that such hours would continue for about a week. Everyone was resolved to the necessity of the schedule.

Friday afternoon, Masters called a meeting of his new staff in the conference room. Immediately, grumblings began to emanate. Basically, the staff felt that they were just too busy to be interrupted. Mike Turner sensed that his staff was already rejecting the "outsider" and did nothing to alter the scheduled meeting. He further suggested complete cooperation with the new manager.

At 2:00 P.M. the meeting was held. Masters introduced himself and spent five minutes describing his background. He then asked each individual to stand, give his name, place of origin, technical area, educational background, and goals. This took one inauspicious hour. Masters suggested, incidentally, that this description begin with Turner.

Next, Masters suggested that the staff, although working hard, had not been creative enough; that more original thinking was required. He suggested that, more than any project group, the crew stations people had to "empathize" with astronauts. One area, he explained, of particular interest was reduced solid-food intake. In order to appreciate the astronauts' dilemma, Masters decided that the entire staff would go on a one-week Metrecal diet. Protestations were loud and adamant. The meeting was adjourned.

It took little time for the meeting results to circulate throughout the XXX Company. The crew stations department was nicknamed the "Metrecal for Lunch Bunch," and were subject to ridicule both on and off the program.

Dr. Masters had responsibility for Life Support on three other advanced-design projects, which he deemed equally as important as, although less exotic than, Athena. Later in the day, he approached four of the crew stations people on the Athena project and offered them added responsibilities on the other programs. He was obviously attempting to gain the acceptance and loyalty of these individuals.

One of the four approached was Dick Harris, the young and unofficial technical leader of the five physicists in the group. Dick was also the undisputed informal group leader. Everyone looked to him for social and administrative solutions to problems. Although not the best technical man in the group, Dick had the ability to chair a meeting, isolate problems, and channel technical discussions into an equitable solution. He was a personal friend of Mike Turner's and Turner was convinced that Dick, more than anyone, was real management caliber and the most valuable member of his staff.

At 4:00 P.M. on Friday, Dick Harris submitted his letter of resignation as illustrated in Figure 3. Within twenty minutes Turner received twenty-one similar letters from other members of the crew stations department. He immediately called on Pete Harley and Harry Delgata with the twenty-two letters in hand and asked, "What should I do?"

TO: Dr. M. Turner

FROM: Mr. R. Harris

COPY TO: Mr. Harry Delgata

DATE: 3 Nov 19__

SUBJECT: Letter of resignation

---

This letter is to inform you of my resignation to be effective immediately. I find that the goals of the XXX Company are no longer in keeping with my own.

Long, painstaking and creative hours have been expended in accomplishing the Athena Program, and I suddenly find myself informed that my work is not "original." Further, I have no intentions of serving as an experimental subject at the whim of an "armchair empiricist," who seems to rate "empathy" as more critical to problem solution than rigorous experimental control.

Up until now, I have enjoyed my tenure with the XXX Company and submit my resignation with some regrets.

Richard Harris

**Figure 3** XXX Company—Dick Harris' Letter of Resignation

# The XYZ Telephone Company

## Part I . . . The Case

In the mid-1960s the XYZ Telephone Company, a large telephone utility, was experiencing a growing problem in its accounting department. The problem was in the department's policy of promoting from within the ranks. The department employed approximately a thousand female clerks, one hundred female first-line supervisors, twenty-five male second-line supervisors, and nine male third-line supervisors. The men in management positions were mostly college graduates who had started their careers in a management training program as second-line supervisors. The first-liners were former clerks. Although obviously not a written rule, there were no female second-liners in the department.

The problem mentioned above resulted from the fact that more and more girls with good intelligence are able to continue their education after high school rather than seeking employment as clerks in large companies. A direct result of this is in the fact that the supply of potential management people within the clerical force was diminishing. To counteract the shortage of female management first-line supervisors of the XYZ Telephone Company started recruiting on the college campuses for a source of first-liners for the accounting department. One of the requirements for the position was that the person must "do well" on the aptitude test for computer programming so that if she does not like her job as a supervisor, she can transfer to the programming staff if she so desires.

The following is the history of one girl who sought such a position, Judy Peters, a graduate of a large university. Her experience points out many of the problems faced by both the employee and the company in trying to put such a program into effect.

Judy, the daughter of an educated and mobile family, had lived in several states during her childhood. Neither of her parents had returned to "live at home" after their graduations from college so it was perfectly natural for her to go someplace other than her small Midwestern "hometown" after her graduation. She chose a large Eastern city "out of pure spirit of adventure." She only knew one girl in that city so wrote and

• Case material prepared by Professor Joel Corman, Suffolk University, as a basis for class discussion. Cases are not designed to present illustrations of either correct or incorrect handling of problem areas. Reprinted by permission.

asked her if she could stay at her apartment a few days while seeking employment and a place to live. Her girlfriend answered her that it would be all right so all Judy had to do then was line up some job interviews for when she arrived in the city. One interview that she had arranged by mail was with the XYZ Telephone Company.

Judy applied for this program, called the Women's Initial Management Development Program, because during her college summers she had had some experience with supervising people and training them for particular jobs in the campus registrar's office. Personnel's description of the position sounded challenging to her: "people" problems, a couple of months learning about a particular unit, and then assignment as supervisor of that unit.

The company offered Judy a salary of $500 per month, which was $75 to $100 a month more than several of her college friends had received for beginning salaries. She considered herself extremely fortunate to be offered such a high salary for a job she would have accepted at a much lower salary. In fact, she was quite pleased with her choice of cities to seek her fortune in—she had a good job, an active social life, and a new apartment to decorate for herself.

At work there were two other girls who had entered the company in the same program (WIMDP) as Judy. One girl, Pat Lauson, had a "staff job," which did not require her to report to anybody. Judy was introduced to Pat on the first day and soon discovered that she (Pat) was most disenchanted with the accounting department in many ways, particularly in its policy of hiring "a man with my background as a second-liner and me as a first-liner." Judy and Pat ate lunch together for about three months discussing every noon the "problems of management."

Judy also met Helen Crawford the other girl in the WIMDP program; however, she "never became very chummy with her." Helen had worked as a clerk in the accounting department on a part-time basis while attending college. Upon graduation she became an accounting office supervisor in a unit she had previously worked in. She spent her first ten months on this assignment in working on the "second shift."

There were twenty other supervisors, in addition to Judy and Helen, who worked in their particular office. The youngest of these was thirty-two with the average age being in the early forties. These "girls" had had a minimum of seven years experience as clerks before they received a promotion to the management level. The maximum salary on their job was $8,800 per annum and only one of the girls had reached it. Judy, on the other hand, was hired for $6,000, a sum which many of her peers had not yet reached or were very near. They all lived at home with their parents in various city suburbs—only one had ever lived away from home for any length of time. Judy observed that the other supervisors consistently remained at work for one to three or four hours after the working day, and thus "used the company as an excuse for their lack of family and social lifc."

The current situation in the accounting department was stressed by Personnel during Judy's job interviews. Personnel's reason for this was to point up the "people problems" involved in the job. Judy stated that this, although making the job appear challenging, made her tend to "clam up on all subjects because I didn't want to mention college or travelling or dates for fear they'd think I was a snob. As a result, I had no friends among the other supervisors who probably considered me a threat to their jobs and a snob anyway."

During her first three months on the payroll, Judy did not report directly to anyone. Mr. George Weitz, a fourth-line supervisor who had interviewed her for the job, gave her her assignments, e.g., an introduction to electronic data processing class for three weeks (consisting of eleven second-liners and herself), "observation" of a supervisor, and several times during that time she was sent home from work by Mr. Weitz because he had nothing arranged for her to do.

On Judy's first working day Mr. Weitz informed her that she was to be the supervisor of a brand-new computer room which would mean that she would be establishing the unit initially and training for staff. However, since the machines had not yet been installed and the second- and third-line supervisors had not been named, the position would not be announced for two or three months. In the meantime, she was informed, she would be going to school to learn computer operations. The only class she did in fact attend was the one mentioned above which did not involve operations but rather just basic concepts. On the six exams given Judy, she maintained "a perfect score of one hundred on each—the best in class."

At the end of three months she was named the supervisor of two units: a machine unit with three girls reporting to her who "ran the machines and felt they were nothing more than factory workers"; and a reports unit consisting of two girls who were responsible for preparing the input to two monthly reports that were produced from a computer.

Since he told her always to come to him with any problem about her job, Judy went to Mr. Weitz for an explanation of why she did not get the computer room position. His explanation was that the office second- and third-liners feel that computer room supervision is considered a "plush job" by the first-liners and it would "lower the morale of the other girls if a college girl got the job."

Mr. Neilson, Judy's third-line supervisor, "rarely spoke to me even though he chatted and was quite friendly with the other three supervisors who also reported to my boss. I'm sure his attitude was "don't rock the boat." He certainly could not afford to be on the wrong side of those girls. With their job knowledge they literally ran the place."

After four months Judy applied for a transfer to the programming staff. "The frustration of being bored all day finally got to me." All the problems that arose in her machine unit during the week "couldn't have filled one day of the week," and the reports unit was busy only the first two or three days of the month. She seldom went on coffee breaks for a lack of someone to go with and spent her lunch hour shopping or making phone calls.

After a three and a half hour debate with her office's fourth-line supervisor, Judy's transfer request went through and became effective two months later.

# The Young Foreman

In the summer of 1955, I was working for the North Harbridge Railway to earn money with which to pay for my next year of college. Quite a few college students in the area worked for the company every summer, doing cleanup work and laying track; but the majority of the men doing this work were permanent employees between the ages of twenty and twenty-five. There were three other college men in the gang I was assigned to, and the four of us became quite close friends. The rest of the gang consisted of eleven fellows about twenty years old, from poor families, most of them without a high school diploma, and all of them tough and hard as nails. Our foreman was a fellow of about thirty-five, who was known around the plant as a taskmaster of the first order. We knew him only by the name Chick. With the exception of our foreman, all of us had been hired at the beginning of the summer and were on the same basis, except that the four of us who were college students did not intend to continue our employment after the end of the summer as did the others.

I always worked with the three other college students, Mac, Jack, and Doc, because we could carry on interesting conversations and swap stories that helped pass the time and make the job more enjoyable. In addition, the rest of the gang seemed fairly tight-lipped, in their own close group, and little, if at all, interested in talking with us. I made an effort to work harder than some of the other fellows, because I had gotten my job through a friend of one of the bosses and felt I had an obligation to him. The summer progressed this way into early August. I frequently talked with the foreman, and we often joked or hurled friendly insults at one another. The rest of the crew did not very often engage Chick in this sort of banter, but they all seemed to get along with him well enough.

Occasionally, when he had messages to deliver to various parts of the plant, or other crews needed an extra man for an emergency job, Chick would send me; but ordinarily I worked with my regular crew and did the same work as they did. On one occasion, Chick sent Mac, Jack, Doc, and me on an emergency job to clean up some track where a "spill"[1] had occurred, and placed me in charge of the group.

Then, in the second week in August, Mac, Jack, and Doc quit working, so as to remain deductions on their fathers' income taxes as dependents. Thereafter, I spent more time talking to Chick, asking him questions about the plant and "shooting the breeze." I was able to do this and still hold up my end of the work, but I noticed some of the others on the crew seemed to resent it and became cooler than usual toward me. I didn't worry about this, as they had never been very friendly, and I was satisfied that I was doing a satisfactory job. Chick sent me on an increasing number of errands and jobs in various parts of the plant, I think, because he knew that I was interested in learning more about the plant. Some of these jobs involved nothing more difficult than walking around oiling switches, which meant I was my own boss for the day. On other occasions the jobs Chick sent me on were emergencies, in which case the work was considerably more difficult than my regular job.

The rest of the crew grew steadily cooler to me and frequently made snide remarks about "getting a soft touch from the boss," even when I was sent out on some of the tougher jobs. Adding to this atmosphere was the fact that when I went on these special jobs, I always had time to wash up before reporting back to the time clock, which the rest of the crew generally did not have the opportunity to do. Seeing me cleaned up when they came in at the end of the day did little to change their opinion of how hard I was working. I continued to ignore their attitude, for I knew I would only be working for another month and then would probably never see any of them again.

One very hot morning, Chick asked me if I would like to go outside the plant during lunch for a couple of beers. This was something he had always forbidden the crew to do; and as it was very hot, I readily accepted. Thereafter, we used to follow this practice about three or four times a week. This only served to make matters worse, and some of the crew became quite hostile toward me in their statements and actions. This bothered me quite a bit, because most of them were bigger than I was and considerably tougher due to the "struggle for existence" type of environment in which they had been brought up. One of them even went so far as to warn me that it might not be wise for me ever to let him catch me alone, or at least "when there weren't any bosses around."

One morning in early September, Chick told me to take four of the crew and the truck to another section of the plant to clean up a load of coke dust that had been spilled on the tracks. I wanted to think of some excuse

[1]Coal had spilled from a car and blocked the track.

for not going, because I was afraid of what might happen or that the men might just refuse to work for me. However, I felt I owed it to Chick to accept the responsibility he had delegated to me. I could think of no logical excuse except the truth, and I refused to lose face in this way. Chick told four of the fellows to get into the truck and go with me, and informed them that I was to be their boss for the remainder of the day. They climbed into the back of the truck, and we set off for our new job. On the way to the other side of the plant, I tried to think of some way to gain their cooperation, but could not. I realized that if I did the wrong thing, we would get little, if any, work done and that I might collect a few bruises for my troubles as well.

When we arrived at the coke spill, I explained to them what we had to do, and we started working. It was a blisteringly hot day, and coke dust is the dirtiest stuff imaginable to work with. The crew didn't like it at all, and it wasn't long before they were spending more time leaning on their shovels than using them. I also heard several remarks relating to what they thought of me and had several sneers passed in my direction. I realized that something had to be done or we wouldn't begin to finish the job, and we might all get in a good deal of trouble. I had continued to work while the others leaned on their shovels. At that moment, one of them made a very nasty remark about me and my relationship with the boss. With this, I completely lost my temper.

Why, you dirty s.o.b's," I yelled. "I don't give a damn what you think of me; but as long as you're working for me, you're going to work your tails off, and anyone who doesn't like it can take his time-card and get the hell out! Now get to work, or get out!" I shouted this at the top of my lungs, and they all stood staring at me. I turned around and began to shovel as hard as I could, half expecting to get a shovel over my head.

# Index